The Moravian Brethren
in a Time of Transition

Historical Materialism Book Series

The Historical Materialism Book Series is a major publishing initiative of the radical left. The capitalist crisis of the twenty-first century has been met by a resurgence of interest in critical Marxist theory. At the same time, the publishing institutions committed to Marxism have contracted markedly since the high point of the 1970s. The Historical Materialism Book Series is dedicated to addressing this situation by making available important works of Marxist theory. The aim of the series is to publish important theoretical contributions as the basis for vigorous intellectual debate and exchange on the left.

The peer-reviewed series publishes original monographs, translated texts, and reprints of classics across the bounds of academic disciplinary agendas and across the divisions of the left. The series is particularly concerned to encourage the internationalization of Marxist debate and aims to translate significant studies from beyond the English-speaking world.

For a full list of titles in the Historical Materialism Book Series available in paperback from Haymarket Books, visit:
https://www.haymarketbooks.org/series_collections/1-historical-materialism

The Moravian Brethren in a Time of Transition

A Socio-Economic Analysis of a Religious Community in Eighteenth-Century Saxony

Christina Petterson

Haymarket Books
Chicago, IL

First published in 2021 by Brill Academic Publishers, The Netherlands
© 2021 Koninklijke Brill NV, Leiden, The Netherlands

Published in paperback in 2022 by
Haymarket Books
P.O. Box 180165
Chicago, IL 60618
773-583-7884
www.haymarketbooks.org

ISBN: 978-1-64259-777-6

Distributed to the trade in the US through Consortium Book Sales and Distribution (www.cbsd.com) and internationally through Ingram Publisher Services International (www.ingramcontent.com).

This book was published with the generous support of Lannan Foundation and Wallace Action Fund.

Special discounts are available for bulk purchases by organizations and institutions. Please call 773-583-7884 or email info@haymarketbooks.org for more information.

Cover art and design by David Mabb.

Printed in the United States.

10 9 8 7 6 5 4 3 2 1

Library of Congress Cataloging-in-Publication data is available.

For Roland

The *task of history*, therefore, once the *world beyond the truth* has disappeared, is to establish the *truth of this world*. The immediate *task of philosophy* which is at the service of history, once the *holy form* of human self-estrangement has been unmasked, is to unmask self-estrangement in its *unholy forms*. Thus the criticism of heaven turns into the criticism of earth, the *criticism of religion* into the *criticism of law*, and the *criticism of theology* into the *criticism of politics*.[1]
    KARL MARX

∴

---

1 Marx 1975, p. 176. Emphasis in original.

Contents

Preface and Acknowledgements XI

Introductions 1
1 To the Marxists 1
2 To Moravian Scholars and Other Theologians 5
   2.1 *Class* 7
   2.2 *Category of History* 11
   2.3 *The Task of History* 19
3 Outline of Chapters 20

1 Introducing Choir Ideology 22
1 Introduction 22
2 From Choir Speech to Choir Ideology 24
3 What Is the Function of a Choir? 28
4 Methodology 31
5 The Choirs as Vanishing Mediators 35

2 The Choirs – A Genealogy 38
1 Introduction 38
2 Overview of the Genealogy 40
   2.1 Bonded Groups (*Banden*) 43
   2.2 *Associations* 44
   2.3 *Classes* 44
   2.4 *Choirs* 45
3 Terminology and the Establishment of the Choirs 46
   3.1 *But First, the Diaries* 46
   3.2 *1736–40* 49
   3.3 *1741* 50
   3.4 *1742* 52
   3.5 *1743* 55
   3.6 *1744* 57
   3.7 *1745* 61
4 The Day of All Choirs: 25 March 81
5 Choir Houses 88
   5.1 *Single Brothers' House* 90
   5.2 *Single Sisters' House* 92
   5.3 *Houses of the Widows and the Widowers* 95
6 Conclusion 97

3 Blood, Wounds, and Class 98
1. Introduction 98
2. Martin Dober's Account 99
3. The Purge in Herrnhut 102
    - 3.1 *The Marriage Document* 102
    - 3.2 *The Sex Scandal in 1744* 107
    - 3.3 *The Meeting Minutes* 113
4. Blood, Wounds, and Authority 118
    - 4.1 *Blood and Wounds* 118
    - 4.2 *Christ, the Chief Elder* 123
5. Conclusion 128

4 The Choir Speeches 129
1. Introduction 129
2. The Saviour: Individual and Collective 131
    - 2.1 *The Saviour* 131
    - 2.2 *Stand* 135
3. Children's Choir 138
    - 3.1 *Relating to the Saviour* 142
    - 3.2 *Seeing/Non-seeing* 143
    - 3.3 *Language* 146
4. Boys' Choir 152
    - 4.1 *Relating to the Saviour* 157
    - 4.2 *History, Gendering and Sexual Systems* 158
5. Girls' Choir 165
    - 5.1 *Relating to the Saviour* 166
    - 5.2 *Presence* 169
6. Single Brothers' Choir 173
    - 6.1 *Relating to the Saviour* 173
    - 6.2 *Governing One's Body and the Role of the Corpse* 181
7. Single Sisters' Choir 193
    - 7.1 *Relating to the Saviour* 195
    - 7.2 *Outer and Inner* 202
8. Widowers' Choir 211
    - 8.1 *Relating to the Saviour* 213
    - 8.2 *Transition* 219
9. Widows' Choir 222
    - 9.1 *Relating to the Saviour* 225
    - 9.2 *Choir* 228
10. Conclusion 232

5 Marriage and Community 234
1. Zinzendorf's Idea of Marriage 234
2. The Problem 239
   - 2.1 *Three Comparisons* 239
   - 2.2 *The Chapel* 245
   - 2.3 *Married Couples' Choir* 248
   - 2.4 *1755–56 and the Separated Choir Speeches* 254
3. After the Synod 259
4. Conclusion 264

6 The State and Its Subjects 265
1. *Stand* as Manifestation of Cultural Revolution 266
2. Gender 269
3. Class Society and the Civic Self 275
4. Individual and Subject 280
5. The Question of Religion 286
6. Conclusion 291

7 Horizons of History 293
1. Times of Change 293
2. Agents of Change or Expressions of Change 296
3. Dimensions of History 299

Appendix 1 305
Appendix 2 318
References 353
Index 374

Preface and Acknowledgements

This book has taken a very long time to write. Not only because I have been distracted by many other tasks and projects, but also because it was such an enormous and daunting task, bedevilled by the ups and downs of life in general, and also the insecurities, challenges, and upsets of scholarly life. Through all of this, Roland Boer has been there, challenging me, supporting me, knowing that I had it in me, especially when I was certain that I didn't. He has been with me to Herrnhut, to Bethlehem, to Halle, and listened to numerous conference papers on the topic, and has seen it all take shape, slowly.

I have worked on this book in our apartment in Newcastle, in my office at Humboldt University, Newcastle University, and the Australian National University in Canberra, where I have enjoyed the hospitality of Julia Wee and Natalie Cooke, as well as Alan and Robyn Cadwallader. I have written sections of the manuscript in my parents' living room in Skodsborg, Pernille Østrem's guestroom in Copenhagen, Käthe von Bose's kitchen in Berlin, Gillian Townsley's living room in Dunedin, Roland's apartment in Beijing, in a former convent in Oslo, in the Widows' House in Bethlehem, Pennsylvania. And, of course, at the Komensky Gasthaus in Herrnhut, where I have stayed almost every time that I have been in Herrnhut these past nine years. I have loved visiting, sometimes for just a week, sometimes for six weeks, working in the archives, walking around in the woods, and enjoying a beer in the Hutberg Keller. I have always felt very welcome in this quiet corner of the world. Thank you to Olaf and Peter; and Jill and Peter for welcoming me into their homes. At the wonderful Archives of the Unitas Fratrum, where so much of the work for this book has been carried out, I have had great help and support from Rüdiger Kröger, Olaf Nippe, Claudia Mai, Frau Wagner-Fiebig and, last but not least, Frau Moreau, who can decipher absolutely everything and has generously proofread all my German transcriptions. Finally, the Zinzendorf society invited me to present this project in 2013, which had a profound effect on the subsequent shape and structure of the book.

The members of the Moravian scholarly community have also been very supportive, and I would like to thank Paul Peucker, Scott Paul Gordon, Katie Faull, Heidrun Homburg, Peter Vogt and Craig Atwood for sharing expertise and work. Paul Peucker has answered every single question I have ever sent him and I have benefited enormously from his expertise both in writing and in person. Paul and Scott have taken the time to read through earlier drafts of chapters and provided valuable feedback for which I am extremely grateful.

During my sojourn in Canberra, the Centre for European Studies was always a welcoming community, and I would like to thank everyone there, in particular Jacquie Lo, Annmarie Elijah, Jane Coultas, Kasia Williams, and Ivana Damjanovic.

At Copenhagen University, I would like to thank Nils Holger Petersen for reading through several chapters with sharp eyes, and his advice on matters big and small. Mette Birkedal Bruun invited me to present my work in her Solitudes project, and she, Kristian Mejrup, and Lars Nørgaard provided suggestions and helpful comments which pushed me further.

Friends and family have been supportive and provided welcome distractions. Since beginning this book, my world has been populated with a nephew and three step-grandchildren, all of whom bring much happiness and many laughs.

Finally, I would like to thank Simon Mussell for copy-editing and proofreading, and Peter Thomas and Danny Hayward at HM for taking this on, and the production team for being so patient with me.

August 2019
Christiansfeld

Introductions

This book brings together two fields: Marxist analysis and the Moravian Brethren. It analyses the socio-historical impact of this particular brand of eighteenth-century Protestant Christianity and shows how a small and seemingly insignificant religious group negotiated the onslaught of a global economy to their utmost advantage, and dissects the class struggles that had to be overcome in order to emerge victorious in the new world. It is not a religious book, but it does analyse a particular manifestation of Protestant Christianity and through close archival work, charts its metamorphosis from peasant piety to early modern citizen via aristocratic excess.

It is as likely that Marxist historians know nothing of the Moravian Brethren as it is that Moravian studies knows little and cares less about Marxist scholarship. I have experienced as much in conferences in both fields. However, these fields do have one thing in common, namely the reluctance to see the Moravians as participating in the transition to capitalism. This pushback is sometimes grounded in different sensibilities (scientific/secular vs. pious beliefs), but both based on an idealistic perception of the role of religion in historical development.

It is, however, my conviction that these fields can be of use and interest to each other, and the present study intends to show how. But first, since these two groups are likely to be unacquainted, introductions are in order.

1 To the Marxists

Meet the Moravian Brethren, also known as the (*Herrnhuter*) *Brüdergemeine* or the *Unitas Fratrum*.[1] It is a religious group and its revered founder was an

---

1 The current English term is the Moravian Church. In this study I will reluctantly use the term Moravian Brethren, since I prefer to use *Brüdergemeine* to emphasise that I am writing about a German group in the eighteenth century. The movement traces its history back to Jan Hus and the Czech Reformation in the fifteenth century, whence the name 'Moravian'. When I will need to specifically distinguish between the overall name of the community from the members who came from Moravia, I will add the German indicator (*mährisch*) to highlight the distinction. This is especially important in Chapter 3. When I use the term Moravian *Brethren* instead of Moravian Church, it is because of the emphasis on the fraternal aspect of the movement, which will become important in Chapter 6.

Another note on my translation of the word 'Gemeine' which is the German word for the community of Brethren, and deliberately spelt without the 'd' as in present German:

aristocrat, an imperial count no less. You may know them from Karl Kautsky's brief and caustic mention in *Forerunners of Modern Socialism*, where he states that they have no significance for general history.[2] I would sincerely urge you to keep reading, because not only is the history of this group nothing short of astonishing, but its source material is fabulous.[3] These features mean that the Moravian Brethren constitute an excellent case study of the socio-economic upheavals in eighteenth-century Eastern Germany, which took a different path from that of Western Europe.[4] The developments and subsequent success of the Moravian Brethren provide a look into how elements of early capitalism emerge within the framework of late feudalism.

A movement such as the Moravian Brethren is highly important for understanding socio-economic shifts, the changing circumstances of household, labour and industry in early modern Saxony, and of course the role of religion in these changes. The prime motivation for such a close analysis of an eighteenth-century group on the cusp of capitalism is following the late Ellen Meiksins Wood and E.P. Thompson, who regarded historical analysis as an important way of thinking in non-capitalist terms. Naturally, this is a tricky venture, given that we are immersed in capitalist conceptual categories, including the relega-

---

Gemeinde. The German word has a broader semantic field than what can be conveyed in English, in that *Gemeine* encompasses both community and congregation. We are thus left with a choice of emphasising either the collective aspect or the religious aspect of the term. For better or for worse, I have chosen the former here, and will translate *Gemeine* as community, well aware that I am blocking out an entire dimension of meaning otherwise associated with the term. My choice is based on what I wish to emphasise in my analysis, namely the non-religious aspect of the Moravian Brethren. There is another choice of translation which is less justifiable, and more aesthetic. In German, the collective term for the brothers and sisters together is *Geschwister*, which has the English equivalent of 'siblings'. While I refer to the individual members as brother and sister, the term *sibling* was for me too tied up with nuclear family terminology, and so I have chosen as a collective term the word *members*. This also excludes an entire dimension of relations in which the brothers and sisters were embedded, but at the very least connects the brothers and sisters firmly to the community and emphasises the level of commitment, but less so the kinship flavouring of that membership.

2 Kautsky 1895, pp. 238–9.
3 The archives were established in 1764 by the synod of the Moravian Brethren, and contain a vast amount of material pertaining to the history of the community, its missionary work within and beyond Europe and thus, by extension, material pertaining to the socio-economic and cultural history of early modern Europe and its colonies. See Kröger, Mai, and Nippe (eds) 2014, pp. 106–53 for an introduction to and overview of the material.
4 Wallerstein 2011, p. 95.

tion of religion to the private sphere, but we can at the very least attempt to, as Meiksins Wood puts it, 'challenge the universality of its constituent categories'.[5]

The main focus of this study is the village of Herrnhut, on the current border of Germany, Poland and the Czech Republic, in the area called the Oberlausitz. This area was renowned for its cloth and linen industry and experienced a flourishing after the 30 Years' War with the immigration of clothmakers from Bohemia and Moravia. The village was founded in 1722 on the estate of count Nikolaus Ludwig von Zinzendorf and Pottendorf, when his estate manager, Johann Georg Heitz, gave permission to a group of refugees from Moravia to settle on the lands of the estate. The first tree from which to build the first house was felled on 17 June 1722 by Moravian carpenter Christian David.

The fields belonging to the estate were already farmed by the peasants of Berthelsdorf, so the Moravian (*mährisch*) settlers, who, apart from some artisans, were mostly peasants, had to find a different way of surviving.[6] This included working as artisans, as well as spinning and weaving. Five years and many, many problems later,[7] the settlers signed the statutes of Herrnhut, which effectively made all the settlers in Herrnhut free subjects in contrast to the enserfed peasants on the estate.[8] This freedom of movement and (in principle) choice of trade meant that the Moravian Brethren from the beginning was a highly mobile workforce that could travel and settle anywhere – a significant advantage in a semi-feudal Europe that was still dependent on agriculture. From these modest beginnings on Count Zinzendorf's estate in the Oberlausitz, they rose to become a worldwide missionary movement with stations and outposts from Greenland to the Cape, and from North America to Australia.

---

5 Wood 1995, p. 13.
6 In his archival study of peasant and master in the Oberlausitz, Willi Boelcke canvasses the excessive population shifts in the Oberlausitz after the end of the 30 Years' War. Encouraged by the masters of the estates and supported by the territorial lord, the settlements of thousands of religious emigrants in the depopulated area provided much needed support for the estate masters over against the Lusatian League towns and their craftsmen, and changed the face of the area. Boelcke 1957, pp. 44–6. Boelcke's examples are from the second half of the seventeenth century and the early eighteenth, and demonstrate that the settlement of Herrnhut was then no exception to the general trends in the area, as Edita Sterik also points out (Sterik 2006, pp. 98–9).
7 The best study of the early years in Herrnhut is Wollstadt 1966. Paul Peucker has recently completed a forthcoming study with the working title, *Herrnhut, 1722–1732: The Early Years of a Moravian Community*, which is a detailed archival study of the make up and conflicts of the early community.
8 Uttendörfer 1925, p. 23. See also Schmidt 1900, p. 56.

What they lacked in numbers, they made up for in willpower, mobility, and above all, an uncanny ability to anticipate and capitalise on global economic developments.[9]

The Moravian Brethren are part of the larger awakening movement known as Pietism which took place after the 30 Years' War in Europe. Pietism emphasised the conversion experience of the individual believer over against church dogmatism, and soon became divided into an institutionalised form in Halle (duchy of Brandenburg) under the leadership of August Hermann Francke, and in various radical formations, such as the Schwarzenau Brethren, the Society of Mother Eve, the Labadists etc.[10] Under government sponsorship Halle sported a university, and under Francke's leadership, it flourished dramatically, and included schools, an orphanage, various entrepreneurial activities, such as trade, bookstore, printing press, papermill, and apothecary.[11] Zinzendorf and his close friend and confidant, Friedrich von Watteville, attended Francke's *paedagogium* for aristocratic boys in the early eighteenth century, and initially intended Herrnhut to be a copy of Halle, but relations between Halle and Herrnhut soured significantly in the 1730s and '40s.[12]

While Pietism may have been a significant innovating force within German orthodoxy at the time, it was still reliant on a state structure, as was the Lutheran Church (as Max Weber notes), and both could be seen as excellent ideologues of mercantilism over against the feudal Catholic Church. However, the extraordinary flexibility of the Moravian Brethren, their geographical spread, and their non-reliance on state structures made them able to penetrate deeper into the decaying social structures of the feudal states and make use of capitalism's global scope in the best possible way.

In this book, I emphasise how the theological developments and communal structure of the eighteenth-century Moravian Brethren functioned as a way to manage class struggle, and in the process became a dynamo of capitalist development and should thus not be dismissed as an emotional or religious aberration to economy and history. I focus on the relation between this context of socio-economic upheaval and what I call choir ideology, which denotes the particular ideology inherent in the hierarchy, organisation, and subjectification practices of the community in the 1740s and 1750s. One of the chief arguments of the book is that the communal organisation of the Moravian Brethren into groups according to gender, age, and marital status (so-called choirs) can be

---

9   See above all Engel 2009.
10 For a recent introduction to German Pietism in English see Schantz 2013.
11 For a recent study into the economic ventures of Francke in Halle see Mejrup 2016.
12 Schneider 2004.

seen as a symptom or ideological precondition of the fledgling abstraction and fragmentation of not only the individual, but also civil society. The role of religion in contributing to these conditions has hitherto only really been addressed by Marx in 'On the Jewish Question',[13] but here, this role will be put to a more comprehensive test.

2   To Moravian Scholars and Other Theologians

Moravian – and other – theologians, the time has come to take a look at what Marxists have to offer.

My many visits to the Unity Archives in Herrnhut have taught me that the destruction of more than half of Herrnhut in the battles between the villagers and the Red Army towards the end of WWII, and the subsequent years within the GDR have not endeared the Herrnhut residents to socialism, and by extension, Marxism. Northern European theologians are, generally speaking, suspicious towards Marxism, and more often than not, see social questions as either irrelevant to theology or historically confined to the wave of liberation theology trending in the 1960s and '70s. History is of course not met with equal hesitation, but theologically palatable history is a certain version of history, which emphasises aesthetic (Renaissance) and idealist (Enlightenment) history and thus serves to emphasise the practice of theology, or theology's influence on practice, rather than theology's social function. However, the history of the Moravian Brethren is so unique and important for understanding European modernity and its socio-economic developments that we need to look at some of its social functions to bring that importance to the fore.

One of the first things at which we need to look is the concept of capitalism. When I have presented my work in your company, several of you have pointed out that Zinzendorf was dreadful with money and left the community in massive debt when he died. For Marxists, however, capitalism is more than just money. It is a socio-economic system which includes organisation of labour, a focus on exchange value, and a global circulatory system of production, distribution, exchange, and consumption and their relations. It also includes a particular understanding of society, civil or bourgeois (*bürgerlich*) society, divided into public and private, as are its citizens. We tend to think of this as natural and universal, but for Marxists, it is important to emphasise that public and private, gender, and civil society all have a specific history and serve a specific

---

13   Marx 1975 [1843].

socio-economic function.[14] This is connected with my insistence that words and concepts have a specific history and function, and thus must be radically historicised to be properly grasped. One of the things I am interested in here is how the Moravian Brethren may have anticipated some of the developments that were to take place, and in some way prepared its members for the massive social upheavals ahead.

As an example of what I have in mind, Gerhard Bondi's article on the contribution of Halle Pietism to the development of economic thinking in Germany notes that

> the particular German development, which generated no groundwork for the emergence of a political economy on German ground, meant that bourgeois economic thinking found its actual expression not in economic theory, but rather, embedded in the most different areas of intellectual life, it presented itself in sometimes unexpected contexts.[15]

By analysing Francke's sermons and the institutions of Halle, Bondi concludes that the doctrines of the Halle pietists played a more significant role in the development of capitalist forms of production and the spread of capitalist thought than the economic theories of the Cameralists – the German science of statecraft that emerged in the early eighteenth century.[16]

In this light, we might look at Zinzendorf's understanding of money again. Because he did seem to intuitively understand what was underway. His aristocratic relation to money as being always to hand could also be seen as connected to the emerging global economy and its logic of credit and abstract value. He certainly was able to work the credit to his own advantage.[17] However, the credit was so tied up to his person and rank, rather than the community, that when he died, the creditors demanded their money back. In terms of other developments of the time, he also understood that mobility was crucial – he himself was a constant traveller, but the leadership in Herrnhut also planned labour and organised its members globally, by sending specific people here (other European settlements) and there (colonies). Finally, his way of solving

---

14 Wood 1995, part 1.
15 Bondi 1964, p. 24. My translation.
16 Gray 2000, p. 91. Gray's study is an examination of Cameralist thinking in the German Enlightenment and its effects on the household structures. See also Tribe 1978; 1988; 1995.
17 See Ward 1987. For an excellent recent article on Zinzendorf, status and money see Becker-Cantarino 2018.

the problems with fractions in the community was to create the gendered choir system, which emphasised gender as the common feature of the members of the community. The importance of such a move cannot be emphasised enough. What he did in such a move was to shift the locus of equality to gender and maintain economic inequality. Because, as we know, while they all *called* each other Brother and Sister, the nobility kept their aristocratic privileges in the community, while the lower orders worked hard. This is the fragmented human being, equal at one level, spiritual or civic, or however we may name it, and unequal at the material level, the level of livelihood and labour. This fragmentation is referred to as alienation, in that humans are regarded as alienated from their true free existence. Not all Marxists subscribe to the theory of alienation, it should be added.[18] But I do. However, whereas I see Christianity as contributing significantly towards this condition, most Marxists would place Christianity at the level of ideology, as a construct designed to keep people from realising their own material misery. Both of these positions may be found in the writings of Marx.

I will now turn to two fairly detailed methodological discussions, since these are assumed as the foundation for the argument of the book. Namely that the history of the community should be understood within the larger transition to capitalism and for this reason, since the older order was breaking down, class struggle was something the community had to deal with rather urgently.

2.1 Class

An issue which serves as an important motor in this work is the question of class. The Marxist concept of class is a somewhat unwieldy one, given that Marx never developed it in any systematic fashion, and also presented differing definitions of the concept. One seemingly static notion is from the *Manifesto of the Communist Party*, which notes that

> The history of all hitherto existing society is the history of class struggles.
> Freeman and slave, patrician and plebeian, lord and serf, guild-master and journeyman, in a word, oppressor and oppressed, stood in constant

---

18   The concept of alienation is a Hegelian concept (*Entfremdung* or *Entäußerung*) which indicates a particular stage in the formation of consciousness. The French Marxist Louis Althusser was insistent on there being an epistemological break between the young Hegelian Marx, and the later mature Marx, and thus that alienation did not constitute an element in Marx's economic theory. He later conceded the presence of Hegelian themes throughout Marx's works. Sayers 2011, pp. x–xi.

opposition to one another, carried on an uninterrupted, now hidden, now open fight, a fight that each time ended, either in a revolutionary reconstitution of society at large, or in the common ruin of the contending classes.[19]

This quotation describes history as the history of class struggle between oppressors and oppressed, which results in the 'epoch of the bourgeoisie' in which the two camps are constituted by the bourgeoisie and the proletariat. However descriptive this may sound, we should take note that these groups reflect different socio-economic formations, and thus all align along the axis of relations and access to means of production as their fundamental principle of organisation. In Marxist thought, class is never a neutral term, nor a merely descriptive one. It is linked to the socio-economic organisation of a society and its ruling and ruled classes.

Another quotation from a later text, *The Eighteenth Brumaire of Louis Bonaparte*, demonstrates a much more complex understanding of class:

The small-holding peasants form an enormous mass whose members live in similar conditions but without entering into manifold relations with each other. [...] Each individual peasant family is almost self-sufficient, directly produces most of its consumer needs, and thus acquires its means of life more through an exchange with nature than in intercourse with society. A small holding, the peasant and his family; beside it another small holding, another peasant and another family. A few score of these constitute a village, and a few score villages constitute a department. [...] *Insofar as millions of families live under conditions of existence that separate their mode of life, their interests, and their culture from those of the other classes, and put them in hostile opposition to the latter, they form a class. Insofar as there is merely a local interconnection among these small-holding peasants, and the identity of their interests forms no community, no national bond, and no political organization among them, they do not constitute a class.* They are therefore incapable of asserting their class interest in their own name, whether through a parliament or a convention. They cannot represent themselves, they must be represented.[20]

---

19   Marx and Engels 1976 [1848], p. 482.
20   Marx 1979 [1852], p. 187. Emphasis added.

This understanding of class is much more Hegelian, in that it relies on both an objective aspect (distinct conditions of existence and mode of life) and a subjective aspect (community, unity, and enemy) to define a class – the classical expression of the difference is class-in-itself and class-for-itself. A class thus is more than the sum of its parts; it is a collective consciousness defined over against a class enemy. The most common examples are the bourgeoisie and proletariat which spring from the conditions of capitalist organisation of labour and production. But these terms do not exist in our archival material of the eighteenth-century Moravian Brethren, given that this organisation of society is in an embryonic stage. Nevertheless, this does not mean that class is an obsolete concept – to which the constant reference to *Stand* (rank) in the source material testifies. So, what I will do in the present analysis is to assume the framework of class struggle, and within this, examine the particularity of the given circumstances in our material.

As the argument unfolds, we will see that there is a class in our material with both objective and subjective characteristics, namely the aristocracy. Indeed, one of the important features of analysis in this book is its attention to the aristocracy in Herrnhut, their influence on theology and community organisation, and the struggles in retaining the upper hand. Feudal society was divided into a number of *Stände* (ranks), the most significant for us here being the aristocracy and peasantry. While Zinzendorf absolved the residents of Herrnhut from their seigneurial obligation to him, this does not mean that the differences in *Stand* disappeared, or that Zinzendorf actively worked to better the lot for the lower classes.[21] Zinzendorf was still an estate owner, and whatever he paid from 'his own pocket' was paid for by the labour of the tenants of the estate.[22] Also, his behaviour and struggles with the Moravian peasants and his exercising aristocratic privilege on numerous occasions are ample evidence of the continued significance of what we will call class. It is thus important not

---

21 Schmidt 1900, p. 55.
22 I would like to thank Heidrun Homburg for fruitful discussions on this point. Wollstadt notes a couple of times that 'Zinzendorf's household' paid for this or that. However, this means that this was paid for from the income of the estate. Especially the orphanage (*Waisenshaus*) was funded by Zinzendorf, and substantial amounts for correspondence. See Wollstadt 1966, pp. 256 and 284. Also Uttendörfer notes that the peasants of the estate were only (!) obligated to work six half days a week (half a day was four hours) which was not enough to rebuild the estate after Zinzendorf purchased it in 1722 and that the Inspector had very little money to work with. Finally, Uttendörfer notes that the first house in Herrnhut was paid for at the expense of the count. Uttendörfer 1925, pp. 146–7. See the whole chapter on the household of Zinzendorf, pp. 144–73.

to fall into the temptation of taking the professed egalitarianism of the community at face value. On the other hand, we also need to take this discrepancy seriously.

In spite of, or maybe because of, these somewhat unchanging class relations in a community of supposed equals, the Moravian community was a relatively safe space in a changing world, because they provided a communal support structure for its members, which roughly aligned with what was underway, as well as including elements from a well-known structure. The community helped prepare its members for an understanding of society where economic inequality was a matter of course, as long as the *commitment* to equality was present. It helped to make the world a smaller place via the networks of the community to its earliest mission fields in the West Indies, Greenland, and North America.[23] And the community helped its members to live and work within a monetary economy. The choir structure, its understanding and production of gender as a self-reflective category, and its use and organisation of labour was a perfect transitional form of living between feudalism and capitalism.

The prevalent position of the aristocracy and the transitional and embryonic features of the Moravian Brethren are connected, I will argue, to the distinct social formation known as the *Gutsherrschaft*, or semi-feudalism.[24] Immanuel Wallerstein, Robert Brenner, and Perry Anderson have in very different ways pointed to the distinct socio-economic developments of Eastern Europe, which did not follow the overt transition to capitalism as in Western Europe for a number of reasons. This is an immensely contested field,[25] and I will hold off on engaging full on with the debate.[26] But, in brief, the main issue is that east of the Elbe river, the transition to capitalism happened *within* the structures of feudalism, in the sense that the feudal structures (estate, serfdom, bonded labour) remained, but were re-contextualised, as it were, within the emerging global economy. Hence, we do not see the processes that characterised the transition in Western Europe, such as enclosures, eviction of tenants, suppression of religious holidays, and restrictions on hunting. Instead, we witness a differ-

---

23   See the full and rich study by Mettele 2009.
24   See Banaji 2010, pp. 79–87.
25   See e.g. the publication which arose as a response to Robert Brenner's initial article, Aston and Philpin 1987. Another article that gives a good idea of what is at stake is Melton 1988. Melton states that he will criticise the model advanced by Brenner and Wallerstein, but only mentions Wallerstein initially, and then focuses on Brenner.
26   Wallerstein does note, however, that the main disagreement is over to what extent this 'second feudalism' or 'semi-feudalism' is to be understood as a form of feudalism or not. Wallerstein 2011, pp. 90–1.

ent means of acquiring control of production and accumulation of wealth. The end, however, to which these means were directed, was the same.

2.2 Category of History

This brings us to the larger and more unwieldy category of history. Very broadly speaking, Marxist history may be content driven or carried out through the theory of modes of production. By content driven, I mean work such as E.P. Thompson's ground-breaking and highly influential book *The Making of the English Working Class* which is, as the title partly indicates, an archival study into the formation of English working-class consciousness in the time of the Industrial Revolution.[27] According to an oft-quoted sentence, Thompson aimed to 'rescue the poor stockinger, the Luddite cropper, the "obsolete" handloom weaver, the "utopian" artisan, and even the deluded follower of Joanna Southcott, from the enormous condescension of posterity'.[28] One might even say amnesia of posterity, since strong is the desire to forget, in Fredric Jameson's words, about 'the fact of labor itself, and the intolerable spectacle of the backbreaking millennial toil of millions of people from the earliest moments of human history'.[29] This we may complement with a quotation from Cambridge classicist G.E.M. Ste. Croix, who in his monumental study on class struggle in antiquity notes that the peasants 'are the voiceless toilers, the great majority – let us not forget it – of the population of the Greek and Roman world, upon whom was built a great civilisation which despised them and did all it could to forget them'.[30] Finally, I will mention another Marxist archival study, a study from 1964 on the class struggle of the Upper Lusatian peasants in the seventeenth century:

> One could accuse us of treating the peasant actions in the Oberlausitz from 1625 to 1720 too extensively. That would, however, be unjustified. In bourgeois historiography much space is devoted to the life and activities of the ruling classes and their individual representatives; whole libraries have arisen from this subject. In contrast, the history of the masses was given a very dismissive treatment.[31]

---

27 Thompson 1966.
28 Thompson 1966, p. 12. I am too young to be able to fully comprehend and appreciate the revolutionary significance of this work. Anything I say should be seen in this light. For a testimony to its importance, see Sewell Jr 1990, pp. 51–3.
29 Jameson 1979, p. 56.
30 de Ste. Croix 1981, p. 210.
31 Leszczynski 1964, p. 8.

In this sense, Marxist history brings out the forgotten and labouring peoples of history, who are eclipsed in historical accounts from Ancient Greece to postmodern Europe.

When reading these various histories, but above all Thompson, I was so impressed by this indignation, the wealth of detail, but above all, the forceful counter-narrative to traditional history these works presented, and wanted to do something similar in respect to Herrnhut. I wanted to look at the role of the Moravian Brethren in the proletarianisation of the peasantry and the worsening of conditions for weavers and spinners in the region. However, when I was sitting with the archival material, I found myself at multiple dead ends. One of the reasons was that capitalism in the Oberlausitz did not develop in the same way as it did in England, which Leszczynski does not explain in great detail. As briefly noted above, the emergence of capitalism in the Oberlausitz took place *through* the feudal structures and not by abolishing them, as was the case in West Germany, France, and England. Another problem with the content-driven approach was that Thompson and Leszczynski focus on archival material *produced* by the classes whose histories they want to write. This could not work for me, because my initial source material, Zinzendorf's speeches to the various choirs in Herrnhut, was produced by an aristocrat and as such did not directly address issues of labour, socio-economic change, and the creation of a new class structure.

So, while I naturally do not regard the *agendas* of Thompson, Ste. Croix and Leszczynski as problematic objectives, it did mean that their analyses could not serve to clarify my own methodological approach. However, I *can* use a discussion of Thompson to clarify some theoretical points and through this, establish my own position.

A deeper problem was Thompson's (and Leszczynski's) way of organising the material, namely presenting the material as something already out there, that then needs to be analysed. This very act of separating material from analysis serves an ideological purpose, namely to disassociate us, our biases and our culpability from the matters at hand, to disassociate us from the making and shaping of history, which then is seen to take place in an otherwise ideologically neutral 'historical sphere'. This is of course curious, given Thompson's desire to show the working class as being present in its own making.

Another problem also amply pointed out by Thompson's critics is his avoidance of addressing structural features, which he regarded as Stalinist. By structural features are meant the theory of class formation and the base-superstructure schema of classical Marxism. The most common Marxist theory of class formation is (as we saw in the quote from *The Eighteenth Brumaire* above) objective and subjective – because it works with classes within capitalism. As mentioned, class formation is objective, in that class struggle is generated by exploitative capitalist economic relations, and subjective, in that it is through class struggle that the proletariat becomes conscious of itself as a class. The base-superstructure schema is another contested and caricatured feature of Marxism. This means, simplistically put, that the economic relations of society constitute the base according to which the superstructural elements of politics, law, consciousness, art, etc. are shaped, as set forth in this polemical quote by Marx and Engels from their early formulation in *The German Ideology*:

> In direct contrast to German philosophy which descends from heaven to earth, here we ascend from earth to heaven. That is to say, we do not set out from what men say, imagine, conceive, nor from men as narrated, thought of, imagined, conceived, in order to arrive at men in the flesh. *We set out from real, active men, and on the basis of their real life-process we demonstrate the development of the ideological reflexes and echoes of this life-process. The phantoms formed in the human brain are also, necessarily, sublimates of their material life-process, which is empirically verifiable and bound to material premises. Morality, religion, metaphysics, all the rest of ideology and their corresponding forms of consciousness, thus no longer retain the semblance of independence. They have no history, no development; but men, developing their material production and their material intercourse, alter, along with this their real existence, their thinking and the products of their thinking.* Life is not determined by consciousness, but consciousness by life. In the first method of approach the starting-point is consciousness taken as the living individual; in the second method, which conforms to real life, it is the real living individuals themselves, and consciousness is considered solely as their consciousness.[32]

What Marx and Engels are saying is that products of thinking are never independent from the people who think them, and are thus always already determined by the material, i.e. socio-economic, situation of these people. The material base, i.e. the mode of production, determines the products of superstructure.

The disagreement concerning the base-superstructure concept consists in the precise relationship between the two, and to what degree this determin-

---

32   Marx and Engels 1972 [1845], pp. 36–7. Emphasis added.

ation works.³³ Some, mostly associated with Soviet Marxism, argue for mechanistic causality, where everything at a superstructural level is reduced to economics.³⁴ The other extreme is the French structuralist Louis Althusser, who placed the economic on par with culture, ideology, politics, which all together make up a mode of production.³⁵

Thompson's own solution was to focus one-sidedly on experience and through this emphasis to dismiss questions of structure. However, as Sewell demonstrated, Thompson *presupposed* both the theory of class formation and the base-superstructure schema of classical Marxism, albeit in an unacknowledged and unexamined fashion. Thompson's point is that class is *not* something independent of experience, as stated in his preface: 'Class happens when some men, as a result of common experiences (inherited or shared), feel and articulate the identity of their interest as between themselves, and as against other men, whose interests are different from (and usually opposed to) theirs'.³⁶ However, as Sewell astutely points out, 'if workers' experiences produce class consciousness, rather than some other sort of consciousness, this is because their experiences are *class* experiences', and 'it seems utterly metaphysical and arbitrary to deny the presence of class in the productive relations yet affirm its presence in the experiences and the consciousness that those productive relations generate'.³⁷ Thompson thus insists that the experiences and consciousness of working people are class experiences and class consciousness, but denies that class exists in the economic conditions of those men.

A similar point could be made about the role of the state in Thompson's book, which is presupposed, yet negated at the same time. It surfaces in his xenophobia (as noted by Hirst in relation to the French, and Boer in relation to the Irish),³⁸ and his exceptionalism, which both are products of the nation state. Thompson's exceptionalism thus presupposes the nation state of England, while negating any overarching theory of the state and the individual, but instead begins with the experience of various workers in England, which then becomes collectivised in the working-class consciousness.

---

33   See the good discussions of this in McLennan 1981, pp. 45–65 and Bottomore 1997, pp. 45–8. I have also benefitted greatly from Wickham 2008, Banerji 2010, pp. 45–101, and Blackledge 2006.
34   A usual punching bag is Plekhanov 1969. See discussion in Laclau and Mouffe, 1985, Chapter 1.
35   Jameson 1981, pp. 7–43.
36   Thompson 1966, p. 9.
37   Sewell Jr 1990, pp. 56–7. Emphasis in original.
38   Boer 2011, pp. 61–2; Hirst 1985, p. 59.

Paul Hirst and Joan Scott criticise Thompson for establishing *experience* and the unified subject as the foundation of historical knowledge – their criticism comes from what we might call an anti-essentialising perspective.[39] However, in light of what lies ahead in the present book, we could also problematise this understanding of the unified subject in the light of the individual within the political state and the public and private persona generated by this formation. By fixating on *English* experience as the fundamental category of his historical narrative, Thompson unwittingly shows that the emergence of the nation state and its relation to capitalism is crucial to his analysis, and evades the point that the individual is produced in accordance with the nature of the political state. I will be giving much more attention to the actual production of the individual in the following chapters.

Haunted by the history of socialism, like many Marxists before and after him, Thompson refused to address issues of structure – be it class or state – as having an impact on the development of working-class consciousness. Indeed, as Sewell points out, *The Making of the English Working Class* and Thompson's other works are characterised by positioning experience and structure as antagonistic principles. In the case of *The Making of the English Working Class*, the structural dynamics of early industrial capitalism nevertheless constitute a hidden dynamo in the narrative. Thompson's narrative is 'untroubled by, yet globally shaped by, the underlying rhythm of a classical Marxist movement from class-in-itself to class-for-itself'.[40]

So, not only are the very nature of the content with which I have been working and Thompson's approach mutually exclusive, but I also do not share his resistance to matters of structure and I am *very* suspicious of the fetishisation of agency. This scepticism is directed more towards the developments in the notion of agency in the last 30 years,[41] rather than Thompson per se. And yet, while Thompson's emphasis on agency is an expression of his vehement reaction against economic reductionism and determination, there is a faint ideological line from his work to the current celebration of the free agent of neoliberalism, unencumbered by anything as vulgar as economic structures.

The thing is, tragically, that Thompson of course agrees with Marx's forceful sentence from *The Eighteenth Brumaire*, that 'men make their own history, but they do not make it as they please; they do not make it under self-selected circumstances, but under circumstances existing already, given and transmitted

---

39 Scott 1991, pp. 71–2.
40 Sewell Jr 1990, p. 57.
41 Barker 2003, pp. 233–9.

from the past'.[42] Nevertheless, because of his politically conditioned disavowal of economic determinism, Thompson cannot find a clear voice, but instead is led 'to deny in his theory, what he is unable to deny in his practice'.[43]

Turning then to the approach to history through modes of production, we here find a more abstract approach, and I offer here only a couple of bare bones, upon which I will build during the book, and then return to in the last chapter, after we have worked our way through the material.

Mode of production (*Produktionsweise*) denotes a given period, in which the forces of production and the relations of production correspond in a specific way. The forces of production are both the actual tools of labour and labour itself, while the relations of production indicate control or ownership of the forces: the owner of the factory owns both the machines and the labour power of the workers. This example of course entails a system within which property rights are fundamental and more broadly available, as in capitalism. In feudalism, only the aristocracy had property rights to the land, its products and producers, while capitalism meant an extension of those property rights to a larger part of the population.

Change from one mode of production to another occurs when contradictions arise between the forces and relations of production, which lead to social revolution.[44] One of the many disagreements within Marxism is the exact nature of the process of change. So-called vulgar Marxism regards the forces as fundamental, and the relations of production as secondary. Change thus arises when developments occur in the forces of production, say the development of new machinery, upon which the older relations of production act as 'fetters'. Bottomore suggests the possibility of seeing it in a more dialectical fashion, namely that the relations are the ones to develop, which causes a development of the forces. These developed forces then react back on the relations but 'in such a way that the effect of relations on forces is multiplied while that of forces on relations is muted'.[45] This constellation would mean that the relations of production would be primary but the maturation of the forces would run up against the 'fetters' which then constitute the contradiction.

This debate echoes the base/superstructure debate referred to above, and gives a good picture of the discussions within Marxism on the primary and secondary nature of economic and cultural phenomena, as well as their relations.

---

42   Marx 1979 [1852], p. 10.
43   Sewell Jr 1990, p. 57.
44   Bottomore 1997, p. 178.
45   Bottomore 1997, p. 179.

Another broader issue with the mode of production is the discussion of diachrony and synchronicity. Are we to understand a mode of production from a diachronic perspective, i.e. as a periodisation of history, or as a synchronic model, where a given mode of production can encompass everything in one massive system or structure (which is what Thompson was resisting)? The understanding of mode of production as diachronic development raises a number of problems, because in practice, a mode of production never quite replaced its predecessor, in that traces of previous modes are always present in the latter.[46]

The process of transitioning from feudalism to capitalism thus took centuries and has in a sense never been totally accomplished. Because of this sedimented nature of modes of production, it has been deemed theoretically necessary to address this analytically in order to highlight the struggles within each mode of production, between past and present modes and those which are to come.[47] One fruitful approach has been that of regulation theory, which breaks down these big blocks of change into smaller processes that highlight the varying distribution of elements in the various modes. For example, while money has been used for millennia, it has only reached its privileged place as absolute embodiment of value within capitalism. And wage labour has also been with us for thousands of years, but only in capitalism has it become constitutive. Conversely, chattel slavery, constitutive of social organisation in antiquity, no longer holds this fundamental position in capitalism. Regulation theory thus breaks up a mode of production into the smaller building blocks of institutional forms and regimes to provide an analytical framework for these primary and secondary elements and their mutual organisation.[48] While I will not be using regulation theory as such, I have taken note of the call to work with much more concrete elements within this unwieldy and abstract concept of mode of production.

Fredric Jameson's work has consistently noted this feature of the modes of production as sedimentations rather than successions and he has worked hard

---

46 See also Banaji 2010, pp. 64–5. A good example is the British Parliament and British property law. England, whose Industrial Revolution often places it in a privileged position with regards to capitalist development, retains, in the twenty-first century, a parliamentary system which divides its representation into a 'House of Lords' and a 'House of Commons'. And these are not only residual *terms*. The House of Lords is constituted by the peerage of England, i.e. the church and the aristocracy appointed by the monarch. Losurdo (2015, p. 52) mentions this as a survival of the ancient regime in nineteenth-century Britain.
47 Jameson 1979, p. 68.
48 For an application of regulation theory to an ancient context, see Boer 2015 and also Boer and Petterson 2017.

towards overcoming the temptation to view a mode of production as a pure synchronous model, which can encompass everything in an iron cage on the one hand, and mechanical assignations of cultural products to a box labelled pre-capitalist or capitalist mode of production.[49] His solution to this two-fold temptation is termed 'cultural revolution' and designates 'that moment in which the coexistence of various modes of production becomes visibly antagonistic, their contradictions moving to the very centre of political, social, and historical life'.[50] Jameson thus approaches socio-economic questions through cultural products, which is a much more promising approach to the present study, given not only the nature of our source material, but the context in which it is embedded. Indeed, the whole concept of the *Gutsherrschaft* impedes any notion of a simultaneous identical transition from feudalism to capitalism and must therefore be considered carefully. If we read our archival material as participating in a struggle, in which the old is vanishing, but the new cannot yet be born (and when it is born, it is not really new, but a conglomerate of old, new, and thinking the old in a new way), then we are regarding our texts as embodying the cultural revolution. But this will be an epistemological struggle for me, given that I am prone to thinking more in traditional transitions, rather than the complex multilayered metasynchronicity which Jameson is advocating.[51] So what we have to do is: (1) not regard a given mode of production, say feudalism or capitalism, as a closed system in itself; (2) not define any given cultural product as being either feudal, pre-capitalist, or capitalist and thereby close off any possibility of seeing it as something else; and (3) not think that instability is exclusively part of the transition, and that once the transition is complete, things will be stable and unchanging until the next transition comes around to shake things up. The point is that the transition is only the surfacing of the struggles that go on all the time, and which are kept down by various mechanisms. And this is crucial, because it is at *this level of struggles under the surface that we need to understand the circumstances and events of early eighteenth-century Herrnhut*. They participate in the larger transitional struggles, but are not the only or even the most significant expression of these struggles. Nevertheless, localising the struggles and their participants might make it more concrete for us to grasp, and to understand the deep effects of socio-economic change on community and consciousness.

---

49   Jameson 1981, p. 75.
50   Jameson 1981, p. 81.
51   Jameson 1981, pp. 82–3.

2.3 The Task of History

Before I turn to a breakdown of chapters, I want to discuss the task of history as pronounced by a younger Marx. The quotation with which the book begins is taken from the introduction to *Contribution to the Critique of Hegel's Philosophy of Law*. Let me just repeat it here:

> The *task of history*, therefore, once the *world beyond the truth* has disappeared, is to establish the *truth of this world*. The immediate *task of philosophy* which is at the service of history, once the *holy form* of human self-estrangement has been unmasked, is to unmask self-estrangement in its *unholy forms*. Thus the criticism of heaven turns into the criticism of earth, the *criticism of religion* into the *criticism of law*, and the *criticism of theology* into the *criticism of politics*.[52]

The context in which it is written is Marx's discussion of the role of religion as the 'heart of a heartless world and the soul of soulless conditions'.[53] This is part of Marx's argument (developed from Feuerbach's position) that religion, rather than being the *cause* of alienation (as, for example, a simplified reading of Max Weber),[54] is the *symptom* of social and economic alienation.[55] Such a position means, of course, that religion cannot be a solution to the problem of social and economic alienation, since it constitutes *part of the problem*. I have touched briefly upon this above, and we will see a similar argument in Marx's essay on the Jewish question with which I will engage in Chapter 6. For now, we need to understand what the tasks of history and philosophy are. They are not simply to analyse this world instead of the 'other world', but to analyse this world from the perspective of *this world* (materialist perspective), rather than from the perspective of the other world (idealist perspective). That is, once we realise that religion is *part of the problem of this world*, that it is a *symptom* of an alienated existence, then we can focus on addressing the alienated existence (the unholy forms of human self-estrangement) in itself, and that which constitutes it, instead of focusing on its symptoms.

---

52 Marx 1975 [1844], p. 176. Emphasis in original.
53 Ibid.
54 Weber's argument in the *The Protestant Ethic and the Spirit of Capitalism* was that Protestantism helped facilitate the development of the capitalist ethos. For a reading which allows for a more complex engagement with Weber, see Jameson 1973, especially pp. 70–9.
55 Boer 2012, p. 130. I have relied heavily on this excellent study to discuss the relationship between Marx and religion.

So, picture this book as squeezed in between the call to analyse this world from the perspective of this world and the realisation that religion is part of the problem, in that I analyse religion from the perspective of this world, and through this, demonstrate how religion is part of the problem. Thus, while my analysis of the Moravian Brethren might place them as a stellar example of being the heart of a heartless world, the role as a symptom is not a feature unique to this community. The Moravian Brethren are useful to understand the social transformations within the context of emerging capitalism, because of their ability to anticipate and negotiate socio-economic change at many different levels. To the residents of Herrnhut and my friends and colleagues within the Moravian community of today, I want to say that I cannot determine how you react to this study, of course. But it has been carried out in deep respect for and ongoing fascination with a most astonishing and under-appreciated history, which I find such an important part of our present world.

3   Outline of Chapters

After Chapter 1, which serves to describe the central term 'choir ideology' and provide some methodological clarification, the argument proceeds in three jumps, which roughly correspond to three larger sections.

Chapters 2–3 look at the emergence of the choir system as a way of overcoming class struggles in the community. Chapter 2 is a very detailed examination of the emergence of choir terminology and how it displaced other understandings of communal organisation. This is carried out chiefly through examination of the handwritten Herrnhut diaries from the mid-1730s to 1745. While this may seem an unnecessarily onerous task, it is a necessary step in my argument, namely that the choirs were not part of the beginnings of Herrnhut, as is sometimes assumed, but rather arose at a specific time, with a specific purpose. This is only possible to demonstrate through tracing in great detail the emergence of choir terminology.

Chapter 3 uses miscellaneous handwritten documents (minutes and correspondence) to look at the struggles that took place in 1744–45. The struggles were chiefly expressed through theological disagreements, and the leadership of the community pushed through the blood and wounds theology, and its focus on the Lamb, which resulted in a large purge of the community. However, this was more than merely theological discord. The victory of this theological line meant a strengthening of certain groups within the community and a weakening of others. Unsurprisingly, these follow class lines, with a weakening of the Moravian (*mährisch*) peasantry, a strengthening of the aristocracy and the upwardly mobile members, Moravian (*mährisch*) and otherwise.

Chapter 4 examines the consequences of this new theology, as expressed in the 'choir speeches', which are a group of 450 handwritten speeches given by Zinzendorf to the various choirs within the community between 1744 and his death in May 1760. The chapter, which is a very long one, is organised according to seven carefully selected choir speeches, which will be used as points of departure to discuss various central themes, such as body, inwardness, gender, marriage, and transition. What I aim to show in these subsections is how these categories are in the making and are part of the overall socio-economic transition to capitalism.

The choir system is a configuration of community, and rests largely on the imagery of the marriage between the Saviour and his church. This has been a very popular research topic, but can also function as a distraction from the actual function of marriage within the community, which was not without problems. Herrnhut consisted of a large number of single members and married couples, and the management of these various groups gave rise to multiple problems. Within socio-economic transitions gender relations and household structures are sensitive to change, and thus an analysis of marriage practice and marriage symbolism is an important part of understanding the disruptions. Chapter 5, then, is an analysis of the role of marriage in the choir ideology, and draws out the contradictions between the idea of marriage and the choir system.

The various points of Chapters 4 and 5 are followed up in Chapter 6, which pulls together these questions of class, community, and self, and discusses the ramifications of these social innovations in relation to the emergence of new understandings of self and statehood underway. This is the more theoretical chapter based on the findings in the preceding analysis, and serves to bring out the socio-economic relevance of archival details.

The final chapter, Chapter 7, is of a more philosophical character, and serves to draw out the historiographical and methodological implications of the argument in the preceding chapters. The thinking and rethinking, writing and rewriting of this book has thrown up numerous questions, especially regarding archival research, which have resulted or matured into a firm commitment to a dialectical, materialist history. What this entails, is better explained following the analysis rather than preceding it. The aim is, following Jameson, to finish in the realm of History, as the ultimate horizon of our experience.

But we begin in Herrnhut.

CHAPTER 1

Introducing Choir Ideology

1 Introduction

Choir (*das Chor*) was the term used by the Moravian Brethren in the eighteenth century to designate a group in the congregation based on its gender, age/maturity, and marital status: children's choir, girls' choir, boys' choir, single sisters' choir, single brothers' choir, married couples' choir, widows' choir, and widowers' choir. The largest and most important choirs were those of the single sisters and brothers, in that these constituted the main workforce of the community. For this reason, the single brothers and sisters lived in communal houses in nearly all the settlements of the Moravian Brethren in Europe. Some settlements also had a house for the widows, and a few had houses for the widowers' choir, and the girls' and boys' choirs. While the European communities were structured according to this system, the choirs were not always used in the colonies mostly due to practical reasons, such as size of congregations, livelihood, and, of course, colonial politics.[1]

The point in this book is that choirs were never only a way of organising a community, nor merely a practical approach to pastoral care, but were rather a significant disruption to material life as it had been known. As we will see, this communal structure challenged the traditional family structure, the guilds, and created a global community in which the individual congregations were embedded. In this sense, the Moravian Brethren took active part in the process

---

1 For example, the mission of the Moravian Brethren in Greenland made use of the choir structure for the first 40 years. In 1748 the first choirhouse was built in Greenland (sisters' house), the brothers' house in 1753, and several years later, the widows' house (and then also big girls' and big boys' houses). In 1783 the houses were discontinued, although the choirs as pastoral groups continued until the general dissolution of the practice in the course of the nineteenth century. In Bethlehem, Pennsylvania the choir houses were the backbone of the General Economy, which was a communal economy that financed the missions to the Native Americans. Before the Seven Years' War, Native converts had been living in the choirs, but during the racial tensions of the war, they were relocated to avoid attracting attention. The General Economy, which had begun in 1741, was dissolved in 1760–62, and transitioned to a German system, where the choirs were independent economic units. The single brothers' choir was dissolved entirely on 16 April 1814. The sisters' and widows' choirs continued until 1844–45, where Bethlehem became a borough through the acceptance of the Act of Incorporation. Engel 2009, pp. 182–90; Levering 1903, p. 688; Erbe 1929, p. 154.

so eminently presented by Isabel Hull in her concise and rich archival study of changes in eighteenth-century German society, where she showed how the emerging state sector strove to break down traditional forms of society, namely community, guilds, and family and from the ruins build the civil society and its distinction between public and private.[2]

The particular focus in the present study is on Herrnhut, which was founded in 1722. Other settlements followed, namely Heerendijk in Ijsselstein (1736), Pilgerruh in the duchy of Holstein (1737), Herrnhaag in the county Isenburg-Büdingen (1738), Niesky in the Oberlausitz (1742), Gnadenfrei in Prussia (1743), Neusalz in Prussia (1743), Fulneck in Yorkshire (1744), Gnadenberg in Prussia (1745), Zeist in the province of Utrecht, the Netherlands (1746), Ebersdorf in the duchy of Reuss-Ebersdorf (1746), Neuwied in the county Wied (1750), Ockbrook in Derbyshire (1750), Neudietendorf in the duchy of Sachsen-Gotha-Altenburg (1753), Sarepta in the Russian Empire (1755), Gracehill in Antrim (1765), Gnadau in Saxony (1767), Christiansfeld in the duchy of Schleswig (1773); Gnadenfeld in Prussia (1780), Fairfield in Lancashire (1785), Königsfeld in Württemberg (1807).

The reason to focus on Herrnhut is because it is the first community and thus the locus of all the early problems, such as the class struggles on which I will be focusing. These issues never quite arose with the same intensity in the later communities,[3] because lessons were learnt from Herrnhut, and the leaders knew what to avoid and where care had to be taken. Also, the hard-won experience of how to work most profitably within the structures of semi-feudal societies meant that newer settlements in underdeveloped regions of Europe, such as Christiansfeld in the duchy of Schleswig,[4] resulted in the Moravian Brethren streaking ahead of their competitors.

The present chapter serves to canvass what is meant by choir, choir speech, choir house, and choir ideology, through the archival material used in the present work. It thus functions as both conceptual and methodological clarification.

---

2 Hull 1996.
3 The following communities were settled with specific populations in mind. For example Niesky (1742) was intended for Bohemian refugees, as was the society in Rixdorf in Berlin. In her book on the Moravian refugees, Edita Sterik also notes that Pilgerruh and Herrnhaag were intended to house Moravians and Bohemians. Sterik 2012, pp. 272–5 and 307. Pilgerruh was disbanded in the late 1740s and sold off in 1751. Herrnhaag quickly became the new nerve-centre for 'enthusiastic youths', displacing the Moravian members. Sterik 2012, p. 325.
4 Fischer 2013. Thank you to Thomas Dorfner for alerting me to this article. See also Petterson 2018.

2 From Choir Speech to Choir Ideology

Between 1744 and 1760, Zinzendorf gave around 430 choir speeches in Herrnhut. Whereas choir (*Chor*) was the designated name for the groups into which the congregation was ordered, choir speeches were speeches given to the individual choirs by the leader of the choir or of the congregation. The context of a choir speech would typically be in connection with a worship service, after which the choirs would gather individually, and Zinzendorf or one of the other leaders would deliver a speech. The nature of the speeches could be reprimanding, encouraging, an exposition of scripture, or on the occasion of a particular celebration, for example a lovefeast.[5] The speeches are commonly headed by a caption noting the choir (e.g. the single sisters' choir), the date, sometimes the occasion (e.g. after the Eucharist), sometimes the location (Herrnhut) and sometimes the speaker (*Papa, Papagen, Jünger* – all names for Zinzendorf).[6] The speeches were not prepared in writing by Zinzendorf, but were written down during delivery. A speech to the widowers on 5 June 1755 notes that the speech which Zinzendorf gave at a lovefeast was from oversight not written down, and 'thus here only is the approximate content of what they noted and afterwards wrote up, and then corrected by the Disciple (*Jünger*)'.[7]

The significance of these speeches in contrast to, for example, the community speeches, is that the choir speeches were conceptualised and intended for internal use and edification, thus differing considerably in style and rhetorical application. Hence, the choir speeches condense the *inner* workings of the community ideology. It is the specific understanding of the community organisation as a choir structure and its subsequent intensification in the genre of choir speeches that I call *choir ideology*.

---

5   The lovefeast, the *agape*, was a simple liturgical meal and constituted one of several community building rituals. See Atwood 2004, pp. 161–3.

6   For example: Chor-Rede der led[igen] Schwestern d. 1 Jul. 1755 in Herrnhuth. gehalten von Papa – Choir speech to the single sisters, 1 July 1755 in Herrnhut, held by Papa (UA R.20.HS48). UA refers to the Unity Archives in Herrnhut. A note on the translation of the texts: Unless otherwise indicated, all translations of the original texts are my own and I have decided to follow the structure of the German original closely so as to bring out the strangeness of the texts, so as to emphasise the different historical context.

7   The full caption reads "Am 5ten Juny [1755] hatte das Wittwer Chor das große Vergnügen den theuren Jünger, in ihrer Mitte, bey einem Vergnüglichen L[iebes]Mahl zu genießen; zu deßen endigung Er eine ausführliche und Solide Chor-Rede an dieselbe hielte, die aber aus Versehen nicht nach geschrieben worden, und also hier nur was sie sich angemerckt, und nachher aufgeschrieben, und als denn vom Jünger corrigirt worden, ungefehr folgenden innhalts ist" (UA R.20.HS31). Paul Peucker notes that Zinzendorf did not write down things himself, but had men write it down, and then went through it afterwards. Peucker 2015, p. 178.

In her memoir (*Lebenslauf*),[8] Elisabeth Maria Lenzner (1730–80) notes that she encountered Zinzendorf's choir speeches during a visit he made to Ebersdorf in 1755 as something very special.[9] Given the extent of the copies of the speeches, their distribution and their redaction and continued use after Zinzendorf's death in 1760,[10] the choir speeches were indeed 'something special'

---

8   The memoirs (*Lebensläufe*) are memoirs of the members of the Moravian Brethren, and they depict, as the name suggests, the description of one's life, conversion and death. Some of the contents are written by the members themselves, with enhancements from others. In other cases, someone else, for example the sisters, whom someone shared a house with, compiled a memoir based on stories they heard. Some are quite long (six pages), while others are very brief, a note or half a page. The most generic type will begin by noting where and when the person was born, and then go on to describe the person's movements, training, conversion, life within the community, marriage, children etc. The main point is always when and how this person encountered 'the Saviour' and joined the community. Atwood 2004, p. 10. The Moravian Archives hold more than 40,000 of such texts which date back to events from the early eighteenth century. For the most important work on the memoirs, see Lost 2006; 2007; 2009. Faull 1997. See McCullough 2015 for a recent discovery of an eighteenth-century memorandum detailing what such a memoir should contain. The practice is traced to Zinzendorf's instruction from 1747 that 'the memoir of the departed person be read at the service of song, or *Singstunde*, on the day he or she was buried in order that one could wish "vale to their soul, just as when as a final gesture one gives a handshake and says farewell"', Faull 1997, p. xxxii, quoted in McCullough 2015, p. 161. Interestingly, I have stumbled upon mentions of this practice five times in the Herrnhut diary, where three of these occur at the funerals of aristocrats (UA R.6.A.b.16.1, 22. February 1743 at the funeral of Lehnel von Seidliz; UA R.6.A.b.17.a.1744.a, 30 July 1744 after the funeral of Brother von Seidliz; UA R.6.A.b.17.a.1745.a, 7 December 1745 at the funeral of Brother [von] Falkenhayn). Of the two remaining occurrences, the events surrounding the death of a Sister Hass is very interesting. Her funeral is noted on 5 February 1745 (UA R.6.A.b.17.a.1745.a, 5 February). What is interesting is that she only arrived in Herrnhut three weeks earlier as the maid of Herr Obristleutnant von Krassow, had never been to the *Saal*, and died with fervent wound-emotion. On 7 February, the diary notes that apart from a detailed account of the memoir, illness, and death of sister Hass, also the description of her blessed and enjoyable state on her sickbed, and of the funeral was sent to her former master, Herr Obristleutnant von Krassaw. This example is curious, in that much ado is made of a stranger. It is most likely that the wound-emotion and her servitude with the Lieutenant Colonel are the reason behind this, and that sending such a detailed account to him was a witness to the faith of the community.

9   Elisabeth Maria Lenzner (UA R.22.63.83).

10 Many of the speeches have a note in the margin indicating their subsequent redaction and use. See the list of speeches which were subsequently edited and distributed by the Unity of Elders Conference in "Register zu Graf Zinzendorfs Reden" (UA NB.II.420.1.II.b) Also, in the various diaries from Bethlehem Pennsylvania, there are frequent mentions of the readings of a choir speech by our dearest *Jünger*. See the diary of the single sisters' choir (MA BethSS) under 23 May 1758, which reads (in German): 'Brother Petrus read us

and, as I will argue, powerful and effective ideological instruments in interpellation and social engineering, producing the embryonic form of the fragmented, alienated subjects of the modern world.

As will become clear in the following chapters, choir is a strong ideological concept, which intended to produce unity, manage social relations and facilitate transition. However, the story did not quite begin in that way, and although I have taken great care to provide a coherent analysis, there might be several occasions where sediments of previous concerns arise. Therefore, I need to explain, briefly, how I arrived at this central category of analysis.

It began with the choir speeches. Focusing on these speeches was the suggestion of the then head archivist in Herrnhut, Rüdiger Kröger, after discussing my interests and objectives, which at the time mainly concerned sexuality and equality. Because they are unpublished, and thus handwritten, the choir speeches had not before been subjected to a comprehensive analysis. However, Zinzendorf was a keen and productive speaker, and the total amount of choir speeches amounts to several thousand. At a rather early stage of the project, when I realised just how many speeches there were, I was faced with the choice of focusing on all choir speeches given to one choir, say, the single sisters (Kröger's suggestion). Or I could choose a set of speeches from all communities within a specific timeframe (my initial approach). However, because I was interested in the socio-economic context in which the speeches arose, and what issues they were trying to resolve, the best solution seemed to be to choose the speeches from one particular location, which would enable me to provide a much more thorough socio-economic backdrop for the speeches than if I had chosen the broader approach. The decision to focus on Herrnhut was based on a naïve supposition that because it was the first community, it would also be blueprint for all others – as Henri Lefebvre said, every analysis begins reductively, and mine was certainly no exception. However, the more I read about the history of Herrnhut, archival and otherwise, I realised that this was not (in hindsight of course) a bad decision. Nowhere in the other communities are the issues of class so prevalent as in Herrnhut. Furthermore, the early social experimentation with groups, individuals etc., took place in Herrnhut.[11] As mentioned earlier, for the Unity leadership, valuable lessons were

---

a wonderful choir speech of the dear *Jünger*'. Also, on the 21 April 1761 we hear that they were read 'our unforgettable *Jünger*'s last choir speech from the 24th April 1760'. MA refers to the Moravian Archive in Bethlehem, Pennsylvania.

11   In her book, *Weltbürgertum oder Gottesreich*, Gisela Mettele does not regard the German context, and thus Herrnhut, as important for the Moravians in general. I shall return to this later, but for now note that she underemphasises this aspect in order to argue for the

learnt from Herrnhut in terms of what to do, and what *not* to do. But at this stage, I had moved outside the speeches, and had started to look at diaries, correspondence, and memoirs.

Then, during a presentation of my work in the Zinzendorf society, one of the members, Gerald McDonald, asked me whether I was interested in the 'choir structure' (which was what I presented) or the 'choir speeches' (which was what I insisted on being my main interest). I shall not bore you with the details of the epistemological crisis generated by this question, but merely indicate that the question eventually pushed me to realise that the choir structure of the community and the choir speeches are *both* products of Zinzendorf and his circle, and not two separate entities, as I had intimated in my presentation. The choir speeches, then, may be seen as an intensification of the ideology already expressed in the concept of the choirs, and as such *in their very form* indicate the socio-economic structures and transformations taking place, namely the emergence of capitalism and the modern state structure.

This potted history of the research process is intended to show how I came from choir speeches to choir ideology. But I need to add something else.

Four hundred and thirty digitised and transcribed speeches later, I had noticed that there were no choir speeches prior to 1744, which made me curious as to whether this was due to material which had been lost in fires, or whether this mode of address only really began there. I had also distilled several significant topics from the speeches (Jesus' corpse, the human body, individual, collective, gender, rank, blood, presence), from which I identified three abstract topics: unity, social relations, and transition. These two issues turned out to be connected, although it would take some time to realise this. So, in an attempt to resolve the first issue, the choir speeches, I combed through the handwritten diaries from 1736 to 1745 to see to what extent choir terminology was present in the daily activities of the community. The results of this exercise are presented in Chapter 2, but for present clarification, choir terminology does not begin to consolidate itself until the early 1740s. Half a year earlier, I had been co-preparing an archival document for publication – the so-called marriage document discussed in Chapter 3 – which had finally attuned me to the class issues between the Moravian (*mährisch*) peasants and the leadership of the community. This document, which testifies to the struggles

---

Moravians as "anti-bürgerlich" and, more importantly, because she sees in these dissenting religious communities the chance for historical analysis beyond the nation state, thereby moving towards a transnational social space (Mettele 2009).

between old and new ways of thinking about marriage,[12] suddenly provided the context and connection between the emergence of choir terminology in the 1740s, and the emphasis on particularly unity and relations in the speeches: The Herrnhut community had been riven by severe conflicts to which the choir speeches were an attempted solution. These conflicts were a tangle of class and authority struggles and were expressed through the emerging choir structure and the theological changes taking place in the community in these years.

In pulling all of this together into a coherent presentation (this book), I have included more material from diaries, correspondence, memoirs, and miscellaneous documents, and less from the speeches, than originally intended. Thus, it is only Chapters 4 and 5 in which the speeches are explicitly analysed. However, as this brief tour of the developments of the project show, the speeches have been absolutely fundamental in discerning the choir ideology, understanding the significance of the choir structure, and fully appreciating the influence of Christianity on the formation of civil society.

3   What Is the Function of a Choir?

There are a number of speeches where Zinzendorf clarifies what a choir is, what the nature of a particular choir is and what the particular characteristics are or should be. Zinzendorf refers to choir at two interconnected levels: the choir sister, who is the individual of the choir, and the choir of which she is a member. In this way, the choir designates a collective as well as a collective of individuals. A good example may be found in the speech to the widows, on 6 September 1755:

> It is true that when many different kinds of people are together, then they can in their different classes[13] among themselves in their own way be blessed. Whoever is faithful, he is perfect to himself and to Him. However,

---

12   Paul Peucker, head archivist of the Moravian Archives in Bethlehem, has been very encouraging and helpful in discussing this and other documents which helped me make sense of this in my analysis. I would like to take this opportunity to express my gratitude for his support and encouragement.

13   Classes are groups within the choirs that separate the members according to degrees of grace, i.e. according to their state of conversion. This means that in their class meetings, such a subdivision enables more targeted conversations dealing with specific problems. We return to this in the following chapter.

if everyone were to be together, imagine what kind of noble and blessed choir they could constitute? [...] Therefore, the choir should in time be constituted by such Hannas,[14] who never leave the temple [...] This, the whole choir, every class, and every soul, of their own experiences with less or more words, should be able to bear witness towards those who request it.[15]

This quotation shows the distinction between an individual believer and the power of the choir. Zinzendorf does not deny that the blessed state can be achieved by the individual, but emphasises that this can be multiplied in the choir, that the choir, as more than the sum of its blessed parts, would be even more blessed. The emphasis is not only on the collective, but also on the individual.

Choirs for Zinzendorf are primarily relations, which he expresses frequently in the speeches: the correct relations with the Saviour (the *Heiland*, i.e. Jesus), with each other, and with the other choirs. The choirs then constitute a group of, say, maidens or widowers,[16] which all relate in their own distinct ways to the Saviour. Each group is addressed according to this principle, and the members' relationship to the Saviour is expounded over and over again. While the speeches all are examples of relating the various choirs to the person of the Saviour, the most powerful imagery and consistent relations appear in the speeches to the single brothers and sisters. The single brothers had close affinity to the Saviour because of the Saviour's identity as a single man. By force of collective (chaste) mind, they are able to summon the presence of 'the Saviour' and engage with him. Their individual ideal is to strive to become like the Saviour's corpse, which means being able to govern one's passions. The single sisters constituted the main symbol in Zinzendorf's conceptualisation of the

---

14 This is a reference to Luke 2:36–38, when Joseph and Mary bring the infant Jesus to the temple in Jerusalem, they encounter (H)anna, the widowed prophetess who worships at the temple day and night.

15 Widows, 6 September 1755 "Es ist wahr, daß wenn mancherley Arten von Menschen beysamen sind, so können sie doch in ihren verschiedenen Classen unter sich auf Ihre Art selig seyn. Wer nur treu ist, der ist *an sich* und auch *Ihm* vollkommen. Wenn aber alle beysamen wären, was kön[n]ten sie nicht für ein ehrwürdiges und seliges Chor ausmachen? [...] Darum soll das Chor mit der Zeit aus lauter solchen Hannen bestehen, die nimmer vom Tempel kommen [...] Das muß das ganze Chor eine jede Classe und eine jede Seele, aus eigner Erfahrung, mit wenig oder mehr Worten, bezeugen können, denen, die darnach fragen". (UA R.20.HS46).

16 Maiden is a translation of the German *Jungfern*, which is more usual in the earlier material. Single sisters is slightly later designation.

ideal believer and the community as a whole, in that their chaste souls became the ideal for which everyone was to strive, and the condition to which everyone was to return in the hereafter, as participants in the collective virgin bride of the Saviour, the eternal bridegroom.

The speeches also demonstrate how the relation to the Saviour is a way of mediating the transition between the choirs. In one of the earliest speeches, Zinzendorf deliberates on how, when a child steps into the rank of boy, 'then it must be given to him what he needs to bring his boyhood to the boy Jesus, in whom he believes and whose name he carries'.[17] The point of this is to highlight the process of identification between 'Jesus the boy' and the boys. When a child becomes a boy in the community (i.e. when he transitions into the boys' choir), he is regarded as carrying Jesus' name, and thus must live up to a certain moral standing.

Another example is from a speech to the single brothers from 1756, where Zinzendorf speaks of the likeness between the Saviour and a brother:

> He was like any human and in behaviour made as a human, in every part from year to year he was like any child, small boy, boy, youngling, a man. [...] The human age goes its proper course without reflection on the circumstances in which one can come from outside, whether one begins a family, or remains for himself, then one becomes a man and finally an old man. Presumably his last days will not be far from a kind of *marasmus senilis*. The Saviour has gone through all this for our benefit. He even gave his Johannes the pleasure that he appeared to him in the form of an old and 90 something-year-old man, whose hair was white like the snow.[18]

---

17 Boys, 5 November 1747, "Sobald einer also in der Gemeine ein Knabe heist, so muß ihm gleich das gegeben werden, was er braucht, seinen Knaben-Stand dem Knaben Jesu, den er bekennt und deßen Namen er trägt, zu Ehren zu führen". (UA GN.C.2 1747).

18 Single brothers, 19 May 1756 "Er war wie ein andere Mensch und an gebehrden als ein Mensch erfunden, in allen Theilen von Jahr zu Jahr war Er wie ein andere, ein Kind, ein Knäbgen, ein Knabe, ein Jüngling, ein Mann. [...] Das Menschliche Alter geht seinen ordentlichen Gang ohne reflexion auf die Umstände, darin man von aussen kommen kann, ob mann eine familie anfängt, oder für sich bleibt, so wird mann ein Mann und endlich ein altvater. Vermuthlich sind seine lezten tage von der Art eines marasmi Senilis nicht fern gewesen. Das alles hat der Heyland durchgestanden uns zu gut. Er hat seinem Johannes noch das Vergnügen gemacht, daß er Ihm in der Gestallt eines alten etlich und 90 jährigen Mannes, dessen Haare weiß waren, wie der Schnee, erscheinen ist". (UA R.20.HS58).

The point is, and we will return to this again and again, that the Saviour has gone through all stages of life, and this for the sake of the individuals as support throughout their lives. He even was an old man, Zinzendorf notes, in reference to Revelation 1:12–16.

Another central motif in the speeches, to which we return in Chapter 4, is the frequent invocation of the body of the Saviour and the constant presence of the Saviour in the choirs. The real character of a choir, Zinzendorf states, is that it places the Saviour 'in his choirshape' in front of its [the choir's] eyes.[19] Zinzendorf uses graphic and affective language to paint the Saviour before the eyes of their listeners and thus make them feel his presence. This is then not the old trope of the community constituting the body of Christ, but with few exceptions, the body of the Saviour standing over against the community as a distinct figure.[20] This then means that the figure of the Saviour no longer serves as that which unites the community, but that this is the function of the choir, whose structure and organisation ensured a fairly tight community identity. As Hanns-Joachim Wollstadt notes in his fine book on the formative years of the congregation: 'By means of the group, the brother and the sister were incorporated (*eingegliedert*) into the community so strongly that they without attachment to a group in no way could have belonged to the collective community'.[21]

These topics will all be expanded upon in the following, but for now I want to emphasise that the choir speeches present the choirs as sites of unity, as a space of learning correct forms of social relations, and as such vehicles of change. Keeping in mind the rapid changes taking place at this time in this part of the world, providing a space within which change can be safely tempered and managed within the cogs of the larger socio-economic shifts was nothing short of a stroke of genius.

4   Methodology

When I began working with the material, I did not know how to find what I was looking for. At first, second, and third glance, the choir speeches displayed a bewildering array of neologisms, bizarre metaphors, foreign words and streams

---

19   Single brothers, 15 April 1748 "Das ist also der eigentliche Character eines Chors das sich den Heiland in seiner Chor-Gestalt so vor die Augen stellt, als wenns wirklich mit ihm lebte" (UA R.20.HS35).
20   See a fuller analysis of the differences in Petterson 2015.
21   Wollstadt 1966, p. 120.

of emotive speech without obvious coherence, and I was not sure how to distil socio-economic change from such material. In other words, what I was looking for was not there directly, and I was not sure what form it would take. Assistance materialised from the quarters of Marxist literary criticism, namely in Georg Lukács and Fredric Jameson.

In his 1936 essay on Johann Wolfgang von Goethe's *The Sorrows of Young Werther*,[22] Georg Lukács makes two observations that are important for the present book. First, he notes the tendency to separate the Enlightenment from the 'Sturm und Drang' of German Classicism and Romanticism, despite the fact that such a separation is tenuous, to say the least. Goethe's *Werther*, from 1774, is commonly associated with the latter, although even 'bourgeois literary historians' are forced to recognise the literary connection with Rousseau and Richardson, who both are regarded as Enlightenment thinkers.[23] Directly connected to this is Lukács' second point, namely that in *Werther*, the 'internal contradictions of revolutionary bourgeois humanism [are manifested] for the first time in world literature in a great poetic creation'. According to Lukács, Goethe staged the conflicts between the emotions of the self and the rules of society, 'the contradictions between human passions and social legality',[24] but this socio-economic aspect was rejected in the reception of the work. Henceforth, the role of *Werther* in 'the universal revolutionary expressions of bourgeois ideology in the preparatory period of the French Revolution',[25] was reduced to a love story, and relegated to the movements of Classicism and Romanticism.[26]

The importance of this for the present work lies in what Lukács calls the 'ideological need' to separate the Enlightenment from German Classicism, and how the narrative of Werther and its staging of conflicts and values *belies* this very separation, and shows how ideologically motivated such a partition actually is. The question which Lukács poses, and with which we should concern ourselves, is: should we analyse 'early modernity' within the ideological parameters set by modernity? If one of the salient characteristics of modernity is the compartmentalisation of human life into supposedly independent spheres of reality (such as sexuality, economy, and religion), should we then approach religious themes in early modern sources (or anywhere) as an already existing

---

22   Lukács 1968, pp. 35–49.
23   Lukács 1968, pp. 35–6.
24   Lukács 1968, pp. 41–2.
25   Lukács 1968, pp. 43–4.
26   The most obvious example is Napoleon, whom Lukács notes (p. 46) reproached Goethe for introducing a social conflict into a love tragedy.

independent field? Or should we assume, following Lukács, that the compartmentalisation, the move that relegates e.g. religion to the private sphere, serves ideological purposes? Furthermore, Lukács' attention to the figure of Werther, as the literary manifestation of these struggles, shows where we might look for tensions and contradictions in material which addresses these things indirectly, namely in the understanding of the person, the subject of the new age. While Lukács thus provided a fruitful way into the material, he did not solve the problem of bridging the gap between the material and its context, between the choir speeches and socio-economic change.

Fredric Jameson's work on form proved to be very useful for overcoming this gap,[27] which, as outlined above, has haunted the project throughout. And the solution, once it appeared, was so obvious that it is almost embarrassing to state it here: *The choir speech as a genre presupposes the existence of choirs.*

I shall return to Jameson and form in the final chapter, where I will use it to draw out the theoretical implications of what I have been arguing in the book and remain at a more concrete level here. The choir structure and the social relations it produces are a significant departure from the feudal household. First of all, in its practical organisation: The entire community envisioned as being one household; each house contained a single gender; and each house contained members of the local aristocracy and peasants from the surrounding countryside as well as from Moravia and Bohemia. This means that whereas before, the feudal household and its familial relations would have the mediating role between individual and society, it is now the community and its choir structure that fulfil this role. Second, while the centre of the household remained patriarchal with the Saviour and/or Zinzendorf at the head, there was an increased attention to the individual and its relation to the larger whole: the choir, the household, and the global community of brothers and sisters, which was growing and with whom connections were maintained through a vast network of communication and information exchange.[28]

Although choir speeches are far from the genre of the novel formidably analysed by Jameson, attention to their formal aspects may yield important insights, as well as support a non-compartmentalised reading. First of all, as mentioned earlier, they were intended for internal use and not published. This meant, at one level, that they were retained in manuscript form and a more uninhibited style,[29] but more importantly, that they presuppose a distinction

---

27 Jameson 1972 and 1981.
28 Mettele 2009, Chapter 3.
29 In his discussion of Zinzendorf's discourses and addresses, Paul Peucker argues that the

between public and non-public usage.[30] This is a significant departure from the practice of Lutheran orthodoxy and Halle Pietism, and I will discuss this further in Chapter 6.

Second, as speeches they intend to affect, and this is where their nature as *choir* speech becomes important, because the intent with the choir structure was precisely to mediate between the gendered individual and the group, which is also evident from the content of the speeches. This has been the overarching focus of the textual analysis of the choir speeches.

I have proceeded as follows. After a number of failed attempts at presenting important topics within the various speeches, I have instead chosen to present a number of different speeches, which include one or two central issues on which I then elaborate. In the back of my mind, this analysis roughly follows three abstract concepts of unification, social relations, and transition, which grew out of the initial analysis. Unification refers to the suppression of class struggle, and the expulsion of thoughts and practices which are not in line with the emerging trajectory. While the speeches serve to consolidate the winning position, and thus do not as such express the struggle directly, Chapters 2 and 3 look at the emergence of the choirs as containing the key

---

       handwritten addresses express Zinzendorf's more unconventional ideas about the disappearance of the differences between the sexes and marriage, because these are seen as special revelations, which are not to be shared with outsiders. Peucker 2015, p. 178.

30   In a choir speech to the widowers in Herrnhut on 31 July 1755, Zinzendorf states that, 'because choir discourses are different from community-speeches, then it is of concern to me that I pitch the subject matter correctly, and would like to see that it has real usefulness for the choir'. Widowers, 31 July 1755: "Weil Chor discourse was anders sind als Gemein-Reden; so liegt mir an, daß ich die Materie recht treffe und möchte, die einen realen Nüzen für das Chor haben könte". (UA R.20.HS31).

       In another speech, to the married choir in Herrnhut from 1757, he spends time deliberating over the damage to the reputation of the Moravian Brethren caused by the publication of a number of speeches given to the married choir. He is horrified that someone would have taken something 'to which he had no right' and then lose it. However, he notes, 'the benefit of this will be that I let be printed all of the spousal-speeches that have given, which thus will come out among people, bringing them out among them was not the intention; but now it is necessary in order to protect against the damage, which can come from incorrect things, since whoever has copied this [even sometimes written something entirely different], or, what he has not had, has supplemented from his head'. Married choir, 9 January 1757: "Der Nuzen wird draus kommen, daß ich alle Ehe-Reden drucken laße, die ich gehalten habe, und also unter die Menschen kommen wird, was nicht die intention war, unter sie zu bringen; aber nun zu Verhütung des Schadens notwendig ist, der aus falschen dingen kommen kan, da, wer so etwas nach geschrieben oder, was er nicht gehabt, aus seinem Kopf supplirt hat". (UA R20.HS 54).

to the struggles. The focus in the analysis of the speeches will be on the constant attempts at unification, most notably in the use of the terms choir and *Stand*.

5 The Choirs as Vanishing Mediators

The choirs themselves are socio-economic structures. With the emphasis on communal, gender-segregated houses, they are a marked deviation from the household structures of the surrounding feudal society, and their social relations.[31] In not adhering to social norms, they provide the opportunity to conceptualise new understandings of relations, gender, self, and community – experiments whose most radical expression was the period of sexual and theological excess known as the Sifting Time,[32] but also had more lasting effects beyond these events. Thus, by comparing the various speeches and their pedagogical undertakings, it becomes possible to discern differing patterns of gender, corporeal relations, and contexts and objectives of self-examination, which then again must be examined in relation to prevailing understandings personhood and the Saviour.

With this in mind, the choirs are best understood as 'vanishing mediators', a concept developed by Fredric Jameson in his analysis of *Wertfreiheit*, rationalisation and religion in the life and work of Max Weber. A vanishing mediator is 'a catalytic agent which permits an exchange of energies between two otherwise mutually exclusive terms', an especially powerful tool for analysing historical change.[33] In the section of Jameson's analysis that deals with the role of religion in Weber's *The Protestant Ethic and the Spirit of Capitalism*, the two mutually exclusive terms are medieval thought and modern thought. What happens, according to Jameson, in Protestantism is first that Luther's attack on the monasteries actually liberates the nascent rationalism (life and work ordered by time) of monastic life, which now is dispersed into everyday life. He thus paves the way for Calvin's inner-worldly asceticism, which means

---

31 For a general description of feudal households in the various estates see Gray 2000.
32 In his formidable book on this enigmatic period in the history of the Moravian Church, Paul Peucker argues that the Sifting Time was a period in which certain groups within the Moravian Church, led by Zinzendorf's son, Christian Renatus/Christel, declared themselves in a state of perfection and sinlessness, and engaged in extramarital sex. Peucker 2015, pp. 104–34.
33 Jameson 1973, p. 78.

that the crucial transformation on the level of means, from a traditional and non-rationalistic organization, to a rational and quantified one in modern times, has been effectuated within the framework, or better still, beneath the cover, of an intensified 'religionalization' of ends [...].³⁴

The separation of means from ends, with which Weber operates, shows that it is in Calvinism that the proper rationalisation of means and religionalisation of ends takes place, and Jameson identifies the crucial point as the change in means – because once the task of opening up for a rationalisation of inner-worldly life has taken place, Protestantism no longer has a reason for being, and 'disappears from the historic scene'.³⁵

Thus, when the usefulness of the mediator is over, it is dismantled and removed – hence 'vanishing'. Turning to the choirs with this in mind, I want to argue that the choir must be seen as part of the larger transitional process to capitalism, where the emerging state is trying to break down the traditional intermediate authorities, namely the community, the guilds, and the household.³⁶ When the transition was 'completed' and feudalism sufficiently dismantled, the choirs dissipated – in the mid-nineteenth century. I will argue that while the motivation for such a communal organisation *could* be seen as 'purely' theological or pastoral, this was enabled by certain non-theological conditions, and furthermore had large ramifications for structuring a society and reshaping it as a collection of individuals.

It will be a constant argument in this book that the Moravian choirs were, above all, vehicles of change. If we estimate that between the 1740s to the 1840s, the choirs were the central organisational framework for most Moravian communities, it is not difficult to see that this structure was in use during some of the most tumultuous years of the modern world. In anticipating the alienated subject of the bourgeois state, the decline of the choirs with the emergence and consolidation of this social structure in Europe should come as no surprise. And yet, such an analysis might still come as a surprise for those who insist on regarding religion from the perspective of modernity and within the parameters of civil society. As should be clear by now, what I want to demonstrate in this book is the possibility of seeing the Moravians as part of the *process* of secularisation, fragmentation and rationalisation that characterised the eight-

---

34 Jameson 1973, p. 76.
35 Jameson 1973, p. 78.
36 This emergence of a new state structure and its destruction of earlier forms is persuasively argued by Hull 1996.

eenth century, instead of relegating the Moravians, and religion in general, to a private, innocuous, and insignificant sphere.

To sum up briefly before moving on to Chapter 2, which traces the emergence of choir terminology, the current chapter has been an attempt to map out the process of interpretative choices and challenges. This has been a necessary clarification, because of the convoluted process of working with this archival material over several years, and the changes in focus, which have left layer upon layer of analysis and argument – some no longer obvious, but nevertheless assumed. The most important feature to grow from this midden is the development of choir ideology as a central component in the history of Herrnhut, and its socio-economic developments. Choir ideology includes the speeches, the organisation, the subjectification (individual and collective) and the houses. Such an ideological structure, which provides the basic needs, namely livelihood and community, created a passage through turbulent times.

CHAPTER 2

The Choirs – A Genealogy

1 Introduction

In the carefully prepared (and successful) application for the World Heritage listing presented to UNESCO by the Moravian settlement in Denmark, Christiansfeld (1773), the report lists the 29 towns which the Moravians built in the years 1722–1807 in Europe and North America. Of the 27 considered in the report, 15 settlements had a minimum of three choir houses, that is, the sisters' house, brothers' house, and widows' house;[1] nine settlements had two choir houses, that of the sisters and that of the brothers; two had only one house and one had none.[2] These statistics indicate that the choir structure and its segregated dwellings were a fundamental feature of the life and practice of the Moravian Brethren in the eighteenth century. This was not the case from the beginning, however. The first Brother-house in Herrnhut was not inaugurated until 1740,[3] and the first Sister-house was built in 1755.[4] So how and why did the choirs begin? Given that the argument of the present book is that the choirs constitute significant ideological and economic units, it is important to trace their emergence, conceptualisation, and function.

While the formation of the town of Herrnhut itself is dated to 1722, the formation of the community as a cohesive unit is dated to 1727. Between 1722 and 1726 Herrnhut had grown rapidly with an influx of more Moravians (*Mähren*) as well as peasants, artisans, and nobles from the German surroundings.[5] The internal tensions of the various groups had come to a head in 1726 and Zinzendorf returned to his estate from Dresden to overcome this 'separatist crisis'.[6] With everyone having 'his head to himself',[7] Zinzendorf faced the task of establishing a community out of these fractions and creating order. This task became

---

1 Namely Bethlehem, Pennsylvania; Christiansfeld, Denmark; Fulneck and Gracehill in England; Sarepta in Russia; Zeist in the Netherlands; Gnadenberg, Gnadenfeld, Gnadenfrei, Neusaltz, all in Poland; Ebersdorf, Herrnhaag, Herrnhut, Königsfeld and Neuwied in Germany.
2 Berg, Marcussen, and Stoklund 2013. For the criteria see p. 315; for the statistical list see p. 325.
3 Uttendörfer 1925, p. 87. Bechler 1922.
4 Uttendörfer 1926, p. 245. Bechler 1922, p. 55.
5 In the much-anticipated study of early Herrnhut mentioned earlier, Paul Peucker deals in great detail with these important early years.
6 Uttendörfer 1925, p. 17.
7 Wollstadt 1966, p. 25.

clear through extensive conversations with the individual residents and the various groups. In his thorough analysis of the early community in Herrnhut in the eighteenth century, Hanns-Joachim Wollstadt illustrates how ideas of smaller groups emerged in these early years (1726–27) as an attempt to mediate between the needs of individuals within the community and the community itself.[8] These bonded groups (*Banden*) or associations (*Gesellschaften*) were loosely structured at first, but would in a couple of years become more formalised.[9] Also the name of the groups changed and their parameters were redefined, as we will see in the present section. By 1744 a full structure was in place, which saw the community organised according to groups now called choirs, into which the congregation was divided according to sex, age, and marital status: children's choir, older girls' choir, older boys' choir, single sisters' choir, single brothers' choir, married sisters' choir, married brothers' choir, widows' choir, and widowers' choir. Even then, however, it would be a mistake to think of it as a fixed structure, since the fluctuations within the choirs continued, and the use of choirs in the different communities differed, as mentioned above. Nevertheless, the choir system was the basic ideological structure of the community until the mid-nineteenth century.

The source of the conflicts of the early community are commonly discussed in religious terms.[10] However, as we will discuss in the next chapter, it would be pertinent also to consider the issue of class in these conflicts, given that the Moravian (*mährisch*) refugees were mainly peasants and artisans, while the German settlers were a mix of nobility, artisans and peasants. Furthermore, the statutes which were drawn up as a kind of constitution do not mention religious conflict, but are more concerned with social cohesion and responsibility for the community. These conflicts were *managed* through the years by shifting and dividing the groups into smaller groups, but they were not resolved. Through the years, the material shows an immense shuffling and reshuffling of the community, especially in 1744–45. These years are particularly interesting, in that the choir structure is intensified in a number of ways: The gender segregation is strengthened and more severely policed. In these years each choir founded a special anniversary day, which was marked with founding myths. And finally, these are the years in which the so-called 'choir speeches', which constitute our main archival material in Chapters 4 and 5, emerge. The following sections will outline these developments, beginning with a summary of the developments from bonded group to choir, followed by a detailed examination

---

8   Ibid.
9   See the excellent and detailed analysis in Schmidt 1909.
10 Meyer 2009, pp. 24–6. Wollstadt 1966, pp. 24–30.

of the vocabulary in the archival material. Then, I trace the coming into being of the Day of All Choirs, an annual celebration held on 25 March, and finish off with a section on the choir houses. All of this serves to demonstrate that the choir system was not a given from the beginning of Herrnhut, that it differs from the organisation and function of the bonded groups, and that it signals a new direction in the community.

2   Overview of the Genealogy

While the idea to organise the community in smaller groups rose at an early stage from the necessity to overcome serious tensions within the nascent community as mentioned above, the word 'choir' did not appear until several years later, namely in 1737.[11] Even then the term was not used exclusively or even frequently in the archival sources until the early 1740s, as we will see. I will argue that the choirs did not seamlessly evolve from the existing smaller groups known as bonded groups (*Banden*) or associations (*Gesellschaften*) in the early community as is frequently claimed, but that the choirs were the result of a later, and partially separate, development.[12]

That something new was taking place shows up in the displacement of the 'apostolic community'. The ideal of the earliest, i.e. apostolic Christian church was imperative in the early days of the community, and undoubtedly connected to the Pietist foundations of early Herrnhut.[13] However, at the Gotha synod in 1740, in a discussion of the choirs, Zinzendorf stated:

> Thus we do not want to pass ourselves off as a Biblical [establishment], but rather as a Moravian Brethren establishment, which they had in old times, only that ours is more refined and orderly than that of the old Brethren, they had not purified it enough. And even if it were neither biblical nor Moravian, the circumstances in which we stand demand it. It is now a whole new world.[14]

---

11   Schmidt notes that Christian David does not use the term in his 'Description of Herrnhut' from 1735. Schmidt 1909, p. 150.
12   Both Wollstadt and Schmidt are appropriately careful in their terminology. Less careful are Uttendörfer 1925, pp. 83–97; Bechler 1922, pp. 47–63; Gollin 1967, pp. 67–89.
13   This was also connected to the Pietist Gottfried Arnold's of the early Christian community in his less famous first book, *The First love: that is, a true Portrait of the earliest Christians according to their living Faith and holy life* from 1696. See Wollstadt 1966, pp. 42–8.
14   "Wir wollens also vor keine Biblische, sondern vor eine Mährische Brüder Einrichtung ausgeben, die hatten sie schon in alten Zeiten, nur daß unsere noch mehr raffinirt und

The new world and new circumstances demand a different social structure, which is neither the biblical/Pietist community structure, nor the cruder Moravian (*mährisch*) community structure, but the distinctive Moravian choir system. The overall argument of this book, as already mentioned, is that the choirs were exceptionally efficient means of transitioning between the old and new worlds, which is why I engage at this level of detail. In my argument, the emergence of the choirs is part of Zinzendorf's increased control of the community and this emergence expresses the shift from Moravian (*mährisch*) theology, its practice and its organisation, to the hierarchical choir structured community under the leadership of the Lamb expressed in a blood and wounds theology. Therefore, it is necessary, as mentioned earlier, to establish precisely when these structures emerged and were strengthened. I have sifted through the handwritten diaries from Herrnhut from 1736 to 1745, in order to trace the development in terminology. But first, as mentioned, a more general overview to situate the more detailed archival presentation.

The year 1736 is my beginning point for the following reason.[15] In his article on the bonded groups and associations in old Herrnhut, Gottfried Schmidt argues that 1736 was a crucial year for the development of the Moravian Brethren and a turning point in the role of the bonded groups, both of which are connected through the banishment of Zinzendorf from Saxony.[16] Zinzendorf's forced exile meant that a new centre was established for the community, namely in the Wetterau in Western Germany, in Herrnhaag. Schmidt's point is that the bonded groups in Herrnhut 'had developed out of very idiosyncratic historical conditions', namely from the desire to build one close-knit community in which trust and intimacy was cultivated and nurtured, as also mentioned by Wollstadt. Schmidt notes that in the communities founded after 1736, the conditions were different, and in these the bonded groups could find no place or use. He sees two ways in which circumstances have changed. First, the sense of community is a given, and does not need to be cultivated. Second, by being released from the local confinement of Herrnhut, the nature, or as Schmidt puts it, its character, underwent a change.[17] The change he connects with Pietism in Halle, and Zinzendorf's gradual distancing from this theolo-

---

  ordentlicher ist, als der alten Brüder ihre; sie hattens nicht ausgeklärt genug. Und wenns auch nicht biblisch noch mährisch wäre, so erforderten es doch die Umstände, in denen wir stehen. Es ist ietzo eine gantz neue Welt" (UA R.2.A.3.A.1).

15 The end year, 1745, is chosen because at this point the choir ideology is firmly in place.
16 Schmidt 1909, p. 192.
17 Schmidt 1909, p. 196.

gical direction.[18] As the quote from Gotha above also shows, he has an excellent case for connecting the changing circumstances with the change in character and for seeing the local disentanglement in relation to Halle. Because the early years have been dealt with in depth by Schmidt, Uttendörfer, and Wollstadt, I have chosen to focus on the period where the term choir began to gain traction from its initial scattered appearances.

In the records from a community, or congregation day (*Gemeintag*) from 5 October 1737, the following structure is outlined by Zinzendorf:[19]

1. On choirs, there are actually 8./ 7 belong to here.[20] Men, women, widows, young men, maidens, boys, girls and 8, the children, the reason for this division is that one can more easily work with them, their workers are the same as them, because they sometimes have issues to speak with each other in confidence and much danger is avoided, what is publicly spoken about and worked though in the choirs.[21]
2. Classes, these are organised on the basis of the amount or degree of grace, for example the manly, childlike, confused, willing, dead, moved, recalcitrant,[22] when it becomes taken for granted it must be abolished at once.
3. Bonded groups or associations (*Banden oder Gesellschaften*) of such people who relate to each other childlike, full of love and trust [...].[23]

---

18   Both Wollstadt and Peucker point to the role of primitive Christianity as presented by Gottfried Arnold in his *Erste Liebe*. Peucker notes that the appeal of this ideal deteriorated in the course of the 1740s, and connects it with Zinzendorf's desire to situate his community as a progression from early Christianity, not a regression thereto. Peucker 2009, p. 28.

19   See also the 'Eventualtestament', which is the will Zinzendorf left behind on his first trip to North America in 1738. Here he also deliberates over the nature of choirs, classes, and *Gesellschaften*. Discussed in Schmidt 1909, pp. 152–3.

20   This formulation is somewhat enigmatic. It probably means that there are eight choirs, but only seven are present in Herrnhut, because the children, who constitute the eighth choir, are in Großhennersdorf.

21   Wollstadt incorrectly reads the sentence 'that one can more easily work with them, their workers are the same as them, because they sometimes have issues to speak with each other in confidence' as referring to the big classes (see below), whereas it here clearly belongs to the definition of the choirs. Wollstadt 1966, pp. 106–7. Admittedly Uttendörfer, from whom Wollstadt is quoting, is less than clear in his presentation of the matter. See Uttendörfer 1912, p. 144.

22   These terms all relate to the level of faith, and whether one is at the beginning (willing), one is totally resistant (recalcitrant, dead), seeking (willing, confused) or advanced (manly, childlike).

23   UA R.6.A.b.13.b, 5 October 1737: 1. Von Cöhren, Es sind eigentlich 8/7 gehören nur hieher. Männer, Weiber, Witwen, Burschen, Jungfern, Knaben, Mätgen, und 8 die Kleinen Kinder, die ursach zu dießer eintheilung ist die, daß man beqvemer an ihnen arbeiten kan, die

THE CHOIRS – A GENEALOGY 43

Here, choir is presented as the overarching structure, within which we find the subgroups of classes and bonded groups/associations. This is indeed what will emerge in Herrnhut, but not for many years. The structural changes took years to implement as we will see in the diaries. But, because of the bewildering nature of the terminology in the diaries, a brief breakdown of the terms and their histories may useful before we emerge ourselves fully into the details of the Herrnhut diaries. Since our main concern are the choirs, I rely mainly on the works of others to ascertain the function of the bonded groups/associations and classes before the advent of the choir system.

2.1 Bonded Groups (*Banden*)

Bonded groups is a term intimately connected with the first years in Herrnhut from their beginning in 1727 until 1736.[24] They were voluntary gatherings within which the members in trust could talk, counsel, pray, and help carry each other's burdens – in short, gatherings of mutual edification.[25] Schmidt identifies a number of functions for the bonded groups, the primary one being an organisation whose purpose was the community's religio-moral education by the members to each other. They are thus not prayer groups, but meetings where one talked with each other, and through these conversations identified and obliterated the old sourdough and fostered obedient and righteous hearts.[26] He notes that corresponding to this purpose and the voluntary nature of the bonded groups, they were constantly subject to change.[27] In contrast to

---

   Arbeiter sind von ihres gleichen, weil sie einerley sachen haben, vertrauter mit einander reden und viel gefahr vermieden wird – was öffentlich geredet, und in Cöhren durch gearbeitet.
   2. Classen, diese sind wegen die Menge oder nach dem Grad der Gnade eingerichtet e.g. die Männlichen, kindlich Confusen, willigen, todten, bewegten, wiederspünztigen Gemüther, wenns aber zur Gewohnheit werden will, mus mans gleich abschatten.
   3. Banden oder gesellschafften solcher Leute die mit einander kindlich, liebreich und vertraut umgehen.

24 Ibid.
25 See the function of bonded groups in early Herrnhut in Wollstadt 1966, pp. 93–9.
26 Schmidt 1909, pp. 153–4. The reference to sourdough comes initially from the Hebrew bible, and is taken up in the New Testament. It refers to the Jewish custom of getting rid of all leavened bread from the houses before Passover each year in remembrance of the escape from Egypt (Exodus 12.15; 13.6–8), and is in the Christian tradition (1 Corinthians 5.7) used as an expression of beginning afresh, as is the case here.
27 Schmidt 1909 has examples on pp. 155–6, footnote 22. See also examples in the diaries from 1736–39 on the organisation of the [married] women's bonded groups – *Weiber Banden*: UA R.6.A.b.13.a.2, 20 January. See also UA R.6.A.b.13.b.3.b.4, where the Sister Siegel bonded group is taken by Sister Wattewille, and the Jud. Rohleder's bonded group falls to the older Nitschmann. See also the re-organisation of management of the leaders of

choir, bonded group and association are often used in conjunction with names. For example, on 19 October 1741, Clothmaker Oertel gave his association and a couple of other brothers a blessed lovefeast.[28]

2.2 Associations

Association is sometimes used interchangeably with bonded groups, as in the 5 October paragraph above, and Wollstadt discusses them together in the same section. In some places, however, it seems to have a distinct function, such as denoting a gathering of Moravians in a non-settlement. Thus, on 1 June, the diary mentions that the Buntzlau people who were converted could fit into the association of Walde, the potter.[29] This is more commonly called *Sozietät*, society.[30] Schmidt argues that after 1736 and the shift in terminology, association came to replace that of bonded groups, because the latter term had been tainted.

2.3 Classes

Classes are also part of the early fabric of Herrnhut, and one which continued within the choir structure. Wollstadt identifies two uses of class: one as an umbrella term according to gender and marital status, which is similar to what will become choirs; and the other a subdivision organised according to spiritual advancement.[31] Schmidt also recognises two uses, one is the same as the subsequent choirs, but the other is subdivided according to age.[32] Both mention the so-called constitution of Herrnhut from March 1733,[33] where eight classes are mentioned (men, women, widows, maidens, young men, boys, girls, and small children), and a song which Zinzendorf had composed in 1728, which mentioned seven classes, all the above bar the children.

---

  the various men's bonded groups – *Männer Banden*: Krügelstein's men's bonded group – *Männer Bande* will be taken over by Watteville in his absence. In Christian David's absence his bonded group will be taken over by Gutbier, who will stay in this bonded group and the young boys/young men – *Purschen* will be taken care of by Jacob Till in Krügelstein's absence.

28 UA R.6.A.b.14, 19 October 1741. See also 29 October 1741, where brother Mathias Schindler's and brother Augustin Beypold's associations had lovefeasts and nightwatch. On 20 July 1741, Rosine's association had a lovefeast.
29 UA R6.A.b.15.a, 1 June 1742.
30 For example, the Society of Brethren in Copenhagen, Amsterdam, Altona, London, etc.
31 Wollstadt 1966, pp. 92–109. esp. pp. 99–102 and pp. 104–9.
32 Schmidt 1909, p. 151.
33 Verfassung der mährischen Brüder-Gemeine, UA R.6.A.a.19.4a.

2.4 Choirs

The first mention of the term choir in the 1737 diary spells it '*Cohr*'.[34] This alternative spelling could be an indication that the term is not fully established, in writing, at least. The provenance of the term is unclear. That it is to be distinguished from a singing choir is indicated by its gender. Whereas singing choirs are gendered masculine (*der Kirchenchor*), the specific Moravian choir is gendered neutral: *das Chor*. In his *Eventualtestament*, a will written before his departure for Pennsylvania in 1738, Zinzendorf explains that the choirs are shaped according to an individual's gender and *Stand*. Two etymologies have been suggested: either *choros* from Greek,[35] or *corps* from French/Latin – where the pronounced word was written down by someone who did not know what it meant, hence the unusual spelling.[36] However unclear its provenance, it signifies a division of the community into sex and marital status. There are exceptions to this organisation; from early on, as I will show below, we have the choir of the hourly intercessionists (*Stundenbeter-Chor*), and in the choir speeches from 1755 we encounter speeches to the priests' choir (*Priester-Chor*).[37]

In a choir speech to the single brothers on 29 August 1756, Zinzendorf notes the following:

> It is today the big day, when the choir took its true beginning 15 years ago, not as if it had not existed earlier, rather while it from then on (because one prefers to name the case with its proper name), only got its character then. [...]
>
> So today it is 15 years ago that something belonging to the ground plan of the choir began to be implemented, that was thought of 18 years earlier, but would have been impossible to implement. We have for 18 years had young men (*junge pürsche*), but in the whole blessed 34 year time in which Herrnhut has been standing, only 15 years of single brothers.[38]

---

34 UA R.6.A.b.13.b, 20 August 1737, the *Burschen* have a gathering, commemorating the ten years in which 56 foreign witnesses have been in their choir: (*Cohr*), followed by a list of names.

35 Peucker 2000, pp. 17–18.

36 Paul Peucker, personal communication. Peucker also drew my attention to a reference in JHD 19 November 1747, where the division of the community into choirs and classes is likened to the division of armies and big corps into regiments and battalions. See full quote in Peucker 2010, p. 196.

37 Peucker notes that in *Summarischen Unterricht* from 1755 Zinzendorf lists up to 25 different choirs. To my knowledge there are no speeches to these choirs in Herrnhut (apart from the *Priester-chor*).

38 Single brothers, 29 August 1756: "Es ist heute der Große Tag, da das Chor vor 15 Jahren

This quotation explicitly names the date of the choir's beginning as 1741, 15 years prior to 1756.

However, as the 1737 quotation showed, choir was already conceptualised as an overarching group earlier. This hiatus matches well what we will see in the diaries, where the increased presence and dominance of the choirs is a slow one.[39]

3   Terminology and the Establishment of the Choirs

After this sketch of the main features, I want to look at the terminological development of the terms bonded groups/associations, classes, and choirs, and their use in structuring the community from 1736 to 1745. While this may seem a somewhat tedious exercise, it shows the growth of the choir structure, how it came to push aside other understandings of community practice, and the connection with economic and theological developments. This chapter is, as mentioned, the lexicographical underpinning of the rest of the argument in this book.

3.1   *But First, the Diaries*

Before we do, however, I need to mention a couple of things on the nature of the material at which we are looking. The diary practice, if one may call it such, of the Moravians is not a researched topic, nor is it easy to grasp. The watershed year is 1740, where Zinzendorf at the winter synod in Marienborn decreed that from the following year, each community should keep their own diary:

> From 1741 the diaries in our communities must be kept properly. They should also record small things, e.g. when a daily watchword (*Losung*[40])

---

seinen wahren Anfang genommen hat, nicht, als wenn es vorher nicht existirt hätte, sondern weil es von da an (denn man nennt die Sach gern beym rechten Nahmen) erst seinen character gekrigt hat. [...] Es ist also heute vor 15 Jahren der Anfang gemacht worden, etwas aus zu führen, was zum Grund Plan des Chors gehört, das aber 18 Jahr vor her gedacht, aber aus zu führen unmöglich gewesen wäre. Wir haben 18 Jahr junge Pursche gehabt, aber in der ganzen seligen, 34 jährigen Zeit daß Herrnhut steht, erst 15 Jahr ledige Brüder". (UA R.20.HS57).

39   Schmidt notes that since the beginning of the settlements in Wetterau (Herrnhaag and Marienborn) in 1736, 'choir' completely (*völlig*) took over the term class. Schmidt 1909, p. 151.

40   The practice of drawing a biblical word to guide the day was a practice in Herrnhut from

fits the community particularly well [the texts in hours, the unlocking and awakenings, the conversions of the souls, the main issues in conferences]. A page will in all cases be used for each day, even if it will not be filled. If one hears anything from other communities, for example that a brother on the same day has arrived here and there, then one writes it to that day, and rectifies it. In the Pilgrim-congregation Gersdorff will do it, in Herrnhaag, Weiss, and Vippach gathers the material for them. The choir elders make their daily diaries and bring them to those, who keep the diaries or tell him in person. Leonhard Dober will notify all the communities about the diary.[41]

These are the individual diaries of the communities, which makes sense of the fact that we in 1741 find the first full diary of Herrnhut. Before then, as we shall see, there were multiple diaries from various hands, many only covering a couple of months. Of interest is the reference to choir elders and their diaries. Is this a command to the choir elders to *begin* keeping a diary? In a folder from 1738, there are diaries from maidens (*Jungfern*) and young men (*Purschen*), married men, and widows; however, these do not all contain choir terminology.[42] In the finding aid from 1904,[43] which includes material lost in

---

1728 and from 1730, they were compiled for the whole year in advance. Peucker 2010, p. 39; Caffier 1980; Gärtner and Motel 1998, p. 44. See also Mettele 2010, pp. 58–60.

41 "Von 1741 sollen die Diaria in unsern Gemeinen ordentlich geführt werden. Sie müßen auch Kleinigkeiten aufschreiben, z.e. wenn eine Losung auf die Gemeine besonders passet, [die Texte in Stunden, die Aufschlüsse und Erweckungen, wie Bekehrungen der Seelen, Hauptsachen in Conferenzen]. Es wird allemahl ein Bogen zu einem jeden Tage genommen wenn er auch nicht voll wird. Wenn man was aus andern Gemeinen höret, z.e. daß ein Bruder an demselben Tage da und da angekommen, so schreibt mans denn an den Tag dazu und holts nach. Bey der Pilger-Gemeine machts Gersdorff; in Herrnhaag Weiß und dem sammlet Vippach die Materien. Die Chor-Aeltesten machen täglich ihre Diaria und bringen sie dem, der das Diarium führen soll, oder sagens ihm mündlich. Leonhard Dober soll es in allen Gemeinen wegen des Diarii melden". (UA R.2.A.4, p. 107). This is from the synod minutes from Marienborn, on 20 December 1740. Paul Peucker discusses this quotation as part of a larger exposition on the Moravian archive in Peucker 2012, pp. 697–8.

42 The term choir does not appear in the diary of the married men (*vereheligten Männer*) and their widows (*Wittiber*) from 19 January–9 February or in the maiden diary. Rather both use bonded groups and classes. In the journal of the workers in Herrnhut, which runs from 4 December 1737 to 25 July 1739, choir appears once, on 14 December 1738, when a big prayer is said at the association conference over the choir and the balance of the heart. However, there are several mentions of associations (such as the reference to the new organisation of the associations on 10 December 1737, the demand to be organised in associations on 25 April 1738; and the many references to association conferences throughout the diary, e.g. 7 December 1738; 1 and 30 March 1739, and 3 May 1739), bonded groups

1945,[44] we see that the first diary from the single brothers' house is from 21 May 1739, a month before the founding of the single brothers' house on 22 June 1739 and more than half a year before this decree.[45] It is not possible to assess whether it is a formal choir diary, or whether it is diary by the elder of the single brothers, as for example Jakob Till's 'private' or personal diary from 1731–38. According to the same finding aid, the first single sisters' diary is from 1743,[46] and here we are more fortunate, given that some sections of these diaries still are extant.[47] Here, the 1744 diary is entitled 'The Diary of the Single Sisters'.

In the same synod minutes (Marienborn, 1740), from the afternoon session on 17 December, there is a post regarding *Gemeintage* – community days:

> The community days shall henceforth be sent to no place, other than where there are workers from us. They shall only be produced in the Wetterau and from there be sent. The other communities send their diaries and extracts from letters in which there are matters of importance, every month to Marienborn and Herrnhaag. And there the completion and sending out of the *Bettage* (prayer days) will be treated as one of the most important matters.[48]

(on 20 December 1737, Nitschmann the cobbler was given the learned bonded group; on 18 January 1738, a bonded group conference was blessed with all kinds of important matters; on 15 February 1738 a bonded group conference was held, and on 7 December 1738 Dober had the bonded group-watch), and classes (on 10 December 1737, Johann Rochke and Mierliche became male nurses for the classes and Jacob Liebig became house-class servant, and Voigt class-superintendent. Also, on 18 October 1738, the positions in the class were distributed). Finally, a fragment from the young men's diary mentions the acceptance of seven of the big boys into the choir of the young men on 17 June 1738.

43   UA R.4.E 28a.
44   There is a compiled diary from the single brothers' house covering selected years 1737–38, 1744–49 and 1758, copied and compiled by archivist Ludwig von Schweiniz (UA R.29.B.79). Paul Peucker makes excellent use of these copies in Peucker 2015.
45   UA R.4.E.28a, Brüderhaus-Archiv-Catalog, Herrnhut, p. 1.
46   UA R.4.E.28a, Schwesternhaus-Archiv-Catalog, Herrnhut, p. 1.
47   There are two 'collections' of sister-house materials. One is what was, for several reasons, not destroyed in 1745. This is the collection known as SHAHt. Here the earliest diary is from 1754–58. The other collection is what was, at some point, handed over to the central archive from the sister-house. This is part of the main archival collection, UA R.4.C.IV, and contains materials from the sister-houses in all of the Herrnhuter communities. It is here that we have the earliest extant diaries, from 1744–47 and 1752–54.
48   "Die Gemeintage sollen hinführo an keinen Ort geschickt werden, als wo Arbeiter von uns sind. Sie sollen nur in der Wetterau gemacht und von da verschickt werden. Die andern Gemeinen schicken alle Monathe ihre Diaria und extracte von ihren Briefen, in denen

Gemein- or *Bettag* was a monthly day when the news and correspondence from other communities was read out loud, and as such this becomes an abbreviated name for the written material. This written material is to be compiled only in the Wetterau (Marienborn and Herrnhaag), and from there sent out to places where there are workers, i.e. a more formal, structured place, than, say, the smaller societies. From 1747, these compilations became the *Gemeinhausdiarium* or *Jüngerhausdiarium* and contained the movements of the pilgrim community, that is, Zinzendorf's entourage, and its gatherings, celebrations, visits, and travel. Furthermore, it contained appendices to each week, where we find speeches, sermons, synod minutes, poems, letters and reports from missionaries, diaries from the various settlements, and short memoirs from deceased members.[49]

So, just to sum up the point of this section, the material is neither uniform nor consistent. It does not cover all years, and it does not follow the same agenda. From early on, there are diary fragments from the different groups, but these do not refer to themselves as choirs. There are diaries from the leaders of the groups, such as the day-books of Poul Münster (older boys) and Jakob Till (single brothers), from elders, such as Martin Dober, but not until 1741 do we have a fuller diary – which is also reflected in the lexicographical examination, to which we now turn.

3.2 1736–40

In these early years, the terminology of groups is not formalised, due perhaps to the ad hoc nature of the various gatherings, the shifting terminology, as well as fragmented diaries. Unsurprisingly, in relation to what was mentioned earlier, the years 1736–40 show bonded groups, classes, and associations as the primary organisational units of the congregation. They are used in connection with names, but also groups divided according to gender and marital status.[50] In Paul Münster's journal, covering the years 1731–43, the termino-

---

Sachen von Wichtigkeit sind, nach Marienborn und Herrnhaag. Und da selbst wird die Verfertigung und Versendung der Bettage als eine der wichtigsten Sachen tractiret". (UA R.2.A.4, p. 88).

49 Mettele 2010, p. 148. See also Peucker 2012, p. 702.

50 On 21 August was the maidens' penance day. The 22 August was a special prayer day for the men's class, on 24 September, the widowers and unmarried (*unbeweibten* – literally unwomaned) men attended a lovefeast in their respective classes (*classeley*). The following day, 25 September, following upon a discussion on 'some unfortunate things' (*ärgerliche Dinge*) among the children, a number of men were placed as helpers among the bigger boys and eight boys were admitted into the class of the middle boys. (UA R.6.A.b.13.b, 25 September 1737, p. 17).

logy of bonded groups and associations is predominant, with 'choir' turning up irregularly from 1738 and with changing spelling (primarily *Cohr* but also *Chor*).[51]

The 1739 fragment from 3 January through to 1 April has two mentions of choir, and otherwise refers to associations. The first mention is of the maidens' choir on January 13, the meaning of which is slightly unclear. The precise wording is: 'the sisters merged (*verbanden sich*), new [women] joined therein. A choir, namely the maidens became more'.[52] The meaning of 'became more' has been corrected and is not completely clear, but it is repeated in Friedrich Sigwart Hark's transcriptions of the diaries from the late nineteenth century.[53] The meaning might be that the merger of the various bonded groups became a choir. The second mention of choir is 9 March, where the diary notes that there was a lovefeast in the entire young men's choir.

In the diary which covers July 1739 through to December 1740, there are a couple of mentions of choir, but association is still more predominant.[54] The use of choir refers to the larger organisation of the community, such as the celebration of 13 August 1739 with a lovefeast in the men's choir and the workers from the other choirs, separate quarters through all choirs (25 March 1740), and finally, the mention of the maidens, widows and women who all had general lovefeasts, each choir unto itself (12 October 1740).

3.3   *1741*

As mentioned above, 1741 is the first year where a full diary is kept, and we see an increase in the use of choir.[55] Fast-forwarding to the end of the year, Lang-

---

51   UA R.6.A.a.37.b. For the use of choir, see 4 April, 7 April, 18 April, 18 May, 12 July 1738, 7 March, 12 May, 22 June, 11 November 1739, 7 April, 19 April, 19 June, 5 October 1740.

52   UA R.6.A.b.13.d. 1, 13 January 1739: "Die Schwestern verbanden sich, neue kamen dazu. Ein Chor neml[ich] dier Jungfern wurde mehr".

53   UA R.6.A.b.6.i.

54   UA R.6.A.b.13.d.2. There is the mention of the establishment of a new men's association (24 January 1740), that Linner had a blessed lovefeast with his association (27 January 1740), that the events of each day were reordered for summer, in which the classes and associations had their place in the evenings (4 April 1740), Hehl took over Rudolph's association and marriage-quarter hour (28 July 1740).

55   This diary is written by three different hands. The first section (1 January–10 July 1741) is written by Martin Dober, the second (11–22 July 1741) by an unknown hand, and the third part (23 July–31 December 1741) is written by Johann Michael Langguth. These three sections also show different emphases, with the section written by Langguth as the most choir intensive.

guth notes, on 21 November, that 'Generally, since 13 November there has been a special time of grace in the community. All choirs, classes, associations etc. are in a particular [state of] blessedness'.[56]

Indeed, the most common organisational terms are choir, class, and associations. Bonded group is not used very much,[57] but choir is also not appearing in places where it will eventually come to dominate. For example, under the entry for 9 April 1741, it is noted that 'classes and societies were organised for the single brothers'. In time, choir will be understood and made explicit as the overall category for the single brothers: 'the single brothers' choir'. This certainly takes place in this diary, for example on 14 August, where it is noted: 'the bonded group-helpers under the single brothers' choir had the nightwatch'.[58] It is just not generally pervasive, and thus I prefer to speak not (yet) of a common ideological framework, but rather of one in the making.

Another interesting feature is the difference in how the term choir is used in the three sections. In the Dober and the anonymous sections, the term is used infrequently. In the Langguth section, however, the term choir explodes with a variety of usages. First we have the usage which also appears in the two previous sections: conjoint with the particular group (*Ehe-chor, Wittwen-chor*, or choir workers).[59] Then we have a couple of usages which appear in Dober and Langguth's sections: conjoint with the particular quarter-hours (*Chor-Viertelstunde*),[60] as a mode of organisation (*Chorweise*),[61] or, standing by itself, as an absolute term, as in: 'the single brothers within their choir', and 'at the moment the choirs present themselves as follows'.[62] Then there are the examples which derive only from Langguth's section. These include a choir lovefeast (27 December), the office of the choir elders (12 and 13 November),

---

56 UA R.6.A.b.14.1, 21 November 1741: "Überhaupt ist seit dem 13 November eine besondere Gnaden-Zeit in der Gemeine. Alle Chöre, Classen, Gesellschafften etc. sind in besondern Seegen".

57 Also, in this diary, bonded group is not used in conjunction with names, as was common in the earlier years.

58 The nightwatch was a significant feature of the bonded group. It was not only to represent the sleeping community to God, but also an edifying and intense experience, since it went through the night. Schmidt 1909, pp. 169–71.

59 UA R.6.A.b.14.1, 1 January, 16 May/17 July, 18 July, 23 July/13 August, 19 August, 23 August, 24 August, 30 August, 27 September, 28 September, 29 September, 20 October, 25 October, 12 November, 13 November, 14 November, 17 November, 19 November, 24 November, 2 December – all 1741.

60 UA R.6.A.b.14.1, 14 April/24 September, 28 October, 13 November, 14 November, 19 November, 25 November, 24 December – all 1741.

61 UA R.6.A.b.14.1, 13 May/22 August, 13 November – all 1741.

62 UA R.6.A.b.14.1, 1 January, 29 July, 11 September, 6 October, 18 November – all 1741.

choir conference (4 September) and then, a significant increase in the plural form, *Chöre*, which only appeared once in Dober (1 January).

It should be noted here – briefly, for we will return to it – that Johann Michael Langguth arrived in Herrnhut to take over the leadership of the single brothers in February 1741,[63] and was one of the chief ideologues of the blood and wounds theology. For his efforts, he was adopted by Zinzendorf's close friend, Friederich von Watteville in 1743, and could then, as Freiherr Johannes von Watteville, marry Benigna, Zinzendorf's oldest daughter in 1746.[64]

3.4   1742

In the diary from 1742, which is also mostly written by Langguth (until 20 May) and Dober, the most prominent words are association and choir. Bonded group and class barely make an appearance, and whereas in 1741, bonded group was still used in connection with the nightwatch, here, in 1742 the nightwatch is now exclusively expressed with the term association.[65] In the 1742 diary, bonded group is only used in connection with the bonded group-conference,[66] except on 28 November, where Sister Langun held a long cordial conversation or *"Herzensbande"* (heart-band), with the minister's wife, which has echoes of the earlier understanding of bonded group as a 'cultivation of an intimate friendship'.[67] Class, which already in the following year will see a large increase, is here used primarily in connection with communion,[68] but also in a couple of cases to subdivide the choirs.[69]

Association, apart from the connection with the nightwatch as noted above, is used in a number of ways. First, and most in line with one of its earlier functions, it is used once as the term to signify a gathering of Moravians in

---

63 Noted in Münster's diary on 28 February 1741. UA R.6.A.a.37.b.
64 Peucker 2015, p. 158.
65 The nightwatch is held every week, on Mondays, by an association of men, who walk around singing until the following day begins. See e.g. entry from UA R.6.A.b.16.1, 15 April 1743, where it says that Hehl and his association had the nightwatch, and that Grassmann and Dober were with them until 2 AM, after which the Gesellschaft went around singing until it became day. ("Die Gesellschaft ging hernach noch singen herum bis es Tag worden"). Schmidt points out that the royal decree from 1737 which banned Zinzendorf from Saxony stated that the term bonded group (*Bande*) was not to be used, and that the Brethren thus changed the name to associations (*Gesellschaften*) to comply with this order. Schmidt 1909, pp. 192–93.
66 See for example, UA R.A.b.15.1, 10 February, 10 March, and 7 April 1742.
67 UA R.A.b.15.1, 28 November. Schmidt, quoting Zinzendorf from a council meeting in London in 1753. Schmidt 1909, p. 201.
68 UA R.A.b.15.1, 9 June, 29 September, and 27 October 1742.
69 UA R.A.b.15.1, 20 May, 31 May, 2 September, and 18 September 1742.

a non-settlement. It is used on a number of occasions to designate groups of specific people: single sisters' and single brothers' associations,[70] the strangers' association,[71] or even more specifically, the association of the workers among the men.[72] Here, the relationship to the choirs is uncertain;[73] it is not entirely clear whether the associations are within, or parallel to the choirs. This terminological unclarity is of course a sign of a greater unclarity in terms of where they exactly belong, and what the function of the association *vis-à-vis* the choirs is. One consistent appearance is in connection with the lovefeasts, where several times we encounter a named person, Brother Weiß or Hehl, giving their associations a lovefeast.[74] And then, finally, the connection between the communicant members and the associations. On a number of occasions, we find the associations mentioned as the group configuration according to which the preparation to communion takes place, which is in line with the earlier functions of bonded groups,[75] and which was one of the functions we identified with classes above.[76] Again, we must emphasise the lack of clear boundaries and functions in the description of these various groups, especially their internal relations.

The choirs, on the other hand, are, with a couple of exceptions, becoming clearer in their configuration, in the sense that the uses are more limited and consistent. First, as in the earlier years we have choir as part of the name of the group: *Wittwen-Chor, ledige Schwestern Chor, Kinder-Chor*.[77] Then there are the usages where it is conjoint with the particular quarter-hours (*Chorviertelstunde*).[78] A couple of mentions of the office of the choir elders,[79] and a very unusual mention of Brother Georg Endter's death as going over into 'the upper choir'.[80] Then, there are two cases of bigger interest, which will relate to topics raised in Chapters 4, 5, and 6. The first is the mention of a new practice:

---

70 UA R.A.b.15.1, 1 September, 11 December, 12 December, 26 December, 30 December 1742.
71 UA R.A.b.15.1, 14 January, 27 May, 26 December 1742.
72 UA R.A.b.15.1, 3 and 9 October 1742.
73 See for example UA R.A.b.15.1, 25 June and 26 December, 1742. In the June example, the choirs have their own associations whereas in the December example, it is next to the choirs, the choirs and the associations.
74 UA R.A.b.15.1, 27 May and 10 November 1742. For other examples, see 17 May; 26 September; 13 November, 22 November 1742.
75 Schmidt 1909, pp. 168–9.
76 UA R.A.b.15.1, 9 June, 4 August, 27 October, 22 December 1742.
77 UA R.A.b.15.1, 4 January; 2 February; 17 April; 24 May; 18 August; 1 September; 13 October; 10 and 24 November; 6, 15, and 24 December 1742.
78 UA R.A.b.15.1, 19 January; 17 February; 1 May; 31 August; 21 December 1742.
79 5 June and 21 December 1742.
80 UA R.A.b.15.1, 21 December 1742: "Nachmittag um ½ 4 uhr gieng auch unser br Georg Endter über ins Obere Chor".

> Today the single brothers began to take a verse from a song about the lamb and his wounds, which every morning the day before will be told the whole choir by one brother. We hope that this arrangement will be of great blessing, and that something from the Lamb stay in the heart of many.[81]

This practice points to the understanding of the choirs as sites of ideological reproduction, where likeness of mind and zeal are cultivated through small everyday practices such as this venture, where a fixed common text is appointed at a daily level within the choir, with which the brothers can connect. This is a subdivision of the daily watchword, which in the diary of 1741 was at the head of each entry. But this serves to strengthen the community of the choir around the theology of the Lamb and his wounds.

The second feature of the choir to which I want to draw attention is the explicit mention of the presence of the Saviour in the choirs during their post-communion talk in the *Saal* in Herrnhut.

> The Saviour was this time very sharp and remained in all choirs. This communion was particularly anointed and blessed by the Lamb. A mild and reverend mercy stirred among us, and we truly felt the dead martyr-corpse of the Lamb and the blood of the wounds, which melts and bends hearts.[82]

The presence of the Saviour in the choirs is something that Zinzendorf will cultivate excessively in the choir speeches. Here it is alluded to in relation to the celebration of communion, but in the choir speeches, it will be extended to be a sign of harmonious life and ideological conformity in the single brothers' choir.

---

81 UA R.A.b.15.1, 20 February 1742: "Die ledigen Brüder fiengen heute an, in ihrer Abend-Viertelstunde allemahl ein Versel aus einem Liede von Lamme und seinen Wunden zu nehmen, welches allemahl Vormittags vorher durch einen Bruder unter dem ganntzen Chore herum gesaget wird. Wir hoffen es soll diese Einrichtung von großen Seegen seyn, und manchen etwaß von Lamm davon im Hertzen blieben".

82 UA R.A.b.15.1, 17 February 1742: "Der Heyland war dßmals sehr scharff und bleiben in allen Chöre sehr viele (meistens von selbst) zurück. Es war dieses Abendmahl gantz besonders gesalbt und geseegnet vom Lamme. es regte sich eine sanffte und gebeugte Gnade dabey u wir fühlten wahrhafftig den getödten marterleibe des lammes und die Bluth der Wunden, die die hertzen zerschmeltztet und beugete".

THE CHOIRS – A GENEALOGY 55

3.5   1743

When we turn to look at the terminological developments in 1743, one thing immediately shows itself. The usage of the word class has increased markedly, taking over semantic fields which were earlier the prerogative of the association. This is especially clear in the cases of the classes as designating specific groups of people: single brothers' classes;[83] single sisters' classes;[84] married classes,[85] strangers' classes,[86] as well as a more general term for subgroups.[87] Of particular interest is the entry from 12 April, where we see the specific subordination of the classes to the choirs: 'the assemblies and classes of the choirs'.[88]

In spite of this marked increase in the appearance of classes, the association terminology is not waning in 1743. The nightwatches are still carried out by associations,[89] and it is also the most common term in connection with lovefeasts.[90]

---

83   UA R.A.b.16.1: 17 and 24 January 1743: a class among the single brothers who had visitors; 3 March: in the single brothers' classes, the brothers were talked to a lot; 21 April: In the afternoon, the two new potter youths were in the new class; 23 April: the single brothers' classes were looked through, and some brothers were moved up, none moved down; 28 April: In the single brothers' quarter-hour, Brother Grassmann took leave of the choir. Afterwards, the 7th class had the opportunity [for a meeting] in the brothers' hall, which they had not been able to hold at noon; 19 May: Brother Grassmann held the single brother classes; 19 June: The class of the new people within the single brothers was particularly blessed.

84   UA R.A.b.16.1: 13 January 1743: the single sisters' classes, which are usually held on Sundays with Sister Augustine; 26 January: the single sisters' class [...] had a lovefeast, 18 class-Sisters were present; 16 June: Sister [Rosine] Gneuß held all the single sisters' classes as a farewell.

85   UA R.A.b.16.1: 5. May 1743: After all quarter-hours, the first marriage-class, the elders and helpers, had a divine lovefeast.

86   UA R.A.b.16.1: 15 April and 10 June 1743, the strangers' class of the women.

87   UA R.A.b.16.1: 11 March 1743, After [the foot-washing], the regular community prayer-hour, the congregating of classes in their places, and then the entire community in the hall; 3 June: After the meal, the Sunday quarter-hours and classes began; 8 June: After [the foot-washing] the classes took place; 29 September: at 7 we chimed in the classes, at 8 in the associations.

88   UA R.A.b.16.1, 12 April 1743, "die Versammlungen und Claßen der Chöre".

89   See UA R.A.b.16.1, 6 January, 13 January, 20 January, 3 February, 10 February, 17 February 1743 and so on, every week.

90   See UA R.A.b.16.1, 1 January 1743: 'Sister Wald gave the bonded group-helpers and a couple of brothers a lovefeast with her association-sisters in the blessed Lord's room on the occasion of her birthday'. See also 15 January (Sister Ikin's association), 17 January (an association lovefeast for the workers among the married sisters), 23 January (the workers' association in celebration of Brother Theil's birthday), 28 January (Sister Augustin had a lovefeast with her association), 5 February (the workers' association gave a lovefeast in celebration of Sister Lorel Gutbiern's birthday), 27 February (Carl Gottfried Knopff gave his association and the brothers connected with him a lovefeast on the occasion of his birthday), 11 March

An example worth mentioning explicitly is 17 January, which was the birthday of Elisabeth Höyer: 'Because grace in such short time had accomplished so much with her, having been such an angry person, and stuck in this for years, her association gave her a lovefeast, on which she made a covenant, to hold the Lamb dear'. In addition to this honour, she was also told that the Saviour had allowed her to come to communion the following day.[91] We shall meet Liese Höyer, as she is also called, in the next chapter, where she, along with her parents, are expelled from Herrnhut in 1744. But for now, we see how the association functions as a support group, offering encouragement and reward for the individual in their progression in faith. We also should note the connection between birthday and lovefeast, which increases dramatically in the 1743 diary – 10 birthday celebrations in connections with associations and lovefeasts are mentioned. Given that this is not an occurrence in earlier diaries, it is a curious and surprising development, and signifies the sudden importance of birthdays.

A final interesting example from 1743 is the lovefeast held on 16 April, which was 'carried out by a number of sisters, mainly noble, at the behest of Frau Ber-

> (Dip gave the entire visiting association a lovefeast in the single brother's house because of his birthday), 16 April (Herr von Heinitz gave his association a lovefeast in Herr von Wittenbach's room, because he had been absent on the last nightwatch), 17 April (Jany, the apothecary pupil gave his association and the workers a lovefeast at noon), 25 April (Brother Geller gave his association a small lovefeast on the occasion of his birthday), 30 April (Wittebach gave his association and the master builder, the master bricklayer and the master carpenter a lovefeast on the occasion of the laying down of the foundation stone for his house), 15 May (Sister Meschler gave the association helpers a lovefeast because of her birthday eight days earlier), 9 June (the helper-association of the single sisters to farewell Rosina Hansch), 12 June (the newly arrived Berthelsdorfer women's *Gesellschaft* had an inaugural lovefeast), 17 June (the worker-association of the single sisters had a lovefeast to farewell Rosina Gneuss), 20 June (a blessed lovefeast was held with the so-called English and some other children of the same age; the small Seifert, whose association this is, had a birthday), 26 June (Geller gave her association a small farewell lovefeast), 12 July (the sisters had a stranger association lovefeast), 1 September (a couple of associations gave brother Jorden a farewell lovefeast), 21 September (Sister Voigt gave a lovefeast to her association because of her inclusion), 25 November (on the occasion of her birthday, Sister Würstbinn took over a young married women's association from David-Hans with a lovefeast).

91 UA R.A.b.16.1, 17 January 1743: "Es war der Anna Elisabeth Hoyer Geburts-Tag, und weil die Gnade in kurtzen so viel an ihr gethan hat, da sie so ein böses Mensch gewesen und viele jahre so geste[c]kt hat, so machte ihr ihre Gesellschaft ein L[iebes]M[ahl] darauf sie einen Bund machten das Lamm lieb zu haben. (Der Hoyer-Li[e]se wurde auch zu ihrem Geburts-Tag zu wißen gethan, daß ihr der Heyland erlaubt hätte übermorgen mit zum Ab[end-]M[ahl] zu gehen.)"

grath von Heinitz. Some brothers were also present'.[92] This entry has an overt reference to class (carried out by noblewomen) as well as a more indirect (at her behest). This is something we will be discussing at greater length in the following chapter.

3.6   1744

When it comes to the year 1744, the full and detailed diaries of the preceding years come to a halt. At some point, the diaries become divided up into a fuller version and a shorter, abbreviated one, which as 'short communication' (*kurtz gefaßte Nachricht*) only notes 'the most notable occurrences' (*merkwürdigsten Begebenheiten*). These abbreviated diaries are intended for distribution among other congregations. In the case of 1744, this short version is unfortunately all that is extant. This does make it a less than useful source for discerning the quotidian life of the community, in that it is produced to project an image of Herrnhut to the rest of the global community.[93] Diary A is divided up into six parts, written by different hands. The first and longest part goes from 1 January to 17 July after which it is noted that from this day on until the end of the year, the diaries are kept in four-week periods (from communal day to communal day) and sent as appendix to the Herrnhut 'communal day' to Marienborn (where Zinzendorf is).[94] The following five parts are then the four-week instalments (17 July to 15 August; 16 August to 12 September; 13 September to 10 October; 11 October to 7 November; and 8 November to 5 December, when the diary ends). Diary B covers the period from 15 August to 12 September, with little variation from A.

What is noticeable in this year is that the classes and associations have receded significantly, or rather that their function is curtailed. Whether this is due to the brevity of the entries will be clarified when we look at 1745, which again is a much fuller diary.

Classes here, in the 1744 diary, denote subgroups under the choirs. We have reference to the classes in the single brothers' choir,[95] as well as the classes in

---

[92]   UA R.A.b.16.1, 16 April 1743: "Hernach war auch ein Liebesmahl welches um der Frau Berg-Rath von Heiniz willen angestellt war, von etlichen Schwestern, sonderlich adelichen, es waren auch einige Brüder dabey [...]".

[93]   It does give an astonishingly full account of the sex scandal in 1744, which will be discussed in detail in the following chapter. This level of detail is perhaps to make an example of the event and its consequences.

[94]   UA R.6.A.b.17.a.1744.a: "Von disem Dato an bis zu Ende des Jahres ist alles successive alle 4 Wochen als ein Anhang des Herrnhutischen Gemein-Tags nach Marienborn geschi[c]kt".

[95]   UA R.6.A.b.17.a.1744.a, 26 January 1744.

the widows' choir.⁹⁶ Then, there is a 'strangers' class' in at least the married couples' choir, which was begun on 26 January,⁹⁷ and there is a reference to a 'strangers' class' among the [married?] men in Herrnhut.⁹⁸ And finally, there is mention of a worker-class.⁹⁹

Associations are mentioned even less. Once as a reference to the association in the town of Leube, which as we saw in 1742 was in line with one of its earlier usages, the gathering of Moravians in a non-settlement.¹⁰⁰ It appears twice as that group to which is given a lovefeast on a special occasion, as in a farewell,¹⁰¹ or a funeral.¹⁰²

One interesting feature which relates to both classes and associations, and which is much more prevalent than earlier, is the emphasis on organisation. On 5 January, the quarter-hours and the classes took place in their order as usual.¹⁰³ The classes of the single brothers were newly organised in January,¹⁰⁴ the servants of the classes were revised on 17 August, the sick-guards on the following day.¹⁰⁵ On 2 September, the new organisation of the various celebrations of communion in a year, i.e. the general ones and the choir ones, were made public.¹⁰⁶ In November, a new organisation of the associations among the married sisters is carried out, and all the married classes were finished and made public.¹⁰⁷ This latter point is an interesting one, because the idea of the associations was based, thus Schmidt, on voluntarism, whereas here, they are re-organised by the leadership.¹⁰⁸

---

96   UA R.6.A.b.17.a.1744.a, 2 February 1744.
97   UA R.6.A.b.17.a.1744.a, 26 January 1744.
98   UA R.6.A.b.17.a.1744.a, 5 April and 21 June 1744.
99   UA R.6.A.b.17.a.1744.a and b, 7 September 1744.
100 UA R.6.A.b.17.a.1744.a, 17 May 1744.
101 UA R.6.A.b.17.a.1744.a, 11 July 1744, where Bruder Kalker and his wife gave a farewell-lovefeast to their *Gesellschaft*s.
102 UA R.6.A.b.17.a.1744.a, 31 July 1744, where Bruder von Seidliz's association gave a lovefeast for some of the main workers, his wife and two beloved sisters after his funeral.
103 UA R.6.A.b.17.a.1744.a, 5 January 1744.
104 UA R.6.A.b.17.a.1744.a, 26 January 1744 it is noted that the newly arranged classes among the single brothers began today.
105 UA R.6.A.b.17.a.1744.a and b, 17 and 18 August 1744.
106 UA R.6.A.b.17.a.1744.a and b, 2 September 1744.
107 UA R.6.A.b.17.a.1744.a, 1 November 1744.
108 See also new organisations of the associations on 19 September 1744 (UA R.6.A.b.17.a.1744.a and b) and 2 November 1744 (UA R.6.A.b.17.a.1744.a). There might have been a lovefeast to celebrate or inaugurate these new divisions, since it is noted on 4 November that Sister Gintowt gave birth to a son, after having been to a lovefeast in her association and evening-song.

On two occasions the associations are mentioned as the only collective. One is on 30 September, where the daily events are put in order for the winter, where association is mentioned as the assembly in the evening.[109] This occurs again on 11 October (in the same diary segment), where it is mentioned that because of the prolonged meeting regarding the sex scandal, there was no time for either association or singing hour (*Singstunde*).[110] This seems a much looser reference to a group gathering of any kind. In these cases, as with the note above on the loss of voluntarism, the term seems to have lost its specificity. In contrast, classes and choirs are more sharply defined.

The emphasis on choir as the central organisational feature of the community is apparent. Choirs are mentioned on some prayer or community day celebrations, where new members, if any, are admitted.[111] Then there is the transition between the choirs,[112] the choir quarter-hours,[113] lovefeasts,[114] the

---

109   UA R.6.A.b.17.a.1744.a, 30 September 1744.
110   UA R.6.A.b.17.a.1744.a, 11 October 1744.
111   The prayer- or community-day (*Bet-* or *Gemeintag*) which mentions choirs in the admittance of new members are 4 January 1744 (UA R.6.A.b.17.a.1744.a), which admits members to the married choir and single sisters' choir, 29 January 1744 (UA R.6.A.b.17.a.1744.a), admitting members to the big boys' choir and sisters' choir, and 10 October 1744 (UA R.6.A.b.17.a.1744.a and b) welcoming new members to the married choir, single brothers' choir and single sisters' choir. Admittance without mention of choir occurs on 25 April, 20 June, and 15 August 1744. Prayer- or community-day without admittance of new members are 29 February, 28 March, 23 May, 18 July, 12 September, 7 November and 5 December 1744. All from UA R.6.A.b.17.a.1744.a.
112   On 2 July 1744, two widows are admitted into the widows' choir (UA R.6.A.b.17.a.1744.a), on 4 October 1744, one widow is admitted (UA R.6.A.b.17.a.1744.a and b). 12 January 1744 on the Big Boys' Day, three boys from the children's choir transitioned into the big boys' choir, and two big boys transitioned into the single brothers' choir (UA R.6.A.b.17.a.1744.a). Also, on 1 January 1744, during the quarter-hours, a special mention was made of those who had arrived, been admitted, and attended communion for the first time, and a verse was sung for each of these groups in every choir UA R.6.A.b.17.a.1744.a. Mention should also be made of Sophia Leopold, a big girl, who died at 9 in the evening of 3 January, 1744. It is remarked that she not even several weeks ago had entered the older girls' choir as a bad and miserable child, and had there embraced the Saviour. UA R.6.A.b.17.a.1744.a, 3 January 1744.
113   Choir quarter-hours on 26 January (UA R.6.A.b.17.a.1744.a) and 25 March (UA R.6.A.b.17. a.1744.a).
114   Lovefeasts in all choirs are mentioned in UA R.6.A.b.17.a.1744.a, 1 January 1744, 26 March, and 24 April in Berthelsdorf. In the widows' choir on 2 February 1744 as a celebration of the Widows' Feast day and a lovefeast given as farewell by Mama Tschirshchy on 29 August 1744 (UA R.6.A.b.17.a.1744.a and b); in the single sisters' choir, marking the fourteenth anniversary of their 'Bund', their covenant, which Anna Nitchmann established among the single sisters in 1730; and in the intersessionists' choir, the hourly prayers on 23 September 1744, the day following their appointment (UA R.6.A.b.17.a.1744.a and b).

Easter celebration,[115] and the frequent mention of choirs in the lead up to and celebration of communion.[116] Finally, we find a couple of miscellaneous items, such as the sending of 120 members from all choirs to Gnadeck,[117] to assist with the establishment of the community there, the mention of leaders, as when Anna Ramsberg was sworn in as vice-elder of the single sisters' choir,[118] or the very interesting meeting of all the choir elders, provosts, and community servants concerning the houses in Herrnhut, where unmarried people of both sexes live at the same time, where it was resolved to get rid of this disorder and indecency.[119] Given the revelation of a sex scandal one month later, in September, it would seem that they were a bit too late. On 11 October, the elders and the provosts receive an angry reprimand from Brother von Peistel, for their failure in monitoring the gender segregation, which resulted in this scandal. Peistel was sent by Zinzendorf and his wife from Marienborn to investigate this mess, and was given the right to punish and reprimand.[120] Another repercussion was that after an examination of the single sisters' choir on the 21 October, around 20 people were advised to leave the community (*consilium abeundi*).[121]

From these examples, the choir structure has taken a hold on the community, in liturgical as well as organisational senses. This is discernible not only in the mention of choirs in various contexts, but also the hierarchical sense which now prevails in the diary, with a bigger emphasis on organisation within the choirs. As we will see in the following chapter, there was a big gap in authority figures from early May till July, during which discipline was loose. The ramifications of the events in September and October of 1744 were deeply felt though 1745, to which we now turn.

---

115   There is mention of the celebration of Easter on the God's Acre (graveyard) on the Hutberg 5 April 1744, when the brothers and sisters stood according to choir, and how the single brothers' choir closed the Easter celebrations by walking around with singing and music (UA R.6.A.b.17.a.1744.a, 7 April 1744).
116   For communion speakings, see married choir on UA R.6.A.b.17.a.1744.a, 8 January 1744; all choirs 17 January 1744; all choirs 22 April 1744; married men's choir 11 July 1744; single brothers' choir and guests, 25 September 1744 (UA R.6.A.b.17.a.1744.a mentions choir, UA R.6.A.b.17.a.1744.b does not); single brothers' choir 26 September 1744. For acceptance into communion see older girls' choir, 15 January 1744 and older girls' choir, 23 April 1744a.

On organisation of choirs in relation to communion see the choir elders' conference in UA R.6.A.b.17.a.1744.a 7 July 1744 and the already mentioned reshuffling and publication of new order on 2 September 1744 (UA R.6.A.b.17.a.1744.a and b); the exclusion of 90 people from all choirs on 13 October 1744.
117   UA R.6.A.b.17.a.1744.a, 31 March 1744.
118   UA R.6.A.b.17.a.1744.a and b, 4 September 1744.
119   UA R.6.A.b.17.a.1744.a, 5 August 1744.
120   UA R.6.A.b.17.a.1744.a, 11 October 1744.
121   UA R.6.A.b.17.a.1744.a, 21 October 1744.

3.7   1745

The diary from 1745 is once again a full one, brimming with choir language and other exciting things.

3.7.1   Classes – Associations – Bonded Groups

As in the earlier years, we see classes as subdivisions of the choirs. An interesting case is presented on 24 January, where it is noted that after the usual marriage quarter-hour, Johann [Nitschmann] presented a fundamental idea on the true sense and qualities of the associations, that

> in order to prevent all pressure, playthings and affectation, very few associations were made, however, the rest of the brothers and sisters were divided into classes, which could serve precisely the same purpose as the associations, but be less prone to abuse, because in the classes there would be the freedom to explain oneself or not, to talk or only to listen, and then the new organisation of the married brothers and sisters in associations and classes was read out.[122]

This quotation posits a difference between classes and associations, namely that the compulsion or pressure to speak in the associations led to amusement and affectation. An attempt was made to overcome this in the classes, where speaking is presented as voluntary. There then is a structural difference between the two modes of organisation, of which we know very little. The married couples' choir, which as we shall see in the next chapter was an unruly one, is in 1745 subjected to three reorganisations. One here, in January, one on 31 May, where the married couples' choir was blessed with a new arrangement in associations and classes, which was commemorated on 4 June with a lovefeast among the workers, and one on 24 November.[123] Also the older girls' choir's associations and classes were rearranged due to some unknown troubles.[124]

---

122   UA R.6.A.b.17.a.1745.a, 24 January 1745: "daß, um alle Zwang, Spielwerk und affectierung dabey zu verhüten der gesellschaften sehr wenige gemacht, die übrige Geschwister aber in Classen eingetheilt worden, die eben zu dem Zweck dienen könnten, wie die Gesellschaften, aber weniger dem Mißbrauch unter worffen wären, weil in den Classen Freyheit wäre sich zu erklären oder nicht, zu reden; oder nun zu hören und denn wurde die neue Einrichtung der ehelichen Brüder und Schwestern in die Gesellschafft und Classe abgelesen".
123   UA R.6.A.b.17.a.1745.a, 31 May, 4 June and 24 November 1745.
124   UA R.6.A.b.17.a.1745.a, 2 December 1745. Note that under the 14 January, the lot is consulted to decide on the organisation of the choir. See below. In UA R.6.A.a.43.4.i, which will be discussed in the next chapter, it is noted that the older girls' choir does not work at all.

Other than that, we have the usual individual classes (the classes in the single brothers' choir,[125] married brothers and sisters[126]) including the strangers' class,[127] the workers' classes,[128] a couple of unspecified,[129] and a mention of the place-classes (*Ortsclassen*).[130] Presumably these refer to the classes arranged according to national provenance. E.g. in 1744, there was mention of the Moravian (*mährisch*) class, and here in 1745, that six Danish sisters had a lovefeast together.[131] However, while classes have made a bit of a comeback in 1745, they are nowhere near as prevalent as they were in the 1743 diary.

With association we have the appearance of it as in the 'company' of,[132] and travel entourage.[133] Then there is the workers' association on several occasions, with one curious expression (22 November) that the workers' association in the single brothers' choir had an unusually useful and hearty association – where association is at the same time the name of the group and the name of the type of gathering.[134] Then we have the association as the locus for some celebration or other, be it birthdays,[135] or e.g. acceptance in the community.[136] Here it is

---

125   UA R.6.A.b.17.a.1745.a, 14 February, 7 March 1745.
126   UA R.6.A.b.17.a.1745.a, 4 March (sisters only), 14 August, 7 October, 13 November (communion brothers only) 1745.
127   UA R.6.A.b.17.a.1745.a, 18 April, 13 May 1745.
128   UA R.6.A.b.17.a.1745.a, 6 March and 20 November 1745 (married choir workers).
129   UA R.6.A.b.17.a.1745.a, 13 May, 23 August 1745.
130   UA R.6.A.b.17.a.1745.a, 22 October 1745.
131   UA R.6.A.b.17.a.1745.a, 11 November 1745 (Danish sisters).
132   UA R.6.A.b.17.a.1745.a, 4 January 1745.
133   UA R.6.A.b.17.a.1745.a, 7 March (Brother (von) Larisch's lovefeast to his travel entourage), 21 May and 3 July (Brother (von) Biberan, left with his travel entourage), 14 November (Dobers and Luzans left with their entourages).
134   UA R.6.A.b.17.a.1745.a, 22 November 1745. For other cases of workers' associations see UA R.6.A.b.17.a.1745.a, 14 February and 13 November 1745.
135   UA R.6.A.b.17.a.1745.a, 11 March (Sister Kohler's birthday in the older girls' association), 10 May 1745 (Sister Meschlern's birthday lovefeast first for the workers and then for her association), 11 May 1745 (double birthday for the von Schweinitz, one for the 'old mother' who celebrated in her widows' *Gesellschaft* and the grandchild in the child's association. This was more extensively celebrated in the antechamber, with a song composed for the occasion). On 7 October 1745, Brother Braths gave a lovefeast on the occasion of his birthday to encourage his association to renewed gravity and faither because of the particular grace which for the moment prevailed in their choir. On 21 October 1745, the old Brother Güttler also celebrated his birthday with his association-brothers and on 25 October 1745, Sister Wäklering had a lovefeast on her birthday with her association-sisters. On 2 July 1745, the married sisters had lovefeast in their associations, although no reason is mentioned.
136   UA R.6.A.b.17.a.1745.a, 31 December 1745, Smith, the baker, gave a lovefeast to his *Gesellschaft* and a couple of workers to mark his happiness at being accepted.

clear that the associations function as subsections of the choirs.[137] Finally, one mention is made of the association in its function as society outside Moravian settlement, namely in Leube.[138]

Bonded groups has with few exceptions all but disappeared. As we saw in earlier years, the nightwatch (*Nacht-Banden-Wache*) is the place where the term sticks.[139] And then a brief mention on 15 November, where it is noted that Liesel Neumann had a lovefeast with her band sisters.[140]

3.7.2 Choir

In some instances, *all choirs* are referred to, sometimes in a summarising fashion,[141] sometimes to explicitly emphasise the unity of the community. In the latter case, we have the entry from 13 June, where the diary notes that 'the dear little flame of marriage blazes very brightly and lovingly between the Lamb and the congregation, so that it manifests itself through *all choirs*, as the wonderful watchword says: He is my husband and he also keeps himself to me'.[142] Also on 13 August we have the implication of all choirs participating in the celebration of this special day,[143] in that it was 18 years ago that the Lambkin proved himself so merciful towards the community, which was celebrated with different choir lovefeasts and a solemn communion.[144]

---

137   See also UA R.6.A.b.17.a.1745.a, 24 January and 31 May 1745 which refers to the association of the married choir, 1 October 1745, where there is a discussion of the association in the single brothers' choir, and 1 December 1745, where the single sisters' classes and association were held.
138   UA R.6.A.b.17.a.1745.a, 27 January 1745.
139   UA R.6.A.b.17.a.1745.a, 9 May, 17 September and 17 October 1745.
140   UA R.6.A.b.17.a.1745.a, 15 November 1745.
141   UA R.6.A.b.17.a.1745.a, 31 January 1745, where different lots were drawn for all choirs; 30 August, where all the newly admitted brothers and sisters had lovefeasts in their respective choirs. 13 November, then the communicants in their respective choirs had separate quarter-hours and there is specific mention of new communicant members in the single sisters' choir. 29 December, all choirs' communicants spoken through for the impending communion.
142   UA R.6.A.b.17.a.1745.a, 13 June: "das Eheflämlein loderte sehr hell und lieblich zwischen dem Lamm und der Gemein, so daß sichs durch alle Chöre bewies, wie die schöne Losung heißt: Er ist mein Mann und Er hält sich auch zu mir".
143   The 13 August 1727 is regarded as Herrnhut's spiritual birthday, in that this was the day of the reconciliation of the community after the divisions and fractions of the first few years. The location of this revelation was at a communion service at the church in Berthelsdorf, where 'Those who had been offended with one another, fell around each other's necks and joined together ... then the community fell down before God and began to weep and sing ... and we went home again ... pretty much out of ourselves. We spent this and the following day in a quiet and amiable contentment and learned love', from the Herrnhut diary, quoted in Sommer 2000, p. 47.
144   UA R.6.A.b.17.a.1745.a, 13 August 1745: "Sonst war dieses der Tag an welchem weyland vor 18

In this 1745 diary, choir terminology is so extensive that I have chosen to approach it differently than in the previous sections. I have not included every reference to choir, and because of the many references to individual choirs, I have divided it choir wise. Nevertheless, apart from the instances mentioned above, there are some general uses which include all choirs, which I have processed below under a couple of subheadings.

3.7.2.1   Choir Activities

One term which turns up often is *Chor-gelegenheiten*, choir activities, and is often used to emphasise the order in which things should be running, and the presence of the Lamb in this order.[145] As an example, the entry on 24 October notes that 'all choir activities in the community are bedewed by the Lambkin in his death sweat'. And once we hear that in all choirs a particular course of grace was felt.[146] Also individual activities are noted, such as lovefeasts[147] and communion.[148] On the Day of all Choirs, the 25 March, which we will look at later in the chapter, all choirs recalled the blessed day, one year ago, when Papa visited and initiated Christel in the single brothers' choir, which is part of the legend building around choirs and memorial days.

3.7.2.2   Stundenbeter

The 'intercessionists' choir' is somewhat anomalous to the general choir structure, in that it consists of members of all choirs that are chosen to be part of the hourly intercessionists (*Stundenbeter*), as we see in the entry on 30 November where, 'according to our lambly mind (*Sinn*), new priests and priestesses from all choirs were appointed for the intercessionists choir' followed by a list

---

      Jahren das Läm[m]lein sich so gnädig an der Gemeine bewiesen und durch verschiedene Chor-LiebesMale und das AbendMal wieder erinnerlich und solenn gemacht". See also on the 18 June 1745, where, 'before we then went to our Husband in the holiest of holies, all choirs first had their lovefeast'.

145   UA R.6.A.b.17.a.1745.a, 2 May; 7 June; 11 July; 5 September; 7 October; 24 October; 3 November; 7 November; 26 December, all 1745.

146   UA R.6.A.b.17.a.1745.a, 7 December 1745.

147   UA R.6.A.b.17.a.1745.a, 7 November, where workers all had a pleasurable lovefeast in the antechamber with various love-ceremonies (*Liebes Ceremonien*), singing of arias and many heartfelt verses because of the dear Mama's birthday.

148   UA R.6.A.b.17.a.1745.a, 23 March 1745, it is noted that the communion members in all choirs are spoken to, followed by a communion conference on the 24 March, where it was decided who could and could not partake in communion, which was conveyed to each choir in the evening. The following day, the day of choirs, is when the big communion takes place and the diary includes a list of the members who went to communion from the first time, listed according to their choirs.

of names according to choir.[149] The *Stundenbeter* idea, i.e. that a member was appointed to pray every hour, is an older one, established in 1727. This fellowship of hourly intercessionists was then, at some point, incorporated into the choir structure.[150]

3.7.2.3 Visit from the Pilgrim Congregation

During a visit (from 26 October to 2 November) from Zinzendorf's entourage, the pilgrim congregation,[151] there was lots of activity in the various choirs, as well as in the community as a whole.[152] I will look at a number of items, because they give a good idea of the opulence in word and celebration which characterise the theology and community at this time, which, I will argue in the course of this book, derives from the world of the aristocracy.

On 28 October, Christian [Renatus, i.e. Christel] spoke with the main workers of the single brothers' choir and all choir communion brothers. Mama [Erdmuth Dorothea von Zinzendorf], Christian and Benigna inspected all the children.[153] On 30 October, there was a special lovefeast for the workers in the single sisters' choir, where Zinzendorf was present and speeches were given, after which the pilgrim members oversaw everyone in their various choir arrangements. Then there was foot-washing and communion in the single brothers' choir, which is described as follows:

> our blessed heart Johannes, Renatus, Steinhofer, Paul, Seebas etc. kindled today's communion hearts in the single brothers' choir through an anointed Pedilavium and thus led to blessed enjoyment of the martyr lamb, after this sacramental sensation and through descent into innermost worship, they still kissed someone who loves this choir above all and spoke to them bloodily and anointed.[154]

---

149 UA R.6.A.b.17.a.1745.a, 30 November 1745: "wurde nach uns Lämmlein Sinn aus alle Chöre neue Priester und Priesterinnen zum Stundenbeter Chor ausgemacht".

150 The choir itself is mentioned UA R.6.A.b.17.a.1745.a, 31 March, 2 July, 19 September (Christel's birthday) and 28 December (Benigna's birthday) 1745. On 2 December 1745 it is noted that new and old members from all choirs came to the intercession.

151 The term arose after Zinzendorf's banishment from Saxony in 1736 as the company which had no dwelling place, but travelled around with him. Peucker 2010, p. 43.

152 There was another visit in early October, which only seems to include Mama and Benigna. See the entry on 2 October, where the single brothers' choir had been very pleased with the visit from Mama, Benignel etc.

153 UA R.6.A.b.17.a.1745.a, 28 October 1745.

154 UA R.6.A.b.17.a.1745.a, 30 October 1745: "unser seeliges Herz Johannes, Renatus, Steinhofer, Paul Seebas, etc. entsündigten im ledigen Brüder Chor die heutigen Abendmals Herzen, durch ein gesalbtes Pedilavium und führten es so hin, zum seeligsten Genuß des Marter-

In summing up, the diary notes that for all choirs it had been a day of much enjoyment. The following day, on 31 October, things continued in the same vein, where the single sisters' choir had a big lovefeast, with hallowed (*gesalbte*) speeches, the contents of which are briefly mentioned:[155]

> Among all the hallowed speeches, the following dear little words captured well the blessed maiden hearts: That which makes a maiden, you have purchased with your blood and it was mentioned that sin in the world has almost abolished all choirs and *Stände*, only in the community can every heart in its choir come again to all mercy and bliss, and to close was sung with the most heartfelt sensation: sanctify for you your people make them into [spoils of the cross][156] for her you buried the sins with you,[157] bless the maidenhood,[158] give them power from the juice of the wounds.[159]

---

lams, nach dieser Sacramentlichen Empfindung und durchs anbeten innigem Versinken küßte sie noch jemand sonderlich der di[e]s Chor liebt ausserordentlich und redete sie sehr blutig und gesalbt an".

155   UA R.6.A.b.17.a.1745.a, 31 October 1745: "Unter allen gesalbten Reden faßten sich sonderlich die seeligsten Jungfr[auen] Herzen dis wörtgen wohl: Daß eine Jungfrau ist, hast du mit Blut erworben und wurde erwehnt, daß die Sünde in der Welt alle Chöre und Stände fast ganz aufgehoben, allein in der Gemeine könte jedes Herz in seinem Chor wieder zu aller Gnade und Seegen kommen, und wurde zum Beschluß mit der innigsten Empfindung gesungen: heilige dir deine Leute, mache sie zur [creutzes-beute etc] der du die Sünde bey dir begraben, seegen die Jungfrauschaft, gib Ihnen Kraft, vom Wunden Saft".

156   See for example *Londoner Gesangbuch* 2, hymn 47 written by Zinzendorf in 1739. The whole stanza is "Heilige du deine leute, mache sie zur creutzes-beute, und durchgehe alle glieder; so krigst du die glieder wieder". Sanctify for you your people make them into spoils of the cross, and go through all members, then you will get the members back.

157   See for example *Londoner Gesangbuch* 2, hymn 72 written by Zinzendorf 1741 and amended in 1744, stanza 33: "Wie muß dein herze nicht mit uns seyn, wenn wir uns deiner menschwerdung freun, und dich innig lieben! willst du das haben, *must du die sünden mit dir begraben*, die an uns seyn". How should your heart not be with us, if we rejoice in your becoming human, and love you dearly! If you want that, you must bury with you the sins, which are in us.

158   See for example Liturgie Buchlein, which is from 1757. The Hymn 44 includes a number of lines which repeat the above (I have only translated the italicised stanzas):

"*Heilige Dir deine leute, Mache sie zur creutzes-beute,*
Laß doch kein einiges unter uns seyn, Das nicht sollte gedeyn,
Das sich nicht nach deinem ganzen sinn, Gäbe hin.
Du weißt, wie lieb wir Dich haben. Heiland der mägde und auch der knaben;
O Haupt, voll Blut, speichel und voller Weh! Segne die heilge Eh;
Segne die Jungfrauschaft; Segne die Witwen auch Kindern gib stimmen von deinem hauch; Und deine Jünglingschaft Werde dahin gerafft Zu deiner ritter-kraft."
Sanctify for you your people make them into spoils of the cross,
O head full of blood, spit and rife with pain. Bless the holy Marriage

THE CHOIRS – A GENEALOGY 67

These random phrases could refer to hymns, or they could be embryonic hymns, which I have indicated in the footnotes. But the important thing about this lovefeast is the emphasis on speeches, and the content thereof, which is very similar to what we will encounter in the choir speeches.

> After this [the sisters'] choir had been overwhelmed with grace and blessing, this also befell to the single brothers' choir, so the dear pilgrim members and also many married brothers invited all to their special celebration and manyfold arrangements, with the sounds of trumpets and trombones. The illumination of their choir houses was resplendent, especially their new dormitory, consecrated on this occasion, which was gorgeously decorated with lights and foliage; during the lovefeast the blessed heart Renatus sang several arias to elegant music, which were especially arranged in light of his dear Mama's impending birthday, the main workers of this choir gave the dear Mama a subservient hand-kiss, before all grace so they can prove against their brothers to this point, our dear heart Papa was thrilled that on the place where our blessed Linner passed away, now an entire choir had been able to build a dormitory, the main reason for this celebration was among others to look at a picture, over which the caption in a green wreath [read]: our holy youthhood, be the wreath of the single brother, underneath this, a picture was painted, which was veiled before, [of] our dear Saviour on the sea, so deep in the ship, sleeping gently and sweetly on small kisses, around him stood bedsteads in which the blessed hearts sung in by the angels with Jesus's screams of anguish and lay thus, as though they smiled at the vision of Jesus' side-hole, over which our dear Papa as seal and latch thereon sang: Sleep in the protection of the Lambkin etc [and] many other bloody verses not to mention hallowed speeches and thus, this month was concluded with inexpressible joy by the single brothers' choir and with fervent blood emotion by the whole community.[160]

    Bless the maidenhood, bless the widows also give the children voices from your breath, and your youthhood will be reaped to serve your knight-power.

159 The 'juice of the wounds' is a popular theme found in several hymns, written by e.g. Zinzendorf (*Londoner Gesangbuch* 1, hymn 2116), Johannes von Watteville (*Londoner Gesangbuch* 2, hymn 177), Erdmuth Dorothea von Zinzendorf (*Herrnhuter Gesangbuch*, hymn 1826), and the count Balthasar Friedrich von Pomnitz (*Herrnhuter Gesangbuch*, hymn 2183).

160 UA R.6.A.b.17.a.1745.a, 31 October 1745: "Nachdem di[e]s Chor mit vieler Gnade und Seegen war überschüttet worden, so wiederfuhr es auch dem ledigen Brüder Chor, so sich

Let me just draw attention to the illumination, the hand-kiss, the music, the blood, and the painting, all of which I will pick up again in the course of the argument as features of the aristocracy, but which we cannot focus on here. But this presence of the aristocracy is emphasised throughout the diary with references to any nobleman, woman or child to set foot in the community,[161] thus for example, the occasions where members of the aristocracy came to inspect the community, their buildings and institutions, which happened on at least two occasions.[162] But to return to the quotation above, the role of the choir and the emphasis on the maiden-hood and disciple-hood are important themes which will recur with numbing regularity in the choir speeches, and appear here, in 1745, for the first time.

On 1 November, the pilgrim congregation dealt with a number of things, great and small: establishment of the community credit, held and organised choir quarter-hours, celebrated brother and sister Haberland's fiftieth anniversary in the married couples' choir, and finally with brother and sister Larisch's lovefeast and accompanying illumination for the pilgrim congregation.

    die theuren Pilger-Geschwister und noch viel verehlichte Brüder zu ihrem besondere Fest und viel artigen Anstalten, mit Trompeten und Posaunen-Schall alle invitirten. Die Ilumination ihrer Chor-Häußer war sehr zierlich besonders ihr Nunmehro durch diese Gelgehenheit eingeweihter neuer Schlaf-Saal, welcher sehr niedlich mit Lichtern und Laubwerck auszieret war. Unterem LiebesMa[h]l sang das seelige Herze Renatus unter artiger Music etliche Arien ab, so besonders auf seiner theuren Mama bevorstehenden Geburtstag eingerichtet waren, die Haupt-Arbeiter dieses Chors gaben der theuren Mama einem unterthänigen Hand-Kuß, vor alle Gnade so sie gegen ihre Brüder biß hieher bewiesen. Unser theures Herz Papa freute sich daß auf der Stelle wo unser seeliger Linner entschlafen, sich nun ein ganzes Chor einen Schlaffsaal hat bauen können. Der haupt Zwe[c]k dieses Fests war unter anderm auf einem Bilde zu sehen, über dem in einen Grünen Cranz die Uberschrift: deine heilige Jünglingschaft, sey der ledigen Brüder Cranz; drunter war auf einem Bilde abgemalt, wie ehedem weyland unser lieber Heyland auf der See so tief im Schiff, auf dem Küßgen sanft und süsse schlief, um Ihn herum stunden Bettstellen in denen die seligen Herzel von den Engeln waren eingesungen worden, mit Jesu Angst Geschrey und lagen so da, als lächtelten sie über dem Gesicht von Jesus Seitenhohl worüber unser theure Papa als zum Siegel und zum Riegel drüber sung: Schlaf ins Lämleins Schü[t]ze etc. vieler andern Blute Verseln gesalbten Reden nicht zu gedenken und so wurde mit unaussprechlicher Freude, vom ledigen Brüder Chor und mit innigem Blut Gefühl von der ganzen Gemeine dieser Monath beschlossen".

161   See for example on 2 October, where two aristocratic birthdays are celebrated: one Sister Christiane von Vippach, who had a birthday lovefeast, where the pilgrim members [Mama and Benigna etc.] were present; and then the celebration of Brother Baron von Schell.

162   UA R.6.A.b.17.a.1745.a, 8 November and 30 December 1745. Perhaps also on the 28 May 1745.

The following day, the pilgrim members held farewell quarter-hours mostly in their own choirs, and then, following many events and lovefeasts, took their leave, and were escorted as far as Guttau by Johann Langguth and Johann Nitschmann.[163]

As may be seen from these brief instalments, the visit was a big event for the whole community even if it primarily was the single choirs which took centre stage. Practically this is also due to the place of Christel in the single brothers' choir, the initiation of which, as mentioned above, was commemorated on 25 March, by all choirs. Likewise, as testimonial to his significance, Christel's birthday, 19 September, is celebrated by the single brothers' choir and the intercessionists' choir.[164] Zinzendorf's daughter Benigna also played a highly significant role in the single sisters' choir, who likewise, along with the intercessionists' choir, celebrated her birthday on 28 December. Her work in the single sisters' choir is mentioned on a number of occasions, three of which will be mentioned here:

On October 3, the diary notes that 'our dear Benignel, thus seeks to decorate her single sisters' choir as a clean bride to the Lambkin, today, after the working through a few days earlier, led her choir to enjoyment of the martyred lamb and after the tender love-kiss, sacramental sensation she finally sank into the dust with her 92 communion sisters with the question? You sisters has it happened, have you kissed the Lamb etc'.[165]

The second example is from 9 October, in the single sisters' choir, where 'all kinds of blessed changes were made because of the visit (?); the dear Benignel inaugurated the newly built garden house with a beautiful verse which she sang from the heart'.[166]

But she is not merely ornamental, in that it is noted that she along with the main workers of the choir brought the question of work for the sisters during winter to the judiciary council.[167] Benigna left Herrnhut a couple of days later,

---

163 UA R.6.A.b.17.a.1745.a, 1 and 2 November 1745.
164 UA R.6.A.b.17.a.1745.a, 19 September 1745.
165 UA R.6.A.b.17.a.1745.a, 3 October 1745: "Unsere theure Benignel so ihr lediges Schwestern Chor, dem Lämlein als ein reine Braut aus zuschmücken sucht, führte heut ihr Chor nach etliche Tage vorher gegangener durch Arbeitung zum Genuß des Marterlamms und nach dem zärtlichen Liebes-Kuß, Sacramentlichen empfinden, sank sie endlich mit ihren 92 Abendma[h]ls Schwestern in Staub dahin, mit der Frage? Ihr Schwestern ists geschehen, habt ihr das Lamm geküßt etc?".
166 UA R.6.A.b.17.a.1745.a, 9 October 1745: "Im ledigen Schwestern Chor wurde wegen des Besuchs allerley gesegnete Veränderungen gamacht, die liebe Benignel weyhete mit einem schönen Versel, das sie aus dem Herzen sang, das neu erbaute Garten Häußgen ein".
167 UA R.6.A.b.17.a.1745.a, 10 October 1745: "die liebe Benignel in ihrem Chor hatte mit den

but her return was announced on 22 October, and she turned up with Zinzendorf's entourage on 26 October.

So, both Benigna and Christel are active participants in the theological innovations taking place in the community, which is something to which we return in the following chapters. For now, we will continue with the choirs of the single brothers and the single sisters.

3.7.2.4 Single Brothers

On 13 February, the single brothers' choir was supposed to have had communion, but they had not received permission from the Saviour (presumably through lot), which distressed the entire choir when they were notified. However, on 6 March, they once again could partake in this union. Apart from the frequent references to communion and the speakings associated therewith,[168] the single brothers' choir has several interesting mentions.

One interesting cluster concerns the new house, which is built this year, along with the dormitory, all of which are related in the diary, but which I will discuss in the last section on choir houses.

Another interesting development in 1745 is the explicit mention of speeches to the choirs. Thus, on 1 January, the single brothers had a choir gathering in the community hall, on their commemoration or celebration (*Fest*) day. 'On this occasion, brother Johann [Nitschmann] spoke about material which until now had belonged to the Litany of Wounds'.[169] On 2 May, the diary notes that in the single brother choir, 'the dear Brother Johannes W spoke of the lamb as the true model for a single brother (in the days of his flesh)'.[170] 'His flesh' could refer both

---

Haupt Arbeiteren noch manche wichtige Sachen zum Beschluß verabredet sonderlich wurde auch heute im Richter Collegio überleget, wie man doch auf den Winter den ledigen Schwestern Arbeit verschaf[f]en kön[n]te".

168 UA R.6.A.b.17.a.1745.a, 13 February, 1745. For the other communion references see 2/6 March, 25 March, 15/16/17 April, 27/28 May (postponed from 8 May due to Brother Paul's absence), 20 August, 23 September, 5/7/8 October, 27/28 October, 12 November all 1745. We will return to 'speakings' later, but they consist of talks between the choir leader and the individual members assessing their spiritual state before their participation in the communion.

169 UA R.6.A.b.17.a.1745.a, 1 January 1745: "11 Uhr, da die ledigen Brüder, weil heute ihr Fest war, aufm Gemein-Saal eine Chor-Versammlung hatten, da bruder Johann die aus der Wunden-Litaney hieher gehörige Materien mit ihnen durchredte ..."

170 UA R.6.A.b.17.a.1745.a, 2 May 1745. Interestingly, 'the dear Brother Johannes W' has been deleted, and the speech changed to passive. We have almost the identical construction a week later on 9 May, where we read that 'incidentally also on this day did the bloody lambkin walk through his track, which was before himself, through all choirs, especially dear Brother Johannes W held a blessed quarter-hour for the single brothers' choir'.

to the brother and to the Saviour, something to which I shall return in chapter 4. Another reference to speaking is on 3 October, where the choir quarter-hour was salted and blessed with Johannes' speech. Finally, there is mention on an occasion on 26 October, where Christel gave a number of speeches, in which the presence of the lamb was strong, which left the entire single brothers' choir mesmerised.[171]

Apart from the quarter-hours,[172] we also find celebrations, such as the burial of Brother Döhner's body, which took place with trombones and hymns on the Hutberg.[173] The single brothers treated this funeral as a celebration because they so seldom had the luck to let someone from their choir into the upper community.[174] Also birthdays are celebrated, such as Johannes von Watteville's birthday on 18 October, which was celebrated by the single brothers' choir with many love testimonies. The gracefulness of the flowers, green twigs and lanterns is difficult to describe, with artistically intertwined letters stating 'you holy trinity, be blessed towards the little Johannes. The musicians proved their artistry and gifts were also given, while some leading workers from the other choirs also partook in their joy. In the antechamber, several from the married couples' choir had also marked the festive occasion with an event.[175] Other birthdays were also celebrated, though with less pomp.[176]

UA R.6.A.b.17.a.1745.a, 8 May 1745 where the 'held' is changed to hatte, and the dative for the Brothers' choir, changed to nominative making them the subject, while Johannes von Waterville has been crossed out: the single brothers' choir had a blessed quarter.

171 UA R.6.A.b.17.a.1745.a, 3 and 26 October 1745: "und in der Abendma[h]ls Viertelstunde, fühlte man an Ihm daß ein dem Lamme innigs Herze die Rede hielt, sein ganzes lediges Brüder Chor war durch Ihn recht aufgelebt".
172 UA R.6.A.b.17.a.1745.a 7 March, 4 October 1745.
173 The Hutberg is the hill in Herrnhut on which the cemetery, the Gottesacker (God's acre), is located. On the morning of Easter Sunday (in 1745 and still to this day), there is a procession to the Hutberg with the brass band after gathering in the Saal. UA R.6.A.b.17.a.1745.a, 18 April 1745.
174 UA R.6.A.b.17.a.1745.a, 17 January 1745.
175 UA R.6.A.b.17.a.1745.a, 26 October 1745: "gegen Abend wurde unsers theuren Johannes Geburtstag mit vielen Liebs-Bezeugungen vom ledigen Brüder Chor gefeyert, die Zierlichkeit von Blumen, grünen Zweigen und Lichtern ist nicht wohl zu beschreiben, mit verzogenen Buchstaben fand man den Ausdrü[c]k: du heilige dreyeinigheit sey vors Johan[n]lein gebenedeyt, die Musici bewiesen ihre Kunst und geschenkte Gabe auch dabey, Einige Haupt Arbeiter aus andren Chören freuten sich mit ihnen zugleich, Im Vorgemach haben auch etliche aus dem Ehe-Chor zur Freude dieses Fest-Tags ein Gelegeneheit gemacht".
176 Thus, on 23 November 1745, Brother Lachman had a birthday lovefeast, first with a couple of workers, then with the whole choir. And on 21 December, four single brothers celebrated their birthdays with a lovefeast.

3.7.2.5 Single Sisters

The entries concerning the single sisters' choir are very focused on its workers and practical issues,[177] as well as people who were coming and going.[178] A couple of times we do hear of an emotional content, though it is not expressed with quite the same pathos as in the single brothers' choir. Thus we twice hear of their connection with the Saviour, once on 1 May, where the diary notes that the single sisters' choir was acknowledged by its blood-groom [i.e. the Saviour] during communion, and once on 7 June where it states that there was much emotional movement (*Bewegung*) in the single sisters' choir and many tears were shed during their activities due to the intimate presence of their bloodgroom.[179] As mentioned, this emphasis on blood, presence, and connection will be absolutely central in the choir speeches which will be analysed in Chapters 4 and 5.

Communion is mentioned a couple of times,[180] as are various celebrations such as their commemoration day on 4 May, a commemorative lovefeast on 13 May to remember the two years since the laying of the cornerstone for their new house, followed by a blessed quarter-hour the same evening for the whole choir. On 19 November, several of the intercessionists in the single sisters' choir

---

177 UA R.6.A.b.17.a.1745.a, 23 April 1745, there was a special celebration commemorating a year since Marianne became choir elderess, and the whole choir was furnished with workers anew. 20 October 1745, the grace during the various activities in the single sisters' choir was palpable to the workers, and also moved the workers in the widows' choir. 1 November 1745, Anna [Nitschmann] and Benignel dealt with blessed organisation in the single sisters' choir. 8 November 1745, different matters were organised in the single sisters' choir. 14 November, Rosina Gneuss and Severin attended to their choirs. 20 November 1745, the workers in their [single sisters'] choir took note in their conference of the blessed founding on the blood and wounds of many souls in a short time.

178 UA R.6.A.b.17.a.1745.a, 9 June 1745, Anna Hotschina, who had been visitor a couple of weeks, left the single sisters' choir. 29 May 1745, in the single sisters' choir, they reflected on a meeting from the day before, where possibly a couple of nobles inspected them. 26 October 1745, the widows' choir received their Sister Grünbeck with love, as did the single sisters' choir with tenderness their dearest Benignel. 28 October 1745, the single sisters' choir witnessed much love and sincerity during the visit of the Pilgergemeine, and the following day 29 October 1745, Anna Caritas delighted, blessed and anointed the single sisters' choir with her presence, affectionate speech, and fervent prayer to the Lamb. Finally, 9 November 1745, Sister Ramsberg held a farewell lovefeast for the choir.

179 UA R.6.A.b.17.a.1745.a, 1 May 1745: "Das ledigen Schwestern Chor wurde von seinem Blut-Bräut[i]gam erkandt durchs heilige Abendmahl". 7 June 1745: "Es war auch eine grosse Bewegung im ledigen Schwestern Chor, und wurden in ihren Gelegenheiten viele Thränen vergossen, wegen der so nahen Gegenwart ihres Blut-Bräutigam".

180 UA R.6.A.b.17.a.1745.a, 1 May 1745, mentioned above, 19 November, the choir was informed of its impending communion. 23 November, Rosina spoke the choir communion sisters through.

had a lovefeast without any specifically mentioned occasion. And then a couple of birthdays, of which the most important one (in light of its celebration) is Anna Nitschmann's thirtieth birthday on 24 November, which we will look at more closely.[181]

> The 24 was the dear Anna Caritas' 30th birthday which, in order to celebrate it with much grace and blessing, the single sisters' choir arranged many activities especially with several lovefeasts. The first was held by 13 workers among themselves, and they left each other with much blessing, then there were several blessed quarter-hours for the choir communion hearts, and the enjoyment of the martyred lamb was saved until today, in order to be bloodier, juicer and more woundy. 82 made up the same heart, which this time experienced the sacramental sensation and cohesion, after the fervent adulation and affectionate lovekiss and the general communion quarter-hour, there was a general lovefeast for all single communion sisters and they were all to be seen in the *Saal* respectable in maidenly dress and in their order ribbons, [the *Saal*] was very illuminated, had a pyramid in the middle and at the side, where the workers from their choir sat, was placed a table with a sweet little lamb. on the wall with golden letters was the noble name and the middle of the C the bridegroom in his glory with the inscription 'Oh my lord Jesus Christ, who so willingly died on the cross, that is our Anna' etc. the musicians sat with orange lutes and sang and played all songs, especially the Aria of our dear Johann N. most pleasantly during the lovefeast. Many members were given to inspect their inner peace and the pleasant view of this choir, the most beautiful was the bloody sheen on the hallowed forehead and the likeness to Jesus' corpse and that so many want to be like Aennel [affectionate diminutive of Anna] thus the girls' choir in heart and kidney, the chosen soul and small hole bee, because now this noble maiden heart, everyone was so fervent and fully immersed and content, the blessed heart Johann N held for the them the last quarter-hour to close so that Jesus's anointment flowed over all words and thus this choir was especially bolted and sealed from all sins and afflictions of the world, especially from the now immediate erupting noise of war.[182]

---

181 Other birthdays include 24 October 1745, Friederica Sieverth, and 3 December 1745, where three satisfied hearts in the single sisters' choir had birthdays.

182 UA R.6.A.b.17.a.1745.a, 24 November 1745: "Den 24ten war der th euren Anna Caritas 30ter Geburtstag, welchen, um ihn mit vieler Gnade und Seegen zu feyern, das gantze ledige Schwestern Chor sich manche Gelegenheit machte, besonders mit etlichen Liebesmah-

One of the interesting things that will be taken up later is the connection between choir and body. First the single sisters' choir and its likeness to the corpse of Jesus. Then the girls' choir in heart and kidney wants to be like Anna Nitschmann. This notion of the choir as a corpse or a body will be taken up in the choir speeches, but with much greater attention to gender segregation than is the case here. Another interesting thing to note is the connection between Anna and Jesus intimated in the inscription and strengthened through the body/corpse idea: As the single sisters' choir holds likeness to the corpse of Jesus, so the older girls' choir as a body strives to be like Anna. I will argue that this is part of a cult of personality which is developing around certain people. The cult is based on Christology and is encouraged precisely through ostentatious birthday celebrations, such as this one, which includes music, a song for the occasion, and an illumination, all things which, as far as the diary tells us, are reserved for birthdays of the aristocracy.

But to return to the choir in its formal structures, what we see is that the 1745 diary represents the choir as an increasingly cohesive unit, with a dress, a celebration day (4 May), and increased organisation and management. There is no doubt that the ceremonial events and activities, as well as the blood and

> len; das erste hatte 13 Arbeiterin[n]en unter sich und giengen mit einem besondern Seegen aus einander. Darauf waren etliche gesegnete Viertelstunden vor der Chor Ab[end]M[ahl] Hertzgen und wurde der Genuß des Marterlamms eben auf heute gespart, um desto blutiger, säftiger und wundenhaftigere zu seyn; 82 waren zusammen derselbigen Herzel, so dis mal das Sacramentliche Empfinden und Verbinden erfuhren, nach dem innigsten Anbeten und zärtlichen Liebeskuß und der allgemeinen Ab[end]M[ahls-]Viertelstunde war ein allegemeines L[iebes]Mahl vor alle ledige Ab[end]M[ahl-]Schwestern und waren alle in Jungfraulicher Kleidung und in ihren Ordensbänden sehr respectirlich in ihrem Saal anzusehen, so gantz illuminiret war, mitten eine Pyramide hatte und an der Seite, wo die Arbeiterinnen aus ihrem Chor sassen, war ein Tisch gesetz mit einem nielidchen Lämmlein an der Wand mit Goldenen Buchstaben der edle Nahme und mitten im C. der Bräutigam in seiner Schöne mit der Beyschrifft: O mein Herr Jesu Christ, der du so willig bist an dem Creuz gestorben, dass unsre Anna ist etc. Die Musicanten saßen unter lauter Orangerie und sungen und spielten alle Lieder besonders die Arie unseres lieben Johann N[itschmann] sehr angenehm ab unter dem Liebesmahl. Es dürften viele Geschwister ihrer innigen Freude und der angenehmen Prospect dieses Chors mit anseh[e]n; das schönste war doch der blut[i]ge Schimmer an den gesabite Stirnen und die Ähnlichkeit der Jesus Leichen und daß doch manches will der Aennel gleichen und so das Mädchen Chor an Herz und Nieren, der außerwehlten Seel und hö[h]le Bienel – weil nun diese edle Jungfräuliche Herzen, alle so innig und eingesunken und vergnügt waren, hielt ihnen das seelige Mertz Johann N[itschmann] die lezten Viertelstunden zum Beschluß so, daß über alle Worte Jesu Salbung drüber floß und so wurde dis Chor besonders vor aller Sünde und Noth der Erden aufs neue verriegelt und versiegelt, besonders vor den nun gleich einbrechenden Kriegs-Geräusch".

wounds theology played a significant part in establishing the internal cohesion, so it is important to recognise these as part of the changes which took place in the early 1740s.

3.7.2.6 Older Girls' Choir – Older Boys' Choir – Children's Choir

The choirs of the children in their various ages are not often mentioned in the diary. There has been focus on the orphanage, but the actual choirs have been in the background. Nevertheless, they do turn up a couple of times, and thus should be mentioned. Especially the passus on the dreadful state of the older girls' choir should be emphasised, because it is a good example of the activity of the lot, indicated in the diaries with an *.

> On 14 January the dreadful state of the entire girls' choir was thought about and considered with sadness, whether anything is to be done in the older girls' choir at all? It stated yes* and then further asked whether the choir quarter-hour should be abolished for a while, 2. whether a special working through them was preferred, 3. whether a penance day was to be held with them, and 4. empty. It fell on the first, namely the choir quarter-hours, then was asked whether the daily house quarter-hours were meant as well, yes*.[183]

We are not informed as to the problems in the choir, but, as indicated earlier, we can see that there are several rearrangements over the year, which undoubtedly attempt to address whatever the problems were.

The two other mentions of this choir concern admissions into the choir, namely on 22 August, where 22 older girls were admitted into their choir at a very important lovefeast. And then Maria Pfautsch from Herrnhaag was admitted on 3 October.[184] As these two examples show, the level of detail from one section of the diary to the next varies greatly, with August being more akin to the abbreviated version, whereas the October section is very full and detailed. And it is usual for the fuller diaries to give names of the people admitted into choirs on the big community days, as is the case here.

---

183 UA R.6.A.b.17.a.1745.a, 14 January 1745: "Es wurde an das Schlechtstehen des gantzen grossen Mädgen Chors mit Wehmuth gedacht und überlegt, ob in dem grossen Mädgen Chor jetzt was zu thun seye? Es heiß ja*; denn weiter gefragt: ob der Chor Viertelstunde eine zeitlang aufzuheben? 2. ob eine besonder durch arbeitung mit ihnen vorzunehmen? 3. ob ein bußtag mit ihnen zu halten u 4. leer. Es traf das erste * nemlich die Chor Viertelstunde, ferner gefragt: ob die täglichel Hausviertelstunde auch damit gemeint ist? Ja *"
184 UA R.6.A.b.17.a.1745.a, 22 August and 3 October 1745.

The older boys' choir is mentioned three times. First, when it is noted that the boys' choir was divided into their quarter-hours, which had taken place already on 25 March, but because of several important occurrences, had remained until now 'and with palpable grace on their hearts was brought about in blessing'.[185] Second, in reference to a lovefeast where their Vice-Elder Metschel was presented, after which they sung their choir song most heartily.[186] The third mention is on 17 October where it is simply noted that 'in the older boys choir an inner breathing of grace was traceable also today'.[187]

The children's choir is mentioned once, on 28 December, the Day of the Innocents where the small choir therefore was given a separate occasion within which this matter, how some from their midst, for the sake of the child Jesus became the first martyrs, was told feelingly and simply by Johann Nitschmann.[188]

By drawing attention to the infrequent mention, I do not intend to indicate that children were insignificant. They are mentioned frequently in the diaries, for example in cases when it is noted that so and so arrived with their children, that this child went to the Saviour, moving in and out of the orphanage or the other children's homes,[189] and the shocking case of the little boy Heinrich Oertel, who was crushed to death in an accident, when a woodpile fell on him.[190] Also, it is mentioned on community days that children become older girls or older boys. But what I have been tracing here is the development of the choir as an explicit organising structure, within which various events take place, where

---

185 UA R.6.A.b.17.a.1745.a, 9 May 1745.
186 UA R.6.A.b.17.a.1745.a, 23 September 1745.
187 UA R.6.A.b.17.a.1745.a, 17 October 1745.
188 UA R.6.A.b.17.a.1745.a, 28 December 1745: "Wegen des Unschuldgen Kinder Tags wurde dem kleinen Chor deshalb eine aparte Gelegenheit gehalten und ihnen diese Materie, wie einige aus ihren Mitteln ums Kindes Jesus willen die ersten Maertyrer geworden, sehr hertzlich und einfältig von Bruder Johann N[itschmann] erzehlt".
189 See for example UA R.6.A.b.17.a.1745.a, 10 February 1745: The boy Ernst Paul, who until now was in training with Brother Franke, left, according to his own will. The sister Stok left with her smallest child for Neusalz to her husband, her two older boys she left here in the institution by Wilhelm (?). [...] there were various discussions because of the children issues, especially concerning the point of punishment, also among the orphanage brothers. On 9 April the two small (von) Seidliz'es from Peilau and the small (von) Gersdorff from Trebus moved from the five remaining small children in the wing, whom they have outgrown, and received their own room in the wing and also their own organisation under the care of the two brothers Gregor and Valentin. A final example from 16 June, where the seigneurial members from Leube brought the rest of their children, namely the two boys to be taken care of by the community.
190 UA R.6.A.b.17.a.1745.a, 12 March 1745.

instruction takes place, and the movement of grace is noted. And at this time, in 1745, all focus seems to be on the single choirs, the married couples' choir, and the widows' choir.

3.7.2.7 Married Couples' Choir

As we shall see in the following chapter, the married couples' choir was bedevilled by problem upon problem in 1744, the ramifications of which may be spotted the following year. And, indeed, the married couples' choir are given frequent mention in this diary, twice in reference to its small size, on 16 July, where the 'small married choir' held its foot-washing,[191] and on 7 September, the so-called Marriage feast, where 'the small married communion choir' celebrated communion.[192]

The problems of the previous year had resulted in a series of expulsions from Herrnhut, as well as redistributions of couples and families to the other communities in the German states. The fact that the leaders in Herrnhut were attempting to begin afresh with the married couples' choir is hinted at in the first two mentions of the choir in the diary.

The first mention is on 11 January, where it is remarked that 'the new married choir had a lovefeast, which took place in the antechamber, and from now the daily early and evening quarter-hour have begun. There was a reverence about this occasion and the quarter-hour is until now continued in respect and wound-emotion'.[193] The increase in morning and evening quarter-hours for the married couples is also noted on 28 April.[194] As we saw in the case of the girls' choir above, they had daily morning quarters, but the evening quarters were not indicated as being a daily occurrence. However, the following entries indicate that a watchful eye is kept on this 'new' choir.[195] For now, however, the desired result, namely respect and wound-emotion, is present.

---

191   UA R.6.A.b.17.a.1745.a, 16 July 1745.
192   UA R.6.A.b.17.a.1745.a, 7 September 1745.
193   UA R.6.A.b.17.a.1745.a, 11 January 1745: "Nachmittags war das Liebesmahl des Neuen Ehe-Chors hier und von jetzt an die täglich Früh und Abend Viertelstunden desselben, im Vorgemach angefangen, es lag eine Ehrwürdigkeit auf dieser Gelegenheit und die Viertelstunden wird bis dato mit einem Respect und Wunden-Gefühl continuirt".
194   UA R.6.A.b.17.a.1745.a, 28 April 1745.
195   On the understanding of the choir as *new*, see also UA R.6.A.b.17.a.1745.a, 29 June 1745, where it is noted that Johannes left, and took leave of a well looked after *young* married choir with a hearty talking through ("So wie das liebe Herz Johannes, bey seinem Abschied gar manch Herz weich machte, so nahm Er sich besonders auch sein apart gepflegtes junges Ehe-Chor unter einem herzlichen durchsprechen herzlich an").

The second mention is on 20 January, where a conference was held on choir matters, especially concerning the arrangement of the classes and associations in the married couples' choir.[196] This is followed up by the entry from 24 January, which was mentioned above as part of the restructurings of the classes and associations, where Johann Nitschmann states that few associations are made to prevent 'pressure, playthings and affectation' and instead classes were used as organisational means, because these, thus Nitschmann, were less prone to abuse, while serving the same purpose.[197]

These two tracks, on the one hand keeping an eye on them, and preaching the 'correct theology', and on the other, the constant reorganising, remain constant for the rest of the year.

In the first category, we see that on 18 February, there was yet another lovefeast with a class of married people randomly chosen for the purpose of Brother Johann (Nitschmann) meeting with them once and telling them his plan. It then follows that a similar one occurred eight days earlier (but not noted in the diary) and that they would continue until everyone had been seen to. It had been as good and blessed as the previous one, and Brother Nitschmann's speech had occasioned many moist eyes.[198] This lovefeast with Nitschmann's speech is not what has been referred to as 'speakings' in preparation for communion, which in the married couples' choir takes place couple by couple.[199] Nor is it the quarter-hours, which take place every morning and every evening. Rather this is a meeting of a group within the group, to which a speech is given[200] which, it seems, lays out the intention, or meaning of it all. The diary reads "s[einer] Sinn", which could refer to Nitschmann's mind, but also to a larger sense of purpose or plan. What we have here, then, looks like instruction in line with a larger scheme, which is shaped by theological changes in the

---

196 UA R.6.A.b.17.a.1745.a, 20 January 1745.
197 UA R.6.A.b.17.a.1745.a, 24 January 1745. For full quote see above, footnote 122.
198 UA R.6.A.b.17.a.1745.a, 18 February 1745.
199 This takes place on 22 February, where it is noted that 38 couples were talked to by Brother Johannes, the Vogts and Dorothea Till. The subsequent communion takes place on 27 February described in some detail. UA R.6.A.b.17.a.1745.a, 22 February and 27 February. There is another communion speaking on 21 April with subsequent conference on 23 April, and communion on 24 April. And communion speaking for the married choir is also noted on 18 May and 7 October, where they were spoken through by Brother von Wattewille, and the Nitschmanns prepared themselves on 8 October, and took communion on the 9 October. Finally, a very blessed communion is mentioned on 14 December, all in 1745.
200 Another speech is noted on 23 May 1745, where the workers from the married choir had a blessed nightwatch after Johann Nitschmann's speech. See also the mention of Anna Nitschmann's speech to the single sisters' choir on 29 October 1745.

understanding of marriage, and the increased emphasis on blood, both of which will be examined in further detail in the next chapter. But here, we may note that in the quarter-hour on 31 May, Brother Johann wished 'the bloody blessing' (*blutgen Seegen*) on the thorough and new division of the married couples' choir.

The final example of instruction takes place on 6 October, where

> Our dear heart Johannes made a couple of remarks to the daily watchword and Lamb text [Deuteronomy 33:18 'Rejoice in your going out' and *Herrnhuter Gesangbuch* 1838, verse 5 'the firstling of our communities still often makes us cry from joy'] 1. what kind of important indictment this gave to our [first] community refugees or strangers, 2. what kind of courteous answer or call from them to us is contained therein. In today's words of the Saviour, he showed the important sense in which the five foolish bridesmaids represent members of the community of whom one cannot say that they will go to hell, however they would obviously be excluded from the enjoyment of the wedding of the Lamb.[201]

This somewhat enigmatic statement could very well refer to the problems of the previous year, which centred upon differing understandings of marriage and resulted in a series of expulsions from Herrnhut. An assessment of the married couples' choir from January 1744,[202] which will be discussed in detail in the following chapter, shows that there were differing understandings of marriage within the married couples' choir, several of which advocated abstaining from intercourse. This understanding of marriage clashed with the new marital mystery, which emphasised marital intercourse coupled with language about enjoyment of the Lamb etc. The new marital mystery alienated especially the ethnic Moravian (*mährisch*) members of the community, the religious refugees.[203] It is not impossible to see Johannes von Watteville's exposition of the watchword in connection with these issues, interpreting the Moravian (*mährisch*) refugees as the foolish bridesmaids, who will not partake

---

201 UA R.6.A.b.17.a.1745.a, 7 October 1745: "Unser liebes Herz Johannes machte bey der heutigen Loosung und Lamms Text wichtige Anmerkungen, 1. was vor eine wichtige Anrede das gäbe zu unsern (ersten) Große Mädgen-Exulanten oder Pilgern, 2. was vor eine artige Antwort oder Zuruf von ihnen an uns darin enthalten, In den heutigen Worten des Heylands, zeigte Er den wichtigen Sinn an, wie die 5 thörichten Jungfrauen Glieder der Gemeine vorstelleten, von denen man zwar nicht sagen könte, daß sie in die Hölle kämen, aber doch of[f]enbar vom Genuß der Hochzeit des Lam[m]s ausgeschloßen wären".
202 UA R.4.C.II.10.1. The document is published and translated by Petterson and Faull 2017.
203 See especially Sterik 2012, esp. pp. 307–60.

in the eschatological copulation with the lamb. Thus, this speech is part of the instruction in that it lays out what *not* to endorse.

3.7.2.8 Widows' Choir

A very significant event took place in early March. On 3 March, it was agreed at a conference that the widows should have their choir communion on Fridays. And thus, on Friday 5 March 1745, they celebrated communion by themselves for the first time, instead of, as had been the custom, celebrating with the single sisters.[204]

Quite a number of lovefeasts are mentioned. One without explicit occasion, namely when Frau General (von) Damniz gave the whole widows' choir a lovefeast on 26 July, but most are stated with the reason. Some are given to celebrate special days,[205] birthdays[206] and some as an occasion to deal with a number of things, as for example the lovefeast given by Sister von Seydlitz for her birthday, which coincidentally had a double usefulness, namely to commemorate that today is one year since Mother Schindler was consecrated into her widow's rank and to take leave of Sister Dörffler as blessed servant of the widows' choir.[207]

Mentions are made of new members,[208] organisational issues,[209] general edification,[210] and visits, as for example the return of Sister Grünbeck, who trav-

---

204   UA R.6.A.b.17.a.1745.a, 3 March 1745. Then follows other communion posts, the speaking on 6 May followed by communion on 8 May, which mentions the presence of their soul-husband; communion on 5 September, 8 October mentions preparation for the sacramental enjoyment of the lamb in the married and widows choir, and the subsequent communion on 9 October. A speaking is mentioned on 11 November and finally, on 16 December 1745, the widow's choir had a blessed communion with 30 people.

205   UA R.6.A.b.17.a.1745.a, 2 February 1745, the widows' day was celebrated with a common lovefeast on the feast of the purification of Mary. 2 May, Sister Dürren gave her widows' choir a lovefeast in remembrance of the day, one year ago, when she was consecrated into the choir (*eingesegnet*). 17 June 1745, the widows celebrated that they moved into their house two years ago.

206   UA R.6.A.b.17.a.1745.a, 21 October 1745, the widows choir took pleasure in the dear heart among them, Sister Grünbecker, and gave her a birthday lovefeast in spite of her absence.

207   UA R.6.A.b.17.a.1745.a, 12 April 1745.

208   UA R.6.A.b.17.a.1745.a, 11 July 1745, Sister Gintownt was admitted into the widows' choir. 7 October, Rosina Hückel was accepted into the widows' choir (*Chor Anstalt*). 12 December, Sister Leopold and Sister (von) Falkenhayn were blessed into the widows' choir. Leopold had arrived a couple of days earlier, on 9 December 1745, despite the unsafe roads (second Silesian war).

209   UA R.6.A.b.17.a.1745.a, 14 October 1745, the offices of servant and sick-helper are renewed because of many patients. On 9 November, reorganisation took place in the widows choir because of the departure of Marcha Micksh. 1 December 1745, the widows' choir bestowed the office of sick helper on sister Gintow.

210   UA R.6.A.b.17.a.1745.a, 3 October, notes a blessed quarter-hour. On 20 October, the work-

elled with the Pilgrim community – and was in Herrnhut in early October,[211] and again late October to early November, where she was received with pleasure on 26 October and the following day notes how busy she was.[212] That she was popular shows up in the occasion taken by the widows' choir to remember her with love.[213]

3.7.2.9 Widowers' Choir

As mentioned earlier, there is an indication in this diary that this is the year of the foundation of the widowers' choir. The entry notes that in the evening of 3 December, the baker, Schmidt, gave a lovefeast to his association and a couple of workers, to express his pleasure at being accepted into the community. On this occasion, Father Dober, as their actual worker, was very pleased that now all the men had been accepted into the community, and thus now he was of the opinion that they constituted a choir. This is slightly strange, in that two years earlier in the description of the celebration of the Day of All Choirs, on the 25 March 1743 (see below), it is mentioned that during the gathering of married couples, Brother Dober and his widowers' choir of nine had occasion to celebrate a small lovefeast.[214]

4 The Day of All Choirs: 25 March

We now turn to look at the Day of All Choirs. In his entry on the choir days in the dictionary of Moravian terms, Paul Peucker notes that the first choir day to be established was that of the married couples' choir on 7 September 1744, followed by celebratory days for the other choirs.[215] The Day of All Choirs, cel-

---

ers in the widows' choir were moved by the palpable grace in the single sisters' choir. 29 October, there was a birthday celebration along with a death of Sister Neumann, and a description of how her soul left her *Hütte* (cottage, tabernacle, i.e. earthly body) a few hours after the blessing of Sister Grünbeck. On 2 December, several activities in the widows' choir were blessed, all in 1745. I have retained the term *Hütte* (rather than body) in the originals to emphasise the oddity of the term.

211 UA R.6.A.b.17.a.1745.a, 10 October 1745 in the widows' choir it is noted that Sister Grünbeck had lot of work and shown warmth at her leave taking.
212 UA R.6.A.b.17.a.1745.a, on 26 October 1745, the widows' choir received their Sister Grünbeck with love, as did the single sisters' choir their dearest Benignel. 27 October notes how occupied the dear Grünbeck was with lots of work.
213 UA R.6.A.b.17.a.1745.a, 10 November 1745.
214 R.6.A.b.16.1, 1743, p. 106.
215 Peucker 2010, p. 19.

ebrated on the 25 March does, however, not have a commencement year. As a survey of the diaries show, it had a very slow coming into being, which I will trace in the following.

The earlier diaries are, as we have already seen, rather fragmented. Martin Dober's diary usually runs through a whole year, and the diary from 1735 is also complete. The rest range from a couple of days to a couple of months, such as the two first ones, neither of which has an entry for the 25 March, in spite of covering the period from January through to August. However, they are written on very few pages, and thus have very sparse entries.[216] Zinzendorf has a diary from 1731, but there are no entries for this day, nor are there any entries between 18 March and 1 April.[217]

In Martin Dober's diary from 1732 we have an entry which notes that on the afternoon of the feast of Annunciation or Lady day, the marriage review was held, namely the speaking – an event which means that the elders speak with the individual couples and assess their situation, conjugal and spiritual. Then, after some notes on different things, we have a nota bene, which adds: 'The young men and women were also spoken with, in which the gracious Lord Count praised the faithfulness of the single *Stand*'.[218] This sounds tantalisingly close to the nature of the choir speeches, in that this is precisely the kind of material they contain, as mentioned in the first chapter, and as we shall see further in some of the following chapters.

There is no entry for 25 March 1733 in Dober's diary,[219] so our next clue is in the diary from 1734, which is taken from a fragment of a diary which covers 23 January to 20 October 1734, where it states that all of the married brothers and sisters followed the example of Mary and went thoroughly through all of the *"Ehestands sachen"* the material of the married *Stand*.[220]

There are two diaries from 1735, with slightly more information. The first is by Michael Jacob von Bagewitz,[221] which states that the day was especially celebrated in Herrnhut because of Mary's example, and the awakening one year ago, when her example was presented to the children, the young men, maidens,

---

216 The 1730 diary covers these eight months on 11 octavo pages (UA R.6.A.b.9a) and the 1731 diary the same period on three folio pages (UA R.6.a.b.10.1).
217 UA R.6.A.b.10.2.1 The last March page is the reverse page of a single folio page and apart from two lines written at the top, is an empty page – apart from the glass ring-mark on the bottom left-hand side. The next page, which begins 1 April is a new folio sheet.
218 UA R.6.A.b.10.4.
219 UA R.6.A.b.11a.4.
220 UA R.6.A.b.11b.1b.
221 A teacher in the Moravian community with a history of sexual offences. See an account of his misdeeds in Peucker 2006, pp. 40–1.

and especially the married people. Bagewitz notes that the marriage material was explained to clarify 1. what the reason for the esteem of the married state is, namely, God's arrangement, appointment and union; 2. what relation the married people had a) among themselves, b) towards God and Christ, c) towards the human species; 3. how to improve the rank (*Stand*) through abstention and discipline.[222]

The other diary from 1735 is Dober's diary. He notes that every class had a quarter-hour to celebrate the Annunciation, in which the [married] men and women in particular were given a speech on the dignity of the married rank, on the means by which one may reach this, and how to keep it sacred. A song was composed on this occasion and Friedrich von Watteville had written it all down.[223]

There are unfortunately only fragmented diaries for the years 1736–39, none of which cover March, save one from 1739, which does not mention any particular occasion on this date.[224] However, the trend with quarter-hours through the groups on 25 March continues in 1740, where one of the diary fragments mentions choir. It is noted that 'a separate quarter-hour was held through all choirs, it was spent in blessedness'.[225] The following year (1741) the entry is also brief, merely noting that it was the Annunciation day, and that the quarter hours were held as is a custom on this day. It was also children's Prayer day, but these events seem to be separated.[226]

---

222   Bagewitz's hand is almost impossible to read. The diaries have been transcribed and compiled by Siegwart Friedrich Hark in the mid- to late nineteenth century, with some amendments. UA R.6.A.b.12.1, 25 March, 1735: "Es ward der Tag in Herrnhut besonders gefeyert wegen des Exempels Mariä, und der vor 1 Jahr da erfolgten Erweckung, da ihr Exempel den Kindern, den jungen Burschen, Jungfrauen, sonderlich den Eh[e]leuten besonders ward vorgestellet. Es ward die gantze Eh[e] Materie abgehandelt 1) was der Grund der Hochachtung des Eh[e]standes, nemlich Gottes Ordnung, Einsetzung und Copulation ii) was die Eh[e]leute vor eine Relation 1) unter sich, 2) gegen Gott und Christum, 3) gegen der Menschlichen Geschlecht hatten iii) wie der Stand zu beßern, durch Enthaltung und Zucht". Thank you to Frau Moreau for help with the deciphering.
223   UA R.6.A.b.12.3 (Dober): "Es wurde jeder Klas[s]e eine Viertel Stunde um des Fests Maria Verkündigung willen gehalten. Denen Männer und Weiber ins besondere eine Rede vom der Würdigkeit des Ehestand[es], von den Mitteln wie man dazu gelangen können. wie heilig er gehalt worden und so es wurde ein Lied darauf gemacht. Das F. von Wattevil[le] hat alles nachgeschrieben".
224   UA R.6.A.b.13.d.1. Indeed, the entry mentions that the new communion members were selected on 25 March, and then that 26 March was the important communion day.
225   UA R.6.A.b.13.d.2, 25 March 1740: "Verkünd[igungs] Tag. wurden die Stundenbeter completirt. und aparte - Viertelstunden durch alle Chöre gehalten es wurde im Seegen verbracht".
226   UA R.6.A.b.14.1, 25 March 1741 "war der Maria verkündigung-Tag. Da wurden die Viertelstunden gehalten wie es dieser tag gewöhnlich nicht ohne Seegen".

In 1742, the Annunciation falls on Easter Sunday, which is celebrated in the morning. The Annunciation is celebrated in the afternoon, where the choirs had lovefeasts with milk-bread and beer or water. At 1pm, the lovefeast of the [married] men and women took place in the big hall, the widowers and widows in separate rooms at 3pm, and after 3pm the single brothers and sisters had their lovefeast in their respective houses, along with the children. The big boys also partook. In the last lovefeast from 5 to 7pm, the usual transition of children from one choir to the next took place, addresses were given and verses were sung for all the children who were accepted into another choir.[227] It is noted towards the end that there are four children's choirs on each side: big boys, middle boys, small boys, small children, and then the babies (*die Säuglinge*), and likewise on the girls' side.

Here things have developed, and a much more defined celebration is described, and the children's Prayer day seems to have been integrated into the Annunciation celebration.

In 1743, it really takes off. A significant clue is that already on 20 March it is noted that the manner of celebration had been discussed and decided through lot (*). The description of 25 March covers more than three quarto pages, and canvasses the entire day from 6 in the morning to 7 in the evening. The main points of the day are:

> 6am: Prayertime on the gospel text held by Hehl followed by a small conference.
>
> 9am: the widows had their gathering in the antechamber, during which a number of important items were discussed: Namely to be a widow from the heart, abstaining from useless gossip especially what concerns marital matters, on sinfulness, and on the connection with the lamb.

---

227 UA R.6.A.b.15.1 "Nachmittags waren wegen des Fests Mariä Verkündigung Chor Liebesmahle, worzu wenig fremde, ja unter den Männer und Weibern nicht einmahl alle die zur Gemeine gehören, genommen wurden. Wir hatten Milchbrödel und Bier oder Wasser. Um 1 Uhr ging das Liebesmahl der Männer und Weiber auf dem gorßen Saal an. Die Wittwer und Wittwen jedes apart auf Stuben von 3 Uhr; Nach 3 Uhr der ledigen Brüder und ledigen Schwestern jedes in derselben Hause und der Kinder dazu auch die großen Knaben kamen von 5 biß 7 Uhr. Bey den letzen Liebesmahle wurde die Gewöhnliche Versetzung der Kinder aus einem Kinder Chore ins andere vorgenommen. Alle Kinder, die in ein ander Chor kamen, wurden zusammen vorgerufen, angeredet und denn wurden ihnen etliche Verse gesungen: War mit einem großen Eindruck vor die Kinder. Sowohl auf der Knaben und Mädel Seite sind 4 Kinder-Chöre 1) Große Knaben 2) Mittel knaben 3) Kleine Knaben 4) Kleine Kinder dazu noch die Säuglinge kommen. So ists auch auf der Mädel seite. Das Lamm war uns bey allen Liebesmahlen innig nahe und seegnete uns".

10am: The older girls gathered in the single sisters' hall, sang some verses, and then Vorwitz spoke on infatuation with the wounds of the lamb. This lasted until 12. The children's hour was also held at 10am. At 12.30pm the single sisters gathered in the large hall and the single brothers at the same time in the hall in the brothers' house. It is noted that the number of the single sisters were 124 communion sisters (*Abendmahlschwestern*) in number, under which were 10 from the older single sisters' choir, and three girls who came over from the older girls' choir. Finally, there were five sisters absent today. The sisters were spoken to about the feeling of a single sister towards the Saviour and about the simple nature towards the lamb. The single brothers were 86 in number, five absent, who all belong to the choir, but who are in Silesia and thus not counted, and two are excluded.[228] They were presented with topics ranging from witnessing to sinfulness, and the destination of a single brother.

At 3pm, both sexes of the married couples' choir came together in the hall and they were spoken to about the importance of the humanisation of the Saviour and the absolution through his blood, the importance of the married *Stand* and which blessings are available in the married state. During this gathering of married couples, Brother Dober had a small lovefeast with the nine widowers.

At 5pm both sexes of the children's choir came together in the hall, where a catechism took place concerning the present day and the importance of the state of the child, given that the Saviour had also been a child. Then they were presented in their classes, each sex in three classes according to year. Each class was given a small verse, and it finished with a prayer over all. This lasted until 7pm. There were 100 boys and 81 girls. Before this congregation of the children, the big boys had their assembly, and were spoken to about the spirit of witnessing.

At 7pm there was a Singing hour, and that was the day.[229]

There are several interesting things here. Once again, we see what looks like choir speeches, or addresses on the particular importance of the moral conduct

---

[228] Since the numbers counted are of the communicant members of the choir, it must be presumed that the excluded brothers are excluded from partaking in the Eucharist, which was a common punishment for a number of offences.

[229] UA R.6.A.b.16.1, 25 March 1743. In the abbreviated diary (UA R.6.A.b.16.2), it is noted that 25 March was Annunciation or Jesus' humanisation day. From all the choirs the communicant members had lovefeasts, and the members were moved up into the next choirs according to their ages, which is also indicated in the full version.

of the members of the choir, and the relation of the brothers and sisters to Jesus as we saw in the brief mention of subjects discussed in the addresses to the widows, the single brothers and sisters, the married couples, the children, and the older boys. Furthermore, we note that the term choir is in full use. Finally, there is the significant expansion in the description of the celebration as well as close attention to the numbers involved. This close attention to planning is indicated in the entry from the previous Wednesday, mentioned above, on consulting the lot to determine the celebration of the day.

In 1744, we note a shift. This is the exact wording of the diary, which while brief, gives an impression of the mood:

> The celebration of the annunciation was an exceptional day of blessing whence blessedness came and remained upon the whole congregation, which will not be forgotten quickly. The dear Papa Zinzendorf held all choir quarter-hours and at the end of the day the big Song-hour, the bloody church-prince with the five wounds was in the Hall and very close to the whole congregation. In the conclusion to the Song-hour, Christian Renatus was made Brother Langguth's helper in his single brother elder-office, and he was consecrated by Papa under many tears and finally the whole community was with priestly blessing placed in the open side crevice. After this was the prayer-hour when the Ave Agnus Dei, or Litany of Wounds (*Wundenlitaney*) was prayed and sung for the first time. The following night, the dear Papa left again.[230]

First of all, Zinzendorf's presence is explicitly mentioned. This celebration takes place during his exile from Saxony, and he arrived the evening before from Silesia and, as noted, left on the night of the 25th, presumably unbeknownst to the authorities. The choir quarters which he held, are undoubtedly what I have determined as the first choir speeches, the addresses given to the wid-

---

230   UA R.6A.b.17a.1744a: "Als am Fest Mariæ Verkündigung war ein ausnehmender Seegens Tag, davon ein Seegen auf die gantze Gemeine gekommen und zurücke geblieben, der nicht wieder wird vergessen werden. Der liebe Papa Zinzendorf hielt alle Chor-4telstunden und zum Beschluß des Tages die grosse Singstunde: der blutige Kirchen-Fürste mit den 5 Wunden war auf dem Saal und überall der Gemeine sehr nahe. Zum Beschluß der Singstunde wurde Christianus Renatus zu Bruder Langguths Gehülffen in seinem ledigen Brüder Ältesten Amt unter vielen Thränen eingesegnet und endlich die ganze Gemeine mit Priesterlichen Seegen in die offene Seiten-Spalte hinein gelegt. Nach dem war das Stunde Gebet da das Ave Agnus Dei, oder den Wunden-Litaney zum erstenmal hier gebetet und gesungen wurde. Die Nacht darauf gieng der lieber Papa weiter fort".

THE CHOIRS – A GENEALOGY 87

ows, older girls, maidens, and the single brothers.[231] Also extant is the address given at Christian Renatus' (Christel[232]) consecration. The lovefeasts did not take place, but the entry from the following day explains that there had not been time for this, wherefore they took place on 26 March – needless to say with great blessing. The language is also more explicit. 'Bloody church-prince', 'open side crevice', and Litany of Wounds are topics not encountered before, but which will be increased in the next years. The presence of the Saviour in the hall has not been mentioned in explicit connection with this celebration, but it was an increasing factor in the diaries after the appointment of the Saviour to chief elder of the community in November 1741, to which we return in greater detail in the following chapter.

In 1745, there is no mention of the annunciation, but the focus is on the community with the Saviour (*Gemeinschaft mit dem Heyland*), rather than the example of Mary. The day begins at 6am with a blessed prayermeeting over the community. At 8 the entire community congregated to the blowing of trumpets for communion, after which the new brothers and sisters were consecrated and then they all went to the church in Berthelsdorf. The whole congregation stood as one heart in front of the Lamb and felt and received his death and bloody blessing. It was divine. The children's events took place in their proper order, where also the children were made to understand the importance of the Saviour becoming human and child. All choirs made a remembrance of this day a year ago, when 'Papa' came to visit and the single brothers' choir made a special remembrance of the consecration of the dear Christel.[233]

---

231   UA R.20.HS1 and HS2.
232   Christian Renatus, von Zinzendorf, the only son of Zinzendorf was known as Christel in the Moravian community. See Peucker 2015, pp. 139–41.
233   UA R.6.Ab.17a.1745a, 25 March 1745: "Den 25ten war früh um 6 Uhr Bethstunde im Seegen von der Gemienschafft mit dem Heyland und dem Liebhaben untereinander und von dem Seegen und Leben, das in den Wunden Jesu liegt und auf die Sünden-Herzen kommt. Um 8 Uhr kam die ganze Gemeine aufs Blasen der Trompeten zu sammen und hatte den Liebeskuß zur Præparation auf den innigen Zusammenfluß zu einem Leib und Geist durch den Genuß des Leichnams und Blut unsers Mannes; nachdem derselbe vorbey und die Gemeine eine Weile auseinander gegangen war, kamen die Geschwister dann wieder zusammen, da wurden die Geschwister die von neue mitgehen durfften, eingesegnet und von da giengen wir miteinander hinein nach Berthelsdorff in die Kirche, da die sämmtliche Gemeine wie Ein Herz vor dem Lamme da stund und seine Tödtung und blutigen Seegen fühlte und empfing; es war was göttliches. [...] Die Kinder Gelegenheiten giengen in ihrer Ordnung, da auch den Kinden das Mensch und Kindlein werden des lieben Heylands wichtig gemacht wurde. Wir erinnerten uns überhaupt in allen Chören des Seegens-Tages, den wir vorm Jahr hier gehabt bey Besuch unsers theuren Papa und sonderlich im ledigen Brüder Chor, durch die Einsegung des liebes Christels".

I will not give detailed descriptions of the following years, but merely note that a shift has taken place, from celebrating the annunciation to the humanisation of Jesus, so that the emphasis is on the connection between the community and the Saviour. In 1746, it seems that the speaking with the various choirs has been pushed to the days before, in preparation for the big day on the 25th. The first two lines from the day are: '25 the blessed congregation of the Lamb celebrated the big salvation minute, when the blessed creator of all things became a creature',[234] continuing this emphasis on the connection between the Lamb and his congregation.

Comparing it with the developments noted in the diaries, we see that the Lamb, Jesus' presence and the blood and wound motifs enter comparatively late in the celebration of the Choir Day, namely in 1744, whereas the diary has it beginning in 1742, albeit slowly. One of the reasons for this discrepancy could be that Johann Langguth, the primary preacher of wounds, was in the Wetterau from August 1742 to August 1743.[235] As we will see in the next chapter, where we will trace this theological development much more closely, there seems to have been a not entirely successful effort to introduce this blood and wounds theology into the community, which may be seen from marriage reports from January 1744.

The point of this section was to show how the Day of All Choirs developed from Lady Day observance, albeit with some pastoral attention, into a large-scale celebration of the choirs and their individual attributes from the year 1743. Coupled with the detailed analysis of choir vocabulary in the diaries, we see that the organisation of choirs was not something which was present from the very beginning of the community, but a particular way of organisation which arose in response to something around the turn of the decade. Before we move on to examining what that is, we need to take a look at the choir houses, since these dwellings became an important locus for cultivating the choir spirit, as the speeches will indicate.

5 Choir Houses

In one of the diary fragments from 1739, we hear of an unexpected problem with the people moving into town, that many young men would be moving into the street where the maidens lived, wherefore the maidens were assigned

---

234 UA R.6.A.b.17.a.1746, 25 March: "Den 25ten feyerte die seelige Lamms-Gemeine die großer Heils-minute, da der seel[i]ge Schöpffer allerding zum Creatürlein worden".
235 Thank you to archivist Olaf Nippe for chasing this up for me.

another house, away from the street.[236] The young men had since 1731 lived in the upper story of the inn, of which they were also in charge. The maidens had lived in Kühnel's house since 1733. This means that they had lived in the same street, separated only by the girl's wing, for six years. In 1739, this was no longer acceptable, and over the next couple of years, the sisters' dwellings migrated across to the other side of the great hall, known as the *Saal*, and the brothers' house was built across the main road.

While segregated dwellings thus had been the practice from the early 1730s, it was not as severely managed as it would become later, with the consolidation of the choir ideology. I suggested above that the idea of the intercessionists, the hourly intercessionists which began in 1727, was co-opted into the choir structure and given a place within this particular system. A similar case may be suggested for the houses. As the above shows, the unmarried men and women of Herrnhut lived in segregated dwellings well before the 1740s which is where I argue the concepts of choirs and choir houses took shape. In extension of the detailed examination in the previous section, we might consider whether 26 young men living together in the left wing in the orphanage is the equivalent of a choir house? Indeed, as mentioned in the beginning of the chapter, it is not a given that the choirs apart from the single brothers and sisters even had their own houses. In a choir speech to the widows' choir, Zinzendorf states that 'in the congregation it is a central feature that every choir goes its own way and become aware of exactly that blessing which lies in that choir'. He adds that it is a 'Commoditaet' if one has a house for this purpose, but that the particularity of the choir lies in the division.[237] The house is then, according to this quotation, merely an external supplement to an ideological ordering of the community.

The present section will look briefly at the developments which led to the construction of the choir houses for the single brothers and sisters, and the widows and widowers. It does seem a bit like 'musical chairs' in that there was a lot of shuffling around for the three latter groups. This means that making

---

236 UA R.6.A.b.13.d.1, 3 March, 1739: "Weil in die Gaße unvermuthet so viele Pursche ziehen müssen, wo die Jungfern auch wohnen, so wurde *Jungfern* (?) ein andre Hauß angeweißen". The reading of the italicised Jungfern is not certain, it has been corrected and cannot be clearly made out on its own. From the context, however, it is the reading that makes the most sense.

237 Widows, 6 June, 1755: "In der Gemeine ist das eine Haupt-sache, daß ein jedes Chor seinen Weg gehe, und just den Segen gewahr werde, der in *dem* Chore liegt. Es ist eine *Commoditæt*, wenn man ein Haus dazu hat: aber eigentlich liegts in der Abtheilung der Chorreigen" (UA R.20.HS46).

sense of which house was where, to whom it belonged, and in what order is not always easy. The single brothers were always in a privileged position, presumable because of their nature as the most productive workforce.

5.1   Single Brothers' House

> He has made the choir house into workshops and poured his spirit over them.[238]

On 22 June 1739 the foundation stone for the single brothers' house was laid in Herrnhut, which was commemorated with a lovefeast.[239] Up until then, they had lived collectively in various quarters, such as the left wing in of the orphanage (*Waisenshaus*), whence they moved in 1728, and, after the rapid growth of the community, the inn (*Gasthof*) in 1731.[240] The house was completed in September, and the young men, now designated 'single brothers', moved in on 16 November 1740.[241] But the community kept growing, and in 1745, on 22 April, with much celebration, the foundation stone was laid for a second single brothers' house.[242] While Bechler mentions that the first house was built at seigneurial expense,[243] the second house was constructed by the brothers, which is mentioned several times in the 1745 diary.[244] During this work, the brothers also acquired another house next door, Kloß's house, where work was commenced on a dormitory in September,[245] and inaugurated on 10 September. On 27 September the first lovefeast took place in the newly built brother-house (by which I think is meant the dormitory), after which the carpenter brothers upholstered the first room. The following day the single brothers moved,

---

238   Single brothers, 9 July 1755: "Er hat die Chor Häuser zur werkstätten gemacht und den Heiligen Geist über sie ausgegossen" (UA R.20.HS51).
239   UA R.6.Ab. 13.d.4: The title of the document in the catalogue is "Purschen-Liebesmahl in Herrnhut zur Grundlegung ihres Hauses" but the document refers to the single brothers' choir.
240   Bechler 1922, pp. 47–8; Uttendörfer 1925, pp. 83–4.
241   UA R.6.A.b.17.a.1745.a, 3 March mentions a birthday celebration in this 'choir house'.
242   UA R.6.A.b.17.a.1745.a, 22 April.
243   Bechler 1922, p. 48. And remember that the seigneurial income came from the estate and the bonded labour.
244   UA R.6.A.b.17.a.1745.a, 9 July, 30 July 1745 where a single brother from Krause, who is a bricklayer, comes to help on the house.
245   UA R.6.A.b.17.a.1745.a, 4 September 1745, Klossen's house, close to the single brothers, was conceded and foundation made for a very necessary dormitory for the brothers at the inn.

accompanied by music, from the inn and had a lovefeast in thankful remembrance of what the Lamb until now had done for them.[246] After the completion of the house, the various trades moved in, but the diary mentions the *posament* makers and the cobblers moving their apprentices into the single brothers house on 16 October and celebrated with a lovefeast on the 20 October with the masters.[247]

Meanwhile, work on the new house continues, and on 21 October the brothers continue working into the night, dragging stones under the half-moon with wonderful music, because they want the building to be ready by winter. Likewise, they work until late at night with music on the building on 25 October. On 31 October, the houses were illuminated for the pilgrims-visit, and we have the presentation of the newly built dormitory as cited above in the section on the pilgrims-visit. So, the three-house complex of the single brothers is under construction from 1739 till 1746, when the three houses are joined by walkways.[248]

This construction of the choir house also meant a considerable reorganisation of labour. In his unsurpassed study of the industrious spirit in Herrnhut from 1743 and onwards, Otto Uttendörfer presents us with the struggle that took place between the masters and the single brothers in 1745. The occasion for this struggle was that 'little by little, the single brothers want to draw the apprentices in all professions from the community to their choir house and to grant each trade a separate room'.[249] Such a move was vehemently opposed by the masters, and the push towards separating apprentices from their masters and loss of control of the labour force occasioned great dispute.

However, as a description of the single brothers' choir house from 1748 shows, the move went ahead, and the leader of the single brothers' choir could show off the house to the government committee:

> through the gallery of one house, where on both sides several large rooms full of skilled craftsmen, shoemakers, linenweavers, cabinetmakers, passementiers, each profession for itself, all fully occupied with work, the rooms incidentally, were very clean and in impeccable order. In the basement of this house is the single brothers' bakery and other arrangements

---

246   UA R.6.A.b.17.a.1745.a, 28 September 1745.
247   UA R.6.A.b.17.a.1745.a, 20 October 1745.
248   Bechler 1922, p. 50.
249   Uttendörfer 1926, pp. 212–14. This study remains the most comprehensive study of social organisation and labour in Herrnhut.

belonging to the household. On the second floor was found several more rather spacious rooms, within which a fair amount of tailors were all fully occupied [...] the committee was led through a covered walkway into the other building and gallery [...] where again on both sides, rooms in which craftsmen of all kinds such as watchmaker, seal-engraver, jeweller, coppersmith, wigmaker, whose cleanly work was especially noticed.[250]

The cohesive nature of the single brothers' choir is undergirded by a magnificent building in which all daily activities were carried out.

5.2 *Single Sisters' House*

The sisters lived in communal houses from 1733, when Anna Nitschmann and a number of unmarried women moved into Friedrich Kühnel's house. In 1739 they moved from there into the right wing of the Orphanage, and from there, in 1740, into three neighbouring houses on Zittauer Strasse, near the archives in today's Herrnhut, which they eventually bought during the early 1740s.[251] In 1748, due to increase in members, they also took over a wing in the adjacent *Vogtshof*, a large Baroque manor-house. These four houses were the sisters' house until 1756, when the single sisters moved into their very own built-for-that-exact-purpose choir house, the foundation stone of which was laid on 24 April 1755.[252] The house was completed in October 1756, and the sisters moved in on 16 October:

---

250 "durch die Gallerie des eines Hauses, da auf beiden Seiten etliche große Stuben voll von Professionisten, Schustern, Leinwebern, Tischlern, Posamentieren, jegliche Profession für sich, alle in voller Arbeit sich befanden, die Stuben übrigens selbst ganz reinlich und in untadelhafter Ordnung waren. In dem Souterrain dieses Hauses ist die ledige Brüderbäckerei und andere zur Ökonomie gehörige Anstalten. In der zweiten Etage fanden sich abermals etliche ziemlich geräumige stuben, darin eine ziemliche Anzahl Schneider, alle in voller Arbeit waren [...] in das andere gebäude und dessen Gallerie [...] da sich wieder auf beiden Seiten Stuben und in denselben Professionisten von allerlei Art als Uhrmacher, Petschierstecher, Juweliere, Kupferschmiede, Perückenmacher befanden, deren reinliche Arbeit besonders bemerkt wurde." Uttendörfer 1926, pp. 225–6. The archival document (minutes from the meeting of the brothers' house, 1748) which Uttendörfer is quoting, is no longer extant.

251 UA R.6.A.b.13.d.2 on 13 October 1740 mentions that the single sisters began moving into their house. UA R.6.A.b.13.d.3, mentions that on 14 November 1740 the move is completed. UA R.6.A.b.13.5.a is Martin Dober's speech on New Year's Eve 1740, where he thanks the Saviour for the brothers' and sisters' houses, and the children's institutions which were established this year. In another, shorter copy (5b), this is not mentioned, but in the Dutch version (5c), which looks like a translation of 5a, it is.

252 UA R.6.A.b.16,1, 25 January 1743.

THE CHOIRS – A GENEALOGY

> Today was the long-awaited day, for which the maiden choir in Herrnhut have sighed for so long and often with tears, when we move into the choir house, newly built not without many difficulties through the grace of our most beloved Lambkin.[253]

Discussions regarding the construction of a new choir house for the single sisters began already in 1743, perhaps as a result of the success of the brothers' choir house. The year begins with a conference on the possible construction of a house for the single sisters.[254] The lot was cast, but with no outcome. Less than a week later, on 10 January, they cast the lot again, asking whether it was urgent, to proceed slowly, or to be done as is. The lot, as many times before, fell blank. It was then resolved not to proceed until more clarity was to be found.[255] Two weeks or so later, the single sisters took a room in Nixdorff's house, within which eight sisters were placed in charge of Sister Hirter with Regina Hansch as helper.[256] It was apparently obvious that something had to give in respect to the single sisters, and so instead of building a house, a dormitory was commenced on 14 February, 1743:

> The single sisters' dormitory, which [...] as a building attached to the present houses connected with corridors across to both ends, so that a large courtyard remains in the middle. The building itself will be 27 ells long, 18 broad and the dormitory itself six ells in height; the lower level built with brick and therein a couple of parlours and small rooms set up for industry (*wirthschaft*), then, the prayer-hall itself under a curb roof and then immediately over the dormitory under the other roof a wash-floor. The wood for this is also identified in these days.[257]

---

253 The only extant diary for 1756 begins on 19 October, thus three days after the inauguration of the sisters' house. The only place I could find the description was in in the GN.C.: "Heute war der längst erwartete Tag, nach welchem sich das Jungfern-Chor in Herrnhut schon so lange und of mit Thränen gesehnt hatte, da wir nemlich das durch die Gnade unsers allerliebsten Lämmleins und nicht ohne manche Schwierigkeiten neu erbaute Chor-Haus bezogen". (UA GN.C.65, 1756, 10, Appendix 20, 349).
254 UA R.Ab.16.1, 4 January, 1743: "In der Conferenz wurde viel über der ledigen Schwestern Haus-Bau deliberirt, sonderlich weil wir 3 Riße darzu hatten, es wollte sich aber nach etlich maligen *en vor dißmal nichts sonderliches ausklären".
255 UA R.Ab.16.1, 10 January, 1743: "Weil es mit dem Ledigen Schwestern Hausbau so gar nicht fort- und zu was positives kommen will, so wurde gefragt * ob geeilt, oder langsam gegangen oder so gemacht werden sollte wie sichs gibt, es war aber, wie schon vielmal, leer. *Dann wurde resolviert, nichts mehr vorzunehmen bis es sich ausklärt".
256 UA R.6.A.b.16,1, 25 January, 1743.
257 UA R.6.A.b, 16.1, 14 February, 1743 "der ledigen Schwestern Schlaff Saal, daß – und wie er

The foundation stone for this dormitory was laid by Sister Augustine on 13 May 1743, at 11am. The event was led by Brother Dober, who spoke, and Brother Grassmann, who prayed, several hymns were sung and many tears were shed.[258]

The consecration of the new dormitory and assembly hall took place at noon on 15 December 1743. The event was led by the head of the single sisters, Anna Marie Lawatsch, who consecrated the assembly hall with prayers and tears in the presence of 226 young women from the single sisters' and older girls' choir, as well as guests. During the lovefeast marking this event, one of the single sisters, Elisabeth Thomas, had died (presumably in a sick-room) and was taken to the death-chamber (*todten Kämmerlein*) in the new house. This was regarded as the Saviour's wish for the consecration of the chapel on the same day. After the lovefeast, they all went to the dormitory, and stood between the beds singing a couple of verses. Then Benignel [Benigna von Zinzendorf] prayed, generating a flood of tears. After some verses, they went back to the assembly hall, where two songs were sung, one by 'the dear Brother Ludwig' [Zinzendorf], the other by Sister Anna Nitschmann, both composed for the occasion. Then followed a penetrating speech by Sister Lawatsch, some more songs and closing prayers by Anna Pisch.[259]

While this complex was not built from scratch, as was the case with the brothers' house, this wing of the sisters' house is a choir house with a dormitory, an assembly hall for their own gatherings, and functional rooms for work, laundry etc., reflecting an increasing concern for co-mingling of the sexes. A reference in the 1741 diary noting that the sisters received 62 Reichsthaler in their house-box, indicates that they were collecting money for the project, and thus they paid for it themselves.[260] As was the case with the single brothers, the house of the single sisters was also both a dwelling place and a work-house. Unrestrained by concerns such as family or household

---

      sollte als ein An- oder Hinter-Gebäude zu ihrem jeztmaligen hause, mit Gängen hinüber an beyden Enden, angefügt werden, so daß in der Mitte ein mäßiger Hoff bleibt. Das Gebäude selber soll 27 Ehlen in die Länge 18 in die Breite und der Schlaff-Saal an und vor sich 6 Ehlen in die Höhe kommen, das unterste Sto[c]kwerk gemau[e]rt und darinnen ein paar zur Wirth-Schafft dienliche Stuben und Cammern eingerichtet, hernach der bett saal selber unter einem gebrochenen Dach, und denn unmittelbar über dem Schlaff-Saal unter dem anderen Dach ein Wäschboden. Das Holtz darzu wurde gleich dieser Tagen auch ausgezeichnet".

258   UA R.6.A.b, 16.1, 13 May 1743.
259   UA R.6.A.b, 16.1, 15 December 1743.
260   UA R.6.A.b.14.1, 6 April 1741.

management, the many unmarried women were free to spin, weave, darn etc. at an unprecedented level.[261]

5.3 Houses of the Widows and the Widowers

The house of Friedrich Kühnel, which, as we saw, had served as the first house for the maidens, was taken off Kühnel's hands by the community in 1739. In this house the community then established a wool factory and gave the widows a parlour and a small room, which they took over in 1740.[262] This is not mentioned in the 1740 diary, nor is it mentioned in Dober's assessment of the year on New Year's Eve. It is mentioned, however, in the diary from 1743, where it is noted that this house was inaugurated as the 'widows' house' on 17 June 1743 and recorded as follows:

> At noon the widows' house was inaugurated with a lovefeast by the entire choir. There were 51 widows present and some guests, it was very blessed and important for the choir.[263]

Short, but sweet. Little space is afforded to record this event; it is one of several events on this day. While Bechler assumes that this is the house in which they had lived since 1740, there is a record in the 1743 diary on 27 May that it was resolved that the widows buy the community-house for their choir.[264] If this is so, then this would be the house inaugurated on 17 June, and in which they lived until the completion of the widows' house on 16 February 1761.

The first house for the widowers of Herrnhut was inaugurated on 28 October 1748 in the place where the large sisters' house complex would be built in 1755. Five widowers moved in, and by the time they moved out in 1754, 34 widowers had lived there, but without any particular choir organisation.[265] From

---

261 See the document UA R.4.C.IV.12 which shows the labour carried out in the sisters' house. It is undated and its location is also unknown, but through the names mentioned on the lists, it may be located to Herrnhut in the years 1740–43.
262 Bechler 1922, p. 59.
263 UA R.6.A.b, 16, 1, 17 June 1743: "Zum mittag wurde das Wittwen Haus von dem ganzen Chor eingeweyht mit einen Liebesmahl, es waren der Wittwen 51 gegenwärtig und einige Gäste, es war sehr gesegnet und dem Chor wichtig".
264 Bechler notes that Kühnel's house was bought by the widows on 27 March 1744 for 600 Thaler, and they expanded and rebuilt it extensively in 1746. Bechler 1922, p. 59. In the document outlining the Status of Herrnhut, dated 1744, there is a paragraph on Kühnel's house, and a thought that it would be ideal for the widows' house due to its size (UA R.6.A.a.58.2, under *Bausachen*) – the Status of Herrnhut must be from the year before, then.
265 Bechler 1922, p. 61.

there, the widowers moved into the widowers' house which was completed in 1754, adjacent to the brothers' choir house complex. The dates of inauguration were 22 and 23 February 1754, where the first day saw the inauguration of the dormitory, and the second day the inauguration of their assembly hall.

> Today and yesterday the widowers moved into their new choir house and would tonight sleep in their new dormitory for the first time. Therefore, Brother Johannes gave a choir speech this evening, welcomed them tenderly in their new house and testified for them his hope that the Lambkin and his spirit in the same, and them in the choir mercy and legitimation in the community over the choirs would be traceable, in addition he notified them a couple of points in regard to the organisation of the house, and that their dear neighbours, the single brothers, had taken over to serve those widowers who wanted to eat together. Then he went with the entire choir to their dormitory, gave another short speech on the temple-nature of our dormitories, the preservation of our *Hütten* through the corpse of Jesus, and our choirs blessed communal sleeping, and then he inaugurated the dormitory with a heartfelt and penetrating prayer, and they slept together so smoothly and blessed through the night, that they the next morning could not express themselves enough thereover.[266]

We will see more of this language when we turn to the choir speeches in Chapter 4, but what I wanted to draw attention to here was the extensive celebration of the inauguration of the house and its choir, which was somewhat more elaborate than what took place in the widows' choir house.

---

266   UA R.6.A.b.19a.1754, 22 February, 1754: "Heute und gestern waren die Witwern in ihr neues Chor-Haus eingezogen, und solten diese Nacht zum ersten mal auf ihrem neuen Schlaf-Saal schlafen, deßwegen hielte ihnen Bruder Johannes abends eine Chor-Rede, bewillkommte sie in ihrem neuen Hause aufs Zärtlichste und bezeugte ihnen seine Hofnung, daß sie das Lämmlein und sein Geist in demselben von Neuen segnen und ihnen in der Chor-Gnade und Legitimation in der Gemeine den andere Chöre nachhelfen würde; zugleich meldete er ihnen noch einige zur Einrichtung des Hauses gehörige Puncte, und daß ihre liebe Nachbarn, die ledigen Brüder, diejenigen Witwer, die gemeinschaftlich zusammen speisen wolten, zu bedienen übernommen hätten. Dann begab er sich mit dem sämtlichen Chor auf ihren Schlaf-Saal, hielte noch eine kurze Rede, von der Tempelhaftigkeit unserer Schlaf-Sääler, der Bewahrung unsere Hütten, durch Jesu Leichnam, und dem seligen Beysammen schlafen unserer Chöre, und dann weyhete er den Schlaf-Saal mit einem herzlichen und durch-dringenden Gebet ein, und sie schliefen die Nacht so sanfte und selig beysammen, daß sie sich den andere Morgen nicht genug drüber ausdrucken konnten."

6 Conclusion

The three sections of this chapter have all served to argue the same point, namely that the terminology of choir did not take hold until the 1740s. The first section has gone through various diaries from 1736 to 1745 and traced the emergence and use of the terms choir, bonded groups, associations and classes, which from the late 1730s were used to designate various groupings within the community. But, as I demonstrate, it is not until 1742 that the prominence of choir is clear; this is coupled with an increase in blood and wounds terminology.[267] The second section traced the development of a commemorative day, the Day of All Choirs, held on 25 March. I show that the big shifts take place between the years 1742–43 and then another big leap to 1744, when the blood and wounds theology also becomes central to the depiction of the special day. Finally, the section on the houses serves to show that while the way of organising the community in gender-segregated housing had been a significant feature of spiritual life in early days, this was strengthened and developed along with the choir structure, and thus co-opted into the choir ideology. The choir houses served as more than just dwellings. They constituted the place for work, dining, sleeping and praying for the single choirs by 1743. This does not mean that there were no communal activities. The diary from 12 April 1745 notes that because the *Saal* was being whitewashed and would be scrubbed on the following day, the community activities were separated and held in the choirs and the choir houses,[268] indicating that there were communal gatherings in the great assembly hall. But the choir houses became the primary units of identification, where choir assemblies were held, and, presumably, where choir speeches were given. They were, then, physical and spatial manifestations of the choir structure, and supported the production of the choir as a unit of and unto itself. The level of detail has been deemed necessary to demonstrate that the choir nomenclature arose at a particular time in the history of the community, and, as I will argue in the following chapter, to deal with a specific situation.

---

267   Schmidt dates the active organisation of the choirs to around 1741. Schmidt 1909, p. 201.
268   UA R.6.A.b.17.a.1745.a, 12 April, 1745. Weil heute der Grosse Mädchen Saal geweißt und den Tag darauf gescheuert wurde, so wurden die Grossen Mädchen-Gelegenheiten getheilt in den Chören und Chor-Häusern gehalten.

CHAPTER 3

Blood, Wounds, and Class

1 Introduction

Under the entry for 1 January 1741, the Herrnhut diary notes the following:

> In the community, many different people made the decision to completely surrender themselves to the Saviour. Hedelhofer weepily requested help of his [peers] in the community to think of his soul. At this time, the choirs present the following figure: Among the men (and women [added later]) there are around three or four whose surrendering one may deny, although many have much to unlearn and forget.[1]

This entry is interesting for a number of reasons. First, it testifies to the awakening within the community, which meant a surrendering to the Saviour. Second, it explicitly mentions the choirs as the framework within which the individual can be helped to reach the desired state of surrender. Finally, only few are thought to be untouched by this awakening, but many need to unlearn and forget.

This process of unlearning and forgetting will increase through the years as we will see in the present chapter. As I traced in Chapter 2, the gradual implementation of what became the choir structure was also followed by a development in the language of devotion in the early 1740s. The blood and wounds theology and the presence of the Saviour became increasingly pervasive, and came to displace the earlier theological focus, which thus had to be unlearned and forgotten.

Blood and wounds theology is usually understood as a given within the Moravian Brethren, with few questioning its actual emergence. One such exception is Paul Peucker who has shown that the blood and wounds theology was a way of creating distance from the Pietism of Halle. He also notes that the increasingly graphic language met with resistance in the community, and

---

[1] UA R.6.A.b.14.1, 1 January 1741: "In der Gemeine machten auch verscheidene viel den Entschluß sich gantz zu dem lieben Heiland zu bekehren. Hedelhofer bat auch sehr wehmüthig seinen in der Gemien zu Hülffe seiner Seele zu gedenken. Die Chöre stehen folgenden Gestalt gegenwartig; unter Männer [und Weiber] sind etwa 3 oder 4 denen man Ihr Bekehrung absprechen kan ob schon bey vielen noch vieles zu verlernen und vergeßen ist".

cites the Moravian (*mährisch*) elder Andreas Grassmann's letter to Zinzendorf in May 1742, complaining about Langguth's blood and wounds preaching as an example of the dissenting position.[2] Despite this initial resistance, Peucker notes, 'blood and wounds devotion soon prevailed'.[3]

In the following, I will trace this resistance, and argue that it was particularly members from Bohemian and Moravian backgrounds who were averse to this new-fangled blood business,[4] and that a veritable purge took place in 1744 ridding the community of the most resistant members. Thus, the blood and wounds theology not only meant a departure from the perceived crusty theology of Halle Pietism, but also created distance from the Moravian and Bohemian members in the community.

2   Martin Dober's Account

As a way into the changes that took place in the 1740s and the developments in language and theology, a good place to begin is a document by Martin Dober, which was discovered among his papers after his death in Herrnhaag in 1748. Dober, while reluctant at the beginning, eventually came to embrace the blood and wounds theology, which is evident from this text. Dober begins by outlining the doctrinal developments from 1725, the year he arrived in Herrnhut, until 1747, after which he compares the first theology with the new theology.

Dober states that the teachings on the wounds and nailmarks of Jesus began in 1734 with Zinzendorf, who taught that Jesus alone was all, and that 'we' were less than nothing, which should be an advance in faith, rather than an impediment to it. He then continues:

> As we are accustomed, this grace increased until it came to the point that one knew nothing more than that a Lamb had been slain. The wounds were soon thereafter preached by themselves. At first it was among a few, when the true free grace made the plan with the preaching of the gospel known, and the method was regulated accordingly. It also became general in the teaching, the Lambkin ushered [us] into the special-grace, which was then choir grace of all the choirs (when only the widowers were left

---

2   Peucker 2015, p. 27. Andreas Grassmann's letter UA R.14.A.14.25, copy in UA R.21.A.52.13.
3   Peucker 2015, p. 27.
4   See Sterik 2012, p. 313.

over), the communion-grace, the taking up and acceptance of the knowledge of the right orders to dispatch. In the year 40, it was the Lamb and the community which were rightfully placed on the throne at the same time, in year 41 it was the dear Saviour as the creator, and, also the special grace toward us, became our elder. Since then, everything went better than before, without comparison – also in the teaching. In the year 1743, all the choirs were even closer to the goal; in the teachings we became even more childlike, especially however, in 1744, when the *Pleura* [sidehole], Brother Lambkin [Jesus], Papagen [Zinzendorf], Mamachen [Erdmuth Dorothea], the dear little church, the mother office, the father office, the bride turned up, when the common prayer was finished, everything with its own particular exquisiteness and with this important insight, its respective grace.[5]

This development corroborates what we saw in the diaries: that the blood and wounds material escalated in the diaries after the early 1740s, and we saw that this particularly took place with Johann Langguth. According to Dober, the community improved greatly through these teachings.[6] Turning to his comparison between the theological language of the earlier years to that of the late

---

5 "Diese Gnade nahm nun, wie wir es gewohnt sind, immer zu, bis es endlich so weit kam, daß man in der That nichts mehr wußte, als daß ein *Lamm* geschlachtet wäre. Die *Wunden* wurden dann bald allein geprediget. Erstlich war es unter einigen, da die rechte freie Gnade bekennet, der Plan mit der Verkündigung des Evangelii, und der Methoden darnach reguliert wurde. Es wurde aber auch unter denen Lehren allgemein, das Lämmlein führte weiter in die Specialgnade hinein, als da sind *Chorgnaden* aller Chöre, (da nur noch die Witwer übrig sind), die Abdmahlsgnade, die Aufnauhme und Annahme, die Kenntniß derer rechten Boten zum Verschicken. Anno 40 war es *das Lamm und die Gemeine* die auf einmal recht auf den Thron gestezt wurde, anno 41 war es der liebe Heiland *als der Schöpfer und auch zugleich die Specialgnade vor uns, daß er unser Aeltester* wurde. (In diesem Jahre die Gemeinlitaney). Seitdem ging alles überhaupt ungleich besser, als zuvor, also auch in der Lehre. Anno 43 legte es sich noch viel näher mit allen Chören zum Ziel, in der Lehre wurden wir noch kindlicher, sonderlich aber 44 kam *die Pleura, Bruder Lämmlein, Papachen, Mamachen* [Wundenlithaney] *Schnürchen, das Mutteramt, das Vateramt, die Sponsa* auf, da der Common-prayer verfertigt wurde; alles mit seiner besondern ausnehmenden und mit dieser wichtigen Erkenntniß accordirenden Gnade". (UA R.24.B.79). There is another version UA R.21.A.2.B.2.

6 Edita Sterik notes that Grassmann's letter, mentioned earlier, was an attempt to intervene in the power struggle which took place between Martin Dober and the 15 years younger Johann Langguth, which went beyond theological dispute, and concerned Langguth's attempts to undermine and usurp Dober. Zinzendorf's reaction to Grassmann's letter was that Dober was displaying envy towards Johannes. Sterik 2012, pp. 313–14.

1740s, we see that everything has been narrowed to focus on the Lamb and the details of its gory appearance.

> Where once the redemption was preached, now it is the wounds and the blood, where once faith was described, now the Lamb is described; then, the foundation, now the elements, in which we live and weave, where we swim and bathe [...] Then, it was told above all the grace God had shown us, now it is told to one another what the little Lamb looks like, how wide the little side [the side-wound] had opened, how it was mistreated, torn, dug out with nails, how one sees in Spirit how it flowed from the loins ...; then, one took pleasure in mainly one's achieved grace, but now, mainly, that one is a sinner. The happiness of a sinner, the being a sinner, the being a little worm, the melting receding small creature was completely forgotten in the beginning!⁷

For Dober, then, there was a large shift in the theological content, which had changed from what could be termed classical theological expressions of redemption and mercy, to that of the evocative and provocative language of blood and wounds. Another point of interest is the direction of teaching. The impression in his quote is that the old teaching was top down ('then it was told') whereas the new one is more lateral (now it is told to one another). A connected topic is his claim that the early theology had paid no attention to the little worm, the individual believer in his or her earthly and sinful condition. This new emphasis on the individual believer will be a focus in the following chapters, in that this really is a new direction with significant consequences for the collective. But for now, we follow the path of victory of this particular theology within the community in Herrnhut.

---

7 "Dazumal predigte man die *Versöhnung*, nun die *Wunden* und das *Blut*; dazumal beschrieb man den *Glauben*, nun beschreibt man das *Lamm*; dazumal den *Grund*, nun das *Elemente, darin* man lebt und webt, *da* man schwimmt und badet. [...]
    Sonst erzählte man von allem dem, was Gott uns vor sonderbare Gnade getan hat, wie weit man gekommen, wie es da und gegangen ist; nun sagt man einander, wie das Lämmlein aussieht, wie weit das Seitchen aufgetan, wie es geschunden, zerricht, mit Nägeln duchgraben wurde. Wie man in Geist sieht, wie's aus der Lende fleußt [...]
    Sonst freute man sich *hauptsächlich seiner erlangten Gnade*, aber nun hauptsächlich, daß man ein Sünder ist. Das Sünder-Glück, das Sünderseyn, das Würmlein seyn, das zerschmoltzene welche kleine Wesen war ganz vergossen in der Erst!" (UA R.24.B.79).

3   The Purge in Herrnhut

In her *Lebenslauf*, Catharina Elisabeth Milditzin (1728–1801) mentions that 'the year of 1745 was a time of sweeping out here in Herrnhut, when many bad people were sent away from the community'.[8]

Indeed, the years 1743–45 were turbulent ones in Herrnhut, and there is not much extant material from these years. Unity archivist in the nineteenth century, Ludwig von Schweinitz, made a number of transcriptions from the communal diary, as well as a version of the material which differs in a couple of details from the communal diary of 1744.[9]

Apart from the communal diary and von Schweinitz's transcriptions, there are three further documents of interest which testify to the unrest of the time, and these are the few bones on which I build my analysis. The first document is a report of the 'speakings' between three workers, namely Andreas Grassmann, Anna Maria Lawatsch, and David Nitschmann (Syndikus) and 84 married couples in Herrnhut and Berthelsdorf held from 7–17 January 1744.[10] The second document is a letter from Carl Heinrich von Peistel to Zinzendorf with details of his actions, dated 11 October 1744. The third document contains the minutes of a meeting held in February 1745, between Anna Maria Lawatsch (Mutter), Rosina Gneuss, and Johann Langguth, concerning the 'Herrnhut Circumstances'. In this section, we will go through these sources in chronological order, beginning with the marriage document, proceed with the surviving diaries and the letter from Peistel to Zinzendorf, and then finish off with the minutes from the 1745 meeting.

3.1   *The Marriage Document*

The Marriage document is a document of 23 folio pages reporting the results of meetings, or 'speakings' with the married couples of Herrnhut over ten days in early January 1744. In this document, it is noted that it was David Nitschmann, Anne Marie Lawatsch, and Andreas Grassmann who spoke with all the couples, and the handwriting in the document is David Nitschmann's (Syndikus). The concept of 'speaking' may be traced back to the early days of

---

8   UA R.22.70.98: "Im Jahr 1745 war hier in Herrnhut eine Zeit des Aufräumens, da viele schlechte Leute von der Gemeine weggeschickt wurden."

9   Peucker 2015, p. 176. In his letter dated 12 October 1744 to Zinzendorf, Jacob Till does not mention any trouble at all, in spite of this date being in the middle of things, as we shall see later. (UA R.6.A.a.42.1.43).

10 See Petterson and Faull 2017. Unless otherwise indicated, the following examples are all taken from the published version of the manuscript. I have changed the translation of 'mystery of marriage' to marital mystery, which I prefer.

Herrnhut, when the leaders of the community spoke with all the members to discern their troubles and misgivings, and of course, their level of faith and commitment.[11] Later, these speakings would be carried out by choir helpers, who would 'speak through' the choir before communion.[12] In the 1741–42 diaries, this was mentioned as a matter of course before communion, and before bigger celebrations, where communion would take place. In this case, no specific reason is given, but on 18 January, the day after the speaking was finished, communion did take place, and the diary mentions that the other choirs had been 'spoken through' on 17 January.[13] In other words, this document could be a communion-speaking, or it could be a special assessment. Whatever the case, we are fortunate that it is recorded in such detail and preserved, giving us rare insight into an important time and its people.

As mentioned, 84 couples are spoken to over ten days. Some of these couples have been married for decades, and others are more recent. Some couples arrived in the community as married couples, while others within the community have been matched via the lot, as was Peter Schütze, Christian Paul and Michael Haberland, who were married in 1742, according to the diary.[14] The objective behind such a conference was to speak with each couple in regards to their marriage and intercourse, and, interestingly for our purposes here, the marital mystery – the *Ehe-Geheimnis*. This mystery is, as becomes clear, a new idea, and involves the husband taking on the role of the Saviour in intercourse, and the wife, the role of the church – we return to this in Chapter 5.[15] Furthermore, by its frequent mention, I suggest that this has been discussed with the individual couples, as a way of checking how far they have come in accepting this new understanding of marriage.

The report lists the couple's name and an assessment of their characters, and to what extent they are receptive to the Lamb, the wounds, and the marital mystery. Lack of receptiveness is usually characterised by the term 'dry',

---

11 Katherine Faull is by far the scholar who has done most work on this; see for example Faull 2009 and 2010. Zinzendorf also mentions this practice in a couple of choir speeches, both to the married choir. In the first, on 21 July 1748, he notes that quarter-hour services are not enough, but that each couple should be addressed personally (UA R.20.HS13). In the second, on 11 December 1750, he says that he himself is too busy to carry out the speaking with each couple, to assess how true they are to the secret (*Geheimniß*) (UA R.4.C.II.12).
12 Faull 2010, p. 157.
13 UA R.A.b.17a.1744.a, 17 and 18 January 1744.
14 UA R.6.A.b.15.1, Haberland on 30 January 1742, Schützen on 6 February, and Paul on 1 May, 1742. They were all spoken to, regarding their impending marriages on 16 January 1742.
15 In Vogt 2011, Peter Vogt describes the developments of Zinzendorf's ideas of marriage and its developments. We return to this in Chapter 5.

which can range from simply 'dry' to 'so dry that one can almost hear the heart rattle'. The entries are cast as the following example shows (emphases added):

> Pet. Schütz
> She has been nursing her child for almost a year.
> NB: these people must certainly be reflected upon; we have treated them very harshly. These are two rather agreeable people; however, they live in constant bickering with each other because of external things. *And ignorant in marital mystery and dry. They said, however, that they would have nothing of marital mystery, in the way that it has been said*, etc.[16]

This example shows that there is a struggle in regard to this marital mystery, and there are several other couples who are resistant to the idea. Thus, the Höyers and the Neußers do not want to speak about it at all, and of the W. Webers, it is stated that 'Dryness is the foundation of the heart against His blood and death, consequently also against marriage';[17] Bayers, the butcher, to whom 'the marital mystery is murky […], dark even, and old habits have made it contemptible to them';[18] a similar description is made of the Lulleyes who 'are (especially him) still in the dark about their whole relationship, but especially concerning the marital mystery'.[19] Bezolds explained himself as having 'enmity against the Savior. I have already often asked him, but he gives me nothing. In my heart I am also still an enemy of the congregation. I can't stand the marital speakings etc';[20] and Procoffs, who are 'blind to the marital mystery, the error is especially his, because he doesn't want to go into it at all'.[21]

There are also references to 'old', which does not (always) seem to indicate age, but rather of the old order, such as the Dippolts, who are characterised as being 'of the old ones, those who belong to the old covenant, where one enthusiastically warms oneself only with false lights, etc'.[22] The Webers also belong to this group, as do the Bertholdts, who are 'fairly agreeable people, however in the old way, who are incapable of the right Lamb marriage'.[23] From another example, we come to understand what this old covenant is:

---

16 Petterson and Faull 2017, p. 69 (German text) and p. 89 (English translation).
17 Petterson and Faull 2017, p. 71 (German text) and p. 91 (English translation).
18 Petterson and Faull 2017, p. 71 (German text) and p. 91 (English translation).
19 Petterson and Faull 2017, p. 73 (German text) and p. 92 (English translation).
20 Petterson and Faull 2017, p. 75 (German text) and p. 95 (English translation).
21 Petterson and Faull 2017, p. 76 (German text) and p. 95 (English translation).
22 Petterson and Faull 2017, p. 71 (German text) and p. 91 (English translation).
23 Petterson and Faull 2017, p. 82 (German text) and p. 101 (English translation).

Hansens: [...] These are people not entirely without hope, however nothing certain can be said about them yet. The marital mystery is not yet clear to him, and one does not know what the dear Lamb will make of them, etc. since they are not yet on the right path, and still hold on to the Moravian (*mährisch*) deceptions and falsehoods, etc.[24]

This denigration of Moravian and Bohemian beliefs is interesting keeping in mind the central role of these beliefs and community structure in the early years of the community. While the first years were coloured by the religious persuasions of the peasants as well as Pietism, this took a turn at some point in the late 1730s to early '40s, as we saw in the diaries as well as in Dober's account.[25] I return to this in the last part of this chapter. The new way, which is being promoted in these interviews, is focused on the blood and wounds theology and the marital mystery, to which several couples are resistant.

As with the Höyers mentioned above, there are couples who abstain from sexual intercourse. The Frödes, for example, have 'not had intercourse for a year. It had become an object of contempt for them; it has become contemptuous especially for him'.[26] The Fritsches are recorded as being abstinent, and it is explained that because their marriage was 'corrupted', i.e. they were married before they joined the community, 'they have come to the point that they for a number of years have completely refrained from intercourse and this from purely God-fearing reasons'.[27] Finally, the Wriedts 'have scruples against the marital mystery, mostly because of Gichtelian principles',[28] which gives us some idea of what is behind their resistance.

Johann Georg Gichtel (1638–1710) belonged to the tradition of early modern spiritualists, in the tradition of Johann Jakob Böhme, and exercised a considerable influence during and after his lifetime.[29] Gichtel's teaching on marriage

---

24   Petterson and Faull 2017, p. 72 (German text) and p. 92 (English translation). See also the case of Joseph Antons, where it is noted that: 'In the evening he brought yet another Bohemian letter, which he had denied today. That is a poor couple, still bewitched'. Petterson and Faull 2017, p. 74 (German text) and p. 94 (English translation). I would translate the term *gebannt* as a negative term, as in mesmerised, spell-bound, and I connect it with the *bömischen Brief*, which in this context most definitely connotes deception and falsehood.
25   Niesky, the settlement intended for the members of Bohemian background, was founded in 1742.
26   Petterson and Faull 2017, p. 78 (German text) and p. 97 (English translation).
27   Petterson and Faull 2017, p. 79 (German text) and pp. 98–9 (English translation).
28   Petterson and Faull 2017, pp. 80–1 (German text) and p. 100 (English translation).
29   Aira Vosa's fine article on Zinzendorf's successor, August Gottlieb Spangenberg, shows the influence of Gichtelian principles on Spangenberg's thought, which were much more influential than previously assumed. Vosa shows how Spangeberg's hesitation towards

was rooted in the influence from Böhme, coupled with his extremely derogatory view of women. For Gichtel, much more so than for Böhme, women functioned as a direct impediment to the connection with Sophia, this heavenly virgin bride, with whom all men should aspire to connect.[30] Thus, any soul who wishes to connect oneself to Sophia must relinquish ties to any earthly woman because, once one is connected to or soiled by a woman, Sophia escapes, and the soul is incapable of loving Sophia.[31] The centrality of Sophia is well-known from Böhme, who taught that Sophia is an androgynous creature, who represents humanity before the fall. S/he is thus also the way for humans to find a way back to a prelapsarian state. This is accomplished through Christ, who at the same time is the way back to this state, as well as one of its manifestations: For single men who strive to reconnect to the divine Christ/Sophia, Sophia appears as a virgin, while for the single women, Christ appears as a chaste man. As Tanner notes, 'we see that Gichtel here replaces Sophia with Christ, or, more correctly, he identifies them [with each other] and uses each one or the other person, according to whether he wants to connect them with men or women'.[32] Thus when one is married, one has already tied oneself to a partner, thus completing the unit at a fleshly level. According to Tanner, Gichtel's teachings thus assume that married couples exclude themselves from copulation with the heavenly bride and groom. He is, however, not willing to say so outright, while such a judgement ultimately is a divine one, thus Tanner.[33] I have only briefly mentioned Gichtel and Böhme here, but there were several other fractions within Pietism with varying views on marriage, which was under recalibration at this moment in time. Lucinda Martin argues that 'Böhme's anthropology led many pietists to believe that sexuality held the key to salvation, whether through celibacy or through the elevation of intercourse to a sacrament'.[34] This is hardly surprising if we bear in mind Karl Kautsky's point that 'every system of production has had a special form of household to which corresponds a special

---

marriage not only preceded his own marriage in 1740, but continued well after. Vosa 2009, pp. 18–19. Indeed, Gichtel's influence is much wider than assumed by e.g. Beyreuther, who sees him as a bad copy of Böhme (Beyreuther 1975, p. 22). However, as Vosa points outs, Gertraud Zaepernick has shown how Gichtel's influence occasioned, or rather gave voice to, a marital crisis between August Hermann and Anna Magdalena Francke. Zaepernick 1982.

30 Beyreuther 1975, pp. 20–1. See also Tanner 1952, pp. 12–19. Sophia is in Jewish thought Wisdom.
31 Beyreuther 1975, p. 25.
32 Tanner 1952, p. 31. My translation.
33 Ibid.
34 Martin 2014, p. 134.

system of family relationship'.³⁵ In this phase of transition between feudalism and capitalism, we see numerous groups experimenting with new family relations, new social relations, and new ways of thinking the individual. The radical pietists' dismissal of marriage is part of this whole transition, as are, of course, the choirs.

There is still much research to be done on sexual practice and views of marriage in early Herrnhut, but reading between the lines of the marriage document and the number of couples who abstained from intercourse, it would seem that there was not yet a firm line or practice when it came to marital intercourse, with the possibility of living within the community and retaining the marital ideologies of radical Pietism's various manifestations. Only in the 1740s would a more streamlined approach emerge, which was much less tolerant of diverse viewpoints.

3.2 The Sex Scandal in 1744

Looking back at the events in the community in September and October 1744, head of the single sisters' choir in Herrnhut, Rosine Gneuss, is reported as

> over this and then over all issues, she became somewhat melancholic, in her *Hütte* she was almost always sickly; the Hitschil-story had added to this, and she and all the workers had become anxious and confused; Peistel had then arrived with sharp orders, and according to him it then became a matter of expulsion, and for a whole month the main issue in Herrnhut became that of clearing out, shaming, punishing, and expelling; the period was no doubt needed, but Rosina felt that it had gone too far.³⁶

These dramatic events refer to the case of Hütschel, the manservant from the inn in Herrnhut who was discovered having had sex with a single sister, Catharina Frank.³⁷ Peistel is the man sent by Zinzendorf to clear up the mess, which caused great disruption in the community, as this quotation indicates. The

---

35   Kautsky 1910, p. 26.
36   "Darüber und auch sonst über allerhand Sachen sey sie etwas melancholisch worden; in ihrer Hütte sey sie fast immer kränklich gewesen, die hitschildishen historien wären dazu gekommen und sie und alle Arbeiter ängstlich und confus worden; Piestel sey darauff mit der scharffen Ordre hingekommen und nach derselben sey es von da an ans Wegjagen gegangen und es sey etliche Monath lang die Hauptsache in Herrnhuth gewesen, auszuräumen, abzuschämen, abzustraffen und wegzujagen; der periodus sey gewiß nöthig gewesen: aber die Rosine glaubt nun selbst, daß es zu Weit gegangen sey" (UA R.6.A.a.43.4.i).
37   The events are reconstructed in both Uttendörfer 1926, pp. 189–91; Peucker 2015, pp. 123–4.

events are surprisingly well recorded in the communal diary, with a couple more details from Ludwig von Schweinitz's notes from the communal diary of 1744–45.

Schweinitz has two versions of the diary. In the first version, Hütschel and Frank were thrown in gaol on 16 September, and the lot was asked whether or not to make it public. The answer was no. On 18 September, two more women were gaoled, because of association with the two persons. The women were Höyer and Kanniek. On 12 October, Sister Susanna Romer and Woheskye carried out the punishment of the three women with rods. The following day, Maria Anton also received her punishment; she had initially refused but relented.

The second version in Schweinitz's notes must be based on the communal diary, for the stories are virtually identical, although slightly abridged in Schweinitz's version, wherefore we follow the fuller event in the communal diary.

Here it is noted, and I am paraphrasing here, that the news of what Hütschel had done with Frank arrived on 16 September, and they were both imprisoned. On 18 September, three further women were apprehended, Canick, Liese Höyer and Anna Maria Anton. On 10 October, Brother [Carl Heinrich von] Peistel arrived with an order in the names of Zinzendorf and the countess, and by the authority of Jesus to resolve the case where Satan, through his unclean spirits and some of his helpers and tools in the community, had begun such a spot of shame and already seduced some souls. The community was very happy that the Saviour had sent someone, which took a load off their minds. The following day (11 October) Peistel addressed the leaders of the community, after which the entire congregation were told that a special assembly would take place the following day instead of the usual communion-quarter-hours. On 12 October, the punishment of the four women was carried out. This is described in extraordinary detail in a letter from Peistel to Zinzendorf, on 11 October 1744, which was undated in regard to year, but which undoubtedly is from 1744 judging from the contents:

> Thus today, immediately after the meal, the punishment of the first three was carried out. Brother Moscherosch and Hansen, and the dear sister Augustine went into the Judicial College building, and let one after the other into a room, one floor down; two dear blessed sisters had voluntarily taken it upon themselves to discipline these poor creatures out of love for the Saviour, the community and for the souls. I [Peistel] went in to assist the lord von Schrautenbach, if the need should arise. Brother Vockel was placed as guard around the house. It all went, praise the Lamb, rather well. Frankin was to receive 300 blows, and the two others around 160 for

the first, and 170 for the second. Frankin had from faintness dropped to the bare ground, and yelled, go ahead and hit. Sister Augustine had with quiet constraint talked to them with great care, and the dear sister Römern displayed unusual heroism, however through the shedding of many tears. After the execution [of the punishment], we immediately sent Brother Gutbiern to see her, he will have her washed with an ointment, we will presumably have to deal with Frankin for some days, to make her well again. Afterwards, they all will each go to farms as maids, where they will come to understand it as grace, which we do hope. The Hoyer Liese must stay until her parents have moved to Berthelsdorf, since they are on the list of people in whose houses unorderly things take place, and they will be told by the Judicial College when to leave Herrnhut at the earliest.[38]

Sister Frank, it seems, was beaten so severely that she needed medical attention for a number of days. We hear no mention of the punishment of Anna Maria Anton, which was otherwise stated in the diary.

Returning to the diary's recording of the events, we hear that in the evening of the 12th, the extraordinary assembly of the entire congregation, excluding boys, girls, and children, took place. Peistel gave a severe admonishment regarding the circumstances in the community. He was sent here by the Countess

---

38 "Also ward nun mit den 3 ersten heut gliech nach Tisch die execution vollzogen. Bruder Moscherosch und der Hansen und die theure Schwester Augustine giengen ins Richtersche Hauß, und ließen eine nach der andern in eine Stube 1 Treppe weiter herunter bringen, es ware 2 liebe selge Schwestern, die es willig übernahmen, die armen Creaturen, aus Liebe zum Heyland, der Gemeine und den Seelen, zu züchtigen. Ich gieng indeßen zu Herrn von Schrautenbach um bey der Hand zu seyn, wenn ich dabey solte nöthig seyn. Bruder Vockel aber bekam die Wache ums Haus herum. Es ist aber alles, dem Lamm sey Preyß, davor recht gut gegangen. die Frankin sol 300 Streiche bekommen, und die 2 andere ohngefehr 160 die eine, und 170 die andre. Die Frankin hat sich vor Ohnmacht auf die bloße Erde gelegt, und geruffen: schlagt nur zu. Die Schwester Augustine hat beym stille halten sehr gesorgt ihnen zugeredet, und die liebe Schwester Römern hat sich ungemien heldenhafft bezeigt, doch unter Vergießung vieler Thränen. Nach der execution schickten wir gleich Bruder Gutbiern hin sie zu besehen, er wil sie mit einer salbe waschen laßen, mit der Frankin werden wir wohl etliche tage zu thun haben, sie wieder zu curiren. // Nachdem kommen sie alle 3 jede auf einen Hoff als Mägde, wo sie es anders als Gnade annehmen, wie wir doch hoffen. Die Hoyer Liese mus etwa so lange bis ihre Eltern nach Berthelsdorf gezogen, denn sie stehen mit unter der Liste von Leuten, da es unordentlich in ihren Häußern zugeht, und denen wird ehistes vom Richter-Collegium angekündigt werden, Herrnhuth zu räumen" (UA R.6.A.a.42.1.44).

My gratitude goes to Frau Moreau, who swiftly transcribed this letter for me, as I could not read Peistel's handwriting (for which he apologises at the end of the letter and trusts that Zinzendorf could read most of it).

[von Zinzendorf] to punish the sinners on behalf of the lordships, to sharpen the holy order of the community, and to let everyone know, that insofar as the sins committed were under secular law, they would be treated as public. Furthermore, should anyone feel further inclined towards sin, they were advised to leave, and that sins committed in fields and bushes should be taken more seriously than those in houses, because the perpetrators thought themselves safe.

On 13 October, the judiciary council (*Richter Collegium*)[39] told five families that because of indecent and disorderly conduct of different kinds they had to leave Herrnhut, namely Höyers (whose daughter, Liesel, was one of the women punished as accessory to the Hütschel case), Frödens, Christian Pauls, Dippolds, and Joseph Antons. Some couples were amicably given the same advice. In addition, 70 brothers and sisters from all choirs were forbidden access to Eucharist. On 14 October, Hütschel was taken away by a company of soldiers, in which he was to serve for two years in place of punishment. The four sisters were settled on farms in Berthelsdorf to work as maids.[40] On 21 October, 20 'new' and 'incomplete' (theologically speaking) people were given advice to leave (*consilium abeundi*). Peistel left for Marienborn (all by himself) on 15 October.[41]

I am particularly interested in the five families who were ordered to leave because of indecent and disorderly conduct *of different kinds*, and what this covers over. Was this connected to the sex scandal, or is it a reference to something else? Fortunately, and hardly coincidentally, we have a testimony on their conduct from the marriage report discussed above. The leaders' testimony on each of the couples sounds as follows (in the order in which they appear in the marriage report).

Höyer
Since one year [presumably relating to intercourse]
They are old corrupted people for whom the marital mystery is still a scandal, about which they do not like to speak. She said, the reasons why

---

39 This council was established in 1729 and had under its powers the right to punish and/or expel deviant members, overseeing admittance of new members, money and business matters, as well as the general maintenance of law and order. Uttendörfer 1925, pp. 31–2. The chairmanship of this council was always in the hands of the aristocracy, Gollin 1967, p. 28. See the paragraph on the *Richterkolleg* in Status of Herrnhut 1744 (UA R.6.A.a.58.2).
40 While the text does not explicitly mention that they are single sisters, but merely speaks of them as 'women', all four are listed in the catalogue of single sisters from 1743 (UA R.27.124.4): Catharina Frank, number 69; Anna Maria Anthon, number 75; Anna Elisabeth Hoyer, number 100; and Susanne Camink, number 106. All four were communion-sisters.
41 UA R.6.A.b.17.a.1744.a, 15 October 1744.

they didn't have intercourse were partly because she had always thought there were enough young people doing it, and they were already too old; and partly because he smokes tobacco in the evenings, and she cannot stand the smell, and third, she sleeps outside and he in the room. We scolded them, and they promised to do better, etc.[42]

Dippolt
For many years, they have led a lawful marriage but have been prepared by the Dobers. But have over time become doubtful again, for the reason that he wanted to sin against the Lamb. Now, however, it is important for both of them, etc. Otherwise, however, they are of the old ones, those who belong to the old covenant, where one enthusiastically warms oneself only with false lights, etc. May God have mercy![43]

Christian Paul
She is an agreeably honest child and exposed her husband quite completely, namely that he wanted intercourse without permitting the seed to enter her. She had not wanted to do it, however, but rather to do it properly and to tell the brothers and sisters before. We scolded him and her roughly. Towards the end, however, she also opened up to us that she sometimes does not deal with him as she should, and is not free from lust, etc.[44]

Joseph Antohns
In the evening he brought yet another Bohemian letter, which he had denied today.
 That is a poor couple, still banned.[45] Especially today they were in the utmost desperation. We confronted them with their latest deed with Gewinn:[46] he asked for forgiveness very much for it and said, he did

---

42   Petterson and Faull 2017, p. 70 (German text) and pp. 89–90 (English translation). I drew attention to Liesel Höyer in Chapter 2, where it was noted that she had a difficult disposition as a child, but that in 1743 she had been improving greatly.
43   Petterson and Faull 2017, p. 71 (German text) and p. 91 (English translation).
44   Petterson and Faull 2017, p. 74 (German text) and p. 90 (English translation).
45   This an amended version of the translation in the published version, where we translated it as 'bonded [to sin]'. However, in light of Josef Anton's history of disobedience and ongoing punishments, I have chosen to understand the term *"gebannt"* as meaning banned (and hence under punishment).
46   In the published document, there is a reference to Jan Vejdělek, who was called Gewinn in German. Sterik 2006, p. 107. Since then, I have found multiple references to Gewinn in the

not regard it as badly as we: Finally, she said: 'My husband had wanted to report it to the congregation but I prevented him from doing it, etc.' Finally, he began to cry and gave up and said: 'Have mercy on us and forgive us for Jesus's sake, we want to do better'. And thus they went their way in tears, etc.[47]

Frödes
These are the Frödes. We truly broke out in a sweat just looking at these people. However, they said that things were going better with them since the brothers and sisters had taken them on. They had not had intercourse for a year. It had become an object of contempt for them; it has become contemptuous especially for him. Their child rearing makes one frightened when they talk about it, etc. In their marriage they only want to be initiated when they, according to their hearts, will have learned to know one another better. They have promised improvement in everything.

In an accounting document from 1745,[48] where it is listed how much they were paid for their houses, it is noted where they went: Höyers with wife and daughter went to Berthelsdorf; Frödens, with wife and son, went to Groß-Hennersdorf; Christian Pauls, with wife and child, went to Berthelsdorf; Dippolds, with wife and two children, to Berthelsdorf; and Joseph Antons left one small child in Herrnhut, and went to Berlin with his wife and another child.[49] Here we should remember that being expelled from Herrnhut also meant being removed from the free subject status which was offered to the residents of Herrnhut. The four sisters, for example, would have re-entered the system of servitude and bonded labour which was still in place in the feudal surroundings.

Joseph Anton and Christian Paul both figure on the list of men who had reported themselves as wanting to take part in the general pardon offered on

---

1742 Herrnhut diary, and found that this refers to his son, bricklayer Matthæus Gewinn, who became a member of the congregation in January 1742, and died in 1781. His memoir states that he was a troubled but constant soul, and, as community gravedigger, he dug 1,000 graves in Herrnhut (UA R.22.16.55). What he and Joseph Anton had been up to, however, has not been possible to ascertain.

47 Petterson and Faull 2017, pp. 74–5 (German text) and p. 94 (English translation).
48 UA R.6.A.a.43.4.m.
49 The community bought their houses, and decided after this exodus to establish an account, which could be used to buy out the houses of people leaving the community (UA R.6.A.b.17a.1744.a, 26 October 1744).

13 November 1741 to anyone who was under punishment or excluded. Thus, there is a history of disobedience with these two.⁵⁰ Also, in the letter from Peistel to Zinzendorf, the list of names of those to be banished are those 'in whose houses, unorderly things take place'. In the case of Joseph Anton, it does not seem to be connected to sex, but rather a generally disagreeable disposition and, more significantly, ongoing unlawful contact with Bohemians, to which the references to the letter and Gewinn above testify. Unorderly (*unordentlich*) thus need not refer to impropriety, but rather to something that goes against the order set down by the community.⁵¹ The reason given to the five couples for being told to leave was 'indecent and disorderly conduct of different kinds', which does not refer exclusively to sexual misdemeanours, but also presumably to disruptions to the community and its smooth running. Resistance to central ideas, then, would not have been a desirable feature in any member, which the blatant pressure on the married couples shows.⁵²

3.3   *The Meeting Minutes*

I have already drawn upon the minutes from the meeting in February 1745, namely Rosina Gneuss's reference to the events in September and October 1744, which left her depressed, sick, and anxious. Here we may return to them in

---

50   Incidentally, they also both have *Lebensläufe*, which in the case of Joseph Anton is not entirely unwarranted, since he is readmitted into the congregation in 1747, after living among the Bohemian Brethren in Berlin for four years. It is, however, unusual that Christian Paul's *Lebenslauf* is in the collection, given that he did not return to the community. He died in Berthelsdorf in 1762.

51   Peucker 2015, p. 25, notes that a strict sense of order was important, and that the Herrnhaag single brothers' diary often has expressions such as 'everything occurred in the most beautiful order'. This mention of order is also common in the communal diary from Herrnhut, where it is noted when 'everything goes in its order', for example UA R.6.A.b.15.1, 11 November 1742: 'The Sunday went in its order in blessed fashion' (Der Sonntag ging in seiner Ordnung geseegnet).

52   There would have been several ways of disciplining individuals. One was, as the above diary excerpts show, to exclude people from partaking in communion. Another one was to strip people of their posts. Such an example could be found in that of Christiane Eleonora Voigt, who was divested of her posts, and excluded from her *Gesellschaft* (UA R.6.A.b.15.1, 8 October, 1741). This could be to punish her husband, in that the 1742 diary notes that on 8 October, that Voigt has 'for the sake of gruesome excesses, committed on the land and in the house, been expelled from here *' (UA R.6.Ab.15.1). The lot, then, has told the community to get rid of him, and he leaves. What these excesses refer to is not clear, but it is interesting that he is expelled, and not his wife, and yet she is encouraged to go with him, only to be welcomed back with open arms after his death some six years later. Her memoir bears witness to her suffering, and also is surprisingly rich in detail about her working life (UA R.22.2b.112).

more detail. The meeting concerns the circumstances in Herrnhut, and the results of what we might call 'centralised' practice. Decisions which affected the community in Herrnhut badly were made elsewhere, with little or no regard for the consequences. In the following quotation, this anger is directed at Herrnhaag, the settlement in the Wetterau, founded in 1738, where Zinzendorf spent some time after his banishment from Saxony. Consequently, it came to be regarded as the new centre of the overall community.

One of the principle items on the agenda of the meeting was the married couples' choir, which had been in trouble for a couple of years, a situation which now seemed rectified.

> At that time, the wounds of the Lamb sparkled bloodily among us, and proved itself in new grace in all choirs. The married choir was mostly old people, and if there was something good among them, it was usually taken away, as was the case just before our arrival, the quintessence of the Herrnhuter married choir, 13 couples of the best were sent to Pennsylvania. If one were to take 13 couples of the most beloved married people from Herrnhaag, what would the rest of the choir look like? No accomplished recruits have come to the Herrnhut married choir afterwards, and so it is no wonder that not many important people in this choir were left. There was one mistake was made in our presence, that our brother, David Nitschmann made it over the entire choir and wanted to suffuse it all at once; by which many were angered and made contrary; it would have been better, if he had first proposed it in its entirety with a few brothers and sisters, and afterwards proceeded. In the meantime, as Rosina testifies, a true and noticeable blessing has remained within the married choir.[53]

---

53   "Die Wunden des Lammes funkelten damahls wahrhatttig recht blutig unter uns und es bewieß sich in allen Chören neue Gnade. Das Ehe Chor war meist ein altes Volk, und war noch gutes unter demselben gewesen, ist immer von Zeit zu Zeit weggenommen worden, wie denn erst kurtz vor unsern hinkommen die quintessens des Herrnhuthischen Ehe Chors, 13 paar von den besten nach Pensylvanien geschickt worden. Wenn man von Herrnhaag 13 paar von den liebsten Eheleuten wegnehmen wollte wie würde es ums übrige Chor aussehen? Keine tüchtige recrouten sind beym Herrnhutischen Ehe Chor nachgekommen, und also ists kein Wunder, daß in diesem Chor nicht so gar viel wichtige Leute übrig geblieben. Ein Fehlers wars auch bey unserm Daseyn, daß sich unser Bruder David Nitschman übers ganze Chor in genere machte und es auf einmahl umgießen wollte; wodurch manche sehr böse und wiedrig worden sind; es wäre am besten gewesen, wenn ers erst mit etlichen Geschwistern aufs ganze angetragen und hernach immer weiter gegangen wäre: indeß ist doch, wie die Rosine bezeuget, ein wahrer und mercklicher Seegen unter dem Ehe-Chore geblieben" (UA R.6.A.a.43.4.i).

Rosina Gneuss is severely critical of the way things have been left in Herrnhut. The community's best citizens are taken from here and used elsewhere (Pennsylvania), leaving only 'old' people in the choir, which has not received new blood for a while. Her criticism is directed at Herrnhaag, in that she asks what their married couples' choir would look like if 13 of their best couples were taken from the community. When Rosina and the other workers then were called away in the beginning of 1744, the community was left with only one person in charge for a three-month period. It did not help that David Nitschmann had insisted on foisting 'something' on the entire choir, which angered many people. From the marriage document discussed in the previous sections, we may surmise that this could refer to the marital mystery, to which many reacted with resistance and refusal. Such an approach, which Rosina regarded as counterproductive, also goes against the practice discussed by Martin Dober in his text discussed above, where he mentions that initially the new teachings were presented to a few and from there seep into the rest of the community.

At a later point in the minutes, it seems as though the leadership realised the problems in Herrnhut after the business with Hütschel and put partial effort into resolving some of the problems. This resulted in the great purge, after which a number of helpers were sent to rebuild the collapsed structures. One person who was sent and who was helpful was Johann Nitschmann, but he would not be staying long, so Rosina was keen to get another 'preacher of the wounds' to teach in the great hall (*Saal*). Another problem with Johann Nitschmann was that he was not part of the married couples' choir [i.e. unmarried], but, because of a lack of personnel, he was in charge. Rosina also felt that he did not have a proper plan for the married couples and was much too harsh. 'If he had his way, then at least half of Herrnhut would have to go'.[54]

In the communal account of the 'sex scandal', it is noted that Peistel opened the elders' conference by showing his orders and mandate from Papa, and after the events had been briefly discussed, the leaders of the choirs and the brothers from the judiciary council were called and given the same introduction.[55] In Peistel's letter to Zinzendorf from 11 October 1744,[56] mentioned earlier, he said that they had a quite angry conference in Rosina's chamber,[57] where he told Vogts, Tills and Hehl of Papa's instructions, and then they summoned Munster,

---

54 "wenns nach seiner Idee gienge, so müßte noch wenigstens halb Herrnhut weg" (UA R.6.A.a.43.4.i).
55 R.6.A.b.17.a.1744.a; 11 October 1744.
56 UA R.6.A.a.42.1.44, Carl Heinrich von Peistel to Zinzendorf, 11 October 1744.
57 Peistel gives a glowing report of Rosina Gneuß's handling of everything.

Kindermann, Moscherosch, Hansen, Otten and Vockel, and Augustine from the sisters. He then states that he spoke to them strongly, especially in regard to why the holy separation of the choirs had been so neglected in Herrnhut, against the written agreement.[58] A look at the minutes puts this talking to in a somewhat different light, in that here it is noted that

> When we went away in the beginning of May 1744 [to the Synod in Marienborn 12 May to 15 June],[59] then Herrnhut was almost completely denuded of workers for almost a quarter of a year, and Graßmann was here completely by himself. And then it was all downhill from there, as it always will, when the community is left without full workers. New workers were supposed to arrive within three to four weeks, but the Synod was delayed into the summer, and after this, Rosina and Christian Vogts finally arrived.[60]

So, all the leaders of Herrnhut were called to Synod,[61] leaving only one person in charge of this unwieldy community, and because the Synod was delayed, the replacement-workers did not come. It is, as the minutes note, no surprise that things got a little out of hand, given that one person was left to enforce gender segregation in seven choirs, with especially the married couples' choir being emptied of all promising material.[62]

---

58   To what this refers has unfortunately not been possible to ascertain.
59   In Peistel's letter, he mentions that Rosina was embarrassed that she had gone with Brother Hehl to the Synod. However, from the minutes it seems that they were all ordered to go.
60   UA R.6.A.a.43.4.i: "Wie wir zu Anfang des May 1744 weggingen, so war Herrnhuth ein Viertel-Jahr fast gantz von Arbeitern entblößet, und Graßman schier ganz allein da. Und da giengs ziemlich wieder berg ein, wie es allemahl gehet, wenn die Gemeinen ohne gantze Arbeiter gelaßen werden. Er sollten in 3–4 Wochen neue Arbeiter hinkommen; der Synodus wurde aber biß in den Sommer hinein verzögert und nach demselben kamen endlich die Rosina und Christoph Vogts hin".
61   Later in the minutes, Rosina is cited as saying that she asks for God's good will, that when the Synod comes, not all will be called away from Herrnhut, but rather that all posts are left properly staffed, so that the damages which arise in the community do not outweigh the benefits the workers may have from the Synod. "Und da bittet sie um Gottes willen, wenn der Synodus kommt, nicht alles von Herrnhuth wegzuruffen, sondern allen [Posten] gut besezt zu laßen, der Schade, darin der Gemeine entstehe, sey größer als der Nutzen, den die Arbeiter vom Synodo hatten".
62   On 7 September 1745, when the marriage celebration took place, it is noted in the diary that the communion group within the married choir was very small (UA R.6.A.b.17a, 1745a, 7 September) from which we could infer that the new blood has either not arrived or not yet taken hold.

The minutes then go on to report the status quo of the community: Who takes care of teaching in the *Saal*, and the various tasks there, who pulls their weight and who doesn't, who is capable and who isn't, what is required and what is desired. Then follows a list of who is in charge of the married couples' choir, who is the elder, who works with and oversees the children, the widows, the single sisters and single brothers, the older girls and the older boys. Which choirs work well (single sisters and brothers), which do not (married couples, widows), and which do not at all (older girls and boys), as well as what is needed and what might be done. Finally, there is a list of institutions and businesses and their state of affairs: the orphanage, seigneurial affairs, the Apothecary (here it is noted that a change is crucial, it is a grievance that it is run by two widows and four single brothers), and the Inn, which Johann Nitschmann would rather have off the premises, having raised a suggestion to the community to build it in a place away from Herrnhut. Finally, a number of points are raised, namely the reimbursement for houses of the expelled couples, which did put the community as a whole in debt; the practice of building must be regulated, so that if one builds without permission, they may not be reimbursed by the community. Reimbursement should from now on only happen when one is given permission to build. Rosina wants certain families relocated and has sent a list to Papa to consider.[63]

This entire meeting dealt with the ramifications of the events in September/October 1744, and outlines how the leaders are trying to avoid anything similar taking place in the future, be it by rearranging the staff in the Apothecary, suggesting building a new inn away from Herrnhut, and manning every choir with three to four workers, who are closely monitored as to their proficiency in nourishing Lamb-like and choir appropriate behaviour.[64]

---

63 I am certain that this is the same document referred to above in footnote 48 (UA R.6.A.a. 43.4.m), where the families who have been expelled are mentioned, as well as the costs associated with buying their houses. The list then continues with 14 more names, but these do no look as though they will expelled as such, two will be going to Niesky after request from the brothers there. Five families from this list are in the marriage document. The second item in the document is a list of 10 families which Rosina would like transferred complete with names, number of children and what houses they have (eight out of ten families are mentioned in the marriage document). Also, the Apothecary and the Inn are on the list to be decided upon and thought through.

64 As an example, we just note the assessment of the brothers in charge of the big boys: 'Among the big boys, we need a Christel and a Hanzsch. After Hanzsch has gone, we are a worker short and things look rather bad. Paul Münster and Ettwein, who have been processing them, are not older boy-ish enough'.

(Unter *den großen Knaben* fehlt ein Christel und ein Hantzes. Seit Hantzes weg ist, fehlts an Arbeitern und es sieht ziemlich schlecht aus. Paul Münster und Ettwein, die sie bearbeitet haben, sind nicht groß Knabenhafftig genug.).

4 Blood, Wounds, and Authority

Disagreements about the interpretation of marriage, a sex scandal and subsequent purge of the community, and minutes from a meeting where the structure of the community is outlined. How does this have any wider social impact, or, put differently, who cares?

In the present section, I will argue that these are expressions of class struggle, in that the struggle against the Moravian (*mährisch*) faith is an ideological struggle between peasant piety on the one hand, expressed by both peasants and some artisans, over against an affected and aesthetic piety displayed by the nobility and embraced especially by those with aspirations, be it leadership and/or class position.

As Dober's overview of the theological developments showed, there is a considerable difference between the old ways and the new, differences which in the marriage notes are articulated in terms of class and cultural provenance, and indicate that the conflicts were far from resolved back in 1727, but rather ongoing. This was evident not only in the theological developments, but also in the change in authority structure which took place in 1741, with the installation of Christ as chief elder of the community. These two developments we now examine more closely.

4.1 *Blood and Wounds*

In 1742, according to the diary, Johann Langguth went to Sorau, presumably to connect with the community of awakened people there.[65] Johannes writes:

> I had instructions to be cordial, and to listen. I learned of the state of the Sorau and found it much worse than I had imagined. They did not know our community at all (as though we were 1,000 miles away from them), and *the matter of the lamb and his wounds is for them a strange and new thing, they regarded it as pretentious and do not know what lies within it.*[66]

---

65 It had been mentioned earlier in the diary that there were many awakened people around in the Lausitz, with whom the Moravian Brethren had no contact – apart from the Bohemians in Zittau (UA R.A.b.15.1, 11 January 1742).

66 UA R.A.b.15.1, 15 January 1742 "Ich hatte Anweisung hertzlich zu seyn, und zu hören, habe den Sorauischen statum ziemlich kennen gelernet und viel schlechter gefunden als ich mir sie vorgestellet. Unsere Gemeiene kennte sie gar nicht [als wenn wir 1000 Meilen von ihnen wären] und die Materie von Lamm und seinen Wunden ist ihnen eine fremde und neue Sache, halten es vor affectirt und wißen nicht waß drinnen lieget".

The Soraus' reaction to the blood and wounds theology as pretentious is extremely interesting, in that it indicates a class issue, not only Langguth's own, but also that of the blood. In other words, when he fails to convince them of the importance of the material on the lamb and wounds, it indicates the distance between the Soraus and the blood, but also, Langguth's inability in this situation to convincingly mediate between the two positions. This is not to denigrate Langguth's preaching abilities per se – indeed, clothmaker Oertel's memoir states that when he visited Herrnhut for the second time in 1741, Johannes was preaching the wounds as the only path to salvation, which went straight to Oertel's troubled heart.[67] But in this case, outside his sphere of influence, Langguth's preaching was not convincing.

4.1.1 In Theory

In the *Will to Knowledge* and his analysis of the bourgeois obsession with sex, Foucault suggests that one of the reasons for this obsession was that the aristocracy had also laid a particular claim to the body, to which the bourgeoisie responded with its own 'classed' body:

> there was a transposition into different forms of the methods employed by the nobility for marking and maintaining its caste distinction; for the aristocracy had also asserted the special character of its body, but this was in the form of blood, that is, in the form of the antiquity of its ancestry and of the value of its alliances.[68]

Foucault connects the aristocracy's focus on blood with its own prestigious pedigree and its alliances, which were above all expressed in marriage.[69] This aristocratic obsession with blood could be connected with the blood and wounds theology in the Moravian community and its appeal for the aristocracy.

---

67 UA R.22.109.9.
68 Foucault 1998, p. 124. I would like to express my extreme gratitude to Lars Nørgaard for connecting this line from Foucault with the Moravians, and for urging me to pursue it.
69 The most recent and ambitious study of blood is Anidjar 2014, which is a study in secularisation. This means that he is governed from the outset by what he calls 'the Eucharistic matrix', which forces him to deny any 'secular' understanding of blood before the early modern period. Anidjar wants to trace modern ideas of racism back to early modern Christianity's obsession with blood, and he is thus critical of suggestions which pertain to class (a secular concept), such as Benedict Anderson's suggestion that racism had its origins in class and the nobility's obsession with pure blood. Anderson 2006. Quoted and dismissed in Anidjar 2014, pp. 63–4.

I return to this in Chapter 6, but will here offer some trajectories which will be followed in the reading of the speeches in Chapters 4 and 5.

In the introduction to her study on blood in late medieval Christianity, Caroline Walker Bynum begins with a very pertinent observation: Blood is not a big deal in early Christianity:

> Although Jerome (d. 420) suggested that all Christ's blood was drained in the passion and referred to the column of flagellation 'dyed with the blood (*cruore*) of the Lord', hence adumbrating the cult of blood relics, it would be several hundred years before blood as object was revered in Western Europe and hundreds more before the bloodbath from an exsanguinated Christ moved to the center of European piety.[70]

Bynum's conclusion is that blood expresses 'peculiarly fifteenth-century anxieties', namely, the issue of holy matter and the issue of access to God.[71] An equally pertinent question would be: Whose anxieties? Bynum does not directly address the role of nobility in promoting the blood cult, but in her narrative we do see the appearance of the nobility as actors in establishing Cistercian convents in the fourteenth century as a way of promoting blood cults in various German principalities.[72] And just as Karl Schmid has insisted that one cannot understand the meaning of noble blood in the Middle Ages without considering the themes of 'child of God' and succession to Christ, both of which were developed in these years,[73] so we should not ignore questions of class when pondering the meaning of blood of Christ, because, as Marx and Engels have taught us, 'the ideas of the ruling class are in every epoch the ruling ideas, i.e. the class which is the ruling material force of society, is at the same time its ruling intellectual force'.[74]

In Moravian scholarship, blood and wounds theology has usually been connected with the Sifting Time, a conflation which has served to reduce the blood and wounds theology to a particular theological aberration, thus containing the actual interpretations of both.[75] Paul Peucker and Craig Atwood have both been instrumental in pointing out this sleight of hand in Moravian historiography and scholarship, and their work shows the fruitfulness of treat-

---

70 Bynum 2007, p. 1.
71 Bynum 2007, p. 7.
72 Bynum 2007, pp. 55 and 57.
73 Schmid 1998, p. 24.
74 Marx and Engels 1972, p. 59.
75 Atwood 2006a; Peucker 2015.

ing the Sifting and the blood and wounds as distinct entities, connected perhaps, but neither synonymous nor synecdochised. Atwood's focus has been on the blood and wounds, and points out that the conflation fails to explain the persistence of blood and wounds theology *after* the Sifting Time, but has served to excise Zinzendorf's influence on Moravian theology.[76] Peucker has focused on the Sifting Time, and has convincingly argued that certain groups within the Moravian Church, led by Zinzendorf's son, Christian Renatus/Christel, had taken Zinzendorf's theology to its logical extremes, and declared themselves to be in their eschatological state of perfection and sinlessness – namely as 'sisters' – and consequently engaged in acts of sexual transgression.[77] Indeed, Peucker notes that Johannes von Watteville[78] specifically uses the blood and wounds theology to refocus attention away from some of those features of the Sifting Time which were regarded as problematic.[79] For our current argument, then, we do well in setting aside the Sifting Time, and focusing on the blood and wounds theology.

As Dober indicated, a significant change in pace took place with the appearance of the so-called 'Litany of Wounds' (*Wundenlitaney*), composed by Zinzendorf, Christian Renatus, and Johann Langguth in 1744. The 'Litany of Wounds' is based on the dying words of Brother Johann Nitsche, who died in Herrnhut in the last week of 1743.[80] Calling upon the wounds of Jesus and seeing the wounds, his 'religious feeling' became, through the subsequent ritualisation, a 'paradigmatic experience of faith and imagination' as noted by Katherine Faull.[81] In the enactment of and participation in the Litany, which was performed antiphonally on a weekly basis, the members of the congregation appropriate the visionary experience of Nitsche and his witness to the wounds.

---

76   Atwood 2006a; 2006b.
77   These transgressive sexual acts are possibly both extra-marital and same-sex activities. Peucker 2015, pp. 122–8. See also Peucker 2006.
78   Remember, this is the former Johann Langguth, who in 1745 became the nobleman Johannes von Watteville.
79   Peucker 2015.
80   The diary notes that 'at the end of the feast day Brother Nitschens from Polish Lissa took blessed and extraordinary leave from us, during a continuous emotion and calling out to the wounds of Jesus' (Den Beschluß der Feyertage machte unsers Bruder Nitschens aus Polnisch Lißa seeliger und merkwürdiger Abschied unter einem continuierliche Gefühl und Anschreien der Wunden Jesu ...) (UA R.Ab.16.1, 27 December 1743). Recall Sister Hass, the maid of Obristleutnant von Krassow who died under great wound emotion in 1745, mentioned in Chapter 1, footnote 8.
81   Faull 1995, pp. 35–6.

Here is an example from the section which adores and prays to the wounds of Jesus, first we have a descriptor and then a reflection on the meaning:

> Softest wounds of Jesus I do love to lye easy and still, and undisturb'd. What do I? I creep to you.
> Ye hot wounds of Jesus Kindle all over, till with your spreading fire and flames you cover the universe.

and so on. The litany ends on this note:

> Our wounds of Jesus All troops of sinners, both young and old, both small and great you traverse, all that have faith.
> My own wounds of Jesus, Mine, mine ye're surely, it is as if you gap'd and was made purely for me alone.
> At the end of all our need, be our unction wounds so red.
> Till then by faith, I'll view his eye streaks black and blue, the clam on mouth and tongue, his corpse with torture wrung, the head which thorns did rack, the furrows on the back. Till in my flesh I see, his body bruis'd for me, whereon so stedfastly we here trust and rely and close to him can greet the prints in hand and feet.[82]

Atwood notes that the vision of the wounds is focused on the individual, which we may see in the syntax and the repeated use of first-person singular, even though (as Atwood also insists) we also have the occurrences of verses with the plural.[83] But the majority of verses portray the wounds of Jesus over against the individual, who over and over again is interpellated or subjectified as Nitsche's 'I'. This individualism expressed in the blood and wounds theology, which sets the individual over against Jesus' seeping wounds, which then conversely confirms the atonement for *me*, will be one of the topics of interest in Chapter 6. Here, we merely want to emphasise its relation to class. Returning to the ideas

---

82 Translation taken from *A Collection of Hymns, with several Translations from the Hymn-Book of the Moravian Brethren*, part 2 (London, 1746), number 398. Thank you to Paul Peucker for this reference and a copy of the English translation. There is a more updated and colourful translation in Atwood 2004, pp. 233–7.
83 Atwood 2004, p. 208.

of the ruling class, one might object that Nitsche was a clothmaker from Polish Lissa, and not an aristocrat, hence his experience of the wounds cannot be 'ruling class ideology'. However, at this point in time, 1743, the blood and wounds theology had already been circulating for a while, dividing the believers and the community. The diary from 1743 mentions clothmaker Winterling, also from Lissa, who had lapsed completely, because of an incensed animosity against the Lamb and his wounds, which he had earlier held in high regard.[84] Furthermore, we do not know the relationship between the words of the dying man and what was expressed in the litany, because the experience of Nitsche did not become paradigmatic until it was set into verse by Zinzendorf, his son, and Johann Langguth. Thus, the fact that Nitsche was a clothmaker and called out to the wounds of Jesus does not necessarily contradict the understanding of the blood and wounds theology as a ruling class idea.

Atwood's attempt at understanding Zinzendorf's blood and wounds theology situates it firmly within a specific theological tradition and a personal piety.[85] Indeed, blood as well as wounds *is* a central theme in medieval mystical piety, as Bynum's work has shown.[86] And, yes, the blood of Christ is commonly connected to the atonement. And yet, this connection between blood and atonement may be emphasised *without* taking it to the level of seeing the believer as a worm swimming in the blood of the side-wound. Also, the theological context does not explain the *shift* to blood and wounds theology in the early 1740s, if such a theology had been part of Zinzendorf's childhood. However, if we understand it as emerging at the time of a power struggle in the community, between a Moravian (*mährisch*) peasant piety and aristocratic sensibilities, then the implementation of the blood and wounds and subsequent ousting of deviants from this line makes better sense. Especially when complemented with the shift in leadership structure and increase in use of the lot.

4.2 Christ, the Chief Elder

In 1741, a significant change took place in the organisation of the larger Moravian community. Leonhard Dober, who had been appointed general elder

---

84 UA R.Ab.16.1, 27 May 1743: "Winterling, ein Tuchmacher aus Polnisch Lißa ist auch auf eine Zeitlang zum Besuch hier, dem ist sein ganzer vermeinter Grund weggefallen, die Feindschafft gegen das Lamm und seine Wunden bricht gewaltig bey ihm aus, da er sich vor so gut angesehen hatte".
85 In the 21 Discourses on the Augsburg confession, Zinzendorf sees himself along the lines of Count Elger, and indeed draws a line from the Herrnhuter back to Count Elger and St Bernard, as Atwood notes. Atwood 2004, p. 96. See also Zinzendorf 1963, pp. 306–7.
86 Bynum 2002; 2011.

of the whole church resigned from his office because of the overwhelming amount of work with the rapidly growing community and its missions. To decide his replacement the lot was used, which revealed that Jesus was to take his place. The day chosen to celebrate this event was 13 November, and to understand the importance of this event, we need to look at an excerpt from the 1741 diary's depiction of the event:

> Here the first part of the community-day began. After a couple of verses, the short notice written to all the communities everywhere concerning the new general elder to whom the lord Count will serve as adjunct was read aloud and the case was explained to the community and then was sung: we kiss you with ardency, you community elder etc. Then, the detailed letter of the lord count to the community was read aloud and after this, the general amnesty and pardon of all, who in the past belonged to our community and are now excluded or are under punishment was made public. What the community thought about his, I cannot really describe. Already at the first letter everyone was astounded at the matter, that the Heyland wanted to overtake the office as elder in his communities [...] After the first astonishment, the tears began to flow, and so thoroughly and persistently through the entire first part that we all could not remember ever have seen or felt such a stirring.[87]

As Dietrich Meyer points out, 'this unusual step meant the transfer of the Zinzendorfian community with Christ onto the constitution of the community, and as a logical consequence thereof, *that the invisible real presence of Christ was taken seriously*'.[88] Meyer explains that this move was deliberate to

---

87 UA R.6.A.b.14.1, 13 November 1741: "Hierauf ging der erste Theil des Gemein-Tages an, din welchen nach einigen Versen erstlich die kurze Nachricht von den neuen General Aeltesten, die der Herr Graf als Adjunctus im Dienst allentalben an alle Gemeinen geschrieben, abgelesen und die Sache weiter der Gemeine deutlich gemacht und gesungen: Wir küssen dich mit Innigkeit, du Aelt[e]ster der Gemeine etc. Dann wurde der ausführliche Brieff des Herrn Graffen an die Gemeine abgelesen und nach demselben die General amnestie und Pardon vor alle, die ehemals zu unser Gemeine gehöret haben und jetzo ausgeschloßen sind, oder die jetzo unter der Zucht sind, publicirt. Was die Gemeine dabey gefühlet hat, kan ich wohl nicht beschreiben. Gleich beym ersten Briefe kam alles in Erstaunen über der Sache, daß der Heyland daß Aelteste-Ammt in seiner Gemeine selbst übernehmen will, [...] Nach dem ersten Erstaunen fingen an die Thränen zu fließen und daß so durchgängig und anhaltend durch den gantzen ersten Theil, daß wir alle uns nie dergleichen Regung gesehen und gefühlt zu haben zu erinnern wißen".

88 Meyer 2000, p. 46. My translation, emphasis added. Indeed, the constitution, which was replaced with this new office of Christ, was that of the original unity of Brethren from

counter the Moravian (*mährisch*) influence in the community, which would have been strengthened with Zinzendorf's impending departure to North America.

Indeed, an important detail in this transferal of power is that this actually displaced the former authority structure of the community, within which the Moravian (*mährisch*) members since the beginning had constituted a significant presence. In 1727, when the community had been growing and left more or less to its own devices which had culminated in a 'separatist crisis', Zinzendorf arrived in Herrnhut to attend to this crisis, and after negotiations with the arguing parties, decided that some communal organization was needed.[89] This resulted in the Seigneurial Precepts and Prohibitions (*Herrschaftliche Gebote und Verbote*) and the Statutes of the Brotherly Agreement (*Statuten des Brüderlichen Vereins und Willkür in Herrnhut*). The first document was binding for all residents of Herrnhut, and placed them under the seigneurial protection of Zinzendorf, while granting them free subject status.[90] The statutes were binding for those who entered into this 'Brotherly Agreement'. Uttendörfter points out, however, that already the following year, from 8 November 1728, this document was no longer signed.[91]

Müller argued that the first constitution which Zinzendorf presented to the community was in line with the constitution of the Lusatian villages.[92] Thus the elder office in Herrnhut should be seen as analogous to the village elders, who assisted the chief justice in administrative matters.[93] From a group of 12 elders, four chief elders were decided by lot, one from each group in the community: the first arrivals (represented by Christian David, carpenter), the members from Zauchtenthal (Georg Nitschmann, cabinetmaker), the members from Kunewald (Melchior Nitschmann, weaver), and the non-Moravians, in this case, a Schwenkfelder (Christoph Hoffmann).[94] The remaining nine general elders also represented each of these groups. Because of the desire

---

Moravia. This practice consisted of a council of 12 elders, and from these 12 were elected four over-elders. In 1730, this structure was rearranged, and the community now only had one chief elder and a deputy elder. When Leonhard Dober took over the chief elder role in 1735, it was changed into the general elder over the entire community, which was growing rapidly. See detailed description of events in Kölbing 1821, pp. 210–52.

89   Uttendörfer 1925, p. 17.
90   Gollin 1967, p. 27; Uttendörfer 1925, p. 23; Wollstadt 1966, p. 30.
91   Uttendörfer 1925, p. 18.
92   Müller 1907.
93   Uttendörfer 1925, p. 25.
94   These names and lists here and in the following are taken from Wollstadt 1966, pp. 148–55 and Appendix 2.

to keep men and women separated, the women also had elderesses, eight in number, which included two aristocrats (the wives of Zinzendorf and Friedrich von Watteville), one from each of the three Moravian groups, a granddaughter of a Bohemian refugee, and two from the German surroundings. The following year, on 18 October 1728, these were re-elected (without lot), and the four groups were still represented – for the non-Moravians, Martin Dober, the potter, along with David Nitschmann, the shoemaker, Johann Nitschmann, and David Nitschmann, the carpenter, the latter was one of the general elders the previous year. On 26 September 1729, the two latter were replaced by Martin Rohleder (Kunewald) and Augustin Neißer (first arrivals). The office of the chief elders was presumably led according to the statutes and instructions of Zinzendorf, as Wollstadt notes. However, two changes took place, which seem to have restricted the office to dealing with spiritual matters. The first was the establishment of a judiciary council for arbitration in April 1729, which was to take over all arbitration, ideally leaving the elders to commit themselves more fully to the brotherly love. This meant that the judiciary council in practice took over all legal issues, such as punishments and permissions, as we saw above in the case of the punishment of the sisters, and the expulsion of undesirable families. The chair and general leadership of the judiciary council was the nobility, in particular Friedrich von Watteville and later von Zaionscheck.[95] The second change was the reduction of the elders to one chief, with a vice-elder. This took place in April 1730, when the single brother Moravian (*mährisch*) baker Martin Linner was elected elder of the community, and Augustin Neißer as vice-elder. Anna Nitschmann (Kunewald) was elected elderess of the sisters, gaining Judith Kloß (Kunewald) as deputy in 1732.[96] Linner held the office for three years, after

---

95   Gollin 1967, p. 28; Uttendörfer 1925, p. 32. Von Zaionscheck is listed as the leader in Status of Herrnhut (UA R.6.A.a.58.2).
96   Wollstadt 1966, p. 150. Judith Kloß, who is also in the marriage document, and her husband and five children were asked to leave Herrnhut in 1744, and moved to Kloster Berge to the Abbot Steinmetz near Magdeburg. They moved to Pilgerruh in the Duchy of Holstein in 1745, because her oldest son had been taken by the soldiers (and returned), but she feared a similar fate for her others. After Pilgerruh fell apart as a community, they stayed for the children's sake, but after the final disbandment, they went back to Kloster Berge in 1748, where her husband died. In 1750, several brothers and sisters came to see the Abbot, including Zinzendorf's successor, August Spangenberg, who took her with him to Barby, because she was a close friend of his wife. In 1751, she and three children returned to Herrnhut, where she moved into the widows' house. This portion of her *Lebenslauf* is printed in Sterik 2012, p. 302. The Kloß family is listed as number six in the document UA R.6.A.b.17.1744.a, from 26 October 1744, mentioned in footnote 63 as one of six families asked to leave. The other five families are the ones of which we have already heard, namely the families which the judiciary council had ordered to leave on 13 October because of vari-

which it was given to Leonhard Dober, and then, as mentioned above, the lot indicated that the Saviour wanted to take over the office. Wollstadt emphasises that the office in the 1730s became a spiritual service, which was to set an example, with the judiciary council and the helpers' council managing all the administrative responsibilities.[97] However, as is clear in the diaries, after the Saviour is inserted in the office, the use of the lot to determine expulsions and permissions increases. This coincides with the decrease in the influence of the judiciary council in 1743 noted by Uttendörfer.[98]

Bit by bit, the Moravian (*mährisch*) members of the community, with notable exceptions, such as Anna Nitschmann and David Nitschmann (Syndikus), were pushed away from positions of authority. Added to this is the following event: On the celebration of the Saviour as Chief elder day, 13 November 1741, the Moravians (*Mähren*) were asked to state whether or not they wanted to be part of the community. As Sterik points out, this group included people who had been co-founders of Herrnhut, who were suddenly regarded as being outside the community.[99] While most turned up, and some in tears, to confirm their desire to belong, four Moravians (*Mähren*) refused to comply. One couple was Augustin and Martha Neusser. Neusser, who had been one of the co-founders and a trusted elder, had actively resisted the new blood and wounds theology propagated by Johann Langguth, provoking, as it were, awkward situations for the leadership, in that two competing theological traditions were preached to potential converts, causing confusion.[100] Neusser, along with his brother Wenzel and cousin Zacharias,[101] left the community in 1746 and moved to Grosshennersdorf, where he died five years later.

Victory to the Lamb and his wounds indeed.

---

ous kinds of indecent and disorderly conduct Höyers, Frödens, Christian Pauls, Dippolds and Joseph Antons. In contrast, Anna Nitschmann was one of the most powerful people in the community, and Zinzendorf's closest ally. They married after the death of his first wife, Edmuth Dorothea. Wollstadt 1966, p. 212.

97 Wollstadt 1966, pp. 154–5.
98 Uttendörfer 1925, p. 32.
99 Sterik 2012, p. 339.
100 Sterik 2012, pp. 340–6.
101 Both are mentioned in the marriage document: Zacharias Neußer as being dry and recalcitrant towards the wounds and marital mystery, and Wenzel Neußer and his wife as a poor and miserable couple, blind to the mystery of marriage and hostile toward the brothers, sisters, and the Saviour.

5 Conclusion

This chapter has looked at several themes which have served to argue a simple point: The choir ideology and its concomitant theological expression emerge as victors in what had been an ongoing class struggle since the inception of the community. The purge in 1744–45, which began with the sex scandal in 1744, served to expel a host of people unwilling to toe the new line of discipline and, it seems, theology. Of the Moravians (*Mähren*) in the community, some were more adaptable to the new conditions than others, and those who showed themselves overly resistant were either excluded explicitly or frozen out. The choir speeches emerge as a way of consolidating this new position, and to these we now turn, to see how the contradictions are managed in this material, and which new problems emerge therein.

CHAPTER 4

The Choir Speeches

1 Introduction

> In a time, in which a revolutionary secularisation of the Christian historical consciousness completes itself and a new world-religiosity breaks through, he [Zinzendorf] tried to develop a new conceptualisation of religiosity, which received its formative powers from the end of history, from the Eschaton. In a turbulent age, determined by centrifugal powers, he sought to create a new security.[1]

With this somewhat laudatory quote, Erich Beyreuther situates Count Nikolaus Ludwig von Zinzendorf and his theological entrepreneurship within a whirlwind of secularisation and dispersion, and summons him as a rock rising above chaos, as attempting to create a new steadfastness in an age in which everything seemed to be dissolving in the face of powers beyond the control of everyday life. The epistemological crisis to which Beyreuther is referring – as 'revolutionary secularisation' – is part and parcel of some of the more far-reaching and long-term developments of capitalist modernity, the emergence of civil society and the implementation of a global economy. The revolution, then, is as Beyreuther states, a religiosity conditioned by the powers of the world, in contrast to which Zinzendorf attempts to create an eschatological religiosity which would function as a new steadfastness.

To some extent I agree with Beyreuther. Obviously, Zinzendorf did create something new and firm in times of trouble. However, the argument here is that the social aspects and economic practice of Zinzendorf's project were very much in the service of this world as it came into being, rather than apart from it. And thus, it must be questioned whether the religiosity really is as otherworldly as Beyreuther suggests. The present book aims to analyse Zinzendorf's role in this 'revolutionary secularisation' rather than placing him outside of it.

---

1 "In einer Zeit, in der eine umwälzende Säkularisation des christlichen Gesichtsbewußtseins sich vollendet, eine neue Weltfrömmigkeit sich Bahn bricht, versucht er eine neue Frömmigkeitsgestaltung auszuprägen, die vom Ende der Geschichte her, von Eschaton her, ihre formenden Kräfte empfängt. In einem aufgewühlten Zeitalter, von zentrifugalen Mächten bestimmt, sucht er neue Geborgenheit zu schaffen". Beyreuther 1963, p. xi. My translation.

One of the main ways in which Zinzendorf participates in this revolutionary secularisation is through *mediation*, of which the choir speeches are prime examples. This means that Zinzendorf articulates something (the mediator) through which something else (humans) must be understood, namely the Saviour, who is the master mediator of all human interaction. But this means that the Saviour himself must undergo a transition, from a heavenly saviour to a human interlocutor. This takes place through explications of gender, body, and corpse by which the Saviour is made earthly and human, while his more intangible qualities are grasped by other means, such as consciousness, senses, presence. And through this relation, the members are subjectified as children, boys, girls, single brothers, single sisters, widowers and widows. This is what I will be analysing in the choir speeches. At another level, I will also be looking at how this mediation generates individuals and collectives. The choirs set in motion a new way of understanding humans and community, and these are important social and epistemological trajectories within the overall changes of eighteenth-century Europe.

The choir speeches are an incredibly complex body of material and consequently confound any simple presentation or discussion. Leaving aside questions of authorship and location, destruction by intent or by disaster, completeness of collection, and transmission, we are faced with a baffling corpus of texts in terms of terminology, inconsistencies, and contradictions. There is no doubt that Zinzendorf was a highly original thinker and that any attempt to understand these streams of thought within our current limitations undercuts this originality to some extent. After much deliberation, I approach the speeches as expressions of dialectical thought, i.e. as experiments with ideological resolutions to real social contradictions. In this process, we find articulations of concepts in the making, and attempts at redefining social patterns and relations.

After a number of failed attempts at structuring, analysing and presenting the material, I have decided to craft the following chapter as a very large whole based largely on one carefully selected choir speech to each choir: children, boys, girls, single brothers, single sisters, widowers, and widows. However, only the children's speech is presented in full, as an example of the genre. The following speeches are summarised with a couple of choice quotations, and the full speech in its German original and English translation is in the appendix. As you will see, the various themes of subjectification (individual and collective), transition, ideology, gender, and marriage are intertwined and fused in multiple ways. This choir-based presentation enables me to demonstrate the progression of address within the choir system as a whole, and thus presents its structural logic in the simplest way.

Before we enter the world of the speeches, I want to draw out two overarching topics as signposts.

2 The Saviour: Individual and Collective

2.1 *The Saviour*

There can be no doubt that the figure of Jesus played a tremendous role in the world of the Moravian Brethren. This is so at a theological level, a personal level, and, most significantly for us, at a social level.

The Saviour, or the Lamb (*Lamm*), the Lambkin (*Lämmlein*) and the martyr-man (*Marter-Mann*) are all terms which Zinzendorf uses for Jesus. This risen martyr-man with broken eyes, pale lips, and perforated hands walks among his people. In this particular state, he is the primary catalyst through which social relations and unity were reconfigured and mediated. However, we should remember that this language was not the general way of speaking about Jesus from day one, as also indicated in Dober's account referred to in Chapter 3. According to Dober, a shift took place from speaking about redemption, faith, and God's grace to the language of Lamb, blood and wounds in the 1740s. Furthermore, as I have been arguing, a distinct shift did take place with the introduction of the choir system, and as we will see, the introduction of the Lamb in his particular role. The choir ideal, then, is much more tied up with the *person* of the Saviour, than the bonded groups, which were more connected to the idea of an apostolic community, as briefly noted in Chapter 2.

As a way of introducing this connection between the Saviour and the choirs, let us take a brief look at the change in emphasis as it is expressed in communion.[2]

---

2 For the non-theologians the case may be outlined as follows: Communion, or the Eucharist, is the ritual of partaking in Jesus' body and blood by ingesting bread and wine. It is based on the last meal of Jesus with his disciples before his death, as recounted in the gospels of Mark, Matthew and Luke. While these three gospels interpret this last meal as an Easter meal, Paul has a version in 1 Corinthians 11, which is not connected with Easter, but has a wording similar to that of Luke. The issue lies in the exact connection between the bread and body, wine and blood. Are they real or symbolic? The Catholic Church's doctrine on transubstantiation was defined and argued by Thomas Aquinas and based on an Aristotelian distinction between substance and accidents. The recital of Jesus' words and the action of the priest transforms the substance of the bread and wine to the body and blood of Jesus, while retaining the accidental nature of bread and wine. Marx alludes to this several times in *Capital* (see Boer 2012). The Protestant Reformation opposed this view, and three positions emerged: Luther's, which holds to the actual presence of the body and blood of Christ, in, with, and under the elements, because of Jesus' words. The two Reformed positions, Zwingli and Calvin hold to more sym-

In the following quote from Christian David in 1731, we see an emphasis on the communion as a communal ritual:

> That they, many each through each other, with his body, to let feed into his body in the eternal and spiritual life, and with his blood to drink to one spirit, that we thus also, as believers in truth from us, through the community-making become one body, one spirit, one heart and one soul, so that we are flesh from his flesh, and bone from his bones, on which, as it is a bread, so also we as many, through the communal love meal, become one body.[3]

As Wollstadt notes, Christian David's emphasis is on the strong effect of the ritual of communion on the life of the community, and Wollstadt rightly connects this with the inner cohesion of the community established and nourished through the image of the community as the body of Christ as a way of overcoming internal strife. As shown in Chapter 2, the community building efforts were carried out through the establishment of the *Banden*, which served to mediate between the individual and the community. Communion as an overarching communal ritual, then, complemented this organisation.

Jumping ahead, some 17 years later, we find a very different notion of communion in Zinzendorf's discourses on the Augsburg confession from 1748, where he speaks of communion as the 'Sacrament of somatic unification', i.e. the unification of 'our sinful nature' with God, 'our true bridegroom and husband'.[4] While the emphasis on the body is retained, the body is no longer a communal one, but an individual one – or at the very least, the idea of the body is no longer purely a collective one. Nor, for that matter, is the unification.

As we will see in the course of the choir speeches, the Saviour takes on multiple figures – single brother, physiological male, corpse, lambkin, side-wound, and martyr-man. These are important names that signify particular relations

---

bolic notions of the relation between bread and body, wine and blood. In the present study, I use 'communion' to refer to the partaking of body and blood of the Moravian Saviour within the community and 'Eucharist' to discuss the doctrinal aspects.

3 "daß sie sich ... ihrer vielle durch ein ander, mit seinem Leibe, zu einem Leibe ins Ewige u. Gestliche Leben, Hinein speißen laßen, u. Mit seinem Blute zu einem geiste tränken, daß wir auch also, alß (73) gläubige in warheit von unß, durch die vergemeinschafftung ein Leib, ein geist, ein Hertz, u. Eine Seele werden, so daß wir fleisch von seinem fleisch, u. Bein von seinem gebeine sein, auf daß gleich wie es ein Brodt ist, wir auch allso vielle, durch daß gemeinschafftliche Liebes Eßen, Ein Leib werden", (UA R.6.A.a.22,1) quoted in Wollstadt 1966, pp. 72–3. My translation.
4 Beyreuther and Meyer 1963, p. 295. My translation.

to the Saviour, and as such, a particular understanding of the member within this relation. There is, however, a fine distinction between the subjectification practices of the brothers and the sisters, which I can articulate here only in a very crude way: While the brothers are instructed to see themselves largely in the image of the Saviour, as well as part of a collective of believers in a choir, for the sisters, it is the other way around. They are primarily subjectified as a collective *Stand*, where the members incidentally also have individual bodies. The brothers are subjectified primarily as individuals within a collective, and the sisters primarily as a collective with individual issues – which will show up in the speeches to the choirs of the boys and girls. As we will see in the material from the girls' choir, there is a theological necessity in the collective understanding of the women, since they represent the community. In other words, the figure of the Saviour is central for understandings of community, gender, and self. This is why we must take seriously and pay close attention to the innovative or unusual features of Zinzendorf's Saviour which made him so central to the individual and collective subjectification practices of the community.

The central Christian dogma of God becoming man in Jesus Christ, means that it is theologically necessary to hold on to the simultaneous divine and human nature in the one person in order to maintain the balance of God's reconciliation with and hence salvation of humanity. The precise nature of the relationship between these two components or natures was a fierce debate in the early church, where a host of 'heretic' understandings of flesh and spirit were deemed unacceptable, and whether Christ was one or two natures.[5] The 'official' Christian position was formulated and decided upon in the council in Chalcedon in 451 in the Chalcedonian Creed: Jesus is 'one and the same Son, the Self-same Perfect in Godhead, the Self-same Perfect in manhood; truly God and truly Man, [...] acknowledged in Two Natures unfocusedly, unchangeably, indivisibly inseparably, the difference between the Natures being in no way removed because of the Union, but rather the properties of each Nature being preserved and concurring into One Person and One Hypostasis' etc.[6] The sig-

---

5 In early modernity, the theological struggles and battles were waged over the Eucharist rather than Christology, although, as we shall see later, the battles over the Eucharist also included disagreements over the presence of Christ, and thus have some Christological component. The importance of all this for the present argument is that in the Renaissance, the importance of the human nature of Christ reappeared, but was not really controversial. Leo Steinberg has noted how artwork tended to emphasise the genitals of Jesus, which indicated, according to Steinberg, an emphasis on his humanisation, becoming human. Given the general interest in the human body and matter in philosophy, medicine, and law at the time, it should not come as a complete surprise that also the human body of Jesus should take centre stage.
6 This agreement was only between the Western and Eastern Churches. The so-called 'oriental'

nificance of the delicate balance between the two natures is that if too much emphasis is placed on the human nature of Christ, his divine efficacy is called into question, i.e. can *he* really save 'us'? If too much emphasis is placed on his divine nature, the object of his salvation is called into question, namely, can he really save '*us*'?

Another important theological issue at stake here is the question of the nature of redemption, and the distinction between objective and subjective redemption. Briefly put, what these forms of redemption signify has also undergone a change from their understanding under feudalism, where objective redemption meant that God received satisfaction for our sins, and, happy with the compensation, reconciled himself to humanity. In objective redemption, where God reconciles himself with humans, the only significant change through the centuries is that the language has shifted more onto the role and sacrifice of Jesus, rather than the litigious nature of God. Subjective reconciliation, however, emphasises humanity's reconciliation with God, and is much more interesting, in that the change here is much more dramatic. From signifying a need for humans to follow in the example of Jesus, as expressed by Pierre Abelard, it becomes, in later Protestant theology, e.g. Schleiermacher, the workings of God in the human, enabling each person to respond to God's grace. What subjective redemption is, changes according to the status of the subject.

Pietism played a significant role in cultivating this idea of subjective redemption, which we then see radicalised in Zinzendorf and the Moravian Brethren. But Zinzendorf also held firmly onto the salvific sacrifice of the Saviour, and claimed that it was *as* the sacrificed lamb that the Saviour could best awaken our response to God's grace, because we could see ourselves in him, and see him in ourselves and our lives. The human Jesus, then, is in perfect extension of our human lives; he died, and he will marry. We are thus the earthly image of the heavenly reality.[7] This is then the specific role of the Saviour in the Moravian Brethren.

As this brief theological discussion shows, concepts such as Jesus and the body are tremendously ideologically burdened.[8] To negotiate this challenge in

---

churches, i.e. the Coptic Church, the Armenian Church and the Syrian Church did not agree to this position and retained an understanding of one nature (Monophysitism) rather than two (Duophysitism).

7 Best expressed in the choir speeches to the married couples, 2 August 1748 (UA R.4.C.II.12) and 4 August 1748 (UA R.20.HS55).
8 In approaching Zinzendorf's very human Saviour and the bodies of the members of the community, I have taken a leaf out of Barbara Duden's seminal book, *The Woman beneath the Skin*

my analysis of the Saviour in the choir speeches, I have endeavoured to suspend any reference to an external 'Jesus Christ' and instead monitor closely what Zinzendorf is doing with the Saviour and how he relates the Saviour to the members of the community, thus emphasising the mediation of religious ideas. This is the reason for retaining the specific signifier 'Saviour', rather than Jesus, except of course when 'Jesus' is used in Zinzendorf's own words.[9]

2.2 Stand

In his speech to the widowers from 7 August 1755, Zinzendorf emphasises that all divisions, – childhood, youth, marriage and widowhood – have their specific covenant with the Saviour. This originated in the incarnation, when the Saviour 'took on our nature and invented his behaviour as a human and experienced the particulars of every rank (*Stand*)'.[10] This is important because of the connection of *Stand* to the human nature of Jesus. We may bolster this with another quotation:

> The children's choirs, the boys and younglings, the older girls, the maidens, the married people, the widowers and widows, in brief, all classes have grace in their grade. And everyone has their own separate blessing from Jesus' humanity. Every single choir can rejoice in its circumstances due to the holy, meritorious humanity of Jesus, and in this, no choir must stay behind.[11]

(Duden 1987). Duden's self-reflective methodology provides a good starting point for working with the Herrnhuter material, in that she shows how she wrestled with how to categorise, understand and interpret the archival sources of the doctor from Eisenach, Johann Storch, whose journals form the basis of her study. Duden notes that in her work with these cases, she kept falling into the trap of either making sense of them in terms of her own anatomical-physiological grid, or according to common categories of eighteenth-century science. She mentions the temptation to interpret Storch's ideas through Ernst Stahl's doctrines, and thus dissolve his work into the larger ideological framework of the doctors in the vicinity of Halle. However, the more she worked with the sources, the more she realised that the primary categories in Storch's work were those he shared with his patients, and not influenced by Stahl, vitalism or Halle. Finally, she realised what it was Storch and his patients held in common: their understanding of the body, *Leib*, an understanding to which Duden has no access, because it was only ever implicit in the sources.

9 I have tried to do something similar in another study of Jesus in the gospel of John (Petterson 2016a). There I argued that releasing John's gospel from a linear reading based on an assumed life of Jesus, it reveals some pre-gnostic ideas and an elite ideology.

10 Widowers, 7 August 1755: "der unsre Natur angenommen und an Geberden als ein Mensch erfunden und eines jeden Standes sein Particulare erfahren hat." (UA R.20.HS31).

11 Single brothers, 4 May 1760: "Die Kinder-Chöre, die Knaben und Jünglinge, die grossen Mädgen, die Jungfrauen, die Ehe-Leute, die Witwer und Witwen, kurz alle Claßen die

As is here stated, not only are all choirs blessed in their particular segment or grade, but every individual is blessed through Jesus' humanity. And Jesus' humanity has conferred circumstances onto each choir, in which the respective choirs may rejoice.

As indicated in Chapter 2, the whole choir idea is tied to the figure of Jesus. Wollstadt notes how in earlier hymns (1728/29), the various groups were presented with Jesus and Mary as examples, an idea which would be fundamental in the later choirs. He continues: 'Every *Stand* should, in its relations and with its gifts, depict a piece of the essence of Jesus'.[12]

The English translation of the German word *Stand* is estate, as in 'estates of the realm', signifying one's position in society. It is, some argue, the precursor of the concept of class, and consequently belongs to a feudal social order.[13] Taking our point of departure in this view, we will focus on the use of *Stand* in the choir speeches and how it is used exclusively to refer to the gendered subjects of the choir speeches. In other words, instead of referring to a metaphysical and theological social order of feudalism, it here refers to the position of each individual in terms of their gender and position *within* the community. In the following two examples, one from a 1750 speech to single sisters, and the other from a 1755 speech to single brothers, *Stand* here refers to different states, which are gendered. In the first example, Zinzendorf is referring to various customs within a gendered *Stand*:

> Thus, customs are also the usual way in which one conforms to a *Stand*, thus the women have their own customs, the widows have their own customs, the children have their separate customs, and the maidens also have their own customs.[14]

In this second, more difficult example, the focus here should just be on the use of *Stand*, which refers to a brother's *Stand* as either a single man or as a married man:

---

haben Gnade in ihrem Grade. Und jedes hat einen Aparten Segen aus Jesu Menscheit. Ein jedes Chor kan sich vor seine Umstände der heiligen verdienstlichen Menschheit Jesu freuen, und darinnen muß *kein* Chor zurück bleiben." (UA R.20.HS57).

12 Wollstadt 1966, p. 107. My translation.
13 Conze 2005.
14 Single sisters, 6 November 1750: "also heißt Sitte auch die gewöhnlich Art, sich in einen Stand zu begehen; da haben die Weiber ihre eigene Sitten, die Witwen haben ihre eigene Sitten, die Kinder haben ihre aparte Sitten, die Jungfern haben auch ihre eigene Sitten". (UA R.20.HS28 and 47).

No brother, who lives in the most difficult married *Stand*, is allowed to do this [i.e. to be God's betrothed], once he has given away what he once had, but he may also not say that it does not often appear to him more difficult for him to maintain his station, than in his free *Stand* and choir. To be blessed and merry, to have his heaven here already, and to fly off into his last end, a single brother needs no further consummation in this time, no change of his *Stand*, no office, no calling among the heathens, rather in the choir house, in his corner, he can be the lovely girlfriend, on which the Saviour's view finds pleasure.[15]

This use of *Stand* to indicate community and difference *within* gender is a way of redirecting struggles pertaining to class, which had been an issue in the community since its inception as we saw in Chapter 3. We will be looking more closely at the issue of gender in the analysis of the speech to the boys, but also in Chapter 6, where we turn to look at the implications of this focus on gender identity, namely in our discussion of alienation. The argument there will be that the unifying function of gender to transcend divisions of class contributes towards the division of human nature into public collective and private individuals, where the socio-economic differences are irrelevant, because the equity is produced at a civic level.

We now turn to the speeches. We begin with the speech to the children which is presented in full to give you a sense of the shape of a choir speech. The following speeches are summarised by me, with a number of quotations and you may find the translation and the transcription of the German original in the appendix. In connection with each speech, I engage selected topics in a theoretical and historical discussion. These will then function as the broad foundation for the more abstract discussions of social change and historiography in the last two chapters of the book.

With these things in mind, we now turn to the various choirs and their choir speeches to see how these various things are articulated.

---

15 Single brothers, 9 July 1755: "Das darf kein Bruder, der in dem allerbeschwerlichsten Ehestand lebt, wenn ers einmal gehabt hat, weggeben; aber er darf auch nicht sagen, daß es ihm nicht oft schwerer ankommt, seine station maintiniren, als in seinem freyen Stande und Chor. Um selig und vergnügt zu sein, um seinen Himmel schon hier zu haben, und sich in sein leztes Ende zu verfliegen, brauch ein lediger Bruder keiner weitern vollendung in dieser Zeit, keiner Veränderung seines Standes, keines Amtes, keines Berufs unter die Heyden, sondern er kan im Chor Hause, in seinem Winkel die *schöne Freundin* werden, daran des Heilands Ansicht ein plaisir findet" (UA R.20.HS58).

3 Children's Choir

The choir speeches to the children are the only ones to have been intentionally edited and published by the Theological Seminary in Barby in 1758.[16] This collection is not exhaustive, however, in that it only contains speeches given between 1755 and 1757 to the children, younger boys (*Knäblein*), and younger girls (*Mägdlein*) in the German communities. The speech I have selected below is unpublished, from 1758, and given to the children in Herrnhut.[17]

The speech refers to the biblical text of the day, the watchword (*Losung*), as well as a painting, which, it seems, depicts Jesus in the tomb.[18] The emphasis throughout is on seeing/visualising the Saviour.

> In the afternoon the children received the following homily on their watchword:
> *My eyes will see Him and greet him close by.*
> There are two beautiful ideas in this together: my eyes will already see Him *here*: 'Blessed are the pure hearts, because they will see God' (Matthew 5.) and 'my eyes will see Him *there*'; David says: 'I will be sated, when I wake up under your image'. But our text is in Job. He said: 'I will see Him myself, my eyes will see Him and no one else in my place'.[19]

Here Zinzendorf is collating a number of biblical texts from Job, Matthew, and an unknown reference, presumably from Psalms, given the reference to David. The watchword text is often made up from a biblical verse and a Moravians hymn or a bon mot, which then interprets the biblical text in a different way.

> Added to that is 'close by' and 'greetings'. Such greetings can also already be obtained here, if the body's eye is *closed*. That one already here in the time can see him standing in front of one's mind, already David has said: 'I always have the Lord before my eyes'. and when he one time didn't have

---

16 Zinzendorf 1965.
17 Children, 11 March 1758 (UA GN.C.78.1758.2).
18 There were three large paintings in the choir houses, and the depiction of Jesus in the tomb was a common one among the general paintings. Which particular painting this speech refers to, is impossible to ascertain.
19 Job 19.27: KJV Whom I shall see for myself, and mine eyes shall behold, and not another; though my reins be consumed within me.

him so, then he asked: 'Why are you hiding your countenance from me, why are you so far away?' Then he fretted in his soul and worried himself daily in his heart until *He* showed himself to him again.

We are then given the meaning of the addition 'greet him close by', which is not part of any of the biblical texts mentioned earlier. It is related to what he calls the eye of the *Gemüth* in distinction to the eye of the body and is given biblical validation through reference to David and Psalm 16:8 on the lord before one's eyes, and Psalm 13:1 on the lord hiding his countenance.

> The *greetings close by* happen in more than one way. The *heart hears* the softest greeting, sometimes it receives a kiss from the pale lips, how strong does that *feel*, sometimes an awareness is *sensed*, as it was to Emmaus, a grave breath, a quiet, gentle breeze from the precious heart-garden of my death (If we are to give off a lily scent, as He likes to smell, then He must first give it to us).

Zinzendorf is asking ('how strong does that feel?') and explaining the nature of the 'greetings' from the Saviour. The pale lips refer to the Saviour's corpse, as does the mention of grave breath and heart-garden of death. The heart is that of the believer, grown in the heart garden of the Saviour's death, and this heart can receive 'greetings' in the form of a kiss or a breeze.

> The older one gets, the more one becomes aware of the corruption in oneself, and sees from near or far, in which way one may once be dissipated, that the soul, the little dove, can fly into the rock-chasm, in his arm and lap.

This is also an amalgamation of biblical allusions and Moravian imagery. The soul, the little dove, could be a reference to John's gospel, where the spirit descends on Jesus like a dove. But the reference to the dove in the rock-chasm refers to both Jeremiah and John's gospel. Jeremiah 48:28 mentions the curse of Moab and says: 'O ye that dwell in Moab, leave the cities, and dwell in the rock, and be like the dove that maketh her nest in the sides of the hole's mouth'. Here we have the dove dwelling in the rock. However, as mentioned in Chapter 3, the side-wound of Jesus is a prevalent image of the Moravians, and comes from John 19:34, where one of the soldiers pierced Jesus' side, and out flowed blood and water. This side-wound is a place of refuge of the Moravians, and here is mentioned as the entry point into salvation, where one will rest in Jesus' arm and lap. The biblical allusions are a backdrop to the imagery, what is important is that the side-wound is a place of refuge, and the believer is encouraged to nestle there as a dove in a rock, when one feels under threat of corruption.

> Until then, one is keen to keep these bones nicely dying, so that he not only redeem one as the child in the cradle, but also in the form of death, in which he redeemed us, and as his eyes blinks in the blindness of all his souls, as long as the world stands, then it will happen to each one of us, as He dispensed his soul and died.

This enigmatic paragraph refers (I think) to the life of the believer following the life of Jesus, which is the foundation of the choir idea, as we will see several times in some of the following speeches. That the Saviour's redemption follows one from cradle to grave, one's form of death connected to the Saviour's form of death, by which the believer is redeemed.

> In the picture, how he lay shrouded in the tomb as a little corpse, one sees him the most and the dearest. And something else is added to this, what you do not have until then, and to which expectation strives: 'you will celebrate more church mystery'. You will get to taste his boils and entire martyred corpse, as though one were held by him in arm and lap, and bit him out of love. This will become for you a true food and drink, by which the heart and body and soul are satisfied.

This is the painting to which I referred above, which also resonates with the first reference to David, which said that he was satisfied when 'I wake up under your image'. This is, for now, where the children are at, to experience the Saviour in full and most dear in imagery. When they get older, they will be further initiated into the mystery of the church, which is communion, the partaking in the body and blood of Christ, which here is given an extra 'fleshiness' in that Zinzendorf speaks of tasting his boils and corpse, an experience which will give them an anticipation of the joys of salvation.

> These are all things that are to be experienced in this time, and which are in the place of the bodily not-seeing and, as it were, reward for it, which shall make it right again, that one has to wait so long for the Seeing, 'because we have, taste, feel, smell, and to crawl to him, into [his] entrails'. In this regard, one can put the Seeing already in his hands until completion.

Here we return to the non-seeing body over against the Seeing, which is the end-time fulfilment, when one sees the Saviour face to face. Until then, one must make do with having, tasting, feeling, smelling and crawling into his entrails (through the side-wound), which are meant to recompense for having to wait for the Seeing.

> But children! if one would like to have it so, here and there, then a pure heart is always part of it; that is, a heart looking for him, Seeing him, which, because it knows nothing above, greater and more blessed than him, would rather let everything in the world go, but him, with whom a dear little hour in in the praises of His wounds, His goodness and loyalty is more important than eating; that even in sleep, he is always at His side, in his friendship wakes up, and thus goes from one hour to the next, and is not afraid of anything except whether he can remain true to Him. That is his ghost, his fear, his sorrow: 'Oh will I remain faithful, will I not grieve you even once?' Certainly, it is true, the Saviour has lost his life for us, what is all our small faith against that, all our diligence, obedience, silence, order, to be small and reverent, what is all this against that? Not only does it not cost us anything, it is also a pleasure and a bliss for us. If we did nothing, then we are not worth the light of the sun, one would not be worthy that He should look upon one, that one be among the children of the community, if not each and every one, as they should, was to rejoice in love with him.

For this to be possible, however, a pure heart, that is always aware of the Saviour and places him above all, is an absolute must. The pure heart is the heart haunted by the fear of not being able to remain true, and the children are admonished that their faith and obedience is a small thing to ask from someone who has sacrificed his life. Not making an effort is making oneself unworthy of the light of the sun, the gaze of the Saviour, and the place in the community.

> But there is nothing difficult in that, except when you have a bad heart, and you do not like it, but such hearts do not belong here. Our soul is a poor sick thing, I say that often, but *sick* is quite different from being wicked and unwilling to love the Saviour. Sickness, misery, weakness, incapability he can well tolerate in us, and his powerlessness and weakliness must do us justice for our weakness: 'good and compassion make us *endurable*'. But He must act very differently with a heart and soul that is not willingly His, which is not attached to Him, for whom 'easy' has more appeal than Him, and who even during the holy activities of singing,

> speaking, and praying about Him, can let his thoughts fare around. Such a mind should not wish that it will be placed in front of His face, for it will be put to shame, for Him in his future. A faithful heart, on the other hand, always wishes and sighs, 'Please look at me, Lord, I pray that you will always find me soft and poor, sometimes even distressed over mistakes and defects and weakness or whatever got in my way, that I cannot be satisfied with myself, but you always find me warm in the heart and loveable, there is always something there that is dear to you, because it comes from you, therefore, look at me, yes, see through me, I fear nothing from your eyes. I know you know me better, than I know myself, but I have also the hope, with [the apostle] Paul, to get to know you again as I am known by you'.

Here we have the contrast between a pure heart and a bad heart, and the difference between a sick soul, which is normal, and a wicked heart, which is wilfully against the Saviour. Again, all focus must be on the Saviour, the children are to mirror themselves in his gaze, and, in direct speech, instructed how to relate, and what to desire. They are to beg of him to look at them, love them, and grant them to know the Saviour as he knows them.

> In the meantime, one always makes blessed and cute representations of Him, and await fervently to see Him face to face. Then one will also see whether one has imagined Him rightly here, and whether our painting is correct.
> Sung: I look after to the heavens, although the only heart stands himself before our gaze, but the eye is closed etc.

The ending speaks of representations of the Saviour, which will only ever be images, and will be tested once they meet him face to face, where they also will be able to assess whether the painting is accurate. The final hymn which they sing also relates to this seeing/not seeing, and the closing of the eye of the body.

There are several significant items in this speech. First, the distinction between seeing and non-seeing, second, the evocative language, and finally, the mode of relating to the Saviour. These are all issues which will resurface in the following speeches, and so we will be returning to them again and again, albeit in different forms.

3.1   *Relating to the Saviour*

One of the ways in which the children are to think as 'selves' is through their relation to the Saviour. Indeed, the whole speech is an instruction into how to relate to him. The emphasis is on the pure hearts of the children, directed solely at the Saviour and cultivating the inner voice of consciousness towards this end, as we saw in Zinzendorf's instruction as to how to feel and think about oneself and one's desire to be seen in a particular way by the Saviour. The Saviour, in turn, is depicted as a corpse, namely by the mention of pale lips and grave breath.

The corpse of the Saviour is an important motif in the choir speeches. While the English term 'body' may refer to a body living or dead, the German term here is *Leichnam*, which means a dead body. Hence the translation 'corpse'.[20] The emphasis is unequivocally on the dead body, and the smell of the grave and the corpse,[21] the broken eyes, the crucified body, the penetrated hands, etc. The emphasis on the corpse of Jesus ranges from the object of one's contemplation: that one 'should and should want to have the martyr man as object with every vein-pulse and draw of breath and every waking and sleeping thought';[22] to one's role model, as we will see below in the speech to the single brothers.

There are a couple of significant points to this near-constant reference to the corpse, and the detailed descriptions of its features (pale lips and broken eyes, blood and bloody wounds). One is that it emphasises the humanity of Jesus. It is the human corpse of Jesus with which the members engage and whom they adore. This then is part of coming to terms with their own death as a mere transition to the presence of the Saviour. This is not a big focus in the speech above to the children, but one that pervades the material at large, both in the diaries, the memoirs, and the speeches. We will return to this at much greater length below, but for now just note that Zinzendorf emphasises the corpse as the manifestation of the Saviour's humanity for the children, as that which is available for them here and now.

3.2   *Seeing/Non-seeing*

The significant baseline in this speech, which is related to the watch-word, is the distinction between seeing and non-seeing, and the eye of the body. The

---

20 In a letter from an English Moravian to Zinzendorf, the letter-writer states: 'That this Nature and likeness be manifest in all my Members, and I believe one great Step towards Effecting this is the Privilege of Partaking of the Corp's + Blood of Jesus in fellowship with this Congregation etc'. Charlesworth to Zinzendorf, sent from Lindseyhouse, 17 May 1754 (UA R.4.CII.11.4).

21 See married sisters, 14 July 1755: 'let yourselves be penetrated by his balsamic air';"von seiner balsamischen Luft durchziehen lassen" (UA R.20.HS42).

22 Single sisters, 6 July 1757: "Warum man sich [...] beschäftigen muß und wünscht, daß ein jeder Adern-Schlag und Othem-Zug und jeder wachende oder schlafende Gedanke den Marter-Mann zum object habe ..." (UA R.20.HS60).

Saviour may be seen in one's mind, if the body's eye is closed. That is not, however, 'the Seeing', for which one longs. Nor is it the representation of the Saviour in paintings. What Zinzendorf calls 'the Seeing' is the face to face meeting with the Saviour, after one's death. Because of the bodily not-seeing, a number of temporary means are in place to experience the Saviour until the Seeing, namely crawling into his side-wound, tasting his corpse at communion, and seeing him in one's mind.[23]

The importance of this at a social level lies in the cultivation of an inner self, which will continue throughout the choirs, albeit with different emphases. Whereas in the adult choirs it will take the form of gender, chastity and desire, here with the children, it takes the form of seeing, or emphasis on the heart within a clean body.[24] A good example of the heart is the speech to the children from 3 December 1755:

> We have behind our body-*hüttlein* something which no one sees; since everything we sing and pray comes not from the hands and feet, but from the *Gemüth*, from the heart. As you are outwardly, so you are also inwardly. The human, who is in the other, must also eat and drink, and rest and observe sabbath, which agrees with the bodily sleep, he must also be holy. An unruly human, who has been separated from his heart and the Saviour, can rattle off prayers and songs with the mouth: but he who understands can hear that it is only the mouth speaking. If it is to be right, then your heart must feel more than your mouth speaks, your soul must sometimes be so joyful in the matter, especially when one goes home [i.e. dies], and the mouth no longer can speak but in the heart it keeps singing; in the heart there is always the life, the spirit and the joyfulness that one can see him, that looks out to the eyes, as well as the sensibility, the warm air from the side of Jesus, while at the same time, the whole body from the outside is cold and stiff.[25]

Here again we see the distinction between the outer (body-*hüttlein*) and the inner (*Gemüth*) human, where the fervency, the joyfulness and sensibility comes from the heart, even after the body is cold and stiff. I will return to this cultivation of consciousness when we have some more examples from the adult

---

23 For other examples of this Seeing, see the choir speeches to the children, 25 March 1756, 9 May 1756, and 30 April 1757 all printed in Zinzendorf 1965 and the choir speech to the girls, 27 February 1758 (GNC 78.1758.2), to which we will return.
24 See 25 March 1756 and 18 April 1756 in Zinzendorf 1965.
25 Zinzendorf 1965, pp. 41–2, my translation.

choirs. But we must keep in mind that while we are quite accustomed to ideas of inner selves, this would not have been common among the ruled classes of early modern Europe – or at least, we do not know, because we have very little material from these classes. Sweeping studies like Charles Taylor's *Sources of the Self* might blind us to the fact that these sources are either products of philosophers and/or period abstractions which are used to speak on behalf of all, such as the Renaissance or the Reformation.[26] As David Sabean notes in his study of village life in early modern Germany,

> by the mid eighteenth century, we can see that 'conscience' had come to mean different things according to one's position in the social structure. There was as yet no notion of the person as a single integrated center of awareness. Indeed, one observer notes that villagers 'did not know how to remember.' Thus conscience, in the terms discussed at the time in elite culture – as a steering mechanism of behavior, linked to consciousness as a consistent unity – would have no meaning.[27]

It is this 'single center or awareness' that is underway in these speeches, and in this speech it is cultivated among the children of the elite and non-elite. The trick is that the modern idea of consciousness has displaced other ways of thinking in Western civilisation, and thus we are faced with the task of understanding a way of thinking which is no longer practiced, and the temptation is to deploy our understandings of this and that to conceptualise patterns of behaviour and modes of thinking. This is of course a well-known problem, but often superficially treated – or addressed in a way which is *thought* to overcome the problem but does not. An example of this is the otherwise interesting study by Ben Morgan,[28] which analyses the understanding of identity as an embedded and collective matter in late medieval mysticism, using phenomenology. I greatly admire the effort to think outside Michel Foucault and Charles Taylor, but question whether Heidegger really is the answer, given that Heidegger's conceptualisation is a community of selves, not a community before there ever were selves.

This shift, from community to community of selves, is what I am trying to trace here in the Moravian material. To illustrate the depth of the problem in more detail, we might look at William Dowling's introduction to Fredric

---

26 Taylor 1989. See also the uninterrupted history of consciousness in Ojakangas 2013.
27 Sabean 1987, p. 35.
28 Morgan 2013.

Jameson's *The Political Unconscious*.[29] In his explanation of how Jameson uses the function of primitive communism, he addresses the problem that due to the changes of capitalism and its forces upon us, we are no longer capable of thinking collectively, in a world where we are shaped as absolute individuals:

> For the unhappy fact is that as creatures of History, locked away in the private and separate and lonely worlds of our own consciousness – the separation and the loneliness having been produced by the implacable market forces of capitalism that constitutes human beings as individual units or 'subjects' in order to function *as* a system – we cannot imagine what it would be like, in the purest sense, to think collectively, to perceive the world as a world in which no such thing as individuals or individuality existed, to think not as 'a member of a group' but *as the group itself*.[30]

The choir speeches are unique insights into how people were instructed to think as individual units, and thus are prime source material into the ideological structures of liberalism which were part of the emergence of capitalism and its particular understanding of community – as a community of selves.

3.3 *Language*

As this speech to the children has indicated, the language of the choir speeches is vivid and highly idiosyncratic. After working through more than half of the speeches, it seems that the strangely evocative, fleshy and sensual vocabulary intends to generate a specific conceptual world. Determining what this conceptual world is will be the topic of this entire chapter, so we will not determine it from the outset, but gain a sense of it in the course of the analysis. However, we may cast a glance at two interesting analyses of Zinzendorf's language, namely Jörg Reichel's analysis of the language and conceptual world in the twelfth appendix to the Herrnhuter songbook, and the chapter on Zinzendorf and de-allegorisation in Burkhard Dohm's study on poetic alchemy.[31]

Our first step is to suspend both studies' emphasis on the Sifting Time as the context for their analyses. As mentioned in Chapter 3, both Paul Peucker and Craig Atwood have convincingly argued that the connection between the Sifting Time and blood and wounds theology is a historiographical legerdemain

---

29 Dowling 1984.
30 Dowling 1984, p. 22, emphasis in original. I have analysed the difference between the community as the body of Christ in Paul's letters (first century) and Zinzendorf's speeches in Petterson 2015.
31 Dohm 2000; Reichel 1969.

which serves to contain blood and wounds theology within a certain period of Moravian history, while it in fact is much broader and deeper than such mystification allows. So, with that reservation, we may appreciate their analyses, without stumbling on this detail.

Reichel characterises the language of the songs from the songbook as difficult to understand because the individual verses contain many different ideas and images which stand next to each other unmediated: 'in a kaleidoscopic manner these images swirl through each other, mixtures of images emerge, and even in individual utterances, several ideas are pressed together'.[32] This sounds familiar in relation to the choir speeches, although as discourses they are not subject to the compact nature and brevity of expression which a hymn is.

Reichel notes that attempts at ordering and defining the compositional principles of the hymns have failed because of the overwhelming nature of the task. He, however, developed the categories by focusing on the hymns which are rewritings of older hymns by Luther, Paul Gerhard, etc., by which the particular Moravian imagery may be distilled. The means by which this is done is, among several things, use of everyday language instead of a religious language, through reduction of general to specific symbols (from passion of Christ to the side-wound), the use of the present tense instead of imperative and future tenses, to make the idea of an afterlife an already present lived reality, and finally, from abstract Christian categories to concrete emotional language (from believe to see, from Jesus gives eternal life to Jesus makes sated forever).[33] Reichel draws on Dober's relation of the shift from traditional theological language to the language of blood and wounds, which we discussed in the previous chapter. Reichel uses this to argue that it is not a question of different content, but of a different way of *expressing* the same Lutheran content, that the two languages ensure the same access to and assurance of the objective redemption.[34] However, as discussed above in the section on the Saviour, there is a shift from a more classical approach to redemption in Pietism, which placed an overriding emphasis on the individual's conversion, and conscious acceptance of Jesus/God. From the more classical expression in the theology of early Herrnhut to the personal piety of the blood and wounds theology, the individual subject has emerged.

As mentioned in Chapter 3, Craig Atwood notes that the vision of the wounds in the Litany of Wounds is focused on the individual, which we may

---

32 Reichel 1969, p. 43. My translation.
33 Reichel 1969, pp. 30–8.
34 Reichel 1969, p. 33.

see in the syntax and the repeated use of first-person singular, even though, as Atwood notes, we also have the occurrences of verses with the plural. But the majority of verses portray the wounds of Jesus over against the individual, who over and over again is interpellated as Nitsche's 'I' through the Litany of Wounds. In addition to Reichel's point on the change from future and imperative forms to present tense, his examples also show that there is an increase in the inclusion of the congregation in the songs, so that the singing person is active in this present tense and thus participates in the divine presence which is manifested here and now.[35] Building on Reichel's analysis, Burkhard Dohm argues that Zinzendorf's aim is, particularly through poetics, to stage or orchestrate divine presence (the numinous) through the use of a simple, non-allegorical, but concrete language.[36] Already Herder had seen this quality in the language, but with an extra interesting twist. He noted that Zinzendorf gave his community 'its own intimate court and heart-language, to speak with their husband and their mother, the spirit, as well as with brothers and sisters among each other'.[37] The language, which Herder noted was conversational, often French-German, but free and frank, is characterised as a language of the court and of the heart, intimate, and used among the members themselves and in their addresses to the Saviour and the holy spirit. There thus is an element of class, with the mention of the court language, conversational language and French, which Dohm ignores, because he is more interested in Herder's observation that it is also a language of the heart and used to communicate both within the community and the divine. Dohm notes that this language which pervaded the community enabled a 'liturgicalisation and sanctification of everyday life to take shape in the Moravian Brethren, which according to the understanding of the count expressed the unmediated nature of Moravian existence to God'.[38] Dohm pays attention to the grave-sensuality of the poetic language, and notes the fascination of the Moravians with the martyred corpse of the Saviour, as expressed for example in the hymn 'O Du wunderschönes Lamm' written by Marianne Ringgold in 1745 for Zinzendorf's birthday. The first verse is as follows:

> Oh you beautiful lamb, yes, you most beautiful among all!
> Your wounds big and small please me; Side-shrine

---

35 Reichel 1969, pp. 30–8.
36 Dohm 2000, pp. 319–41.
37 quoted in Dohm 2000, p. 282 n. 3, my translation.
38 Dohm 2000, p. 284. My translation.

Your colorful martyr-signs charm me.
You are beautiful, my lamb![39]

In his analysis of the hymn Dohm shows how the emphasis on 'me' and 'my' in the first verse serve to associate the beauty of the depicted lamb with 'the subjective perceptive and sentient experience of the speaking I'.[40] But otherwise Dohm does not enter into the subjective appropriation of the wounds in that he is more interested in the presence of the divine in the community, and how Zinzendorf's language is an attempt to effect this presence. And I have no objection to this interpretation. Indeed, his analysis of the rest of the hymn is excellent, and I agree completely that this is without a doubt what Zinzendorf does with his language. But I do not wish to eclipse the subjective experience from our line of questioning, since there is also no doubt in my mind that this affective language intends to generate a response, individual as well as collective. There is an individualism inherent in the blood and wounds theology, as noted by Dober, which sets the individual over against Jesus' seeping wounds and conversely confirms the atonement for the *me*.

The blood and wounds language, then, creates a world which has its focus on the Saviour and his martyred body, and its connection to the individual believer. That this is cultivated from early on in the believer's life is seen in the speech above, where the children are to anticipate the celebration of more church mystery, where they will taste the boils and corpse of the Saviour.

What I have indicated here will be pursued through the rest of the speeches, namely seeing Zinzendorf's linguistic innovations as experimenting with a form of affective language, which intends to call into being an object, through which subjective transformation takes place. An example of the first, which we can regard as an extension of the emphasis on the corpse, is that the choir speeches advocate the presence of Jesus in the choirs. I mentioned earlier, in

---

39 Du wunderschönes Lamm, ja, du schönster unter *allen*! mir ge*fallen*
    deine wunden groß und *klein*; Seiten*schrein*
    mich scharmiren deiner *leichen* ihre bunte marter-*zeichen*.
    Schön bist du, *mein* Lämm*elein*!

   Quoted in Dohm 2000, p. 319, number 2144 in the *Herrnhuter Gesangbuch*. My mangled translation, which only intended to bring out the 'me' of the song, has not done justice to the rhyme of the song, here noted by italics. It was precisely this mesmerising quality of slow singing with embedded rhymes which enthralled the Indigenous population of Greenland, and still influences their singing today.

40 Dohm 2000, p. 322.

Chapter 2, that the real character of a choir is, according to Zinzendorf, the fact that it places the Saviour 'in his choirshape' (*Chor-Gestalt*) in front of its [the choir's] eyes, as though it [the choir] really lived with him.[41]

Katherine Faull calls this particular technique of language 'painting a word picture'.[42] Zinzendorf uses this technique often, namely, making use of simple, graphic and affective language to paint the Saviour before the eyes of his listeners, to make his (the Saviour's) presence felt.[43] Zinzendorf insisted that an unmediated presence of the divine was possible through simple non-allegorical language. And while Dohm connects this use of language with liturgy,[44] it is worthwhile to consider the choir speeches as another example of this speech, which intends to summon and make manifest the body of Jesus.

An example of the second aspect of Zinzendorf's linguistic style is the constant subjectification strategies which we also saw in the children's speech, strategies which introduce a particular awareness of the self. To this will be added ideas of body and gender in the older choirs. The men are encouraged to identify with and take on the corpse of Jesus as well as to imagine themselves as possessing female souls. The sisters are encouraged to imagine themselves as brides of Christ, and as inhabiting the body which suckled Jesus. These are well-known tropes from the history of Christianity, but in Zinzendorf's speeches they function specifically as a way of emphasising congruence between the believers' bodily existence and their souls and thus call into being that which the words describe.

This rhetoric of presence, or painting word pictures, is connected with the rediscovery of *ekphrasis* in the Renaissance. In her excellent book on ekphrasis in antiquity, Ruth Webb begins by explaining the shift in the meaning of the term from antiquity to today.[45] One of the reasons for this shift is the gradual detachment of *ekphrasis* from its rhetorical background, and its subsequent appropriation by disciplines such as art history and archaeology; disciplines which connect it exclusively with descriptions of works of art, thus giving it

---

41 Single brothers, 15 April 1748 (UA R.20.HS35).
42 Faull 1995, p. 50. This is also called *ekphrasis* (Preston 2007) and/or *enargia* (Plett 2012), two rhetorical concepts that were taken up with enthusiasm during the Renaissance. While *ekphrasis* signifies descriptive speech that brings the thing vividly before the eyes, *enargia* is the rhetorical term for the ability to create a vivid presence through language (Plett 2012, pp. 12 and 26).
43 The success of this approach among the missionaries is particularly evident in the missions to the Native Americans, see Atwood 2006b, p. 32 n. 2.
44 Dohm 2000, p. 291.
45 Webb 2009, p. 1.

the commonly assumed meaning of the term today as a text which engages with visual arts.[46] Another reason for the shift in meaning of *ekphrasis* is the change in the understanding of language, and its relationship to reality and the immediate context of communication. Comparing the theory of description by French literary theorist Philippe Hamon with Quintilian's understanding of *enargia* as an 'unfolding' or 'opening up', she concludes:

> The two differ so radically in their approaches that it is clear that they are speaking from very different worlds. Where Hamon sees only words, Quintilian sees words as the communicable aspect of mental images which are crucial to the formation and reception of those words. Quintilian and Hamon are working with radically different conceptions of language, and of the relation of words to external reality on the one hand, and to their speakers and audiences on the other.[47]

The shift in the meaning of *ekphrasis*, then, is not only due to disciplinary decontextualisation, but also, and more significantly so, due to the fact that not only have the function of language and the world at large changed, but so too has the relationship between them. A concept like *ekphrasis*, which, as Webb makes clear, is contingent on an understanding of language as a force acting upon the world, must be redefined if it is to be deployed in a present context, where language is representation. And this alerts us to the obvious fact that language is not a meta-historical spirit, but a socially embedded signification practice which responds to socio-economic change.[48] As Valentin Vološinov emphasised, it is necessary to locate any analysis of the sign in its specific social intercourse and that the word is 'the most sensitive index of social changes'.[49] And, as Marx and Engels remind us, thoughts and language 'are only *manifestations* of actual life'.[50] Part of our considerations, then, should be to think of language as socio-historically embedded, and how changes may be discerned in the use of language, or what Fredric Jameson concisely called 'a theory of

---

46 Webb notes that the modern sense of ekphrasis as descriptions of art only became prominent in the late nineteenth century. Before this, on the rare occasion that the term ekphrasis appeared, it retained its classical sense. She then refers to a couple of occasions where the term appears. (Webb 2009, p. 6).
47 Webb 2009, p. 106.
48 Vološinov 1973. See also Marx and Engels' scattered comments on language in Marx and Engels 1972, pp. 36, 44, 426, 446–9.
49 Vološinov 1973, p. 19.
50 Marx and Engels 1972, p. 447.

language through the mode of production'.[51] We shall continue this in the section on the speech to the girls' choir and the exploration of presence. But first, to the boys.

4 Boys' Choir

The occasion of the selected speech to the boys is a special choir day, where new boys are admitted into the choir.[52] Unsurprisingly, then, Zinzendorf focuses explicitly on what it means to 'become a boy'.

In the world, i.e. outside the community, becoming a boy means being sent to learn a trade, and taught to be servile and useful, a disposition which is in extension of his growing up and helping his father either in the fields or at home. This is a contrast to the Moravian boys. The community of Herrnhut has its own etiquette and divisions, and these are what the child now comes to encounter, when he enters into the serious *Stand*. As already mentioned earlier, *Stand* is usually translated into English with estate or rank, and denotes one's place in the social order. In the choir speeches, Zinzendorf uses it almost exclusively, and very frequently, to refer to the choir's gendered structure and its transitions – as we see here. This particular transition, from child to boy, is a difficult one and should be overseen with forbearance and not resentment. For the child, the consolation is that Jesus also went through this, and so the boy can identify with him.

> Now what is then the difference between a child and a boy? I just want to tell you, dear children, perhaps you will not find any difference in the first, second, third year, and you will think: why was I put among the boys? I am and remain a child, I can still think and act, happy and blissfully like a child, nothing occurs to me that depresses me, I know nothing of new or difficult circumstances, why did not I remain among the children? Answer: It does not have to go so quickly with us, we must always maintain the last [stage], and meanwhile, as long as we can, be prepared for the new circumstances.

The difference will be explained below, but I just want to draw attention to the way Zinzendorf poses and then answers the question, or objection. The

---

51 Jameson 1981, p. 31.
52 Boys, 14 January 1760 (UA, R.20.HS.52).

objection arises rhetorically from the children who are placed in the boys' choir, yet cannot see any difference in themselves, and thus wonder why they were moved. To this, Zinzendorf responds that the change does not take place overnight, and that the transition takes a long time to prepare, because the former stage must be drawn into the new circumstances. We shall return to this, but the question of transitioning between the choirs means maintaining a delicate balance between constancy and change, between a nature acquired in the former *Stand* and choir, which must be brought into the new circumstances, and understanding what is to be left behind.

> Some of you may still remain children for three and six years. I congratulate him therewith and will rejoice in this. For whom it is so, always think thus: as long as God pleases his heart, it is well with him, and he stands in childish simplicity, honesty, and openheartedness. The moment, however, when he first feels that he is reflecting on something, that he wants to say something, he could be asking something, or that a hesitation comes to mind for the first time, then immediately think: yes indeed, you are a boy, you are no longer a child, and regard that as a scar from the fall, and keep the following day as a penitence day. It is not necessary to speak much about it, it can be done quietly. And when the supervisors notice and ask what is wrong with him, then he can only say: I have fallen from the *Stand* of innocence, I have wanted to speak and ask something, and haughty thoughts have occurred to me, what will one think of me, when I say so.

Here we are given the difference between the nature of a child, and that of a boy. The childish nature is one of simplicity, honesty and openheartedness, whereas the nature of the boy is one of reflection – when the directness of experience is mediated by something, then one has become a boy. This is to be marked with penitence, and quietly communicated to the supervisors of the choir. The whole transition is characterised as heritage (scar) from the fall, i.e. the fall of man in the garden of Eden, when Adam and Eve disobeyed God, and were cursed and expelled from the garden. The becoming a boy is described as having fallen from the state of innocence, where one begins to question things, and think independently. The following section elaborates:

> If you come up with something that looks and seems good, looks different than usual, something external, a piece of cloth, if you have written a line that pleases you extraordinarily, or you have made one more beautiful than the other; the first thought and *reflection* about yourself, the *compar-*

ison and equation that you make between yourselves and others, when two of you have made something beautiful, and one thinks, his is better, or is ashamed if his is worse, when he can't help it, then it is not a flush of sinner's shame, but vexatious and self-loving, and no longer childish. The glory of childishness consists in *simplicity, naivety,* and sanguinity, since one can always confidently look someone in the face,[53] and no lateral thoughts of himself and others come to one. All lateral thoughts, whatever their names or their actions, are not childlike. If you have already experienced that in childhood, you are already boys, and you have been *tolerated* only until your year draws near. A child must feel nothing but love, felicity, grace, and peace of God in his heart, and yet feel intensely what he cannot express with his senses and cannot connect in his mind, otherwise he is no longer a good child, but already a tainted one.

This way of reflecting is here named 'lateral thoughts' (*Quer-Gedanke*) and consists in reflection and comparison, reflection upon one's achievement, and comparison with the achievements of others. Note that vexation and self-love are not equated with sin. Sin is the self-realisation of the believer in his or her relation to the Saviour, while the mentioned faults are self-absorbed and unproductive. The nature of a child is connected with the heart, and a boy with the senses and the mind. The shift is one from simplicity to complexity, and the difference is thus one of disposition and not of bodily changes.

> Well, with you it is as follows: if you are constantly trying to be people who are not satisfied, but are plagued with reason and thoughts that go through the head hundreds of times, and you cannot change anything, and have no help against this from the Saviour, then you would be very miserable. But there is much help from His humanity; in His meritorious boyhood, there is advice for all, if only you are faithful, straightforward hearts, in no circumstance let the *simplicity* be taken from you, but overcome all false shame, and ask from the Saviour: Preserve me in straightforwardness and truth that I speak no word, but the truth.

Zinzendorf instructs them in how to make use of the Saviour in this new stage of life, and how to ask for his support. The main issue, and we will see this again and again, is to avoid obsessing about things in private (plagued with reason and thoughts that go through the head hundreds of times), and instead, one

---

53   'under the eyes', see Grimm DWB, Auge 5 Bd. 1, Sp. 792.

should ask the advice of the Saviour, who has been through this stage himself. They need to maintain simplicity and ask the Saviour to preserve one in truth, faith, and straightforwardness, and not give in to fancies of the mind. The way to go about this is, for example, when noting a change in disposition (*Gemüth*), the boy is to articulate this change to the Saviour, and once it has been put into words, the boy should then go to his choir workers. By self-monitoring in this way, the boy should be able to notice and communicate the change. Again, the concerns are articulated by Zinzendorf, and the result guaranteed: if you are faithful, everything will be fine, and you will receive proper guidance.

> as soon as you notice the slightest change in the disposition which was not usual in the previous class, of which you have no example, immediately go to your best friend, the Saviour, let words bring in his presence what appears new to you, and when you have done that, tell it to the faithful people, to whom you are accustomed; such and such it is with me, I have felt and noticed this and that, what do I do, or what should I not do?

Note the mention of class here, which as we saw in Chapter 2, is a subdivision within the choirs, according to spiritual maturity. Within the boys' choir, then, as with all choirs, the boys were divided into classes, and transitioned between them according to their inner developments.

> Admittedly, your matters will become more serious, more relevant and more important from year to year, and you get closer and closer to the community grace and church mysteries. To this end you have rich influx from Jesus' salvific blood and boy-merits, it gives what you need, and your soul and *Hütte* are sprinkled with new grace in blood. And if you are faithful, then finally one church mystery arrives after the others that you have not yet experienced, that will complete you and prepare you for the whole future humanity and clothe you with *Jesus-ish-ness* from within and without.

That everything is as it should be does not mean that everything will remain the same. The issues one faces will become more serious, as one grows older and draws closer to the centre of the community life and rituals. Jesus' life and death will support and guide the individual boy through this time and initiate him further into the grace and mysteries of the community. And if they are faithful, they will encounter the most important mystery of all, where they will ingest the blood of the Saviour in communion, and thus also internally bathed in his blood. This experience will complete them and prepare them for the whole future humanity and 'clothe you with *Jesushaftigkeit* (Jesus-ish-ness) inside and out'.

Everyone must have a bloodied heart, i.e. a heart which is sprinkled with the sacrificial blood of the Saviour,[54] and thus sanctified and in line with what is required by the community. If at this time, there is a boy who does not have that, then he has not made full use of his childhood time, which is now over without anything to show for it. Added to this grave issue is the problem that they would have been in the children's choir with such an unblessed nature, setting a bad example for the others, leading children astray who should have been following the Saviour. Such behaviour would mean that the choir would be happy to be rid of them into the next stage.

> If that serves to make such a child as small as a speck of dust, and upon entry into the young boys' choir, he is totally quashed, smashed, and as the holy scripture expresses it, made into a humble and defeated spirit, then it might still be his blessing. But we do not reckon with you that your childhood should have been neglected – that should be extraordinary examples, but that you all, or most, may enter your new *Stand* today with a bleeding heart, may pass through the years in beauty with a bloodstreak, and may you delight the heart of your superior and fellow-brothers and, most peculiarly, the heart of the boy without sin, the boy for you.

All is not lost, however; there is the hope that the celebration of his leaving the choir would make the boy feel small, and then, when in the boys' choir, his unruly nature will be broken, and from it arise a humble and defeated spirit. But this example is of course an extraordinary one, the boys present here today would not have neglected their childhood. And so, it is wished that the boys on the threshold of their new *Stand* will enter into the boys' choir with the desirable bloodied heart, and there be a delight to his superiors, to his brothers, and the heart of the Saviour (the boy without sin, the boy for you).

---

54 Zinzendorf often uses temple imagery to convey the significance of the Saviour and this particular letter was a great favourite of Zinzendorf's. Hebrews Chapters 9–10 make good use of temple imagery and the sacrifice of Jesus is depicted as superior to all the sacrifices of bulls and goats that took place there earlier. Thus, here we might see an allusion to the letter to the Hebrews (10, 19–21): 'Therefore, brothers, since we have confidence to enter the sanctuary by the blood of Jesus, by the new and living way that he opened for us through the curtain (that is, through his flesh), and since we have a great priest over the house of God, let us approach with a true heart in full assurance of faith, with our hearts sprinkled clean from an evil conscience and our bodies washed with pure water'.

4.1 Relating to the Saviour

This is a tremendously interesting speech because it is quite specific as to what the characteristics of the boys' choir are, and we see how this takes place in relation to the Saviour. We also see how the relation to the Saviour becomes a way of mediating the transition between the choirs. In one of the earliest choir speeches, Zinzendorf deliberates on how, when one steps into the *Stand* of boy (is named a boy), 'then it must be given to him what he needs to bring his boyhood to the boy Jesus, in whom he believes and whose name he carries'.[55] The point of this is to highlight the process of identification between Jesus and the boys. When a child is named a boy in the community, he is regarded as carrying Jesus' name, and thus must live up to a certain moral standing. In this present speech, one of his last, Zinzendorf points out that when one becomes a boy with the Moravians (enters into the boys' choir), then he is entering a serious rank (*serioser Stand*), which differs markedly from the carefree life of children, and that their only comfort is that Jesus had been through this time as well. It is thus highly important that the likeness is drawn between the individual boy and Jesus' boyhood, and how the latter can serve as an example of how best to be one in this complex stage of selfhood. As mentioned, the fact that Jesus took on human form and lived a human life in order to know all of its particulars, means that he can be used as male role model in the walk of life of a Moravian brother, starting here, with boyhood. Male transition, then, was managed by relating it to the physical developments of the Saviour. I also want to draw attention to a quotation from a community speech which Zinzendorf gave in Gnadenfrey (in present-day Poland) in 1747, which Craig Atwood has used to show the connection between the choirs and Christ:

> One just grows up with the Saviour: he is everything to whatever one is at that time: is one a child, so he is a child to him; is one a boy, so he is a boy to him; is one a youth, so he is a youth to him; is one a man, so he is a man to him. For the sisters, it is the same; for them he is a maidenly heart, with a particular tenderness and a special knowledge. And so one grows up with him into male age and he is always just so to each.[56]

---

55 Boys, 5 November 1747: "Sobald einer also in der Gemeine, ein Knabe heißt so muß ihm gleich das gegeben werden, was er braucht, seinen Knaben Stand dem Knaben Jesu, den er bekennt und deßen Nahme er trägt, zu Ehren zu fuhren" (UA GN.C.2 1747.1).

56 "Man wachst eben mit dem Heilande auf, Er ist einem alles, was man gerade ist: ist man ein Kind, so ist Er einem ein Kind; ist man ein Knabe, so ist Er einem ein Knabe; ist man ein Jüngling, so ist Er einem ein Jüngling; ist man ein Mann, so ist Er einem ein Mann. Den Schwestern ists eben so, mit einer besondern Zartlichkeit und specialen Erkenntniß,

I have modified Atwood's translation slightly to bring out the explicitly gendered nature of the person growing up, and his connection to the Saviour. Because it is clear that we are talking about a male figure to which one is to relate, and that this growing up and relating to the Saviour as one grows up is the provenance of the male members of the community.

We see here something which will become clearer when we move through speeches to the other choirs, namely that women relate to the Saviour as an object of their affection, while men are to strive for analogy with the Saviour.

Another point of interest is the change in disposition. The change becomes visible in the act of comparison – what he calls cross, or lateral, thoughts (*Quer-Gedanke*), which children are incapable of, due to simplicity and naivety. All of these thoughts must not develop into private obsessions, but must instead be confessed to the Saviour, in whose humanity the boys can take refuge and solace. His servile boyhood-time (*Knaben-Zeit*) is advice for all and the example to follow, which means to have a true heart, speak the truth, speak of bad feelings, and to let your best friend – the Saviour – know of the smallest change in disposition. The children's *Stand*, then, is the state of innocence, which is gone as soon as one commences self-reflection, and thinks of oneself as distinct. *Stand*, in this conceptualisation, is the sign of burgeoning individualism, a kind of Lacanian mirror stage, or self-othering,[57] and thus a position which implies self-awareness. When one reaches a time of self-awareness, one is moved into the choirs of the older girls or boys respectively. Once this self is manifested, it must be brought under control, and directed in a particular way, which differs for brothers and sisters. It is thus firmly tied to the understanding of gender, which is the main topic from this speech to which we will turn our attention.

4.2   History, Gendering and Sexual Systems

The choirs may be understood as a sexual system. This term comes from Isabel Hull's study on the reconfiguration of the sexual system in three South-Western German states in the long eighteenth century in order to document 'a general picture of the official sexual system in Central Europe'.[58] By sexual system, Hull means 'the patterned ways in which sexual behaviour is shaped and given

---

daß Er fur sie ein Jungfraulich Herz ist. Und so wachst man an Ihm heran ins mannliche Alter hinein, und Er ists einem immer gar." Zinzendorf 1970, p. 225. Quoted in Atwood 1997, pp. 28–29.

57   Gayle Rubin gives a good account of this in Rubin 1975, pp. 92–4 and I return to her article in Chapter 6.

58   Hull 1996, p. 2.

meaning through institutions'.⁵⁹ Her reason for using this term is due to historical accuracy. Sexuality, in its common usage, refers to 'individual sexual potential or sexual subjects generally'. But this is a conceptualisation precisely in the making in the material at the heart of Hull's study, as she notes with reference to Foucault's analysis of the emergence of sexuality as the bourgeoisie's attempt at self-definition over against the nobility and the lower classes.⁶⁰ Hull also does not want to demand that the reader recalls Foucault's definition every time one reads 'sexuality'.⁶¹ Already in 1979, Robert A. Padgug noted that 'the most commonly held twentieth-century assumptions about sexuality imply that it is a separate category of existence (like "the economy", or "the state", other supposedly independent spheres of reality)'.⁶² However, if academic discourses take their cue from Foucault, *without* including the socio-economic provenance of the discourses of sexuality, then, as Padgug correctly notes, such a surprising lack of a properly historical approach to the subject of sexuality has allowed a fundamentally bourgeois view of sexuality and its subdivisions to prevail.⁶³ If so, then it is our task to ensure that this false universal is unmasked, which is what Hull is doing in her careful use of terminology, and what we must endorse.

While there are other studies that are attentive to differing historical attitudes to sex, gender is another category of analysis which is surprisingly ahistorical.⁶⁴ Hull notes, following Joan Scott, that gender usually refers to the 'culturally determined differences between men and women'.⁶⁵ But such a definition is a *fait accompli*; it does not explain how various cultures came to produce 'gender' or embrace understandings of male and female that then can become a 'category of analysis'. Indeed, in her ground-breaking article, Scott calls for historians to 'examine the ways in which gendered identities are substantively constructed and relate their findings to a range of activities, social organiza-

---

59   Hull 1996, p. 1.
60   Foucault 1998. It should be noted that Foucault returned to this question in later works, exploring the theme in antiquity, thus implying that the question of the modern self and sexuality could not be resolved by recourse to class analysis. Thanks to Matt Chrulew for discussions and clarification of this problematic.
61   Hull 1996, p. 6.
62   Padgug 1979, p. 8.
63   Padgug 1979, p. 5.
64   For studies on Moravian gender and sexuality, see Atwood 1997; 2011; Faull 2013; 2011a; 2011b; Fogleman 2003; 2007; Peucker 2006; 2007; 2011a; 2011b; 2015; Schmid 2002; 2004; Vogt 2006b; 2009; 2015. For studies into subjectivity, see in particular Schmid 2009.
65   Hull 1996, p. 7. Hull also draws attention to the fact that the difference between sex (commonly understood as biologically charged) and gender (culturally determined) cannot be distinguished in German, which uses *Geschlecht* for both.

tions, and historically specific cultural representations'.⁶⁶ I am curious as to why the 'activities' and 'social organisations' are not specified as historically specific in the way that 'historically specific cultural representations' are, but I will return to this after taking a brief look at Scott's definition of gender. Scott's call is for a theorisation of gender that navigates between feminism, which she finds ahistorical, Marxist feminism, which she finds reductive and, it seems, too historical, and psychoanalysis, which she finds most ahistorical. What emerges is a two-pronged definition, where the first part sees gender as a constitutive element of social relationships based on perceived differences between the sexes. This first part of the definition contains four interrelated elements: culturally available symbols; normative concepts; social institutions (kinship, economy, and polity); and subjective identity. The above quotation on gendered activities which are substantively constructed etc. appears as a conclusion to this part of her definition. Then follows the actual theorisation of gender, where she notes that 'Gender is a primary field within which or by means of which power is articulated'.⁶⁷ Scott is not explicit about whether this is so for modern Western history or for all of history. She mentions several examples of analyses of the legitimising function of gender with reference to the work of Pierre Bourdieu, Gayatri Spivak, Natalie Davis, and Caroline Walker Bynum, within which she uses masculine and feminine to describe what it is that these examples do. To this, she concludes that

> sexual difference is a primary way of signifying differentiation. Gender, then, provides a way to decode meaning and to understand the complex connections among various forms of human interaction. When historians look for the ways in which the concept of gender legitimizes and constructs social relationships, they develop insights into the reciprocal nature of gender and society and into the particular and contextually specific ways in which politics constructs gender and gender constructs politics.⁶⁸

As you can see, we are not given a specific historical context for these sweeping assertions, and therefore such a statement appears to me to be reductionist. If Scott is referring to the eighteenth century and the emergence of gender and the body as the key identity markers of a modern human, then I cautiously

---

66   Scott 1986, p. 1068.
67   Scott 1986, p. 1069.
68   Scott 1986, p. 1070.

agree with the first part of her gender definition and its four constitutive elements. If the overall definition is historically contextualised, then it follows that the constitutive elements are part of that context. But I am not entirely sure that this is the case. Especially since the second part of her definition reduces social organisation, political power, and change to gender. If, however, this theorisation and deployment of gender is limited to capitalist social relations and the organisation of the bourgeois state, then it is historicised and of course placed in relation to socio-economic organisation. However, judging by Scott's absolute emphasis on gender as primary and as an independent analytic category, this treating-gender-as-by-product-of-changing-economic-structures is precisely what she is trying to avoid.[69]

I have spent some time with this article because it has been defining for historical gender studies,[70] and important for showing how gender is understood, or rather not understood, as a historicised category. For example, in Michael Thomas Taylor's otherwise historiographically sensitive study on Moravian sexual heterodoxy, the term 'existing gender hierarchies' appears a couple of times without any qualifier, as that against which the Moravian understanding of marital sex should be understood.[71]

Another example of generic gender is the article on Christology and gender in Zinzendorf's writings by Peter Vogt.[72] Vogt looks at the fundamental role of gender in the community and indicates three levels on which gender is prevalent: Organisation; Subjectification; Theology. The choir system and its gender segregation constitutes the particular organisation of the community; gender has a role in constituting individual subjects and subject-experiences, which he sees expressed in the Moravian memoirs; and finally gender is at the forefront of theological reflection in the community, exemplified for example in the emphasised masculinity of Jesus, which plays a central role in the soteriology of the community.

Vogt's article is mainly concerned with the latter, namely the emphasised masculinity of Jesus which he rightly sees as a dominating feature of Zinzendorf's Saviour, and as fundamental in organising the community. Vogt also notes that an important locus for mediating this understanding of Christologically conditioned gender was the choir quarter-hours. However, Vogt only refers to the printed choir speeches, namely those in Johann Gottlob Seidel's 1755 publication, *Haupt-Schlüssel zum Herrnhutischen Ehe-Sacrament* (Master-

---

69 Scott 1986, p. 1061.
70 Canning 2006, pp. 8–9.
71 Taylor 2015, pp. 113 and 14.
72 Vogt 2015.

key to the Moravian Marriage Sacrament),[73] which was a publication of 79 speeches given by Count Zinzendorf to the married couples' choir within the congregations of Herrnhaag, Marienborn and Herrnhut in the late 1740s. As Vogt notes, 'here there is very extensive evidence as to what it meant, according to Zinzendorf's opinion, for a member of the Moravian Brethren to be a man and a woman respectively'.[74] In his conclusion, Vogt urges that a more in-depth analysis which takes account of the differences from and likenesses with the sex/gender structure of civil society (*bürgerlichen Lebenswelt*) is needed. Earlier in the article, Vogt notes that Zinzendorf is conscious of absolutely contradicting 'conventional sex/gender-roles'.[75] The quote which is used to demonstrate 'conventional sex/gender roles' is from the public community speeches from 1747, which were published in 1748, and states:

> In the world it is completely the other way round, because one has obligated women to such services, to such regards, occupations and vexations with their husbands, that in many places they can think of almost nothing but how they may please the husband and serve him, and one calls this a good wife.[76]

The text goes on with the different structure in the Moravian marriage, where the man is at the service of his wife due to the holy spirit. The point is, however, where such an understanding of gender comes from – the one from the quote above? For those of us with feminist sensibilities, it sounds very recognisable and indeed conventional, but our historical knowledge should make us pause, given that this is, as I will argue later, a feature of bourgeois society which was still in the making, and thus not a convention in 1747.[77] Far more likely is that Zinzendorf is drawing on his aristocratic experience of roles within a marriage.[78]

---

73   Seidel 2000.
74   Vogt 2015, p. 83. My translation.
75   I use sex/gender as a way of translating the German *Geschlecht* because Vogt's use distinguishes between gender as a theoretical concept and *Geschlecht* as that which the concept clarifies.
76   "In der welt ist es sehr umgekehrt; denn man hat die frauen da obligirt zu solchen diensten, zu solchen regards, beschäfftigungen und plagen mit ihren männern, daß sie an manchen orten fast an nichts denken können, als wie sie dem manne gefallen und ihn bedienen mögen, und das heißt man eine gute frau [...]". Beyreuther and Meyer 1963, p. 129. See also Seibert 2003, p. 104.
77   As Lukács notes, the first bourgeois revolution was the French Revolution but the effects of that did not reach the German states until Napoleon. Lukács 1975, pp. xxiii–xxiv.
78   See Gray 2000, pp. 26–9.

There is no doubt that Vogt is correct in noting that the choirs are the prime locations for the inculcation of new gender norms; however, the more pertinent question, as to why this is necessary, is not even posed. This is not surprising given that Vogt relies on 'gender-perspectives' which, as I will demonstrate through the following chapters, is a compartmentalised and dehistoricised category of analysis which necessarily leaves the results of its operations as merely descriptive.[79]

Instead, I would argue that the understanding of gender was not a given. What we see in these speeches is a move from seeing men and women as people with various roles to play in society, to a much more self-reflective and pervasive understanding of oneself *as a man or a woman*. What we see here is the process of *gendering*, of bringing into being a gendered consciousness, which is connected to a gendered *body*. Connecting this with Joan Kelly-Gadol's point that sex is always relational,[80] which Scott also strongly advocates,[81] I will follow Knopp and Lauria and insist that sex/gender relations are *always* social relations.

This is not only the case with the members, but with the Saviour as well. Because, while the preceding Christian tradition does not use the masculine gender to further any particular point,[82] Zinzendorf placed an enormous emphasis on the Saviour's maleness and put it to specific use, as Vogt also observes.[83] As mentioned above, the more human the Saviour is made, the more the human body is needed to articulate this humanity. For this reason, the male nature of the Saviour is intertwined with the male nature of the brothers and placed in elaborate relation with the sisters. The gender of the Saviour is not a given either.

In his book on embodiment and Christianity, Ola Sigurdson suggests that human subjectivity plays a crucial role in the difference between historical and modern Christologies.[84] What this means is best understood through his

---

79   As Hegel notes in a different context, by separating the categories of reason from the living and moving totality of the world, non-dialectical thought merely reflects the fragmentation of philosophy. Lukács 1975, p. 262.
80   Kelly-Gadol 1987.
81   Knopp and Lauria 1987. Scott quotes Natalie Zemon Davies (as does Kelly-Gadol) for saying that it makes as little sense analysing one gender as it does analysing one class by itself (Scott 1986, p. 1054).
82   Once we reach modernity and questions of gender arise, Jesus' maleness is used to legitimate a number of things, but this was relatively unquestioned beforehand. See Steinberg 1983.
83   Vogt 2015, p. 79.
84   Sigurdson 2016, p. 94.

discussion of Friedrich Schleiermacher. Without going into too much theological detail, Schleiermacher reformulated the historical discussions of Jesus' two natures (divine and human) and strongly emphasised the human dimension of Jesus coupled with a 'God consciousness'.[85] We should note here that this Christology divides Jesus up into a person with a human nature and a divine consciousness, which of course coincides with contemporary developments in understanding individual humans as consisting of body and consciousness. Salvation occurs when believers participate in Christ's 'God consciousness' which is experienced in the fellowship of believers.[86] Sigurdson's problem with Schleiermacher is a dogmatic one, but we may use it for historical gain, in that his issue with Schleiermacher is that he 'sets up contemporary human subjectivity as a superordinate norm and starting point for his Christological thought', and thus risks 'becoming a legitimizing ideology both for the God consciousness of the time and for the science and church of the time'.[87] The question is, though, whether 'contemporary human subjectivity' and 'God consciousness of the time' were really such developed thoughts, or whether Schleiermacher was part of defining these understandings of humanity. Another interesting point is that the more Jesus' humanity is emphasised, the more his maleness comes to the fore, which becomes evident in feminist theology's reaction against a theology which uses patriarchal Christology to produce subservient women.[88] Both of these points will be discussed further, in that for Zinzendorf, Jesus' humanity is crucial to developing the network of believers and their social relations, and in this endeavour, Jesus' maleness is of equal importance. Finally, I did not pounce on Schleiermacher randomly to pester the reader with theological niceties. Schleiermacher was, in fact, educated within the Moravian Brethren, in Niesky.[89] Thus, similarities in thoughts about the humanity of Jesus, divine consciousness, and the shaping of members towards such an understanding of self are not entirely coincidental. I will return to the topic of gender as a category of analysis in Chapter 6.

---

85   Regin Prenter, a Danish theologian, accused Schleiermacher of an Ebionitic Christology, that is, a Christology that emphasises the humanity of Christ at the expense of the divine nature. Prenter 1998, p. 431.
86   Sigurdson 2016, p. 97.
87   Sigurdson 2016, p. 102.
88   See brief discussion in Sigurdson 2016, pp. 128–40.
89   Seibert 2003, pp. 46–63.

5 Girls' Choir

The speech to the girls' choir is from 1758 and the main topic is presence, which is related to the watchword of the day.[90]

Zinzendorf begins by speaking about the omnipresence of the Saviour (*Dasein*) and his closeness or special visits (*Nahsein*) as two different things, and that his special visits are so significant that Zinzendorf wishes for more. His omnipresence means that he is present everywhere, even at the ends of the world, and even if it is a thousand miles from the localities he loves (such as Herrnhut).

> However, what *I* actually mean here by His presence and visits is what in Revelation is called a stroll between his lampstands. Such house-calls He pays in bodily person, as the human Jesus Christ with the *Hütte* which He has not yet shed, in the figure of a holy devotee, the tortured man, He stands there, walks through his congregation, choir houses, and children's institutions, surveys his people, and notes whether they stand in the expectation of his personhood, whether they are allowed to be *with Him under four eyes*, and to know how to treasure this, even when they don't immediately see Him with physical eyes.

The Book of Revelation in the New Testament is a lengthy vision of the end of the world experienced by John of Patmos. His vision begins with a vision of Christ, who first speaks to John behind him. When John turns around, he sees seven golden lampstands and standing in the midst of them was 'one like the Son of Man', presumably another name for Jesus in the New Testament, borrowed from the Jewish tradition.[91] What Zinzendorf means here, then, is the physical and manifest presence of the Saviour on earth, 'among the lampstands'. These house-calls, through which he inspects his congregation and their buildings (choir houses and institutions) are to assess whether or not 'his people' stand in the correct relation, and may engage with him one on one, a relation they will treasure even when he is not immediately apparent. These visits take place in the flesh, so to speak, in the crucified and martyred body which is not yet shed.

In a flowing paragraph, the logic of simultaneous absence and presence is extended to sisters and brothers who are no longer among the living, but still

---

90 Girls, 27 February 1758 (UA, GN.C.78.1758. 2).
91 For a good overview of the Son of Man tradition, see Müller 2008.

retain a palpable presence within the community, and so constitute part of the girls' community. This means that the collective is made up not only of the members on earth, but also of those who are no longer living – we return to this in the speech to the single brothers. The intimate relationship with these brothers and sisters can be used to understand the nature of relationship with the Saviour, who embraces them as a collective choir and as individuals girls.

The visits from the Saviour may be expected any time, because they are planned at his discretion and because he has both omnipresence and a chariot of cherubs. This means that he is not confined to one place, or even one continent, given that he can be in Herrnhut and Bethlehem, which is the settlement in North America, on one day.

> Thus, each heart can stand in daily expectation of such a dear visit, a new protection through His embrace, a new enthusiasm and incorporation in Him, even beyond the same great, solemn, and communal [ones], that are not unknown to some of you.

Here Zinzendorf distinguishes between the individual daily connection with the Saviour through his visit, embrace, and becoming one with his body (*Einleibung*), and the communal connections with which some of the girls would be familiar. This may be liturgies, and most certainly communion, which, as mentioned earlier, had a new emphasis as a sacrament of somatic unification with the Saviour. Once this has taken place, the soul will experience a yearning for the presence of the Saviour. What we should note is the speech assumes the physical presence of the Saviour, and not just a feeling or spiritual presence. This presence, however, should never stop them thinking of his corpse and it is the last breath that should be at the centre of their longing.

5.1 *Relating to the Saviour*

The main topic in this speech is how to relate to a transcendent Saviour, who is nevertheless present in the community. A contradiction is presented, which consists of the Saviour's omnipresence on the one hand, and the special visits in the flesh on the other. I will return to this contradiction below, and here focus on how the presence or 'special visits' are manifested as a particular kind of relation. The girls are told that the Saviour assesses whether they expect his presence or the manifestation of his person, the extent to which they can be with him one on one, and whether they are able to treasure this. In this speech, it is not especially clear what is meant by this, but from other, more admonishing speeches, it is possible to get closer to uncovering its meaning. In a speech from 1751, Zinzendorf is lecturing the girls on the correct relation to the Saviour, which is connected to their relation to their own flesh, or *Hütte*.

> For many years I have been thinking about your choir and the bad condition in which many in the older girls' *Stand* have found themselves; is that dreadful thing something which is brought over you in alteration? Since if one could see that the tenderness, which is found in your childhood years, still is there in twelfth and fourteenth [year], even continues in fifteenth and sixteenth, and even increases rather than diminishes, then one could be emotional and content with you. The opposite example, however has meant that one has grown sad about your *Stand*, and thought: your souls are not chaste, you are not direct enough to your superiors, to tell them the smallest change which takes place in your *Hütte* sometimes in your disposition at the right time, when you could be assisted immediately, but when you save up, for days and weeks, when a change has taken place, and your disposition has been thrown into perplexity or licentiousness, and you can listen for three to four hours and in the *Singstunde* open your mouths to the Saviour and sing along to the most loved truths and blessings, and speak with the mouth, when the disposition really isn't part of it: then you are hypocrites, and when you then out of fear after much interrogation finally say how it was a month or quarter of a year ago, then it is not the same as when you had come and told, how it was with you this minute or this hour.[92]

---

92 Older girls, 25 March 1751: "Ich denke nun schon viele Jahre über eure Chor, und der schlechte Zustand, worinnen sich manche im großen Mädgen Stande befunden haben; ist das schlime Ding das einem in alteration über euch bringt, wenn man sähe daß die zärtlichkeit, die sich in euren Kinder Jahren findet, auch wohl in 12ten und 14ten noch da ist, noch in 15ten, 16ten so fort ginge, und sich ehe vermehrte als verringerte; so könte man seelig und vergnügt über euch seyn. Die Exempel des gegentheils aber haben gemacht daß man sich über euren stand betrübt und denkt, eure Seelen seyn nicht keutsch, ihr seyd nicht grade genug gegen eure vorgesezten, Ihnen die geringste veränderung, die in eurer hütte bey der gelegenheit in eurem gemüth vorkomt zu sagen, und das zu rechter Zeit, den[n] da wäre euch gleich gehollffen, wenn ihr aber zusammen Spart, von Tagen und wochen, da euch eine Veränderung vorgekommen da euer Gemüth in perplexitaet oder leichtsinn gekommen, und könnet 3 4 stunden anhören und in den singstunden euren Mund zum Heylande auf thun, die Allerliebsten Wahrheiten und seeligkeiten mitsingen, und mit dem Munde aussprechen, da doch das gemüth nicht recht mehr damit ist = So seyd ihr heuchler und wenn ihr den auch aus angst nach vielen ausfragen, endlich sagt; wies euch vor einen monath oder vi[e]rteljahr gewesen ist, so ists nicht das, als wenn ihr kämet und sagtet, wies euch entweder diese Minute oder diese Stunde war" (UA R.20.HS32).

This very long quote about the *Stand* of the older girls' choir is significant for a number of reasons. *Stand* is used as a way of collectively admonishing the girls for individual transgressions. The condition of the girls' *Stand* itself, in 1751, is dreadful; it has given rise to concern, because the girls do not notify their supervisors of bodily changes and the associated distress. Zinzendorf has been trying to understand the change in disposition of the girls, and wonders whether this is connected with the 'alteration', which sounds like the onset of puberty. The tenderness which was characteristic of them as children does not necessarily have to disappear, but in this case it has, leading to withholding information and private obsessions. If they feel this on the inside, while partaking in worship of the Saviour, they are hypocrites, according to Zinzendorf, and he says that the situation is not abated when the information is dragged from them months after the events. In the choir speech to the older girls from 5 November 1747, Zinzendorf notes that if they had been single sisters, or children, then it would be a *Stand* which could be easily organised, but that in this present one, they are being prepared for the maiden *Stand*, and therefore need particular care.[93] The children have not yet deviated from their object, and the single sisters are already in order, but the older girls are in intermediate circumstances, where it could go either way – and judging by the admonishments in 1751, it did not go well.[94]

So, from this improper way of relating to the Saviour, we can now return to our 1758 speech, where they are told how this is supposed to feel: 'My soul is in awe, an unspeakable power of His personality, my heart feels something intimate of Him, my sympathy and harmony with Him, my temperament, which has gone over into His element, feels a weak riveting and that is His'. Note that these things are to be felt even if one does not see the Saviour, but merely feels his presence acutely. In contrast to what we saw in the speech to the boys, we see here that the girls are to position themselves differently in relation to the Saviour. Zinzendorf is invoking a sensual intimacy, which is different from the intimacy which arises from likeness, as was the case with the boys. The girls are to sense the presence of the Saviour and a somatic union which is expressed in terms of soul, heart, and temper as touched by his presence. What lies behind this is Zinzendorf's idea of the cosmic marriage, where the Saviour is copulated

---

93   See also older girls, 25 March 1744, where it is noted that if girls do not surrender themselves to the joyful playfulness and birdlike *Stand* of the choir, then it is better to leave them as children, so that they do not begin to act as girls when they do not have the heart thereto (UA R.20.HS1).

94   Recall the 1745 diary discussed in Chapter 2, which mentioned the dreadful state of the older girls' choir, and the leadership consulting the lot for advice on how to proceed.

with his church, and these roles are instilled in the everyday lives of members. This is presented in an early speech to the married couples where Zinzendorf has the following to say in terms of ensuring the ideological reproduction of this understanding of marriage:

> That is why in a community, the small maidens, from childhood [lit. children's legs] should be raised to a community, to a person who resembles the community, and our small boys shall from childhood be acquainted with their priestly character, and hold on to it, and let them see something venerable in that part, just as the girls are given to see something inclined, something affable, something acquiescent, and if such a preparation has taken place with the children, then the community-marriage suffers no need, it makes it by itself.[95]

If girls are raised to see themselves as similar to the community, or collective, and its emphasis on affability and acquiescence, and the boys as individual priests, with the character traits of venerability and gravitas, then there is no need for constant handholding and management later in life, since the preparatory work will ensure the self-perpetuation of the idea.

The present speech to the girls cultivates an intimacy with the Saviour. And one of the tasks in the management of the children is precisely to encourage and nurture this intimacy. The children are to think of him constantly and relate every aspect of their lives to him. In the case of the female members, this will move towards a spousal connection – individual as well as collective – which is not yet articulated in the present stage of life. What we have in this speech is a cultivation of the intimacy as a physical presence, which is a crucial feature of the community and its general self-understanding.

5.2 *Presence*

As mentioned in the last chapter, the presence of Jesus was used by Zinzendorf to bypass the authority structure of the Moravian church, which had been followed up until September 1741. We saw how the office of general elder in the

---

95 Married choir, 26 October 1747: "Darum sollen in einer gemeine die Mägdlein von kindes Beinen auf zu einer gemeine zu Personen die der gemeine ähnlich sehen auferzogen werden, und unsrer Knäblein sollen von Kind auf ihren priesterlichen c[h]aracter kennen lernen und darüber halten, und etwas ehrwürdiges in dem theil, so wie die Mädgen was gebogenes was leutseliges was ergebenes an sich blicken laßen, und wenn eine solche praepartion mit den Kindern vorgegangen so hats darnach freilich mit den GemeinEhen keine Noth, die machen sich von selbst" (UA R.4.CII.12).

larger Moravian community was taken over by the Saviour in 1741 as a replacement for Leonhard Dober, who had resigned. The replacement was decided by lot and indicated to the community that it was the Saviour's own wish to take over the office as general elder. This also had repercussions at the ideological level in that the diaries, as we saw, display an increase in the comments on the presence of the Saviour from 1742, as well as the decisions made by lot. Of interest to us in the present context, we recall how Dietrich Meyer pointed out that the transfer of the office of general elder onto the Saviour meant that 'that the invisible real presence of Christ was taken seriously'.[96] Indeed, the Saviour's presence is a distinct and pervasive topic in the choir speeches,[97] and firmly connected to the blood and wounds theology, as we see in this speech to the girls, where the martyred corpse of the Saviour pays visits to the various institutions and buildings in the community.

One of the central points in the speech to the girls is the idea of the presence of the Saviour as simultaneously omnipresent and local. Interestingly, this is an important extension of Luther's understanding of the Eucharist and the idea that Christ is both everywhere (ubiquity) and specifically in the elements of the Eucharist in all locations. Indeed, Craig Atwood sees everyday experiences of the body and blood of the Saviour as an enhancement of the significance of the Eucharist.[98] As point of departure I will consider Atwood's understanding as centripetal, as an attempt to reduce everything to theological master signifiers, such as the Eucharist, whereas I want to try and think of the theological innovations as part of a larger semantic shift. While I agree that the Eucharist or communion indubitably plays a role in understanding the presence of Saviour in the community, I want to dig a little deeper into the understanding of presence itself, in that this was a key issue in the Reformation. The question is, then: can the struggles over the understanding and definition of the Eucharist be understood more broadly as a shift in semantics, ontology, metaphysics, in brief, as a revolution in ideology?

---

96 Meyer 2000, p. 46.
97 In the speech to the single sisters, 1 February 1758, Zinzendorf says, 'one comes and asks: is the Saviour in the community? Does the Saviour keep himself especially to the place? Then the real answer is "yes indeed, because there is a blessed sisters' choir there".' "Man kommt und fragt: ist der Heiland in der Gemeine? Hält sich der Heiland besonders zu dem Ort? So ist das eine reale Antwort: Ja freylicht, denn es ist ein seelig Schwestern Chor da". (UA R.20.HS60). See also single brothers, 1 February 1758 (UA R.20.HS57); single sisters, 31 March 1751 (UA R.20.HS28); single sisters, 1 July 1755 (UA R.20.HS47); married choir, 17 February 1758 (UA R.20.HS54); single brothers, 29 August 1757, (UA R.20.HS57); and widowers, 17 July 1755 (UA R.20.HS31).
98 Atwood 2004, p. 165.

The French philosopher Louis Marin has suggested that the Eucharist can be seen as 'a particular instance of the problem concerning signs and words in their relation to things and ideas'.[99] This observation gains significant momentum when we consider the shifts in the production of meaning that took place in the fifteenth and sixteenth centuries and which are embodied in struggles over and engagement with the Eucharist by, for example, Luther,[100] Leibniz,[101] and the Port-Royal Logic.[102] If the Eucharist is a prism for the production of meaning and exploring the relation between sign and presence, then the displacement of the presence of Jesus to the everyday as we see in the choir speeches is momentous. I will suggest that this presence serves to refract ideas of sacredness and spiritualism from Jesus to the individual, producing a new understanding of a human being and its relation to the world. I will do this in a number of steps, beginning with an analysis of language and presence in Luther's later Eucharistic theology and language, moving on to language and signification, and ending up in presence.

In an article on the figures of speech in the language of Martin Luther's theology, Danish theologian Nete Enggaard notes the narrow connections between Luther's understanding of the Eucharist and his attempts at forging a new language:

> With the strange fleshy vocabulary of the texts, an original treatment of the contemporary language and conceptual world develops, which makes it possible to see Luther's linguistic innovations as tied to a larger cluster of theological motifs, namely as experimenting with a new language: *nova lingua*.[103]

Enggaard argues that Luther used the innovative metaphors to articulate the *real presence* of Christ in the elements of the Eucharist. Whereas the tradition after Luther saw a danger of reifying, containing, and objectifying God's presence in Luther's insistence on Christ's corporeal presence in the Eucharist, and hence regarded Luther's later Eucharist writings as vestiges of a medieval sacramental realism, Enggaard argues that this is a conscious attempt by Luther to express Christ's *presence* in the elements over against both the transubstan-

---

99   Marin 1989, p. xvi.
100 Hörisch 2000.
101 Dascal 1987.
102 Marin 1989.
103 Enggaard 2011, p. 334. My translation.

tiation doctrine of the Catholic Church, as well as Zwingli's spiritualist understanding of the symbolic presence of Christ in the Eucharist. Enggaard argues that:

> Because the sacrament and presence for Luther is insistently founded on the incarnation, he cannot accept an understanding of sign or language which works on the basis on the ontological primacy of the interior, spiritual (the signified) over the exterior, material (the signifier). That is why the corporeal becomes so important in the later Eucharist writings.[104]

Enggaard examines the implications of this new language for the question of Christ's presence, but we may extend her line of questioning and consider to what extent such a shift in the understanding of the presence of Christ means for the understanding of presence in general.

In his cultural study on the Eucharist,[105] Jochen Hörisch argues that Luther 'defined anew the sacramental relation of the *signa* and *res*, the word and the thing, the symbolic and the real' by sharpening the focus on the words of Jesus so as to substantiate the coincidence of being and meaning in the Eucharist – essentially what Enggaard argued.[106] Hörisch distinguishes between semontology, which signifies 'the certainty of the real that determines the value of the sign' and ontosemiology, namely 'words that give the real signs their value'. The important point in this is that both Enggaard and Hörisch argue that with Luther's ontosemiology, a new understanding of language takes place, which is seen to unite what had been divided earlier. This all takes place to refute the Catholic doctrine of transubstantiation, and the more symbolic understanding of bread and wine of the Reformers (Zwingli in particular) as mentioned above.

These discussions over signification and language must be connected to the discussion of immanence and revolution flagged earlier. The shift of language so as to be a more immanent means of relation, and the idea of presence that such a change effectuated, are important in assessing the innovative aspect of Zinzendorf's Saviour and the presence of him in the Herrnhut community.

---

104   Enggaard 2011, p. 336. My translation.
105   Hörisch 2005, p. 119. I would like to thank Sven Rune Havsteen for recommending this work to me.
106   In another work, Hörisch writes: 'The technical term "ontosemiology" may refer to the problem that countless religions, philosophies, theories and worldviews expressly or implicitly claim to solve, and which every social formation (if in very different ways) actually assumes to have mastered: how to prove or establish a correlation between being (*Sein*) and meaning (*Sinn*) in such a way that the question of whether this established view has in fact intersubjective validity does not come up at all'. Hörisch 2000, p. 22.

What we are seeing, and trying to capture into words, is what Derrida characterises as the moment when 'the determination of absolute presence is constituted as self-presence, as subjectivity'.[107] In Herrnhut, as we have seen in the first three choir speeches, this takes place through the mediation of the Saviour and his flesh, as the means by which the members become gendered flesh, singular presences, and subjects.

6 Single Brothers' Choir

6.1 *Relating to the Saviour*

The speeches to the single brothers emphasise above all the affinity between the Saviour and the single brothers. This is an extension of what we saw in the speech to the boys, and the primary way in which the men, especially the single brothers, of Herrnhut were to relate to the Saviour. In several speeches, as we will see below, this understanding oneself in the image of the Saviour is cultivated through the emphasis on government of the body and its limbs. In the speech I focus on here, the issue is how such a government is to be achieved; how can a brother become like the corpse of the Saviour, in order to please him?[108]

The speech used as point of departure begins with the daily watchword and the collect:

> Do you not know that your members are Christ's members and every member achieves resemblance to the corpse.

The first clause is a rewriting of 1 Corinthians 6:15a: 'Do you not know that your bodies are members of Christ?' The difference is in the replacement of 'your bodies' in Corinthians with 'your members' in Zinzendorf's quote. This is quite a significant modification in that it shifts the meaning from one of participation (your bodies are members of Christ) to one of resemblance or identification (your members are Christ's members). This is strengthened in the modification of the collect taken from hymn 37 in the *Londoner Gesangbuch* II, which reads: 'every *look* achieves resemblance to the corpse'.[109] With the change to 'member' we thus have a strengthening of the modified bible text, and an over-

---

107 Derrida 1976, p. 16.
108 This was one of Zinzendorf's last speeches, given less than two months before his death. Single brothers, 19 March 1760 (UA R.20.HS52).
109 *Londoner Gesangbuch* II, hymn 37: "ein jeder blik erreiche die ähnlichkeit der leiche".

all emphasis on the resemblance between the body of a single brother and the body of the Saviour.

The body of a single brother is the overriding focus of this speech, of which I present a paraphrase here.

A thorough understanding of the body is required, because the body is created as part of the plan of creation. The more one understands movements in the body, the more one understands the difference between what is natural, what is sin, and what is Jesus-like. Natural body movements are not to be feared or give cause for unnecessary distress. That there is a propensity for worry is due to the Fall, the disobedience of Adam and Eve, and the expulsion from the Garden of Eden as well as our simplistic approach to things as human beings. Whether or not bodily movement is natural or sinful is a decision, which must be based on understanding.

In the single brothers' choir (the choir of the Saviour), the same strictures apply as in the other choirs. It is thus not enough to lead an impeccably moral and lawful life, one must also cherish and hold sacred not only all the blessings which the Saviour's person has achieved for one, but also his arrangements, i.e. the structure of the community. In addition to this, one must also regard one's limbs and bones as belonging to the Saviour. This does not just mean hygiene and medicinal care, but a thorough knowledge of the *Hütte* and its movements, in order to understand the quality of the soul's regime of the body.

The workers were appointed to each choir to care for the members and ensure adherence to the community line. In the case of a good brother, not much work is required. However, a brother who leads an unwise regime over his body must be shown the way, patiently, and 20 times if necessary. Such a brother is an extreme example, though. Choir brothers, who per definition are selected by the Saviour (by lot), must study the principles and practice of the choir idea and how to live by these principles and with these practices. He must monitor his temperament, his health, etc., not for his own sake, but for the sake of the community, which ultimately is for the sake of the Saviour, whom one does not want to distress, but rather always please.

A single brother's properties, then, do not just entail meaning well, abhorring sin, the shame of his flesh, and being embarrassed by practices or bad habits; they also involve leading his way surely, happily, and in the nature of Jesus. A ruler of his body and a servant of the Saviour. This idea of being both a ruler and a servant is a necessary component of being a complete single brother, and may result in three different paths: worker, i.e. choir worker, a person with a trusted office within the community; messenger, i.e. missionary; and 'marriage-angel', i.e. a husband, where he would become servant of the soul and *Hütte* of his wife, who has a different constitution from him. When one of these offices has enabled the brother to achieve a state of blessedness, and his body and *Gemüth* also release him, and the Saviour also wishes to confer upon him this state of calm, then he will rise above, so to speak, issues that would have caused concern many years earlier. Then he will understand the aim of the 'choir path'.

The speech continues here with a meditation on the corpse and what this means. It is not in the sense of an actual corpse, in which everything evaporates and only dryness is left. Because in the kind of corpse we are talking about here, there is still salivation, blood movement, excretions, etc., it is just that the soul only engages with what is reverential, and Jesus-like, and thus distances itself (externalises itself) from anything which cannot be used to this effect, and in the end one's *Hütte* will become oblivious to these movements.

There are, then, sensations, and there are fleshly sensations. The fleshly sensations are the sensations which are non-corpse-like, that is, sensations that give rise to impure thoughts or desires. Sensations, without the 'fleshly' qualifier, are those natural things that occur, but under the governance of a proper attitude do not cause reverberations in the soul. The 'need' in the soul, which has power through natural inclination of the *Gemüth*, the mind and spirit, is cut off and thus weakens the drive for sin, to the extent that this desire, this power, this need becomes worthless remains over against our *Hütte*, and is thus, as mentioned above, externalised. From this point on, all things corporeal and physical must be examined and their provenance, divine or diabolical, determined. If it is neither temptation, evil sorcery, or self-will, then one may be satisfied and attend to one's body in this issue and in all, as a matter of Christ. The natural condition of a child of god is to draw from the Saviour day and night, to be one whose spirit, soul, and limbs only serve to please Jesus.

While the emphasis on the body is individual, the address itself is to the choir, and this is mentioned a number of times. First, early on, where Zinzendorf speaks of the choir of the Saviour, which refers to the idea presented in other speeches that the Saviour was 'the first single brother', and as such the founder of the single brothers' choir.[110] Further, a single brother must study the choir principles and practices in order to understand how to temper his body and soul. Finally, once the brother has matured, he will realise the truthfulness and purpose of the choir path. These three points are important and interwoven. The last two points show that there are principles and practices in

---

110   On choir relatives, see single brothers, 5 March 1760 (UA R.20.HS52); the Saviour as a single brother unto death is also in 26 October 1750 (UA R.20.HS22), 29 August 1757 (UA R.20.HS57) and 1 June 1758 (GNC 80.1758.4) and 2 January 1760 (UA R.20.HS52). See also married couples, 17 August 1757 (UA R.20.HS54).

a given choir, and that there is an idea of a path on which to tread. This path is following the life of the Saviour, which is what the present choir and its practices indicate, as the first two points mention. We will return to the path below, when discussing transition in the case of the widowers. Here I focus on the practices and principles of the choir.

In an earlier speech, Zinzendorf notes that:

> When the choir is of one mind to be one spirit with Him and upholds his vessel in sanctification and honour, to honour His limbs and to permit no external life, then the Saviour, with the pervasive knowledge of the choir point, will hinder no soul, but encourage and will encourage what is required of you to the completion of this practical truth.[111]

Here we see a number of overlapping ideas with our present speech, namely the concern for limbs, the avoidance of external influences, and the support of the Saviour to the 'choir point' which may be connected with the state of peace in our speech, where the brother is given the cross of the Saviour and understands what the choir path was all about. Each choir has a point, and these points make up a path in life. Another important item in this paragraph is that it articulates what is required of the choir; namely to become one spirit with the Saviour, to uphold his (Saviour's or the brother's) vessel in sanctification and honour, and to honour his limbs and to permit no external life. When the choir is in one mind to make this happen, then the Saviour will reward the brothers by helping them reach this noble goal.

Going back to the *Losungs*-text, there is more of importance here. As noted, the first clause – 'Do you not know that your members are Christ's members?' – is a rewriting of 1 Corinthians 6:15a: 'Do you not know that your bodies are members of Christ?' I noted that this was a very significant modification because it changed the emphasis from participation to resemblance. Instead of the believers being the members of Christ's body (participation), the believers' bodies themselves are now to be identified with the body of the Saviour. This emphasis on the physical resemblance between Jesus and the men of the congregation instead of the usual membership model is congruent with another important trope in Zinzendorf's theology, namely the production of two *distinct* bodies:

---

111 Single brothers, 5 March 1760: "Wenn das Chor Eines Sinnes ist, zu seyn mit Ihm Ein Geist, und sein Faß im Heiligen und Ehren zu behalten, die Glieder Sein zu ehren und kein fremdes Leben zu zulassen; so hält der Heiland mit der durchgängigen Erkenntniß vom Chor-Punckte keine Seele auf, sondern fördert und wird fördern, was zur Completirung dieser practischen Wahrheit bey Euch erfordert wird" (UA R.20.HS52).

that of the community over against that of Christ.¹¹² This was also the case in the ideal of the choir spirit: the single brothers must become a collective body in will and thought.

The vessel that is to be upheld is the penis, but whether it refers to that of the Saviour or the single brother is not straightforward. This 'vessel' idea relates to our speech in that the *Losungs*-text (Do you not know that your members are Christ's members? And every member achieves resemblance to the corpse) would also include the penis. Given the overall emphasis on governing desire, perhaps the focus is especially on the penis. The men in the community are, by way of their physical likeness to the Saviour, blessed, in that there is no member on the body of a brother that was not present on the body of the Saviour. In another speech, Zinzendorf calls this 'membership' (*Gliederschaft*), which refers to the collective body, but given Zinzendorf's common references to the member of Jesus, and its significance for the brothers, membership could also be taken to refer to the penis, as a certain common feature of the Saviour and the men of the community.¹¹³ In yet another speech, Zinzendorf refers to this as the member of difference, the "*Unterscheidungsglied*".¹¹⁴

While Zinzendorf on the one hand places great emphasis on the penis, on the other hand he also tries to emphasise that the penis itself is not important:

---

112   I have analysed the differences between the collective body in 1 Corinthians and the collective body of Zinzendorf's in Petterson 2015.
113   Single brothers, 27 April 1757 (UA R.20.HS57).
114   Single brothers, 26 October 1750: 'On the question of what makes a young man a *Jüngling*: The member of difference does not make one a *Jüngling*, since this is carried by the child, the boy, the young man, the man and the widower'; "die Unterscheidungs-Glieder machen einen nicht zum Jüngling, denn die trägt das Kind, der Knabe, der Jüngling, der Mann, der Witwer" (UA R.20.HS22).

From other choir speeches (e.g. workers, single brothers, 17 April 1751) we understand 'that the member, they [the brothers] carry for the sake of distinction, by no means is a member, which must be confused with nature and flesh, because it is merely a sign of honour, which they carry upon order of the Saviour'; "daß der Glied, das sie zur Distinction tragen, im geringsten kein Glied ist, das mit Natur und Fleisch vermengt werden muß, weil es ein Bloßes Ehren-Zeichen ist, das sie auf Ordre des Heilands tragen". Later, he also notes that 'what is called our member has no particular concurrence with this; it serves the single brother nothing more than for the benefit of distinction and worth, as a sign of honour'; "was man unser Glied nennt, das hat damit keine speciale concurrenz das dient einem ledigen Bruder zu weiter nichts, als zur distinction und Würde, zum Ehren-Zeichen" (in GN.C.21.1751.5).

The concept of covenant-member (*Bundes-Glied*) in reference to the penis is abundant in the 12. *Anhang zum Herrnhuter Gesangbuch*, along with the focus on Jesus' circumcision. Reichel 1969, p. 58.

... the distinction-member does not make one a youngling (*Jüngling*), since also the child, the boy, the youngling, the man, the widower carries it. The youngling-trait must thus reside in something else. And that is also certain that the youngling-trait is nothing else but the virginal (*Jungfräulich*) mind in a man's image, which turns a child into a youngling.[115]

To be a youngling, then, is Zinzendorf's term for a true brother, one who has taken upon himself the nature and meaning of living as the companion of Jesus, and who possesses the mind of a female virgin. This is also something which may be part of the single brothers' selfhood and is an interesting counter-point to the equally significant emphasis on him as a corpse, as we will see in the quotation below. In essence, they amount to the same thing, a chaste mindset that governs the body and its urges and surges. As Zinzendorf notes, that is *the* necessary question for all brothers and sisters, but particularly for the single brother choir and *Stand*.[116] This state is either maiden-like or corpse-like, or both, as in this quotation:

> If one looks at the issue in Jesus' heart, according to the mind of our Immanuel [Jesus[117]], the first choir brother, the arch elder of the single brothers' *Stand*, and one is a maiden heart, a corpse-compeer, an imprint of the singular maiden man, and martyr for us, the broken eyes therefore look out of one's eyes, because the whole Christ-mind is in the heart, then the idea appears as commonplace, then every single brother prepares oneself thereto, that were it possible, to remain in the Saviour's choir organisation, and therein, to be his follower.[118]

---

115 Single brothers, 26 October 1750 (UA R.20.HS22).
116 1 August 1755: 'How far one must acknowledge and tolerate the life of the limbs and to what extent one should and can eliminate it; that is a question that is very necessary for our entire course, and in particular in the single brothers' choir and *Stand*'; "Wie weit man das Leben der Glieder agnosciren und toleriren soll und wie weit mans gantz abschaffen soll, und kan, das ist eine question die unserm gantze[n] Gange, und in Specie im Ledigen Brüder Chor und Stand sehr nöthig ist" (UA R.20.HS58).
117 Immanuel is the name of the young woman's son in Isaiah 7:13 (Look the young woman is with child, and shall bear a son, and shall name him Immanuel), which is repeated in Matthew 1:23 as a prophecy of the birth of Jesus.
118 Single brothers, 29 August 1757, "Wenn man die Sache aber im Herzen Jesus ansieht, nach der Denckweise unsers Immanuels, des Ersten Chor-Bruders, des ersten Chor-Bruders, der Erz-Aeltesten des ledigen Brüder-Standes, und man ist ein Jungfräuliches Herz, ein Leichnams Genoß, ein Abdruck des Einigen Jungfräulichen Mannes, und Märterers für uns, die Gebrochne Augen sehen einem darum aus den Augen heraus, weil der ganze Christus-

And a bit later in the same speech:

> And that is what, brothers, always falls upon my heart during choir communion. I do think that the Saviour and the merit of his *Stand*, shall not only make the single brothers to true maidens, but also give them the diacritical mark, the characteristic, what one could call the special and exceptional nature of the a choir brother; that they not only will become pure, holy and immaculate souls, but that they also realise and understand the felicity, the privilege, the prerogative, the levity and leisure of their present *Stand*, how highly a single brother is favoured by God, and to what extent he has a distinct blessedness, which no maiden, widower or man who hasn't passed that choir have experienced.[119]

This exceptional status of the *Stand* of the single brothers is not only given by the Saviour (make them true maidens, give them the characteristic nature of a choir brother), by which they become pure souls. It is because the Saviour himself was a single brother, and thus gives privilege to their *Stand* which should be reflected upon and fully experienced, so that they understand their favoured position above all others in the eyes of God.[120]

Sinn im Herzen ist, dann sind einem die Idee gäng und gäbe; da richtet sich ein jeder lediger Bruder drauf ein, wenns möglich wäre, ins Heilands Chor-Einrichtung zu bleiben, und darin sein Nachfolger zu seyn" (UA R.20.HS57).

119 Single brothers, 29 August 1757: "Und das ists, Ihr Brüder! was mir bey Chor-Communionen allemal aufs Herz fällt. Ich dencke nemlich, der Heiland und das Verdienst seines Standes solte die ledigen Brüder nicht nur zu wahren Jungfrauen machen, sondern ihnen auch die notam diacriticam, das characteristicum, was man die specielle und exceptive Natur eines Chor-Bruders nennen kan, *dazu* geben; daß sie nicht nur reine, heilige, unbefleckte Seelen überhaupt wären, sondern daß sie auch die Glückseligkeit, das Privilegium, das Vorrecht, die Leichtigheit und Gemächlichkeit ihres gegenwärtigen Standes gründlich erkenneten und verstünden, wie hoch ein lediger Bruder von Gott begnadigt ist, und in welchem Theil er eine aparte Seligkeit hat, die keine Jungfrau, Witwer oder Mann die *das* Chor nicht passiert sind erfähret" (UA R.20.HS57).

120 This is also emphasised in single brothers, 4 May 1760, the last speech Zinzendorf gave before he died on 9 May: 'Our single brothers know the special grace which they enjoy ahead of the other choirs. That they have the sacred youngling *Stand* of the head of the community, who in this world also was a single brother in front of them and regard themselves as his choir relatives, and should let themselves be made similar to him in body and soul'; "Unsre ledigen Brüder kennen die special Gnade, die sie vor den anderen Chören zu genießen haben, daß sie den heiligen Jünglings Stand des Hauptes der Gemein, der in dieser Welt auch ein lediger Bruder war, *vor sich* haben, und sich als Seine Chor-Verwandten ansehen, und nach Leib und Seele Ihm ähnlich machen lassen sollen" (UA R.20.HS57).

The mention of the brothers as maidens ('one is a maiden heart, an imprint of the singular maiden man' and the Saviour will 'make them true maidens') in the two paragraphs just quoted is an element of a larger understanding of marriage. We shall return to this in much greater detail when we discuss the married couples' choir in the following chapter, but here we may look at the element at hand, namely the identity of brothers as maidens. This is, I think, part of Zinzendorf's attempt at producing a collective body as *distinct* from the Saviour, to which the community can relate, namely the bride of the Saviour. It is in this particular understanding that Zinzendorf can speak of the brothers as maidens:

> The brothers are blessed, when they arrive in the blessed sisterhood and one believes that this will happen to them, if they remember that they are the souls, sisters and virgins of Jesus Christ and that the member, they carry for the sake of distinction, by no means is a member, which must be confused with nature and flesh, because it is merely a sign of honour, which they carry upon order of the Saviour.[121]

While marriage on earth is a representation between the Saviour and his church, it takes on a different relation in the hereafter. In eternity, the brothers of the congregation will return to their *original female state* and relate to Christ as women towards the one true man.[122] According to this quote, the corporeal reality of men is an anomaly. The physical reality of being a man has no corresponding spiritual component but will morph into the blessed sisterhood in eternity. This is somewhat at odds with the otherwise heavy emphasis on the physical likeness between the Saviour and the brothers which, as we have seen, is such a common feature of the choir speeches to the male members. Per-

---

121   Workers, single brothers, 17 April 1751 (UA GN.C.21.1751.5) "Die Brüder sind glückselig, wenn sie in die seligen Schwesterlichkeit kommen und mans ihnen glauben kan, wenn sie sich besinnen, daß sie Seelen, Schwestern, Jungfrauen Jesu Christi sind und daß das Glied, das sie zur Distinction tragen, im geringsten kein Glied ist, das mit Natur und Fleisch vermengt werden muß, weil es ein Bloßes Ehren-Zeichen ist, das sie auf Ordre des Heilands tragen".
122   The common reference is from Zinzendorf's speech in Zeist on the wedding of Henrietta Benigna von Zinzendorf to Johannes von Watteville in 1746 (Zinzendorf 1963, p. 208): 'All human souls are generis foeminini, and the soul of our Lord Jesus Christ is the only one generis masculini', quoted in Faull 2011, p. 61. Seidel also quotes this in a footnote (2000, p. 43) and wonders icily who has made this revelation to the Count. There are, however, multiple examples throughout the choir speeches. See for example single brothers, 5 November 1747 (UA R.20.HS34) and workers, single brothers, 17 April 1751 (UA GN.C.21.1751.5). See also Petterson 2014.

haps this is why there is reference to the Saviour as a singular maiden-man, the original of which the brothers are an imprint, to hedge that particular interpretation as well. Whether the brother is a maiden, a corpse or a man, all of these are copies of Jesus. However, the corpse and the man are individual subjectification techniques, while the maiden-ideal is conceptualised collectively. As we shall see, this is in line with how the female members are subjectified, namely, as a collective.

6.2 Governing One's Body and the Role of the Corpse

In the speech above, we saw several instances of the idea that the soul is the ruler of the body. Zinzendorf spoke of how 'the attending to limbs does not only mean washing one's face and hands, taking medicine when one is sick (although that is part of it), rather it consists in the thorough study of one's entire *Hütte* in a clear idea of whether one has a soul which governs the body wisely, or whether it still leads an ignorant regiment'. He also insisted that all the mechanisms of nature would not stop in the body of a true brother, salivation takes place, blood will circulate, the body excretes and so on. Furthermore, desire, and whatever else is useless in making one's body into a service to the Saviour, is to be externalised and will appear outside, or over against the body as a lifeless matter, *caput mortuum*. We thus have three things in operation here: the soul, the purified and governed *Hütte*, and the externalised desire for sin, which constitutes the makeup of a true brother.

What Zinzendorf is wrestling with are well known contradictions from the history of Christianity, but in lieu of the different historical context, they are cast in new skins, so to speak. What is the relation between the body and soul, when the body, and this life, takes on increased importance? How can the soul be used in the production of the body as a tool? And how does one temper the body, if one of the key symbols is eschatological copulation with the Saviour?

The attention to the *Hütte* is a pervasive one in the speeches. The members are encouraged to monitor change, to report everything, and to learn how to be comfortable in ones 'dying bones'. At one level, the historical significance of this focus is that in these years, society was undergoing dramatic changes, with older forms of collectivity and social order eroding and new forms emerging, as succinctly pointed out by Isabel Hull:

> Where collective estate, or *Stand*, had once organized society, the individual citizen now founded civil society. Stripped of social status and regional inflection, the individual citizen had to be based on universal principles adhering to the only distinguishing feature he had left: his body. ... the degree to which this model citizen was based not on (bourgeois)

class but on gender can be seen if one analyses the successive steps by which the older male sexual model was refashioned, or if one carefully examines in practice the defining characteristic of relations between civil society and the state, namely the split between public and private.[123]

As this quote from Hull shows, the individual body and gender came to take on the role as the main unit of society. It is thus within these developments that we should find the extensive deliberation on bodies in the choir speeches important.

It seems to be a general assumption that Zinzendorf had a positive assessment of the human body.[124] And we do find many examples of this in the speeches. For example, as when Zinzendorf declares that 'the Saviour and his mother carried *Hütten* no different from those of other people. He, the Saviour, bore a male *Hütte*, and she had formed his *Hütte* in her maiden body (*Leibe*)'.[125] 'He [the Saviour] was born with exactly the pain, haemorrhage, and all that can take place in a physical birth'.[126] The members of the Herrnhut community carried the limbs of the Saviour and those of his mother.[127]

By now we should realise that it is not quite that simple. There are four reasons for this. First, the understanding of the male *Hütte*. As I have mentioned earlier, one of the components in Zinzendorf's cosmic marriage is that the brothers will return to their original female souls at some undefined point, and be part of the church, which is then the spouse of the Saviour. There are multiple examples of this, but a couple will suffice:

> But a single brother has his *Hütte* for no other reason than to learn what a woman also has. Everything, which he experiences with the *Hütte*, what relates to diet, health, illness, smell, evacuation [defecation and urination], he experiences not as a single brother, but as a human. The inner structure of his *Hütte* makes a difference in the concoction and movement of the things, especially also in the manner that there is more fire, sulphur and cholera in him, than with a sister. Because the *Hütte* of the

---

123 Hull 1996, p. 5. See also Canning 2006, p. 177.
124 Atwood 1997, p. 29.
125 Single sisters, 26 July 1757: "der Heiland und seine Mutter haben keine andre Hütten getragen als andere Menschen. Er der Heiland hat eine Männliche Hütte getragen, und sie hat seine Hütte formirt in ihrem jungfräulichen Leibe" (UA R.20.HS60).
126 Married Sisters, 25 December 1755: "Er ist mit eben der Schmerzen, Blutsturz und allem, was bey einer leibliche Geburt vorgehen kan[n], geboren worden" (UA R.20.HS42).
127 See also single sisters, 5 Sept 1755, 'we partake in his humanity'; "Wir haben Theil an seiner Menschheit" (UA R.20.HS47).

brothers are set up more for the nature of a soldier, thus so also the movements by him are stronger, more solid, more brief, but more violent, because the *Hütte* has been built and inaugurated a long time ago. However, what is called our member has no particular concurrence with this; it serves the single brother nothing more than for the benefit of distinction and worth, as a sign of honour.[128]

It is important how there is a distinction between the afterlife (the blessed sisterhood) and the current state with its physical experiences of the *Hütte*, which are related to being human. In another speech to the men in the community, Zinzendorf begins by noting that 'we men are an anomaly in nature, we are a *Stand* which has no place in eternity, time is our fixed appointment, after which our anomaly ceases to exist, and we go, *jure post liminii*[129] into the right we have as another creature, as another human soul'.[130]

According to these examples, the corporeal reality of men is an anomaly and only serves for men to experience what women also experience. Furthermore, the penis ('member') is a symbol of distinction and not connected with nature or the flesh. The physical reality of being a man has no corresponding spiritual component but will morph into the blessed sisterhood. In line with Zinzendorf's understanding of men as a vice-Saviour, there seems to be an incarnational logic behind this arguing, since the nature taken on in the *Hütte* is different from the spiritual reality, while there is a correspondence between

---

128 Workers, single brothers, 17 April 1751: "Aber ein lediger Bruder hat seiner Hütte nach nichts anders zu erfahren, als was eine ledige Schwester auch hat. Alles, was er an der Hütte erfährt, was zur Diaet, Gesundheit, Kränklichkeit, Ausdünstung, Evacuation gehört, das erfährt er nicht als ein ledige Bruder, sondern als Mensch. Die innere Structur seiner Hütte kan eine Differenz machen in der Concoction und Bewegung der Dinge, sonderlich auch in der Art und Weise, daß mehr Feuer, Schwefel und Cholera bey ihm ist, als bey einer Schwester. Denn weil die Hütten der Brüder mehr aufs Soldaten-Wesen eingerichtet ist, so sind auch die Bewegungen bey ihnen stärcker, solider, kürzer, aber gewaltsamer, denn die Hütte ist auf länger gebauet und eingerichtet. Aber was man unser Glied nennt, das hat damit keine speciale Concurrenz das dient einem ledigen Br zu weiter nichts, als zur distinction und Würde, zum Ehren-Zeichen". (UA GN.C.21.1751.5).

129 The expression *jure post liminii* [reprisal/act of taking back] is an expression from international law and/or laws of war.

130 Married men, 5 November 1747: "Wir Männer sind ein Anomalion der Natur, wir sind ein in die Ewigheit nicht gehöriger Stand, unser Termin ist die Zeit, darnach hört unsere Anomalie auf, und dann gehen wir Jure post liminio in das Recht, das wir als eine andere Creatur als eine andere menschlichen Seele auch haben" (GN.C.2.1747.2). See also married men, 8 December 1756: 'I have said many times and stand by it, that our *Stand* is an artificial Stand'; "Ich habe vielmahl gesagt, und bliebe dabey, daß unser Stand ein künstlicher Stand ist". (UA R.4.C.II.12).

women's spiritual and corporeal reality. Thus, physical men are the product of a 'becoming', of moving into a radically different *Stand* which is marked by the penis. Interestingly, Michael McKeon has argued that one of the features of the modern sex-gender system was the new focus on anatomical difference and the associated emphasis on genitals and penetrative sex.[131] This adds further weight to the argument regarding the masculinity of Jesus and his male genitals as a constituent feature of modern humanity.

The second issue is Zinzendorf's distinction between inner and outer human, which we will have occasion to discuss in more detail when looking at the speech to the single sisters below. Here, Zinzendorf emphasises that the inner human is the constant and this is where one's true connection with the Saviour is, while the outer human is subject to change and transition. The outer human should be characterised by obedience to the will of the Saviour, and this obedience grows out of the inner relationship.

In both of these two cases, then, there is a constancy in the inner human, and change in the outer, which is where the *Hütte* belongs. This is connected with the understanding that the deceased are still present as the community above. Zinzendorf mentions, for example, how all the single brothers are so blessed in their choir that all they want to do is, 'as single brothers to leave the *Hütte* and … to reach the upper rows of maiden-people, to our blessed Christel,[132] and to so many other choir relations in the community up there'.[133] In the suggested amendments to the statutes of the community drafted in 1755, it is declared that because the God's Acre in Herrnhut is in no way an ordinary graveyard, but simply 'a continuing choir house and dormitory', no outsiders to the community should be buried there without permission.[134]

---

131   McKeon 2012, pp. 792–3. See also Thomas Laqueur's contribution in the same issue (Laqueur 2012).
132   Zinzendorf's only son, who died in 1753.
133   Single brothers, 4 May 1760: "wenn auch alle ledigen Brüder in ihrem Chor so selig sind, daß sie sich nichts anders wünschen, als daß sie als ledige Brüder aus der Hütte gehen, und in den obere Reigen der Jungfräulichen Leute zu unserm seligen Christel, und zu so vielen andern Chor-Verwandten in der Gemeine droben gelangen möchten" (UA R.20.HS57). See also widows, 9 May 1756: "obere Gemeine" and how widows have more a glimpse into the realm of spirit (*Geisterreich*) than other members who are working (UA R.20.HS46).
134   UA R.6.A.a.39.1: "Weil der Gottes-Acker zu H[errn]huth blos ein continuirendes Chor-Haus und Dormitarium ist, keines weges aber ein allgemeiner Kirchhoff, […] daß wer in der Zeit außer der Specialen H[errn]hutschen Banden- und Chor-Pflege ist, und aus der Zeit geht, ohne ein vor dem gantzen Gemein-Rath resolvirtes Special-Decret, auf dem Gottes-Acker in H[errn]huth nicht begraben werden soll".
      Gottesacker/Godsacre is the specific name of the graveyards and cemetaries of the Moravian Church. They are characterised by the separation of the sexes on either side

On the other hand, however, we have the extreme importance attached to the *Hütte* and the dying bones. This is evident not only in the near constant obsession with *Hütte* and its 'circumstances', observation, understanding, explaining its movements and stirrings, but also in the already mentioned unprecedented emphasis on the human body of the Saviour.

This is not only a thematic contradiction in the speeches, but also a struggle within the realm of each person. In the speeches, the *Hütte* is usually in the company of some or all of other elements, namely soul (*Seele*), spirit/mind (*Geist*) and the 'inner' (*Gemüth*). And the relationship between them is far from clear.

In a speech to the single sisters from 1755, Zinzendorf says that the incarnation of the Saviour is proof that a *Jungfer* has grace and that her creator has ensured that

> if her *Hütte* is not *perturbed* by the wickedness of her soul, but rather that a chaste soul lives in the dying bones, then a grace-endowed *Hütte* will be generated from this blessed and innocent body, and create no impediment in their advancement toward the bridegroom.[135]

Here we see that the soul has an effect on the *Hütte*, that the soul is able to perturb the *Hütte*, if the soul is not governed properly. The matter of *perturbation* (turbas, turbire) is a very interesting one, not least because its understanding is one of independent forces working on and within the limits of a *Hütte*.

A similar situation appears in a longer quote from a speech to the married couples' choir in Herrnhut from 25 March 1756:

> We ought to search for all good and evil in the soul (*Seele*), and not lay down our heads until we know that our soul (*Seele*) is chaste, that the exorcism of all wickedness, deceit, crookedness, false shame, secrecy, concealment and hiddenness of the spirit is spoken out, and all the evil spirits, who knows, where to? are cursed. If we then always carry our soul in hands, and with the assistance of the Saviour are placed in possession of the regiment, of the priestly kingdom over the soul (*Seele*), then we should

---

of the central axis, and identical slabs for all members. In Herrnhut, there are eight larger graves on the central axis, which belong to Zinzendorf and some members of his family (including his two wives) and Friedrich von Watteville.

135   Single sisters, 25 December 1755: "daß wenn ihre Hütte durch keine Argheit ihrer Seelen *turbirt* wird, sondern eine keusche Seele in einem sterbenden Gebeine wohnt" (UA R.20. HS47).

> become friends with our dying bone (*sterbende Gebein*), be its keeper, and be less afraid of it as a united choir because we are in the profession of procuring for him blessed, liturgical, wholesome, occupations, invented by our Creator himself.[136]

The quote is in two parts, the first deals with making the soul chaste by exorcising wickedness, deceit, false shame, etc. Then, the brothers and sisters are, with the help of the Saviour, put in charge of the regiment, and are able to place the priestly kingdom in charge of the soul. This in place, they can then befriend and take care of their dying bones, from which they as a united choir have little to fear, because they as a choir are able to give the bones blessed, liturgical and wholesome occupations, as instructed by the Saviour.

The course of action is as follows: the Saviour puts the brothers and sisters in charge of the regiment over their souls that then, properly governed, can take charge of the dying bones. It is the Saviour who can ensure the proper state of being which is characterised by blessedness, courage and happiness, as indicated in this excerpt from a 1756 single sisters' speech.

> that only His blessing, healing hand can sweep away everything, and that His blood can wash away what makes us dismal, what shifts our goal, what hampers our joyfulness, what interrupts the virgins' continuous blessedness, valour, courage, and true rapture of the heart and perturbs the spirit.[137]

---

136 Married couples, 25 March 1756: "Wir sollen eigentlich alles gute und böse in der Seele suchen, und unsern Kopf nicht eher sanfte legen, bis wir wüßten, daß unsre Seele keusch gemacht ist, daß der Exorcismus über alle Argheit, Tücke, Krümme, falsche Scham, Räzelhaftigkeit, Geists-Verborgenheit und Versteckheit aus gesprochen ist, und alle die bösen Geister, wer weiß, wohin? verwünscht sind. Wenn wir dann unsre Seele immer in Händen tragen, und durch des Heilands Beystand in die Possess des Regiments, des priesterlichen Königreichs über die Seele gesezt sind, dann solten wir uns mit unserm sterbenden Gebein befreundschaften, sein Pfleger seyn, und uns weniger vor ihm fürchten, als einiges Chor, weil wir in dem Beruf sind, ihm selige, liturgische, heilsame, von unserm Schöpfer selbst erfundene occupationen zu verschaffen" (UA R.20.HS54).

137 Single sisters, 21 May 1756: "daß seine segnende, curirende Hand nur alles so weg streichen und daß sein Blut hinweg schwemmen kan was uns trübe macht, was unser Ziel verrückt, was unsre Freudigkeit hemmt, was den Jungfrauen ihre continuirliche seligkeit, Muth, Courage und wirkliche Frö[h]lichkeit des Herzens interrumpiren und den Geist turbiren kan. Denn das ist unsre große Absicht mit beym Sacrament, wenn Er sein Blut über uns regnen und seinen Schweiß auf uns triefen läßt, so kan uns nicht beßers auf Erden segnen" (UA R.20.HS47).

Note here how the body and mind are something acted upon from the outside,[138] that there are things which can perturb the mind/spirit and shatter or interrupt the joy of the heart. These examples show that humans are not from the outset in control of their own *Gemüths*. Indeed, particularly the sisters have areas in their body and soul which they themselves cannot access nor improve.

> A sister has more hidden, more gentle and thus more dangerous circumstances in nature than what is called a brother. The female sex has its own angles in soul and *Hütte*. They can only be found with difficulty by themselves and therefore not easily straightened.[139]

This ironing out of internal folds is thus the task of the Saviour and the workers of the choirs. The important role of the choir in managing these things can be seen in the following quote from a speech to the single brothers from 1748, where Zinzendorf notes that the aim of the choirs is to cultivate this state of peace and bliss through daily and hourly undertakings of the mind (*Gemüths-geschäft*):

> There [in the sidehole] one is dead to all other things, estranged and out of any connection with the things that do not fit therein, and one is soulful and well, and if one stands well with one's Lord, and He looks at one kindly, and He is satisfied with one, then nothing in the world is able to perturb one's peace and blessedness. Much work is going in to this, this is the aim of the choirs, and if this is not the daily, even hourly mind-undertaking (*Gemüths-geschäft*) in the choirs, in all external work, in every physical illness of the *Hütte*, if the daily inclusion of mind (*Gemüth*) and blood in Jesus's blood does not always take place, then shame on such a choir, which is not worthy of the effort that is called a choir.[140]

---

138 This notion of being open to being acted upon is what Paul Scott Gordon calls 'glad passivity', and he notes that while this is not unique to Moravians, it was lived out very intensely in the North American settlements. Gordon 2018, p. 26.

139 All sisters 13 March 1760: "Eine Schwester hat verborgenere, sachtere und also gefährlicher Umstände in der Natur, als was man einen Bruder nennt. Das Weibliche Geschlecht hat ganz eigne Winkel in Seel und Hütte. Sie können von ihnen selbst schwer ausgefunden und also auch nicht so leicht ausgegleicht werden" (UA R.20.HS52).

140 Brothers, 10 May 1748: "Da ist man allen andere Dingen abgestorben, fremde und außer aller Connexion mit den Sachen, die dahin nicht einpassen, und man ist seelich und wohl und wenn man mit seinem Herrn gut steht und der sieht einen freundlich an, und der ist zufrieden mit einem, so ist nichts in der Weld im Stande, jemanden seine Ruhe und

The state of oblivion is for the single brothers often likened to the Saviour's corpse and how to attain corpse-ness. In a speech to the single brothers from 28 January 1751, Zinzendorf deliberates over the corpse and as a leadup to this, there are a couple of paragraphs on how to reign over one's body:

> When one wants to bring one's body into order, then more than one thing is needed. Paul speaks in view of his *Hütte*, he keeps his body in a bridle, lets it know that it has a skilful rider, and yields no ground for excess. In German it says: *I punish my body*. I seek no further meaning in the word than keeping a tight rein, not granting anyone too much will. This is confirmed through another idea from the same Apostle when he says, 'make no provision for the body to gratify its desires, allow its needs, but not *too much*'.[141]

First, Zinzendorf refers to Paul's approach to his body, how he keeps it in a bridle and lets it feel that it has a skilful rider and gives it no occasion for extravagance. The main quote is from 1 Corinthians 9:27, (he cites the Luther bible), but the supporting allusions, which refer to bridles and reins, are from James 3:2–3. The first half of the other idea from the apostle is of course from Romans 13:14, but the second half (allow its needs, but not *too much*) is Zinzendorf's addition, which actually ameliorates the quote from Romans by allowing for its needs in a limited fashion. This is one of Zinzendorf's main points, that not all movements of the flesh are bad, but that the body has its urges and movements. For Zinzendorf, dwelling on and obsessing over this and that sensation, not the sensation itself, is sinful, which is what he is reading into the quote from Romans.

Seeligkeit zu turbiren. Darauf wird nun loß gearbeitet, darauf wird eigenlicht gezielet in den Chören, und wenn das nicht das tägliche ja stündliche Gemüths-geschäfte ist in den Chören bey aller äußerlichen Arbeit, bey allen phüsicalishen Kränkeln der Hütte, wenn die täglich Einsprengung des Gemüths und Geblüts mit Jesu Bluts nicht immer fortgehet, schade vor ein solches Chor, das ist nicht der Mühe werth, daß mans ein Chor nennt" (UA GN.C.5.1748.3).

141 Single brothers, 28 January 1751: "Wenn man seinen Leib in Ordnung bringen soll, so ist mehr als einerley dahin gerhörig. Paulus spricht in Ansehung seiner Hütte, er halte seinen Cörper in Zaum, laße ihn fühlen, daß er einen geschickten Reuter habe, und daß er ihm keine Extravaganzen machen dürfe. Im teutschen stehet: *ich betäube meinen Leib*. Ich suche weiter keinen Sinn in dem Wort, als im Zügel halten, jemanden nicht zuviel Willen laßen. Das wird durch eine andere Ideé deßelben Apostel bekräftiget, da er spricht: Wartet des Leibes, doch also, daß er nicht geil werde, gebt ihm seiner Nothdurft, aber nicht *zu viel*" (UA R.20.HS35).

That is one method to deal with one's *Hütte*, according to which one must adjust oneself in the extreme need, especially if one were a worker. For if one were already a worker, and still did not have a whole heart, and one did not yet have grace and forgiveness of sins, and has not yet been washed in the blood of the Lamb, and has not the privilege of becoming as holy as Jesus' wounds, then one must, if one is to be an honourable human, give one's body to one's reason as a rider, and keep it in order, to become a kind of Nazarean,[142] like Samson, that one might not preach to others while being condemnable.[143]

This first method is especially good for those who want to be workers, or choir helpers, since they need to show outwardly that they have their bodies under control, so that they live as they preach. Here we see the 'holiness code' of Zinzendorf, which involves having a whole heart, holding on to grace and forgiveness of sins, being washed in the blood of the Lamb and becoming as holy as the wounds of Jesus.

However, he continues,

The selfsame apostle has given us another blessed overture: *it is no longer I who live, but it is Christ who lives in me*. That is an even better method, one does not need half as much reasoning and still something comes out of it, it happens as if not paying attention, without saying a word (*quasi aliud agendo, sans mot dire*); more is done than said, the belief in him who loved us, *before he even speaks, he has already done*.[144]

---

142 Nazarean is someone who comes from Nazereth, but what Zinzendorf might mean, which may be inferred through the reference to Samson, is Nazarites. These were men or women consecrated to God, but not connected to the priesthood. The commandments are to be found in Numbers 6. Cross and Livingstone 2005, p. 1141.
143 Single brothers, 28 January 1751: "Das ist eine Methode mit seiner Hütte umzugehen, da man freylich im äußersten Nothfall, zumal wenn man ein Arbeiter wäre, sich drein richten müste. Denn wenn man eben schon ein Arbeiter wäre, und doch noch kein ganzes Herze, und hätte noch nicht Gnade und Vergebung der Sünden und wäre noch nicht gewaschen in Blute des Lamm[e]s und hätte noch nicht das Privilegium, so heilig zu werden als Jesu Wunden, so müste man doch, wenn man ein ehrlicher Mensch seyn solte, seinem Leib an seinem Verstande einen Reuter schaffen und ihn in Ordnung halten, eine Art eines Nazaraeers werden, wie Simson, damit man nicht andere predigte und selbst verwerflich würde" (UA R.20.HS35).
144 Single brothers, 28 January 1751: "Aber eben derselbe Apostel hat uns noch eine selige Ouverture gemacht: ‚Ich lebe aber nicht ich, sondern Christus lebet in mir'. Das is noch eine beßere Methode, da brauchts nicht halb so viel raisonnirens und es komt doch

While the 'method' advocated by Paul in Romans actually says something similar to Galatians, Zinzendorf juxtaposes them as two distinct methods of governing the body, with the latter one from Galatians 2:20 as the preferable one. This he can do because he modified the meaning of the Romans text and relaxed its severity.[145] Here the body acts as willed by Christ rather than by oneself, the right thing is done without even thinking about it or saying a word – as is possible for the Saviour.

The best way to achieve this is to attain a corpse-like nature. The emphasis on the corpse of Jesus is a very consistent one, and ranges from the object of one's contemplation – that one 'should and should want to have the martyr man as object with every vein-pulse and draw of breath and every waking and sleeping thought' –[146] to one's role model:

> Wherein, then, is the difference between a corpse and a body? Therein, that the corpse is not aware of all the things which takes place in it, that a precious soul does not worry about this, and the *Hütte* does not know what pain is, or that, which one in the world calls lust, and does not know what happens in it, [...] That is the point that through the touch of the Jesus' corpse on a human in his dying *Hütte* will receive, that is the corpse-kind.[147]

Those who have embraced the Saviour in truth and are close to his corpse (*Leiche*) take part in the sourdough and are touched by the corpse (*Leichnam*), have made their *Hütte* corpselike. Through the enjoyment of Jesus' corpse (communion), the individual will be transported into corpse-like state, obli-

---

was heraus, es geschi[e]ht quasi aliud agendo, sans mot dire, es wird mehr gethan als gesagt, der Glaube an den, der uns geliebt hat, ehe er noch sagt, hat er schon gethan" (UA R.20.HS35).

145 Interestingly, the first method is also applicable to the single sisters in single sisters, 17 August 1756 (UA R.20.HS47).

146 Single sisters, 6 July 1757: "[Warum man sich] beschäftigen muß und wünscht, daß ein jeder adern-schlag und Athem-zug und jeder wachende oder schlafende gedanke den Marter – Mann zum object habe ..." (UA R.20.HS60).

147 Single brothers, 28 January 1751: "Worin besteht denn die Differenz eines Leichnams und Cörpers? Darin, daß der Leichnam von alle dem, was in ihm vorgeht, nichts gewahr wird, daß sich eine kostbare Seele nicht drum bekümmert, und die Hütte nicht weiß, was Schmerz oder was das ist, was man sonst in der Welt Lust nennt, und weiß nicht was in ihr vorgeht, sondern steht in einem Tiegel und wird fertig. Das ist das Pünctgen, das durch die Berührung des Leichnams Jesu bey einem Menschen in seiner sterbens-Hütte erhalten werden soll, das ist die Leichnams-Art" (UA R.20.HS35).

vious to nature's movements of the body, as a person under the influence of opiates during surgery. This particular state is advocated as a role model in choir speeches to the single men's choir.[148]

This is not to say that the idea of the corpse was not significant to the other choirs, as we saw in the speech to the children. This corpse is the focus of the community, it is a central part of the understanding of marriage and is emphasised in large paintings in the community buildings as well as the language of the various liturgies – as for example the Litany of Wounds discussed in the previous chapter. This means that death is not a disturbing or disgusting event, but a familiar one, and one which is given a particular understanding in relation to the Saviour, since this is the moment of coming to rest in his arms and lap – a very common expression in the speeches.

As a transition to the next section, which is that of the single sisters, we should note that in spite of the fact that Zinzendorf at times mentions the corpse and the chaste maiden nature in one breath, the corpse is not generally for women to emulate.

With Zinzendorf, however, there is always an exception, such as the following quote from a single sisters' speech (1756), which is in the context of how to prepare one's body for the future union with the Lambkin:

> that the soul has been made chaste, put on his corpse-like nature, committed to attaining corpse-likeness; that we kill sin, but what we live, we live for him, so that we do not partake in any drop of blood, any stirring or movement that is not according to his mind and kind.[149]

The more usual connection between single sisters and the corpse, however, is, for example, participation in the corpse through the communion;[150] they can see themselves as contributors, in that Mary as a maid shaped Jesus's body, hence corpse, in her womb,[151] that they might attain the corpse in the here-

---

148   See also single brothers, 9 July 1748 (UA R.20.HS35).
149   Single sisters, 20 May 1756: "da die Seele keusch gemacht worden ist, auf seine Leichnams-Beschaffenheit angetragen, und darauf angestel[l]t, daß wir Leichnams-Art kri[e]gen; daß wir der Sünde sterben zu einem mal, was wir aber leben Ihm leben. Daher wir auch an keinem tropfen Blut, an keiner Regung und Bewegung, die nicht nach seinem Sinn und Art ist, einigen Antheil nehmen" (UA R.20.H47).
150   Single Sisters, 20 September and 26 September 1755; single sisters, 22 March and 25 March 1756 (UA R.20.HS 47).
151   Single sisters, 13 November and 8 December 1755 (UA R20.HS47 and HS60).

after,[152] or hold it as an object of their adoration.[153] Some of these options are expressed in this quote from a speech to all sisters:

> because apart from that his dear presence is our daily fortune and new every day, apart from that we with the air and breath feed into the leaven of his corpse and have the sprinkling of his blood's nectar, and become one spirit with him, that, if that were not a daily matter, our soul could not subsist nor could life be retained, then we still come together bodily, the corpse, the true martyred body, which is given for us, will be transformed in our bones and flesh every month, we will be kneaded together with him, essentially, sacramentally, corporally, bodily, and the blood, which ran from the marks, will be drunk with thirsty souls, and with no less certainty than if we stood under his cross, placed our mouths on the sidehole and sucked.[154]

The sisters can enter into the leaven of his corpse, they can have the sprinkling of his blood's nectar, they can become one spirit with him at a daily level. Once a month, at communion, they can then experience how his corpse is changed (*verwandelt*) into their flesh and bones, they can come together with the corpse and will be kneaded together with it, they will drink the blood running from the wounds as though they were sucking from his sidehole. This understanding of communion echoes what we saw in the beginning of this chapter, namely communion as the 'sacrament of somatic unification', which was the unification of the members with their 'true bridegroom and husband'.[155]

The main aim of this section, however, was to gain an understanding about the bewildering relations of almost trinitarian proportions of the interrelation of *Gemüt*, soul and *Hütte*. While we did not reach any conclusions, it was clear

---

152   Single sisters, 2 July 1748 (UA R20.II628), single sisters, 5 September 1755 (UA R20.HS47), 20 May 1756 (UA R20.HS47).
153   Single sisters, 10 July 1748 (UA R20.HS28 and HS60) and single sisters, 2 August 1748 (UA R20.HS28).
154   All sisters, 14 May 1758: "Denn über das, daß seine liebe Nähe unser tägliches Glück und alle Morgen neu ist, über das, daß wir mit der Luft und Othem seines Leichnams Sauerteig einziehen und seines Blutes Saft und Besprengung haben, und Ein Giest mit Ihm werden, daß, wenn das nicht eine alltägliche Sache wird, unsre Seele nicht bestehen noch Leben behalten kann; so kommen wir ja auch noch cörperlich zusammen, der Leichnam, der ware Marter-Leib, der für uns gegeben ist, wird in unser Gebein und Fleisch alle Monate verwandelt; wir werden mit Ihm zusammen getaigt, wesentlich, Sacramentlich, cörperlich, leiblich, und das Blut, das aus den Maalen rann wird mit durstiger Seele getrunken und nicht mit weniger Gewißheit, als wenn wir unter seinem Creutze stünden, den Mund an der Pleura angesezt hätten und daran saugten" (GN.C.20.1758.4).
155   Beyreuther and Meyer 1963, p. 295.

that this testified to a not entirely worked out composition of what constitutes a human. While the sovereignty and freedom of our bodies and selves are regarded as inviolable rights and matters of course in modern Western culture, we can see from this section that this was not the case in Herrnhut in the mid-eighteenth century. Here, the body was still a mystery, the 'self' not yet fully formed, and the relation to forces outside still not completely severed. In this sense we can see Zinzendorf's attempts at achieving a proper balance between mind and body as one out of several contributors to the eighteenth-century medical and philosophical debates over the interrelationship between body, soul and mind, and the nature of their connection with the divine.

Importantly, though, for Zinzendorf, the Saviour is a key player in these relations. In contrast to the brothers and sisters, the Saviour, having experienced the same feelings as humans during his time in body and soul, knows how to govern himself, and this is the model that should be copied. Zinzendorf's Saviour is the arch-other through which all of our social relations should be mediated within the choirs. The result we saw in one of the first quotes, where the priestly kingdom is to be placed in charge of the soul, after which the body, or dying bones can be attended to, and through the work of the choir given blessed, liturgical and wholesome occupations.

7   Single Sisters' Choir

One of the main points in this choir speech to the single sisters in Herrnhut, from 3 April 1758,[156] is to correct a misunderstanding in relation to their choir identity. The collect, from no identifiable source, is 'become it, and remain, until we see the one in which we believe'. Zinzendorf takes hold of the sentence 'become it and remain' and says that this carries different meanings for young single sisters, older single sisters, widows and married women. The three latter groups know the different meanings of this word, but younger single sisters cannot be blamed for innocently thinking that the Saviour intends for them to stay in the state, i.e. single sisterhood, in which he planted them. This is, however, not the case.

> Remaining does not mean that I will remain single, [that] I will remain on the outer maiden-point (*Jungfernpunkt*), because I have arranged myself so well. You know well, my sisters, that I have often praised the blessed-

---

156   Single sisters, 3 April 1758 (UA R.20.HS60).

ness and the corporeal co-habitation in your choir houses and in your choir offices. I know this bliss, I can understand it, it has nothing artificial in it, for it is a natural rose garden of my dead one, where it is not wonderous at all, if one is always well.

Zinzendorf emphasises that 'remain' does not refer to being single for the rest of one's life, and here he refers to the 'outer' maidenpoint, which means the 'being single'. As we will see below, there is an outer singleness which is circumstantial and an inner singleness which is essential. Here he is refuting the circumstantial and continues to praise the choir houses and the administration of the choir (the choir offices, *Chorberuf*). He knows the particular state of bliss associated therewith, it is simple and easy to feel at home there. The mention of 'rose-garden of my dead one' refers to the Saviour's corpse as a rose-garden around which the believers buzz as bees.[157]

He then continues to talk about the correct disposition in mind and soul which keeps the *Hütte* in a pure state where it may be taken to heaven at any time. This disposition means to let oneself be filled with the bridegroom, i.e. the Saviour, and imbibe the air of the cross to the extent that one's whole body is taken over by his death. This is intensified in communion, or the monthly embrace, which functions as an antidote to any idle thought.[158] Should one be tempted to stray away from this path into idle thoughts, then these dispositions should, along with the Spirit, help kill off any improper obsession.

When the Saviour calls, be it death, choir duty, or marriage, they must obey and not lock themselves into their outer place. What this means, is that if it is decided by lot that Sister X should marry, she might have some objections against the set time or the chosen partner that may be taken into consideration, but the marriage itself is not up for questioning, because that is the essence of

---

157   Indeed, one of the more innovative ways in which the members can relate to the Saviour's corpse as a collective is Zinzendorf's understanding of the members as "Leichnams-Bienen", single sisters, 6 April 1751: 'Corpse-bees, who are drawn to the corpse of the Saviour and use him as their best rosegarden'; "Leichnams-Bienen, der zieht sich zum Leichnam des Heylands und bedient ihn als seinen besten Rosen garten". (UA R.20.HS28, also in HS47 and SHAH64). See also 11 September, 1755 (UA R20.HS28), 26 October 1750 (UA R20.HS28), single brothers, 15 October 1750 (UA R20.HS28).

158   A good example of this is to be found in the choir speech to the single sisters from 2 June 1751 also catalogued as 22 June 1757, where Zinzendorf speaks of earlier days 'when one did not yet live in the wounds of the Saviour, and was not yet as deeply immersed in him' which meant that 'one could think more about oneself', which led to questions regarding the usefulness of the *Hütte*. What we see in the speech above, is this immersion which (almost) precludes any useless thoughts (UA R.20.HS28).

the matter, and that toward which she must be obedient. This would entail her changing *Stand*, namely civil status, and choir. Both *Stand* and transition are crucial features of the choir structure and will be discussed in relation to the speeches to the widows and widowers. This then deals with the outer path, in which the sister has little say. In relation to the inner essence, he continues:

> the remain, 'become it, and remain' surely is meant in relation to your maiden hearts, your choir mind, your chaste mercy, the eternal maiden wreath of your souls, but not in relation to the circumstances in which the present time can be divided, and in regard to the many scenes therein that you will represent, which no one knows, but Him.

Zinzendorf connects the 'remain' from the collect with the inner qualities of a maiden, that is to remain constant in their path through life and choirs. The hearts, mind and chaste souls will remain their essence throughout their lives, and this is what is meant by 'remain', rather than the differing periods of life. The outer path is determined by the Saviour alone.

Zinzendorf continues and assures the sisters that it is no embarrassment to be asked to transition into a new phase of life, it is not an evil sign, nor is it a degradation. It is an expression of need, they are needed somewhere else, whether it is as missionaries in Greenland, establishing a new choir in Neuwied, or working as a nanny in the household of a baroness. These are all decisions of the Saviour and are not up for discussion. So, if one has pledged herself to belong to the Saviour, this is what she has signed up for.

7.1 *Relating to the Saviour*

In this speech there is a range of ways in which the single sister relates to the Saviour. He can appear as bridegroom, master, father and lord. Thinking back to the speech to the girls' choir, we see here a more concrete manifestation and detailed exposition of how the single sisters are to relate to the Saviour in a variety of circumstances. More particularly, we see how the maleness of the Saviour comes to the fore in his various roles of power, interpellating the sisters as bride, maid, and daughter. While the main issue in the present speech is obedience, we should not lose sight of the inner connection which is depicted in the bridegroom relation. Indeed, the inner consistency is crucial because of its representative function. The single sisters are the representatives of the community in the marriage symbolism, which holds the entire community together in a large union.[159] That is what is meant by references to 'maiden heart' and

---

159 Single sisters, 7 January 1756: 'You have nothing else to take care of except as maiden hearts

the 'eternal maiden wreath of your souls'. This is the chaste bride of the Saviour. The constancy of this relation is maintained in the inner person and in inner dialogue with the Saviour.[160] Naturally, one must also be in harmony with the wishes of the Saviour in external matters, given that he knows all, within and out.[161]

In an earlier speech, from 1756, Zinzendorf reflects on the causes behind female respect for men. There are two kinds of respect, one without 'attachment', which seems to indicate a non-personal relation of the sexes, as it appears in patriarchal society at large. This is described in the first paragraph. Zinzendorf sees this general superiority of men as the illegitimate claiming of leadership at the expense of women, whereas he sees the more proper relation (true respect and attachment) as being divinely anchored:

> In the female sex there is a certain respect towards and attachment to the male sex. As far as mere respect without attachment is concerned, men have actually taken care of that, because from the beginning they have taken all offices and functions, everything which could be called venerable things, out of the hands of women, and usurped it for themselves, so that in the rest of the world no one thinks that it is possible for sisters to lead, direct, and teach one another, it is to them such an astonishing, strange and so inconceivable thing that no nun-Abbey without male confessors, male director and other male spiritual cloister officials remain, and yet a quite different cause is whence comes the true respect and attachment to the male sex which the Creator has also placed in the women.
>
> The cause is twofold: the outward, that the women have corporeal fathers and grandfathers, or spiritual fathers. That is the natural reason why they have special respect toward the male sex; but the inner and original cause, the most cherished, most heartfelt cause, [is] that of the *only Maiden Man*, for it is not enough for him to be loved as a spectre, rather he wants to be loved as the *bone of our bones*, he wants to be considered,

---

in a constant representation of your bridegroom and his beloved presence'; "Ihr habt vor nichts zu sorgen als vor Jungfräuliche Herzen in einer beständiger Representation eures Bräutigams und Seiner lieben Nähe" (UA SHAH64).

160   See single sisters, 25 March 1744 (UA R.20.HS1), 1 July 1755 (UA R.20.HS47), 3 February 1756 (UA R.20.HS47), 21 May 1756 (UA R.20.HS47), 4 May 1757 (UA R.20.HS47), 15 March 1758 (UA R.20.HS60), 5 May 1758 (UA R.20.HS49), and 11 March 1760 (UA R.20.HS60).

161   Single sisters, 4 September 1755 (UA R.20.HS47), 20 September 1755 (UA R.20.HS47) and again, 11 March 1760 (UA R.20.HS60).

as a true human, as a human who is beautiful, whose beauty does not consist in the mixture of the colours of the face, or in a certain external tenderness, but prides himself on the true beauty which the spirit makes, which the heart and the inward mercy makes, of which not all men have understanding, but whoever has understanding, can find beauty in an otherwise misshapen person, and can regard a juxtaposed famous world-beauty with the greatest contempt and disdain, if not even with aversion caused by the inner human, from whom all the enchanting, praiseworthy, heart-affected beauties are determined.[162]

The true respect and attachment to men is divinely instilled in women and has an external and internal cause, with the internal cause being the source of the external cause. Zinzendorf is thus moving from the outside into the inward relation between women to the Saviour.

What is important in this quote is that it draws out what is otherwise implied in most of the speeches, namely that the Saviour functions as mediator for

---

162   Single sisters, 12 January 1756: "Es liegt in dem weiblichen Geschlecht ein gewißer Respect gegen, und attachement ans männliche Geschlecht. Was den bloßen Respect ohne attachement betrift, da haben die Männer wol eigentlich davor gesorgt, sich den zu machen, weil sie von Anfang an alle Aemter u Verrichtungen, was ehrwürdige Dinge genennt werden können, aus den Händen der Weibs-Personen heraus genommen, und sich etwas selbst angemaßt haben, daher in der übrigen Welt niemand denckt, wies möglich ist, daß Schwestern einander selbst führen, dirigiren und lehren können, das ist ihnen eine erstaunliche, wunderbare und so unbegreifliche Sache, daß keine Nonnen-Abtey ohne Beicht-Väter, Directores und andre geistliche Closter-Beamten bleibt, die Manns Personen sind, und doch ists eine ganz andre Ursach, woher der wahre Respect und das attachement an das männliche Geschlecht kommt, die der Schöpfer auch in die Frauensleute gelegt hat. Die Ursach ist zweyerley: die äußerliche, daß die Weibs-Personen leibliche Väter und Groß-Väter, oder geistliche Väter haben. Das ist die natürlichste Ursache, warum sie vor dem männlichen Geschlecht eine besondre Achtung haben; aber die innere und Original-Ursache, die gefühlichste, herzlichste Ursache von dem einigen Jungfräulichen Mann, denn dem ists nicht genug, daß Er als ein Gespenst lieb gehabt wird, sondern Er will lieb gehabt seyn als Bein von unsern Beinen, Er will considerirt seyn, als ein wahrhafter Mensch, als ein Mensch, der schön ist, dessen seine Schönheit nicht in der Mischung der Gesichts-Farben, oder in einer gewißen äußerliche Zärtlichkeit besteht, sondern Er piquirt sich von der wahren Schönheit, die der Geist macht, die das Herz und die inwendige Gnade macht, davon nicht alle Menschen Verstand haben, aber wer Verstand hat, der kan eine Schönheit finden, in einer sonst ganz ungestalteten Person, und kan neben derselben eine berühmte Welt-Schönheit sehen mit der grösten Verachtung und Dedain, wo nicht gar mit einer aversion, die der inwendige Mensch verursacht, dem der alle die hinreißenden löblichen Herz-afficirnden Schönheiten determinirt." (UA R.20.HS47).

women's relations to men. The Saviour wants to be loved as a human being, not just as a spiritual entity. *For a sister, this means to love him as a man – which then becomes the original relation for a sister's relation to all men.*

In our 1758 speech, Zinzendorf again moves from the external to the internal, positing the internal as that to which the text applies:[163] 'the remain [...] surely is meant in relation to your maiden hearts, your choir mind, your chaste mercy, the eternal maiden wreath of your souls, but not in relation to the circumstances in which the present time can be divided'. He thus denies that the text applies to outer circumstances. Of interest here is the division between inner and outer circumstances. While the inner is characterised by connection to the Saviour, the outer is characterised by submission to the Saviour. In the speeches to the sisters, the question of obedience is most often connected with that of *Stand* as we will see in a number of examples in the following.

In a speech to the single sisters from 5 June 1755, Zinzendorf mentions *Stand* several times and explicitly connects it to obedience and submission to the will of the Saviour:

> If you submit yourself to his will, and look at your inward state, at your communion with the Saviour, and know how you stand with Him, and can say with truth: You are His, His wretched, insignificantly small, imperfect, but His and that is enough for you, could you wish to be in a happier *Stand* if you understand Him correctly? Could you leave your *Stand*, except out of obedience, out of resignation [...] Therefore, regard your blessedness highly, for this reason it goes on in this manner in the Herrnhut choirs, that you are true children of God, that you as true maids of God make your bodies an offering to Him, if He calls you from your *Stand*, and does not call you home, because if He calls you home, then your *Stand* does not change, but then that happens when you sacrifice yourselves to Him in marriage, and do not say what I want but what you want, because to be a maiden, if you are a child God is, needs no skills.[164]

---

163   Interestingly, in the single brothers' choir on the same day, Zinzendorf speaks on the previous day's text, which is Jeremiah 31:21 (KJV): 'set thine heart toward the highway [actually, the opened way]' and emphasises that the meaning of the text is straightforward, to which there is an internal and an external application. The internal one is that the individual must find his way if he has lost it, while the external application is a collective sense, where the members will yearn for the reappearance of the Saviour. Single brothers, 3 April 1758 (UA R.20.HS57). In the canonical gospels, the idea of 'preparing a way for the Lord' (from Isaiah 40:3) is voiced as prophecy of Jesus' appearance on earth. See Mark 1:3; Matthew 3:3; Luke 3:4; John 1:23.

164   Single sisters, 4 June 1755: "w[e]nn Ihr euch daß nur seinet willen gefallen laßt, und

The maiden, or *Jungfer-Stand* as it is expressed here, is characterised by submissiveness to the will of the Saviour, an open interconnectedness with him, and simplicity by virtue of being unchanged. When a single sister goes home [i.e. dies], she does not change choir or *Stand*, but simply comes to manifest what has been implied all along, namely her paradisal state. In the speech of 15 June 1755, he notes that they are 'in the privileged *Stand*, since you can easily and unimpeded go to meet your friend and bridegroom'.[165]

A single sister's *Stand* is thus not changed in death (home-calling), but it changes in marriage, be it with a brother on earth, or when she submits herself to the Saviour in marriage. The Saviour can call a sister out of her *Stand* as single into earthly marriage, to which she must obey and enter with resignation.

So, in what does this maiden-*Stand* consist? In the first quote above, it was characterised as submissiveness. In this speech from 17 August 1757, we come a little bit closer to the contents.

> proving your faith to the Saviour does not mean thinking: I will never for the rest of my life leave my choir, I will stay forever in my choir house, I will not let my blessed situation be disturbed in my life. And if a sister really would go so far that she places nothing in change, then she should not afterwards think, now I am complete. Because that can be for 100 reasons, and is, according to my perception no accomplishmen, since s/he who has understood it rightly, would not wish to remain in their *Stand* forever, and not want to leave for the rest of their lives. You must precisely become complete people in this school, you must receive a maidenly character, a maidenly heart, a maidenly *Hütte*, a maidenly mode of thought, a maid-

---

sehet auf Euren inwendigen Zustand auf eure Comunication mit dem Heiland, und wißt wie Ihr mit Ihm steht und kön[n]t mit Wahrheit sagen: Ihr seyd Seine, Seine Elende, Unansehnlich kleinen, Mangelhaftig aber Seine, und das ist genug vor euch, könnt Ihr euch da wol in einem seligeren Stand wünschen wenn Ihr Ihn recht versteht? Könnt Ihr wol aus dem Stande gehen, anders als aus gehorsam [...] Darum achtet eure Seligkeit ja recht hoch, darum geht alle darauf loß, in den Herrnhuthschen Chore, das Ihr wahre Kinder Gottes seyd, das Ihr als wahre Mägde Gottes Ihm eure Leiber zu einem Opfer hingeben mögt, wenn Er euch aus eurem Stande rufft, und euch nicht heimruft, denn wenn Er euch heimruft, so verändert ihr eure Stand nicht, aber als dann geschiechts wenn ihr euch Ihm aufopfert in die Ehe, und sagt nicht was ich will, sondern was du willst, denn Eine Jungfer zu seyn, wenn man ein Kind Gottes ist, das ist keine Kunst" (UA R.20.HS48).

165 Single sisters, 15 June 1755: "Ihr seyd in dem priviligirten Stande, den ihr fein und ungehindert eurem Freunde und Bräutigam entgegen gehen könnt" (UA R.20.HS48).

enly impression, in this your present *Stand*, which endures in all cases, through all times and circumstances and changes and lasts until his arm and lap.[166]

The *Jungfern-Stand* is a disposition in character, heart, body, and will endure through all changes, in that it is something which the individual sister possesses. This is one of the many cases of individual subjectification, where the individual is urged to take on certain traits, and through this, shaped as an individual.

In another example (9 March 1758) where Zinzendorf has been talking about the slow realisation of children as they come to experience the Saviour, he warns them not to imagine that all is well, once they have turned to the Saviour, which is also the point in the above quotation.

But however beautiful they make it, however blissfully everything goes with them, in the little maiden's *Stand*, in the young sister's *Stand* and the rest of her whole life, through to the matron *Stand*, then they are not free, then and now from debasing themselves, as long they cannot say, 'we have Christ's mind', from which we recognise that we remain in him because he has given us from his spirit.[167]

This quotation also mentions the *transitional aspect of Stand*, to which I drew attention above. Indeed, this is one of the most pervasive uses of *Stand*, be it

---

166 Single sisters 17 August 1757: "daß eure gröste Treue, die ihr dem Heiland beweist, nicht darin besteht, daß ihr denckt: ich will mein Lebtage nicht aus meinem Chor gehen, ich will immer in mienem Chor-Hause bleiben, ich will mich mein Lebtage nicht aus meiner seligen Situation verrücken laßen. Und wenns eine Schwester wircklich so weit hat, daß ihr an einer Veränderung gar nichts liegt, so muß sie darnach nur nicht denken: Nun bin ich vollendet. Denn das kan 100 Ursachen haben, und ist nach meiner Erkenntnis gar keine Kunst, denn wers recht verstehet, wer würde sich nicht ewig in seinen Stand zu bleiben wünschen, und sein lebtage nicht wieder Heraus wollen. aber ihr müßt eben *gantze* Leute werden in dieser Schule, ihr müßt einen Jüngfräulichen Character, ein Jungfräulich Herz, ein Jüngfräuliche Hütte, eine Jüngfräuliche Denkweise, eine Jungfräuliche Impression kriegen in deisem eurem ietzigen Stande der allenfalls durch alle Zeiten und Umstände und Veränderungen aushält und fort dauret bis in seinem Arm und Schooß" (UA GN.C.59 1756, 4).

167 Single sisters, 9 March 1758: "Aber wenn sies nun noch so schön machten, wenn alles noch so selig mit ihnen gienge, im kleinen Jungfern Stand, im jungen Schwestern Stande und ihr übriges ganzes Leben durch, bis in den Matronen Stand: so sind sie so lange nicht frey, sich noch als denn zu prostituiren, wenn sie nicht sagen können: *Wir haben Christi Sinn*, daran erkennen wir, daß wir in Ihm bleiben, weil Er uns von *seinem* Geist gegeben hat" (UA R.20.HS60).

THE CHOIR SPEECHES   201

in discussions of resisting change (as above, 17 August 1757) and in our main speech where Zinzendorf says that the sister has nothing to judge but to be obedient, in that 'He is Father and Lord, who can command, whether His child is to married off, or stay on its own'. The change of *Stand*, which in the case of this choir means marriage, is something the Saviour decides, and to which the single sisters must respond with obedience.

> [Before the Saviour appeared on earth] there were no choir communities, or *Stands*-divisions, chapels or sacristies, within which Mary's disposition could be handled as profitable, from which the Saviour probably takes out this one and that one, and urges them into marriage, but their disposition, like all and one, has simply one object, namely, the man who is the necessary bridegroom of the human soul and remains eternal, and admits no other image into her soul if they change their *Stand* according to his will and enter into these for them indisputably unfamiliar circumstances, and must enter into ideas and plans, of which they either do not know how to make a conception, or lost the once-owned notions a long time ago.[168]

This change in *Stand* does not mean a change in disposition, in that the object of their entire lives and thought (i.e. the bridegroom) will remain unchanged.

I have drawn attention to these quotes primarily to show the connection between *Stand* and change, but of course we can also see the intense formative aspect of the discourse, and its emphasis on obedience and submission to the eternal bridegroom as a central feature of the *Jungfer-Stand*. *Stand*, as it is used here in the speeches to the single sisters, is characterised by transition, expressed in both constancy and change, which correspond to two different but related points. Change in *Stand* refers to the relationship with an earthly man: one is either a single sister, married sister, or widow, what in the nineteenth century will be commonly known as *Zivilstand*, marital status. The constancy in *Stand* refers to the Saviour, at two levels. First, as the correct disposition towards him, submissiveness, adoration, full focus of one's life, etc. We could call this

---

168   Single sisters, 17 May 1756: "Aber das waren keine Chor-Gemeinen, oder Stands-abtheilungen, und Capellen, und Sacrysteyen, darinnen der Maria ihr Sinn als Gewinn gehandhabt wird, aus denen der Heiland wol einmal diese und Jene heraus nimmt, und in die Ehe nöthigt, aber derer ihr Sinn, wie aller und jeder, Simplement ein Object hat, neml. den Mann, der der nothwendige Bräut[i]gam der Menschen-Seele ist, und Ewig bleibt, und kein ander Bild in ihre Seele einläßt, wenn sie auch nach Seinem Willen ihren Stand verändern und in diese ihr unstreitig Fremde Umstände hinein gehetn, u in Ideen u Plane entriren muß, davon sie sich entweder keinen concept zu machen weiß, oder die etwa gehabte Notiones lange weider verloren hat" (UA, GN.C.13 1750, 4).

a behavioural relation (the proper *Jungfer*-heart, body and mind). Second, in one's connection with the Saviour, which is fixed through the gender of a sister. This means that the changes which characterised *Stand* in its earthly manifestation is at the spiritual level constant, as in the speech from 9 March 1758, where the women are to realise across all choirs that 'we have Christ's mind'. Again we see *Stand* as both an individual and collective concept. Individual in terms of one's relationship to the earthly man, and collective in terms of the relation to the Saviour.

7.2 Outer and Inner

As the speech demonstrates, there is a difference between the outer and inner nature of a sisters' life. The outer single sisterness is circumstantial, and the inner, in this speech understood as 'maiden hearts', 'choir mind', 'chaste mercy', and 'the eternal maiden wreath of your souls' is essential and eternal. The following example is from one of Zinzendorf's last speeches before his death, given to all the sisters in Herrnhut:

> I think there is little difference in *the point* of purity, obedience, chastity, and manner of thinking, whether you are currently in the maidens' choir, or in marriage, or have come back from marriage, into the *reiterated* maidenhood, into the specially *modified* maiden classes, which one calls the widows. Your souls have little *difference*, they can more or less stay in *status quo*, and always alike in mind to what Jesus' soul was. There may be a *difference* in the operation of the dying bones. By that I do not mean the *difference* of which the *Stand* and external circumstances, the passages in office consist, but rather the operation of one's bones in the close, inseparable *connection* with the soul.[169]

Here Zinzendorf notes that the sisters' souls are all more or less the same no matter which *Stand* they are in, be it maiden, married sister, or widow. The difference in which he is interested here is not the external differences of *Stand*

---

169 All Sisters, 13 March 1760: "Ich denke, es ist wenig Unterschied in puncto der Reinigkeit, Lauterkeit, Keuschheit und Denck-Art, ob sie actuell im Jungfrauen-Chor, oder in der Ehe sind, oder aus der Ehe zurück gekommen, in die reiterirte Jungfrauschaft, in die besonders modificirte Jungfrau'n Classen, die man die Wittwen nennt. Ihre Seele hat wenig Differenz, sie kan ziemlich in Statu quo bleiben und immer desselben gesinnt, was Jesu Seele auch war. Es mag eine Differenz seyn in Bedienung des sterbenden Gebeins. Ich meine damit nicht, die Differenz, die der Stand und äusserliche Umstände, der Amts-Gang an sich selbst macht sondern die Bedienung seines Gebeins in der nahen, unzertrennlichen Connexion mit der Seele" (UA R.20.HS52).

and duties of office, but rather the difference in the relationship between soul and bones. What he means is that there are different disciplinary measures to be taken depending on one's *Stand* as a maiden, which is where you learn how to manage your body, its flows and desires, married sister, where these things have to managed in relation to sexual intercourse and the role of the Husband and the Saviour in this ménage,[170] and finally, widowhood, where these things have to be readjusted in relation to the Saviour alone. We will return to this later, and instead keep our focus on the distinction between inner and outer.

There is also a difference between outer and inner in the speeches to the single brothers. This following quote repeats the connection between the brothers and the Saviour as well as continuing the idea of the inner self introduced in the speech to the children.

> This is my idea of Christ in us, that the inner human who is there and from the child into the whole age grows into Christ, sees the Saviour in person, possesses, speaks and experiences, thoroughly smells of him, is penetrated by Him, and becomes Jesus-like (*Jesushaft*), so that when reason and the powers of the mind (*Gemüth*) are weak, as in sickness or in sleep: the Saviour's internal existence and operation in the inner human exerts an even greater power. When it says: you will have dreams and see visions:[171] then the idea is that your inner human will enter into such a continuous, accurate conversation with me [i.e. the Saviour], that – when they rest from their outward transactions and distractions that occur throughout the day, find a bit of quiet to oneself, their senses quenched, and let hands and feet rest, my operation, which during the day, because of it all, even good undertakings, cannot come to full power – as soon as they get their free run, and they have nothing more to do but give more room and space to the joys and games of grace, the games of the Lord with his human.[172]

---

170 See e.g. married sisters, 27 January 1756 (UA R.20.HS54).

171 An amended version of Joel 2:28: 'Then afterward I will pour out my spirit on all flesh; your sons and your daughters shall prophesy, *your old men shall dream dreams, and your young men shall see visions*'. This quote also appears in the Acts of the Apostles, 2:17 on the day of Pentecost. In this Joel text, God is the speaking subject, which is why Zinzendorf continues in the first person, he is speaking on behalf of the Saviour.

172 Single brothers, 2 July 1755: "Das ist meine Idee von *Christus in uns*, daß der inwendige Mensch der doch da ist und vom Kind an bis ins ganze alter Christi hinein wächset, den Heiland in Person sieht, hat, spricht und erfährt, durchrochen von Ihm, durchgangen und Jesushaft wird, so das wenn der verstandt und die gemüths Kräfte schwach sind, als in Krankheiten oder im Schlaaf: des Heilands inwendiges da seyn und operation in den

The inner human is totally saturated by the Saviour, who thus can exert greater power when the mind is weak or when the body ceases to be preoccupied with things such as work. When a person enjoys some quiet time, withdrawn and meditative, the inner person can indulge in games of grace, in interaction with the Saviour. As with the sisters, also the brothers are subject to the will of the Saviour and obedience in external matters. However, once the inner connection is in place, this is not an issue, as the following quotation illustrates:

> When they have become acquainted with his heart, and become true and whole brothers, and are as similar as possible to His person, that one can think of a single brother without a headache, so it was with the Lamb on earth: thus one thereafter lets Him preside surely over what He wants to do with their choir and every person among them. *Preside, God, wherever one goes*;[173] one in his arm and lap, the other over the sea into a distant lands, the third into marriage, the fourth in the office of his choir externally or internally, and the fifth in a profession (*Beruf*) here or there, as instructed to him.[174]

---

inwendigem Menschen eine desto grössere Macht exerirt. Wenn es heist: Sie sollen träume haben und gesichte sehen: so ist die idee die: Ihr inwendige Mensch in eine solche Continuirliche genaue Conversation mit mir kommen, daß wenn sie von ihren äusserlichen Geschäften und Distractionen, die den Tag über vor kommen, ein bisgen Ruhe kriegen vor sich sind, ihre Sinnen stillen, und Hände und Füsse rasten lassen, meine operation die am Tage durch aller hand ander auch gute geschäfte nicht zur vollen kraft kommen können. Als bald ihrem freyen lauf, und sie weiter nichts zu thun haben, als dem Freuden und gnadespiel, dem spielen des Herrn mit seinem Menschen desto freyere Raum und Platz zu lassen" (UA R.20.HS51).

[173] From hymn 2277, verse 8 in the *Herrnhuter Gesangbuch*. The hymn is called "Nun hör, du Creuz-Luft-Völkelein!" ('Now listen you Cross-air-little-bird') and is one of Zinzendorf's best-known words for the members, which evokes movement.

[174] Single brothers, 2 February 1756: "Wenn sie sich mit seinem Herzen bekannt gemacht, und zu rechten ganzen Brüdern und seiner Person so ähnlich als möglich worden sind, daß einem bey einem ledigen Bruder ohne Kopfbrechen einfallen könne: *so wars Lamm auf Erden*: so läßt man darnach in dem, was Er mit ihrem Chor und jeder Person unter ihnen machen will, Ihn sicher walten. *Walts Gott, whoin man fahre*; der eine in seinen Arm und Schoos, der andre über die See in ferne Lande, der dritte in die Ehe, der 4te in Aemter seines Chors äußerlich oder innerlich und der 5te in sonst einen Beruf, der ihm da und dort angewiesen wird" (UA R.20.HS57). See also single brothers, 20 May 1758: 'For he calls one either in work or in marriage, or in his arm and lap, to the transformation of your entire externally created species, not only to be one spirit with him, but to his undying she. The preparation thereto he understands better than we'; "Denn Er ruft sie entweder in die Arbeit oder in die Ehe, oder in seinen Arm und Schoos, zur Verwandlung ihres ganzen äußerlichen Geschöpfs Art nicht nur zu Einem Geiste mit Ihm, sondern zu seiner unsterblichen Sie; Die zubereitungen dazu zu Versteht Er besser, als wir" (UA R.20.HS50).

The target is, then, to be a true and whole brother, which means to be as similar as possible to the Saviour, so that this or that brother does not cause headache to his superior, but rather acts just as the Lamb (the Saviour) did, when he was on earth. When such a connection has been established, then it is no matter to let the Lamb have his way with the choir and the members of the choir, be it death, missionary, marriage or a profession here in Herrnhut or, say in Niesky. A good example of this is demonstrated in the *Lebenslauf* of Gottlieb Oertel (1714–1767). Oertel was a clothmaker. According to his memoir,[175] he was born in 1714 in Steinkunzerdorf in Silesia, current Poland. After his conversion experience on the way to church service in Berthelsdorf during his second visit in Herrnhut, he was accepted into the community on 16 July 1741.[176] He returned to his hometown where he was released by his landlord. He wrapped up his affairs within four weeks, and left for Herrnhut. In the 26 years of his membership, he established three factories for the Moravian Brethren, but he himself wanted to do something different, more meaningful or innerly (*innerlich*) in contrast to the external business (*äußerliche Dinge*), to which he was being put to use. He eventually came to understand his own wants as sinfulness, but was still a grumpy man when he died.

This discrepancy between his own sense of calling, and the use to which he was being put, follows for the rest of his life, and this is precisely the kind of self-determination which is undesirable in the community. A brother must follow the path the Saviour has set out for him. There is an emphasis in the speeches on the equality between the various offices, be it marriage or evangelisation, that these are all in service of the Saviour:

> All sorts of things are good: for example, the external breakthrough, and undertakings and evangelisation and also marriage can be both for him and for someone else the Saviour's plan for him and a real thing for him.[177]

---

175   UA R.22.109.9 and then also amended and printed in *Nachrichten Aus Der Brüder-Gemeine* (Gnadau: C.E. Genft, 1825), pp. 771–80.

176   A diary entry mentions plans for him and a factory less than a week after his arrival in Herrnhut. UA R.6.A.b.14, 21 August. 'When we have paid Göbel the current debts, then all should be forgiven and he should be an example and warning to others on debt, and be allowed to move to Berthelsdorf. We want to do something similar with the Hantzchens, as soon as he has sold his house, which is propositioned for Brother Oertel and his factory'; "Wenn wir dem Göbel die jetzigen Schulden völlig bezahlt haben, so soll ihm alles gelaßen werden und er soll anderen zum Exempel und zur Warnung, sich vor dergleichen Schulden zu hüten, nach Berthelsdorff ziehen. Und so wollen wirs auch mit Hantzchens machen, so bald er sein Haus verkaufft, welches vor dem ledigen Bruder Oertel und seine Fabric in Voschlage ist".

177   Single brothers, 7 August 1755: "Es sind allerhand dinge gut: Z[um] E[xempel] das äusser-

External breakthrough may refer to the spread of the Moravian Brethren in the world, and the subsequent commercial success.[178] So here, we hear that this success, commercial undertaking, evangelisation, and marriage are all cogs in the machine of the divine plan, and that the Saviour may have this or that plan for this or that person. It is just as important to be married in Neuwied as it is to be building an oil-mill in Bethlehem or sent out as a missionary to Paramaribo. The significant thing is the inner relation to the Saviour:

> Christ must take shape in us, we will become Jesus-like, we will come close to his corpse, we emerge from the atmosphere of the tomb of Christ, all of our undertakings and external activities do not alter anything in the matter, in our heart's foundation.[179]

In fact, one's duties may minimise one's blessed state, because one is so busy with all kinds of things that the inward relation to the Saviour must suffer as a result:

> Of course, many undertakings, internal as well as outward, also make a difference to you. No supervisor [lit. room-overseer] can be as blessed as her other sisters; some of her joy and pleasure, the embrace-sensation, the daily delicate, joyful enjoyment, must be sacrificed in her ministry.[180]

So, leadership is a sacrifice of the pleasures connected to this inner enjoyment of the relation to the Saviour.

The inner/outer issue deals with the members' place within the community, and is, as I will argue, constitutive of the entire community. The choir speeches are a case in point, in that they are conceptualised for the members, and not

---

liche Durchkommen und Geschäfte und Bothschaften und auch das Heirathen kan bey diesem und ienem des Heilands Plan über ihn und eine reale Sache für ihn seyn" (UA R.20.HS51).

178 See a good analysis of the change in perception of the Moravians from 'evil sectarians' to industrious entrepreneurs in Dorfner 2018.

179 Single brothers, 3 November 1750: "Christus muß in uns eine Gestalt gewinnen, wir werden Jesushaft, wir kommen seinem Leichlein nah, wir kommen aus der Atmosphær des Grabes Christi her, alle unsere Geschäfte u äußere Verrichtungen alteriren nichts [geringste] in der Sache, in unseres Herzens Grunde" (UA R.20.HS23).

180 Single sisters, 1 December 1755: "Viele geschäfte, innerliche so wol als äußerliche machen freylich auch bey euch einen Unterschied. Es kan keine Stuben-Aufseherin so selig seyn, als ihre anderen Schwestern, es muß eine jedwede etwas von ihrer Freude und Vergnügen, von der Umarmungs-Sensation, von dem täglichen empfindlichen, frö[h]lichen Genuß, ihrem Amt aufofpern" (UA R.20.HS47).

for the public. The effects of the transgression of this boundary is seen in a choir speech to the married couples' choir in Herrnhut on 9 January 1757, briefly mentioned in Chapter 1, where Zinzendorf spends time deliberating over the damage to the reputation of the Moravian Brethren caused by the publication of a number of speeches given to the married couples' choir. He notes the following:

> Something that has happened and I regard as impossible has not been completely removed from my inner (*Gemüth*). I had not thought that a brother or sister was able to discuss their grace of marriage with outside people. No peasant, no beggar gossips from the marital bed, let alone a brother or a sister. To be sure, one can from spiritual bliss become a fool. But that has not happened, rather what has taken place is the beginning of the Sifting and the biggest carelessness from the world, of which one has not made much. I can also not yet complete the matter, since the spousal-speeches through a person, who had no call to do so, were copied and lost, and were hereafter printed in the world. The possibility does not excuse the affair. Since I cannot imagine – of any reasonable person – that he would seize something to which he had no right or permission, and then keep it so negligently that he would lose it. The benefit of this will be, that I let be printed all of the spousal-speeches that have given, which thus will come out among people, bringing them out among them was not the intention; but now it is necessary in order to protect against the damage, which can come from incorrect things, since whoever has copied this [even sometimes written something entirely different], or, what he has not had, has supplemented from his head. I am saying this, so that you see what it is, the special concerns that I have held back until now.[181]

---

181   Married Couples, 9 January 1757: "Etwas das geschehen ist und ich für unmöglich gehalten ist mir noch nicht ganz removiert aus meinem Gemüth. Ich habe nicht geglaubt, daß ein Bruder oder Schwester capabel wäre von ihrer Ehe-Gnade mit aus wärtigen Leuten bande zu halten. Kein Bauer kein Bettelmann schwäzen aus dem Ehe bette, geschweige ein Bruder oder Schwester. Man kan zwar von Geistlicher freude ein Narr werden. Aber das ists nicht gewesen, sondern es ist der Anfang der Sichtung und der gröste Leichtsinn von der Welt gewesen, aus dem man sich nicht viel gemacht hat. Ich kan auch mit dem Casu noch nicht fertig werden, da die Ehe-Reden durch einen Menschen, der keinen Ruf da zu gehabt, abgeschrieben und verloren und hernach in der Welt gedruckt worden sind. Die Möglichkeit ist keine Entschuldigung der Sache. Denn ich kan mir von keinem verständigen Menschen vorstellen, daß er ein Depositum, das er sich ohne Erlaubniß angemäßet, so liederlich besitzen solte, das ers verlieren könte. Der Nuzen wird draus kommen, daß ich alle Ehe-Reden drucken laße, die ich gehalten habe, und also unter die Menschen kommen wird, was nicht die intention war, unter sie zu bringen; aber nun zu Verhütung des

Zinzendorf is obviously not impressed with this 'someone' who had copied the speeches without permission and then lost them, causing great damage to the community's reputation. The publication of the speeches is only part of a larger matter on the topic of marriage and the relation to outsiders in the speech, the issue being that the spousal ideology of the community had been leaked to the outside, which astounds him, since he had not envisioned that brothers or sisters would maintain bonds with outsiders, let alone gossip about the 'spousal bed', something which not even peasants and beggars do. And finally, he is dismayed by this unauthorised publication, because – according to Zinzendorf – it is full of mistakes and nonsense.[182]

What he is referring to is presumably Johann Gottlob Seidel's 1755 publication, *Haupt-Schlüssel zum Herrnhutischen Ehe-Sacrament* (Master-key to the Moravian Marriage Sacrament),[183] which was a publication of 79 speeches given by Count Zinzendorf to the married couples' choir within the congregations of Herrnhaag, Marienborn and Herrnhut in the late 1740s. Zinzendorf's problem with this publication is twofold. First, that the handwritten choir speeches were never intended for public consumption ('bringing them out among them [the people] was not the intention'), but for internal edification. Second, there is the matter of 'the Sifting'. The quotation above mentions 'the beginning of the Sifting' which generally means a time of tribulation, when the false believers will be sifted from the true believers.[184] There are two other appearances of the term in this speech, however, which relate to a different sifting, one in the past. One speaks of a grace, which could not find its place 'until the Sifting was over', and the second appearance is in a string of challenges, with which Zinzendorf had to deal in the past: 'I was weighed down with the Sifting time, I had the defence of the people on my list, I dealt with the parliament and the nation', etc. These two occurrences of 'Sifting' refer to the period in the late 1740s, which, in spite of the fact that sifting is used for other periods

---

Schadens notwendig ist, der aus falschen dingen kommen kan, da wer so etwas nach geschrieben† oder, was er nicht gehabt, aus seinem Kopf supplirt hat. Ich sage das darum, damit ihr seht, was es ist, das mich von der special Sorge bis her zurück gehalten" (UA HS.20.HS54).

182 See also Spangenberg 1838, p. 444: 'It therefore appeared, and in such a manner that the numerous errors in the manuscript were increased by a multitude of typographical errata, not to speak of the places which the publisher had been unable to read, and where he has made interpolations which were quite unsuitable'. The German original has the interpolations 'make no sense at all'. Spangenberg 1772, vol. 7, p. 2004.
183 Seidel 2000 [1755].
184 The term comes from Luke's gospel, 22:31, where Jesus says to Simon that 'Satan has asked to sift all of you as wheat'.

of trial and tribulation, is known as 'The Sifting Time'. We have already dealt with the detail and intricacies of this time and its significance in Chapter 3, but what is important here is that a major concern of 'The Sifting Time' is *reputation*. To recap, Paul Peucker argues that the Sifting Time was a period in which certain groups within the Moravian Church, led by Zinzendorf's son, Christian Renatus/Christel, declared themselves in a state of perfection and sinlessness, and engaged in extramarital sex.[185] These developments occurred simultaneously with anti-Moravian material circulating and effecting a change in public opinion, and Zinzendorf and his agents seeking recognition for the Moravian Church in Saxony as well as by the British Parliament.

In other words, at the same time as the elector of Saxony in Dresden was deliberating on whether to allow Moravian congregations in his realm or to follow the example of what the electorate of Hannover had done, namely to expel them, and while the British Parliament was deliberating on what was to become the 1749 Act of Parliament,[186] things were getting out of hand in Herrnhaag, where reports of wantonness, indecencies, and licentiousness were emerging. Especially the publication *Revealed Secret*,[187] by the former Moravian Alexander Volck, caused trouble for Zinzendorf's agent negotiating with the electorate in Dresden.[188] Volck's descriptions of the goings-on outside the public eye were not only too close to the truth, but also had an impact on public opinion.

So, to return to Seidel's publication, the speeches in it were from this critical time in the life of the community, but published more than five years later. Thus, they never really endangered the prospects of the Moravians, who by this time had been recognised as desirable, industrious entrepreneurs. Nevertheless, Zinzendorf felt that he had been presented as inarticulate and nonsensical, and more importantly for the present argument, the publication of the speeches made public what was never intended to be so. This distinction between material intended for outsiders and insiders is not limited to the choir speeches. In his publication of Zinzendorf's 'Seventeen Points of Matrimony', a document dated to 1740, Peter Vogt discusses the difference between 'public and non-public modes of Moravian discourse on this sensitive topic [i.e. marriage]'.[189] The article discusses and compares the Seventeen Points and the pub-

---

185   Peucker 2015, Chapter 6, pp. 104–34.
186   Podmore 1998, Chapter 8 and 2007, pp. 43–6.
187   Volck 1748–51.
188   For these events see Peucker 2015, pp. 47–50. For an analysis of Volck's text, see Miller 2014.
189   Vogt 2011, p. 39.

lished 'Manual of Doctrine' from 1742,[190] which is a catechism of Moravian beliefs, in which there is a section on marriage. Vogt's analysis shows that the 'Seventeen Points' expresses the transition from a more traditionally Pietist expression of marriage to the innovative *Ehe-Religion*, which marks the Moravian community from the late 1730s, and indeed is what we find in the choir speeches. Vogt's comparison also shows that the points in the published manual are elaborated through reference to biblical texts, while the 17 points in internal instructions are not, but rather elaborate a position on marriage which includes theology and the everyday practice of being a married couple (intercourse, conception, etc.). Vogt argues that the scriptural framework of the Manual is implicitly expressed in the 'Seventeen Points' and thus emphasises continuity in content, despite difference in form.[191] While this may be so in the case of these two documents, is this a general condition of Moravian communication? In his discussion of Zinzendorf's discourses and addresses, Peucker insists that the handwritten addresses express Zinzendorf's more unconventional ideas about the disappearance of the differences between the sexes and marriage, because these are seen as special revelations, which are not to be shared with outsiders.[192]

This split between internal and external materials, as well as Zinzendorf's efforts with the various governments, should alert us to something distinct about the Moravians, when comparing them with other early radical formations. The concern with reputation is connected with a desire for recognition by the state, to become part of the state, rather than working against it – or the state working against the Moravians. E.P. Thompson already noticed this when he observed that 'the Moravian tradition seems to dilute the antinomian vocabulary; it lacks an "intellectual" or doctrinal anti-intellectualism found in obscurer sects'.[193] The Moravians, then, are not to be understood as quite as anti-establishment and radical as many of the other groups of the time. This will be discussed further in Chapter 6.

---

190 *A Manual of Doctrine: Or, a Second Essay to Bring into the Form of Question and Answer as Well the Fundamental Doctrines, as the Other Scripture Knowledge of the Protestant Congregations Who for 300 Years Past Have Been Called the Brethren* (1742).
191 Vogt 2011, p. 43.
192 Peucker 2015, p. 178.
193 Thompson 1993, p. 57.

8 Widowers' Choir

The main matter of the speech is bereavement.[194] Zinzendorf notes that because 'going home', i.e. dying, is such a central feature of the community (a blessing and a new degree of life), these things are easier to cope with for the Moravians than for others. Zinzendorf refers to the death of Sarah and Abraham's grief from Genesis 23:1–2. Curiously, the following verse from Genesis 23:3, where Abraham rose from beside Sarah's corpse after weeping and mourning, has here been rewritten so that it is a *male* body from which Abraham rises. There is very little doubt that this refers to the Saviour's corpse as the following paragraph makes clearer:

> Because Jesus' corpse is our consistent object, because we keep the order of our marriage *Stand* with the image and have not turned our gaze away from the dug-out hands, we are already so familiarised with the cadaverousness, that what is so odious about death for natural people, disappears for us.

Because of the constant focus on the corpse of Jesus, and even so throughout a marriage, as the basic order of that arrangement, the Moravians are so well acquainted with death, and thus are not repelled by it, as are 'natural people'. In contrast to Abraham, the widowers only need to think of their usefulness within the community, which at this stage in life is reduced to enjoyment, given that they are released from their marital obligations, their children are in the care of the community and the choirs, and they enter into a new *Stand*:

> But with us a new *period* begins, one enters into a new class, and the singular object of each *Stand* is, as often as one enters a new class, modified anew. The widowers, who have risen from their corpses, and have come to terms [lit. given themselves to peace] with the departure of their helpers, throw themselves *a corps perdu* into the Saviour's arms, 'we want to be helpers in your blessed difficulties, until we rest with each other'. The Saviour begins a new *connexion*. Before he was the third man, since two were gathered in his name. After He has taken the one with Him behind the curtain, He is now the second. Before that, one always had to be on guard, that one did not consider Him superfluous, therefore it was not necessary, because one would be otherwise alone and bereft.

---

194 Widowers, 28 August 1755 (UA R.20.HS31).

For the Moravian widowers, a new period begins. With a change in *Stand*, a widower enters into a new class, by which the object changes, or has to be remodified. This is spelled out here, in that as soon as the widower has risen from the corpse of his spouse, he throws himself, body and soul, into the arms of the Saviour, ready to stand by him, until the end comes. The death of a spouse thus means that the widower steps into a new connection with the Saviour, in that the Saviour now can take the place of the second, whereas he was the third wheel when the couple was still a couple. This makes remarrying difficult precisely because of the experience gained in the first marriage and the role of the Saviour within the marriage. The following paragraph explains further:

> For no other than a husband can speak of the intimate cabinet meeting, where two people are brought into the most exact *connexion* by the Saviour, who knows them best among all humans, and are in a way transformed one into the other's soul and body, however, the Saviour knows the means to place himself as the middle-point so that he concentrates *within himself* the tender *connexion*, and through himself only makes it more tender, whole, and sacramental.

The 'cabinet meeting' is Zinzendorf's term for having sex. In his article 'In the Blue Cabinet: Moravians, Marriage, and Sex', Paul Peucker shows through archival sources how the (blue) cabinet is a place where people in a communal dwelling can have private, intimate intercourse.[195] In some sources it refers to a specific room off one of the assembly halls in the Marienborn complex,[196] while in other sources, such as songs and poems, it refers to 'the general term for the place where sexual intercourse takes place'.[197] Zinzendorf is still trying to explain the precise relation between a married couple and the Saviour, and what role he assumes within a marriage as well as intercourse. So, the Saviour, who knows them both best, connects them with each other, whereby they somehow are transformed into each other in a two-become-one scenario. However, the Saviour knows the means (*Mittel*) of embodying the 'connexion' between the two, and therefore can make it more tender and sacramental. It is very interesting how the Saviour inserts himself as the mediator between the two, in that this is one of the chief functions of Zinzendorf's Saviour as we have

---

195 Peucker 2011a, pp. 19–24.
196 The manor at Marienborn in the Wetterau was leased by the Moravians from 1738–79. Peucker 2000, p. 39.
197 Peucker 2011a, pp. 20 and 23.

seen in several examples above. I will pull this together in the conclusion to the chapter and am just drawing attention to it here.

Zinzendorf closes the speech by stating that being a widower is a degree, by which he means a station in the life of a Moravian Christian. This role, as with all roles in the community, is one within which one grows and comes to understand the particulars of one's *Stand*, and whatever connection with the Saviour that is appropriate to this *Stand*. If one is not able to capitalise upon these privileges, then he must be lacking.

8.1 *Relating to the Saviour*

Earlier in this chapter I referred to the speech to the widowers from 7 August 1755, where Zinzendorf claimed that childhood, youth, marriage and widowhood had their specific covenant with the Saviour due to the incarnation in which the Saviour 'took on our nature and invented his behaviour as a human and experienced the particulars of every rank (*Stand*)'.[198] Now it is time to look at how the Saviour has experienced widowhood: 'First, he has seen himself as alone and left by his people, "He looked down from heaven on humankind, there was not one, who thought of God, who sought him, not even one, they had all fallen away, they had all neglected their marriage-right"'.[199]

This neglect of their marriage-right refers back to the cosmic wedding theme between the Saviour and the congregation. We thus see not only a rewriting of the psalm which places Jesus in the subject position, thus taking the place of God, but also inserting the specific Moravian theme of marriage between the Saviour and his people to argue for the Saviour's status as a widow. However, the Saviour is not only such a half-widower (*halber Witwer*), but became a real widower when death came over Adam and Eve, and God's spirit returned to

---

198 Widowers, 7 August 1755: "der unser Natur angenommen u an Geberden als ein Mensch erfunden und eines jedem Standes sein Particulare erfahren hat" (UA R.20.HS31).

199 Widowers, 7 August 1755: "Er hat sich allein und von seinem Volck verlaßen gesehen ,Er sahe vom Himmel auf die Menschen Kinder, da war nicht ein einiger, der an Gott dachte, und nach Ihm fragte, auch nicht einer, sie waren alle abgefallen, sie hatten alle ihre Ehe-Recht verwahrloset'" (UA R.20.HS31). This is an adaptation of Psalm 53:2–3 or 14:2–3: 'God looks down from heaven on humankind to see if there are any who are wise, who seek after God. They have all fallen away, they are all alike perverse; there is no one who does good, no, not one', albeit with two significant modifications. Instead of God as the one who looks down from heaven, Zinzendorf inserts a 'he', which refers to Jesus. This is consistent with Zinzendorf's Christocentric theology, which regards Christ as the Covenant-God, the Creator-God, the Father and the Son. Atwood 2004, pp. 77–85. The other modification is to connect this to marriage.

him. The bride was dead and the Saviour was *"revera Witwer"* – albeit one who has since remarried his people.[200]

So, following this argument, the Saviour has indeed experienced every (male) *Stand*, and the brothers of the community can seek a new connection which he establishes in each *Stand*, as the member transitions from one *Stand* to another. We saw this above, where Zinzendorf notes that the object of every *Stand* is modified from the beginning and that the Saviour begins a new connection.[201]

Apart from the Saviour's experience of widowhood, the primary concern of the *Stand* is, according to Zinzendorf, managing the sexual experience gained in the married *Stand*, as we see in this excerpt which urges the deactivation of the member and this experience:

> therefore, he must take great care that this memory does not degenerate into a useless, hence damaging memory, because it is outside his calling; rather that the members, which in the single brothers *Stand*, gradually died off, which however through the marriage calling from the Saviour Himself again was set to a certain activity and revived, with the widowers through a new mercy and degree, completely rectified through an anointing and cure taken from the humanisation of Jesus, whereby they can again be locked away […].[202]

The interpellation of the widowers as single brothers, then, is a way of producing chaste widowers albeit with privileged knowledge.[203] This knowledge

---

200 This could possibly be a reference to 3 Enoch 5, and the separation of the Shechina from Adam and its return to God – supported by Zinzendorf's moderate use of Shechina as God's spirit in several choir speeches from the period. See e.g. married couples, 4 March 1758 (GN.C.78.1758.2); single sisters, 9 March 1758. (GN.C.78.1758.2); and married couples, 6 March 1760 (UA R.20.HS 54). Thanks to James Harding for the reference to 3 Enoch. A similar logic behind the Saviour's experience of the widower *Stand* is presented in the speech to the widows from 18 March 1756 (UA R.20.HS 46).

201 See also the mention of a new covenant with his heart in the new *Stand* in widowers, 13 September 1755 (UA R.20.HS31).

202 Widowers, 25 March 1756: "Darum muß er desto genauer auf sich acht geben, daß dieses Andencken nicht degenerire in ein unnützes und darum schädliches Andencken, weils außer Beruf ist, sondern daß die Glieder, die im ledigen Brüder Stande nach und nach absterben, die aber durch den Ehe-Beruf vom Heiland selbst wieder in eine gewiße activitæt gesetzt worden, und reviviscieren, beym Witwer durch eine neue Gnade und Grad, durch eine aus der Mensch-werdung Jesu hergenommenen Salbung und Cur gänzlich rectificirt werden, damit sie wieder können verschloßen werden" (UA R.20.HS31).

203 See e.g. widowers, 5 June 1755 (UA R.20.HS31) and 29 April 1756 (UA R.20.HS31).

makes the difference between their *Stand* as widowers and that of the single brothers, in that the single brothers do not quite understand the concept of marriage, when their hearts are being prepared thereto, while the widowers have the experience of the *Ehestand*.[204] While Zinzendorf does not want this knowledge to be used for unsavoury thoughts, he also doesn't want it to be forgotten:

> I wish that you walk your course not without making room for return and reflexion. I do not give this advice to the widows, whom I usually counsel that they should forget as much as possible of their previous *Stand* and perhaps have a feast once a year where they remember the servant of the Lord who led them, but apart from that, they should forget that they ever were in other circumstances than what they are now. With you it is different. You have been officiants and have held active worship.[205]

By active worship, Zinzendorf means sexual intercourse. In another widowers' speech from 1 December 1755, Zinzendorf explains that the man is unchanged because he has not had a liturgy enacted *on* him, as the sister has, therefore a widower is unchanged after marriage, while a widow is not.[206] We should also note the difference from the widows' speeches, in in that in the

---

204 Widowers, 25 March 1744 (UA R.20.HS1).
205 Widowers, 29 April 1756: "Ich wünsche, daß ihr euren Gang gehet nicht ohne Retour und Reflexion zurücke. Den Witwen geb ich den Rath nicht, denen pflege ich zu rathen, sie sollen so viel möglich ihren vorigen Stand vergeßen und vielleicht des Jahrs einmal einen Festtag halten, da sie sich an den Knecht des Herrn erinnern, der sie geführt hat, aber außerdem sollen sie vergeßen, daß sie jemals in anderen Umständen gewesen, als sie nun sind. Mit euch ists anders. Ihr seyd Liturgi gewesen und habt active Gottesdienst gehalten" (UA R.20.HS31).

See also widowers, 10 November 1755, where the merits of the current *Stand* are described as waiting for the bridegroom with burning lamps (UA R.20.HS31).

206 Widowers, 1 December 1755: 'that is the difference between you and the sisters, who *hoc respectu* have not become again what they were, the brothers however are entirely back in status quo, because liturgy was not carried out on them, rather they have carried such one out; which is to be made clear in the difference between anyone who is appointed to the office, passive, and the one who appoints, active; between the ordinatore and the ordinato, the Consecratore and the consecrated person etc.'; "Das ist der Unterschied zwischen ihnen und den Schwestern, die hoc respectu nicht wieder werden, was sie waren; die Brüder aber sind völlig wieder in statu quo, weil nicht an ihnen Liturgie verrichtet worden, sondern sie solche verrichtet haben: Welches klar zu machen ist mit dem Unterschied zwischen einen jeden, der in ein Amt gesezt wird passive, und dem der einsezt, active; zwischen dem Ordinatore und dem Ordinato, dem Consecratore und der consecrirten Person" (UA R.20.HS31).

present choir, Zinzendorf does *not* counsel them to forget as much as possible, but rather to cultivate it towards and understanding of their union with the Saviour.

The question of remarriage turns up in these speeches as well, and Zinzendorf explains that if a widower wants to remarry without the Saviour calling him thereto, or without one's outer circumstances compelling him thereto, then it is inappropriate and lusting against Christ (*Geil werden wider Christum*). Zinzendorf notes that it is possible for a widower to be incomplete in his former *Stand*, and not really grasping the correct concept of marriage, which leads to an inability to fully appreciate the blessedness of the choir and the house.[207]

Such an abuse of the *Ehestand* is discussed in the speech from 17 July 1755, where Zinzendorf notes that a marriage in which the Saviour is not put above all is less preferable than the *Stand* of the widows and widowers:

> It [i.e. the separation from the spouse] is, however, nothing against the alarm and obsession of the mind, when one still lives in such a marriage, where one is not on both sides conscious that one lives for the bridegroom alone, and that between him and us comes nothing. Such a married *Stand*, where one is conscious of the slightest obstacle from the other, is much more unpleasant and muddy than the widowers' and widows' *Stand*. I would soon bring forth the subsequent confession from several members in your choir whom I know, if they do not desist out of modesty.[208]

This last sentence gives us a hint of one of the functions of the choir, to discuss one's spiritual state in the realm of the choir, in this case using examples from one's own marriage to understand the correct and incorrect ways of the

---

207 Widowers, 5 June 1755 (UA R.20.HS31). Another discussion of remarriage is in 23 August 1755, where the widower must consider a number of things, whether he wants to take oneself to the new covenant belonging to his present stand, or according to the Saviour's mind, accept another legation. This does not concern those who were recently called into the widows' rank and who appreciate the attention to their own souls, but rather the brothers, who have come to realise that there is a blessing in the marriage (UA R.20.HS31).
    See also widowers, 22 September 1755 (UA R.20.HS31) and 3 January 1760 (UA R.20.HS52).
208 Widowers, 17 July 1755: "Es ist aber doch nichts gegen der Beängstigung und Besezung des Gemüths, wenn man noch in einer solchen Ehe lebt, da man nicht auf beyden Seiten gewiß ist, daß man dem Bräutigam alleine lebt, und daß zwischen Ihn und uns nichts kommt. Ein solcher Ehestand, da man sich der allergeringsten Hinderung von einander bewußt ist, ist viel unangenehmer und trüber, als der Witwer- und Witwen-Stand. Das Nach-Bekenntniß wolte ich von etliche Geschwistern in eurem Chor, die ich kenne, bald heraus bringen, wenn sies nicht aus modestie unterließen" (UA R.20.HS31).

union. However, while Zinzendorf knows that there are members whose marriages could be useful in pointing out the 'don'ts' of marriage, it seems that the members are free to refrain from sharing.

This self-examination is important both at a personal level and at a choir level:

> But we have it so good in the community, that we can organise our access to him according to the church divisions and *Ständen*, within which we find ourselves. Therefore, it is a necessary part to be acquainted with one's *Stand*, know who one is, to what end one has been pardoned by him. According to the ordinary course of our community places, a widower is a single brother returned home, a youngling who has been released from his office, whether he was in the choir or not. He is, if God married him, called out from his single *Stand* and became the superior of another person, it has been tried with him for a while in a ministry and liturgy, and after his release from his office, he is yet again what he was before.[209]

Stand is thus a means of organising access to the Saviour within the community, and thus includes its own coherence and connection. Getting acquainted with the purpose of one's *Stand* and one's role in the larger scheme of things is a necessary part of life in the community, and demands self-reflection and examination:

> He who has found for himself mercy and peace, and is a child of god and a compeer of Jesus' corpse, from him the Saviour will then also demand choir sense and choir faith, and what he demands, he has already given, so that I believe, that the least true brother among you, who holds a true heart for his choir, unfailingly knows more of the *Stande* and was is fitting, the good and blissful therein, than what I in an entire week can conceive.[210]

---

209 Widowers, 1 December 1755: "Aber wir habens in der Gemeine so gut, da wir unsere Zugang zu Ihm auch nach den Kirchen-Divisionen und Ständen, darin wir uns befinden, einrichten können. Daher ists ein nothwendiges Stück, seinen Stand kennen, wißen, wer man ist, wozu man von Ihm begnadigt ist. Nach dem ordinariren Gang unsere Gemein-Orte ist ein Witwer ein zu Haus gekommener lediger Bruder, ein von seinem Amt dimittirter Jüngling, er sey in dem Chor gewesen oder nicht. Er ist, wenn ihn Gott verheyrathet hat, aus seinem ledigen Stand heraus gerufen und einer andere Person vorgesezt gewesen, es ist mit ihm probirt worden eine Zeitlang in einem Dienst und Liturgie, und nach seiner Dimission von seinen Amt ist er wieder was er zuvor war" (UA R.20.HS31).

210 Widowers, 17 July 1755: "Wer aber für sich Gnade und Friede gefunden und ein Kind

Finally, the correct aim of a widower is to reach a certain state of mind, where the former and latter experiences converge, which is called the 'patriarchal *Jünglings*-point' where the maiden-like *Stand* in the marriage and the experience of latter come together:

> when one in the marriage seeks to maintain one's maiden *Stand*, to follow the lamb where it goes, when you bring the experience to the previous principles, then emerges such a blessed, complete patriarchal *Jünglings*-point, which he could not have had in the previous time. For this reason, I do not want that you, when it with the new *Jünglings*-point could be at its highest, forget the historical circumstances of your previous *Stand*, and neglect the thoughts, on what you have become, what has been placed upon you, what mercy and priestly office has been administered through yourselves.[211]

This sedimentation of experience and inner connection with the Lamb is an important part of all brothers and sisters in Herrnhut as the choir speeches have shown. The individual member sees him- or herself in their present *Stand*, and understands its purpose within a larger scheme, but is also encouraged to remember, or carry with oneself, the previous experiences, which means that one (ideally) gains a fuller understanding of the parts within a community and how they all come together. The individual has a place within the choir and the community as a whole and can move safely therein. In a world where everything was groaning and transition and flux would soon be commonplace, choir life was a good preparation.

Gottes und Genoße des Leichnams Jesus ist, von dem fordert der Heiland dann auch Chor-Verstand und Chor-Treue, und was er fordert, das hat Er erst gegeben, so daß ich glaube, daß der geringste wahre Bruder unter euch, der ein treues Herz für sein Chor hat, von dem Stande und was das Prepon, das gute und selige darin ist, unfelhbar mehr davon weiß, als ich in einer ganzen Woche ausdenken kan" (UA R.20.HS31).

211 Widowers, 31 July 1755: "wenn man in der Ehe seinen Jungfräulichen Stand bewahren will, dem Lamm nach zu folgen, wo es hingeht, wenn ihr *die* Erfahrung zu den vorigen principiis bringt, so wird ein solcher seliger, ganzer Patriarchalischer Jünglings-punkt daraus, als er in der vorigen Zeit nicht hat seyn können. Ich wolte darum nicht, daß ihr, wenns mit dem neuen Jünglings-punkt aufs allerhöchste kommen wäre, die Historischen Umstände eures vorigen Standes vergäßet, und den Gedanken, was ihr gewesen, was auf euch gelegen hat, was vor Gnade und Priester-Amt durch euch verwaltet worden, negligirtet" (UA R.20.HS31).

8.2 Transition

As we have seen in several examples, the choir speeches deal with the concept of transition in various ways. Indeed, one of the chief functions of the choir structure in my interpretation is mediating transition. The choir speeches articulate transition at a microlevel which serves not only to prepare the brothers and sisters for transitory life, but also to articulate transition as such. Again, we need to bear in mind that feudalism in general was not given to transition and flux, in that the feudal social structure was based on fixed ranks and a stationary life. Given the free subject status of the members in Herrnhut, the outward conditions for breaking with this form of life were given. The internal shaping of this new mindset, I argue, took place in the choirs, and through the speeches. Again, this is carried out with the Saviour as the mediating, transitional figure, against which the progression of members through life are measured and determined. In other words, the relation to the Saviour becomes a way of mediating the transition between the choirs.

As we have seen in the case of the male members of the community, the men relate to the Saviour through identification. The physical likeness to the Saviour's human manifestation is fundamental. The Saviour also provides the men of Herrnhut with a moral example and shows them how to act. Recall how Zinzendorf stated in one of the earliest speeches, how when a child steps into the '*Stand* of boys' he must relate to 'the boy Jesus' and is regarded as carrying Jesus' name, and thus must live up to a certain moral standing. In the speech to the boys' choir I analysed, Zinzendorf points out that when a child enters the boys' choir in Herrnhut, he is entering a serious *Stand*, where the boy can take comfort in the fact that he is now the age Jesus was, when he appeared as a boy, with reference to Luke's Gospel. One of the reasons for the exceptional status of the *Stand* of the single brothers and their favoured position in the eyes of God, lies in the fact that the Saviour himself was a single brother.

For the married men, the relation moves to a different level. For while they are still men and as such can mirror themselves in the manhood of the Saviour, the Saviour himself did never marry:

> I am exempt from the small detail, says the Saviour, but I have had to regard the whole human race for four thousand years as an adulteress; I have led a difficult marriage, and still lead it, learn my disposition and principles, think about your sisters, as I do about the whole human race *a priori* and *posteriori*, then you will find that you have a gentler yoke and a lighter burden than me. So, there is a profoundness in the matter that the Saviour has not stepped in our *Stand*, and was able to marry *one* person,

because He is the bridegroom of *all* human persons *ad unam omnium*, and thus not willing to make differences among them.[212]

Zinzendorf, speaking on behalf of the Saviour, explains that the reason that the Saviour has not entered into the physical married *Stand* is because that would reduce him to being connected with only one person, when in fact he is the bridegroom of all. The Saviour has led a difficult marriage with the adulterous human race and encourages them – thus Zinzendorf – to learn his mind and his principles, and that men should think about their wives as the Saviour thinks about the whole human race.

At one and the same time, this excerpt says that the Saviour did not marry and yet leads a difficult marriage. Zinzendorf has to deal with the self-imposed challenge that the Saviour died a single brother, yet is someone who all men in their different *Stände* can relate to, which creates an issue in respect of the married men and the widowers. This is where the Christian heritage of Zinzendorf comes in handy in undergirding the institution of marriage with the more abstract bridal mysticism that regards the Saviour as eternal bridegroom, and in that way sets an example for the *Stand* of the married men and the widowers. I will have much more to say on marriage in the following chapter.

So, just to repeat, we see that generally men relate to the Saviour through likeness, whereas the women primarily relate through marriage. This is expressed in the following quote from a widows' speech given in August 1755:

> A child who holds the Saviour dear, a girl who is the Saviour's, a maiden who knows the Saviour, a woman who has experienced something from/ of the Saviour: these are all gradations; the happy soul steps towards the happy wedding. And the walk into *the* chamber, into *the* antechamber, into the next antechamber before his chamber, where He is, where the throne of marriage is: That is the widows' *Stand*.[213]

---

212 Married men, 8 December 1756: "Von dem kleinen detail bin ich dispensirt, sagt der Heiland, aber ich habe das ganze Menschliche Geschlecht 4000 Jahre als eine Ehebrecherin an mir zu consideriren gehabt, ich habe einen schweren Ehe-Stand geführt, und führe ihn noch, lernt meinen Sinn und Principia, denkt über eure Schwestern, wie ich übers ganze Menschliche Geschlecht a priori und posteriori denke, so werdt ihr finden, daß ihr ein sanfters Joch und eine leichtere Last habt, als ich. Es stekt also eine Teife in der Sache, daß der Heiland darum nicht hat in unsern Stand treten, und sich mit *einer* Menschlichen Person vermählen können, weil Er *aller* Menschlichen Personen, ad unam omnium, ihr Bräutigam ist, und einigen Unterschied unter ihnen zu machen nicht willens hat" (UA R.4.CII.12).

213 Widows, 16 August 1755: "Ein Kind, das den Heiland lieb hat, ein Mädgen, die des Heilands

Both of these quotations deal with the question of the various stages in the lives of men and women, stages which constitute the choirs in the community. The differing stages in a man's life are regarded as analogous to the developments of the Saviour as a human male, while the stages of the woman's life are mapped out according to how intimately acquainted she is with the Saviour. Thus, behind the statement on the [married] woman (*Frau*) having experienced something of the Saviour, and the happy soul stepping towards the blessed wedding lie Zinzendorf's notion of the 'Procurator-marriage', touched upon in Chapter 3. So, women and widows will both, through their experience of sexual intercourse, know of the Saviour in ways that girls and maidens do not. While the life of a male member of the community progresses *as* Jesus, that of the female member is divided into her relationships *with* Jesus, which mature and become sexualised the older she becomes, and are all steps on the way to final copulation with Jesus, with the widow's rank being the penultimate step of this progression.

The transitional aspect of the choir and *Stand* which shines through in the talk about passing through one *Stand* to the other, and the experiences a widow takes with her in her transition, are also mentioned in the speech to the widows from 22 September 1755. Zinzendorf states that theirs is

> a completed *Stand*, you stand after it, you have it front of you. You can go through one after the other and think them through, and the take into account the state of soul and *Hütte* to the different times, and know how have understood the thank worthiness and suffering of the Saviour in each and every one of these *Stände*.[214]

---

ist, eine Jungfrau, die den Heiland kennt, eine Frau, die was vom Heiland erfahren hat: das sind alles gradationen: bis zur frohen Hochzeit schreitet eine Seel. Und das Gehen in *die* Kammer, in *das* Vorgemach, in das nächste Vorgemach vor seiner Kammer, wo Er ist, wo der Ehethron ist: das ist der Witwenstand" (UA R.20.HS46).

214 Widows, 22 September 1755: "Es ist ein vollendeter Stand: ihr steht dahinter, ihr habts vor euch. Ihr könnt eins nach dem andern durchgehen und durchdenken und die Beschaffenheit der Seele und der Hütte zu den differenten Zeiten dazu nehmen, und wissen, wie ihr in einem jeden von diesen Ständen des Heialnds Verdienstlichkeit und Leiden verstanden habt" (UA R.20.HS46). See also the speech to the widows, 23 August 1755, where Zinzendorf talks sbout their choir ribbons, white with blue stripes, 'to remind you of your previous married *Stand*, partly without the selfsame to the ones, which as of now, suitably forget all, because they place their weidding day in front of their eyes'; "Das *weisse* Band ist euch gegeben, theils mit dem blauen Streifgen, zur Erinnerung des vorigen Ehestandes; theils ohne dasselbe denjenigen, die nunmehr billig alles vergessen, weil sie ihren Hochzeittag vor ihre Augen zu setzen, keinen Anstand mehr haben" (UA R.20.HS46). Also, widows,

What he means, I think, is that this is the last *Stand* in the human existence, and that as a widow, one can think through all of the previous *Stände*, and the varying relationships of body and soul, but that the one central point is understanding the precise role of the Saviour in each *Stand*. Thus, the widow knows everything, and knows what lies ahead.

What all of these movements between *Stand* and choir cultivate is a more general openness towards transition. Both at an individual level, as well as within the larger plan and purpose.

9 Widows' Choir

In the speeches to the widows' choir, Zinzendorf often has to wrestle with the less than flattering portrayal of the widows in the biblical texts as well as older understandings of widows.[215]

In the selected speech,[216] Zinzendorf argues that the bad social standing of the widows was because the doctrine of the marriage to the Saviour was not known. This doctrine means that the widows are the highest class within the four classes of women, which apart from the married women also includes the girls, maidens, and widows. To the already mentioned ideas of the widows' choir as the crown of all choirs, and their protection by the Saviour, is added the idea that they are the reconstituted maiden choir – a very common widow trope in Zinzendorf's speeches. With the death of her spouse, the widow is presented to the Saviour as 'his maiden' presumably upon entering the choir. When the Saviour does his thing among the choirs, the widows are honoured and shown respect. It is on this respect and honour that the congregation must build, i.e. that the place of the widows must be understood in the larger whole, and to this, rests a significant task by the widows, to make themselves *Hochwürdigen*, to be regarded with great esteem. This all requires that they are 'real widows' which is a reference to 1 Timothy 5, where Timothy is told to distinguish between real widows who are faithful and devoted, and younger widows who only think of remarriage and gossip.[217]

---

29 August 1755 emphasises the other side of marriage, childbirth and knowledge of intimacy with the Saviour as reasons for demonstrating a certain vivacity in their *Stand* (UA R.20.HS46).

215 In the present speech, Zinzendorf first mentions the understanding of a widow as a person on the outer side of a life already lived. Then, Zinzendorf refers to the idea of the grass-widow, in its older usage designating a woman with a child out of marriage, followed by a number of stories from the Hebrew Bible.

216 Widows, 15 July 1755 (UA, R.20.HS.46).

217 1 Timothy 5:5–6, 'The real widow, left alone, has set her hope on God and continues in sup-

To be a child of God, a sister, and a choir sister: that is not the same thing; these are two different issues. The latter is what one calls the choir point. Married members, who recently came into marriage from the single choirs, wrote me that they still hold firmly on to their choir point. This is incorrectly spoken, as they understand it. Of course, one does not relinquish the blissful and obedient heart, which one acquires in his choir, when one comes into another *Stand*. But that is not the choir point; that is the issue of all the children of God. Rather, that everyone is content in his *Stand*, and is so blissful about the self-same division, that it constitutes the bliss of life; this is the choir point. When one, against one's will, conscience and thinking, is placed in another *Stand* by the Saviour, and it directly affects a Sister who is strengthened in grace, then the loss of her previous *Stand* can only be experienced as painful.

There is a difference between being a child of God and a choir sister. Being a child of God means having a blissful and obedient heart through all *Stände*. There are some who confuse this with the choir point, such as the married members who wrote to Zinzendorf. The choir point means that one submits to and takes seriously the division and adapts herself in whatever *Stand* she is placed in, in complete accordance with its logic, and finds bliss therein. He realises that some sisters, who have settled into a choir, and are suddenly thrown into new circumstances where they have to start over might find this difficult because all the conditions are now different. While the transitions into other choirs would always have been if not expected, then at least carefully prepared, the transition into the widows' choir is more serendipitous. The rest of the speech concerns the transition.

> The choir point of a single cannot be the choir point of a widow. If a widow thinks maritally, she is disturbed in the head; if a wife thinks unmarried, then she is, to use Paul's expression, corrupted in her mind;[218] if a wife would like to become a widow, then judging her favourably, she is also disturbed in this point. To this belongs a sacred guidance, to this belongs the Saviour's utterance, the fact that the Saviour removes the man, and He

---

plications and prayers night and day; but the widow who lives for pleasure is dead even while she lives'. This text is discussed in widows, 20 June 1755 (UA R.20.HS46), to which he is probably referring, see also choir speech widows, 28 April 1756 (UA R.20.HS46).

218 2 Corinthians 11:3. Paul is talking about other preachers encroaching on his territory: 'But I fear lest by any means, as the serpent beguiled Eve through his subtilty, so your minds should be corrupted from the simplicity that is in Christ'.

embraces his released one as returning to his special care, into his hand. Only then does a sister understand the choir point, and receives thoughts that she should not, nor could have had a few days earlier. So, to see oneself as a renewed maiden of the Lamb, that is where it concerns you.

Because the choir points relate to specific choirs, they cannot be the same for the various choirs. The choir points indicate different ways of relating to the Saviour, and a single sister, who has not had sexual intercourse, cannot see herself in relation to the Saviour in the way a widow can. All of these examples of taking over the wrong choir point is regarded as wrong and disturbed. To ensure that they stay in the right mind and that their lives correspond to their respective choir points, they need the guidance of the Saviour, which consists in: 1. his utterance (a bible verse, perhaps the one we have already discussed, the claiming of a people as his property); 2. that the widow understands that the Saviour has taken the husband; and 3. that the widow understands that in doing so, the Saviour claims the sister as returning to his care. When this is grasped, then the widow can see herself from the choir point of view and may begin to think about her new stage in life on its own conditions. So, for a widow, the task is to 'see oneself as a renewed maiden of the Lamb'.

So, all of the women in the widows' choir have moved from maiden to married woman to widow, be it in the world (outside the community) through disorder,[219] or through the community. Whatever circumstances they come from, they are now back in the hands of the Saviour. Now he addresses the choir regarding the new members, who have arrived in the widows' choir, received a choir sign (perhaps the coloured ribbon,[220] indicating the new *Stand*) and have now come to live with the choir, and will get to know what the *Stand* is through living in the house. She will (i.e. should) seek to understand the difference of this *Stand* from the former one, and also try to gauge the stage of blessedness of

---

219 I am not sure what this means. Perhaps Christiane Eleonora Voigt is (1705–1780), mentioned in Chapter 3, is an example of what is in mind: In 1742, after 11 years in Herrnhut, her husband decides to move to Nieder-Rennersdorf because of animosity against the community. The following year he then moved to Berthelsdorf. In the 1742 diary, on 8 October, however, it is noted that he was expelled. His wife was not expelled, but encouraged to go with him, which she does, very reluctantly. After his death six years later, she is welcomed back with open arms, and moves back the day after being granted permission. She is a widow, but the path taken was somewhat disorderly.

220 All sisters had ribbons on their caps indicating their marital status. Peucker 2000, p. 18. The widows' ribbon was white with blue stripes, blue being the colour of the married sisters, and thus retaining the memory of the previous *Stand* in the present one. See Zinzendorf's discussion in widows, 23 August 1755, mentioned above. See also Uttendörfer 1926, p. 264.

her fellow choir sisters by their accounts. She will then learn to discern the 'holy without bloodstreaks' from the Mary Magdalen-ish holies, who are repentant sinners and the ones whose example one should follow, seating herself at the feet of the Saviour and remembering with shame the times when the husband's needs were placed ahead of those of the Saviour. This is an understanding that can only come after the transition.

9.1 Relating to the Saviour

A common topic in the widows' speeches is in respect to *Stand* and concerns their release from the covenant of the married women, and their return to the single sisters' choir where they constitute the most noble class. Their marriage is characterised as an 'an interim time', 'a parenthesis', which represented the future, or even proleptically grasped what was to come in the marriage covenant with the Saviour. Released from their former *Stand*, they have returned to a free *Stand*, and now pursue the Saviour along with the other maidens:[221]

> You have passed through the married *Stand*, and [are] now again maidens, choir maidens of the Lamb. This idea is connected with another. You see, when you have become warm in your choir, and have spent 50 nights in your dormitory or otherwise, but still in the widows' grace, as His restored maidens in his arm and lap, then firstly it must be incredibly well for you, second, the experience, which you have had in the *Zwischenstand* (middle *Stand*) in various ways, has made you a notably distinguished persons among His people.[222]

There are, however, two additions to the *Stand* of a widow from that of the maiden, which is expounded in a summary of a speech given on 30 June 1755. First, 'the blessedness of the sacristy [intercourse], which she has usefully experienced in marriage, and the traces of mercy which she has received from

---

221 Especially widows, 5 November 1747 (GN.C.2.1747.6), see also widows, 6 June 1755 (UA R.20.HS46) for this understanding of the widows as restored maidens, brought back into the *Stand* from which the Saviour took them.

222 Widows, 19 May 1758: "Ihr seyd durch den Ehestand passirt, und nun wieder Jungfrauen, Chor-Jungfrauen des Lammes. Diese Idee ist mit einer andern verknüpft. Wenn ihr nemlich in eurem Chore warm worden seyd, und habt auf eurem Schlaaf-saal, oder sonsten, aber doch in der Wittwen Gnade 50 Nächte, als seine restituirte Mägde in Jesu Arm und Schoos verbracht, so muß euch dabey vors erste erstaunlich wohl worden seyn, vors andere mach euch die Erfahrung, die ihr in dem Zwischen-Stand auf verschiedene Art gehabt, du besonders ausgezeichneten Personen unter seinem Volk" (GN.C.80.1758.4).

conceiving, bearing, and raising children'.²²³ Second is that for a widow, relations with the sisters is not enough, because she now desires a more intimate conference with the Saviour defined as 'Enochic relations' and 'cabinet relations'. These do not consist of many words, and can take place in a corner or in the chamber of one's heart. As already discussed above in the section on the widowers, the cabinet relation refers to intercourse with one's husband, who in the case of the widows, is the Saviour. If that is not possible because one cannot find a quiet corner for this purpose, then there is the possibility of an Enochic relation. In consideration of the apocalyptic nature of the material attributed to Enoch in the apocryphal tradition,²²⁴ it is perhaps not unreasonable to see the concept of an Enochic relation as corresponding to closing oneself in the chamber of one's heart and enjoying a more revelatory, visionary experience of one's Saviour.²²⁵

There are a couple of speeches with a very surprising twist. On 25 March, the Feast of the Annunciation, Zinzendorf talks about Mary, which, given the occasion, is not totally surprising. However, he speaks of Mary as being part of the *Stand* of the widow:

> There is hardly a widow's *Stand* that has passed with such deep yet sinful, yet gracious reflection, as with the mother of the Lord, when she had reflected upon that she, when He lived in her body, became the first temple of god, the cathedral of all human *Hütten*, and, as often as her pulse beat His life, even every drop of sweat steamed the forgiveness of sins.²²⁶

---

223 Widows, 30 June 1755: "daß der Name einer *Witwe*, der von den vorigen Umständen herrühre, da die Krone von ihrem Haupte gefallen, eine Standes Erhöhung, und eine Restitution, dem Namen und Stande nach, in ihr voriges Jungfrauen Recht mit sich bringe: Zu dieser Gnade kommen noch ein Zusatz, nemlich die Sacristey-Seligkeiten, die sie in der Ehe mit Nutzen erfahren haben, und die Gnadenspuren, die sie vom Kinder-Empfangen, tragen und Erziehen bekommen haben, und nicht von ihnen genommen werden" (UA R.20.HS46).

224 Enoch appears in the genealogy in Genesis 5 as the son of Jared. He lived 365 years, and then, 'Enoch walked with God; then he was no more, because God took him' (Genesis 5:24). This enigmatic sentence has been taken to mean that Enoch did not die, but entered heaven alive, and thus was in a position to testify to the truths of heaven. The figure of Enoch has thus given a name to a series of early Jewish and Christian apocalyptic and visionary writings, which claim to be revelations to Enoch.

225 Thanks to Kristian Mejrup and Søren Holst for discussions which helped clarify this point.

226 Widows, 25 March 1756: "Es ist wol kein Witwenstand mit solcher tiefen obwol sünderhaften, doch anmuthigen Reflexion vorbey gegangen, als bey der Mutter des Herrn, wenn sie sich besonnen hat, daß sie, da Er in ihrem Leibe wohnte, der erste Tempel Gottes, die

This connection between Mary, Jesus, and widowhood is taken up again in May 1756, where Zinzendorf explains:

> If, however, only one person may have shared in this grace, and only one in her widowhood has been able to pride herself on that she was predestined to be a mother, there still is, always and properly so, an impression of this widow in your choir. For she was in your choir, and was recommended as your choir sister by the dying Saviour to the disciple. She has begun your choir in Christendom, and has been followed by a lot of her equals. We do not know much about her marriage, but of her brief maiden days and her widow *Stand*, Scripture has kept for us the most solid and complete, how she had been among the apostles, and when revelations of the Son of Man took place among them, certainly she experienced them. Hers is certainly the guise in whom He has redeemed her and the whole human race, and which she has been able to regard so closely, (for she has been there) ever remaining, until her own departure. Now the figure shall also stay with you until your mouth pales in His arm and lap.[227]

What was hinted at on 25 March is taken further here, namely that the death of Jesus left Mary a widow. This was in fact ordered by him as he was dying on the cross, when he gave her over to the disciple.[228] What is surprising is less

---

Cathedral aller menschlichen Hütten gewesen, und so oft ihr Puls Sein Leben geschlagen, zugleich jeder Schweißtropf Vergebung der Sünden geraucht hat" (UA R.20.HS46).

227 Widows, 21 May 1756: "Ob nun wol dieser Gnade nur eine Person theilhaftig worden, und nur Eine sich in ihrem Witwenstande hat rühmen können, daß sie auserkohren worden, Mutter zu seyn: so ist doch noch immer, und billig, ein Eindruck von dieser Witwe bey eurem Chor. Denn sie ist in eurem Chor gewesen, und als eure Chorschwester von dem sterbenden Heilande an den Jünger empfohlen worden. Sie hat den Anfang eures Chors in der Christenheit gemacht, und ist von einer Menge ihres gleichen nachgefolget worden. Von ihrem Ehestande wissen wir nicht viel: aber von ihrer kurzen jungfräulichen Zeit und ihrem Witwenstande hat uns die heilige Schrift das solideste und ganzeste aufbehalten, wie sie unter den Aposteln mitten drunter gewesen, und wenn unter ihren Offenbarungen des Menschensohnes vorgekommen sind, gewiß auch was davon erfahren hat. Ihr ist gewiß die Gestalt, darin Er sie und das ganze menschliche Geschlecht erlöst hat, und die sie so nahe hat betrachten können (denn sie ist dabey gewesen) immer geblieben, bis zu ihrem eigenem Heimgang. Nun die Gestalt soll euch auch bleiben, bis eure Mund erblasset in seinem Arm und Schoos" (UA R.20.HS46).

228 This is a reference to John 19:25–27 (NRV): 'Meanwhile, standing near the cross of Jesus were his mother, and his mother's sister, Mary the wife of Clopas, and Mary Magdalene. When Jesus saw his mother and the disciple whom he loved standing beside her, he said to his mother, "Woman, here is your son". Then he said to the disciple, "Here is your mother". And from that hour the disciple took her into his own home'. Naturally, there is no men-

the fact that Zinzendorf is claiming that this was the admittance of Mary into the widow's choir, or that we know of her widow *Stand*. What is surprising is that her widowhood is connected with the death of Jesus, and not her husband. What does this entail for the widows of Herrnhut? On the one hand, Zinzendorf uses Mary as an identifier for the female choirs. Not constantly, but fairly frequently. This makes sense in the single sisters' choir, where the lowly maiden accepts the will of the Saviour, and for married women she is the paradigm of motherhood. In that sense it is not unusual for Zinzendorf to try and press Mary into a mould for widows to follow. However, it is also interesting because of the implications for men. With such a reading, all men become Jesus, and we see how this understanding is implemented in the women's speeches. Indeed, this is also a common feature throughout the choir speeches as we will see in the next chapter on subjectification and marriage, but here it is presented in an oblique manner, with the implications only gradually sinking in.

9.2   *Choir*

Choirs for Zinzendorf are primarily relations, which he expresses frequently in the speeches: the correct relations with the Saviour, with each other, and with the other choirs. After working our way through all of these choir speeches, we may now appreciate the extent to which the whole choir idea is tied to the figure of the Saviour and how fundamental the gendered subjectification practice is to this structure. As such, the choirs are what Hull called a sexual system, namely 'the patterned ways in which sexual behaviour is shaped and given meaning through institutions'.[229] The reason I have placed such an emphasis on the choirs is that we have to analyse Moravian Christianity in its institutions in order to understand its specific social relations,[230] which are presented as relations of gender. These gendered relations were transported into settings even where choirs were not the main institution, as was the case in most missions.

Both *Stand* and choir refer to gender. But where *Stand* indicates the position within the order (individually and collectively), choir is the order itself. As indicated in Chapter 3, this sexual system emphasises gender as the significant common feature, as a feature of unity. Importantly, however, the understand-

---

tion of either widows or choirs, but Zinzendorf's interpretations of the biblical texts are nothing if not original. And this would not be the first time that someone has read their contemporary situation into the biblical past.

229   Hull 1996, p. 1.
230   One of Marx's criticisms of Feuerbach is that the latter abstracts religious essence from its institutions, and human essence from its relations. See Rosenberg 2011, p. 5 and endnote 7 on page 186.

ing of gender was not a given. What we see in these speeches is a move from an understanding of man and woman as people with various roles to play in society, to a much more self-reflective, and pervasive understanding of oneself *as a man or a woman*. What we see here is the process of *gendering*. With the reduction of *Stand* to that of sexual system, the process of gendering is both individual and collective.

The near constant evocation of the body motif serves the dialectic between individual and collective, as demonstrated in this quotation on the collective nature of the single men's choir:

> To this [end] the houses must first become one man, and the heart, disposition, idea and the natural capacity of each be inserted into the whole, in the *spiritum generalem*, in the spirit of its choir, and then the Lord will build the blessing and life above it. When the brothers dwell so harmoniously together, one spirit with Him and having become one soul among themselves, then, even if afterwards the limbs seem torn like a catoptric body and one hardly knows where to bring eyes, hands, legs together, so they are before Him the one man, He who filled the ground with fruit.[231]

This excerpt explains the ideal of the choir spirit: the single brothers must become a collective body in will and thought in order to imagine (lit. place before oneself) Jesus as the one man. A significant function of this staging of Jesus' body in front of the congregation, is to make visible how the members are to negotiate their own bodies and members. In another speech, Zinzendorf declares:

> And when we have the true disposition of the soul, then it is biblical and not fantastic to say: I have placed the Lord in front of my eyes [...] This is thus the real character of a choir: that it in its choir form places the Saviour thus in front of its eyes, as though it really lived with Him, walked around with him, promenaded, walked out and in, ate and drank, let alone that at

---

231   This quote is taken from single brothers, 3 March 1758: "Dazu muß erst der Hausen ein Mann werden und Herz, Gemüt, Idee und die natürliche Kapazität eines jeden sich ins Ganze, in den spiritum generalem, ins Genie seines Chors hineinzufügen, und dann gebeut der Herr dem Segen und Leben über ihm ganz besonders. Wenn die Brüder so einträchtig beisammen wohnen, ein Geist mit ihm und eine Seele unter sich worden, und wenn auch hernach die Glieder zerrissen scheinen wie ein katoptrischer Körper, da man kaum weiss, wo man die Augen, Hände, Beine zusammenfinden soll, so sind sie doch vor ihm der einige Mann, der den Erdboden mit Früchten erfüllet" (UA R.20.HS50). Also quoted in Uttendörfer 1926, p. 260.

the time of the Saviour only 12 or 13 people had the good fortune and nowa-days all brothers and sisters have the [occasion] at certain times and hours to eat Him and partake in His corpse, not only eat *with* Him, rather that whoever eateth me, says the Saviour, he shall live for my sake.[232]

As these examples show, the choirs are at the same time sites of unification and individualisation. Since all members, brothers and sisters, were instructed to see themselves in relation to the Saviour, it is necessary to emphasise the Saviour as a mediating figure for the individual. Every single member had to think about, understand, and articulate his or her personal and physical relation to the Saviour, and share this understanding with their choirs. The members woke up with the Saviour, worked with him, ate, breathed, slept, and died with him. The great and unusual emphasis which Zinzendorf placed on the Saviour's humanity meant that for the Moravians the Saviour could empathise with all of these earthly things, because he had lived through them himself. The Saviour, in Zinzendorf's understanding, sanctified the earthly and human existence of all Moravian Brethren.[233]

As has been pointed out multiple times, the emphasis on the Saviour's humanity as the basic order of the choir system generated a necessary gendering of the members. The idea of growing up with the Saviour, the notion that the choir enables the Saviour to appear in front of the eyes of its members, and attaining corpse-like disposition are features that only appear in the speeches to the brothers. The sisters, on the other hand, are instructed to relate to the Saviour as women to a man: either as mother or wife. Thus, the ongoing gendering takes place in specific relation to the Saviour. The choir speeches thus forge the gendered individual, the individual choir and through these, the entire congregation, all with a significantly christological hammer.

As we saw in the choir speech to the widows, there is a difference between being a child of God and a choir sister. Being a child of God is what, in the section on the single sisters' choir, we related to the inner person, the level of constancy. In the speech to the widows, this was characterised as having a bliss-

---

232   Single brothers, 15 April 1748: "[...] da es biblich und nicht phantastisch ist, zu sagen: Ich hab mir den Herre vor die Augen gestellt [...]". "Das ist also der eigentliche Character eines Chors das sich den Heiland in seiner Chor-Gestalt so vor die Augen stellt, als wenns wirklich mit ihm lebte, herumginge, wandelte, aus und eininge, äße und trünke, zu geschweigen, daß zur Zeit des Heilands nur 12 13 Personen das Glück hatten, und heut zu Tage habens alle Geschwister] daß sie zu gewißen Zeiten und Stunden ihn eßen und seines Leichnams theilhaftig werden, nicht nur *mit* ihm eßen, sondern, Wer mich ißet, sagt der Heiland, der wird leben um meinet willen" (UA R.20.HS35).
233   See also Atwood 1997.

ful and obedient heart which would remain through all *Stände*. The choir point, on the other hand, is relative to one's *Stand* and requires that one lives one's life in the choir point of one's *Stand* and choir. To this end, they need the guidance of the Saviour, and the help of the choir workers and sisters and brothers.

For us, living in socio-economic conditions of which the splitting of a person into a private and public individual is a constituent feature, such a division of a person is perhaps not particularly noteworthy. However, bearing in mind that self-reflection and its associated agonies of soul was a ruling class privilege, and most people were focused on surviving and creating conditions of survival for their children, this was not a common feature of the ruled classes in feudal society. Seeing with inner eyes, cultivating an inner consciousness, and thinking about what it actually means to be an individual man or woman, and how one may engage with one's body as a separate entity are all features of early modernity and the fledgling separation of inner and outer selves.

In Herrnhut, the outer institutions which framed this understanding were the choirs, and to these corresponded the revamped notion of *Stand*, which was used in the following ways:

- as a transitional concept, which encompasses the earthly level, while constancy is guaranteed by inner connection to the Saviour;
- as an individualising concept, which defines one's position in the social order, cultivated from early on;
- as a collective concept, in that it relates to the order of the community, as the social position within the various choirs of which one is a part and into which one may enter.

Stand, as used by Zinzendorf, is tied to choir, the gendered social order, and used almost exclusively in the choir speeches in reference to this order. In contrast, when Luther spoke of *Stand*, e.g. 'the three estates of chastity: the widow-*Stand*, the married *Stand*, and the maiden-*Stand*',[234] it was framed within an understanding of society as a *Ständesordnung* with a fixed order of social class, namely within an understanding of a society that was divided into three estates, the so-called *Drei-Stände-Ordnung*. This order divided society into clergy (*Lehrstand* – teaching estate, and often *geistliche Stand*, spiritual Stand), ruling class (*Wehrstand* – weaponed estate, i.e. the aristocracy) and peasants and townspeople (*Nährstand* – nourishing estate).[235] Luther's use of

---

234 "die drey stende der keuscheyt, nemlich den wydwinstand, den ehlichen stand und den jungfrauenstand" from his sermon on 1 Corintians 7 (1523), W 12, p. 103.

235 See for example Luther's *Weihnachtspostille* from 1522 (W 10 I 1), where he uses *Stand* mostly as an indicator of an outward order of society, and several times to denote the rank of maiden, marriage, and widow.

Witwen Stand and *Jungfern Stand* were thus embedded in a larger social order of *Stand*, within which it was not possible to move freely. As Hull notes, in a different context, 'Like noble, bourgeois, peasant, and clergy, the category married/unmarried/widowed formed an axis along which every inhabitant found his or her proper place, an axis neatly dividing the prescribed from the proscribed'.[236]

As we saw in the speeches, Zinzendorf's use of *Stand* is understood within the choir order, meaning that there is an element of mobility and transition in the Herrnhut social order. It was possible to go from *Jungfern-Stand* to a married woman, and from there to the widow's *Stand*. This was also the case with Luther. However, as mentioned above, the social order and the sexual system were separated in Luther's context, which meant that the transition was only within the sexual system, whereas in Herrnhut and its collapse of sexual and social system, they were one and the same, so that a transition in the sexual system was a social transition. But it also means that, to some extent, the *ständisch* society, albeit with significant moderation, was retained in a smaller setting. The implications of this will be followed up in Chapter 6.

10   Conclusion

As mentioned in the first chapter, I have worked through these speeches by reading and transcribing them. Through this labour-intensive process, I have drawn out a number of concrete topics, which have then been used to reread the speeches and on which my analysis is based. While I have been focused on the development of the individual's relation to the Saviour, and how this relation generated an inner and outer person, I have also wanted to emphasise the particulars of each choir, in that this is where unity was produced – a unity which ultimately relied on gender and is most notably expressed in the use of the terms choir and *Stand*. Unification refers to the suppression and redirection of class struggle, and the expulsion of thoughts and practices which are not in line with the emerging trajectory. While the speeches serve to consolidate the winning position, and thus do not as such express the struggle directly, I have suggested in the previous chapters that the emergence of the choirs was the key to the struggles.

The present chapter, then, has worked with the assumptions with which the last chapter finished. The present chapter is an important element of the

---

236   Hull 1996, p. 77.

overall argument which insists that the choir ideology can be understood as a response to socio-economic struggles, and presented a solution so ingenious that it anticipated the solutions offered by civil or bourgeois society years later. This means that while the choir speeches in one sense are expressions of a situation when the 'real business' is over, they are also part of what Lukács calls the 'ideological preparation of the bourgeois-democratic revolution'.[237] Thus the parameters for the struggles were set by the early 1740s, but the struggles themselves continued – to which the speeches testify.

Producing unity, of course, does not mean that opposition disappears. As Marx and Engels point out in *The Communist Manifesto*, to which we will return, the emergence of bourgeois society did not mean an end to social antagonism; it merely meant a different way of ordering groups within society and managing social relations. Consequently, the dissolution of the logic behind the feudal social order meant that social relations had to be reconfigured and redirected in a new and meaningful way, in other words in a way so as to best minimise discord and secure the appearance of stability. As economic, philosophical, and theological debates of the time show, this task is not unique to the Moravian Brethren. However, because they are a small group and present us with a concrete attempt at resolving the contradictions which emerge at the time, they are an ideal case study to examine not only the recalibration of social relations between collective and individual, but indeed the resignification of the terms and conditions of collective and individual. Examining how the choir speeches express both unification and individualisation is an important contribution to our understanding of how bourgeois society and its alienated citizens were crafted.

This is not to say that the Moravian communities were perfected bourgeois societies before such a thing existed. But they did encounter and dealt with the same contradictions of the emerging state structure, and their solutions display, if in embryonic form, some of the solutions that would be characteristic of this new social formation. The Moravian communities of the eighteenth century thus enact the transition between two modes of production in a way that astutely anticipates the requirements of the modern world, while providing some sort of communal and material support system for those about to leave the old.

237 Lukács 1968, p. 42.

CHAPTER 5

Marriage and Community

As we saw in the last chapter, marriage as a symbolic relationship held a privileged place in the choir system as a whole. The notion of 'mystical marriage' was the unity from which the choirs gained their respective roles and placed them into relation with the Saviour, thus forging an overall purpose in which all choirs participated. However, as we saw in Chapter 3, the marriage document which recorded the 'speakings' with the marriage choir revealed the difficulty in implementing the *mystery of marriage* among the married couples in Hermhut. Many of the couples found this somewhat bizarre and were not completely convinced of the applicability of such a teaching in their marriages. The document demonstrated how the leadership derided the resistant members as too simple and coarse to appreciate the sophistication of this doctrinal innovation, but whether we take the point of view of the leaders or the members, what appears is the problem between idea and implementation.

This chapter is based on the assumption that marriage has a specific configuration and purpose which is connected to its socio-economic context. Marriage was a continuation of former household practices and would outlive, in a different shape, the choirs, and continue into the developing socio-economic structure. As already mentioned in Chapter 3, Karl Kautsky argues that the household form and its system of family relationships is relative to the system of production of which it is a part.[1] And so the Moravian experimentation with new family relations in the transition between feudalism and capitalism is hardly surprising, nor exclusive to the Moravians as also indicated in Chapter 3.

Here, we begin with a more general overview of Zinzendorf and marriage, which has been a topic of scholarly interest since the earliest twentieth century and move on to looking at some of the problems in the implementation of marriage in a community with a strong collective focus.

1 Zinzendorf's Idea of Marriage

In the choir speeches, and in many other texts as well, Zinzendorf developed a theology of marriage in the course of the 1740s, which has been the focus

---

1 Kautsky 1910 [1892], p. 26.

of much scholarly attention.[2] This theology of marriage intended to unite the community by assigning everyone a place in the cosmic copulation between Christ and his church. At the spiritual or theological level, his ideas of marriage were coherent. The problem however, turned up at the level of practice, namely, how to relate these ideas to choir life. This side of the matrimonial equation has not attracted the same level of analysis,[3] partly due to availability of sources, but perhaps also due to the colourful and distracting nature of the symbolic level which covers up the contradictions.

'Bridal mysticism',[4] 'marital theology',[5] 'mystical marriage',[6] and 'procurator marriage'[7] are all concepts which refer to the imagery or symbolism of marriage, the central feature of which is the eschatological event of the copulation between the bride, i.e. the community/church with its heavenly bridegroom, the Saviour. A central feature in this event was the transformation of earthly men into their original state as sisters in the hereafter whereby they would join the collective of the bride of the Lamb, something which is regularly presented in the choir speeches, as we saw in the previous chapter. This copulation between the eternal bridegroom and his bride is copied and enacted in marriages between men and women in the Moravian Brethren, where the man represents the Saviour and the woman represents the church, a configuration of the earthly marriage known as the 'procurator marriage':

> that everything the members do and think, do and think in God, and when they say something to each other, especially the brothers to the sisters, the latter should be able to think and assume as though our Lord Jesus Christ Himself was engaging with them, and the brothers, when they hear their sisters' mind, can feel the spirit of the church: towards this we are aiming, and are not quite there yet.[8]

---

2 Beyreuther 1975 [1963]; Tanner 1952.
3 But see Paul Peucker's work on the events in Herrnhaag during the Sifting Time, which addresses the consequences of a literal interpretation of bridal mysticism. Peucker 2006; 2011b; 2015. Peucker also notes the need for looking at practice in 2011a, p. 14. See also the resistance to the new ideas in Petterson and Faull 2017.
4 Peucker 2011b.
5 Faull 2011; Vogt 2011.
6 Atwood 2011; Peucker 2015.
7 Petterson 2014.
8 Married couples, 20 May 1758: "daß die Geschwister alles was sie thun und denken in Gott thun und dencken, und wenn sie einander was sagen, sonderlich die Brüder den Schwestern, leztere denken und es so annehmen können als handelte unser Herr Jesus Christ mit ihnen selber, und die Brüder, wenn sie ihrer Schwestern Sinn hören, den Geist der Kirche fühlen können: Daran machen wir noch immer, und ist noch nicht ganz" (UA R.20.HS54).

Here Zinzendorf is explaining how a brother and a sister may think of each other in a marriage. The man must act towards the woman as would Jesus, and the woman must regard her husband's dealings with her, as were he Christ himself. In a different speech, he notes that

> God is the original and we are depicted thereafter, in the beloved God and his revelation lies the original wherefrom we are badly produced copies. Thus also with the Saviour's eternal marriage with the soul, the true original of all marriages and of which our marriages are a copy [...][9]

The importance of this scenario lies less in its importance for the married couple as such, and more in its function to include all the members, married and unmarried into its orbit. Because the single members did make up a substantial part of the community.

In his article on homosexuality, mysticism and Moravian brothers in the 1750s, Paul Peucker draws attention to the minutes from a meeting between Zinzendorf and two of his co-workers known from Chapter 3: Johann Nitschmann (the former leader of the married couples' choir) and Carl Heinrich von Peistel (Zinzendorf's brother in arms). Here it is apparent that the leadership realised that not all members were suitable for marriage. Zinzendorf noted:

> One should by all means examine the brothers if they are capable of wedlock before one unites them in marriage, because when a dear sister would get a brother who is unsuitable for the sacramental act of matrimony and who is not capable of having carnal knowledge of his wife, then this would make an unpleasant marriage, although our sisters are beyond the flesh and do not marry for such reasons. A sister would think, 'I might just as well have remained single as living a celibate life within marriage'. For intercourse is an essential part of marriage, and no brothers and sisters should be given in marriage who are not capable of that.[10]

---

9   Married couples, 4 August 1748: "Gott ists original und wir seyn darnach Gebildet, in dem lieben Gott und seiner offenbahrung liegt das original wovon wir schlecht gerathene Copien sind. Und also liegt auch in des Heylands seiner ewigen Ehe mit der Seele, das wahre original aller Ehen und unsere Ehen sind eine Copie davon [...]" (UA R.20.HS55).

10 Johann Nitschmann Jr. [1712–83], UA R.21.A.115.b: "Mann solte die Brüder allemal erst untersuchen, ob sie zur Ehe im Stande wären, ehe man sie verheyerathete, denn wenn eine liebe Schwester hernach einen Bruder kriegte, der zur sacramentischen Handlung der Ehe untüchtig und nicht im Stande seine Frau ehelich zu erkennen, so mache daß, obgleich unsere Schwestern über das Fleisch weg und aus keinen solchen Ursachen heyerathen, eine unangenehme Ehe. Eine Schwester dencke: ich hätte eben so wohl ledig

Peucker argues that Zinzendorf is referring to couples who do not have sex, because the husband [or wife – given the last sentence] is incapable of or disinterested in sexual intercourse.[11]

A sad case is the example we find in the *Lebenslauf* of Rosina Nitschmann, born Schindler.[12] It is based on Zinzendorf's remarks about her spoken on a Remembrance day of the dead on 12 December 1753. After praising her dedication to his family and her hard-working nature, he says,

> She was, however, a bad spouse, and never showed the proper respect and love towards her husband. The reason was, that it was one of the Bertheldorfian marriages, where they married by themselves, without the community. Therefore, she did not know whether she rather should have remained single. This futile sorrow, when one is already married with three children, she could have spared herself and could have been as a wife towards her husband if her heart didn't have to break constantly over this, but rather rejoice.[13]

This echoes the sentiment in the previous quote, namely that if they had been married according to community principles, both would have undergone examination as to whether or not they were suitable for marriage, and this whole heartbreak could have been avoided. As it was, they married, and the marriage was not a good one – even though Zinzendorf later notes that she did make an effort sometimes.

Another interesting point in Rosina Nitschmann's *Lebenslauf* is the 'Bertheldorfian' marriage, which, it seems, indicates that this is a marriage which the couple themselves decided. David Nitschmann (Bishop) and Rosina Schindler

---

bleiben können, als ehlose in der Ehe leben. Denn die Vereinigung sey ein wesentliches Stück der Ehe und es solten keine Geschwister verheyerathet werden, die darzu nicht im Stande wären". Quoted and translated in Peucker 2006, p. 43. See also speech to married couples, 20 May 1758: 'it is certain that many sisters and many brothers must not marry' (GN.C.80.1758.4).

11 Peucker 2006, p. 44.
12 Rosina Nitschmann was the first wife of David Nitschmann, the bishop. He remarried the following year in Pennsylvania after Rosina's death.
13 "Aber sie war eine schlechte Ehefrau, und hat gegen ihren Mann niemals den gehörigen Respect und Liebe bezeugt. Der Grund war, weils eine von den Berthelsdorfischen Heirathen war, die sich selbst verheirathet, ohne die Gemeine. Daher war sie ungewiß, ob sie nicht hätte sollen ledig bleiben. Diese unnütze Sorge, wenn man schon verheiratet ist und 3 Kinder hat, hätte sie sich ersparen und gegen ihren Mann als eine Frau sein können, darüber sich sein Herz nicht so oft hätte brechen sondern erfreuen müssen". (UA NB.I.R.4.291.C.2.30).

were married in 1726 in the very early years of the community. Another couple married in that year and of their 'own will' is David Nitschmann (Syndicus) and Anna Helene Anders, a marriage to which we return below. In his points, or description of early Herrnhut, Zinzendorf notes that Nitschmann approached him and requested a suggestion for a helper, and Zinzendorf suggested Anna Helene. Later, it is noted that they were engaged, but no lot is mentioned. When exactly the lot began to be used for selection of marriage partners is not known, but not at this early stage.[14]

The lot-practice, which consisted in asking the Saviour for an answer by drawing or throwing lots with the options yes, no, or blank was used to decide many issues ranging from the names of places, to marriage partners. This meant that coupling was arranged marriages, with the leadership presenting a pool of options (say five single sisters from which one is to marry the single brother who is now destined for missionary work in St. Thomas, for example) between which the lot is cast. Thus, the brother and sister did not know each other and had to be helped in matters of marriage, such as sex, co-habitation, child-rearing and so on. On the surface, the only thing they would have had in common from day one was their service to the Saviour, be it setting up a new factory in Gnadenfrei, going to Bethlehem to bolster the married couples' choir there, or travelling as missionaries to Paramaribo, but the leader of the choirs did take pains to match couples, not only with eye to the future plans for them, but also with each other. Nevertheless, massaging two persons into a married unit would have taken some work, and inevitably meant a focus on the couple, as we will see.

Matrimony, then, was not a must in the Moravian Brethren, the significance of which in the mid-eighteenth century we should not overlook. It offered people the possibility to live unmarried by offering a livelihood independent of marriage.[15] Unmarried brothers or sisters could easily find a role in the con-

---

14   However, Paul Peucker drew my attention to a letter from Zinzendorf to his wife Erdmuth from 1723. While on the road to attend the coronation of Charles VI in Prague, Zinzendorf and Friedrich von Watteville are discussing Watteville's future marriage partner. Watteville was supposed to (and did) marry 'Hannchen' or Johanna von Zezschwitz, but they started drawing lots and Zinzendorf writes, 'But now we have just drawn a piece of paper and he has twice pulled the Joh[anne?] of Hennersdorf; which will give him other ideas. If he could get her and has faith enough, because she has nothing, it would be fine. She should be a dear sister to me and the Z[ezschwitz?] would be spared many circumstances'. However, Zinzendorf still thought that Zezschwitz was the right person and he asked his wife to carefully ask her if she was interested. Zinzendorf an Erdmuth Dorothea Reuss, 'Quell' in Tschechien 16 September 1723 (UA R.20.B.22.b.206). I thank Paul for sharing this reference with me.

15   In his analysis of the transitions between the household of the agricultural communit-

gregation,[16] which is testified by the numerous autobiographies left behind by unmarried brothers and sisters.

But for this to work, a larger structure of unity had to be forged, and this relied on the idea of marriage between Christ and his church as found in several New Testament writings.[17]

2 The Problem

In a nutshell, the relation between the Moravian theology of marriage and the choir structure is problematic. The difficulties are less due to recalcitrant members as discussed in Chapter 3, but rather that a contradiction emerges between the understanding of a choir as a collective and a married couple as a unit. However, the background to these problems run much deeper, which should not surprise us given the nature of marriage as a social institution.

To set the scene, we will look at three comparisons which serve to define the precise nature of the marriage in Moravian understanding. They are between worldly marriage and Moravian marriage, early Herrnhut and later Herrnhut, and finally, other radical Pietist movements and Herrnhut.

2.1 *Three Comparisons*
2.1.1 Worldly Marriage and Moravian Marriage

In the earliest extant speech to the married couples' choir, held on 20 October 1747,[18] Zinzendorf deliberates on the difference between marriage in the Moravian community and outside. The particular nature of marriage in the Moravian Brethren is defined as follows:

---

ies and the bourgeois family and the shifts in understandings of gender, historian Marion Gray shows the significance of marriage and household practice in pre-capitalist social formations (Gray 2000).

16 Married sisters, 25 December 1755: 'Therefore (because of the sanctity and importance of marriage) it is a big deal for a single sister to know whether she should enter into this liturgy, whether her soul and *Hütte* is served with the liturgy and care, which is called marriage, or whether she in her singleness can arrive at exactly the same grace'. "Darum ists eine große Sache für eine ledige Schwester zu wißen ob sie in diese Liturgie eingehen soll, ob ihre Seel und Hütte mit der Liturgie und Pflege gedient ist, die man die *Ehe* nennt, oder ob sie in ihrer Ledigkeit zu eben der Gnade kommen kan" (UA R.20.HS54).

17 See this argument unfolded in more detail in Petterson 2015.

18 UA R.4.CII.12: With few revisions, this is identical to the speech from 26 October 1747 (UA R.20.HS55).

> In the marriage matter, less reflection should henceforth be given to the begetting of children etc. than on the similarity which a man in his marriage has with the head of the community, and that which a wife in the marriage has with His [i.e. the Saviour's] community.[19]

The quotation states that emphasis should now be on the married man's likeness to the head of the community [i.e. the Saviour], and the married woman's likeness to the community. This is, to repeat, the mystical marriage, the marriage between the Saviour and his church, which is here reproduced in the marriage between a man and a woman in the community. The contrast between begetting children as the main point of marriage over against the deeper understanding of marriage is more fully expounded in a speech from 11 December 1750. Zinzendorf begins:

> There is nothing more difficult in the world than to treat people, who are not made for mysteries, with material in which mysteries flow.[20]

Mysteries are not for everyone and must be revealed, and Zinzendorf uses this as an entry point into the understanding of marriage. If, he says, a human being is convinced that procreation is the most venerable and serious deed that the human being is capable of, then there is no longer any mystery. This idea, that procreation is the most important thing in a human's life is very common, but Zinzendorf says that a marriage cannot be reduced to this. Instead:

> with every look we give one another, as often as we touch each other, we become close, really see each other, speak with each other, think about each other, and are always counted to be introduced to the mystery with the same humble knowledge and feeling of our happiness, that the Saviour has given us to understand the matter of a man with his wife, to know that image of the church must appear against him as his against a wife, must appear between both, constantly constitute the subject of the whole mystery of the Saviour and His daughter the church, so that her domestic doings, their daily discourses, their sweet nightly

---

19   Married couples, 20 October 1747: "es soll in der Ehesache nicht mehr so vohl reflectirt werden aufs Kinderzeugen etc. als auf die ähnlichkeit, die ein Mann in seiner Ehe mit dem Haupte der gemeime und die eine Frau in der Ehe mit seiner gemeine hat" (UA R.4.CII.12).
20   Married Couples, 11 December 1750: "Es ist nicht schwerers in der Welt, als den selben Materien die in die Geheimniße laufen, mit Leuten zu tractiren die zu Gehemnißen nicht gemacht sind" (UA R.4.C.II.12).

sacristies, their sleep temples, their marital doings, their marriage liturgies are always governed by the same influences, that of the head in His members, in His body, that the man be proportionally powerful, and his wife proportionately blessed in the Saviour and in His companionship, so that when married brethren are seen acting in the Saviour's business [sex], they may perhaps be seen as more deliberate and less heroic, but one may be promised and expect an anointed solidity and certainty from them.[21]

The Saviour has given the correct understanding of marriage, which is that the married couple represents the image of the Saviour and his church, in all aspects of the marriage. This understanding should also govern the feelings of the couple, so that they share this knowledge and know it in all mutual interaction. It becomes their common project. And when the couple have sex, the husband should be seen as fulfilling a purpose, from which one may expect (anointed) reliability. So, in comparison with views on marriage which emphasise procreation as the pinnacle of human achievement, Zinzendorf emphasises the representational aspect of marriage as the mystery of marriage, and that which is revealed to the initiated.

2.1.2   Early Herrnhut and Later Herrnhut

The second contrast is from 14 May 1748, where Zinzendorf contrasts the old 'simplistic' understanding of marriage in the community with the new. The difference is that earlier there was no real connection between earthly marriage and spiritual marriage, which was a transcendental, external thing. But then, 22 years ago on this day, a wedding took place, which changed the way of view-

---

21 Married couples, 11 December 1750: "So daß wir bey einem jeden Blik, den wir auf einander thun, so offt wir einander beruhren, nahe werden, einander recht besehen, mit einander sprechen, über einander denken, allemal angethan sind mit derselben demüthigen Erkenntnis und Gefühl unsers Glücks in das Geheimniß eingeleitet geworden zu seyn, daß es uns der Heiland gegeben, die Sache eines Mannes mit seiner Frau zu verstehen, zu wißen, daß das Bild der Kirche gegen Ihn und seines gegen eine Frau zwischen beiden erscheinen muß, das subject des ganzen Geheimnißes des Heilands und siener Tochter der Kirche beständig aus zumachen, so daß ihr häußlich Geschäffte, ihre tägliche discourse, ihre nächtliche Sacristeygen, ihre Schlaf-Tempel, ihre Ehe-Geschäffte, ihre Ehe-Liturgien immer von den selben Influenzen regieret werden, des Hauptes in seine Glieder, in seinen Leib, daß der Mann proportionirlich mächtig, und sein Weib proportionirlich seelig sey im Heiland, und in seiner Gemeinschafft, so daß wenn man geheuratete Brüder ins Heilands Geschäfften handeln siehet, man sie vielleicht mehr bedächtlich und weniger Heldenhafft sehe, aber sich eine gesalbte solidität und Gewißheit von ihnen versprechen und erwarten könne" (UA R.4.CII.12).

ing the union, and hence a new understanding of marriage developed, one that saw the mystical marriage from Ephesians 5 as embodied in all married couples in Herrnhut.

The marriage to which Zinzendorf is alluding is that between one David Nitschmann and Anna Helene Anders, a milkmaid from Berthelsdorf. This context is given in the *Jüngerhausdiarium*, where it is stated that the foundational nature of their marriage was to be found in their class difference.

> After this, the first class of the married people had a lovefeast in the new hall, at which the *Ordinarius* [Zinzendorf] sang a heartfelt song, and then reminded [us], that it was today, 22 years ago that the community marriage was begun through the marriage of Brother Nitschmann (syndicus) to the blessed Anne Lene who was a, according to external appearance, simple, unsightly, unpleasant, sickly, very poor and old dairy maid in Berthelsdorf, but thoroughly converted. The then young, handsome and rich burgher in Herrnhut, David Nitschmann had obstinately demanded this woman in marriage, upon which she was sent from Berthelsdorf with these words: You are our sister, grow in many thousands. After this, she became the most respectable, most pleasant, happiest, most active, wisest, and most venerable person in the whole place, and directed high and low with applause for eight whole years.[22]

Their marriage became the 'founding marriage' of the congregation, according to Zinzendorf, in that it connected a simple, sickly, old maid with a young, wealthy *Bürger* (citizen) of Herrnhut, a couple which went on to become a virtual power couple in the congregation.

Zinzendorf's appraisal of this marriage as a founding feature of a new marriage theology is undoubtedly cast in glorious hindsight. However, there is no

---

22   Married couples, 14 May 1748: "Nachher hatte die erste Classe der Eheleute in dem neuen Saal ein LiebesMahl auf welchen ihr der Ordin[arius, i.e. Zinzendorf] ein hertzliches, niedliches. Liedgen sang und so dann erinnerte, daß sich heut vor 22 Jahren, eigentligch die Gemeine Heirathen durch die Ehe des Bruder Nitchmanns (Synd[icus]) mit der seligen Anne Lene angefangen, welche eine dem äußerlichen Ansehen nach, einfältige, unansehnliche, unangenehme, kränkliche, sehr arme und alte Vieh-Magd in Berthelsdorf gewesen, aber gründlich bekehrt. Die habe der damals junge, schöne und reiche Bürger in Herrnhut, David Nitschmann obstinat zur Ehe begehret, worauf sie mit den Worten von Berthelsdorf dimittirt worden: Du bist unsere Schwester, wachse in viel 1000. Sie sey aber die ansehnlichste, angenehmste, munterste, activeste, klügste und venerabelste Person in ganzen Orte worden, und habe hoch und niedrig mit applausu diritigirt, 8 ganzer Jahre" (UA, GN.C.3 1748, 1).

MARRIAGE AND COMMUNITY 243

doubt that the marriage at the time had a tremendous social significance in terms of mending breaches and forging alliances – a very aristocratic approach to marriage, in fact.

2.1.3 Other Radical Pietist Movements and Herrnhut

The final comparison is found on 4 August 1748, where Zinzendorf mentions the difference between the Moravian view on marriage, and that of the followers of Gichtel and the old 'Anachoreten', i.e. hermits, presumably celibates. The context is concrete human gender relations and how they reflect heavenly realities.

> This is why all the other sects, the Gichtelians, and the old hermits have stumbled over the issue, since they have not understood to deduce any sacredness or importance from the matter, and have, as philosophical spirits swung away from it, who did not want to wish to lower themselves into such bodily matters. Had they only led the holiness of the marriage out from the office of the men from the holiness of the *Hütte* of Christ, [i.e.] from their correct principles, then they and their marriages would never have been the object of ridicule, and then the atheists and the deists would not have been able to laugh themselves to pieces over the bad condition of Christian marriage.[23]

What Zinzendorf is doing is establishing a connection between heaven and earth, which the Moravians have understood, but the other sects have not, a misunderstanding which has made Christian marriage the laughing-stock of the enlightened world. We should not underestimate the presence of the Commisariorum Theologians at this speech,[24] and Zinzendorf's attempt to cast the Moravian Brethren the last defender of Christian marriage. While Zinzendorf for this reason is interested in showing up the difference between the Gichteli-

---

23 Married Couples, 4 August 1748: "Daher ists gekommen, daß alle übrigen Secten die Gichtilianer und die alten Anachoreten über der Sache gestolpert sind, denn sie haben keine heiligkeit und wichtigkeit aus der Sache zu deduciren gewust, und haben als philosophirte Geister sich über die Sache weg geschwungen, die sich nicht in solche Cörperliche Sachen herunter laßen mögen. Hätten sie nur die Heiligkeit der Ehe aus dem Amt der Männer aus der Heiligkeit der Hütte Christi hergeführet, als aus ihrem rechten principio so wären sie sie mit ihrer Ehe nicht zu einem Spott geworden und so hätten die Atheisten und Deisten über den schlechten Zustand der Ehe der Christen sich nicht so zerlachen können" (UA R.20.HS55).
24 The occasion of the speech notes that the marriage quarter-hour takes place in the presence of the lords of the theological commission.

ans and hermits and the Moravian Brethren, it also gives us a glimpse of the positions. In contrast to the Gichtelians and others, who separate heaven and earth, and *sever* any connection between sacredness and body, Zinzendorf advocates the *connection* between heavenly sacredness and bodily matters. Indeed, he posits that the heavenly sacredness constitutes the correct principles for the marriage as it is conceptualised in the Moravian Brethren.[25]

These three examples help define the trap which Zinzendorf sets for himself. The worldly understanding of marriage as being all about the procreation of children is tied to inheritance and securing one's future – peasant and noble alike. This is not relevant for the non-aristocratic citizens of Herrnhut, because there is no land to secure, and one's future is all taken care of within the community.[26] One does not have to marry or have children in order to provide for one's old age. In dismissing procreation as the central feature of marriage Zinzendorf is advocating a change in *purpose* of the institution of marriage, one that infuses it with mystery. From the procreation of children to the representational ideal, and instead of a horizontal, social understanding of marriage, he emphasises a vertical relation, where the couple constitutes the image, the imprint of the divine original.

The second example reinforces this vertical dimension, while also emphasising the socially transgressive nature of Moravian marriage. The marriage between David Nitschmann (Syndicus) with Anna Helene Anders is presented as one transcending social boundaries, in that Nitschmann would later become a high-ranking member of the community. At the time of their marriage, however, he was a failed entrepreneur, who had attempted to set up a linen-workshop in his house but was deeply in debt. After giving up on this venture, he became the private secretary of Zinzendorf and from there, chief negotiator of the Moravians. For our purposes here, it is relevant that the marriage is interpreted as uniting both heaven and earth and indicating the (relative) insignificance of social class, by uniting a wealthy citizen with an old milkmaid.

The final example further strengthens the vertical dimension, and indeed sees this vertical dimension as presenting the truly divine aspect of marriage, over against the radical pietist sects, who regard it at as a fleshy, contaminating institution. Zinzendorf is convinced that his interpretation of Ephesians 5 and

---

25   This connection between heaven and earth, and that 'we' are copies of a heavenly original, is also a theme in the speech from 2 August 1748 (UA R.4.C.II.12).
26   For the aristocratic members, the preservation of the estate and fortune was still important, and it was not common to see older single brothers of rank in the same way as with the aristocratic single sisters.

its manifestation in the married couples in Herrnhut is a proper Christian marriage. It is an imprint of the heavenly marriage and, as such, a prefiguration of what is to come.[27] Here, then, we see the moves that are made to insulate Moravian marriage from any external considerations or influences.

2.2 The Chapel

The consequence of the use of the lot and the attempted avoidance of external influences is an overriding focus on the married couple as a unit, and the relation to the heavenly marriage. This comes through in the following quote, where the reason for humanity's division into two sexes is rooted in the eschatological copulation between the Saviour and his community, represented by the two people in a marriage.

> The Saviour wants to see such a small *familie* in the marriage more or less in the same way as He would be with the soul, and therefore has divided the whole of the human race into two parts, of which one part shall be priest, and the other the community.[28]

The reconfiguration of marriage as constituting a distinct liturgical space is confirmed in the addresses to the married couple, where this is emphasised repeatedly.

The most common way of expressing this is designating the marriage between a brother and a sister as a sacristy, a chapel, and/or a church within the church.[29] A good example of this is the summary of the speech from 15 April, which observes the following about marriage:

> But this [the difficulty of marriage] does not make the marital *Stand* worse, but all the more venerable, [it makes it in] to a special *Stand*, to a *statu in statu* in the community, to a chapel or sacristy in the great church, where a distinct worship service and liturgy always is held.[30]

---

27 Married couples, 3 June 1748 (GN.C.1 1748 (excerpt)), 2 August 1748 (R.4.C.II.12), 4 August 1748 (UA R.20.HS55), 16 August 1748 (R.4.C.II.12).

28 Married couples, 26 October 1747: "der Heiland will in der Ehe eine solche kleine familie sehen, wie ungefehr er seyn würde mit der Seele, und hat desvegen daß ganze menschliche geschlecht in 2 theile getheilt, davon der eine theil Priester der andere die gemeine seyn soll" (UA R.4.CII.12).

29 See also 2 July 1748 (GN.C.3.1748 (excerpt)), 21 July 1748 (UA R.20.HS 13), 11 June 1751 (UA R.20.HS54) and 14 June 1751 (GN.A.15:2).

30 15 April 1748: "Das mache aber den Ehestand nicht schlechter, sondern desto ehrwürdiger, nur zu einem speciellen Stand, zu einem statu in statu in der Gemeine, zu einer Capelle

Zinzendorf claims that the marital *Stand* is a privileged *Stand* within the community, as a chapel in a large church, so the marriage is its own holy space with its own distinct worship service and liturgy (i.e. intercourse) within the community as a whole. He continues:

> This is a *status complicatus*, and is connected with the obligation of the representational and with a kind of art and skill, hence not so convenient, as if one were still single. For indeed, the other part, the Levite or deacon of this chapel, i.e. the sister, must really have reason to recognise her husband as her priest. She must feel it, it must harmonise with her sound mind. This requires a gift of grace that not everyone has.[31]

This is, he says, complicated, for the reason that it is *representative* surely referring to the relation between the Saviour and the community, which is easier with the single brothers and sisters. This means that there is a gravity connected with the relation, namely that the sister (the Levite or deacon) must be able to see her husband as the priest,[32] which places a certain expectation on his behaviour in general, and towards her in particular. And this behaviour must be genuine, it must match her mind. For this match to occur, and his behaviour to be of the correct nature, an intervention from the Saviour, a 'gift of grace', is required, because this is not endemic to human nature as such. Zinzendorf

---

oder Sacristey in der großen Kirche, wo allemal ein eigener Gottesdienst und Liturgie gehalten werde" (UA, GN.C.3 1748, 1).

[31] 15 April 1748: "Das sey ein status complicatus und mit der Obliegenheit des repræsentirnes und mit einer Art von Kunst und Geschicklichkeit verknüpft, mithin nicht so commode, als wenn man noch einzeln sey. Denn da müße der andere Theil, der Levite oder Diaconus dieser Capelle i.e. die Schwester, würklich Grund haben, ihren Mann für ihren Priester zu erkennen. Sie muße es fühlen, es müße mit ihrem gesunden Verstande harmonieren. Dazu werde nun eine eigene Gnaden-Gabe erfordert, die nicht ein jedes habe".

[32] Interestingly, here the internal dynamic of the marriage is that between a priest and his deacon, or Levite. This is also temple language, where the temple of God in the Hebrew Bible is in Zion, or in some strands of the New Testament Zion is in heaven. The temple imagery for the married couple is very common. An example for the married men can be found in the speech from 5 November 1747: 'Therefore, to step up to the [married] *Stand* requires a great measure of mercy and a separate sprinkling with man-blood, a personal consecration and sanctification, for there is no man who should not at the same time be a priest of God'; "Darum gehört freilich in den Stand zu treten, ein großes Maaß Gnade, darzu eine eigene Besprengung mit Mannes-Blut, eine eigene Weihung und Heiligung, denn es gibt keinen Mann der nicht zugleich ein Priester Gottes seyn soll" (GN.C.2.1747.1). Also, the five to seven speeches to the priests' choir in 1758 (all in GN.C.78.1758.2) are probably to the married men in the congregation.

then goes on to argue that the holy spirit works best if a soul is given free rein to engage with its bridegroom in all the other choirs. Not so in the married couples' choir:

> But in view of the marriage choir and its nexus with the workers and servants in the house of the Lord, be it otherwise. There, a continuous connection is necessary from one day to the next, a constant assistance, subservience to each other's gifts, and to serve the other with his experience in this important circumstance. 'God be comforted with the couples', is the desire and the pleading of the workers for each married couple.[33]

The work with the married couples is very 'hands on', in that the relation between the husband and wife must be managed, and a particular connection fostered and encouraged at a daily level. This is the task of the workers of the married couples' choir, which also means that the leadership of this choir differs from that of the others, which has a more *laissez faire* approach. We get an understanding of what this entails from the minutes of the preparatory meeting to the marriage synod 1756/57 in Herrnhut on the 22 December 1756. In the midst of assigning blame as to the present state of the married couples' choir, Johannes von Watteville notes,

> it is lacking in management. Papa has since then [1746] not done in the married choir what the Mother [Anna Nitschmann] has done among the single sisters, and I among the single brothers. There has been no regular married choir correspondence. Papa has not done it, and neither I nor anyone else have had the mandate to do this, I have only begun dabbling from the side, without any married choir worker under me, as was the case in the single brothers' choir, where I could demand he report to me from his choir.[34]

---

33   15 April 1748: "Aber in Ansehung des Ehe-Chors und deßen nexus mit den Arbeitern und Dienern im Hause des HErrn sey es anders: da sey eine continuirliche Connexion nöthig von einem Tage zum andern, eine beständige Gehülfenschaft, einander seine Gaben zu subministriren und mit seiner Erfahrung dem andern zu dienen in dieser wichtigen Umständigkeit. *Tröst dich Gott mit dem Paare*, sey der Wunsch und das Flehen der Arbeiter für ein jedes Ehe-Paar. Das mache di[e]s Chor gleichsam zu einer aparten Gemeine, die eine von allen andern Chören ganz unterschiedene Führung habe, und dadurch ein Bild des *Ganzen* werde, ein Focus, wo sich alle die andern Strahlen fangen und wieder heraus brechen können, so daß, wenns in *dem* Chor gut gehe, es einen gewißen Einfluß ins Ganze habe." (UA, GN.C.3 1748, 1).

34   "Es fehlt unterdessen doch an einer Direction und Papa haben das zeither beym Ehe Chor

Choir management entails regular correspondence,[35] choir workers, and information gathering and exchange. The leaders also discuss choir workers and whether there are deviations within the workers' group as to the application of the theory. Johannes says that in dogma they are united but in the actual application of the principles there is sure to be violations and that Papa is needed to instruct the choir workers in the understanding of the principles and their correct application.

Returning to the speeches, we see that it was already noted in 1748 that the result of this different government is the distinct nature of the married couples' choir:

> This makes this choir like a distinct congregation, which has a completely different leadership from all other choirs, and thereby becomes a picture of the whole, a focus where all the other rays can be caught and break out again, so that, if it goes well with the choir, it has a certain influence in the whole.[36]

Because of the distinct nature of this choir, it is an image of the whole, i.e. the congregation, the focal point and prism of the other choirs, whose harmony and wellbeing will rub off on the other choirs.

2.3 Married Couples' Choir

However, the emphasis on the marriage unit in effect undermines the choir logic in that the married couple is conceived of as a unit unto itself. The problems in this are mentioned in a choir speech to the single brothers in 1748, where Zinzendorf notes:

---

nicht gethan, was die Mutter bey den ledigen Schwestern, und ich bey den ledigen Brüdern gethan habe. Es ist keine reguläre Ehe-Chor Correspondenz gewesen. Papa habens nicht gethan und weder ich noch jemand sonst haben keinen Auftrag dazu gehabet, ich habe nur so angefangen von der Seite zu stümpern, mich aber bey keinem Ehe-Chor-Arbeiter unterstanden, was ich mich bey einem ledige. Brüder Arbeiter unterstehe, zu fordern daß er mir referire von seinem Chor" (UA R.4.C.II.9, 5, p. 6).

35 Peucker's article on the blue cabinet uses a collection of letters addressed to Johann Nitschmann held in UA R.4.C.II.1.65, Peucker 2011a.

36 Married couples, 15 April 1748: "Das mache di[e]s Chor gleichsam zu einer aparten Gemeine, die eine von allen andern Chören ganz unterschiedene Führung habe, und dadurch ein Bild des *Ganzen* werde, ein Focus, wo sich alle die andern Strahlen fangen und wieder heraus brechen können, so daß, wenns in *dem* Chor gut gehe, es einen gewißen Einfluß ins Ganze habe." (UA, GN.C.3 1748, 1).

The choirs of the single members have quite undoubtedly something in advance in the method for the happy execution of this purpose. It is quite natural that their blush of shame will be even greater if they do not achieve the purpose. In the married couples' choir the leadership is difficult for two reasons, because in itself there are already two persons and because the two persons can experience that 100 come from them and therefore the same concern, the connection that one has with the two persons, must spread out too much and finally flies from the hands of the two people, so that they are no longer able to govern the cart: Since, according to the Saviour's approval, no *cura generalis* is required of them, but their children must, according to the Saviour's way of thinking, be distributed into their various choirs, in order to enjoy there a kind of care which the parents cannot give them. The married choir is thus an irregular choir that never stays together. By contrast, the single brothers' choirs can be rightly regarded as though they were an individual that exists unto itself.[37]

There is a submerged contradiction between Zinzendorf's idea of 'procurator marriage', where the intercourse between husband and wife represents the copulation between the Saviour and his church, and the choir structure, where the choirs represent the actors in the mystical marriage.[38] In this quote, Zinzendorf notes that the married couples' choir is an 'irregular choir' and that it is more difficult to regulate and lead due to the fact that there are two people in a unit rather than one as in the single choirs and that the care given to two has to be extended to all of the others in the choir, thus leaving the couples to themselves. Not only does Zinzendorf struggle with this in the speeches, because he real-

---

37 Single brothers, 10 May 1748: "Die Chöre der ledigen Geschwister haben ganz unstreitig was voraus in der Methode zur glücklichen Außführung dieses Zweckes. Es ist ganz naturell, daß ihre Schamröthe auch desto größer wird, wenn sie den Zweck nicht erhalten. Im Ehe-Chor wird aus 2 Ursagen die Führung schwer; weil es an sich selbst schon 2 Personen sind, und weil die zwo Personen erleben können, daß 100 aus ihnen werden, und weil also dieselbe Sorge, die Connexion, die man mit den 2 Personen hat, sich zu sehr ausbreiten muß, und den 2 Personen endlich aus den Händen komt, daß sie nicht mehr im stande sind den Wagen zu regieren: da denn auch nach des Heilands Billigkeit keine cura generalis von ihnen soll gefordert weden, sondern ihre Kinder müßen nach des Heilands denkweise wieder in ihre diverse Chöre vertheilt, um daselbst einer aparten Pflege zu genießen, die ihnen die Eltern nicht geben könne. Das Ehe-Chor ist also ein irreguläres Chor, das niemals beysammen bleibt. Hingegen die ledigen Brüder-Chöre kan man mit allem Recht ansehen, als obs ein Individuum wäre, das vor sich selbst bestünde" (GN.C.5 1748, 3).
38 This is also discussed and agreed upon in the preparatory meeting to the marriage synod. UA R.4.C.II.9, 5. The discussions over the married couple as a liturgical unit is on pp. 4–5.

ises that marriage was fundamentally *un*choirly, and, we might add, because it represented a different household structure.

The organisational difficulties are mentioned several times. On 21 July 1748, Zinzendorf notes that the married couples' choir have not had its quarter-hour, which the other choirs have had on weekly basis. This is not from neglect, but rather because of considerations as to how this may be organised.[39] After a couple of considerations on his own role and the correct understanding of marriage, he finishes off with two points. One is the consideration to separate the choir, and have separate quarter-hour for the brothers and sisters, which, in light of the matter would be good. However, this is up to the Saviour. Second, it is not only necessary to hold quarter-hours, but also that every couple be addressed personally, since: 'every couple is a church … when I see a single choir, I see a community, and when I see a married couple, I also see a community'.[40]

The important point here is the consideration to separate the couples and address them as brothers or sisters instead of together. This will take place in 1755–56, but here, in 1748, we see that the matter is put 'to the Saviour', i.e. the lot was used to decide. His second point for consideration is that it is necessary, beyond the group meetings, to meet every couple individually. We saw an example of this in the 'marriage document' mentioned in Chapter 3, where the choir charges had spoken to each couple to assess the extent of their understanding of the marital mystery in 1744. Whether this practice had been suspended we do not know, but Zinzendorf here is advocating the practice, the reason being that each couple constitutes a church and a community, and thus contains the whole in itself.

In 1750, Zinzendorf gives three speeches to a small group within the married couples' choir.[41] Two of these mentions organisational considerations. In the first speech from 12 November, Zinzendorf notes that

> We are a collective, within which it is not suitable to be preached to in a communal gathering, rather we must see, speak, and get to know each other distinctly and apart, and yet at times be able to add a few others,

---

[39] This is also discussed at length at the synod in 1756/57, where it is noted that there are no classes within the married choir and no hall or room to hold these meetings, a problem mentioned several times.

[40] Married couples, 21 July 1748: "Wenn ich ein lediger chor sehe so sehe ich eine Gemeine und wenn ich ein paar Eheleute sehe so sehe ich auch eine Gemeine" (UA R.20.HS 13). Thank you to Frau Wagner-Fiebich for sharing her transcription.

[41] The dates are 12 November, 22 November, and 11 December. They are preserved together in UA R.4.C.II.12.

who are not used to being treated according to the species of room and chamber, so that they also hear something good and blessed and receive good news.[42]

Here we see deliberations as to the mode of address and gathering. Zinzendorf believes that the particular form of community which the married couples constitute are not suited for collective address but must be primarily engaged at smaller levels. The select group here is chosen (which he notes following this excerpt) because they are all at the same level in faith, and thus may be addressed at the same level. A group such as this such ideally now and then incorporate couples who are not 'in the know' to offer them the benefit of the more elevated address.[43]

I will make an effort, my brothers and sisters, to get these gatherings going. We must form classes, with whom I speak in my room, and have a weekly general gathering. So, we have to ask the Saviour that he gives us mercy, to seek out for the couples which would match well in classes. That is the innocent and simple-minded coming together.[44]

Zinzendorf wants to begin these smaller congenial classes within the choir, supplemented by a general weekly meeting. The marriage document from 1743 discussed in Chapter 3 had as an appendix a list of the classes for the married couples. And as we saw in the diaries, the married couples' choir did have classes earlier. When and why this practice was discontinued is not known, but from Zinzendorf's zeal here, it is to be taken up again.

---

42   Married couples, 12 November 1750: "Wir sind eine Gesellschafft, da sichs nicht schikt, sie zu einer Gemein-Versamlung werden zu laßen darinnen gepredigt wird, sondern wir mußen einander distincte und apart sehen, sprechen und kennen lernen, und doch auch manchmal ein paar andre hinein mengen können, welche nicht nach Stuben und Cammer-Art [behandelt zu werden] gewohnt sind, damit sie doch auch was gutes und seeliges hören, eine gute Nachricht bekommen" (R.4.C.II.12).
43   This approach sounds like Dober's considerations which we saw in Chapter 3. Dober spoke of a gradual implementation of the new teachings, where it at first was among a few, and then the plan was clearer, the method was regulated accordingly.
44   Married couples, 12 November 1750: "Ich werde mich nun befleißigen, mein Geschwister erst nur in Gang zu bringen zu dergleichen zusammenkünften. Wir müßen Classen formieren, die ich auf meinem Zimmer spreche, u wöchentlich eine General zusammenkünfft haben. Wir müßen also den Heiland bitten, daß Er uns Gnade gebe, die Paare wohl aus zusuchen, wie sie sich in Claßen zusammen schiken. Es sind das unschuldige und einfältige zusammenkünffte" (UA R.4.C.II.12).

The third speech in this cluster is from 11 December 1750, whose contents we have already touched upon. Here, in the consideration of the practical matters for the married couples' choir, I just want to mention the conclusion of the speech, where Zinzendorf explains that there is no time for him to speak with everyone as to assess the truth of the mystery because of his heavy schedule:

> The time has not yet present, that I can proceed *en suite* in the matter; my concerted business does not permit me to speak with every couple myself [to find out] how faithful it is to the mystery. But if it has begun, then it will continue, and then they will come to us from other choirs, once grace prevails again. Because we must receive special grace contractions to which the Saviour has His times and hours.[45]

Zinzendorf's keenness to get things going has abated a bit, due to the workload required and the time available to him. But he has confidence that once the material is grasped and the couples are faithful to it, it will proceed, and grace will prevail in this choir again. This will attract members from the other choirs, the Saviour will see to that.

As we have seen, there is thus a logic which runs from heavenly marriage to earthly manifestation, from earthly manifestation as an individual nexus, which fits in with the representational status. But what about the married couples' *choir*? In a speech held in 1751, on 11 June, Zinzendorf expresses concern over the difficulty in cultivating a choir spirit in the married couples' choir.[46]

The speech is divided into two halves. The first half is to the whole choir, the second half to the men only. The first half deals mostly with the relations between the husband and wife and their relationship to the Saviour and the

---

45 Married couples, 11 December 1750: "Die Zeit ist noch nicht da, daß ich en suite in den Materien forthandele, meine concatenirten Geschäffte laßen mich nicht zu, daß ich jedes paar selbst sprechen kan, wie treu es dem Geheimniß ist. Wenn es aber ein mal angeht, denn wirds fortgehen, denn werden auch aus andere Chören, welche zu uns kommen, wenn die Gnade erst wieder recht walten wird. Denn wir müßen ein apartes Gnaden-Wehen dazu kriegen, dazu der Heiland seine zeiten und Stunden hat" (UA R.4.C.II.12).

46 Married couples, 11 June 1751 (UA R.20.HS54). Also at the synod, Johannes von Watteville complains about the lack of plerophoria (exaltation over the side-wound): 'I cannot say that I had as much plerophoria from the Saviour in the married choir as I had in the single choir to act in the whole' / "kan aber nicht sagen daß ich vom Heiland soviel plerophorie hätte im Ehechor so wie im ledigen Chor ins ganze zu agiren" (UA R.4.C.II.9, 5).

balance between them. Of interest, however, is the second half, directed to the married men, in that this is where some of the organisational challenges are addressed.

> In one thing, however, the married choir is ripe, and the members may discuss this. The single brothers have their choir activities, the single sisters and the widows likewise; in this, however, the married choir is not yet communally organised. The evening blessing up until now is not yet sufficient for the choir grace of the married couples. They should have been led just as it happens in the single brothers and sisters in their choirs, otherwise our young married couples may become annoyed and think that they have lost something of their choir grace.[47]

While the other choirs, such as the single brothers, single sisters, and widows have activities for the given choir, this is not the case in the married couples' choir, which is 'not yet communally organised'. This means that whatever individual grace is present, however a fervent sister or brother one may be, this does not translate into a communal cohesion. The evening blessing is probably a choir event, i.e. everyone is present, but they are not a group, and *as a group* they do not possess 'choir grace', i.e. the grace that comes from being in a given choir. This needs to be cultivated and articulated in the choir, just as it is in the single choirs, so that the younger married couples do not feel that they have been set back by getting married.

> ... It makes a big difference whether one talks to a man or a woman, one cannot always talk with them both at the same time, neither apart nor in the whole. It used to be that one held classes, where men and women were together to prevent the gossip and the resulting damage if they had the opportunity to talk about and against each other in front of the members. But we are rather far from that.[48]

---

47 Married couples, 11 June 1751: "In einer Sache aber ists Ehe-Chor reif, und darüber mögen sich die Geschwister besprechen. Die ledigen Brüder haben ihre Chorgelegenheiten, die ledigen Schwestern und Witwen desgleichen; darinnen aber ist das Ehe Chor noch nicht Gemeinmäsig eingerichtet. Der bisherige Abendsegen ist noch nichts genugsam zur Chorgnade der Eheleuten" (UA R.20.HS54).

48 Married couples, 11 June 1751: "Und es ist doch ein grosser Unterschied, ob man mit einem Mann oder Frau redet, man kan nicht allezeit mit beyden zugleich reden, weder apart noch ins ganzen. Ehedem wars so, daß man Classen hielte, wo Mann und Frau beysammen waren, um die Klatschereyen, und den daheraus kommenden Schaden zu Verhüten, wenn

Earlier in Herrnhut, the married couples' choir was divided into classes, where there was opportunity to discuss with each other in front of the rest of the class. This group 'therapy' was regarded as a way of preventing gossip, but is not, apparently practiced anymore. At present, it would seem, it is a worker or leader who speaks with the couple both by themselves because it is difficult to address men and women at the same time, both at the level of individual couple and at the level of the choir.

> So now the men should come together separately in order to strengthen themselves in their husband's duty and become strong and complete men; and so also the sisters, to strengthen themselves in their daughter's duty or rather daughter-bliss; and only together communally a couple of times a week.

Therefore, the brothers and sisters will now gather separately, to strengthen their respective duties, and only occasionally every week meet all together. That the sisters are to be strengthened in their daughter duty goes back to the speech to the couple, where the women are to humble themselves, regard themselves as daughters to alleviate their doubt in their husbands, as well as their husband's self-doubt as to his ability to act as the Saviour in their marriage. The husband should also look to this deference to understand how they are to act over against the Saviour.

Zinzendorf left Herrnhut in June 1751 and went to Barby and Ebersdorf and from there to England on 21 July through Switzerland and France. He stayed in England from August 1751 to March 1755 and returned to Herrnhut in June 1755.[49]

2.4   *1755–56 and the Separated Choir Speeches*

Between 25 June 1755 and 14 June 1756, Zinzendorf gave 13 speeches to the married couples' choir and 16 speeches to the Married Men and Married Women respectively. The separated speeches were especially intense in the period from mid-November 1755 to early February 1756, where 11 of these separated choir speeches are held. I will take a look at the speeches, to distil the relevant points of the separate speeches and the speeches to the married couples' choir.

---

sie Gelegenheit bekämen, vorm Geschwister von und gegen einander zu reden. Darüber sind wir aber wohl ziemlig weg" (UA R.20.HS54).

49   Peucker 2000, pp. 8–9.

The speeches to the married women focus on the understanding and negotiating the proper relation between herself and the Saviour and herself and the husband.[50] This is the married sister's greatest challenge (17 November).[51]

> do not let business or trouble, or anything else, deter you from having an attentive *Gemüth* on your main plan, from speculating on your marriage-Lord, from treating your deputies [husbands] with all respect, but always only as messenger of your Lord, as people who do not lead home, but only lead right.[52]

In relation to the Saviour, she is the direct object of the collective bridegroom (17 November). In relation to her husband, they are partners,[53] except in intercourse, where they have defined roles (13 November, 1 December), which is also expressed as 'communal sex' (22 August).[54] When she has sex with her husband, she is the church and he is the Saviour. This is how intercourse is to be understood and hence is a sacramental act.

The speeches to the married men focus on their relation to the Saviour and their relation to their wives. In regard to the Saviour, this includes regarding themselves as the artificial *Stand* or, the interim state (8 December, 25 December), however the emphasis is less on what will happen in the hereafter,[55] and more on how they in their present state represent the Saviour:

---

50   Married Sisters, 14 July 1755 (UA R.20.HS54), 22 August (UA R.20.HS54). 1, 12, 27 January 1756 all in UA R.20.HS54.
51   Married Sisters, 8 December 1755 (UA R.20.HS54). See also the prayer held over the married sisters on 26 March 1756 (UA R.20.HS54).
52   Married sisters, 17 November 1755: "laßt euch weder durch Geschäfte noch Beschwerlichkeit, noch irgend etwas abhalten, ein attentets Gemüth auf euren Haupt-Plan zu haben, in euren Ehe-Herrn zu speculiren, eure Deputirten zu tractiren mit allem Respect, aber alle mal nur als *Boten* eures Herrn, als Leute die nicht heimführen, sondern nur zurecht führen" (UA R.20.HS54). This is also expressed in the speech to the married men on 24 November 1755 (UA R20.HS54).
53   See the interesting speech to the married sisters from 7 January 1756, where he talks about married women in missionary service, which shows that 'a sister must not think that she is made for staying at home'. This is qualified, however, given that not only did a missionary sister had to be married for service, but she also had to 'man up' for missionary service 'regardless of all natural weakness learn to act like a man' / "aller natürlichen Schwachheit ungeachtet als ein Mann handeln lernen" (UA R.20.HS54).
54   Also married men, 8 December 1756, when they give their wives a foretaste of what is to come, and if not, then it is not a 'communal marriage' (UA R.4.CII.12).
55   But see 27 January 1756, where it is mentioned (UA R.20.HS54).

> Every man who is a child of God is an angel of the Lord and represents our Lord Jesus in person.
>
> ...
>
> But if we bear in mind that our co-believers and our compeers of the corpse of Jesus look upon us with such respect, that they picture something of the Saviour in us, and think, that is my head, as Christ is his head, then we cannot really deny it, and ultimately go against the Saviour's basic principles and formal edicts, but it places us in an apprehension: Dear Saviour, am I really equal to my office? Can I maintain Your and my honour, and prove myself in every measure to my wife, children, and family, as if our Lord J[esus] C[hrist] Himself acted with them?[56]

and another,

> Your incarnation has served the male sex and enabled that it is able to represent Your place; we sin against Your human soul and *Hütte* if we do not allow ourselves the mind of a man.[57]

The *similarity* between a brother and the Saviour is not confined to intercourse, as we saw in the last chapter – the similarity with Jesus is the foundation of all the male choirs. But here it also looks as though the 'standing in' or 'acting on behalf of' the Saviour goes beyond intercourse. Indeed, the expression 'as if our Lord Jesus Christ himself acted with them' is mentioned frequently without

---

56 Married men, 2 February 1756, "Ein jeder Mann, der ein Kind Gottes ist, ist ein Engel des Herrn und repraesentirt unsern Herrn Jesum in Person. [...] Aber wenn wirs uns bedencken, daß unsre Mit-Christinnen und Mitgenoßen am Leichnam Jesu uns mit solchem Respect ansehen, sich was vom Heiland an uns was vorstellen, und dencken, das ist mein Haupt, wie Christus sein Haupt ist: so können wir ihnen das zwar nicht ganz verwehren und schlechterdings gegen des Heilands Grund-Principia und sanctionem pragmaticam angehen, aber es sezt uns in eine apprehension: Lieber Heiland, bin ich meinem Amt auch gewachsen? werde ich auch deine und meine Ehre mainteniren, und mich in allen Stücken bey Frau, Kindern und Familie so beweisen, als handelte unser Herr J[esus] C[hristus] selber mit ihnen?" (UA R.20.HS54). See also married men, 27 January 1756: 'O dear man! give us, by grace, an ever-present spirit, similar to you, the ghost of openheartedness towards our sisters, in short, such a change in which, after all, something of equality can be seen'; "O lieber Mann! schenke uns aus Gnaden einen immer praesenten, dir ähnlichen Geist, den Geist der Offenherzigkeit gegen unsre Schwestern, kurz, einen solchen Wandel darin sich doch was von diener Gleichheit sehen läßt" (UA R.20.HS54).

57 Married brothers, 26 March 1756: "Deine Menschwerdung hat dem Männlichen Geschlecht verdient, und verschaft, daß es deine Stelle vertreten kan; wir versündigen uns an deiner menschlichen Seele und Hütte, wenn wir uns nicht den Geist eines Mannes geben laßen" (UA R.20.HS54).

specific mention of intercourse:[58] with reference to various dealings in a marriage (24 November 1755), as the ground for sisters not acting wilfully against their husbands (17 November 1755).[59]

Even the married sisters are told that 'a man has a difficult office in the marriage, because he has a regal, prophetic and priestly calling towards a daughter of God, even in the smallest details, to treat her in the name of Jesus Christ, as if Jesus Christ Himself dealt with you. But this does not affect the character of his soul'.[60]

In other married brother speeches, however, it is mentioned that they are partners in life, and that it is only in intercourse that they are the Saviour.[61] This is most evocatively mentioned in 21 August:

> we should bring them under the sceptre of our bridegroom, and maintain our authority to a certain degree, in the hours, where we with dignity must represent.[62]

and again 14 July, albeit less poetically:

> you shall use your members as the members of Christ, and do to your sister what her husband ahead of time cannot and does not yet want to do to her, but will do.[63]

There is also mention of their task or commission,[64] namely

---

[58] I have tried to find where this comes from, given that it sounds like a fixed expression. In the married brothers' speech, 14 July 1755, Zinzendorf mentions that it is alluded to in the catechism (UA R.20.HS54).

[59] For two more examples without intercourse see 14 July 1755 (UA R.20.HS54) and 27 January 1756 (UA R.20.HS54). For an example with intercourse see 26 March 1756 (UA R.20.HS54).

[60] Married sisters, 17 November 1755: "Ein Mann hat darin ein difficiles Amt, daß er einen Königlichen, prophetischen und priesterlichen Beruf, obgleich im wenigen und kleinen, an eine Tochter Gottes hat, sie im Namen Jesu Christi so zu behandeln, *als handelte unser Herr Jesus Christus mit ihr selber*: aber das afficirt den Charachter seiner Seele nicht" (UA R.20.HS54).

[61] Married brothers, 13 November 1755 (UA R.20.HS54).

[62] Married brothers, 21 Auust 1755: "wir sollen sie unter unsers Bräutigams Zepter bringen, und unsere autoritaet gewißer maßen mainteniren, in den Stunden, da wir mit Dignitaet repraesentiren müßen." (UA, R.20.HS.42).

[63] Married brothers, 14 July 1755: "du soltest deine Glieder als Christi Glieder brauchen, und an d[eine]r Schwester thun, was ihr Mann vor die Zeit noch nicht an Ihr thun kan und will, aber thun wird." (UA, R.20.HS.42).

[64] See also married sisters, 27 January 1756, married brothers, 1 January 1756 (UA R.20.HS54).

to act in the name of the Saviour and protect and sanctify and bring him as a pure virgin one from the sex, which the Saviour chose as a production site for His humanisation.[65]

The brother's connection to the Saviour and his wife are of course intertwined, and to articulate this connection, Zinzendorf draws on the New Testament trope of head-ship, most famously from 1 Corinthians 11:3, where Paul states that 'Christ is the head of every man' and in verse 7, where man is 'the image and glory of God' – in Zinzendorf's hands changed to the 'glory of Christ'.[66]

Both the married brothers and married sisters have to negotiate the relation to the Saviour and to their spouse – and the intricacies of these machinations are, it would seem, as difficult to explain as to understand. For women, this means that while she must regard her husband as a representative of the Saviour, with duties towards her, she must not mistake him for the Saviour himself, but reserve the true deference, obedience, love, desire, etc. for the Saviour. In other words, her actions towards her husband should only *mirror* or reflect her engagement with the Saviour. Apart from this challenge of keeping husband and Husband apart, the inner life of a sister is easy, because she merely has to continue on her inner path of representation cultivated from when she was a girl.

For the married brother, however, he has to negotiate the heavy burden of acting on behalf of the Saviour. As a single brother, he was like the Saviour and could strive for similarity with his corpse, but now he *has to be* the Saviour in the copulation with his wife, the church. He should also be her head, shape her into a maiden for the Saviour, take care of her, protect her, but also see her as a partner, an equal.

We should not underestimate the significance of treating each married man as the Saviour and the distinction it places on a married brother. While most aristocratic men in the eighteenth century would probably find this distinction congruent as well as appropriate to their class, we should also consider the effect on the much larger group of men, artisans, peasants, and aspiring merchants, who thus are raised into a level distinction, to which they would not have been accustomed.

---

65 Married brothers, 8 December 1755: "ins Heilands Namen zu agiren, und eins aus dem Geschlecht, das der Heiland zur Werckstatt seiner Menschwerdung erwehlt hat, zu hüten, zu heiligen, und Ihm als eine reine Jungfrau zu bringen" (UA R.20.HS54). Also, married brothers, 17 November 1755, where it is mentioned that a married man has the means and method 'to make a sister, as the Saviour wants her'; "eine Schwester zu machen, wie sie der Heiland haben will" (UA R.20.HS54).

66 Married brothers, 13 November 1755, married brothers, 1 December 1755 (UA R.20.HS54).

All the non-logics of the incarnation are transferred onto the married brother, splitting him into two. In relation to his wife, he represents the Saviour, but in relation to the Saviour, he is, as are all the other male members and husbands-as-Saviours, part of the future bride. He is instructed to see himself as occupying different roles corresponding to different contexts. To repeat, for us, born into the constituent logic of public and private in bourgeois society this is not necessarily a challenge, but for most people in the eighteenth century, this would take some effort not only to understand but to implement in one's social relations.

The sisters, on the other hand, are merely to be subservient both here and there, and their duty is to distinguish between masters. Their challenge thus is in a relation to someone outside of themselves, whereas the challenge for the men is within themselves, and how to comprehend themselves as being a divided human being.

3 After the Synod

The marriage synod of 1756/57 revealed a number of problems in the conceptualisation and management of the married couples' choir, such as the lack of harmony within the choir, jealousy between the choirs, and Zinzendorf's crisis in the understanding of marriage, a crisis which began in 1746 and was amplified in 1755 by the publication of the married couples' choir speeches by an enemy of the Moravian Brethren. I will not go into too much detail here, but merely note that the lack of harmony within the choir was seen as connected to the idea of the married couples' choir as a unit unto itself: 'the married choir is no choir, rather every family is a small church unto itself, but all of these small churches together surely do make up a whole'.[67] To this is added in the margin 'must however stand in a particular connection, and be subordinated such as the whole community stands under one hierarchy'.[68] What is taught in the *Saal*, about the princess-nature of the sisters, and the servant-nature of the brothers has been misunderstood or exaggerated. To this Johannes adds, 'all choir workers agree in the theory, that priestly-ness, liturgy and sanctity must be enacted

---

67 "Zuweilen kommt auch das Sentiment vor, daß das Ehe Chor kein *Chor* sey, sondern eine jede Familie ein kirchlein für sich. Aber alle diese Kirchlein zusammen machen doch ein ganzes aus" (UA R.4.C.II.9, p. 4).
68 "müßen [doch] in einer gewissen Connexion und wie die gantze gemeine unter einer Hierarchie stehen und Subordinirt seyn" (UA R.4.C.II.9, p. 4).

in the marriage'.⁶⁹ This element is characterised as a jewel, a *'kleinod'* in the church of the Brethren, and is the result of Zinzendorf's blessed work in the years 1744, 1745 and 1746. With this work, it is noted, the eternal foundation was laid which sustained the married couples' choir through the Sifting Time, and which meant that this choir was not ruined, as was partially the case in the other choirs. This foundation and its practice give the married couples' choir an advantage over the other choirs, and they agree that this is worth building upon.

Jealousy between the choirs is mentioned by Johannes who states that the married couples' choir feels discarded when it is observed how much time and effort Zinzendorf spends on the other choirs – something of which he himself is accused in this synod. He would rather, so it seems, have stayed in the single brothers' choir, where he spends most of his time and energy. It is pointed out, that his role was actually to facilitate transition of brothers from the single choir to the married couples' choir and be supportive of the newly married couples. These newly married brothers have felt very much neglected by Johannes.

Finally, Zinzendorf's crisis. It is noted at the synod that he withdrew from marriage affairs after Johannes and Benigna's marriage in 1746, and it is suggested that this was due to the stream of defamatory publications that were the result of the publicised marriage theology of the Moravian Brethren.⁷⁰ This flared up again after Seidel's publication of more than seventy speeches to the married couples' choirs of Herrnhaag, Marienborn, and Herrnhut from the late 1740s, mentioned in Chapter 4.⁷¹ Zinzendorf acknowledges as much in a speech from January 1757, which we touched upon in the previous chapter. While Zinzendorf was not present at the first three days of the synod, he read the minutes from the two first days, added a heap of comments, which were discussed on the third day, and then showed up on the fourth. However, he did not address the gentle criticisms or provide solutions there and then, but, judging from the choir speeches the following years, the problems and his role in them were taken to heart.

This shows up in the choir speeches to the married couples' choir held after January 1757 in three interconnected ways. There is less emphasis on the single couple as a unit or jewel, and more focus on their symbolic roles as Saviour and Church. Furthermore, the married couples' choir is mentioned much more,

---

69 "Und in der Theorie, daß in der Ehe Pristerlich, liturgistch und heilig gehandelt werden muß sind alle Chor Arbeiter eins" (UA R.4.C.II.9, p. 4).
70 For analyses of selected publications relating to the topic of marriage during the Sifting Time, see Miller 2013 and 2014; Peucker 2015.
71 Petterson 2015 and 2016.

and the challenges within this particular choir are articulated and brought to the fore. Finally, the balance or harmony in the wider community of Herrnhut is promoted by addressing the complementary roles of the choirs. These are intertwined, but we may get a sense of it through a couple of select quotations:

> That's the real essence in marriage, if they are to be and remain as a liturgy, that the heart readily believes all the things which makes them a liturgy. Hence marriage is a certain division of the congregation, whence one, when one enters, works as if one had a heavenly hierarchy before oneself.[72]

and in another speech:

> From each marriage must come a silent heaven, a temple-order, and a peace-chapel, on which the Saviour can graze, a solitude for the holy trinity, a small model of what the whole church of the Saviour looks like on a large scale.[73]

Both of these quotations retain echoes of marriage as a unit by using words such as liturgy and chapel, but both quotations also include the larger community as a reference point. At the end of a longer speech which is more focused on the couple, Zinzendorf ends with the following words:

> But to say what does not fit, that is not my business, I cannot rightly say that, and must leave it to others; I really have nothing to say but what fits the plan of the Saviour, to which we and the community are in understanding together, where everyone may ask themselves: Why is there a married couple in the community?[74]

---

72 Married couples, 29 April 1757: "Das ist der eigentliche Ikker in der Ehe, wenn sie eine Liturgie seyn und Bleiben soll, daß das Herz an alle die Dinge, die sie zur Liturgie machen, gerne glaubt. Daher ist die Ehe eine gewiße Abtheilung der Gemeine, davon man, wenn man hinein komt, arbeitet, als wenn man eine himmlische Hierarchie vor sich hätte" (UA R.20.HS54).

73 Married couples, 17 August 1757: "es muß aus einer jeden Ehe wircklich so ein stiller Himmel, Tempel-Ordnung und Friedens-Capelle werden, woran sich der Heiland selber weiden kan, ein secessus für die Heilige DreyEinigkeit, ein Modellgen wie die ganze Kirche des Heilands im Großen ausseiht" (UA R.20.HS54).

74 Married couples, 17 February 1758: "Aber zu sagen was *nicht paßt*, das ist nicht meien Sache, ich kan das nicht recht, und muß es andern überlassen, ich weiß eigentlich nichts zu sagen, als *was sich paßt*, den Plan des Heilands, wo zu wir und der Gemiene zusammen ver-

There the matter is more clearly in the foreground. The presence of married couples in a community may seem odd, but is not for 'us' to question, when 'we' have committed ourselves to the plan of the Saviour.

The mention of the married couples' choir may be seen in the speech to the married couples' choir from 27 December 1759, where Zinzendorf repeatedly speaks of 'us and our choir', 'our choir grace, our choir path, and choir knowledge', and

> that our marriage choir here is noticeably, visibly and undeniably accustomed to being blessed, person by person, and as it is said, 'that every one should not only learn to keep his vessel in sanctification and honour', but also to see everyone according to his manner, each as complete as is his neighbour, as the (hundred) couples, which the holy spirit has taken into its care and direction, so that the most complete which is underneath the whole is even the hundredth, because there is no difference among the souls.[75]

Here there is a focus on the choir, and the choir members as a collective. This is also the case in an earlier speech, where Zinzendorf wishes,

> I wish that the members would build on the other married members, and that they would find the choir in which they come, that they should not repent because they could not see what they should see that they have at home: the choir spirit, the liturgical graces, the simplicity of the heart, the Awe, the choir way of thinking, and the sinner-holiness.
>
> We are not yet so far in our marital affairs as the four other choirs, and the two children's choirs, the boys and girls. This is true.
>
> But the difference among the people is much bigger with us than with the other choirs. There may be very bad people in the other choirs, but what is good and reliable, that is twice as much; what has a plan, has a plan. But that cannot be so in marriage. Good souls, faithful hearts, whole

---

standen sind, da mag sich eben jedes selbst fragen warums ein Ehe-Paar in der Gemeine ist?" (UA R.20.HS54).

75 Married couples, 27 December 1759: "daß sich unser Ehe-Chor hier merklich, sichtlich und unleugbar hinein gewöhnt ins selig seyn, Person vor Person, und wies dort heist, 'daß ein jegliches nicht nur lerne, sein Faß zu bewahren in Heiligung und Ehren', sondern auch ein jegliches in seiner Art ganz zu sehen, ein jedes so ganz, als sein Nachbar ist, als die (hundert) Paare, die der Heilige Geist in seine Pflege und Direction genommen, daß so ganz der ganzeste darunter ist, auch der hunderste sey, weil kein Unterschied ist unter den Seelen" (UA R.20.HS54).

people, may be bad married people before the Saviour, over against half as blessed and faithful hearts.[76]

Here, the newly married couple should follow or build upon the members of the married couples' choir, who can demonstrate the fullness of one's choir life and married life. Zinzendorf admits that the married couples' choir still has a long way to go, which is connected to the more complicated nature of the married couples' choir and the extra layers of roles and personhood.[77] The idea that a true heart can be a bad spouse is connected to the idea of not everyone being cut out for marriage, and the examination that goes before coupling.[78]

This leaves room for the single choirs, and these later speeches do demonstrate how the single and married couples' choirs complement each other, rather than compete. For not all people are cut out to be 'anakoreten' or single people, and not all are cut out for marriage. The single choirs are meant to prepare people for a correct understanding of marriage that a select group can then transition into.[79] This transition is not easy either, as the speech on 12 April 1757 makes clear, and needs both preparation as well as care – which was lacking before.

Thus, in the end, the unity of the community prevailed, and it was finally realised, that if the community was to survive, then the marriage must be built on community principles which must be cultivated in the choirs.[80]

---

76   Married couples, 20 May 1758: "Ich wünsche, daß sich die Geschwister an den andern Eh-Geschwister erbauen und daß sie das Chor, drein sie kommen so finden mögen, daß ihnen keine Reue an komme aus dem Grunde, weil sie etwa nicht sehen solten, was sie zu Hause hatten, den Chor-Geist, die liturgischen Gnaden, die Einfältigkeit des Herzens, die Awe, die Chor-denkweise, und die Sünder-heiligkeit.

  Wir sind in unsrer Ehe-Sache noch nicht so weit, als die 4 andern Chöre, und die 2 Kinder-Chöre, der

  Knaben und Mägdgen. Das ist wahr. Aber der Unterschied unter den Leuten ist bey uns auch viel größer als bey den andern Chören. Es können in den andern Chören recht schlechte leute seyn, was aber gut und zuverläßig ist, das ist wieder doppelt so, was Plan hat, das hat Plan. Das kan aber in der Ehe nicht so seyn. Es können gute Seelen, Treue Herzen, ganze Leute vor den Heiland schlechtere Eheleute seyn, as andre nur halb so selige und Treue Herzen" (UA R.20.HS54).

77   See also the speech to married couples from 3 February 1758, where Zinzendorf mentions the different conditions for a single member and a married one, and the extra commitment and responsibility which comes with marriage (UA R.20.HS54).

78   In the speech to the married couples from 4 March 1758, he designates people who are extraordinarily called into marriage as a 'certain type' of people who are called into this sacramental choir (UA R.20.HS54).

79   Married couples, 10 April 1760 (UA R.20.HS54). See also 24 February 1758 (UA R.20.HS54).

80   Married couples, 6 March 1760 (UA R.20.HS54).

4 Conclusion

In this chapter, I wanted to show how marriage as an institutional form clashed with the collective emphasis of the choir system, and how the symbolic marriage was meant to overcome this problem. This was carried out both to engage the scholarship on the topic, which is vast, but also to problematise the lack of engagement of marriage as an institutional form of gender relations. I return to this in the following chapter. As should be very clear by now, the choir system was not simply a system of pastoral care groups and religious supervision. They enabled new forms of gender and gender relations in that this household structure offered a way of life which was not tied to the semi-feudal social structure and the expectations and conditions associated with this mode of production.[81] Thus individuals did not have to marry, and married couples were not compelled to have children. The choir system provided the framework as well as the means of implementing these new understandings of gender relations. However, as the former chapter also demonstrated, and as repeated in this one, the men were subjectified as copies of the Saviour;[82] while the women were subjectified as spouses, via the idea of the congregation as a bride, and consequently, could be seen as the true image of the congregation.[83] These examples indicate that in spite of the relative freedom offered by the choir structure in terms of actual marriage and childbirth, the imagery used in the choir speeches was useful in producing spousal ideology independent of an actual marriage.

81 See the more developed argument in Petterson 2014.
82 My favourite example is this quote from a speech to the single brothers on 8 June 1757: 'And a single brother should seek the soul of Christ every day ... and there seek his comfort, and call upon him and ask him, that in the manner of which the oil flows from the head of the high priest onto his entire gown, that he likewise let the anointing oil of his holy humanity (*Menschheit*) flow and thoroughly embalm the choir, every individual and his *Hütte*, and sanctify the brother's *Hütte*, as a God's tabernacle of a choir kin of the Lamb'; "Und ein lediger Bruder hat sich alle Tage nach Christi Seele um zu sehen [...], seinen Trost da zu suchen, sich darauf zu beruffen und Ihn zu bitten, daß wie von der Hohen priesters Haupt das Oel auf sein ganzes Kleid gefloßen ist, Er so das Salb Oel seiner heiligen Menschheit aufs Chor, auf ein jedes individuum und deßen Hütte fliessen laßen, durch gehen, Balsamiren und zu einer ledigen Bruder Hütte, zu einer Gottes Hütte eines Chor Verwanten des Lamms heiligen soll" (UA R.20.HS57).
83 A good example is this quote where Zinzendorf describes the sister houses as 'Dwellings of peace and blessing, heaven on earth, the courtyards of the lord, which only need the walls to be removed, then the bridal chamber stands there with the bridegroom within' Single sisters, 8 June 1757 (UA R.20.HS60).

CHAPTER 6

The State and Its Subjects

We return to that formidable text known as *The German Ideology*, where Marx and Engels insist that[1]

> the ideas of the ruling class are in every epoch the ruling ideas, i.e. the class which is the ruling material force of society, is at the same time its ruling intellectual force. The class which has the means of material production at its disposal, has control at the same time over the means of mental production, so that thereby, generally speaking, the ideas of those who lack the means of mental production are subject to it. The ruling ideas are nothing more than the ideal expression of the dominant material relationships, the dominant material relationships grasped as ideas; hence of the relationships which make the one class the ruling one, therefore, the ideas of its dominance.[2]

In a period of transition, such as the one in which the present analysis is situated, it should not come as a surprise that there are competing ideas. At present, the ruling ideas of capitalist society may be regarded as the ideological basis of that self-same society, that which renders it legitimate and coherent. But this was not the case in the eighteenth-century eastern German states, something of which analyses of historical material should be acutely aware. To avoid using liberal ideology to analyse social formations and relations in pre-capitalist settings, I have been thinking with Fredric Jameson's concept of 'cultural revolution' mentioned in the Introduction. Jameson defined it as that moment in which competing modes of production and their obvious antagonisms have moved to the centre of political and social life,[3] and I mentioned reading our archival material as taking part in a struggle between the old world and its impending transformation. This is what I have been working to draw out in Chapters 4 and 5, where I focused on ideas of inner selves, presence, signification, gender, and body as expressions of new understandings of human nature as well as of social relations, individual and community, in an attempt to follow Ellen Meiksins Wood's call to 'challenge the universality of its [i.e.

---

1 Sections of this chapter have been published in Petterson 2019.
2 Marx and Engels 1972, p. 59.
3 Jameson 1981, p. 81.

capitalism's] constituent categories'.[4] Now the time has come to lift this up to the next level and explore the socio-economic change which lends particular salience to these archival observations.

To articulate one obvious antagonism between 'old' and 'new' ways of thinking, we return to the concept of *Stand*, after which I turn to the questions of gender and class. We then move on to the emergence of the individual, and then finish up with the question of religion and the emergence of the modern state.

1 *Stand* as Manifestation of Cultural Revolution

> The history of all hitherto existing society is the history of class struggles. Freeman and slave, patrician and plebeian, lord and serf, guild-master and journeyman, in a word, oppressor and oppressed, stood in a constant opposition to one another, carried on an uninterrupted, now hidden, now open fight, a fight that each time ended, either in a revolutionary reconstitution of society at large, or in the common ruin of the contending classes.
>
> In earlier epochs of history, we find almost everywhere a complicated arrangement of society into various orders, a manifold gradation of social rank. In ancient Rome we have patricians, knights, plebeians, slaves; in the Middle Ages, feudal lords, vassals, guild-masters, journeymen, apprentices, serfs; in almost all of these classes, again, subordinate gradations.
>
> The modern bourgeois society that has sprouted from the ruins of feudal society has not done away with class antagonisms. It has but established new classes, new conditions of oppression, new forms of struggle in place of the old ones.[5]

We also return to *The Communist Manifesto*. As this quotation indicates, class antagonisms have not disappeared in modern bourgeois society, but take on a different shape. In this chapter we will explore a crucial feature of the Moravians in the transition to modernity, namely, their communal structure as an attempt to neutralise or divert class struggle. In the speeches we saw how the feudal foundation of *Stand* was redefined and used to signify one's relation in the gendered order, rather than as a socio-economic characteristic. What is the socio-historical significance of this?

---

4 Wood 1995, p. 13.
5 Marx and Engels 1976 [1848], pp. 482 and 485.

As mentioned several times, *Stand* was, broadly speaking, the fundamental principle of order in pre-modern Europe.[6] However, after a series of social upheavals in early nineteenth century Germany, characterised by Werner Conze as a dismantling of the corporate order, a shift in the proportions between groups in society, and the dissolution of the social and moral universe,[7] *Stand* was replaced by the individual citizen and social classes along new lines. As mentioned in the previous chapters, Isabel Hull observes that this individual citizen was defined by the universalism of the body, as the only distinguishing feature left, and as such became the foundation of civil society. As we have seen, Zinzendorf's own sexual system and process of gendering provides a good insight into this process.

At a terminological level, the concept *Stand* underwent two contradictory developments from the middle of the eighteenth century according to Conze.[8] On the one hand, he notes the disuse of the term because of its legitimisation of the outdated social order and its base in metaphysics and theology.[9] On the other, he points to its continued usage, but in new clothing. For some, *Stand* was a useful concept to reconfigure what I would determine as social relations in accordance with new socio-political parameters. As an example of disuse Conze mentions Kant, whose insistence on the (formal) equality and natural rights of the individual (aided by the French Revolution) delivered the political deathblow to *Stand* as socio-political organisation and its foundation in birth, inheritance and aristocratic privilege. As an example of the revamped version Conze points to the parlance of the cultured classes (*gesittete Stände*), which covered the nobility and the new bourgeois class, who sought to distance themselves from the lower classes through reference to culture.[10] Conze sees this usage as a way of redefining the term by using it within other areas of life, such as education. Here, with its emphasis on consciousness and self-definition, its use is much closer to 'class' than the older understanding of *Stand*.

In his study on 'enlightened Protestantism', Ulrich Barth mentions the fate of the three-estate structure in the period from Luther to Schleiermacher. He notes that Schleiermacher used his ethical structure of state-church-family as

---

6   Kocka 1990, p. 33. See also Gray 2000, pp. 25–39.
7   Irmline Veit-Brause has helpfully translated Conze's concepts of *Dekorporierung, Dispropotionierung* and *Entsittlichung* in Veit-Brause 2003, pp. 337–8. These concepts appear in Conze 1962, p. 248 with explanation on pp. 249–61.
8   Conze 2005.
9   At a philosophical level, theories of natural law and social contracts (he mentions Hobbes, Spinoza and Pufendorf) had done away with the social differentiation privileges based on and associated with *Stand*. Conze 2005, p. 211.
10 Conze 2005, pp. 216–17.

a replacement for the 'old Protestant three-estate structure' as a part of his efforts to adapt Protestantism to the changing social conditions. Luther's adaptation of the three-estate structure had consolidated itself as a coherent theory for 'Christian society', but in the social upheavals of the German Revolution, where it became obvious that the three-estate structure was not compatible with modernity, a new model of socio-cultural reality was required, which was what Schleiermacher offered.[11]

Within this timeline, Barth notes that despite the fact that Spener and Francke (after Luther, and before Schleiermacher) attempted to neutralise the effects of differences in estate in the religious sphere, they did not see the need to reconceptualise Christian social teaching as such, precisely because the three-estate structure was still reckoned with in the early eighteenth century.[12] Barth does not mention the Moravian Brethren in this context,[13] but as we have seen, he would have been justified to do so, in that Zinzendorf went much further than Spener and Francke in his use of *Stand* and at a time when the three-estate structure was in a further state of dissolution. What is significant here is the implications of the use of *Stand* in Zinzendorf's speeches and how to understand this frequent occurrence and its different emphasis. Because Zinzendorf does not use *Stand* as an explicitly class related concept, we should place him in Conze's second trend, namely that of the reconceptualisation along different parameters, thus continuing a process already evident in Francke which reaches its apex in the cultured classes, as suggested by Conze above. However, the two examples posited by Conze (Kant and the natural rights of the individual, and the cultured classes) poses yet another problem, in that both examples concern two crucial features of civil society, namely the inalienable rights of the individual and the universalisation of a particular middle-class perspective. Within both developments Zinzendorf falls short, because these are features which belong to a slightly later period. Nevertheless, Zinzendorf's emphasis on gender certainly makes him a precursor of both these developments. First, the implementation of gender awareness anticipates the modern alienated subject, and second, it provides an identity which is common and universal, and as such can transcend differences based on class.

---

11   Barth 2004, pp. 163–4.
12   Barth 2004, p. 164.
13   He mentions them only as background to Schleiermacher's early theological training (p. 263), and then in the context of Schleiermacher's ideal church and animosity towards established churches (p. 287). However, as we saw in Chapter 4, Schleiermacher's background in the Moravian Brethren played a significant role in his Christology, and thus it is not inconceivable that the understanding of *Stand* also would have played a role.

These two aspects are obviously related in that the transcending of class differences necessitated an emphasis on the *individual* subject and its civic nature, which corresponds to the dismantling of the social order of which *Stand* was the organising principle.

Stand, then, would ordinarily signal the old world order and its privileges, but here, in Herrnhut, it is used freely as an indicator of the choir order of the community, at a time when the old order characterised by *Stand* was unravelling. One of my main understandings of the choirs, is that they function as a site within which social relations are reconfigured, but because of the choirs' gendered order, there is the danger of seeing gender as the only feature of the choirs. However, gendering is also subjectification, both individual and collective, to which the choir speeches testify. The choir speeches, then, use *Stand*-as-gender to collectivise *and* individualise. And while gender relations are a good place to commence analysis, it must be emphasised that gender relations are a particular form of social relations, in that gender relations also express the socio-economic structures of which they are a part.[14]

Using *Stand* to understand new ways of expressing gender and social relations is part of the trajectory from Francke to the cultured classes, and testifies to the gradual separation of the term from its socio-economic function. Here, in the mid-eighteenth century, however, it still has a function, in that it is still connected to its original socio-economic context, which was crumbling, thus releasing the word and enabling it to be redeployed in different contexts. Its frequent usage in Zinzendorf testifies to its ideological importance at this time. Only decades later will it be gradually reduced to having a mere 'civic' function.

However, in Herrnhut, *Stand* in its older sense also plays a significant structural role, in that the role of the aristocracy in Herrnhut was fundamental – both in economics and ideology. This should not be surprising in that at this time, the aristocracy still was the ruling class, albeit weakening. So, what we are witnessing is an instance of Jameson's concept of cultural revolution; it is clear that there are competing claims to the means of production and antagonistic understandings of organising society and social relations. As should be clear by now, I see Herrnhut as a prime example of such a moment, and the archival material demonstrates these contradictions and antagonisms in different ways.

2   Gender

Let us continue with the issue of gender. In scholarship, the Moravians are without exception seen as challenging prevailing understandings of gender

---

14   Knopp and Lauria 1987, p. 51.

and marriage as noted in Chapter 4. However, keeping in mind the concept of cultural revolution, and that mid-eighteenth-century Eastern Germany was in a time of transition between socio-economic systems and their corresponding organisation of people, then what existing gender hierarchies should we take as the one challenged by the Moravians?[15] Did they challenge feudal household organisation or capitalist gender hierarchies? This is an interesting point, and also the point at which I have met the most fervent resistance, namely in my suggestion that the Moravian understanding of gender was aligned with the emerging structures of capitalism. The most common opinion is that the Moravian choir system *challenged* some vague ahistorical understanding of gender. Upon further questioning, this shows itself as bourgeois understandings of gender, which from a historical point of view did not really exist as an independent and firm structure at the time of the Moravian challenge. We are, in other words, dealing with a false universal, something which bourgeois ideology is infinitely capable of producing.[16]

In her article on gender and history already discussed in Chapter 4,[17] Joan Scott assesses a number of approaches to gender which may or may not be useful for historians. Here, Gayle Rubin's article, 'Traffic in Women',[18] is mentioned as an example of work which articulates the usefulness of psychoanalysis for understanding the reproduction and enculturation of gender. Scott continues,

> But the universal claim of psychoanalysis gives me pause. Even though Lacanian theory may be helpful for thinking about the construction of gendered identity, historians need to work in a more historical way. If gender identity is based only and universally on fear of castration, the point of historical inquiry is denied.[19]

For anyone who has worked at length with Rubin's article, this is a curious – but effective – reduction of a sophisticated argument. Scott states that historians cannot base their work on universal claims, and certainly not psychoanalysis's proclivity for castration.

Scott continues,

---

15   Kate Carté asked me this question in reference to my project, and I found it so fruitful in terms of clarifying assumptions that I shamelessly appropriate it here.
16   McKeon 1995, p. 306.
17   Scott 1999.
18   Rubin 1975.
19   Scott 1999, p. 1068.

Moreover, real men and women do not always or literally fulfil the terms either of their society's prescriptions or of our analytic categories. Historians need instead to examine the ways in which gendered identities are substantively constructed and relate their findings to a range of activities, social organisations, and historically specific cultural representations.[20]

She emphasises biographies of nineteenth- and twentieth-century women as 'the best efforts in this area'.

Do not get me wrong, I am not a fan of psychoanalytic approaches to history. This is, however, less due to their castration narrative, and more due to their overriding focus on the individual.[21] Nevertheless, for Western culture, gender has become a fundamental master narrative through which everything is assessed and rewritten. It is such a matter of course that gender is part of our own identities and shapes how we see the world. That this was not always so is far from obvious. There have always been men and women, and in most historical reconstructions, there has always been oppression of women. But the implications of gender are intimately connected to that of subjectivity, which again is historically connected with psychoanalysis. In dismissing Rubin's article so quickly, Scott also ignores or overlooks a number of very important observations therein. To demonstrate this, I need to borrow some points from Lukács's exposition of the problems of history.[22]

Paraphrasing Marx, Lukács points out that bourgeois historians work within parameters set by social institutions, and leave the principles of society untouched – indeed, this is my problem with Scott's article. Rather, Lukács insists that 'history is precisely the history of these institutions, of the changes they undergo as institutions which bring men together in societies'.[23] This means that bourgeois historians operate with laws that are only useful 'within the framework of the historical context which produced them and which in turn is produced by them', while the task of history is rather to analyse the parameters and the historical contexts.[24]

---

20   Scott 1999, p. 1068.
21   Petterson 2016c.
22   I am referring to the chapter 'Class Consciousness' in 1990, pp. 46–82.
23   Lukács 1990, p. 48. See also Lukács 1975, p. 314, where Lukács notes that specific social institutions come into being and acquire their object nature as a result of externalisation. It is thus the *process* which should be analysed, and not the objectified institutions.
24   Lukács 1990, p. 49. See also Lukács 1975, p. 395, where Lukács points out that Hegel breaks up and challenges 'human thought which had been ossified by the habit of metaphysics' and posits dialectical thought as a way beyond this habitual thinking.

Rubin is not a historian, but an anthropologist. Her argument rests on a 'sex/gender system' by which she means a set of arrangements by which a society transforms raw material, i.e. biological sexuality, into products of human activity. This is empirically observable in kinship systems, which are 'made up of and reproduce concrete forms of socially organised sexuality'.[25] If kinship is the culturalisation of sexuality at a social level, psychoanalysis describes the enculturation of the individual into such a given social contract.[26] What Rubin is doing in her article, is analysing psychoanalysis as a framework of modernity to examine the particularity of the gender relation of this given period. In other words, she is not letting herself be confined by the parameters of history but includes them in her analysis.[27]

A more philosophical approach to the same question of whether the modern notion of 'gender' has a specific history is found in Carole Pateman's *The Sexual Contract*. In this dense study, Pateman argues that social contract theory marks the transition from classical patriarchal thought to modern patriarchy which structures capitalist civil society. Social contract theory is a way of explaining the relation between state and individual, and Pateman astutely notes how it also produces ideas of men and women in its articulation: 'To tell the story of the sexual contract is to show how sexual difference, what it is to be a "man" or a "woman" and the construction of sexual difference as political difference, is central to civil society'.[28] Pateman wants to pinpoint the structures of modern patriarchy and therefore refuses to regard patriarchy as universal, in that it then is too easy to dismiss as a feudal relic. Instead, she examines the distinct nature of modern patriarchy and the shift in male power over women as it is expressed in the social contract theories:

---

25 Rubin 1975, p. 82.
26 Rubin 1975, pp. 92, 95.
27 It would take us too far away from our line of questioning to analyse the curious tango with Marx/Engels that takes place in Rubin's argument, but a couple of points might be useful down here in the footnotes. While there are some examples to the contrary in the article, the main thrust seems to be a reluctance to conceive of the sex/gender system as a part of economic developments, and instead a preference to create a political economy of sex: 'Levi-Strauss and Freud's work enables us to isolate sex and gender from "mode of production" and to counter a certain tendency to explain sex oppression as a reflex of economic forces' (Rubin 1975, pp. 101–2). Presenting gender relations as a distinct and independent system of relations from the relations of production is what is known as the 'dual systems' theory, of which Iris Young was particularly, and justifiably, critical (Young 1981).
28 Pateman 1988, p. 16.

Modern civil society is not structured by kinship and the power of fathers; in the modern world, women are subordinated to men *as men*, or to men as a fraternity. The original contract takes place after the political defeat of the father and creates modern fraternal patriarchy.[29]

The father figure, the hierarchical power figure of traditional/classical patriarchy, has been stripped of his power, making the idea of the contract necessary.[30] Thus, Pateman notes, one kinship term has replaced another, with this new term signalling 'community, solidarity or fellowship', instead of the crusty, obsolete hierarchical power structure of yore.[31]

This idea of patriarchal power transforming from a hierarchical structure to a contracted power of the brotherhood is not uninteresting in our current context, especially not bearing in mind the emphasis on 'brethren' in the various names of the Moravians: *Unitas Fratrum, Herrnhuter Brüdergemeine*, Moravian Brethren.[32] Of immediate interest is rather what this means for the shift in gender, namely men *as men*.

From the field of English Literature, Michael McKeon suggests that 'the form of modern patriarchy depends upon the structural separation of the genders: that the emergence of modern patriarchy is coextensive with the emergence of gender difference, which is therefore historically specific to the modern era'.[33] Thus the rise of modern patriarchy entails a process of differentiation at various levels. Elements which formerly had been understood as part of 'an integral whole' were now being separated out. It is in this larger process that McKeon sees the emergence of gender difference. Drawing on Thomas Laqueur's work, McKeon notes that 'it was only in the eighteenth century that female bodies ceased to be seen as aberrant versions of a unitary male body, and were viewed instead as physically and naturally different'.[34] This argument is furthered in a special edition of the journal *Signs* in 2012, introduced and edited by McK-

---

29 Pateman 1988, p. 3.
30 Pateman 1988, p. 77. Pateman distinguishes between traditional patriarchy and classical patriarchy, where traditional patriarchy signifies the authority of the father as the metaphor and the family as the model for authority relations. Classical patriarchal thought is connected with Robert Filmer and is a deliberate conflation of paternal and political power, and brings together notions of political right and political obedience. This was a very short-lived form and was superseded by modern patriarchy. Pateman 1988, pp. 24–5.
31 Pateman 1988, p. 78.
32 The American province prefers Moravian Church as the current name.
33 McKeon 1995, p. 300.
34 McKeon 1995, p. 301. The reference is to Laqueur 1990.

eon with contributions from Laqueur and others.[35] McKeon and Laqueur both situate the emergence of modern gender and modern sex within the revolutions of the eighteenth century, the changes in production and consumption, politics and the emergence of civil society, as the conditions which enabled these reframings of sexuality and gender relations.[36]

This was already noted by Jameson, who points out that when sexuality was part of social life, as was, for example, eating, it was merely 'a banal innerworldly event and bodily function'.[37] Once it was released from this social field and isolated, it was possible to grant it endless symbolic possibilities, as in Freudian psychoanalysis – which Rubin used to show the particularity of modern gender subjectification.[38] The conditions, thus Jameson, 'become visible, one would imagine, only when you begin to appreciate the extent of psychic fragmentation since the beginnings of capitalism, with its systematic quantification and rationalisation of experience, its instrumental reorganisation of the subject just as much as of the outside world'.[39] Indeed, the basis of Freudian analysis 'lies in the preliminary isolation of sexual experience, which enables its constitutive features to carry a wider symbolic meaning'.[40]

Drawing these potted analyses together, then, 'gender' becomes a feature of capitalism's particular and fragmented way of conceptualising sexual difference and gendered consciousness. It is not difficult to see this expressed in the choir speeches, where a gender consciousness is cultivated at nearly all levels. Gender is thus explicitly produced as part of the individualisation process, but also a sense of collectivity based on gender. The one thing that all of these 430 speeches to women and men in their various stages of life have in common is

---

35 McKeon 2012.
36 Laqueur 2012, p. 806. Rubin touches upon this briefly in her observation that there was a time when sex and gender 'had functions other than itself', namely the organisation of society, whereas now, 'it only organises and reproduces itself'; see also her remark that kinship 'has been systematically stripped of its functions – political, economic, educational and organisational'. Rubin 1975, p. 99.
37 Jameson 1981, p. 49.
38 Joan W. Scott is concerned with psychoanalysis's exclusive fixation on 'the subject' and its universalisation of 'the categories and relationship of male and female'. She sees this as providing historians with a reductive reading of the past, and thus does not 'permit the introduction of a notion of historical specificity and variability'. Scott 1999, p. 1064. I agree with her criticism, but as argued above, I find the making of a subject a useful process for understanding the emergence of self, which corresponds to the heavy emphasis on gender. I am also not entirely sure that she escapes this criticism herself.
39 Jameson 1981, p. 47.
40 Jameson 1981, p. 49.

their demonstrating and explaining their relationship to their Saviour, which is always carried out in terms of gender. The men are to explore and understand how they can become like the Saviour, in full control of their bodies and desires, and the women are instructed and encouraged to relate to the Saviour as a wife, and how to take on the appropriate submissiveness.

Instead of regarding gender as something given and the choirs as a convenient way of managing random men and women, I have focused on what the focus on gender and gender relations actually serves in this particular historical setting, namely overcoming class conflict. However, as indicated, class conflict does not simply vanish, but resurfaces in a set of new tensions that must be overcome. In other words, by placing the emphasis on gender as the common denominator, the problem of socio-economic inequality is not solved; it is merely displaced, and left to continue – which it did, and still does. This focus on gender, and its use as a symbol, is a step towards the production of fragmented existence of humans in capitalist civil society.

3   Class Society and the Civic Self

As discussed in the Introduction, one of the salient features of capitalist society is the emergence of class consciousness, namely those of the bourgeoisie and, of course, the working classes, the latter formidably demonstrated by E.P. Thompson. What this entails, as argued by Marx in the *Eighteenth Brumaire*, is both an objective aspect (distinct conditions of existence and mode of life) and a subjective aspect (community, unity, and enemy) to define a class. A class thus is more than the sum of its parts, i.e. in itself; it is a collective consciousness defined over against a class enemy, i.e. for itself.

However, as I have argued, one of the key features of the speeches was to cultivate self-reflection as well as a choir identity in and for itself. Since this is well before Hegelian dialectics and Marx's use thereof, we need to look elsewhere for a source for this type of thinking. And here we should look to the ruling class, because the ruling class has always been in its various manifestations, a class *for* itself. Ruling class consciousness is a thing which serves to distinguish the ruling classes from the ruled, as noted by George Simmel:

> While the nobility, in its purest historical manifestation, unite the life values of the individual with unique strength in its collectivity, and while on the other hand, its development aims with unconditional unanimity at the formation, growth and independence of the individual, the nobility

provided a historically unique solution to the balance between the whole and the individual, the predetermined realities and the personal arrangements of life.[41]

Ruling class consciousness, as demonstrated in the aristocracy, is both individual and collective consciousness and perhaps played a bigger role in the emerging self of modernity. Indeed, James van Horn Melton's critique of Habermas's theory of the public sphere is that the latter overlooks the participation of nobles in the public realm, which to Melton suggests that

> to focus solely on the subversive dimensions of the Enlightened public sphere overlooks the resilience and adaptability of Old Regime society and institutions, which were quite capable of recognising the communicative potential of the public sphere. ... Moreover, if the practices of sociability nurtured in salons or masonic lodges tended to dissolve boundaries that had traditionally distinguished noble from bourgeois, the impact was not necessarily subversive. To the contrary, one might just as easily see the social intermingling of noble and bourgeois as having contributed to a progress of social integration, fusing the propertied classes of society into a new elite by creating new criteria for social distinction and exclusion based on education and taste. In this respect the Enlightened public sphere betrayed a fundamental paradox: while bridging the social and cultural divide separating noble and non-noble, it simultaneously widened the distance between propertied and plebeian.[42]

Melton notes that Habermas's notion of the public sphere and the dissolution of the distinctions between noble and bourgeois is not necessarily subversive, because, given the 'resilience and adaptability' of the aristocratic ruling class, there is the distinct possibility that they have actively participated in the re-organisation of society and the configuration of a new ruling class based on aristocratic cultural principles (Conze's cultured classes, mentioned earlier), and creating a distinction over against the 'plebeian'. Melton's study goes on to study the emergence of public opinion, and its manifestations in writings, salons and coffee houses, so we may leave him here, but take note of this important point, namely that the aristocracy did not just go away.[43]

---

41 Simmel 2009, p. 651.
42 Melton 2001, pp. 11–12.
43 See also Brinkmann 1926. Brinkmann looks at the segments of the aristocracy who did

The aristocracy of the eighteenth century was not, in other words, merely wigs, gold, and colour. It was a ruling class rapidly losing power, as the social structure on which their privileges and income was dependent was crumbling. Some managed the transition, and some did not. Both Halle Pietism and the Moravian Brethren were helpful in mediating the transition for the aristocracy to the new world of commercial power, in that they provided classical roles of patronage for the various counts and countesses *within* the respective communities, and in this way alleviated the impending redundancy.

Even a superficial glance at documents from the history of the community demonstrate the significance of the aristocracy in Herrnhut. For example, Uttendörfer recounts the early debates over clothing in Herrnhut between 1731 and 1744, where there were countless complaints over brothers and sisters who imitated the dress and mannerisms of the nobility and dressed above their station. Several regulations were implemented to avoid this social malady.[44] Another example is our social entrepreneur Johann Michael Langguth, who was married to Zinzendorf's oldest daughter, but not before he was adopted by Zinzendorf's old friend and co-worker Friederik von Watteville in 1745 and granted the title of Freiherr/Baron Johannes von Watteville.[45] A final example is from 1744, when Zinzendorf's entourage (*Pilgergemeine*) consisted of 53 members of his household and 30 servants.[46] In relation to this practice, Paul Peucker mentions the 'religious court culture' that emerged in the 1740s and 1750s within the Moravian community, which 'mirror[ed] the secular courts and set them [the Moravians] apart from other religious movements of the early modern period'.[47]

---

not want to engage in capitalist business, and the segments which could not, he identifies the segment which were won over to new business practices and 'either dissolved or preserved the aristocracy' (p. 28).

44 Uttendörfer 1925, pp. 40–4.
45 Grosse 1914, p. 58.
46 Paul Peucker refers to the document from Marienborn, October 1744, where there is a list of the household and its guests, and which has a special section on *Domestiquen der Gäste*, with 15 unnamed servants in the guesthouse, five in the kitchen, and then follows a list of some named servants, such as Schneider the footman, Weinecke the postman, the host, Herchenhahn and his wife. Furthermore, two single men are mentioned (Matthias Seybold and Gottfried from Canada) with no specific function, a married woman, Bonn from Canada, and finally three married couples (Bernicke, Kilian and Lehr) also with no mentioned function (UA R.27.292.33). See also Becker-Cantarino 2018, pp. 168–9, who apart from mentioning the size of the *Pilgergemeine* also draws attention to the size of the household in Berthelsdorf.
47 Peucker 2015, p. 24.

Uttendörfer drew repeated attention to the increased aristocratisation of Herrnhut, beginning in the late 1730s:

> In 1739, only one noble homeowner is present, apart from Zinzendorf; now in 1741 Frau von Tschirschkz and Herr von Seydliz want to buy houses, which, however, was prohibited by the lot. But on February 3, 1743, Moscherosch writes: 'It is now right that Herr von Wiedebach will have a large, handsome house built, whereby our poor brothers can again earn something,' and in fact the aristocratisation of Herrnhut now sets in.[48]

And this was not just restricted to dress, mannerisms, or housing, but eventually led to theological innovation:

> The sentimental, joyful religiosity of the new brethren, with their enjoyment of the Saviour's love, appears in general as a permeation of aristocratic piety over against the narrow gravity of petty-bourgeois Pietism, and the more this type of piety emerged the winner under Zinzendorf's leadership, the more the attraction of the Brethren appealed to higher, especially noble circles.[49]

This aristocratic air of Herrnhut has long been recognised especially due to the work of Schmidt and Uttendörfer.[50] The past decades have seen a surge of research on the aristocracy in general,[51] which also has endowed Herrnhut with reflected glory.[52] A good survey of older positions is found in Peter Vogt's article on Zinzendorf's 'paradoxical pietist-aristocratic identity'.[53] Vogt suggests four theses: First, he looks at the already mentioned study of Theodor E. Schmidt, who, according to Vogt, emphasises Zinzendorf's aristocratic background as fundamental for his agency. Zinzendorf could not *not* act as a count. However, also his pietism served as stimulus to the 'ideal of a binding Christian social order'.[54] The second thesis is that of Hans Walter Erbe,[55] who argued that Zinzendorf was part of the pious nobility of his time, and that the conflict with Halle was not due to the blood and wounds theology; rather his

---

48   Uttendörfer 1925, p. 59.
49   Uttendörfer 1926, p. 14.
50   Schmidt 1900; Uttendörfer 1925; 1926.
51   Düselder, Weckenbrock, and Westphal 2008; Weckenbrock 2014.
52   Albrecht et al. 2018; Schattkowsky 2013.
53   Vogt 2018.
54   Vogt 2018, p. 102.
55   Erbe 1928.

churchly activism and ordination was seen as compromising the dignity of the rank. The third is that of Uttendörfer, and the increasing aristocratisation of the Moravian Brethren, which led to an increase in aristocratic influence on communal life. This prompted the already mentioned imitation of dress and mannerism, which led to a downturn in the production output of the community, because lifestyle expenses increased, while the will to work decreased. The Sifting Time was a natural outcome of this influence, and the corrective measures taken afterwards placed a greater emphasis on difference of *Stand* than previously. Fourth is Peter Zimmerling,[56] who argued that Zinzendorf's theology generated a 'democratisation of aristocratic ways of life' which meant the import of elements of court life into the liturgy and everyday life of the community, thus leading to egalitarianism. These four examples lead Vogt to conclude that in Zinzendorf we can identify a double movement: 'On the one hand he removed himself from the conventions of the nobility, on the other hand, he brought the influence of the nobility to bear on the Moravian Brethren'.[57] Vogt defines this as the 'paradox of pietist-aristocratic identity' in Zinzendorf. However, there is one issue which I think needs unpacking. As our examination in Chapter 2 demonstrated, there was a shift in the understanding of the nature of the community which may be dated to the synod in Gotha, where Zinzendorf states that 'we' will move away from the ideal of the apostolic community and instead carve a new path for a new world. While Vogt several times does note that Zinzendorf's disavowal of the aristocratic *Stand* as part of the apostolic ideal and 'republican constitution' were part of the beginnings of the Moravian Brethren, he nevertheless implies that this 'impulse' remained alongside Zinzendorf's appreciation of his aristocratic background, hence the paradoxical identity. I find a more plausible explanation one which acknowledges the shift from an older idealistic, and indeed egalitarian community, to a hierarchical choir-based baroque extravaganza. This also has the benefit of focusing on the community, where the increase of nobility generated a penetration of aristocratic culture into the community as a whole. The 'democratisation of aristocratic ways of life' is not, in my interpretation, connected with Zinzendorf's theology, but his class and his position in the community, which, as Uttendörfer noted, attracted other aristocrats. In his monograph on the Moravian Church in England, Colin Podmore draws attention to not only the imposing buildings, but also Zinzendorf's love of architecture, music, and painting, which 'brought an aristocratic attitude to life as a whole'.[58] And, as I

---

56   Zimmerling 1991.
57   Vogt 2018, p. 104.
58   Podmore 1998, pp. 150–2.

have demonstrated in Chapter 2, birthdays and the reading of one's *Lebenslauf* at the funerals of members were all aristocratic events which eventually made their way into the lives of community members. There were many members from the first generation of Moravian and Bohemian immigrants who did not know their birthdate, only a year.[59] Of course, birthdates later become a fundamental part of civil registration, but here in eighteenth-century Herrnhut, it is for celebration and patronage. As the diaries demonstrated, the birthdays of the aristocratic members of Herrnhut and leaders were celebrated in pomp, music and colour, in Marie-Louise Hopf-Droste's words, a cultic celebration.[60] And, as discussed in Chapter 3, the blood and wounds theology of the 1740s engaged the aristocracy at an emotional level.

4 Individual and Subject

Another important transformation of the time is the appearance of individuals. In the chapter on the choir speeches, I showed how a number of features were cultivated in the members from very early on. These included the production of an inner self, a reflective consciousness, and attention to one's body, to name a few. Furthermore, in these choir years, we also need to remember that these are the years in which the Saviour is conceptualised as a subject, and a much more present one than what has earlier been the case. These features are part of a process of individual subjectification, and articulate a new mode of interacting with the world, different from that inherent in the three-estate structure. One indicator of this emerging individualism is the emphasis on smell, which we saw mentioned in the speech to the children, as well as in many others. We recall the description of communion as tasting the boils of the Saviour in the speech to the children. Smell is, of course, along with sight, taste, hearing, and touch, one of the five senses. And, as Jameson points out with reference to Marx, the senses are 'the results of a long process of differentiation even within human history'.[61] In his 'Economic and Philosophical Manuscripts', Marx writes

---

59   In the catalogue of the named sisters interned in the Gottesacker, of the 37 who do not have an assigned date of birth, 20 are from Moravia. Some have a year, others no indication (*Der Gottesacker zu Herrnhut* 1822).
60   Hopf-Droste 1979, p. 236. Hopf-Droste's analysis sees the emergence of the modern birthday as the expression of individualism and a linear conception of time over against the name-day and pre-modern birthday celebrations which were mainly for the upper classes, and also did not focus on age. This only became a feature in the course of modernisation and its obsession with individualisation and quantification.
61   Jameson 1981, p. 62.

that man is 'affirmed in the objective world not only in thought but with *all* the senses'.⁶² The senses, then, are a particular way of relating to the world,⁶³ and this way is not a given, but conditional, and for Marx, related to subjective experience.

Another indicator is the make-up of a human being as consisting of a *Hütte* and a host of inner entities, such as soul (*Seele*), *Gemüt* and *Geist*, the three of which form the inner life of a human being in no apparent fixed order or hierarchy. As we saw, these inner entities are connected to external forces, which can make them enact undesirable effects on the *Hütte*. All of these opaque connections between the various entities means that we cannot in any meaningful way speak of a unified self, much less an autonomous self. We are thus far from the sovereignty and freedom of our bodies and selves, which are regarded as inviolable rights and matters of course in contemporary Western culture. The choir speeches are clearly from a time when this was not so; when the body was still a mystery, the self not yet fully formed, and the relation to external forces still not completely severed. These issues were not only debated in both European medicine and philosophy, but, as we see, entered the everyday lives of the Moravian Brethren.

Here, we may latch on to the dense and not always comprehensible study on enthusiasm by Jordana Rosenberg. She identifies enthusiastic discourse as a 'uniquely dialectic encounter with the key features of early modernity',⁶⁴ and connects this discourse with historical thinking, sovereignty, and capitalist accumulation:

> the fantasies of immediacy long articulated in the rhetoric of enthusiasm, give shape to the ideologies of autonomy that attend the birth of commodity culture and the relations of capital accumulation. Furthermore, these fantasies [...] are discursively reconfigured to articulate ideas of state sovereignty and the autonomous, self-regulating subject of that state.⁶⁵

---

62   Marx [1844] 1975, p. 301, emphasis in original.
63   This might be traced in Goethe's relationship to Kant as expressed in the preface to his *Farbenlehre*, but that is the topic of another study. See Sepper 2009. See also Rosenberg's observation that 'sense experience and aesthetic appreciation both exist by virtue of a larger structure that guides the parts into their proper places and *is* the placement of these parts. The subject's introspection, in Mary Poovey's words, "yields understanding of the proper relation between the self and the whole, of which the individual is but a part"'. Rosenberg 2011, p. 47. The Poovey quotation is from Poovey 1998, p. 178.
64   Rosenberg 2011, pp. 3–4.
65   Rosenberg 2011, p. 25.

This immediacy or experience of unmediated communion with God is also something we encountered in the choir speeches, where the direct experience of the Saviour's presence among his people was emphasised, and articulated in terms of senses, but also vividly represented in the language of the speeches (which of course is mediation, but is nevertheless presented and experienced as direct communication with the divine). This enthusiasm is thus 'religious autonomisation' and is expressed in an autonomous subject within capitalist relations of production and its sovereign state. This is essentially what I am arguing here, namely that the articulation of self we encounter in the choir speeches is part of a larger drive towards the individual of the modern state, and that in the course of this articulation, the relations between self and community are reconfigured. Where I depart from Rosenberg is my emphasis on the divine as actor and mediator in this, namely my stress on the Saviour as mediator.

As an aside, we may note Rosenberg's reading of enthusiasm in Shaftesbury. Unlike Locke, but in extension of Hume, Shaftesbury saw how 'enthusiastic passion [...] became a way of describing the individual's relation to the social whole itself' – and that passions, not unlike what we have seen above, 'mark an individual subject's calibration with an objective order that exceeds them'.[66] In her reading of *Sensus Communis*, Rosenberg demonstrates how this emphasis on enthusiasm as self-regulation had the effect of introducing competing sovereignties, namely the individual over against the state, and how Shaftesbury resolved this in the early eighteenth century. How, is not really an issue here, what interests me is *that* Shaftesbury encountered this contradiction, and endeavoured to resolve it.

Both Shaftesbury and Zinzendorf wrestle with a contradiction which they try to mediate. This is a *precursor* to the contradiction of civil society where the individual is divided, and where the civil society enters into a new contradiction with the state. They are both wrestling with the individual and the whole once it is released from its aristocratic confinements. In this breakdown of forces and relations of production which have to be dealt with in a new process, issues of *Stand* are individualised, and become issues of class. It is thus an economic question (following Marx) rather than, as Hegel, a political one.

Wrapping up this focus on the individual, we might briefly look at Etienne Balibar's analysis of the emergence of the 'citizen subject' after the French Revolution. Here, Balibar sets forth different ways of being a subject in the

---

66   Rosenberg 2011, p. 45.

history of philosophy, of which the modern citizen subject is one in a longer line of relations between the philosophical subject and sovereignty.[67] Balibar begins with the distinction between *subjectus* and *subjectum*, with *subjectus* indicating subjection to something else, and *subjectum* indicating a sovereign subject, bearer of consciousness. The point of this is to understand *when* the *subjectum* emerged. Heidegger, according to Balibar, argued that this began with Descartes. Balibar, on the other hand, denies that we see in Descartes' thinking thing, the *res cogitans*, a transcendental subject, in that Descartes' individual is made up of body and soul, and thus not a transcendental subject, *and* because Descartes' individual is subjected to divine sovereignty and its earthly representative rather than founded in its own reason. This means, in brief, that Descartes' individual is a *subjectus* rather than a *subjectum* and that the concept of individual subjectivity – as self-consciousness – does not appear until Locke, and then Kant. While Shaftesbury understood the relationship of individual and community as holistic, this social outlook is not one that encumbers either Locke or Kant. However, the holistic attitude is also characteristic of Zinzendorf's experimentations, where, as we have seen, the choir speeches perform individualising strategies on the one hand, while constantly presenting the choir as the community to which this individual belongs. In this dialectic of producing the community and the individual, what takes place is a similar process to the one Rousseau some decades later outlines in *On the Social Contract*:

> Whoever dares undertake to establish a people's institutions must feel himself capable of changing, as it were, human nature, of transforming each individual, who by himself is a complete and solitary whole, into a part of a larger whole, from which, in a sense, the individual receives his life and his being, of substituting a limited and mental existence for the physical and independent existence. He has to take from man his own powers, and give him in exchange alien powers, which he cannot employ without the help of other men.[68]

A similar observation in our direct context is the already mentioned quotation from Hanns-Joachim Wollstadt's study on the formative years of the congregation: 'By means of the group, the brother and the sister were incorporated (*eingegliedert*) into the community so strongly that they without attachment

---

67   Balibar 1991.
68   Quoted in Marx 1975 [1843], p. 167.

to a group in no way could have belonged to the collective community'.[69] While Wollstadt is talking about the earlier years before the choir structure, this tendency would only have been strengthened with the implementation of this structure.

We have now moved from individual to collective. As I have mentioned on several occasions, I see the Moravians as participating in breaking down the communal features of feudal society, such as guilds, household, and local community, and creating a new form of community. The most successful form of the new community is that of the choir, in that it here is possible to focus on gender as the defining feature of the individual as well as the community to which this individual belongs. But what does this mean for the idea of community? In the above-mentioned article on the Citizen Subject, Balibar notes that

> the citizen is unthinkable as an 'isolated' individual, for it is his active participation in politics that makes him exist. But he cannot on that account be merged into a 'total' collectivity. Whatever may be said about it, Rousseau's reference to a 'moral and collective body composed of as many members as there are votes in the assembly', produced by the act of association that 'makes a people a people', is not the *revival* but the *antithesis* of the organicist idea of the corpus mysticum (the theologians have never been fooled on this point).[70]

The difference between the corpus mysticum and Rousseau's 'moral and collective body' is precisely the role of the individual, because Rousseau's body is a collection of individuals, who, thus Balibar, can never be wholly body, nor wholly individual, while the corpus mysticum is an entirely different way of thinking group, before the notion of individual. Thus, while they both may be collective bodies, their understanding of what makes up the collective body differs radically, to which we now return.[71]

In the early pages of his introduction to *The Political Unconscious*, William Dowling uses the body to explain the function of 'primitive communism' (unfallen social reality) in Jameson's thinking, and how to imagine collective thinking in an individualist world. Dowling first outlines the paradox of the inability to think collectively (already quoted in Chapter 4):

---

69 Wollstadt 1966, p. 120.
70 Balibar 1991, pp. 51–2. Emphasis in original.
71 The following is taken from Petterson 2015.

For the unhappy fact is that as creatures of History, locked away in the private and separate and lonely worlds of our own consciousness – the separation and the loneliness having been produced by the implacable market forces of capitalism that constitutes human beings as individual units or 'subjects' in order to function as a system – we cannot imagine what it would be like, in the purest sense, to think collectively, to perceive the world as a world in which no such thing as individuals or individuality existed, to think not as 'a member of a group' but *as the group itself*.[72]

Dowling is using the body as an analogy to the kind of group thinking which is conceived of in that social reality before alienation and estrangement, primitive communism. He is here drawing attention to the radical difference of collective thinking which existed before capitalism. This is the kind of collective body which is in operation in the notion of the collective body of Christ in the New Testament, where the collective is presupposed as an absolute horizon – even though many biblical scholars do their best to individualise and christologise the collective. As we have seen, Zinzendorf's speeches exhibit a dialectic between the individual and the collective, which, while emphasising the community, nevertheless does so through the individual. Zinzendorf's use of the body of the Saviour is not only the ultimate horizon, but his body of the Saviour has also been radically individualised in order to serve as mediator between the individual sisters and brothers and the collective.[73]

Accessing the pre-capitalist understandings of collective is, however, impossible, because our language belongs to the fallen reality and thus cannot articulate this collectivity: 'In primitive communism as Jameson conceives it no concept of the group as such could exist, any more than I can consider my arms, my legs, and other parts of my body a group, as though I were to say "the whole group of us ran away: my legs did the pumping, my arms did the flailing, my eyes did the navigating," etc.'[74]

Zinzendorf's community of individual gendered members, connected via intermediate institutions such as the choir, meant that the choir structure was the central ideological feature of the community, which facilitated all practices in the community and served to mediate between the individual and the com-

---

72 Dowling 1984, p. 22. Emphasis in original.
73 Recall the change in the language of the Eucharist mentioned in Chapter 4, where Christian David in 1731 spoke of the believers becoming 'one body, one spirit, one heart and one soul' through the Eucharist, which in 1748 had changed to the sacrament of somatic unification, namely the connection of 'our nature' with that of the bridegroom.
74 Dowling 1984, p. 23.

munity. It is precisely in their mediating function that it is possible to detect the early stages of alienation characteristic of the modern state. This brings us back full circle, to the conceptual categories of capitalism in which we are so fully immersed that thinking as a body is virtually unthinkable.

5   The Question of Religion

So, what we are approaching is the question of alienation and the contradictions of bourgeois society, and in the last section of this chapter, I want to discuss the role of Christianity in this process. One of the results of Weber's attempted correction of the relationship between the Protestant ethos and the spirit of capitalism, is that Protestantism has been placed on the outside of capitalism, endowed with an agency with which it can act upon early capitalist thinking. However, as should be clear by now, I argue that the Moravian Christianity should be seen as part of the process.

When Georg Lukács describes the antithesis between the fullness of life of human beings and the one-sided human beings in bourgeois society who are deformed and reduced to automata in *Der junge Hegel*, he mentions Goethe's *Wilhelm Meister* as an excellent example of a work which deals with this particular issue. It is, Lukács states,

> typical of the state of Germany at the time that Goethe does not entirely reject religious solutions to these contradictions. The life of the canoness described in the Confessions of a Beautiful Soul gives a moving account of such a solution in which a sensitive woman holds herself aloof from ordinary life with the aid of religion, while through love she sustains a living human relationship with her fellow human beings. Of course, the religious solution is by no means Goethe's final word. On the contrary, the canoness is compared unfavourably with those who enter into the ordinary life of the capitalist world.[75]

What is interesting about this quote is not only the role of religion as one way of attempting to overcome the alienation of the individual, but the reference to 'the canoness' as the figure who embodies this role. The 'Confessions of a Beautiful Soul' are widely regarded as being inspired by the aristocratic woman Susanne von Klettenberg, who, apart from being an inspiration for

---

75   Lukács 1975, pp. 114–15.

Goethe's 'canoness', also had close affiliation with the Moravian Brethren, and the confessions in Wilhelm Meister are thus seen as an adaptation of her writings.[76]

Another interesting feature of this quote is the role of religion. Where Lukács otherwise shows great suspicion of what he calls the 'ideological need' to erect a 'Chinese wall' as a strategy of containment, he seems to fall into this trap himself when it comes to religion. As mentioned in Chapter 1, Lukács shows how the tendency to separate the Enlightenment from the 'Sturm und Drang' of German Classicism and Romanticism, enables literary historians to associate Goethe's *Werther* with the latter, reducing this embodiment of the struggles of pre-revolution bourgeois ideology to a love story. By showing how the narrative of Werther stages conflicts and values of bourgeois humanism, he demonstrates how Werther dramatically *belies* the wall constructed between Enlightenment and Classicism, and the ideological motivation of such a partition.

Surprisingly, however, Lukács seems to be following a similar pattern here in respect to his treatment of religion as something *outside* the contradictions between individual and community, which can or rather, cannot, function as a solution.

However, later in the same book, when discussing Hegel's criticism of Kant, Lukács then makes the following observation:

> The point at issue is the problem of 'the whole man'. In German idealism, the capitalist division of labour, particularly in its primitive, pre-revolutionary, ascetic phase, is reflected as the division of man into qualities of mind and the senses. This division is the heritage of religion, but its implications in the initial stages of classical German philosophy do not stem from religion in general, *but from the religious asceticism of those sects that embodied these ideological tendencies at an early stage of capitalism when its ideological and economic development was still rudimentary.* We must remind ourselves of the role of the sects in the Peasant War in Germany, the War of Liberation in the Netherlands and even in the English Revolution. And it would be a mistake to overlook the very significant elements of this tradition in Rousseau's ascetic idealism and in a number of his Jacobin disciples, such as Robespierre.[77]

---

76 Boyle 1992, pp. 75–8. Kormann 2018.
77 Lukács 1975, p. 150, my emphasis.

Here Lukács quite happily gives a role to sectarian Christianity as the progenitors of the fragmentation of man and connects it to the capitalist division of labour, without clarifying fully how that connection is to be understood.

To begin with the matter of sectarian Christianity, what Lukács is saying is that it is not religion per se which has laid the groundwork for German idealism, but rather that it is to be found in a number of sects which embodied the fragmentation at an early stage of capitalism. These sects, as well as early capitalism, are connected with asceticism, which, certainly in the cases of the Peasant War and the English Revolution, sounds highly curious. What this does sound like, however, is an echo of Max Weber's argument in *Protestant Ethic and Spirit of Capitalism*,[78] and the role of ascetic Christianity in the development of the early capitalist ethos.

Another issue is fragmentation. Following this quotation above is a sentence which repeats the point: 'In addition the reality of the capitalist division of labour itself led to specialization, the separation of the particular human qualities and faculties from each other and the overdevelopment of one at the cost of crippling the others'.[79] This fragmentation refers to the separation of the mind from the senses, which is another sweeping characteristic of sectarian Christianity that does not necessarily fit well with the Peasant Revolution or the English Revolution. It rather belongs to Enlightenment sensibilities and the posed contradiction between reason and emotion.[80] I am not entirely sure what is going on here, in part because it is difficult to trace when Lukács is glossing Hegel and when he himself is offering an explanation of the role of fragmentation. This current discussion appears, as mentioned, in the presentation of Hegel's disagreement with Kant, where Lukács notes that Hegel's objections 'are based on what Hegel thinks of as Kant's tendency to freeze the various moments of modern bourgeois fragmentation, to turn them into absolutes and thus to perpetuate the contradictions in a primitive, rudimentary state in which they can no longer be superseded or transcended'.[81] Kant's human, thus Hegel, is a 'soul-sack', 'stuffed full of "faculties" arbitrarily separated from each other'.[82] And I agree that the forerunner of this is to be found in some smaller sects, but

---

78 This is not discussed in Tarr 1989, but the connection between the two is argued in the article. Lukács, however, did engage Weber in his *Destruction of Reason* (Lukács 1980, pp. 601–19).
79 Lukács 1975, p. 150.
80 For a discussion of this in light of the Moravian Brethren, see Faull 1995; Bredsdorff 2003.
81 Lukács 1975, p. 150.
82 Lukács 1975, p. 148.

a more appropriate context for the separation of the mind from the senses than the German peasants or the True Levellers in England in the sixteenth and seventeenth centuries, is, in my opinion, the Moravian Brethren.[83]

Staying with the topic of fragmentation and the role of religion, Lukács states that Hegel initially saw religion as that which could unify man fragmented by capitalism. And it would seem that Lukács is trying to argue against such a position by pointing out the role of religion in that fragmentation. In that we agree, the disagreement is at the level of historical detail.

This role of religion, or more specifically Christianity in the fragmentation of human life is also, as mentioned in the introduction, the argument of Marx in the early essay 'On the Jewish Question'. In his disagreement with Bruno Bauer over the nature of emancipation, Marx argues that Bauer is already speaking from within the logic of the modern state and can as such only argue for political emancipation, not true human emancipation. While Bauer believes that political emancipation entails the individual and the state's abolishment of religion, Marx argues that true emancipation entails the abolishment of the division of humans into public and private. What Bauer does not see is that the state simply relegates religion to the individual sphere:

> The division of the human being into a *public man* and a *private man*, the *displacement* of religion from the state into civil society, this is not a stage of political emancipation, but its *completion*; this emancipation therefore neither abolishes the *real* religiousness of man, nor strives to do so.
>
> The *decomposition* of man into Jew and citizen, Protestant and citizen, religious man and citizen, is neither a deception directed *against* citizenhood, nor is it a circumvention of political emancipation, it is *political emancipation itself*, the *political* method of emancipating oneself from religion.[84]

Consequently, modern citizenship constitutes a person as living two lives: a person is an individual at the level of civil society as well as a citizen within the political state. This is the nature of political emancipation, which divides soci-

---

83   E.P. Thompson already noticed this when he observed the Moravian dilution of antinomian vocabulary as mentioned in Chapter 4 above (Thompson 1993, p. 57). The Moravians, then, are not to be understood as quite as anti-establishment and radical as many of the other groups of the time, which is why I think we need to distinguish between the various sects and their direct or indirect roles in the establishments of civil society and their citizens.

84   Marx 1975 [1843], p. 155, original emphasis.

ety into civil society and political state. So, Bauer's notion of emancipation is, despite its intended universality, extremely narrow, according to Marx, because it operates within the parameters of the modern state, and does not endeavour to liberate humans from the divided and alienating existence.

As should be discernible from the previous five chapters, my analysis of the Moravian Brethren has taken place within this line of questioning, and assuming an important role for this particular brand of Christianity in the changes underway. What has been of interest to me has been the contradiction between individual and community, and emerging alienation in the archival material, well knowing, of course, that we are situated before Goethe and before the full emergence of the civil society and its contradictions. However, as the history of the community has shown, the leaders and especially *male* members were from early on faced with the contradiction of individual and community, which they attempted to resolve. The ultimate embodiment of this contradiction results, as we all know from Hegel and Marx, in alienation. But I want to argue that the Moravian Brethren should be seen as *part of* the problem of alienation, rather than, as in Lukács's first position, a possible solution to a problem posed separately from the sphere of religion. While the motivation for the choir structure of the Moravians *could be seen* as 'purely' theological or pastoral, the emergence was enabled by certain non-theological conditions to which it responded at a very early stage. This in turn had significant ramifications for structuring of a society and reshaping it as a collection of individuals.

This relation between socio-economics and religion represents a significant adjustment of Max Weber's thesis on the role of Protestant Christianity and the emergence of capitalism. Not only is Weber's collapse of Pietism and Moravian Christianity problematic, given the significant differences between them,[85] but our chief concern is with his ideal typical construction of capitalism, which emerges as a reductive obsession with money and profit, with little or no concern for its social disruptions, its ideological import and its effect on social relations. In other words, Weber is not concerned with capitalism as a mode of production, and his analysis is already determined by the logic of cap-

---

85 Weber needs Pietism as a contrast to the rationality of Methodism in order to argue for a de-emotionalisation or increase in rationalisation in the movement from Pietism to Methodism, which thus sheds the problematic emotional nature of Pietism. Not only is Weber so governed by opposing rationality and emotion that he misses the dialectical point that the emotional nature of his ideal type of Pietism has a rationality behind it; a more historical problem is that using Zinzendorf as a key figure of Pietism enables Weber to import emotive content from the Moravian church into Pietism as a whole – which certainly in the case of Francke's Halle is a misnomer.

italism and its fragmentation of life into distinct and externalised categories of 'economy' and 'religion'. His idea of religion then can abstractly act as a force upon society.

The relegation of religion to the private sphere as characteristic of the civil state has the effect that religion is often analysed as a compartmentalised feature of society, with no bearing on or relation to socio-economic developments. What I have been urging throughout this book on this particular religious formation is to foreground the possibility of seeing the Moravians as part of the *process* of secularisation, fragmentation, and rationalisation that characterised the eighteenth century. In such a framework, the changes in religious practice in the eighteenth century must be seen as means to an end, rather as an end in itself.

6   Conclusion

As indicated in the introduction, it is the task of this book to understand the Moravian Brethren within the context of the transition from feudalism to capitalism and the emergence of the modern state and its innovations. Chapters 4 and 5 looked at how the choir speeches articulated these trends through the important reuse of the concept of *Stand*, the understanding of choir, and the production of individuals and collective. The present chapter assessed the political, philosophical, and socio-economic implications of these analyses and the interconnectedness of gender, collective, marriage, transition and individual members.

As we saw in Chapter 4, the choir speeches exhibit, as one of their most central features, an ongoing dialectic between individual and community. This fostering of groups and individuals was, as discussed in Chapter 2, already attempted as a solution in the early years (1722–27) of the community, as a way of resolving the differences as well as creating a sense of collectivity. As the records show, such a process is far from easy, in that the people joining the community were already, so to speak, embedded in social relations, from which they had to be disentangled, and then re-embedded in this new communal web. This did not take place without a struggle, and our focus up until this chapter has been on the attempted solutions.

The present chapter continued the argument initiated in the first chapters and demonstrates that the choir structure is not merely an exclusively religious practice, but a socio-economic form. As I showed in Chapter 4, the choir ideology produced a new understanding of community and a new understanding of self, and in the present chapter, I have discussed the ramifications of the new understanding of community and self in the making and analysed it in relation to the emergence of new understandings of self and statehood underway.

Does the Moravian community have a function within the developments that led to the emergence of the political state? I want to see the Moravians as contributing to the erosion of the feudal social structure, and some of its fundamental features, for example the estate structure and the guilds. What emerged in its place is the choir structure, which, as a feature of the individual congregations, meant that all Moravian communities worldwide shared this social structure. So, on the one hand, it is possible to claim that the choirs meant that the members still stood in a 'relation of separation and exclusion' from others, a feature characteristic of the feudal order. However, on the other hand, the global scope of the community meant that an abstracted level of allegiance, characteristic of modern society, was emerging.

CHAPTER 7

Horizons of History

1   Times of Change[1]

I have been focused on what would be characterised as superstructural expressions of socio-economic change. We have thus not been looking at the increasing growth of the estates of the landed aristocracy in the Oberlausitz and the deterioration of living and survival conditions of the peasants.[2] As I said in the Introduction, the particular nature of the source material does not lend itself well to this kind of analysis. But such a focus should by no means make us forget that class struggles were peaking around the Oberlausitz and in Saxony. The reason it has not played a great role in our material is that the Moravians were aristocratised, and so largely on the 'winning' side of the class struggle. At the very least, we are presented with a ruling class perspective. The aristocratic members of Herrnhut might have been dear brothers and sisters, but they were also members of a class engaged in squeezing out the most they could from the peasant villages and farms. Current analyses of nobility tend to analyse the aristocracy not as a class, but as individuals of status, which obscures their responsibility for the impoverishment of the peasants and the increase in exploitation. In this, von Zinzendorf, von Watteville, von Reuss, von Peistel, von Gersdorf, von Schweinitz, von Heinitz, von Promnitz, von Hayn, von Kalkreuth, and all the other aristocratic brothers and sisters of Herrnhut were no exception. However pious their intentions and actions within the Moravian Brethren, the income of their estates was derived from the exploitation of the peasants and day-labourers on their estates. The generosity shown towards their brothers and sisters in the Saviour was enabled through wealth created by the work of others.[3]

The ability of the aristocracy to hold on to power in the Oberlausitz is connected with the *Gutsherrschaft*, the particular nature of the advent of capit-

---

1   Parts of this section have been published in Petterson 2016b.
2   But see Boelcke 1957 and Leszczynski 1964.
3   In a long letter to Zinzendorf after a synod in 1754, Friedrich von Watteville complained about members merely living off the goodwill of others. By his harsh remarks on the poor lordships who are robbed and suffer neglect at the hands of the malicious serfs, we may gather that he is not referring to the aristocracy and their relation to their servants and serfs, but to members who have no right to live off the wealth of others. *Beilage für Jüngerhaus* (UA R.2.A.34.2.3).

alism in eastern Europe. Commonly known as the second serfdom, this semi-feudal socio-economic system of Europe east of the Elbe continued until the early twentieth century. In distinction from the feudalism of the Middle Ages, which was characterised by being embedded in a local subsistence economy, the feudalism of sixteenth-century Eastern Europe was part of an emerging capitalist world economy in that the production on the estates were sold on the emerging market. So, while on the surface things may seem the same in terms of bonded labour and taxation, the context and the competition had expanded significantly.[4]

An expression of this is found in the introduction to Johann Gottlob Seidel's publication of Zinzendorf's choir speeches in 1755, already mentioned in previous chapters. Seidel was pastor in Rennersdorf, a neighbouring village of Berthelsdorf. In this introduction, Seidel charges the community of Herrnhut and its obnoxious leader, Zinzendorf, not only with professing a perverse theology, but also with conducting business in a manner which contributed to the deterioration of local industry. The publication of the speeches was Seidel's attempt to draw the authorities' attention to Zinzendorf and the effects of the Moravian Brethren on the local community of the Oberlausitz. Seidel's introduction provides us with a good look into the socio-economic consequences of the entrepreneurial activities of the community in the region, in that it contains a range of issues which indicate the emergence of a larger economic context.

Seidel points to a number of Moravian ventures that cause problems for the local industry. He mentions Zinzendorf's cloth trade with the English and Dutch, which puts the domestic products at a disadvantage. Equally problematic is Zinzendorf's monopolization of the trade in silk, calico, and other precious linens, spices, cotton, and leather goods. Another issue for Seidel is that Zinzendorf is ruining the local calico and linen printers through his ability to obtain the best artists for the printing (at little cost, but 'through much flattery'). Likewise, the wax bleaching industry and the brewing of spirits ('Brandewein'), as well as the wine trade with overseas partners, are all firmly in Zinzendorf's grasp. Seidel points out that this has serious consequences for the otherwise blooming trade in Zittau and other neighbouring towns. Such overseas connections enable Zinzendorf and the Brethren to establish other ventures under other 'Sovereigns', which also has an effect on the local economy.

Another important issue for Seidel is that the brethren are undermining the guilds by not recognising the specialised labour needed, because in Herrnhut

---

4   Wallerstein 2011 [1974], pp. 225–6.

and other congregations, the individual is taught – in a mere 14 days – the trade which is convenient within the congregation. With such an army of labourers, Zinzendorf also has a considerable amount of leverage, according to Seidel:

> And here the Count Zinzendorf appears in his total grandeur, that he has a state within the state (*statum in statu*) and at his nod either gradually draws the best manufacturers from our land to other lands, or if one does not agree with him in everything, probably even threatens to let all his cross-air-birds fly out along with the best manufacturers. So formidable has he made himself.[5]

Seidel has now shown Zinzendorf in his magnitude: he has such astonishing revenues at his fingertips from so many sources (which are beyond what comes in from the estates of Hennersdorf and Berthelsdorf), and a very wide network of communities at his beck and call. These communities are not only destinations to which he can send the best manufacturers within 24 hours. They also make up several thousand of the most exquisite manufacturers, which in no time at all may be significantly multiplied and yet again sent out wherever need might be. Seidel even suggests that Zinzendorf uses these circumstances to get his way, threatening to leave and take his communities and manufacturers with him should his demands not be satisfied.

Seidel's laments range from undermining the guilds to the opulent lifestyle of 'the Lord Count', the appropriation of funds from the apothecary, seminary, and orphanage, and the command over and orchestration of a considerable number of manufacturers. However, what is of interest here is the presence of an overseas market whose currents, as Katherine Carté Engel has convincingly shown, the Moravians utilised at a very early stage.[6]

As indicated above, however, these issues are more than just the effects of Zinzendorf. These elements all indicate a significant shift in the socio-economic system and the consequences of this for the institutions that undergird it.[7] Not surprisingly, these are the institutions that Seidel sees as being under attack.[8] Seidel's text, then, gives us insight into some of the consequences of the socio-economic shifts of the time, such as global trade and profit mar-

---

5 Seidel 2000 [1755], Introduction.
6 Engel 2009.
7 In Richard van Dülmen's study on the various societies of Enlightenment Germany, he notes and proceeds to analyse how the various elements of the old world corroded in the course of the Enlightenment and the role that (secret) societies played in this. Dülmen 1986, p. 14.
8 Hull 1996, pp. 29–52.

gins. Seidel sees a connection between the more mobile and global business practices of Zinzendorf and the consequences of this for the Oberlausitz. But he seems to understand it as a local problem and attacks it at what he sees as its most basic feature, the sacrament of marriage. In other words, Seidel has sensed that something is amiss and that change is underway. From his immediate perspective, the signs of change are everywhere. Yet, the problem of his immediacy is that he is unable to see the larger picture, leading him to regard a single man – Zinzendorf – as the cause of the problem.

With the benefit of a wider socio-economic perspective that is removed from such immediacy, we can see that Herrnhut's choir structure and its understanding of marriage are ideological features, which complemented the complex and overlapped transition from feudalism to capitalism in Eastern Europe. The choir structure and the mobility it ensured, combined with the missionary endeavours of the Moravians, which took them all over the globe, placed the Moravians in a unique position to make the most of the early flows of capitalism and direct these flows into Herrnhut in the Oberlausitz, where all Seidel could do was rage fruitlessly against the 'plague of Zinzendorf'.

2   Agents of Change or Expressions of Change

> Behind the history of the state, between the storms of war, and throughout other public events, flow quieter sources of life, often deeper and more powerful than what the revealed world shows the eye, and which nevertheless continue, powerfully erupting in state, church and literature. In particular, peculiar forms of piety and morality have always had their own places and paths in the little-noticed circles of society, among artisans and peasants, and indeed among despised outcasts. If one finds higher education, penetrating talent, or noble rank (*Stand*) on a ground of such strong emotional drive, then something extraordinary will come to life which will astonish the world.[9]

---

9 Im Rücken der Staatsgeschichte, zwischen den Stürmen des Krieges und andern öffentlischen Ereignissen hindurch, strömen stillere Quellen des Lebens, eines oft tieferen und kräftigeren, als die offenbare Welt dem Blicke zeigt, und welches weiterhin dennoch wohl in Staat, Kirche und Litteratur mächtig ergreifend ausbricht. Besonders haben eigenthümliche Gestaltungen der Frömmigkeit und der Sitteneinrichtung in den wenig beachteten Kreisen der Gesellschaft, unter Handwerkern und Landleuten, ja unter ganz verachteten Ausgestoßenen, von jeher eigne Stätten und Bahnen gehabt. Findet sich auf diesem Boden zu solch starken Gemüthstriben höhere Bildung, durchdringendes Talent oder vornehmer Stand, so kommt leicht Außerordentliches an den Tag, das der Welt zum Erstaunen wird. Ense 1846 [1829], p. 3.

Thus begins Karl August Varnhagen von Ense's biography on Zinzendorf, which he sent as a gift to no other than Hegel in 1830.[10] With this poetic introduction, Varnhagen shows that he understands the Moravian Brethren as the result of superiority of education, talent or rank harnessing the emotional drive of the lower orders and their direct line to the unnoticed, but powerful religious current which has always existed throughout history, and runs through the world.

As the quote suggests, but does not make explicit, religion has throughout history provided a useful, and at times politically legitimate, outlet for desperation and rage caused by poverty, exploitation, and deep socio-economic iniquity.[11] But this is only when it runs its own ways in the channels of the lower orders of society. Properly harnessed, it brings something extraordinary to the world. However, as I have been arguing throughout this book, in respect of the emerging social order, the Moravians were never revolutionary or anti-establishment, which, as mentioned several times, E.P. Thompson also pointed out.[12]

As the most obvious example of this emotional drive and its eruptions, Ernst Bloch would most probably have directed us to Thomas Müntzer and the Peasants' War of 1525 in Germany – and indeed, there is something in Varnhagen's quote which sounds *almost* Blochian.[13] However, Bloch's concept of history is vaster and deeper than what Varnhagen expresses, as this quote from Bloch displays:

---

10   In a letter dated Berlin, 23 May 1830, Hegel wrote to Varnhagen, thanking him for the two gifts, which, judging from the content of the letter, were two biographical books. One a biography of Johann Benjamin Erhard, and the other the biography of Zinzendorf. Hegel apparently read all night, and declared himself 'thoroughly moved by the multiple excitations': "Ich thue dieß jedoch mit mattem Kopfe, den ich habe die wunderbare Anschauung, die Sie uns dargereicht, vergangene Nacht noch verschlungen, das Meiste gelesen, so daß ich von den vielfachten Erregungen durchbewegt bin." Hegel and Hoffmeister 1969, p. 302.

11   This forcefield of anger, injustice, and apocalyptic fervour has also been captured and conveyed in Luther Blissett, *Q* (2003).

12   Thompson 1993, p. 57.

13   I refer to Bloch's mesmerising book on Thomas Müntzer (Bloch 1960). Bloch of course has sentences which surpass that of Varnhagen in both depth and power, as for example: '[History] is not, as in Spengler, a crumbling sequence of images, not even, as in secularised Augustinianism, a solid epic of progress and salvation-economic providence, but tough, vulnerable journey, in suffering, roaming, erring, searching for the hidden homeland; full of tragic desolation, boiling, bursting from cracks, chips, lonely promises, discontinuously loaded with the conscience of the light'. Bloch 1960, p. 13. Translation from the German by myself, Li Yahzi, and Roland Boer.

> [These pages, i.e. the book on Müntzer] bring together the everyday, the coming days, the early stirrings, half-forgotten, barely conscious thoughts. Certainly and obviously the present work is, its empirical infrastructure notwithstanding, essentially concerned with philosophy of history and religion. According to this [view], not only our lives but everything grasped from him [Müntzer] continues its work and thus he does not remain in his own time, nor is everything enacted inner-historically, but continues to act as a witnessing figure in a meta-historical field.[14]

This quote shows how Bloch's philosophy of history transcends history. Properly grasped, events are not only to be understood inner-historically, as only referring to or giving meaning to their own time and place, as a sort of diachronic dislocation, but rather continue to work and bear witness to life at a meta-historical level.

Another important difference here is that Bloch sees Müntzer as embodying a meta-historical field, whereas Varnhagen sees Zinzendorf and the Moravians as being agents of the events and of history.

It seems to me that Varnhagen has only grasped history as such and Zinzendorf in an inner-historical sense, which, judging by Hegel's response to the book, is a fair assessment. Hegel writes:

> [...] in Zinzendorf the interior from early youth decides without development, almost without deception and struggle, and he is only this individuality, without individuality being a ready-made instrument of his steadfast highest [...].[15]

This brief sentence in the midst of an abundance of gratitude points to an understanding of Zinzendorf as pure subjectivity, which echoes Hegel's critique of Schleiermacher's understanding of religion as a subjective experience.[16] As I have been arguing throughout the analysis of the choir speeches

---

14 Sie mischen in den heutigen, in die kommenden Tage frühes Bewegen, halb vergessene, nur noch abgemattet bewußte Gedanken ein. Gewiß doch und selbstverständlich ist die vorliegende Arbeit, unerachtet ihres empirisches Unterbaus, wesentlich geschichts- und religionshistorisch gehalten. Diesem entsprechend, daß nicht nur unser Leben, sondern alles von ihm Ergriffene fortarbeitet und derart nicht in seiner Zeit oder überhaupt innergeschichtlich beschlossen bleibt, sondern als Figur des Zeugnisses weiterwirkt, in ein übergeschichtliches Feld. Bloch 1960, pp. 12–13. Translation by myself, Li Yahzi, and Roland Boer.
15 Forster and Boumann 1835, p. 531.
16 Crouter 1980, p. 24.

and in the previous chapter, Zinzendorf was a complex and dialectical thinker, and the assessment of him in this letter is inaccurate, however correct it may be on the basis of Varnhagen's book.

It is this difference between inner and meta-history which I want to pursue in this final chapter, in that I have been trying to break out of inner-historical and one-dimensional thinking in this book, and present the history of the Moravian Brethren in a fuller context, which demonstrates not only their own role in European (and hence, colonial) history, but also the depth of socio-economic change in the transition from feudalism to capitalism. This is the final matter, to which we now turn.

3   Dimensions of History

At a conscious level, I have been working at three interconnected surfaces in the writing of this book. First, the archival material, which, although I have endeavoured to put as much of my work on display as possible, still only represents a fraction of the time and labour which went into transforming these metres of handwritten documents into a coherent argument. Then there is the surface constituted by the epistemological assumptions of scholarship and its neat compartmentalisations. This mainly finds expression in secondary literature on the Moravians, where I have been struggling with the categories of analysis, universalising perspectives, as well as the ideological containment of the Moravians from the real action of the eighteenth century. Finally, there is the broader historical context of socio-economic change in which the Moravians constitute a tiny piece. The interaction of these three surfaces eventually made me realise that I was also exploring a fuller or three-dimensional understanding of history and the role of the Moravians in it. This became clear through the resistance to my analyses, the battle waged on surface three, which entailed a reluctance or even rejection on the part of many to accept the intermingling of religion and history – this from people both with and without religious commitment of various kinds. Such arguments are deliberately reductive, in that they not only serve the ideological purpose of relegating religion to the private sphere, but also function to dismiss the larger concerns, without having to address them directly. It is, in other words, a way of protecting the ideological particularity of capitalism, and treating it as *the* ultimate interpretative horizon.

The multi-dimensional approach which I have been seeking, i.e. my archival methodology, has been based on the three horizons of interpretation as outlined and demonstrated in the *Political Unconscious*. Jameson's interpretative code posits that the enlargement of the inert givens and materials of a particular text must take place within three concentric frameworks, which mark out the widening of the sense of the social ground of a text through three horizons: political history, society and history.[17]

From early on in the research process, I wanted to situate the material within the transition from feudalism to capitalism, and naively thought that it would be clear how the material would yield its context. But, as noted earlier, the material does not immediately lend itself to economic analysis, but must be coaxed to surrender its socio-political unconscious.[18] The texts instead spoke of wounds and the Saviour, chaste souls, broken eyes, penises, etc. Thus, in the end, I realised that what I had at the beginning were only fragments of a bigger picture, and that I needed to work my way through these interpretative horizons and the deeper ideological shifts, before being able to return to the archival material and articulate its unconscious.

In terms of presenting my material, I indicated this hierarchy of horizons by charting the contours of the third horizon (history and mode of production) in the Introduction, and my own path through the horizons in Chapter 1. Chapter 2, then, demonstrates the first horizon, that of the political or literal level, where history is understood narrowly as punctual happenings in time. In Chapter 2 we looked at the historical development of choir terminology and how it increased in the early 1740s and was part of a restructuring of the community which emphasised hierarchy and structure, instead of the more informal, voluntary practices of the early days. The leadership structure changed, placing all authority in the hands of the Saviour. The theological shift accompanying this structural transformation moved away from communal expressions of devotion to personal encounters, from being the body of Christ, to encountering the corpse of the Saviour. Gendering the community became highly pronounced and increasingly monitored, and marriage symbolism began to take centre stage. Finally, a large number of members were expelled, and some chose to leave.

These various elements by themselves do not tell a full story, but drawing them together demonstrates a much larger and deeper change, which goes way

---

17   Jameson 1981, p. 60. I have not followed this to the letter, and you will not have found a progression through these levels and concentric frameworks in a 1:1 fashion. But the framework is nevertheless a crucial structure without which this product would never have reached its consummation.

18   This is due to not only the material itself, but also the method, which, as Roland Boer notes, was 'developed largely for studying the cultural productions of capitalism', and thus had to be modified somewhat to take the specific context into consideration (Boer 1996, p. 87).

beyond what is usually characterised as the 'Sifting Time'. As mentioned in the first chapter, a presentation in the Zinzendorf society of my research project gave rise to an epistemological crisis. My presentation had focused on the choir structure, while insisting that the speeches were my main interest, which was pointed out during the discussion. This made me realise, eventually, that the choir structure of the community and the choir speeches were *both* products of Zinzendorf and his circle, and not, as I had initially presumed, two separate entities. As noted in Chapter 1, the choir speeches thus constitute the concentrated form of the ideology expressed in the choir structure, and are thus in form and content a symptom of changing understandings of community and household, as well as introducing self-reflection and gender. At this stage, we have already transitioned into the second horizon, that of the social, where the disparate fragments are understood within a widened horizon.

During the first 40 years in Herrnhut, the main problem was as follows: How do you bring together people from different ranks and make them feel part of the same group with the same target? This task can be difficult enough today, without the compounding factors of the eighteenth century such as the given hierarchies of *Stand* and the rapid socio-economic change affecting both the aristocracy and the peasantry. It was the beginning of the end of the world as they knew it. The solution to this problem was, as we have seen, social engineering, breaking *Stand* and creating units of individuals that then could reconvene as brothers and sisters with a singular focus on the Saviour. These were not the random inventions of the Moravian Brethren, but were very definite problems of the age.[19] That we should then find a similar general shape of the problem at a larger level in the transition to capitalism, should come as no surprise. Also, here we see the construction of a new social order on the ruins of the old. This was the focus of Chapter 6. As such, the choirs indicate the changes in the social fabric and socio-economic transformations and contradictions characteristic of the birth pangs of capitalism and its social forms.

However, the Moravians are not normally seen as participating in the birth pangs of the new world. The main reason for this, I think, is the agenda set by Weber more than a century ago. By this I do not mean the denial of Pietism as having any impact on the spirit of capitalism, but rather the framing of the question and the assumptions of his parameters. What Weber does, and the shift is almost imperceptible, is to externalise religion. A Marxist understanding, such as the one Bondi is advocating, sees Pietism as an expression of

---

19   I am here paraphrasing Lukács, who makes this observation in relation to Hegel's *Phenomenology of Mind*. Lukács 1975, p. 445.

bourgeois economic thinking, or perhaps to put it a bit more broadly, we may say that Christianity takes the form of a particular socio-economic ideology. In other words, religion is situated within a socio-economic entity with a particular function (as for example the heart in a heartless world, soul of soulless conditions, etc.). By arguing for the influence of the Protestant ethos on the spirit of capitalism, Weber is placing religion as an external factor with a force to act on society, which places religion in an outside position. We noted this in Lukács as well. Religion is thus compartmentalised. And while scholarship has worked to disprove his thesis, for example in refuting the lack of influence of Pietism, as e.g. Hinrichs,[20] or the importance of the Moravians (Mettele, and me),[21] they accept the parameters and follow the line of questioning defined by Weber, which is the fragmented and externalised view of religion characteristic of modern capitalist society.[22]

This is a generally accepted place for religion, and one followed by most secondary literature, as a comfortable compartmentalisation which is unable to encompass both the historicity and contingent nature of the concepts and forms, and unable to resist these containments and transcend the disciplinary categories of academia. Such fragmented histories, of enlightenment, religion, the early modern period, gardens, emotions, etc., all work within a complacent view of the world as it is, and ultimately serve to protect the ideological particularity of capitalism, treating it as *the* ultimate interpretative horizon.[23]

One of the main objectives of *The Political Unconscious* is to develop a proper Marxist hermeneutic. To this end, Jameson uses the medieval allegorical system, which he appropriates in order to show the various levels leading toward the totality of human history. Within the development of his own method, however, he moves through Northrop Frye, who also made use of this medieval allegorical *Vorlage* and its levels of literal, typological, moral and anagogical interpretation – the literal level being the historical or textual referent, the Hebrew Bible, followed by the allegorical or typological key or code, which is the New Testament, or the life of Christ. This is then enhanced by the moral or individual reading and culminates in the political reading, which indicates the collective meaning of history. But while Jameson's own appropriation seeks

---

20   Hinrichs 1971.
21   Mettele 2005; Petterson 2018.
22   George Comninel also draws attention to the capitalist nature of Weber's ideal types (Comninel 2013, pp. 34–5).
23   This may well be a 'necessary and practical way of gaining understanding' as Robert W. Cox points out, but he also notes that such a subdivision of reality 'correspond to the ways in which human affairs are organised in particular times and places' (Cox 1981, p. 126).

to emphasise the totality of human history as the final horizon of interpretation, Frye, in his opinion, *recontains* the possibilities for collective and social interpretation and reinscribes the logic of desire prevalent in psychoanalysis and its privileging of the individual human body. Frye inverts the collective and individual realms, whereby the individual realm becomes the end of interpretation,[24] whereas Jameson insists that the socio-economic must always be the final horizon of interpretation. This is where Jameson appears as his most Marxist, and, one might argue, most Hegelian.

Jameson's final horizon of interpretation is that of history, namely

> history now conceived in its vastest sense of the sequence of modes of production and the succession and destiny of the various human social formations, from prehistoric life to whatever far future history has in store for us.[25]

This is the viewpoint from *within* the absolute, once we have passed through the fragments of the social and have gradually understood the larger context in which we, our social contexts, our ideologies, and our institutions are to be comprehended. At this stage, we can now understand the entire picture of which we are a part. On the one hand, this sounds very Hegelian, in that the *Phenomenology of Spirit* demonstrates the process of the gradual integration of the individual consciousness within the world spirit. And with Jameson, we have moved through history on its inside to its more expansive horizons, transcending the inner-historical limitations, and following it to a meta-historical field, which gives us a new perspective.[26] Thus, after realising that the archival fragments are part of a larger social history, we have gone back to the beginning and put together this argument from the viewpoint of the whole. This is where we realise that we are connected to a reality larger than ourselves and our everyday lives. That reality is History, a reality in which we are entirely immersed and to which we are fully accountable. As Marx wrote in *Capital*, quoting Horace, 'de te fabula narratur', it is of you that the story is told:[27]

---

24 Jameson 1981, p. 57.
25 Jameson 1981, p. 60.
26 Such a perspective is usually caricatured by Foucauldians as a 'supra-historical subject', but it is important to point out that for both Hegel and Jameson, the subject position is never on the outside, but is rather part of the whole which the subject is now regarding as a whole rather than from fragmented epistemes. For a good overview of Foucault's understanding of history and its caricatures, see Falzon 2013.
27 Marx 1976, p. 90. The quote, from Horace's Satire 1.1, is in the Preface to the first German edition as a comment to the German workers who would think that what is analysed in

A Marxist hermeneutic – the decipherment by historical materialism of the cultural monuments of the past – must come to terms with the certainty that all the works of class history as they have survived and been transmitted to people by the various museums, canons and 'traditions' of our own time, are all in one way or another profoundly ideological, have all had a vested interest in and a functional relationship to social formations based on violence and exploitation; and that, finally, the restoration of the meaning of the greatest cultural monuments cannot be separated from a passionate and partisan assessment of everything that is oppressive in them and that knows complicity with privilege and class domination, stained with the guilt not merely of culture in particular but of History itself as one long nightmare.[28]

There is history and there is History; history with a small h is an objectifying fragmentation of life, which serves to disassociate us from our place in it, mollify the consequences of our actions, and make invisible our accountability. History with a big H, however, is the History of the Manifesto and of the political unconscious, the History in which we all are implicated, of which we are all products, and where class can never be dismissed as empty or unimportant. Remember, the history of all hitherto existing society is the history of class struggles, whether it explicitly says so or not. *De te fabula narratur.*

Capital is only relevant for workers in England. A biblical equivalent would be 2 Samuel 12:7, where Nathan rebukes David with the words 'You are the man'.

28 Jameson 1981, p. 289.

Appendix 1

This is a full list of the choir speeches consulted for this study. Speeches marked with * are printed in Seidel. Unless otherwise indicated, all speeches are handwritten. Versions copied into the communal diaries (GN or JHD) are only indicated if this is their only location. In cases where the HS version is *not* the main one consulted, the HS reference is in parentheses.

Choir	Date	Archival location
Single sisters	4 January 1735	UA SHAH64
Single sisters	25 March 1744	UA R.20.HS1
Widowers	25 March 1744	UA R.20.HS1
Older girls	25 March 1744	UA R.20.HS1
Single brothers	25 March 1744	UA R.20.HS33
Married couples	20 October 1747	UA R.4.C.II.12
Married couples	26 October 1747	UA R.4.C.II.12 (HS55)
Single brothers	5 November 1747	UA R.20.HS34
Boys	5 November 1747	UA R.20.HS42 and HS46
Older girls	5 November 1747	UA R.20.HS42
Single sisters	5 November 1747	UA R.20.HS42
Brothers	5 November 1747	UA GN.C.2 1747, 2 (HS42)
Sisters	5 November 1747	UA R.20.HS42
Widows	5 November 1747	UA GN.C.2 1747, 6 (HS42)
Single brothers	19 November 1747	UA R.20.HS34
Married couples	15 April 1748	UA GN.C.3 1748, 1 (HS55)
Single brothers	15 April 1748	UA R.20.HS35
Single brothers	10 May 1748	UA GN.C.5.1748.3
Single sisters	12 May 1748	UA R.20.HS60
Married couples	14 May 1748	UA GN.A.4.1748.2, 23
Single brothers	20 May 1748	UA GN.A.4.1748.2, 25a*
Sisters	20 May 1748	UA GN.A.4.1748.2,25b*
Single brothers	27 May 1748	UA R.20.HS35
Single sisters	28 May 1748	UA R.20.HS28
Married couples	3 June 1748	UA GN.A.4.1748.1: 332–3 (excerpt)

(*cont.*)

Choir	Date	Archival location
Single sisters	3 June 1748	UA R.20.HS28
Single brothers	3 June 1748	UA R.20.HS35
Single brothers	2 July 1748	UA R.20.HS35
Single sisters	2 July 1748	UA R.20.HS28
Married couples	2 July 1748	UA GN.A.3.1: 406 (excerpt)
Single brothers	9 July 1748	UA R.20.HS35
Single sisters	10 July 1748	UA R.20.HS28[1] and HS60
Single brothers	16 July 1748	UA R.20.HS35
Single sisters	17 July 1748	UA R.20.HS28 (twice)
Married couples	21 July 1748	UA R.20.HS13[2]
Single sisters	24 July 1748	UA R.20.HS28 (twice) and HS60
Single brothers	26 July 1748	UA R.20.HS35
Single sisters	2 August 1748	UA R.20.HS28
Single brothers	2 August 1748	UA R.20.HS35
Married couples	2 August 1748	UA R.4.C.II.12
Married couples	4 August 1748	UA R.20.HS55
Single sisters	4 August 1748	UA R.20.HS13[3] and HS28
Single brothers	6 August 1748	UA R.20.HS35
Single brothers	15 August 1748	UA R.20.HS35
Married couples	16 August 1748	UA R.4.C.II.12
Single sisters	17 August 1748	UA GN.A.3.1748.1: 604–5 (sum)
Single brother	15 October 1750	UA R.20.HS28
Single sisters	17 October 1750	UA R.20.HS28; HS47; HS49
Single brothers	21 October 1750	UA R.20.HS22
Single sisters	22 October 1750	UA R.20.HS28 and HS49
Single sisters	26 October 1750	UA R.20.HS28 and HS47
Single brothers	26 October 1750	UA R.20.HS22
Single sisters	27 October 1750	UA SHAH65
Single brothers	3 November 1750	UA R.20.HS23
Single sisters	6 November 1750	UA R.20.HS28 and HS49
Single brothers	10 November 1750	UA R.20.HS23

1 Double with 10 July 1751.
2 Transcribed by Katrin Wagner-Fiebig.
3 Transcribed by Katrin Wagner-Fiebig.

APPENDIX 1

(cont.)

Choir	Date	Archival location
Married couples	12 November 1750	UA R.4.C.II.12
Single sisters	13 November 1750	UA SHAH65; HS28; HS47; HS49
Single sisters	22 November 1750	UA R.20.HS28; HS47; HS49
Married couples	22 November 1750	UA R.4.C.II.12
Single brothers	22 November 1750	UA R.20.HS23; HS35; HS51b; HS57
Single sisters	24 November 1750	UA SHAH65
Children	29 November 1750	UA R.20.HS28
Single brothers	8 December 1750	UA R.20.HS23
Single sisters	8 December 1750	UA R.20.HS24; HS47; HS49
Married couples	11 December 1750	UA R.4.C.II.12
Girls	17 December 1750	UA R.20.HS23
Single sisters	28 December 1750	UA R.20.HS28; HS47; HS49
Single brothers	1 January 1751	UA R.20.HS35
Single sisters	12 January 1751	UA R.20.HS28; HS47; HS49
Single brothers	13 January 1751	UA R.20.HS35
Single brothers	18 January 1751	UA R.20.HS35 and HS51b
Single sisters	21 January 1751	UA R.20.HS28; HS47; HS49
Single sisters	26 January 1751	UA R.20.HS28; HS47; HS49
Single brothers	28 January 1751	UA R.20.HS35
Widowers and widows	2 February 1751	UA GN.A.18.1751.4, 12
Single sisters	9 February 1751	UA R.20.HS28; HS47
Single brothers	11 February 1751	UA GN.B.11.1751.1
Single sisters	19 February 1751	UA R.20.HS28; HS47; HS49
Single brothers	23 February 1751	UA GN.B.11.1751.1
Single sisters	24 February 1751	UA R.20.HS28 and HS47
Single sisters	3 March 1751	UA R.20.HS28 and HS47
Single brothers	4 March 1751	UA GN.B.11.1751.1
Single sisters	10 March 1751	UA R.20.HS28; HS47; HS49; and UA SHAH64
Single brothers	16 March 1751	UA GN.A.11.1751.1
Single sisters	18 March 1751	UA R.20.HS28; HS48 and HS49
Single brothers	23 March 1751	UA GN.A.11.1751.1
Single sisters	24 March 1751	UA R.20.HS28 and HS47
Older girls	25 March 1751	UA R.20.HS32
Single sisters	25 March 1751	UA R.20.HS28 and HS47

(cont.)

Choir	Date	Archival location
Single brothers	31 March 1751	UA GN.A.15.1751.2
Single sisters	31 March 1751	UA R.20.HS28
Single sisters	6 April 1751	UA R.20.HS28; HS47; and SHAH64
Single brothers	7 April 1751	UA GN.A.15.1751.2
Single brothers	8 April 1751	UA R.20.HS35
Single brothers	13 April 1751	UA GN.A.15.1751.2
Single sisters	13 April 1751	UA R.20.HS28 and HS47
Single brothers	14 April 1751	UA GN.A.15.1751.2
Workers, single brothers	17 April 1751	UA GN.C.21.1751.5
Single sisters	4 May 1751	UA R.20.HS28; HS47; and HS49
Married couples	24 May 1751	UA GN.A.20.1751.39
Single brothers	27 May 1751	UA GN.A.15:1751.2
Single sisters	28 May 1751	UA R.20.HS28; HS47
Single sisters	2 June 1751	UA R.20.HS28
Single sisters	10 June 1751	UA R.20.HS28 and HS49
Single brothers	10 June 1751	UA GN.A.15.1751.2
Married couples	11 June 1751	UA R.20.HS54
Married couples	14 June 1751	UA GN.A
Single sisters	4 June 1755	UA R.20.HS47; HS48; HS60
Widowers	5 June 1755	UA R.20.HS31
Single brothers	5 June 1755	UA R.20.HS51
Single brothers	6 June 1755	UA R.20.HS51
Widows	6 June 1755	UA R.20.HS46
Single sisters	15 June 1755	UA R.20.HS47 and HS48
Single brothers	18 June 1755	UA R.20.HS51
Pregnant sisters	19 June 1755	UA R.20.HS42 and HS54
Widows	20 June 1755	UA R.20.HS46
Single sisters	23 June 1755	UA R.20.HS47 and HS48
Single brothers	25 June 1755	UA R.20.HS51 and HS58
Married couples	25 June 1755	UA R.20.HS42
Widows	30 June 1755	UA R.20.HS46
Single sisters	1 July 1755	UA R.20.HS47 and HS48
Single brothers	2 July 1755	UA R.20.HS51 and HS58
Older girls	2 July 1755	UA R.20.HS32
Younger girls	2 July 1755	UA R.20.HS32

APPENDIX 1

(cont.)

Choir	Date	Archival location
Widowers	7 July 1755	UA R.20.HS31
Single brothers	9 July 1755	UA R.20.HS51 and HS58
Married sisters	14 July 1755	UA R.20.HS42 and HS54
Married brothers	14 July 1755	UA R.20.HS42 and HS54
Single sisters	15 July 1755	UA SHAH 64
Widows	15 July 1755	UA R.20.HS46
Single brothers	16 July 1755	UA R.20.HS51 and HS58
Widowers	17 July 1755	UA R.20.HS31
Widows	29 July 1755	UA R.20.HS46
Widowers	31 July 1755	UA R.20.HS31
Single brothers	1 August 1755	UA R.20.HS58
Married couples	1 August 1755	UA R.20.HS42
Single brothers	6 August 1755	UA R.20.HS58
Widowers	7 August 1755	UA R.20.HS31
Single brothers	7 August 1755	UA R.20.HS51
Married couples	8 August 1755	UA R.20.HS42
Widows	9 August 1755	UA R.20.HS46
Widowers	15 August 1755	UA R.20.HS31
Single brothers	15 August 1755	UA R.20.HS58
Married couples	15 August 1755	UA R.20.HS42
Widows	16 August 1755	UA R.20.HS46
Single sisters	18 August 1755	UA R.20.HS47 and UA SHAH 64
Married brothers	21 August 1755	UA R.20.HS42
Married couples	22 August 1755	UA R.20.HS54
Single brothers	23 August 1755	UA R.20.HS58
Widowers	23 August 1755	UA R.20.HS31
Widows	23 August 1755	UA R.20.HS46
Single brothers	27 August 1755	UA R.20.HS58
Widowers	28 August 1755	UA R.20.HS31
Widows	29 August 1755	UA R.20.HS46
Single sisters	30 August 1755	UA R.20.HS49
Single sisters	31 August 1755	UA R.20.HS47 and HS49
Single sisters	2 September 1755	UA R.20.HS47 and HS49
Single sisters	4 September 1755	UA R.20.HS47
Single sisters	5 September 1755	UA R.20.HS47
Single sisters	6 September 1755	UA R.20.HS47

(*cont.*)

Choir	Date	Archival location
Single brothers	6 September 1755	UA R.20.HS58
Widowers	6 September 1755	UA R.20.HS31
Widows	6 September 1755	UA R.20.HS46
Single sisters	11 September 1755	UA R.20.HS28 and HS47
Widowers	13 September 1755	UA R.20.HS31
Single brothers	13 September 1755	UA R.20.HS58
Widows	13 September 1755	UA R.20.HS46
Single sisters	20 September 1755	UA R.20.HS47
Young sisters	20 September 1755	UA R.20.HS32
Widowers	22 September 1755	UA R.20.HS31
Widows	22 September 1755	UA R.20.HS46
Married couples	22 September 1755	UA R.4.C.II.12
Young sisters	24 September 1755	UA R.20.HS32
Single sisters	26 September 1755	UA R.20.HS47
Widowers	29 September 1755	UA R.20.HS31
Widows	29 September 1755	UA R.20.HS46
Married couples	29 September 1755	UA R.20.HS54
Single sisters	30 September 1755	UA R.20.HS47
Widowers	10 November 1755	UA R.20.HS31
Widowers	13 November 1755	UA R.20.HS31
Single brothers	13 November 1755	UA R.20.HS57
Single sisters	13 November 1755	UA R.20.HS47 and HS60
Widows	13 November 1755	UA R.20.HS46
Married brothers	13 November 1755	UA R.20.HS42 and HS54
Married sisters	13 November 1755	UA R.20.HS42 and HS54
Single sisters	17 November 1755	UA R.20.HS47 and HS60
Widows	17 November 1755	UA R.20.HS46
Single brothers	17 November 1755	UA R.20.HS57 and HS58
Married sisters	17 November 1755	UA R.20.HS54
Married brothers	17 November 1755	UA R.20.HS54
Married brothers	24 November 1755	UA R.20.HS54
Married sisters	24 November 1755	UA R.20.HS54
Single sisters	24 November 1755	UA R.20.HS60
Single brothers	24 November 1755	UA R.20.HS57
Widowers	24 November 1755	UA R.20.HS31
Widows	24 November 1755	UA R.20.HS46

APPENDIX 1

(cont.)

Choir	Date	Archival location
Single sisters	1 December 1755	UA R.20.HS47 and HS60
Widowers	1 December 1755	UA R.20.HS31
Single brothers	1 December 1755	UA R.20.HS57 and HS58
Married sisters	1 December 1755	UA R.20.HS42 and HS54
Married brothers	1 December 1755	UA R.20.HS42 and HS54
Single sisters	8 December 1755	UA R.20.HS47 and HS60
Single brothers	8 December 1755	UA R.20.HS57 and HS58
Married sisters	8 December 1755	UA R.20.HS42 and HS54
Married brothers	8 December 1755	UA R.20.HS42 and HS54
Single brothers	25 December 1755	UA R.20.HS57
Single sisters	25 December 1755	UA R.20.HS47 and HS60
Widowers	25 December 1755	UA R.20.HS31
Widows	25 December 1755	UA R.20.HS46
Married sisters	25 December 1755	UA R.20.HS42 and HS54
Married brothers	25 December 1755	UA R.20.HS42 and HS54
Married brothers	1 January 1756	UA R.20.HS54
Married sisters	1 January 1756	UA R.20.HS54
Widows	1 January 1756	UA R.20.HS46
Widowers	1 January 1756	UA R.20.HS31 and HS62
Single sisters	1 January 1756	UA R.20.HS47 and HS60
Single brothers	1 January 1756	UA R.20.HS57
Widowers	5 January 1756	UA R.20.HS31 and HS62
Single brothers	5 January 1756	UA R.20.HS57 and HS58
Married brothers	5 January 1756	UA R.20.HS54
Single sisters	6 January 1756	UA R.20.HS60
Widows	7 January 1756	UA R.20.HS46
Married sisters	7 January 1756	UA R.20.HS54
Single sisters	7 January 1756	UA R.20.HS28 and UA SHAH 64
Single brothers	12 January 1756	UA R.20.HS57 and HS58
Married brothers	12 January 1756	UA R.20.HS54
Married sisters	12 January 1756	UA R.20.HS54
Single sisters	12 January 1756	UA R.20.HS47 and HS60
Widowers	12 January 1756	UA R.20.HS31
Widows	12 January 1756	UA R.20.HS46
Widowers	26 January 1756	UA R.20.HS31

(*cont.*)

Choir	Date	Archival location
Widows	27 January 1756	UA R.20.HS46
Single brothers	27 January 1756	UA R.20.HS57
Single sisters	27 January 1756	UA R.20.HS47 and HS60
Married sisters	27 January 1756	UA R.20.HS54
Married brothers	27 January 1756	UA R.20.HS54
Widowers	2 February 1756	UA R.20.HS31 and HS62
Married brothers	2 February 1756	UA R.20.HS54
Married sisters	2 February 1756	UA R.20.HS54
Single brothers	2 February 1756	UA R.20.HS57
Single sisters	2 February 1756	UA R.20.HS47 and HS60
Widows	2 February 1756	UA R.20.HS46
Widows	12 February 1756	UA R.20.HS46
Married couples	12 February 1756	UA R.20.HS54
Single brothers	12 February 1756	UA R.20.HS57
Single sisters	12 February 1756	UA R.20.HS47 and HS60
Widows	20 February 1756	UA R.20.HS46
Widows	28 February 1756	UA R.20.HS46
Widowers	29 February 1756	UA R.20.HS31
Married couples	29 February 1756	UA R.20.HS54
Single brothers	29 February 1756	UA R.20.HS57
Single sisters	29 February 1756	UA R.20.HS60
Married couples	18 March 1756	UA R.20.HS54
Widows	18 March 1756	UA R.20.HS46
Single sisters	18 March 1756	UA R.20.HS47 and HS60
Single brothers	18 March 1756	UA R.20.HS57
Single sisters	22 March 1756	UA R.20.HS47
Single brothers	25 March 1756	UA R.20.HS57 and HS58
Single sisters	25 March 1756	UA R.20.HS47 and HS60
Widowers	25 March 1756	UA R.20.HS31
Widows	25 March 1756	UA R.20.HS46
Married couples	25 March 1756	UA R.20.HS54
Girls	25 March 1756	UA R.20.HS32 and HS60
Young sisters	25 March 1756	UA R.20.HS32 and HS60
Young sisters	26 March 1756	UA R.20.HS32 and HS60
Widowers	26 March 1756	UA R.20.HS31
Married sisters	26 March 1756	UA R.20.HS54

(cont.)

Choir	Date	Archival location
Married brothers	26 March 1756	UA R.20.HS54
Single sisters	26 March 1756	UA R.20.HS47 and HS60
Single sisters	28 March 1756	UA R.20.HS47
Single sisters	19 April 1756	UA R.20.HS47
Single brothers	20 April 1756	UA R.20.HS57 and HS58
Single sisters	24 April 1756	UA R.20.HS47 and HS60
Widows	28 April 1756	UA R.20.HS46
Widowers	29 April 1756	UA R.20.HS31
Married couples	29 April 1756	UA R.20.HS54
Widowers	9 May 1756	UA R.20.HS31
Widows	9 May 1756	UA R.20.HS46
Single sisters	9 May 1756	UA R.20.HS47 and HS60
Married couples	9 May 1756	UA R.20.HS54
Single brothers	9 May 1756	UA R.20.HS57 and HS58
Single sisters	17 May 1756	UA R.20.HS47 and HS60
Single brothers	19 May 1756	UA R.20.HS57 and HS58
Single sisters	19 May 1756	UA R.20.HS47 and HS60
Single sisters	20 May 1756	UA R.20.HS47 and HS60
Married couples	20 May 1756	UA R.20.HS54
Widowers	21 May 1756	UA R.20.HS31
Widows	21 May 1756	UA R.20.HS46
Single sisters	21 May 1756	UA R.20.HS47 and HS60
Married brothers	3 June 1756	UA R.20.HS54
Married sisters	3 June 1756	UA R.20.HS54
Widows	14 June 1756	UA R.20.HS46
Single brothers	14 June 1756	UA R.20.HS57
Married couples	14 June 1756	UA R.20.HS54
Single sisters	17 June 1756	UA R.20.HS60
Single brothers	19 June 1756	UA R.20.HS57
Single sisters	30 June 1756	UA R.20.HS60
Single brothers	21 June 1756	UA R.20.HS58
Widows	6 August 1756	UA R.20.HS46
Single sisters	17 August 1756	UA R.20.HS47 and HS60
Single brothers	29 August 1756	UA R.20.HS57
Single brothers	19 September 1756	UA R.20.HS57 and HS58
Single sisters	16 October 1756	UA R.20.HS60

(cont.)

Choir	Date	Archival location
Married couples	8 December 1756	UA R.4.C.II.12
Married couples	25 December 1756	UA R.4.C.II.12
All sisters	1 January 1757	UA R.20.HS47
Married couples	9 January 1757	UA R.20.HS54
Married couples	12 April 1757	UA R.20.HS54
Single brothers	27 April 1757	UA R.20.HS57 and HS58
Single sisters	28 April 1757	UA R.20.HS47 and HS60
Married couples	29 April 1757	UA R.20.HS54
Boys	2 May 1757	UA R.20.HS58
Single sisters	4 May 1757	UA R.20.HS47 and HS49
Widowers	19 May 1757	UA R.20.HS62
Single brothers	28 May 1757	UA R.20.HS57 and HS58
Single sisters	8 June 1757	UA R.20.HS60
Single brothers	8 June 1757	UA R.20.HS57 and HS58
Single sisters	22 June 1757	UA SHAH 64
Single sisters	6 July 1757	UA R.20.HS60
Single brothers	6 July 1757	UA R.20.HS57 and HS58
Married couples	8 July 1757	UA R.20.HS54
Single sisters	27 July 1757	UA R.20.HS60
Single sisters	17 August 1757	UA R.20.HS60
Single brothers	17 August 1757	UA R.20.HS57
Married couples	17 August 1757	UA R.20.HS54
Single brothers	29 August 1757	UA R.20.HS57 and HS58
Single brothers	1 February 1758	UA R.20.HS50 and HS57
Single sisters	1 February 1758	UA R.20.HS60 and UA SHAH64
Widows	2 February 1758	UA GN.C.77.1758.1
Widowers	2 February 1758	UA R.20.HS62
Girls	3 February 1758	UA GN.C.77.1758.1
Married couples	3 February 1758	UA R.20.HS54
Single brothers	15 February 1758	UA R.20.HS50 and HS57
Married couples	17 February 1758	UA R.20.HS54
Children	20 February 1758	UA GN.C.78.1758.2
Widows	22 February 1758	UA GN.C.78.1758.2
Single brothers	24 February 1758	UA R.20.HS50 and HS57

APPENDIX 1

(cont.)

Choir	Date	Archival location
Single sisters	24 February 1758	UA R.20.HS60 and SHAH64
Married couples	24 February 1758	UA R.20.HS54
Single brothers	25 February 1758	UA R.20.HS50 and HS58
Girls	27 February 1758	UA GN.C.78.1758.2
Single brothers	3 March 1758	UA R.20.HS50 and HS57
Single sisters	3 March 1758	UA R.20.HS60
Widows	3 March 1758	UA GN.C.78.1758.2
Married couples	3 March 1758	UA R.20.HS54
Widowers	3 March 1758	UA R.20.HS62
Children	4 March 1758	UA GN.C.78.1758.2
Married couples	4 March 1758	UA R.20.HS54
Priests	9 March 1758	UA GN.C.78.1758.2
Single sisters	9 March 1758	UA R.20.HS60
Single brothers	10 March 1758	UA R.20.HS50 and HS57
Priests	10 March 1758	UA GN.C.78.1758.2
Married couples	10 March 1758	UA GN.C.78.1758.2 (HS54)
Children	11 March 1758	UA GN.C.78.1758.2
Widowers	12 March 1758	UA R.20.HS62
Single sisters	12 March 1758	UA GN.C.78.1758.2
Single brothers	14 March 1758	UA R.20.HS50 and HS57
Priests	14 March 1758	UA GN.C.78.1758.2
Single sisters	15 March 1758	UA R.20.HS60
Single sisters	17 March 1758	
Priests	18 March 1758	UA GN.C.78.1758.2
Girls	18 March 1758	UA GN.C.78.1758.2
Brothers	25 March 1758	UA GN.C.78.1758.2
Girls	25 March 1758	UA GN.C.78.1758.2
Sisters	25 March 1758	UA GN.C.78.1758.2
Children	3 April 1758	UA GN.C.79.1758.3
Married couples	3 April 1758	UA R.20.HS54
Single brothers	3 April 1758	UA R.20.HS50 and HS57
Widows	3 April 1758	UA GN.C.79.1758.3
Widowers	3 April 1758	UA R.20.HS31
Single sisters	3 April 1758	UA R.20.HS60 and UA SHAH64
Single sisters	5 May 1758	UA R.20.HS49 and HS60
Priests	9 May 1758	UA GN.C.79.1758.3

(*cont.*)

Choir	Date	Archival location
Single brothers	10 May 1758	UA R.20.HS50 and HS57
Priests	11 May 1758	UA GN.C.79.1758.3
Priests	12 Maj 1758	UA GN.C.79.1758.3
Brothers	14 May 1758	UA GN.C.20.1758.4
Sisters	14 May 1758	UA GN.C.20.1758.4
Sisters	19 May 1758	UA GN.C.80.1758.4
Brothers	19 May 1758	UA GN.C.80.1758.4
Widowers	19 May 1758	UA R.20.HS31
Single brothers	20 May 1758	UA R.20.HS50 and HS57
Married couples	20 May 1758	UA R.20.HS54
Girls	23 May 1758	UA GN.C.80.1758.4
Girls	24 May 1758	UA GN.C.80.1758.4
Single brothers	1 June 1758	UA GN.C.80.1758.4
Single brothers	7 June 1758	UA R.20.HS50; HS57; HS58
Single brothers	25 June 1758	UA R.20.HS50 and HS57
Single sisters	26 June 1758	UA R.20.HS49; HS60; UA SHAH64
Widows	28 June 1758	UA GN.C.81.1758.5
Single sisters	30 June 1758	UA R.20.HS60
Single brothers	1 July 1758	UA R.20.HS50; HS51 and HS57
Single brothers	10 July 1758	UA R.20.HS58
Single sisters	17 September 1759	UA SHAH 64
Married couples	27 December 1759	UA R.20.HS54
Single sisters	29 December 1759	UA R.20.HS60 and UA SHAH 64
Single brothers	2 January 1760	UA R.20.HS50; HS52; HS57; HS58
Widowers	3 January 1760	UA R.20.HS52
Boys	14 January 1760	UA R.20.HS52
Widowers and widows	2 February 1760	UA R.20.HS52
Sisters	4 March 1760	UA R.20.HS52
Single sisters	4 March 1760	UA R.20.HS60; and UA SHAH 64; UA SHAH 64b
Single brothers	5 March 1760	UA R.20.HS50; HS52; HS57; HS58
Married couples	6 March 1760	UA R.20.HS52 and HS54
Single sisters	11 March 1760	UA R.20.HS52; HS60; UA SHAH 64
Sisters	13 March 1760	UA R.20.HS52

APPENDIX 1

(cont.)

Choir	Date	Archival location
Brothers	13 March 1760	UA R.20.HS52
Single brothers	19 March 1760	UA R.20.HS50; HS51; HS52; HS57; and HS58
Single sisters	25 March 1760	UA R.20.HS60
Older girls	25 March 1760	UA R.20.HS52
Sister	25 March 1760	UA R.20.HS52
Brothers	25 March 1760	UA R.20.HS52
Married couples	10 April 1760	UA R.20.HS52 and HS54
Single sisters	24 April 1760	UA R.20.HS46; HS52; HS60
Single brothers	5 May 1760	UA R.20.HS57

Appendix 2

This appendix contains all seven choir speeches analysed in Chapter 4, transcribed[1] and translated by me.

1 Children

1.1 *Transcription*
Homilie an die Kinder, Sonnabend, den 11. Marts 1758

Nachmittags bekamen die Kinder folgende Homilie über ihre Loosung:
Meine Augen werden Ihn schauen und in der Nähe grüßen.

Darinnen sind 2 schöne Idéen beysammen; meine Augen werden Ihn schon *hier* sehen: *Seelig sind die reines Herzens sind, denn sie werden Gott schauen.* (Matth. 5.) und meine Augen werden Ihn *dort* sehen; David sagt: ich will satt werden, wenn ich erwache nach deinem Bilde (*).[2] Unser Text aber steht im Hiob. Der sagte: „ich werde mir Ihn selbst sehen, *meine* Augen werden Ihn schauen und kein anderer an meiner Stelle." Dazu kommt noch das in der Nähe noch grüßen. Solche Grüße kan man aber auch hier schon bestellen, wenn gleich das Leibes-Auge *zu* ist. Daß man Ihn schon hier in der Zeit vor seinem Gemüth kan stehen sehen, hat bereits David gesagt: „Ich habe den Herrn immer vor Augen"; und wenn er Ihn einmal nicht so hatte, so fragte er: „warum verbirgst du dein Antliz vor mir, warum trittst du so ferne?" Da sorgte er dann in seiner Seele und ängstigte sich täglich in seinem Herzen, bis *Er* sich ihm wieder zeigte.

Das *in der Nähe grüßen* geschicht auf mehr als eine Wiese. Das *Herze hört* den sachtsten Gruß; manchmal krigts einen Kuß von den blaßen Lippen, wie kräftig *fühlts* den; manchmal *spürts* ein Gewehe, wie das zu Emmaus war, eine Grabes-Lufft, ein stilles, sanftes Wehen aus dem Herz-Gärtlein meines Todten, (wenn wir einen Lilien-Geruch, wie Er ihn gern riecht, von uns geben sollen, so muß Er ihn uns erst zuwehen).

Je älter man wird, je mehr wird man von der Verweslichkeit an sich gewahr, und sieht von nahen oder fernen, worüber man einmal aufgelöst werden wird, daß die Seele, das Täubgen in die Stein-Kluft fliegen kan, in seinen Arm und Schoos. Bis dahin hat mans ganz gern, daß dis Gebeine hübsch sterbend erhalten werde, und daß Er einem nicht nur als das Kind in der Wiege, sondern auch in der Tods-Gestalt, worinn Er uns erlöste, und wie ja seine Augen im erblinden allen seinen Seelen winckten, die, so lang die

---

[1] They have been proofed, as have all the German texts in the manuscript, by Elke Moreau.
[2] (*) welches eben alleweil der Casus von Bruder Bartschen im Witwer Hause und nicht lange nachher vom Josua Nitschmann, Joh. Episc. 2ten Sohne im Cathrinenhof.

Welt steht, seelig werden; so geschahe es just auch einem jeden von uns, da Er seine Seele ausbließ und verschied. In dem Bilde und wie Er als Leichlein in Grabes-Tücher eingehüllt gelegen, sieht man Ihn am meisten und am liebsten. Und da kommt noch etwas dazu, was euch bis dahin noch fehlt, und worauf die Vermuthung zielet: „ihr würdet mehr Kirchen-Geheimniße halten"; Ihr krigt nehmlich seine Beulen und ganzen Marter-Leichnam zu kosten, als ob man Ihn würklich in Arm und Schoos hielte und für Liebe in Ihn biße. Das wird einem zu einer würcklichen Speise und Tranck, da sezt sich Herz und Leib und Seele und stillt sich.

Das sind lauter Sachen, die man in dieser Zeit erfährt, und die an der Stelle des leiblich nicht sehens und gleichsam der recompens dafür sind, der es wieder gut machen soll, daß mans *Sehen* so lange werwarten soll, „weil wir haben, schmecken, fühlen, riechen, und Ihm bis ins Eingeweide kriechen". Darüber kan man das *Sehen* schon in seine Hand stellen bis zur völligen Fertigmachung.

Aber, Kinder! wenn man das gerne so hätte, hier und dort, so gehört allemal ein *reines Herz* dazu, das ist ein darum nach Ihm aussehendes und sehnendes Herz, das sich, weils nichts höhers, größers und seeligers weiß, als Ihn, lieber alles in der Welt fahren ließ als Ihn, dem ein Stündgen, im Umgang mit Ihm und im Lobgesang seiner Wunden, seiner Güte und Treue wichtiger ist als eßen und trincken; das auch im Schlafe Ihm immer zur Seite ist, in seiner Freundschaft aufsteht und so hingeht von einer Stunde zur andern, und sich vor nichts fürchtet, als ob es Ihm auch treu bleiben wird. Das ist sein Gespenste, seine Angst, sein Kummer: „ach werde ich auch treu bleiben, werde ich dich nicht einmal betrüben?" Freylich ists wahr, der Heiland hat sein Leben für uns gelaßen, was ist all' unser bißel Treue dagegen? all' unser fleißig, gehorsam – still – ordentlich, klein – und herzlich seyn, was ist das dagegen? es kostet uns nicht nur nichts, sondern ist noch dazu eine Freude und Seeligkeit für uns. Wenn wirs nicht thäten, so wären wir nicht werth, daß uns die Sonne beschiene; man wäre nicht werth, daß Er einen ansähe, daß man unter den Kindern in der Gemeine wäre, wenn nicht ein jedes Ihm zu Liebe mit Freuden seyn wolte, was es soll.

Doch darinnen ist auch gar nichts schweres, außer, wenn man ein böses Herz hat und mag nicht; aber solche Herzen gehören auch hieher nicht. Unsere Seele ist wol ein armes krancks Ding, das sage ich immer, aber *kranck* ist ganz was anders als boshaftig und unwillig, den Heyland lieb zu haben. Kranckheit, Elend, Schwachheit, Unvermögen kan Er gut an uns vertragen, und seine Ohnmacht und Schwächlichkeit muß uns unsere Schwachheit selbst recht machen; „gutes und die Barmherzigkeit machen uns hier *erträglich*".

Ganz anders aber muß Er mit einem Herzen und Gemüth handeln, das nicht williglich sein ist, nicht an Ihm hängt, dem leicht etwas beßer gefällt als Er, und das wol gar unter den heiligen Handlungen des von Ihm singens, redens und betens, seine Gedancken wo anders herum fahren laßen kan. Solch ein Gemüth wird nicht wünschen, daß es ihm vors Gesicht gestellet werde, denn es wird so genug zu Schanden werden, für Ihm in seiner Zukunft. Ein treues Herz hingegen wünscht und seufzt immer: „Sieh doch auf mich, Herr, ich bitt' dich, du findest mich wol allemal blöd und arm, ja manchmal noch dazu betrübt über Fehl und Gebrechen, und Schwachheit oder sonst etwas, das mir in den Weg gekommen, da ich mit mir nicht zufrieden seyn kan: aber du findest mich doch allezeit warm im Herzen und liebhabend, es ist doch immer was da, das dir lieb ist, denn das ist von dir her, darum siehe auf mich, ja siehe mich durch, ich fürchte mich nicht vor deinem Anblick. Ich weiß, du kennest mich beßer, als ich mich selbst kenne; ich habe aber auch mit Paulo die Hofnung, *dich* noch einmal so kennen zu lernen, wie ich von dir erkannt bin." Inzwischen macht man sich immer seelige und niedliche Vorstellungen von Ihm, und erwartet sehnlich, bis man Ihn sieht von Angesicht. Da wird man denn auch sehen, ob man sich Ihn hier recht vorgestellt hat, und ob unsere Mahlerey zutrifft.

Gesungen: Ich blicke nach der Höhe, wiewol das Ein'ge Herz steht selbst vor unsrer Sähe – das Auge ist nur zu etc.

1.2 *Translation*

In the afternoon the children received the following homily on their watchword:

My eyes will see Him and greet him close by.

There are two beautiful ideas in this together: my eyes will already see Him *here*: Blessed are the pure hearts, because they will see God. (Matthew 5.) and my eyes will see Him *there*, David says: I will be sated, when I wake up to your image (*).[3] But our text is in Job. He said: 'I will see Him myself, my eyes will see Him and no one else in my place'.[4]

Added to that is 'close by' and 'greetings'. Such greetings can also already be obtained here, if the body's eye is *closed*. That one already here in our time can see him standing in front of one's mind, already David has said: 'I always have the Lord before my eyes'. and when he once did not have him so, he asked: 'Why are you hiding your countenance from me, why are you so far away?' Then he fretted in his soul and worried himself daily in his heart until He showed himself to him again.

The greetings close by happen in more than one way. The *heart hears* the softest greeting, sometimes it receives a kiss from the pale lips, how strong does that *feel*, sometimes an awareness is *sensed*, as it was to Emmaus, a grave-breath, a quiet, gentle breeze from the precious heart-garden of my death (If we are to give off a lily scent, as He likes to smell, then He must first give it to us).

---

3 (*) which for example was the case with Brother Bartschen in the widowers' house and not long after, Josua Nitschmann, Biship Johann's second son in Cathrinenhof.

4 Job 19.27: KJV Whom I shall see for myself, and mine eyes shall behold, and not another; though my reins be consumed within me.

The older one gets, the more one becomes aware of the corruption in oneself, and sees from near or far, in which way one may once be dissipated, that the soul, the little dove, can fly into the rock-chasm, in his arm and lap. Until then, one is keen to keep these bones nicely dying, so that he not only redeem one as the child in the cradle, but also in the form of death, in which he redeemed us, and as his eyes blinks in the blindness of all his souls, as long as the world stands, then it will happen to each one of us, as He dispensed his soul and died. In the picture, how he lay shrouded in the tomb as a little corpse, one sees him the most and the dearest. And something else is added to this, what you do not have until then, and to which expectation strives: 'you will celebrate more church mystery'. You will get to taste his boils and entire martyred corpse, as though one were held by him in arm and lap, and bit him out of love. This will become for you a true food and drink, by which the heart and body and soul are satisfied.

These are all things that are to be experienced in this time, and which are in the place of the bodily not-seeing and, as it were, reward for it, which shall make it right again, that one has to wait so long for the Seeing, 'because we have, taste, feel, smell, and to crawl to him, into [his] entrails'. In this regard, one can put the Seeing already in his hands until completion.

But children! if one would like to have it so, here and there, then a pure heart is always part of it; that is, a heart looking for him, Seeing him, which, because it knows nothing above, greater and more blessed than him, would rather let everything in the world go, but him, with whom a dear little hour in in the praises of His wounds, His goodness and loyalty is more important than eating; that even in sleep, he is always at His side, in his friendship wakes up, and thus goes from one hour to the next, and is not afraid of anything except whether he can remain true to Him. That is his ghost, his fear, his sorrow: 'Oh will I remain faithful, will I not grieve you even once?' Certainly, it is true, the Saviour has lost his life for us, what is all our small faith against that, all our diligence, obedience, silence, order, to be small and reverent, what is all this against that? Not only does it not cost us anything, it is also a pleasure and a bliss for us. If we did nothing, then we are not worth the light of the sun, one would not be worthy that He should look upon one, that one be among the children of the community, if not each and every one, as they should, was to rejoice in love with him.

But there is nothing difficult in that, except when you have a bad heart, and you do not like it, but such hearts do not belong here. Our soul is a poor sick thing, I say that often, but *sick* is quite different from being wicked and unwilling to love the Saviour. Sickness, misery, weakness, incapability he can well tolerate in us, and his powerlessness and weakliness must do us justice for our weakness: 'good and compassion make us *endurable*'.

But He must act very differently with a heart and soul that is not willingly His, which is not attached to Him, for whom 'easy' has more appeal than Him, and who even during the holy activities of singing, speaking, and praying about Him, can let his thoughts fare around. Such a mind should not wish that it will be placed in front of His face, for it will be put to shame, for Him in his future. A faithful heart, on the other hand, always wishes and sighs, 'Please look at me, Lord, I pray that you will always find me soft and poor, sometimes even distressed over mistakes and defects and weakness or whatever got in my way, that I cannot be satisfied with myself, but you always find me warm in the heart and loveable, there is always something there that is dear to you, because it comes from you, therefore, look at me, yes, see through me, I fear nothing from your eyes. I know you know me better, than I know myself, but I have also the hope, with [the apostle] Paul, to get to know you again as I am known by you'. In the meantime, one always makes blessed and cute representations of Him, and await fervently to see Him face to face. Then one will also see whether one has imagined Him rightly here, and whether our painting is correct.

Sung: I look after to the heavens, although the only heart stands himself before our gaze, but the eye is closed etc.

2 Boys

2.1 *Transcription*

Chor-Rede des Jüngers an die *Knaben* in Herr[n]huth gehalten, zu ihrem Chor-Feste den 14. Jan. 1760 über den Text vom Fest Epiphanias her:[5]

Das Kind wuchs und ward stark im Geiste voller Weisheit und Gottes Gnade war bey Ihm. Am Tische stand die Collecte dazu: *Deine heilige Knaben-Zeit heilige die Tage unsrer Knaben.*

Jezt geht nun bey Euch die Zeit an, da sich ein Knabe in der Welt determinirt. Da läßt mans was lernen, da schickt mans aufs Handwerk, da lernts schon so auf eine Art das Dienen, es fängt an dem Vater zu helfen in der Feld- oder Haus-Arbeit, und wird gewöhnt ein brauchbarer Mensch zu seyn, der das, was an ihm gewendt ist, wieder vergilt, daß man wieder einen Nutzen von ihm habe. Das sind nach der Welt-Art nützliche und nöthige, aber freylich mit mancher Gefahr verknüpfte Dinge. Aber darum bekümmert sich weiter niemand, wenn nur der Zweck erhalten wird.

Die Gemeine ist in gewißen Stücken eine eigne Welt, die Welt Gottes, die Familie Jesu, Sein Hausgesinde auf Erden. Da haben wir auch unsre etiquette, Classen und Abtheilungen. Und wenn eins ein Knäbgen bey uns wird, so geht da ein serioser Stand an, da man den Kindern nicht übel nehmen kan, wenns ihnen anfangs schwer wird.

---

5 Chor-Rede des Jüngers an die Knaben in Herr[n]huth gehalten, zu ihrem Chor-Feste den 14. Jan. 1760 (UA, R.20.HS.52).

Ihr einziger Trost ist das *Alter* Jesu, „ich trete izt ins Alter Jesu, da Er das erstemal als ein Knäbgen erschienen ist", nach dem gestrigen Sonntags-Evangelio. Nun was ist dann der Unterschied zwischen einem Kinde und Knaben? Da will ich euch nur sagen, liebe Kinder, vielleicht werdet ihr im ersten, zweiten ja dritten Jahr noch keinen Unterschied finden und denken müßen: wie komme ich doch unter die Knaben? ich bin und bleibe ein Kind, ich kan noch denken und handeln, frölich und selig seyn, wie ein Kind, es fällt mir nichts ein, das mich drükte, ich weiß nichts von neuen oder beschwerlichen Umständen, warum bin ich nicht unter den Kindern geblieben? Antwort: Es muß nicht so hurtig gehen mit uns, wir müssen immer das lezte bey behalten und inzwischen, so lange wir können, auf die neue Umstände zubereitet werden. Es kan mancher unter euch vielleicht noch 3 und 6 Jahr ein Kind bleiben. Ich gratulire ihm dazu und werde mich drüber freuen. Wems so ist, das denke immer so, so lange Gott sein Herz erfreut, ihm wohl ist, und es in kindlicher Einfalt, Gradigkeit und Offenherzigkeit steht. Den Moment aber, da es das erstemal merkt, daß es sich über was besinnt, es will was sagen, es solte über was fragen, oder es fällt ihm zum erstenmal eine Bedenklichkeit ein, da denke es nur gleich: Ja so, du bist ein Knabe, du bist kein Kind mehr, und sehe das an, als eine Narbe vom Fall, und halte den Tag darauf einen kleinen Buß-Tag. Es braucht nicht viel davon zu reden, es kans in der Stille thun. Und wenns die Vorgesezte merken und fragen, was ihm fehle, so kan es nur sagen: ich bin aus dem Stande der Unschuld gefallen, ich habe etwas reden und fragen wollen, und es ist mir der hochmüthige Gedanke eingefallen, was wird man von mir denken, wenn ichs sage. Wenn euch was einfällt vom gut stehen und aussehen, von anders aussehen, als sonst, was äußerliches, ein Kleid, wenn ihr eine Linie geschrieben habt, die euch extraordinair gefällt, oder daß ihr die eine schöner gemacht habt, als die andere; der erste Gedanke und reflexion über *euch* selber, die Comparaison und Vergleichung, die ihr zwischen euch und andere macht, wenns ihrer zwey schön gemacht haben, und der eine denkt, seins ist beßer, oder schämt sich, wenn seines schlechter ist, wenn er nicht dafür kan, da ists nicht sünder schamroth, sondern krицklich und eigenliebisch, und nicht mehr kindlich. Die Ehre der Kindlichkeit besteht in der Simplicitaet, naivitaet und Trostmüthigkeit, da man einem immer getrost unter die Augen sehen kan und einem kein Quer-Gedanke bey sich und andern kommt. Alle Quer-Gedanken, sie mögen Namen haben, welche sie wollen, und handeln, wovon sie wollen, sind nicht kindlich. Wenn ihr die in der Kindheit schon erfahren habt, so seyd ihr schon Knaben gewesen und man hat euch nur tolerirt, bis eure Jahr heran kommen. Ein Kind muß lauter Liebe, Seligkeit, Gnade und Frieden Gottes in seinem Herzen fühlen und was es mit seinen Sinnen nicht ausdrücken und im Gemüth nicht zusammen hängen kan, doch innerlich fühlen, oder es ist kein gutes Kind mehr, sondern schon ein verdorbenes. Nun bey euch ists so: wenn ihr beständig Leute seyn müstet, die nicht vergnügt, sondern mit der Vernunft und Gedanken geplagt wären, denen hunderterley durch den Kopf ginge, und ihr köntets nicht ändern und keine Hülfe vom Heiland dagegen haben, so wäret ihr sehr miserable dran. Aber da ist viel Hülfe aus Seiner Menschheit, in Seiner verdienstlichen Knaben-Zeit ist Rath für alles, wenn ihr nur treue, gerade Herzen seyd, euch die Simplicitaet nicht nehmen laßet auf keine Art, alle falsche Schaam überwindet und euch vom Heiland ausbittet; Erhalte mich in der Gradheit und Wahrheit, daß ich kein Wort rede, als was wahr ist und so, wie ichs rede, daß, wenns schlecht steht in meinem Gemüth, und mich jemand drum fragt, ich schmerzlich antworte: es steht schlecht, und wenns gut steht, ich demüthig gestehe: es geht gut, und keinen solchen Einfall in mein Gemüth einlaße: izt bringst du dich in Miscredit, oder: izt lobst du dich, wie schickt sich das; sondern daß ich alles nach der Warheit sage; nur allemal, wenns schlecht ist, kindlich hoffend, und wenns gut geht, kindlich gebo[r]gen. Wenn ihr das voraus setzet, und so bald ihr im Gemüth die geringste Veränderung merkt, die euch in der vorigen Classe nicht gewöhnlich gewesen, davon ihr kein Exempel habt, gleich zu eurem besten Freunde, dem Heilande geht, es da euch in Seiner Gegenwart in Worte bringen laßt, was euch neues vorkommt, und wenn ihr das gethan habt, es dem *treuen* Menschen sagt, an den ihr gewohnt seyd; so und so ist eines, das und das habe ich gemerkt und wahrgenommen, was mache ich, oder was mache ich nicht? wie bewahre ich meine Gnade, die mir übrig gebliebene und aus Gnaden gelassene Kindlichkeit? wie helfe ich mir, daß ich so lange es möglich ist, ein Kind bleibe, ich fürchte mich dafür, rathe mir; so wird euch nach dem Herzen des Heilands und aus Erfahrung gerathen werden. Und wenn ihr nur treu seyd, so wird alles bald selig vorüber gehen, und ihr werdet euch drein finden, wies seyn soll. Freylich wird eure Sache serioser, wichtiger und importanter von Jahr zu Jahr, und ihr komt den Gemein-Gnaden und Kirchen-Geheimnissen immer näher. Dazu habt ihr auch aus Jesu Heils-Geblüte und Knaben-Verdienste reichen Zufluß, es wird auch geschenkt, was ihr dazu braucht, eure Seele und Hütte werden mit neuer Gnade im Blut besprengt. Und wenn ihr treu seyd, so kommt dann endlich ein Kirchen-Geheimniß nach dem andern, das ihr noch nicht erfahren habt, das macht euch zur ganzen künftigen Menschheit fertig und bereit und kleidet euch mit Jesushaftigkeit ein von innen und aussen.

Eine Haupt-Erinnerung muß ich euch geben, die ihr izt ins Knaben-Chor tretet. Ich will nicht hoffen, daß einer drunter sey, der kein Kind Gottes ist. Wenn ich auf einer Canzel stünde, so würde ich das nicht sagen, aber in der Gemeine solte man erwarten können, daß keiner drunter wäre, der nicht Vergebung der Sünden hätte, der nicht bekehrt und ein Kind Gottes wäre. Sonst trätet ihr ja in eine Ordnung, die nicht für Euch paßte, und ihr hättet vor eine Weile nicht als Kinder und Knaben der Gemeine behandelt werden müssen: denn man kan der Kinder Frölichkeit nicht genießen, und der Knaben Andacht nicht inne werden, wenn man kein Gnaden-Kind ist. Eure Jahre fangen an, geschwinder zu gehen, es geht auf den künftigen Gebrauch oder Misbrauch eurer Seele und Hütte los, oder der Heiland nimmt einen lieber zu sich, ehe man Ihm nichts nütze wird, und bringt einen in seine Sicherheit. Zu dem allen aber gehört ein beblutetes Herz, sonst ists nichts. Wenn ein und andrer das noch nicht hat, die haben freylich Ursach, ihre Kinderzeit zu beweinen, daß sie sie nicht mit mehr Segen angewendet haben, daß nun eine Classe vorbey ist, dafür sie dem Heiland nicht Rechenschaft geben können; zu geschweigen, daß ihre Minen, ihre Trägheit, Unganzheit, unbegnadigtes Wesen vielleicht zum Anstoß anderer Kinder gereicht hat, daß, wenn sie sie angesehen, sie, statt den Heiland drüber anzubeten, und sich ein Exempel dran zu nehmen, sich ihre Ungezogenheit angewöhnt, oder doch ein verdriesliches Andenken von ihnen haben und dem Heiland danken, daß das Kind ein Knabe worden ist und sie nun seiner los sind. Wenn das dazu dient, daß es ein solches Kind stäubleins klein macht und beim Eintritt ins junge Knaben-Chor ganz zermalmt, zermanscht und wie die Heilige Schrift ausdruckt, zum gedemüthigten und zerschlagenen Geist macht, so kan es ihm noch hinten nach zum Seegen werden. Darauf rechnen wir aber bey euch eben nicht, daß ihr eure Kinderzeit sollt verwahrlost haben, das sollten außerordentliche Exempel seyn, sondern daß ihr alle, oder doch die meisten, mit einem bebluteten Herzen in euren neuen Stand heute eintreten, in einer Schönheit mit dem Blut-Strich die Jahre durch passiren und das Herz eurer Vorgesetzten und Mit-Brüder und absonderlich das Herz *des Knaben ohne Sünde*, des Knaben für euch, erfreuen möget.

2.2 *Translation*

Choir speech of the Disciple given to the Boys in Herrnhut on their Choir feast on 14 January 1760 on the text from Epiphany:

The child grew and became strong in spirit, full of wisdom and the grace of God was with him.[6]

On the table stood the Collect thereto: May your holy boy-time sanctify the days of our boys.[7]

Now the time approaches for you, when a boy is decided in the world. One is taught something, one is sent to a craft, there one learns a way of serving, and it begins with helping one's father in the field or housework; one becomes accustomed to being a useful person, how, whatever skill is given to him, is returned, that one has use of him

---

6 Luke 2:40: 'And the child grew, and waxed strong in spirit, filled with wisdom: and the grace of God was upon him'. The child is Jesus, and Luke is the only canonical gospel which presents a story of Jesus as a child. Other apocryphal gospels, which are the texts not included in the canon of the New Testament, have stories about Jesus as a child, the most important one being the Infant gospel of Thomas.
7 Collect is the prayer connected to the reading, here from the 1757 Liturgybook, number 21. The same combination of this biblical text with that collect is in the metadata for hymn 2282 in the *Herrnhuter Gesangbuch*, which notes that this hymn was written for these two texts on the boys' feast day, 27 April 1747.

again. These are, according to the nature of the world, useful and necessary things, but admittedly associated with many dangers. But no one cares about it, if only the purpose is served.

The community is in certain ways its own world, the world of God, the family of Jesus, his household staff on earth. Here we also have our etiquette, classes, and divisions. And when one becomes a young boy with us, then a serious *Stand* begins, where one cannot resent the children, when it is difficult for them at first. Their only consolation is the *age* of Jesus, 'I am now entering the age of Jesus, when He first appears as a young boy', according to yesterday's Sunday Gospel. Now what is then the difference between a child and a boy? I just want to tell you, dear children, perhaps you will not find any difference in the first, second, third year, and you will think: why was I put among the boys? I am and remain a child, I can still think and act, happy and blissfully like a child, nothing occurs to me that depresses me, I know nothing of new or difficult circumstances, why did not I remain among the children? Answer: It does not have to go so quickly with us, we must always maintain the last [stage], and meanwhile, as long as we can, be prepared for the new circumstances. Some of you may still remain children for three and six years. I congratulate him therewith and will rejoice in this. For whom it is so, always think thus: as long as God pleases his heart, it is well with him, and he stands in childish simplicity, honesty, and openheartedness. The moment, however, when he first feels that he is reflecting on something, that he wants to say something, he could be asking something, or that a hesitation comes to mind for the first time, then immediately think: yes indeed, you are a Boy, you are no longer a child, and regard that as a scar from the fall, and keep the following day as a penitence day. It is not necessary to speak much about it, it can be done quietly. And when the supervisors notice and ask what is wrong with him, then he can only say: I have fallen from the *Stand* of innocence, I have wanted to speak and ask something, and haughty thoughts have occurred to me, what will one think of me, when I say so. If you come up with something that looks and seems good, looks different than usual, something external, a piece of cloth, if you have written a line that pleases you extraordinarily, or you have made one more beautiful than the other; the first thought and *reflection* about yourself, the *comparison* and equation that you make between yourselves and others, when two of you have made something beautiful, and one thinks, his is better, or is ashamed if his is worse, when he can't help it, then it is not a flush of sinner's shame, but vexatious and self-loving, and no longer childish. The glory of childishness consists in *simplicity*, *naivety*, and sanguinity, since one can always confidently look someone in the face, and no lateral thoughts of himself and others come to one. All lateral thoughts, whatever their names or their actions, are not childlike. If you have already experienced that in childhood, you are already boys, and you have been *tolerated* only until your year draws near. A child must feel nothing but love, felicity, grace, and peace of God in his heart, and yet feel intensely what he cannot express with his senses and cannot connect in his mind, otherwise he is no longer a good child, but already a tainted one. Well, with you it is as follows: if you are constantly trying to be people who are not satisfied, but are plagued with reason and thoughts that go through the head hundreds of times, and you cannot change anything, and have no help against this from the Saviour, then you would be very miserable. But there is much help from His humanity; in His meritorious boyhood, there is advise for all, if only you are faithful, straightforward hearts, in no circumstance let the *simplicity* be taken from you, but overcome all false shame, and ask from the Saviour: Preserve me in straightforwardness and truth that I speak no word, but the truth and thus, as I speak when my *Gemüth* is bad and someone asks me about it, I answer painfully: it is bad, and if it good, then I humbly confess: it is well, and let no such fancy into my *Gemüth*: [i.e.] 'now you bring yourself in disrepute', or, 'now you praise yourself', how is that proper; rather that I say it all according to the truth, only whenever it is bad, to hope as a child, and when it is good, hide it as a child. If you presuppose that, and as soon as you notice the slightest change in the Gemüth which was not usual in the previous class, of which you have no example, immediately go to your best friend, the Saviour, let words bring in his presence what appears new to you, and when you have done that, tell it to the faithful people, to whom you are accustomed; such and such it is with me, I have felt and noticed this and that, what do I do, or what should I not do? How do I preserve my grace, and the childishness granted from grace? How can I help myself to remain a child as long as possible, I am afraid of it, advise me; then you will be advised according to the heart of the Saviour and from experience. And if only you are faithful, everything will soon pass by blessedly, and you will find yourself as it should be. Admittedly, your matters will become more serious, more relevant and more important from year to year, and you get closer and closer to the community grace and church mysteries. To this end you have rich influx from Jesus' salvific blood and boy-merits, it gives what you need, and your soul and *Hütte* are sprinkled with new grace in blood. And if you are faithful, then finally one church mystery arrives after the others that you have not yet experienced, that will complete you and prepare you for the whole future humanity and clothe you with *Jesus-ness* from within and without.

I have to give you a main reminder, you who now enter into the boys' choir. I do not want to hope that someone among you is not a child of God. If I stood on a pulpit, I should not say so, but in the community, one should expect that there would be no one among you, who did not have the forgiveness of sins, who is not converted and a child of God. Otherwise, you would be stepping into an order that does not suit you, and you should not have been treated as children and boys of the community for a time, because one cannot enjoy the children's frivolity, and enter into the boys' reverence, if one is not a child of grace. Your years are beginning to go quickly, it will turn on the future use or abuse of your soul and *Hütte*, or the Saviour would rather take one to him, before one becomes of no use to him, and brings one into his safety. To all, however, belongs a bloodied heart, otherwise it is nothing. If someone else does not yet have that, they certainly have cause to weep for their childhood-time, that they have not used it with more blessing, that a class is now over, but they cannot give an account of it to the Saviour; to say nothing of the fact that their expressions, their indolence, disingenuousness, and unblessed nature may have been detrimental to other children, so that, if they looked at them, they, instead of asking the Saviour, and take example thereof, they would get used to naughtiness, or at least a vexed memory of them, and thank the Saviour, that the child has become a boy, and being rid of them. If that serves to make such a child as small as a speck of dust, and upon entry into the young boys' choir, he is totally quashed, smashed, and as the holy scripture expresses it, made into a humble and defeated spirit, then it might still be his blessing. But we do not reckon with you that your childhood should have been neglected – that should be extraordinary examples, but that you all, or most, may enter your new *Stand* today with a bleeding heart, may pass through the years in beauty with a blood-streak, and may you delight the heart of your superior and fellow-brothers and, most peculiarly, the heart of the boy without sin, the boy for you.

3   Girls

3.1   *Transcription*

Montag, den 27ten Febr. 1758[8]

Nachmittags bekamen die Mägdgen auf ihrem Saal folgenden Homilie über die heutige Loosung:

Ich bin bey dir (Gesch. 18) *bist du da? ich dencke ja!* Das *dencken, daß Er da ist*, meine Kinder, ist ein eignes Pünctgen für euch.

Sein wahrens *Daseyn* ist freilich allemal so vest gesezt als sein *Nahseyn*, wiewol doch ein so großer Unterschied ist zwischen seiner *Allgegenwart* und seinen *speciellen Visiten*, daß ich freylich wünschte, daß Er weiter herum zu reisen und mehr Orte zu besuchen hätte, als ich noch ausdencken kan. Als Gott und Schöpfer aller Dinge hat man Ihn, wo man um Ihn weint. Und wenn man tausend Meilen von seinem geliebten Pläzgen ist; so ist sein Geist da, wies im Psalm heist: Er ist *auch da*. Wenn jemand fliegen könte wie die Morgenröthe, die an aller Welt Ende reicht, so würde *Er* auch da seyn.

Was *ich* aber hier eigentlich mit seinem Daseyn und Besuchen meyne, das heist in der Offenb[arung] Joh[anni] *ein Wandeln zwischen seinen Leuchtern*. Solche Haus-Besuche stattet Er in leiblicher Person ab, als der Mensch Jesus Christus mit der Hütte, die Er noch nicht abgelegt hat; in der Gestalt des seeligen Liebhabens, der Marter-

---

8   Homilie an die Mägdgen, Montag, den 27ten Febr. 1758 (UA, GN.C.78.1758. 2).

Manns steht Er da, durchwandert seine Gemeinen, Chor-Häuser und Kinder-Anstalten, besieht sich seine Leute und merckt, ob sie in Erwartung seiner Personalitaet stehen, ob sie das *unter 4 Augen mit Ihm* seyn dürfen, auch recht zu schäzen wißen, wenn sie Ihn auch gleich mit leiblichen Augen nicht sehen.

Ihr wißt, meine Kinder, daß ihr schon manche liebe Music und Gesang gehört habt von Geschwistern, die mit euch und über euch und ihr mit ihnen seelig gewesen, und die unter euch im Geist herum gewandelt sind, ob ihr *sie* gleich in specie so wenig gesehen habt, als ihr *Ihn* sehet. Ihr habt eben vor ihnen gesessen oder gestanden, oder sie sind vor euch hergegangen, oder ihr seyd in euren Stuben und sie sind auf dem Plaze gewesen, und ihr seyd dadurch so bekannt damit worden, als mit euren übrigen Freundinnen und lieben Herzen. So weit können wirs auch mit unserm ungesehenen all-gemeinen Freunde, dem Patriarchen unsrer Religion, dem *Kinder-Vater über alles*, bringen, daß Er uns an Sein Herz und Wunden drücke, in gewißen sehr seeligen Stunden so wol das Ganze als die Theile und jede Person insonderheit. Und weil das nie ist ohne ein *Wehen, wies zu Emmaus war*, so verräth sich sein Anblick bald, ob er gleich noch so inimitable und seine leibliche Gestalt dabey noch so *ungesehen* bleibt, es geschicht einem, wie in dem schönen Liede steht: „Daß ich o Liebster dein Daseyn vermercke". *Wie Er das macht, wenn* und *wie* Er so disponirt und wie Er sich sein Jahr zu solchen Haus-Visiten eintheilt, das bliebt Ihm befohlen. Er kan alle Tage rum kommen, wenn Er will, in unsern Gemeinen.

Die Cherubim stehen Ihm alle zu Dienste, Ihn in ihrer Litiere nach Bethlehem und H[errn]huth in Einem Tage zu tragen, daß ER seine *göttliche* Allgegenwart nicht zu Hülfe zu nehmen, nöthig hat; Ihr könt euch also ohne praejudiz und Nachtheil eurer übrigen Freunde und Freundinnen *tägliche* Besuche von Ihm ausbitten und erwarten, alle Tage Sabbath halten aus der Ursach: *der Herr ist da. Ist Er da? ich dencke ja.* Woran denckst dus denn? meine Seele steht in Awe, einer unaussprechlichen Gewährung seiner personalitaet, mein Herz fühlt was innig nahes von Ihm, meine Sympathie und Harmonie mit Ihm, mein Temperament, das nun in sein Element übergegangen ist, spürt ein *schwächliches Geweh* und das ist *seines*. So heists schon dort in der alten Oeconomie: *„Es kam ein stilles sanftes Saufen*, da merckte Elia, *daß der Herr da war* und bückte sich".

So kan ein jedes Herz in täglicher Erwartung so eines lieben Besuchs stehen, einer neuen Beschämung durch sein Umarmen, einer neuen Begeisterung und Einleibung in Ihn auch außer derselben großen, solennen und gemeinschaftlichen, die etlichen unter euch auch nicht unbekannt ist. Darnach kan sich jede Kinder-Seele sehnen und nach Gelegenheit von Herzen drum weinen: „Laß meine Seele Schritt vor Schritt mit deiner Seele ziehn" und wenn sie merckt, seine menschliche Person geht wieder ab, für dasmal ist sie wider von uns und weiter gegangen, so sieht man ihr so sehnlich *nach* im Geist des Gemüths, als Ihm die Apostel gen Himmel nachsahen, „es verlöhr' sich Muth und Säh' *gerne* mit der lezten Zäh"; so lang noch ein Spizgen von Ihm zu erreichen und noch ein Schein von Ihm zu haben ist, möchte es nichts davon verpaßen. Bey dem allen, bey dem zärtlichen Umgang mit Ihm in Person und seiner Beschauung im Geist eures Gemüths, recommendire ich euch vor allen andern, „euch immerdar zu sehnen, sein leztes Athemstehn, die lezte Perl der Thränen euch eingeflößt zu sehn". Seine persönliche und leibliche Gegenwart, seine Gegenwärtigkeit im *Leben* muß euch nie aus der Meditation bringen *von Seinem Leichlein*.

3.2 *Translation*

In the afternoon, the Girls received the following Homily in their Saal, on the daily watchword: *I am with you (Gesch 18)*[9] *are you there? I think yes!*[10] the *thinking that He is there*, my children, is a particular point for you.

His true *being there* is, of course, as fixed as is his *closeness*, however big the difference between his omnipresence and his special visits that I, of course, wished that He would travel further and would have more places to visit than I can think up. As God and Creator of all things, one has Him where one cries for Him. And when one is a thousand miles from his beloved small places, his spirit is there, as the Psalm says, He is *there too*. If anyone could fly like the dawn that reaches out to all ends of the world, then *He* would be there too.

However, what *I* actually mean here by His presence and visits is what in Revelation is called a stroll between his lampstands. Such house-calls He pays in bodily person, as the human Jesus Christ with the *Hütte* which He has not yet shed, in the figure of a holy devotee, the tortured man, He stands there, walks through his congregation, choir houses, and children's institutions, surveys his people, and notes whether they stand in the expectation of his personhood, whether they are allowed to be *with Him under four eyes*, and to know how to treasure this, even when they don't immediately see Him with physical eyes.

You know, my children, that you have already heard much dear music and singing from brothers and sisters who have been blessed with you and over you and you with them, and those among you who have wandered about in spirit, whether you have seen them equally individually as little as you have seen *Him*. You have just sat or stood in front of them, or they have gone in front of you or they are in your rooms, and they have been in the places, and you have become so well acquainted with this, as with your other friends (feminine plural) and dear hearts. We can also bring this to bear on our invisible common friend, the patriarch of our religion, the ultimate *father of all children*, that he presses us to his heart and wounds, in certain very blessed hours, the whole as well as the parts and each person in particular. And because that never

---

9 Jeremiah 1:8.
10 *Londoner Gesangbuch*, volume 2, number 44.

is without a *sigh, as it was to Emmaus*, then his gaze soon betrayed itself, even though he remained as special and in respect to his bodily form just as *unseen*, it happens to one, as the beautiful song says: 'That I, o beloved, feel your presence'. *How* He does that, *when* and *how* He arranges [it] and how He divides his year for such house visits, that is at his command. He can come around any day, if He wills, in our communities.

The cherubs are all at His service, to carry Him in their chariot to Bethlehem and Herrnhuth in one day, that He may not need to make use of His *divine* omnipresence; you may also daily ask for and expect *daily* visits from Him, without prejudice and detriment of your other friends and friends (feminine plural), keep Sabbath every day for the reason: *the Lord is here. Is he there? I think so.* How do you think about this? My soul is in awe, an unspeakable power of his personhood, my heart feels something intimate of him, my sympathy and harmony with him, my temperament, which has gone over into his element, feels a *weak riveting* and that is *his*. Thus it was expressed even in the old economy: *'There came a quiet, soft sighing,*[11] when Elijah felt, *that the Lord* was there and bowed'.[12]

Thus, each heart can stand in daily expectation of such a dear visit, a new beholding through His embrace,[13] a new enthusiasm and incorporation in Him, even beyond the same great, solemn, and communal [ones], that are not unknown to some of you. Thereafter every child-soul can yearn and according to the occasion cry from the heart thereof; 'Let my soul draw with your soul step by step' and when she feels his human person leaves again, for this time, it has again gone from us, and moved on, then one looks so eagerly after it, in the spirit of the mind, as when the dear apostles looked to heaven for him, 'courage was lost and would like to see with the last tear',[14] as so long as a point of him was to be reached, and as long as it was possible to catch a glimpse of Him, it was not to be missed. By all this, by the tender dealings with Him in person and his beholding in the spirit of your *Gemüth*, I recommend you ahead of all others, 'always to long for his last breath, to see the last pearl of tear flow for me'.[15] His personal and bodily presence, his presence in life, must never bring you out of the meditation of His corpse.

---

11   The German word is *Saufen* which means liquid. I have translated as though it says *Seufzen*.
12   Perhaps an allusion to 1 Kings 19:12–13 where Elijah hears a small voice after an earthquake and a fire. When he hears the voice, he wrapped his face in his mantle.
13   Here I have translated *beschauung* (beholding), instead of *beschämung* (embarrassment). *Beschauung* occurs a couple of lines down.
14   Quote from hymn 2345 in the *Herrnhuter Gesangbuch*, vers 7, line 4.
15   Ich kan mich wirklich sehnen Sein letztes Athem-stehn/Die letzte perl der Thränen Mir eingeflößt zu sehn, from the Herrnhuter version of Paul Gerhardt's popular hymn "O Haupt voll Blut und Wunden", see the Liturgienbuch 1757, 15, verse 10.

4 Single Brothers

4.1 *Transcription*

Chor-Rede an die ledigen Brüder in Herrnhuth. den 19ten Mart. 1760[16]

Wisset ihr nicht daß eure Glieder Christus Glieder sind, und jedes Glied erreiche die Aehnlichkeit der Leiche.
Das hat einen doppelten Sinn ob er gleich ziemlich auf eins hinaus läuft. Erstlich ist freilich der grosse Haupt-Sinn allemal, daß das Heilige AbendMahl seinen realen effect habe, und daß unsre Hütte nach und nach Seiner Leiche immer ähnlicher werde, eh sie Seinem erklärten Leibe ähnlich wird. In dem Sinn heißts: denkt euch nicht satt, ihr Seelen, ans Lämmleins Todes Noth, ich steh den Leibes-Hölen fürs Leben aus dem Tod. Es ist aber darnach noch was drinne, davon ich nicht weiß, obs die Bruder sehr observirt haben. Es explicirt eine gewisse materie, die mir erstaunlich am Herzen liegt, und die ich allemal lieber vons Heilands Seiner Menschheit und Leichnam her deducire, als sonst weit herhole. Es ist nemlich ein gewisser Misverstand in puncto der Pflege des Leibes, da man negligirt, diejenigen Dinge, die der Heiland in Leib und Seele gelegt hat recht kennen zu lernen. Wenn man leichtsinnig ist, so übersieht man was schlecht ist, und denkt, es ist natürlich; ist man ängstlich so macht man was unschuldiges zur Sünde, und denkt, es ist was unjesushaftes. Diese idéen muß man nie ohne Grund fassen. Man muß von keiner natürlichen Sache denken, sie kan *passiren*, wenn man nicht Schrifft-Grund hat, so zu denken, und man muß von keiner Sache denken, sie ist *schlecht*, wenn man nicht Grund dazu hat. Die *Vorsichtigkeit* komt aus unsrer billigen Furcht, vor den Folgen des Falls her; die *Einfältigkeit* in dem, das man annimmt, aus dem Plan des Schöpfers, uns nicht Engel, sondern Menschen seyn zu lassen. Das decisum muß aus dem Plan der Lehre genommen werden. Es geht mit *dem* Chor des Heilands, wie mit den andern. Es ist nicht genug, daß man endlich ein ordentliches, gesetztes, unsträfliches und ein solches Leben führt, da einen sein Gewissen nicht drüber nagt, sondern man muß auch alle die Seeligkeiten, die einem des Heilands Person zu wege gebracht, und Seine Ordnungen lieb und werth ja heilig halten, und was an Seele und Hütte consecrabel ist, ohnfehlbar heiligen und consecriren; das heist: sein sterbendes Gebeine *bedienen*, weil mans anzusehen hat, als *Seine*. Das Bedienen der Glieder besteht nicht nur im Gesicht und Hände waschen, im Arzney nehmen, wenn man krank ist, (das gehört zwar auch dazu) sondern es besteht eigentlich in dem gründlichen studio seiner ganzen Hütte in einer klaren idée, ob man eine Seele hat, die den Cörper weislich regirt, oder ob sie noch ein unverständig Regiment führt. Ein weiser Diener des Heilands, der mit einem Bruder redt, der ein weises Regiment führt,

---

16   Chor-Rede an die ledigen Brüder in Herrnhuth. den 19ten Mart. 1760 (UA, R.20.HS.52).

wird niemals einem solchen Bruder viel dicentes machen, sondern sich über seinen Gang freuen, und aus einem discours von der Art mehr Liturgie als Predigt machen. Einen Bruder der allerdings ein unweises Regiment führt, muß man freilich zurecht weisen, Geduld mit ihm haben, und ihm eine Sache das 20te mal repetieren, wenn er sie zum 19ten mal noch nicht verstanden hat. Es ist aber allemal ein Fehler. Wen der Heiland gewürdiget hat, ein Chor Bruder zu seyn, der muß seine Chor principia und Chor-praxin zu des Heilands Füssen gründlich studiren, und so wol seine Seele aus dem Grunde kennen lernen, als sein Fuß behalten lernen in Heiligung und Ehre. Er muß den Zeiten nachspüren, seinem Temperament, Krankheit oder Gesundheit, seiner Capacitaet, seinen Fehlern oder Gebrechen, seinen Gaben, nicht um Gefallen oder Misfallen an sich selber zu haben, sondern um alles mit einander *der* Ansicht dessen zum plaisir zu reguliren, den man so gern erfreut, und den man so ungerne das Herz über sich klopfen macht. Es gehört also zu einem ledigen Bruder nicht nur, daß ers gut meint, daß er die Sünde haßt, sich seines sündigen Fleisches schämt, und betreten, bekümmert und verlegen ist, wenn ihm gewisse Gewohnheiten oder Unarten anhängen, davon er sich nicht nach seines Herzens Wunsch so gleich entschütten kann. Das ist gut und treu gedacht; aber es gehört noch dazu, daß er seinen Gang sicher, frölich und jesushaft führt, und also ein weiser Regent und zugleich Diener ist: denn das ist sehr gut compatible mit einander: dienen und regieren. Das er das lernt, gehört zu einem completen ledigen Bruder und hat allemal 3erley effect. Einer von den dreyen, ich möchte sagen von den vieren, ist, entweder die Habilitirung eines ledigen Bruders zu einem Arbeiter oder Boten, der ohne Schaden hingeschikt werden kann, wo es auch ist, in alle Gefahren und Unbequemlichkeiten, die sonderlich die Wanderschafft der Heiden mit sich bringt, und der als ein ganzer und gesetzer Mann hingeht; oder die Habilitirung eines ledigen Bruders zum Ehe-Engel, zum Diener einer Seele und Hütte, die anders als die seine modificirt ist. Und wenn endlich einer von den Dreyen seelig zu stande ist, oder seine übrige Beschaffenheit des Leibes und Gemüths ihn davon dispensiren, und der Heiland ihm den Cranz geben will, den keuschen Cranz in Seinem Arm und Schoos, ohne viel von ihm zu fordern, so wird er sich, wenn er treu gewesen ist, peu à peu so ruhig, ordentlich unbekümmert und unincommodirt finden, von den Dingen, darüber er etwa vor 10, 12 Jahren geseufzet hat, daß er sehen wird, was der Chor-Gang, der treue Chor-Gang für ein seelig Ende nimmt, auf eine oder die andre Art. Daher ist es mein Wunsch, daß das mag hübsch in unsrer Brüder Herzen klar werden, und so klar werden, daß sie sich drüber freuen können, wies in der heutgen Losung heist, daß sie sich so sehr gefreut haben, denn, heist es, sie hätten die Worte verstanden.

Ich will noch was von den *Leichen* sagen. Der Leichen ihre Art ist nicht, daß sie keine Feuchtigkeit mehr hätten, und daß nicht das und jenes von ihnen ausdünstete, und weg ging: denn die ganze Verwesung ist nichts, als ein continuirliches Ausgehen: sondern eine Leiche ist tod zu dem allen, die ganze Salivation geht ohne ihr Wissen vor, ohne daß sie notiz davon nimmt. Also steht auch das Blut nicht stille in den Kindern Gottes:

die Natur hört nicht auf zu würken, die nöthigen Excretionen cessiren nicht, aber die Seele melirt sich nur mit dem, was jesushaft, liturgisch und der Seele awfull ist und seyn kann. Was ihr zu keiner Liturgie dienen kan, deren entäussert sie sich, und endlich wird noch die Hütte indolent. Alle Dinge, die mit ihr vorgehen und bey ihr geschehen, der Natur-Ordnung nach, werden ziemlich auf gleichem Fuß tractirt. Was man vor diesem *Empfindung* genant hat, das bleibt noch Empfindung, es wird nur der Zusaz *fleischlich, anhänglich,* davon genommen. Der Hang in der Seele wird weggenommen, die Krafft die es aus der Neigung des Gemüths her hat, wird ihm abgeschnitten; dadurch wird die Lust zur Sünde entkräftet, und wird endlich zu einem entgeisterten, entsalzenen Wesen vor unsere Hütte, was man eaput mortuum nennt. Wenns so weit ist, so werden darnach alle natürliche Dinge, die zur Krankheit und zur Gesundheit gehören, allemal examinirt, obs Schöpfer Einrichtungen sind, ob die Zauberey der Sünde und des bösen Feindes draus gebannt ist, ob der eigne Geist sich nicht drein sezt, und ob keine Versuchung die der Apostel Jacobus ganz auf den Menschen geschoben hat, dahinter ist. Wenn das alles nicht ist, so ist man darüber zufrieden gestellt, und bedient das sterbende Gebeine in gesunden und kranken Tagen, auch in diesem Theil, und in allen Umständen wie einer, der das alles ansieht, als Christi Sache.

Ich recommendire aber dabey nochmals das, was man gewissermassen meine marotte, meinen Tikk und privat-Meinung nennen könnte; daß ich nemlich gar keine *Schwierigkeit* in den Sachen finden kan, weil ich nicht begreife, daß ein Herz, das des Heilands ist, sich eine Sache anders, als unter einem jesushaften Bilde vorstellen kan. Es ist das Gegentheil nicht naturell. Denn wenn man verrückt im Kopf ist; und ist ein Kind Gottes, so redt man wol verrükt, aber doch jesushafft, es hängt wol nicht zusammen, aber es ist allemal *das* gemeint. Die Verrükung macht nicht, daß man *anders* denkt, und *anders* will, daß man sein Vergnügen und Liebe *verändert,* und ein anders object kriegt, sondern nur, daß mans nicht recht zusammen kriegen kan, daß man sich die Sache wild, unordentlich und unverständig vorstellt, weil man wol weiß, was man will, aber nicht wie mans will, und daß wenns affectirt beschreibt. Man phantasirt nichts böses, sondern immer das Gute, nichts unseeliges, sondern immer das seelige. Ein Kind Gottes, das phantasirt, phantasirt keine Comoedien, keine Gedancken des bösen Feindes, kein Sauf-Gelag, sondern den Heiland, seine Brüder, *eine Stunde,* oder eine hübsche Sache, dabey es immer ein Kind Gottes bleibt, daran man sieht, was man sonst sagt: in vino veritas; Narren reden die Wahrheit: denn es ist allezeit Wahrheit, und der fond des Herzens. Das ist eine festgesetzte Idée bey mir, die ich mir nicht anders, als mit sehr soliden Gründen könnte ausreden lassen, wenn ichs anders glauben sollte. Wenn unsre Seele mit Seiner Seele zieht Tag und Nacht, so ist es gar kein apart Meisterstück und miracul, sondern der natürliche Zustand eines Kindes Gottes, den Geist, die Seel und Glieder, nur dazu zu leihen, Jesum zu erfreuen.

4.2 Translation

Choir Speech to the Single Brothers in Herrnhut, 19 March 1760.[17]

Do you not know that your members are Christ's members and every member achieves resemblance to the corpse.[18]

That has a double sense, even if it runs out in the one.

First, the big main sense is always that the holy communion has its real effect, and that our *Hütte* gradually becomes more like His corpse, before it becomes like His glorified body. In that sense it is said: *don't think yourselves sated, you souls, from the distress of the Lambkin's death, I stand [in] the body-cavern for life from death.* There is however more therein, which I do not know if the Brothers have observed much. It explicates a certain matter, which is surprisingly at my heart, and which I always rather deduct from the humanity and corpse of the Saviour, rather than bring from afar. It is, you see, a big misunderstanding in the point of the care of the body (*Leibe*), that one neglects to get to know properly those things, which the Saviour has laid in body and soul. When one is reckless, then one overlooks something bad, and thinks that is natural; when one is anxious, then one makes something innocent into a sin, and thinks it is something un-Jesus-like. One must not have such ideas without reason. One must not think about anything natural, as though they can *happen*, if one does not have the scriptural ground to think in this manner, and one must not think of anything, that it is bad, without having reason thereto. This *carefulness* comes from our rightful fear of the consequences of the fall; the *simplicity* in whatever one takes on, from the plan of the creator, to let us be humans, not angels. That decision must be taken from the plan of teaching. It goes with *the* choir of the Saviour as with the others. It is not enough that one finally leads a proper, lawful, unpunishable and such a life, at which one's conscience does not gnaw, rather, one must also hold dear and worthwhile, indeed, sacred, all the blessings which the Saviour's person has achieved for one, and his arrangements, and infallibly sanctify and consecrate what is consecrateable in soul and *Hütte*, that means, to *attend* to ones dying bones, because one regards them as *His*. The attending to limbs does not only mean washing one's face and hands, taking medicine when one is sick (although that is part of it), rather it consists in the thorough study of one's entire *Hütte* in a clear idea

---

17 This speech is extant in five copies, which testifies to its importance. In two versions, the two clauses are clearly distinct on two separate lines (HS 50 and HS 58). In two other versions, the two are less clearly distinct, and written on the same line, but separated by a question mark after the first clause, and a break in the underline (HS 51 and HS 57). Finally, in HS 52, the two clauses are written together as one, with no separation.

18 The first clause looks like a rewriting of 1 Corinthians 6:15a: 'Do you not know that your bodies are members of Christ?' The collect is taken from *Londoner Gesangbuch*, volume 2, number 37 which reads that every *look* achieves resemblance to the corpse (*ein jeder blik erreiche die ähnlichkeit der leiche*).

of whether one has a soul which governs the body wisely, or whether it still leads an ignorant regiment. A wise servant of the Saviour, who speaks with a brother who leads a wise regiment, will never make much speaking with such a brother, rather rejoice in his path, and from a discourse of the kind, make more liturgy than sermon. A brother, who however leads an unwise regiment, one must freely show him correctly, have patience with him, and repeat a case for the twentieth time, when he has not yet understood it the nineteenth time. He is, however, always a mistake. He whom the Saviour has honoured to be a choir brother, he must study the choir principles and choir praxis thoroughly at the Saviour's feet[19] and learn to know his soul on this foundation as well as learn to keep his feet in holiness and honour. Through time, he must trace his temperament, sickness and health, his capacities, his mistakes or transgressions, his gifts, not to have pleasure or displeasure in himself, rather to regulate all with each other to pleasure in the sight of the one, one always wants please, and whose heart one does not want to make race on account of one. It thus belongs to a single brother, not only that he means it well, that he hates sin, is ashamed of his sinful flesh, and is embarrassed, worried and constrained when certain practices or bad habits persist, from which he cannot from his heart's desire shake off so easily. That is well and truly thought, but there is more to it, that he leads his path surely, happily, and Jesus-like and thus is a wise ruler and also servant; because these are very compatible with each other: to serve and to rule. Learning this is part of becoming (belongs to) a complete Single Brother and has a triple effect. One of the three, I would like to say of the four, is either the habilation of a Single Brother to a worker or a messenger, who without harm may be sent to places, where it also is, in all dangers and discomforts, which especially the wanderings of the heathen brings with it, and which goes against him as a complete and lawful man, or the habilation of a Single Brother to a marriage-angel, to a servant of a soul and *hütte*, which is modified differently from his. And when finally one of the three has achieved blessedness, or the remaining condition of body and *gemüth* will release him therefrom, and the Saviour wants to give him the cross, the chaste cross in his arm and lap, without demanding much from him, then he will, if he is *true*, bit by bit (peu á peu) find himself calm, orderly, unworried, and uninconvenienced, from the things, over which he had sighed 10, 12 years earlier, that he will see, what kind of blessed end the choir-path, the true choir-path takes, in one way or the other. That is why this is my wish, that it become beautifully clear in the hearts of our Brothers that they may rejoice thereover, as it says in the watchword of today, that they have rejoiced so much, because, it says, they had understood the words.

---

19   Perhaps an allusion to Luke 10:38–42 and the story of Mary and Martha, where Mary sat at Jesus' feet and learned from him.

I want to say more about the corpse. The type of corpse is not that it would have no further moistness, and that not this and that is emitted from it and goes away; for the entire decomposition is nothing but a continued going-out; rather a corpse is death to all, the entire salivation takes place without you knowing it, without it taking notice thereof. Also, the blood does not stand still in the children of god; nature does not stop working, the necessary excretions do not cease, but the soul only occupies itself with what is Jesus-like, liturgical, and what is and may be awful to the soul. What you cannot serve as a liturgy, it will externalise itself from it, and finally, the *hütte* will become indolent. All things which pass over and happen to it, according to the order of nature, will be treated on the same foot. What one has named these *sensations*, the sensations remain, only the *fleshly*, *clingy* addition will be taken away from it. The need in the soul is removed, the power, which it has from the inclination of the *Gemüth*, are cut off from him, through this desire for sin is weakened, and will finally become a dispirited, desalinated entity over against our *Hütte*, what is called caput mortuum (worthless remains). When it has come this far, then all natural things, which belong to illness or health, will be examined every time, if it is the creator's design, or the sorcery of sin and the evil enemy is banned to the outside, whether the own spirit does not sit therein, and whether no temptation, which the apostle James has pushed entirely onto to humans, lies behind. If all of this is not the case, then one is made satisfied therewith, and attends to the dying bones in healthy and sick days, also in this part, and in all circumstances as one who sees it all, as Christ's issue.

I nevertheless recommend once more what one normally would call my marotte, my tick, and private opinion; namely that I cannot find any *difficulty* in the matter, because I fail to see that a heart, which belongs to the Saviour, can visualise a matter in any other way than in a Jesus-like image. The contrary is not natural. For if one is disturbed in the head, and is a child of god, then one speaks disturbed, but nevertheless Jesus-like, it does not make sense, but *that* is always intended. The disturbance does not make one think *differently* and want *differently*, that one *changes* one's enjoyments and love, and receives another object, rather only that one cannot properly get it together, that one imagines the case wildly, unorderly and unreasonably, because one knows what one wants, but not how one wants it, and that one describes it as affected. One does not fantasise evil, rather always the good, nothing unholy, rather always the holy. A child of god who fantasises, does not fantasise comedies, no thoughts of the evil enemy, no drinking-binge but rather the Saviour, his brother, *an hour* or a beautiful matter, wherewith one always remains a child of god, whereby one sees as is said: in vino veritas, fools speak the truth, for it always truth, and the heart's foundation. That is a fixed idea in me, which I could only be talked out of by very solid reasons, if I had to think otherwise. When our souls draw with His soul day and night, then it is no separate masterpiece and miracle, but rather the natural condition of a child of god, whose spirit, soul and limbs only lend themselves to please Jesus.

5 Single Sisters

5.1 *Transcription*

Homilie an die Ledigen Schwestern den 3ten Apr. 1758 (in H[errn]huth)[20]

Ich habe dich gepflanzet zu einem ganz recht schaffenen Saamen.
Gesungen: *Werdens auch bleiben bis wir den sehen an den wir gläuben.*
Es muß wol gar modest gesagt werden: *Werdens auch bleiben,* wenn man im eurem Chor und in den Jahren ist, da man noch nicht so lustig seyn kan, wie die Alten Jungfräuelein, die des Kummers End entgegen sehn; (denn da hat freilich eine Wittwe und eine Matrone was voraus in der Trostmüthigen Aussprache des Worts: Werd's auch bleiben). Wir könnens euch aber doch nicht verdencken, daß ihr in aller Demuth *so* denckt. Denn unser Heiland hat doch keinen andern Zweck gehabt, da Er euch gepflanzt hat, als *daß ihr bleiben sollt.* Das *Bleiben* heißt nun nicht, ich werde ledig bleiben, ich werde auf dem äußern Jungfern Punct, da ich mich so gut ein gerichtet, vest stehen. Ihr wißt wohl, Meine Schwestern, daß ich euch viel mal die Seligkeit auch des leiblichen Wohnens in euren Chor-Häusern und in eurem Chor-Beruf herzlich an gepreißt habe. Ich kenne diese Seligkeit, ich kan sie begreifen, sie hat gar nichts Künstliches in sich, denn es ist ein naturaller Rosen-Garten meines Todten, da es gar nicht wunder bar ist, wenn einem immer wohl ist. Man kan auf den Gängen eures Hauses sagen: „Kommt lasset uns Spaziren gehen, der Gaßen Herrlichkeit zu sehn"; denn es fehlt doch nichts am Jerusalem das droben ist, als die Unbeweglichkeit, sonst wüßte ich nicht, wie ihr Ihm nicht köntet eure Gänge und Stuben so niedlich machen, daß Er immer appetit bekäme zu einer Haus Visit nach der andern von Zeit zu Zeit; es stört euch nichts Ihm zu arbeiten, zu schlaffen und zu wachen; und was die Kinder im Mädgen Hause Täglich erfahren, das könnt ihr allenfalls hier fort sezen, denn seit dem die Kinder auch leiblich Arbeiten, ist zwischen euch und den Kindern kein Unterscheid; vor diesem wars vielleicht anders. Ihr habt auch nicht sehr Ursach ans elende Leben zu dencken, in Ansehung eurer Hütten; denn die sinds, die den Brüdern das Leben eigentlich schwer machen, und eine Differenz zwischen ihren frühen und späten Zeiten bey ihnen verursachen. Das ist bey euch nicht; es sind rare Fälle, da euch eure Hütte drückt, anders als natürlicher Schmerz und Beschwerlichkeiten, die man Ihm nach trägt, der auch ein kranck Persöngen war, und darinn man Ihm ähnlich seyn kan. Wenns nicht Dinge sind, darin ihr Ihm und der Jungfrau Maria, die Ihn Trug, nicht ähnlich seyd, sonst habt ihr keine so gar große Noth. Wenn eure Seele voll Bräutigam ist, in seiner Creuzes-Luft lebt, wenn jeder Puls sein Verscheiden und jeder othem sein Leiden bezeugt und den Frieden, den uns darauß kommen ist, kurz, wenn ihr in einer beständigen Con-

---

20 Homilie an die Ledigen Schwestern! den 3ten Apr. 1758 in H[errn]huth (UA.R.20.HS.60).

nexion und suite seines Lebens und Leidens bleibt und eure Seelen nicht mit eiteln vergeblichen Gedancken bemüht, oder wenn sich eure Seele dahin lenckt, durch den Geist, der gleichen Geschäfte zu rechter Zeit zu Tödten: o so könt ihr bey jeder monatlichen Umarmung, und bey dem jedes mal zurück bleibenden Gegen-Gifft und Arzeney wieder alles Verderben, eure Hütten so rein, keusch und heilig bewahren, daß sie alle Minuten lebendig gen Himmel geholt werden könnten auf Elias Wagen. Ihr dürft euch nicht schämen in seiner Gegenwart, weil alles was Er euch zu schickt, und was an die Hütten Umstände attachirte und ihr ein naturte Beschwerlichkeiten sind, vor Ihm ein Heiligthum ist, denn sie sind geheiligt worden durch seine Menschwerdung; und durch seiner lieben Mutter empfangen, Tragen und Gebähren des Marter-Manns, sind alle die äußerliche Regungen und Bewegungen im Geblüthe und alles übrige, was sich in einen Cörper samlet und daher transpirirt, reichlich geheiligt, begnadigt und angenehm gemacht in dem Geliebten und gar nicht incompatibel mit dem Geruch seiner Salbe und der Narde, deren ihr beständiges Liebliches riechen, wie Ers gern hat, wie Er euch immer gerne sieht und uns mit euch.

Man kans nicht leugnen, das Paradies eines ledigen Schwestern Chors ist evident und ganz unleugbar, und es müste einer wieder die Sonne reden, wenn ers diffitirte und disputirte, denn wem nicht wohl unter euch und in eurem Hause ist, das ist eben eine unglückselige Seele, der auch im Himmel nicht wohl wäre, wenn sie nein käme. Aber ich meine darum doch keine Gefangenschaft und Nothwendigkeit, in dem äußern Gange fort zu gehen, wenn euch der Meister rufft, denn ob Er euch zu sich oder in Ämter, oder in einen andern Stand rufft, daß muß euch einerley seyn, weil ihr Seine Creaturen seyd. Da habt ihr nichts drüber zu urtheilen als gehorsam zu seyn. Wenn ihr wieder Umstände was habt, das könt ihr allemal sagen; Aber wieder die Sache selbst könt ihr nichts haben, die habt ihr nicht zu beurtheilen, denn Er ist Vater und Herr, der erwehlen kan, ob sich Sein Kind vermählen, obs einsam bleiben soll; darüber ist einer Schwester gar keine Versicherung zu geben. Folglich ist das *Bleiben* „werdens auch bleiben", wol auf eure Jungfräuliche Herzen, auf euren Chor-Sinn, auf eure Keusche Gnade, auf den ewigen Jungfern-Cranz und Seegen eurer Seele gemeynt, aber nicht auf die Umstände, darinn die gegenwärtige Zeit eingetheilt seyn kan, und auf die mancherley Scenen, die ihr darinnen repraesentiren solt: denn die weiß niemand als Er: Es ist keine Schwester, die der Heiland nicht aus dem Chor rufft, im Geringsten darum verlegen, denn es ist kein böses Zeichen, es gehört unter Seine Special-Disposition und in seinen Verstand, Er exercirt seine ganze Weisheit und Treue darin, weil Er seine Leute am besten kennt, und wenn Er eine rufft, so ists wieder keine degradation, sondern der Herr bedarf ihr, das ist die Sache.

Ihr könnt Ihm also ohne alles Bedencken und Besinnen und ohne die geringste Furcht vor künftigen Vorfällen, alle Stunden die Hände geben, *daß ihr bis an das Ende wolt seine Treue Seelen seyn.*

5.2   *Translation*

Choir speech to the single sisters in Herrnhut, 3 April 1758.

I have planted you as a new very righteous seed.[21]

Sung: Become it, and remain, until we see the one in which we believe.[22]

'*Become it and remain*' must be said demurely, when one is in your choir and in the years when one cannot yet be as joyful as the old maidens, who see the end of grief before them (for in that a widow and a matron has something in advance of the comforting delivery of the word: 'become it and remain'). We cannot blame you for thinking *thus* in all humility. For our Saviour had no other purpose, when He planted you, than *that you should remain.*

Remaining, however, does not mean that I will remain single, [that] I will remain in the outer maiden-point (*Jungfernpunkt*), because I have arranged myself so well. You know well, my sisters, that I have often praised the blessedness and the corporeal co-habitation in your choir houses and in your choir offices. I know this bliss, I can understand it, it has nothing artificial in it, for it is a natural rose garden of my dead one, where it is not wonderous at all, if one is always well.

One can say in the corridors of your house, Come let us go for a walk, to see the grandeur of the streets, which lack nothing in the Jerusalem which is above, apart from the immobility, otherwise I would not know how you could not make your passages and dwellings so nice that He always receives appetite to make one house visit after another, from time to time; it does not bother you to work, to sleep and to watch for Him; and what the children in the girls' house experience daily, you can in any case continue, since the children also work corporeally there is no difference between you and the children, perhaps it was different before that.

You also do not really have reason to think of wretched lives in regard to your *Hütten*, whereas for the brothers they make life difficult and cause a difference between their early and late times with them. That is not so with you, there are rare cases, when your *Hütte* presses you, beyond natural pain, and difficulties which one bears with Him, who was also a sick person, and within which one may resemble Him. If they are not things, that do not resemble Him and the Virgin Mary who bore Him, you have no distress at all. When your soul is full of bridegroom, lives in His cross air, when every pulse testifies to His passing every breath His passion, as well as the peace that has come to us from

---

21   This verse is amended from Jeremiah 2:21 here quoted in the King James Version as the closest English translation of the Hebrew *zarah emet*, trustworthy, righteous seed: Yet I planted thee a noble vine, wholly a right seed.

22   As far as I have been able to ascertain, this is not from any of the printed Moravian hymns from the time. It is not in the *Herrnhuter Gesangbuch*, the *Kinderoden*, the *Kleines Brüdergesangbuch*, the *Liturgienbuch* (1757), or the *Londoner Gesangbuch* 1–2.

these, in short, if you remain in a continual connection and in suite of His life and suffering, and if your souls are not encumbered with vainly futile thoughts, or if your soul directs itself thereto, is killed in time through the Spirit and similar occupations, then you can, at every monthly embrace and its subsequent antidote and remedy against all depravity, keep your *Hütte* so clean, so chaste and so holy, that it would be able to be taken alive to heaven any minute by Elijah's chariot.[23]

You are not to be ashamed in His presence because everything he sends you and what circumstances belongs to the *Hütte*, and natural inconveniences, are for him a sanctuary, because they were sanctified, through His incarnation through His dearest mother's receiving, carrying and giving birth to the martyred man. All the external impulses and movements in the blood, and whatever else is gathered in a body, and therefore transpires, is amply sanctified, pardoned and made pleasing in the beloved, and not at all incompatible with the aroma of his oil and ointment which you constantly smell with pleasure, how he always likes to see you, and us with you.

One cannot deny that the paradise of a single sisters' choir is evident and quite undeniable, and one would have to be speaking against the sun if he denied or disputed this, for whoever is not well among you, and is in your house, that is just an unhappy soul, who also would not be well in heaven, should she enter. However, by that I don't mean imprisonment and necessity to continue on the external path when the master calls you. Because whether He calls you to him or to an office, or into another *Stand*, that must be the same to you, because you are His creatures. You have nothing to judge thereover, but to be obedient. If you have something against the circumstances, you can always speak up, but against the matter itself you cannot have anything against it, that is not for you to judge, since He is father and lord, who can choose, if His child marries, or if it should remain single.

Apart from this, there is no assurance for a sister. Consequently, the *remain*, 'become it, and remain' surely is meant in relation to your maiden hearts, your choir mind, your chaste mercy, the eternal maiden wreath of your souls, but not in relation to the circumstances in which the present time can be divided, and in regard to the many scenes therein that you will represent, which no one knows, but Him.

There is no sister whom the Saviour does not call out of the choir, who is the least embarrassed thereby, because it is not evil sign, it belongs to His special discretion, and in His reason, He exercises His entire wisdom and faith in this, because He knows his people best, and when He calls one, it is again not a degradation, rather that the Lord needs you, that is the thing. So, you can without any apprehension or consideration, and without the slightest fear of any future incidents shake hands on it, *that you want to be his faithful souls till the End.*

---

23 Possible allusion to 2 Kings 2:11 where Elijah is picked up by a whirlwind accompanied by a chariot of fire.

6 Widowers

6.1 *Transcription*

Chor-Rede an die Witwer in Herrnhuth d. 28en August 1755

Darnach starb Sarah und Abraham beweinte sie.
Denn ihr aus seinem Gesicht verscheiden macht' der
Gewohnheit ein bittres Leiden.

Es ist was remarquables, daß die Gewohnheit unter allen menschlichen Dingen das vesteste und starkeste ist, und über alle andre Arten der persuasion und des Eindrucks geht. Es ist kein Vergleich zwischen der Verliebtheit eines natürlichen jungen Menschen, der ein Object in die Augen kriegt, das ihm seinen Verstand so benebelt, daß ers für seinen Gözen hält, und sich für die glückseligste Creatur hielte, wenn ers hätte, und zwischen der Liebe, Herzlichkeit und Vertraulichkeit zweyer Eheleute, die sich 50 Jahr gehabt haben. Wenn sie (wies unter der natürlichen Leuten ist) eine Menge Verdrießlichkeiten, Contrariæten und Objecte zu Zorn und Wiederwärtigkeit gehabt, wenn sie einander wegen gewisser aversionen vor dem nicht leiden können, wenn die Neben-Absichten, um derer willen sie einander genommen, aufhören, und nichts übrig bleiben solten als degout, wenn sie einander 30 Jahr nicht haben leiden können, und man sieht sie in 15 Jahren wieder, so sieht man die vergnügtesten, attachirtesten und vertraulichsten Menschen. Sie sind zusammen gewohnt. Der selige Doct Petersen hat, da ihm seine Frau im 81ten Jahr heimging, in einem lateinischen Gedicht eine große lamente angestellt, wie verlaßen er nun sey, und wie ihm alles in der Welt zuwider wäre: Barbarus ego illi, barbarus ille mihi.

Ich zweifle nicht, daß sich Kinder Gottes in 5–6 Jahren so zusammen gewöhnen können, und wenn sie das Heimgehen nicht für so eine große Seligkeit und neuen Grad heilten, so würden sies nicht so bald vergeßen können: aber der gestrige Text macht, daß es sich bey ihnen eher als bey andern Leuten gibt. *Abraham stund auf von siener Leiche.* Er hatte was zu thun bey der Sache und muste seine Klage suspendiren. Aber weil Jesu Leichnam unser bleibendes Object ist, weil wir mit *dem* Bilde unsern Ehestand in Ordnung erhalten, und unsern Blick nicht gewendet haben von dem durch grabenen Händen, so sind wir mit der Leichenhaftigkeit schon so familiarisirt, daß das bey uns ganz wegfält, was beym Sterben der natürlichen Leute so odiös ist. Wir haben also in der Gemeine nichts als unserm Nuzen zu consideriren, und der reducirt sich aufs Vergnügen. Denn weil die Witwer in der Gemeine zu der Zeit gemeiniglich los werden, was ihnen in der Ehe aufgelegt war, weil ihre Kinder besorgt sind, und ihre Handthierung sich ändert, so treten sie zugleich in einen neuen Stand.

Es ist nicht wie mit Abraham, der an seiner Frau das Haupt der Familie nach ihm verlor, und sich, obgleich mit noch so treuen Gesinde behelfen muste, denn die Kinder galten nichts, so lange der Vater lebte, der mache mit ihnen, was er wolte, und verheyrathete sie ungefragt, sie waren die ersten und grösten Knechte, wies noch mit den Prinzen vom Geblüt ist, die an ihrem Exempel zeigen müssen, wie sich ie unterthanen verhalten sollen. Der Sohn wurde also nicht als das Haupt des Hauses angesehen, folglich war Abraham einsam, und wuste sich mit fremden Leuten behelfen.

Bey uns aber geht ein neuer Periodus an, man kommt in eine neue Claße, und das einige Object eines jeden Standes wird, so oft man in eine neue Claße tritt, von neuem modificirt. Die Witwer, die von ihrer Leiche aufgestanden sind, und sich über den Abgang ihrer Gehülfen zufrieden gegeben haben werfen sich nun a corps perdu ins Heilands Arme, „wir wollen uns Gehülfen werden in deinen seligen Beschwerden, bis daß wir mit einander ruhe". Der Heiland fängt eine neue Connexion an. Vorher war Er der dritte Mann, da 2 versamlet waren in seinem namen. Nachdem Er das Eine mit ich hinter den Vorhang genommen hat, so ist Er der zweyte. Vorher muste man immer auf der Huth seyn, daß man Ihn nicht für entbehrlich hielt, davor hats nun nicht noth, denn man wäre sonst gleich allein und verlaßen. Alle andere Geschwister und Freunde, die Kinder nicht ausgeschloßen, sind in dem Ehebande, wo 2 versamlet sind in seinen Namen, und Er mitten unter ihnen, gar nicht in dem Computo. Wenn eins weg ist, so kan kein andrer Freund in deßen Stelle treten, sondern der Heiland bleibt von dem Bund und Collegio der dreye, das zweyte übrig. Und es wird wol niemand sagen, daß er zum Heiland noch einen dritten nöthig hat. Wer sich zu dem Paar, das man mit Ihm ausmacht, noch eine Gesellschaft von der engen Art, mit einer gewißen Ausschließung aller andern Creaturen dazu suchen soll, daß es weider ein Collegium von dreyen werden soll, den muß der Heiland dazu nöthigen, er muß viel schwerer dran gehen, als da er zu erst in ein solches genaues Band eingeflochten wird, da er zwar auch den Heiland hatte, aber noch nicht erfahren hatte, was es ist, wenn zwey eins werden in seinem Namen und er sich dazwischen colirt. Denn von der engen Cabinets conferenz kan niemand als ein Ehe-Mann reden, da 2 Menschen vom Heiland in die genauste Connexion gebracht werden, die sich unter allen Menschen am besten kennen, und auf eine Art eins in des andern Seele und Leib verwandelt werden, der Heiland aber doch Mittel weiß, sich in den Mittel-Punct davon hineine zu bringen, so daß er die zärtliche connexion in *sich* concentrirt, und durch sich nur noch empfindlicher, ganzer und und sacramentlicher macht. So bald nun der Tertius, der Liebhaber, der Amicus Communis die 2 Leute wieder aus einander bringt, so muß ers leiden, daß man sich darnach in Ihn vollends hinein denkt und verliert, in seinem Verdienst und Gemeinschafft sich weidet, auf eine vorher noch nicht erfahrne Weise. Denn der Heiland muß einem immer was beßers schaffen. Man dient bey Ihm nicht zurück, sondern was man hat, das behält man, und kriegt was schönes dazu. Es ist ein grad des Christenthums, ein Witwer seyn. Und wer in dem Grade nicht wächst, daß ers selber sagen kan und andre es sehen können, daß er durch die Veränderung zu neuer Pracht zu recht gemacht ist, an dem muß es selber fehlen.

6.2 Translation

Choir speech to the Widowers in Herrnhut, 28 August 1755[24]

After that, Sarah died and Abraham wept.[25]

For her departing from his sight makes the habit into a bitter suffering.[26]

It is something remarkable that habit among all human things is the firmest and strongest, and goes beyond all other kinds of persuasion and impression. There is no comparison between the love of a natural young man who acquires an object in front of his eyes, that so dulls his mind that he thinks of it as his idol, and would regard himself the happiest of creatures, if only he possessed it, and between the love, cordiality and confidentiality of two married people who have had 50 years.

If they (as it is among the natural people) have had a lot of annoyances, oppositions, and objects leading to anger and obnoxiousness, if they cannot stand each other because of certain aversions, if the by-intentions for whose sake they had taken each other stopped, and nothing remains but disgust, if they have not been able to stand each other for thirty years, and you see them again in fifteen years, you see the happiest, the most committed, and the most trusting people. They are used to each other. The late Doctor Petersen has, when his wife went home in her eighty-first year, carried out a huge lament in a Latin poem, about how abandoned he felt, and how everything in the world seemed to be against him: *Barbarus ego illi, barbarus ille mihi*.[27] I do not doubt that children of God would be able get used to each other in 5–6 years, and if they did not regard 'going home' as such a great blessing and new degree, they would not be able to forget so quickly: but yesterday's text shows that it is so with them rather than with other people: *Abraham rose from his corpse*. He had something to do in the matter and had to suspend his lamentation. Because Jesus' corpse is our consistent object, because we keep the order of our marriage *Stand* with the image and have not turned our gaze away from the dug-out hands, we are already so familiarised with the cadaverousness, that what is so odious about death for natural people, disappears for us.

We thus have in the community nothing to consider apart from our usefulness, and that reduces itself to enjoyment, since the widowers in the community are generally

---

24 Partially printed in Zinzendorf, 1763, pp. 383–6.
25 Genesis 23:1–2 which retells in the briefest of words of Sarah's death and Abraham's grief.
26 From *Herrnhuter Gesangbuch*, number 1733, amended from 'For your departing from our sight makes habit into bitter suffering' ("Denn dein aus unserm gesichte voerscheiden macht der gewohnheit ein bitteres leiden").
27 The Latin poem written by 'the late Doctor Petersen' is presumably a reference to Johann Wilhelm Petersen, the husband of Johanna Eleonora Peterson. The poem, however, seems to be written in the late 1670s by Constantijn Huygens and the object from which he is estranged is Latin, not his wife. I have not been able to establish a connection between Petersen and Huygins. Blom 1998, pp. 202–3.

released from their obligations in marriage, because their children are taken care of, and their handling has changed, and thus they enter into a new *Stand*.

It is not like Abraham, who lost the subsequent head of the family to his wife, and had to manage, albeit with so faithful a servant, for the children were regarded as nothing, as long as the father lived, he did with them, what he wished, and married them off unasked, they were the first and foremost servants, as it still is with the princes of the blood, who must show by their example how the subjects should behave. The son was thus not considered to be the head of the house, consequently Abraham was lonely, and had to make do with strangers.

But with us a new *period* begins, one enters into a new class, and the singular object of each *Stand* is, as often as one enters a new class, modified anew. The widowers, who have risen from their corpses, and have come to terms [lit. given themselves to peace] with the departure of their helpers, throw themselves a corps perdu into the Saviour's arms, 'we want to be helpers in your blessed difficulties, until we rest with each other'. The Saviour begins a new *connexion*. Before he was the third man, since two were gathered in his name. After He has taken the one with Him behind the curtain, He is now the second. Before that, one always had to be on guard, that one did not consider Him superfluous, therefore it was not necessary, because one would be otherwise alone and bereft.

All other members and friends, not excluding children, are in the Married *Bande*, where two are gathered in his name, and He is among them, not at all in [which is not?] the final accounting. When one is gone, no other friend can step into that spot, rather the Saviour remains as the second, from the covenant and collective of the three. And surely no one would say that he still needs a third person in addition to the Saviour. Whoever seeks to add to the couple which one makes with him, another companionship of the intimate kind, with the certain exclusion of all other creatures, in order once again to become a collegium of three, must be compelled by the Saviour to do so, he must go to this much harder than the first time he was woven into such an exact ribbon, because, while he then also had the Saviour, he had not yet experienced what it is when two become one in his name and he intervenes between them. For no other than a husband can speak of the intimate cabinet meeting, where two people are brought into the most exact *connexion* by the Saviour, who knows them best among all humans, and are in a way transformed one into the other's soul and body, however, the Saviour knows the means to place himself as the middle-point so that he concentrates *within himself* the tender *connexion*, and through himself only makes it more tender, whole, and sacramental.

As soon as the Third, the lover, the Amicus Communis separates the two again, then he must suffer, that one hereafter completely thinks and loses oneself into him, and takes delight in his merit and community in a way not previously experienced. Because the Saviour always has to obtain something better for one. One does not serve Him back, but what one has, one keeps, and receives something wonderful on top. It is a degree of Christianity to be a widower. And whoever does not grow in this degree, that he can say to himself and others can see that he through change has been rightly made to new splendour, in him the self-same must be lacking.

7 Widows

7.1 *Transcription*

Chorrede an die Witwen in H[errn]huth. den 15ten Jul. 1755.[28]

Gesungen: Ich grüß euch ehrerbietiglich vons Heilands seiner Sie; von der, die in die Kammer schlich, und von der, die noch hie.

In der Idee des gestrigen Gesangs, des Brautgesangs, da die Töchter hier und die Schwestern droben in genauer Harmonie sind, und in Consequenz der gestrigen Losung: „Du bist ein heilig Volk Gott deinem HErrn, dich hat Gott, dein HErr, erwehlt zum Volke des Eigenthums aus allen Völkern, zu seyn ein Volk, das Gott gefallen, ein Volk, damit sein Schöpfer pranget, das ihm gar sauer worden ist;" will ich auch das sagen, was ich bey den *Witwen* gern zu stande hätte.

Es steht im 146ten Psalm: *Er erhält die Witwen*. Es ist da ein Wort gebraucht, wenn jemand fallen will, er ist ausgeglitscht, und man richtet ihn auf, und *erhält* ihn. Und man kanns den Gläubigen Alten Testaments nicht übel nehmen: der Schutz, das Aufrichten war ihnen genug; Gott solte sie bey der Hand halten, ihr Stecken und Stab seyn; das allein begehrten sie, und nichts weiter. Und in dem Liede: O du meine Seele singe etc. heist es: „Er ist der Fremden Hütte, die Waisen nimt Er an, erfüllt der Witwen Bitte, wird selbst ihr Trost und Mann," der sie schützt, wie ein Mann seine Frau; ihre Protection, ihre Bedeckung ist von ihr genommen, und nun ist Gott dazu da. *Die* Idee ist *uns* nicht genug. Sie ist nicht neutestamentisch. Der Sinn und Context ist auch eigentlich der: „Der HErr behütet die Fremdlingen und Waisen, und die Witwen will Er groß machen, die will Er erhöhen, die will Er ehren." Und wenn ein jedes mit seinem Rang in Ordnung seyn wird, so wird ein gemeinschaftlich Hallelujah in seinem Tempel erschallen. So sind alle Stände durch gegangen, und mit den Witwen wird beschlossen, daß sie sollen zu Ehren kommen.

Mit der Ehre der Witwen ists so. Die alte Idee war blos: Eine Witwe ist eine separirte Person, die mit der Welt nichts mehr zu verkehren, die ausgelebt hat, und auf die Seite geht. Das Pünktgen, das euch ehedem hat revoltiren wollen, nemlich daß man Personen, die ausser der Ehe Mutter worden, Witwen heist; war damals der ordent-

---

28   Chorrede an die Witwen in H[errn]huth. den 15ten Jul. 1755 (UA, R.20.HS.46).

liche Gang. Der Thamar nicht zu gedenken, die nach dem letzten Concubinat mit ihrem Schwager Onan in ihres Vaters Hause Witwe blieb, ob sie gleich schon Braut mit Selah war: so ist von der Tochter Davids aufgezeichnet, daß sie, ohngeachtet sie genothzüchtiget, und also nach dem Gesetz unschuldig war, doch als eine Witwe, χηρεύσσα, in ihres Bruders Hause blieb. Auch wird von Davids Weibern noch bey Lebzeiten ihres Herrn gesagt, daß sie als Witwen gelebt.

Die Sache ist bey uns auch so gemeint: nicht aus Geringschätzung eures Chors, wie im alten Testament; noch aus Geringschätzung gegen sie, bey der Gemeine zumal, da man an die alte Welt nicht mehr gedenkt, da man eines jeden sein Thun und Wesen im Naturgange nicht erst lange nachsucht, wenn es ein Kind Gottes wird; sondern weil es für ihr Herz so am convenabelsten, und weil ihre mütterliche Treue von ihren Kindern mit mehr Respect aus dem Witwen Chor, als aus dem ledigen Schwesternhause, angenommen wird.

Wie es sich aber mit der Dignitaet eures Chors nach und nach gemacht hat: das wollen wir sehen. Damals wars also schlecht. Wenn eine Witwe zu sehr verachtet wurde, das wurde desapprobirt; wenn eine zu hart gedruckt wurde, das wurde getadelt: aber die Lehre von der Ehe mit dem Heiland, und daß die Ehe ein Interims-Stand ist, daß sich das weibliche Geschlecht in 4 Classen befindet, die erste ist der Mädgen, die zweyte der Jungfern, die dritte der Weiber, und die 4te und höchste Classe ist der Witwen; das war damals noch nicht bekant. Aber davon sind wir jetzt genugsam unterrichtet. Mein Text ist eine Verheissung, daß im Neuen Testament, im Tempel des neuen Bundes, die Witwen den ersten Rang haben, die ersten unter den Geschwistern seyn werden. Da ist nicht von Gemeinämtern und Gemeingange die Rede; sondern nur was die Geschwister überhaupt sind. Die Witwen sind ein Fürsten Chor; sie sind in des Heilands eigene Hut, das restituirte Jungfern Chor. Der Mann, oder, wenn es der Mann nicht gethan hat, der heilige Geist, hat die Schwester Christo als seine Jungfrau wieder überliefert. Wenn Er nun sein Amt thut an allen Chören, an dem Volk des Eigenthums, das dem HErrn heilig ist; so *ehret* Er seine Witwen, und wendet ihnen Respect zu.

Darauf muß gearbeitet werden in der Gemeine des Heilands. Darauf begrüßte ich euch, in Expectation, daß ihr euch werdet zu solchen *Hochwürdigen* machen lassen. Freilich wird erfordert, daß ihr *rechte Witwen* seyd; wovon ich auch zu euch geredet habe.

Ein Kind Gottes, eine Schwester, und eine Chorschwester seyn: das ist gar nicht einerley; das sind 2 unterschiedene Sachen. Das letztere ist das, was man den Chorpunkt nennt. Es haben mir Ehegeschwister, die aus den ledigen Chören kürzlich in die Ehe gekommen, geschrieben, daß sie noch fast über ihrem Chorpunkt halten. Das ist unrichtig geredet, wie sies verstehen. Man legt freilich das selige und lautere Herz, das man in seinem Chor acquirirt, nicht ab, wenn man in einen andern Stand kommt. Das ist aber nicht der Chorpunkt; das ist die Sache *aller* Kinder Gottes: sondern daß jedes in seinem Stande zufrieden, und just über derselben Abtheilung so ganz selig ist, daß das mit die Glückseligkeit des Lebens ausmacht; das ist der Chorpunkt. Wenn eins vom Heiland wieder seinen Willen, Wissen und Denken, in einen andern Stand gesetzt wird; und es trift gleich eine Schwester, die in der Gnade noch so erstarkt ist: so kann doch der Verlust ihres vorigen Standes ihr nicht anders als schmerzlich fallen. Denn davon verändern sich die agrémens. Der Chorpunkt einer Ledigen kann nicht der Chorpunkt einer Witwe seyn. Wenn eine Witwe ehelich denkt, so ist sie verrückt im Kopf; wenn eine Ehefrau ledig denkt, so ist sie, Pauli Ausdruck zu brauchen, in ihren Sinnen verrückt; wenn eine Ehefrau gern eine Witwe würde, so ist sie, aufs gelindeste zu urtheilen, in dem Punkt auch verrückt.

Dazu gehört eine heilige Leitung, dazu gehört des Heilands Ausspruch, das Factum, daß der Heiland den Mann wegnimmt, und Er seine Freygelassene umarmt, als wieder zurückgekommen in seine Special-Sorge, in seine Hand. *Dann* versteht erst eine Schwester den Chorpunkt, und kriegt Gedanken, die sie wenig Tage vorher nicht hat haben sollen, noch können. Also, sich als eine erneuerte Jungfrau des Lammes ansehen, darauf kommts bey euch an. Ihr seyd durch den ordinairen ehelichen Gang in der Welt, oder durch Unordnung, oder durch den Gemeingrad (das sind sehr differente Wege) aus eurem Jungfernstande gekommen; auf dem dritten Wege, nach dem Gemeinsinn, als Mägde des Heilands. Das nennt die heilige Schrift: *nach der Jungfrauschaft mit einem Manne leben.* So wird die Hanna beschrieben. Wer nun also aus einem dieser 3 Umstände wieder in des Heilands Hand zurückgekommen, in euer Chor genommen, und eins von euren Chorzeichen gekriegt hat, um mit euch zu wohnen, und sich respectirlich zu tragen um der Engel willen: die soll *lernen*, was ihr Stand ist, bey ihren Schwestern im Hause, bey ihren Gespielen sich erkundigen, was Witwengnade ist, worinnen sich ihre Gnade von der Gnade anderer Chöre distinguirt; sie soll sich die Gnade, die ihr erzehlt wird, ansehen, ob sie unblutig ist oder besprengt. Und rencontrirt sie eine Heilige ohne Blutstrich; die kann sie wol respectiren, aber sie wird nicht ihre Nachfolgerin, sondern sieht sich nach Sünderstirnen um, die Marie-Magdalenelich heilig seyn, die mit thränenden Augen zu den Füssen des Heilandes sitzen, mit einem gleichwol kummerhaften Andenken der vielleicht in dem vorigen Stande verletzten jungfräulichen Ehren; weil, ob sie schon gewust haben, wie weit das Recht des Mannes von *Seinem* Recht unterschieden ist, es doch manchmal zu Seinem Nachtheil ausgefallen, und mit einem damit gemischten schamrothen Witwenblick. *Solche* Herzen sieht man sich zu Exempeln aus, und erbaut sich an ihnen, dem Statui denkt man nach, da denkt man sich hinein, und läßt sich vor allen Dingen mit Ysop besprengen, mit dem Myrrhenbüschel aus *seiner* heiligen Seite. Denn der muß uns doch in alles hinein heiligen und reinigen, und zu allem restituiren, was versäumt worden.

Darnach geht man in die Gelegenheiten, in alle Liturgien, mit einem wahren *Witwengefühl*, das ich nicht beschreiben kann; so wie ihrs köntet und soltet haben, und billig von seiner Treue kindlich erwartet.

7.2 Translation

Sung: I greet you respectfully, she who belongs to the Savior; from she who crept into the chamber and from she who is still here.[29]

In the idea of yesterday's song, of the bride's song, where the daughters here and the sisters above are in perfect harmony, and in consequence of yesterday's Losung: 'You are a holy people [of] God your Master, God your Master has chosen you as his property out of all peoples,[30] to be a people pleasing to God, whereby their Creator is exalted, which has been made sour',[31] I will also say what I would like to see happen with the widows.

It is written in the 146th Psalm: *He upholds the widows*.[32] There a word is used, when someone will fall, he has skidded off, and one sets him upright and *upholds* him. And one cannot blame the faithful of the Old Testament: the protection, the setting upright was enough for them; God would hold them by their hand and be their stick and staff; that was all they wanted, and no further. And in the song: 'O you my soul sing etc.',[33] it is said, 'He is a hut to the stranger, he embraces the wise, he fulfils the widows' request, he himself becomes her consolation and husband', who protects her as a husband protects his wife; her protection, her consideration has been taken from her, and now God is there for that. *This* idea is not enough for *us*. It is not of the New Testament. The meaning and context is actually this: 'the Lord preserves the strangers and orphans, and he wants to make the widows great, he wants to exalt them, he wants to honour them'. And when each one with his rank is in order, a communal Hallelujah will sound in his temple. So, all the *Stände* have been examined and it was decided that the widows should come to honour.

With the honour of widows, it is like this: The old idea was only: a widow is a separated person, who does not truly engage with the world, she is run out [lit. lived out], and walks on the side. The small point, against which you wanted to revolt long ago, is that once, it was the proper course, that persons who became mothers outside marriage, were called widow. Not to mention Thamar, who after the last concubinage with

---

29 *Londoner Gesangbuch* 1, 2168, verse 4.
30 From Deuteronomy 7:6: 'For thou art an holy people unto the LORD thy God: the LORD thy God hath chosen thee to be a special people unto himself, above all people that are upon the face of the earth'.
31 Hymn by Karl Friedrich Lochner (1634–97), called "Was gibst du denn, o meine seele", the English version known as 'Soul, What Return Has God, Thy Saviour' printed in *Herrnhuter Gesangbuch*, number 640. The songbook version speaks of the heart as that which exalts the Creator, which has here been shifted to a collective 'people' which will exalt their Creator.
32 Psalm 146:9: The LORD preserveth the strangers; he relieveth the fatherless and widow.
33 "Du meine Seele singe" ('You my soul sing') is a hymn written by Paul Gerhard (1607–76), based on psalm 146.

her brother-in-law Onan remained widowed in her father's house, although she was already a bride with Selah:³⁴ it is recorded of the daughter of David that although she is raped, and therefore innocent by law, she remained a widow, χηρεύσσα, in her brother's house.³⁵ It is also said of David's wives, during the life of their master, that they lived as widows.³⁶

Among us, the issue is also meant like this: not out of contempt for your choir as in the Old Testament; nor out of contempt for you, especially in the case of the congregation, where one no longer remembers the old world, where one does not long for one's doing and being in nature once it becomes a child of God; but because it is so most appropriate for her heart, and because her motherly fidelity is accepted by her children with more respect from the widows' choir, than from the single sisters' house.

However, let us look at how the dignity of your choir gradually changed. At that time it was bad. If a widow was despised too much, that was disapproved, if she was pushed too hard, that was admonished; but the doctrine of marriage to the Saviour, and that marriage is an interim state, that the female sex is in four classes, the first is the girl, the second the maiden, the third the wives, and the fourth and highest class is the widow; that was not known then. But we are so well informed now. My text³⁷ is a promise that in the New Testament, in the temple of the new covenant, the widows have the first rank, they will be the first among members. There, we are not talking about community offices or community affairs; but only what the members are.

The widows are a princely choir; they are under the Saviour's own protection, the reconstituted Maiden Choir. The man, or, when the man has not done so, the Holy Spirit, has redelivered the sister to Christ as his maiden. When He carries out his office (*Amt*) upon all the choirs, upon the people which are his property, which are holy to the Lord, he honours his widows, and gives them respect.

Thereupon work must be done in the congregation of the Saviour. Thereupon I greeted you, in expectation, that you will let yourselves be made *magnanimous*. Of course, it requires that you are *real widows*;³⁸ of which I have also spoken to you.

---

34 The story of Tamar, who was married to Er, and after him, his brother Onan is from Genesis 38. Both men were killed by God for their evil ways. She was held in the house of her father-in-law, Judah, who had promised her to his third son Selah, but did not want to fulfil the promise.

35 Tamar is also the name of the daughter of King David. She is raped by her brother Amnon in 2 Samuel 13 and afterwards lived in her brother Absalom's house.

36 This is a reference to the ten concubines of David, whom he left in charge of the palace, and upon his return 'put them in a house under guard, and provided for them, but did not go in to them. So they were shut up until the day of their death, living as if in widowhood' (2 Samuel 20:3).

37 'My text' could refer to the watchword.

38 'Real widows' could be a reference to 1 Timothy 5, where Timothy is told to distinguish

To be a child of God, a sister, and a choir sister: that is not the same thing; these are two different issues. The latter is what one calls the choir point. Married members, who recently came into marriage from the single choirs, wrote me that they still hold firmly on to their choir point. This is incorrectly spoken, as they understand it. Of course, one does not relinquish the blissful and obedient heart, which one acquires in his choir, when one comes into another *Stand*. But that is not the choir point; that is the issue of all the children of God. Rather, that everyone is content in his *Stand*, and is so blissful about the self-same division, that it constitutes the bliss of life; this is the choir point. When one, against one's will, conscience and thinking, is placed in another *Stand* by the Saviour, and it directly affects a sister who is strengthened in grace, then the loss of her previous *Stand* can only be experienced as painful, From then, the agrémens change. The choir point of a single cannot be the choir point of a widow. If a widow thinks maritally, she is disturbed in the head; if a wife thinks unmarried, then she is, to use Paul's expression, corrupted in her mind;[39] if a wife would like to become a widow, then judging her favourably, she is also disturbed in this point.

To this belongs a sacred guidance, to this belongs the Saviour's utterance, the fact that the Saviour removes the man, and He embraces his released one as returning to his special care, into his hand. Only then does a sister understand the choir point, and receives thoughts that she should not, nor could have had a few days earlier. So, to see oneself as a renewed maiden of the Lamb, that is where it concerns you. You have come out of your maiden Stand through the ordinarily married path in the world, or through disorder, or through the community rank (these are very different ways); on the third path, according to community mind, as maids of the Saviour. That is what the scriptures call: *to live with a man after the maidenhood*. This is how Hanna is described.[40] So whoever has come back from one of these three circumstances back into the Saviour's hand, taken into your choir and received one of your choir-signs, in order to dwell with you, and to carry herself for the sake of the angel, she shall *learn* what your *Stand* is, with her sisters in the house, inquire at their games (*Gespielen*), what a widow's grace is, how her mercy distinguishes itself from the grace of other choirs; she should inspect the mercy which is told her, whether it is bloodless or sprinkled. And should she encounter a holy

---

between real widows who are faithful and devoted, and younger widows who only think of remarriage and gossip.

1 Timothy 5:5–6: 'The real widow, left alone, has set her hope on God and continues in supplications and prayers night and day; but the widow who lives for pleasure is dead even while she lives'.

39 2 Corinthians 11:3. Paul is talking about other preachers encroaching on his territory: 'But I fear lest by any means, as the serpent beguiled Eve through his subtilty, so your minds should be corrupted from the simplicity that is in Christ'.

40 Anna/Hanna in Luke 2:36. An old widow who 'had lived with a husband seven years from her virginity' (KJV).

without bloodstreaks, she may well respect her, but she will not be her follower, but she will look around for sinners brows, who are holy in the manner of Mary Magdalene, who with tearful eyes sits at the feet of the Saviour, with an equal-minded memory of the possibly damaged virginal honour of the previous Stand, for although she already knew how far the right of the husband is from *His* right, it has still sometimes turned out to His disadvantage, and with this a blush of shame is mixed into the widow's gaze. *Such* hearts one looks towards as examples, and builds oneself upon them, one contemplates that state, therein one thinks oneself, and above all, lets oneself be sprinkled with hyssop, with the tufts of myrrh from *His* holy side. For He must sanctify and cleanse us in everything, restore everything that has been neglected.

After that one participates in the occasions, in all liturgies, with a true *widowed feeling* that I cannot describe; it is how you could and should have it, and appropriate to his faithfulness, childishly expected.

References

1 Archival References

1.1 *Unity Archive, Herrnhut* (UA)
1.1.1 Diaries

R.6.A.b.9a	1 January to 3 March 1730
R.6.A.b.10.1	1 January to 22 August 1731
R.6.A.b.10.2	1. January to 24. Oktober 1731
R.6.A.b.10.4	Martin Dober's journal 25 August 1731 to 31 December 1732
R.6.A.b.11a	1733
R.6.A.b.11b	1734
R.6.A.b.12.1	1 January to 19 November 1735
R.6.A.b.12.3	Martin Dober's private diary, 1 January to 25 September 1735
R.6.A.b.13.a.1	16 April–6 May 1736
R.6.A.b.13.a.2a–b	January–February 1736
R.6.A.b.13.a.3a–3d	11 April–3 May; 8 May–28 May; 6–27 June; and 2–24 July 1736.
R.6.A.b.13.b.1	13 August–9 November 1737, and 17–28 November 1737.
R.6.A.b.13.b.2	December 1737 and beginning of 1738.
R.6.A.b.13.c.1	Mathias Schindler's diary, 1 January–2 August 1738.
R.6.A.b.13.c.2	Married men and widowers, 19. Januar–9. February 1738
R.6.A.b.13.c.3	Workers diary, 4 December 1737, all of 1738 until 25 July 1739.
R.6.A.b.13.c.4	Excerpts from 1738
R.6.A.b.13.c.5	November 1738
R.6.A.b.13.c.6.a.–d	Diaries from the orphanage, single sisters and brothers.
R.6.A.b.13.d.1	3 January–1 April 1739.
R.6.A.b.13.d.2	Abbreviated version, 26 July–26 December 1740.
R.6.A.b.13.d.3	Notices for prayer day, 11. November 1740
R.6.A.b.13.d.4	Description of the celebration of the laying of the foundation stone for the single brothers' house on 22 June 1739.
R.6.A.b.13d.5–c	Martin Dober's speech on New Year's Eve 1740
R.6.A.b.13.d.7.a	1 January 1739, summary of the achievements of the Lamb in Herrnhut in this year.
R.6.A.b.13.d.7.b	1–6 October 1740.
R.6.A.b.14.1	Complete diary of 1741 written by Martin Dober and Johannes von Watteville
R.6.A.b.15.1	Complete diary of 1742 written by Johannes von Watteville and Martin Dober
R.6.A.b.16.1	Complete diary of 1743

R.6.A.b.16.2	Abbreviated diary of 1743
R.6.A.b.17.a.1744.a	1 January to 5 December, 1744
R.6.A.b.17.a.1744.b	15 August to 10 October, 1744
R.6.A.b.17.a.1745.a	Complete diary of 1745
R.6.A.b.17.a.1746	Complete diary of 1746
R.6.A.b.19a.1754	Complete diary of 1754
R.6.A.a.37.b	Paul Münster's diary from Herrnhut
R.6.A.b.6.i.	Combined diary from Herrnhut (1738–1739 and 1744–1751) copied by Sigw. Friedrich Hark

1.1.2   Choir Speeches

GN.C.2 1747, 1	Boys, 5 November 1747
GN.C.2 1747, 2	Brothers, 5 November 1747
GN.C.2.1747.6	Widows, 5 November 1747
GN.C.3 1748, 1	Married couples, 15 April 1748
GN.C.5 1748, 3	Single brothers, 10 May 1748
GN.C.21 1751, 5	Workers, single brothers, 17 April 1751
GN.C.59 1756, 4	Single sisters, 17 August 1756
GN.C.78.1758.2	Girls, 27. Februar 1758
GN.C.78.1758.2	Married couples, 4 March 1758
GN.C.78.1758.2	Single sisters, 9 March 1758
GN.C.78.1758.2	Children, 11 March 1758
GN.C.80.1758.4	All sisters, 14 May 1758
GN.C.80.1758.4	All sisters, 19 May 1758
GN.C.80.1758.4	Married couples, 20 May 1758
GN.C.80.1758.4	Single brothers, 1 June 1758
R.4.C.II.12	Married couples, 20 October 1747
	Married couples, 26 October 1747
	Married couples, 2 August 1748
	Married couples, 16 August 1748
	Married couples, 12 November 1750
	Married couples, 22 November 1750
	Married couples, 11 December 1750
	Married men, 8 December 1756

REFERENCES

R.20.HS1   Older girls, 25 March 1744
                   Single sisters, 25 March 1744
                   Widowers, 25 March 1744

R.20.HS13   Married couples, 21 July 1748

R.20.HS.22   Single brothers, 26 October 1750

R.20.HS23   Single brothers, 3 November 1750

R.20.HS28   Single sisters, 2 July 1748
                   Single sisters, 10 July 1748
                   Single sisters, 2 August 1748
                   Single brothers, 15 October 1750
                   Single sisters, 26 October 1750
                   Single sisters, 6 November 1750
                   Single sisters, 31 March 1751
                   Single sisters, 6 April 1751
                   Single sisters, 2/22 June 1751
                   Single sisters, 11 September 1755
                   Single sisters, 7 January 1756

R.20.HS31   Widowers, 5 June 1755
                   Widowers, 17 July 1755
                   Widowers, 31 July 1755
                   Widowers, 7 August 1755
                   Widowers, 28 August 1755
                   Widowers, 13 September 1755
                   Widowers, 22 September 1755
                   Widowers, 10 November 1755
                   Widowers, 1 December 1755
                   Widowers, 25 March 1756
                   Widowers, 29 April 1756

R.20.HS32   Older girls, 25 March 1751

R.20.HS34   Single brothers, 5 November 1747

R.20.HS35   Single brothers, 15 April 1748
                   Single brothers, 9 July 1748
                   Single brothers, 28 January 1751

R.20.HS42	Married brothers, 14 July 1755
	Married sisters, 14 July 1755
	Married brothers, 21 August 1755
	Married sisters, 25 December 1755
R.20.HS46	Boys, 5 November 1747
	Widows, 6 June 1755
	Widows, 30 June 1755
	Widows, 15 July 1755
	Widows, 16 August 1755
	Widows, 29 August 1755
	Widows, 6 September 1755
	Widows, 22 September 1755
	Widows, 18 March 1756
	Widows, 25 March 1756
	Widows, 28 April 1756
	Widows, 9 May 1756
	Widows, 21 May 1756
R.20.HS47	Single sisters, 1 July 1755
	Single sisters, 4 September 1755
	Single sisters, 5 September 1755
	Single sisters, 20 September 1755
	Single sisters, 26 September 1755
	Single sisters, 13 November 1755
	Single sisters, 1 December 1755
	Single sisters, 8 December 1755
	Single sisters, 25 December 1755
	Single sisters, 12 January 1756
	Single sisters, 2 February 1756
	Single sisters, 22 March 1756
	Single sisters, 25 March 1756
	Single sisters, 17 May 1756
	Single sisters, 20 May 1756
	Single sisters, 21 May 1756
	Single sisters, 17 August 1756
	Single sisters, 4 May 1757
R.20.HS48	Single sisters, 4 June 1755
	Single sisters, 15 June 1755
	Single sisters, 1 July 1755

REFERENCES 357

R.20.HS49   Single sisters, 5 May 1758

R.20.HS50   Single brothers, 3 March 1758
                Single brothers, 20 May 1758

R.20.HS51   Single brothers, 2 July 1755
                Single brothers, 9 July 1755
                Single brothers, 7 August 1755

R.20.HS52   Single brothers, 2 January 1760
                Widowers, 3 January 1760
                Boys, 14 January 1760
                Single brothers, 5 March 1760
                All Sisters 13 March 1760
                Single brothers, 19 March 1760

R.20.HS54   Married couples, 11 June 1751
                Married brothers, 14 July 1755
                Married sisters, 14 July 1755
                Married couples, 22 August 1755
                Married brothers, 13 November 1755
                Married sisters, 17 November 1755
                Married brothers, 17 November 1755
                Married brothers, 24 November 1755
                Married brothers, 1 December 1755
                Married brothers, 8 December 1755
                Married sisters, 8 December 1755
                Married sisters, 25 December 1755
                Married brothers, 1 January 1756
                Married sisters, 7 January 1756
                Married sisters, 27 January 1756
                Married brothers, 27 January 1756
                Married brothers, 2 February 1756
                Married couples, 25 March 1756
                Married sisters, 26 March 1756
                Married brothers, 26 March 1756
                Married couples, 9 January 1757
                Married couples, 29 April 1757
                Married couples, 17 August 1757
                Married couples, 3 February 1758

	Married couples, 17 February 1758
	Married couples, 24 February 1758
	Married couples, 4 March 1758
	Married couples, 20 May 1758
	Married couples, 27 December 1759
	Married couples, 6 March 1760
	Married couples, 10 April 1760
R.20.H S55	Married couples, 4 August 1748
R.20.H S57	Single brothers, 2 February 1756
	Single brothers, 29 August 1756
	Single brothers, 27 April 1757
	Single brothers, 8 June 1757
	Single brothers, 29 August 1757
	Single brothers, 1 February 1758
	Single brothers, 3 April 1758
	Single brothers, 5 May 1760
R.20.H S58	Single brothers, 9 July 1755
	Single brothers, 1 August 1755
	Single brothers, 19 May 1756
R.20.H S60	Single sisters, 8 June 1757
	Single sisters, 6 July 1757
	Single sisters, 27 July 1757
	Single sisters 17 August 1757
	Single sisters, 1 February 1758
	Single sisters, 9 March 1758
	Single sisters 15 March 1758
	Single sisters, 3 April 1758
	Single sisters 11 March 1760

1.1.3   Letters

R.4.C.II.11.4	James Charlesworth to Zinzendorf, 17 May 1754
R.6.Aa.42.1.43	Jacob Till to Zinzendorf, 12 October 1744
R.6.A.a.42.1.44	Carl Heinrich von Peistel to Zinzendorf, 11 October (1744)
R.14.A.14.25	Andreas Grassmann to Zinzendorf, 4 May 1742
R.20.B.22.b.206	Zinzendorf to Erdmuth Dorothea Reuss, 16 September 1723

1.1.4 Memoirs

R.22.2b.112	Christiane Eleonora Voigt
R.22.16.55	Matthæus Gewinn
R.22.63.83	Elisabeth Maria Lenzner
R.22.70.98	Catharina Elisabeth Milditzin
R.22.109.9	Gottlieb Oertel
NB.I.R.4.291.C.2.30	Rosina Nitschmann

1.1.5 Miscellanea

GN.C.65 1756, 10, Appendix 20	Single sisters' description of the move to their new choir house in Herrnhut on 16 October 1756.
R.2.A.3.A.1	Minutes from synod in Gotha, June 1740
R.2.A.4.1	Minutes from synod in Marienborn, December 1740.
R.4.C.II.9	Marriage synod in Herrnhut 22 December 1756–10 January 1757
R.4.C.II.10.1.	Married couples, 7–17 January, 1744.
R.4.C.IV (SHAHt)	Remains of the archive from the sisters' house.
R.4.E 28a	Finding aid for Herrnhut community archive.
R.6.A.a.19.4a	Constitution of the Moravian community of Brethren.
R.6.A.a.22.1	Christian David's Description of Herrnhut (1731)
R.6.A.a.39.1	Documents belonging to the Herrnhuter statutes.
R.6.A.a.43.4.i	Conference concerning the Herrnhut circumstances, February 1745.
R.6.A.a.43.4.m.	Notes on a couple of main issues 1745 or 1746.
R.6.A.a.58.2	Status of Herrnhut 1744
R.27.124.4	Catalogue of single sisters, 1743.
R.27.292.033	Members' list, Wetterau – Marienborn – All Choirs.
R.29.B.79	Ludwig von Schweiniz's collection of documents pertaining to the Sifting Time (1745–1750). Includes the diaries from the single brothers' house 1737–38, 1744–49 and 1758 and Martin Dober's description of the developments in Zinzendorf's teaching (1725–47).
NB.II.420.1, IIb.	Register to the speeches of Count Zinzendorf

1.2 Moravian Archives Bethlehem (MAB)

MAB BethSS	Diary of the single sisters' house.

2 General References

Albrecht, Ruth, Ulrike Gleixner, Corinna Kirschstein, Eva Kormann, and Pia Schmid (eds) 2018, *Pietismus und Adel. Genderhistorische Analysen*, Hallesche Forschungen 49. Halle: Verlag der Francheschen Stiftungen.

Anderson, Benedict 2006 [1983], *Imagined Communities: Reflections on the Origin and Spread of Nationalism*, London: Verso.

Anidjar, Gil 2014, *Blood: A Critique of Christianity*, New York: Columbia University Press.

Aston, T.H., and C.H.E. Philpin (eds) 1987, *The Brenner Debate: Agrarian Class Structure and Economic Development in Pre-Industrial Europe*, Cambridge: Cambridge University Press.

Atwood, Craig D. 1997, 'Sleeping in the Arms of Christ: Sanctifying Sexuality in the Eighteenth-Century Moravian Church', *Journal of the History of Sexuality*, 8, no. 1: 25–51.

Atwood, Craig D. 2004, *Community of the Cross: Moravian Piety in Colonial Bethlehem*, University Park: Pennsylvania State University Press.

Atwood, Craig D. 2006a, 'Interpreting and Reinterpreting the Sichtungszeit', *Neue Aspekte der Zinzendorf-Forschung*, edited by Martin Brecht and Paul Peuker, Göttingen: Vandenhoeck & Ruprecht.

Atwood, Craig D. 2006b, 'Understanding Zinzendorf's Blood and Wounds Theology', *Journal of Moravian History*, 1: 31–47.

Atwood, Craig D. 2011, 'The Union of Masculine and Feminine in Zinzendorfian Piety', in *Masculinity, Senses, Spirit*, edited by Katherine M. Faull, Lewisburg: Bucknell University Press.

Balibar, Etienne 1991, 'Citizen Subject', in *Who Comes after the Subject?*, edited by Eduardo Cadava, Peter Connor and Jean-Luc Nancy, London: Routledge.

Banaji, Jairus 2010, *Theory as History: Essays on Modes of Production and Exploitation*, Leiden: Brill.

Barker, Chris 2003, *Cultural Studies: Theory and Practice*, London: Sage.

Barth, Ulrich 2004, *Aufgeklärter Protestantismus*, Tübingen: Mohr Siebeck.

Bechler, Theodor 1922, *Ortsgeschichte von Herrnhut mit besonderer Berücksichtigung der älteren Zeit*, Herrnhut: Verlag der Missionsbuchhandlung.

Becker-Cantarino, Barbara 2018, 'Zur Bedeutung der *Oeconomia* im Engagement adliger Frauen im Pietismus: Erdmuthe Dorothea von Zinzendorf', in *Pietismus und Adel: Genderhistorische Analysen*, edited by Ruth Albrecht, Ulrike Gleixner, Corinna Kirschstein, Eva Kormann and Pia Schmid, Halle: Verlag der Franckesche Stiftungen.

Berg, Annemette Løkke Borg, Lene Lindberg Marcussen, and Karen Stoklund, 2013 (eds), *Christiansfeld: A Danish Moravian Settlement*, Kolding.

Beyreuther, Erich, and Gerhard Meyer (eds) 1963, *21 Discourse über die Augsburger Konfession*, Zinzendorf Hauptschriften 6, Hildesheim: Georg Ohlms Verlag.

Beyreuther, Gottfried 1975 [1963], 'Sexualtheorie im Pietismus', in *Zweiter Sammelband über Zinzendorf*, edited by Erich Beyreuther and Gerhard Meyer, Hildesheim: Georg Olms.

Blackledge, Paul 2006, *Reflections on the Marxist Theory of History*, Manchester: Manchester University Press.

Blissett, Luther 2003, *Q*, London: Heinemann.

Bloch, Ernst 1960, *Thomas Münzer als Theologe der Revolution*, Berlin: Aufbau-Verlag.

Blom, Frans R.E. 1998, '"What Has Been My Weight on Earth": The Autobiography of Constantijn Huygens', in *Modelling the Individual: Biography and Portrait in the Renaissance*, edited by Karl A.E. Enenkel, Betsy de Jong-Crane, and Peter Liebregts, Amsterdam: Rodopi.

Boelcke, Willi A. 1857, *Bauer und Gutsherr in der Oberlausitz: Ein Beitrag zur Wirtschafts-, Sozial- und Rechtsgeschichte der ostelbischen Gutsherrschaft*, Schriftenreihe des Instituts für Sorbische Volksforschung, Bautzen: Domowina-Verlag.

Boer, Roland 1996, *Jameson and Jeroboam*, Atlanta: Scholars Press.

Boer, Roland 2011, *Criticism of Theology: On Marxism and Theology III*, Leiden: Brill.

Boer, Roland 2012, *Criticism of Earth: On Marx, Engels, and Theology*, Leiden: Brill.

Boer, Roland 2015, *The Sacred Economy of Ancient Israel*, Louisville: Westminster John Knox.

Boer, Roland, and Christina Petterson 2017, *Time of Troubles: A New Economic Framework for Early Christianity*, Philadelphia: Fortress.

Bondi, Gerhard 1964, 'Der Beitrag des Hallischen Pietismus zur Entwicklung des ökonomischen Denkens in Deutschland', *Jahrbuch für Wirtschaftsgeschichte*, 5, no. 2–3: 24–48.

Bottomore, Tom 1997, *A Dictionary of Marxist Thought* (2nd edn), Oxford: Blackwell.

Boyle, Nicholas 1992, *Goethe: The Poet and the Age*, Oxford: Oxford University Press.

Bredsdorff, Thomas, 2003, *Den brogede oplysning. Om følelsernes fornuft og fornuftens følelse i 1700 tallets nordiske literatur*, København: Gyldendal.

Brinkmann, Carl 1926, 'Die Aristokratie im kapitalistischen Zeitalter', in *Grundriss der Sozialökonomik IX: Das soziale System des Kapitalismus. 1. Teil: Die gesellschaftliche Schichtung im Kapitalismus*, edited by G. Albrecht, G. Briefs and C. Brinkmann, Tübingen: J.C.B. Mohr.

Bynum, Caroline Walker 2002, 'The Blood of Christ in the Later Middle Ages', *Church History*, 71, no. 4: 685–714.

Bynum, Caroline Walker 2007, *Wonderful Blood: Theology and Practice in Late Medieval Northern Germany and Beyond*, Philadelphia: University of Pennsylvania Press.

Bynum, Caroline Walker 2011, *Christian Materiality: An Essay on Religion in Late Medieval Europe*, New York: Zone Books.

Caffier, Wolfgang 1980, 'Wie das Losungsbuch Entsteht. Konzeptionelle und redaktionelle Überlegungen', *Unitas Fratrum*, 7: 42–52.

Canning, Kathleen 2006, *Gender History in Practice: Historical Perspectives on Bodies, Class and Citizenship*, Ithaca: Cornell University Press.

Comninel, George C. 2013, 'Critical Thinking and Class Analysis: Historical Materialism and Social Theory', *Socialism and Democracy*, 27, no. 1: 19–56.

Conze, Werner 1962, 'Das Spannungsfeld von Staat und Gesellschaft im Vormärz', in *Staat und Gesellschaft im deutschen Vormärz, 1815–1848*, edited by Werner Conze and Theodor Schieder, Stuttgart: E. Klett.

Conze, Werner 2005, 'Stand, Klasse VII: Zwischen Reformtion und Revolution', in *Geschichtliche Grundbegriffe: Historisches Lexicon zur politisch-sozialen Sprache in Deutschland*, edited by Otto Brunner, Werner Conze and Reinhart Kosselleck, Stuttgart: Klett-Cotta.

Cox, Robert W. 1981, 'Social Forces, States and World Orders: Beyond International Relations Theory', *Millennium*, 10, no. 2: 126–55.

Cross, Frank Leslie, and Elizabeth A. Livingstone 2005, *The Oxford Dictionary of the Christian Church* (3rd edn), Oxford: Oxford University Press.

Crouter, Richard 1980, 'Hegel and Schleiermacher at Berlin: A Many-Sided Debate', *Journal of the American Academy of Religion*, 48, no. 1: 19–43.

Dascal, Marcelo 1987, *Leibniz, Language, Signs, and Thought: A Collection of Essays*, Philadelphia: J. Benjamins Publishing Company.

Der Gottes-Acker zu Herrnhut: Bei der Einhundertjährigen Jubel-Feier des am 17ten Juny 1722 begonnenen Anbaues Böhmisch-Mährischer Brüder der Evangelischen Brüdergemeine, gewidmet von einigen hierzu vereinigten Freunden, Hirschberg, 1822.

Derrida, Jacques 1976, *Of Grammatology*, translated by Gayatri C. Spivak, Baltimore: Johns Hopkins University Press.

Dohm, Burkhard 2000, *Poetische Alchimie: Öffnung zur Sinnlichkeit in der Hohelied- und Bibeldichtung von der protestantischen Barockmystik bis zum Pietismus*, Berlin: De Gruyter.

Dorfner, Thomas 2018, 'Von „Bösen Sektierern" zu „Fleißigen Fabrikanten": Zum Wahrnehmungswandel der Herrnhuter Brüdergemeine im Kontext kameralistischer Peuplierungspolitik (ca. 1750–1800)', *Zeitschrift für historische Forschung*, 45, no. 2: 283–313.

Dowling, William C. 1984, *Jameson, Althusser, Marx: An Introduction to the Political Unconscious*, London: Methuen.

Duden, Barbara 1987, *Geschichte unter der Haut. Ein Eisenacher Arzt und seine Patientinnen um 1730*, Stuttgart: Ernst Klett Verlag.

van Dülmen, Richard 1986, *Die Gesellschaft der Aufklärer: Zur bürgerlichen Emanzipation und aufklärerischen Kultur in Deutschland*, Frankfurt am Main: Fischer.

Düselder, Heike, Olga Weckenbrock, and Siegrid Westphal 2008 (eds), *Adel und Umwelt: Horizonte adeliger Existenz in der frühen Neuzeit*, Köln: Böhlau.

Engel, Katherine Carté 2009, *Religion and Profit: Moravians in Early America*, Philadelphia: University of Pennsylvania Press.

Enggaard, Nete Helene 2011, 'Nadver, kød og krop – Luthers udspil til et nyt teologisk sprog', in *Kroppens teologi – teologiens krop*, edited by Kirsten Busch Nielsen and Johanne Stubbe Teglbjærg, Copenhagen: Anis.

von Ense, Karl August Varnhagen 1846 [1829], *Leben des Grafen Ludwig von Zinzendorf*, 2nd edn, Berlin: G. Reimer.

Erbe, Hans-Walter 1928, *Zinzendorf und der fromme hohe Adel seiner Zeit*, Leipzig: Eger & Sievers.

Erbe, Hellmuth 1929, *Bethlehem, Pa. Eine kommunistische Herrnhuter Kolonie des 18. Jahrhunderts*, Stuttgart: Ausland und Heimat Verlags-Aktiengesellschaft.

Falzon, Christopher 2013, 'Making History', in *A Companion to Foucault*, edited by Christopher Falzon, Timothy O'Leary and Jana Sawicki, London: Blackwell.

Faull, Katherine M. 1995, 'Faith and Imagination: Nikolaus Ludwig von Zinzendorf's Anti-Enlightenment Philosophy of Self', in *Anthropology and the German Enlightenment: Perspectives on Humanity*, edited by Katherine M. Faull, Lewisburg, PA: Bucknell University Press.

Faull, Katherine M. 1997, *Moravian Women's Memoirs: Their Related Lives, 1750–1820*, Syracuse: Syracuse University Press.

Faull, Katherine M. 2009, 'Girl Talk: The Role of the "Speakings" in the Pastoral Care of the Older Girls' Choir', *Journal of Moravian History*, 6: 77–99.

Faull, Katherine M. 2010, 'Speaking and Truth-Telling: Parrhesia in the Eighteenth Century Moravian Church', in *Self, Community, World*, edited by Heikki Lempa and Paul Peucker, 147–67, Bethlehem: Lehigh University Press.

Faull, Katherine M. 2011a, 'The Married Choir Instructions (1785)', *Journal of Moravian History*, 10: 69–110.

Faull, Katherine M. 2011b, 'Temporal Men and the Eternal Bridegroom: Moravian Masculinity in the Eighteenth Century', in *Masculinity, Senses, Spirit*, edited by Katherine M. Faull, Lewisburg, PA: Bucknell University Press.

Faull, Katherine M. 2013, 'Masculinity in the Eighteenth-Century Moravian Mission Field: Contact and Negotiation', *Journal of Moravian History*, 13, no. 1: 27–53.

Fischer, Ole 2013, 'Wirtschaftliche Prosperität und religiöse Erweckung. Das Handwerk in der Herrnhutersiedlung Christiansfeld', in *Aus der Mitte des Landes. Klaus-Joachim Lorenzen-Schmidt Zum 65. Geburtstag*, edited by Detlev Kraack and Martin Rheinheimer, Neumünster: Wachholtz Verlag.

Fogleman, Aaron Spencer 2003, 'Jesus is Female: The Moravian Challenge in the German Communities of British North America', *The William and Mary Quarterly*, 60, no. 2: 295–332.

Fogleman, Aaron Spencer 2007, *Jesus is Female: Moravians and Radical Religion in Early America*, Philadelphia: University of Pennsylvania Press.

Forster, Friedrich, and Ludwig Boumann 1835, *Georg Wilhelm Friedrich Hegel's vermischte Schriften*. 2. Georg Wilhelm Friedrich Hegel's Werke 17, Berlin: Duncker und Humblot.

Foucault, Michel 1998 [1976], *The Will to Knowledge. The History of Sexuality 1*, London: Penguin.

Gärtner, Burkhard, and Hans-Beat Motel 1998, 'Die Entstehung der Losungen', *Unitas Fratrum*, 44: 133–41.

Gollin, Gillian L. 1967, *Moravians in Two Worlds: A Study of Changing Communities*, New York: Columbia University Press.

Gray, Marion W. 2000, *Productive Men, Reproductive Women: The Agrarian Household and the Emergence of Separate Spheres During the German Enlightenment*, New York: Berghahn Books.

Grosse, Johannes 1914, *Studien über Friedrich von Watteville: Ein Beitrag zur Geschichte des Herrnhutertums*, Leipzig.

Haymann, Johann Gottfried, and Carl Gottlob Dietmann 1750, *Neue Europäische Staats- und Rejsegeographie worinnen kürzlich alles was zur Geographischen, Physikalischen, ... und Topographischen Kenntniß eines Staates Gehöret, Nach und nach Vorgestellet ... werden soll*, 16 vols., Vol. 1, Leipzig: Richter und Compagnie.

Hegel, G.W.F., and J. Hoffmeister 1969, *Briefe von und an Hegel: 1823 bis 1831*, Meiner.

Hinrichs, Carl 1971, *Preußentum und Pietismus: Der Pietismus in Brandenburg-Preußen als religiös-soziale Reformbewegung*, Göttingen: Vandenhoeck & Ruprecht.

Hirst, Paul Q. 1985, *Marxism and Historical Writing*, London: Routledge.

Hopf-Droste, Marie Luise 1979, 'Der Geburtstag. Ein Beitrag zur Entstehung eines modernen Festes', *Zeitschrift für Volkskunde*, 75: 229–37.

Hörisch, Jochen 2000, *Heads or Tails: The Poetics of Money*, translated by Amy Horning Marschall, Detroit: Wayne State University Press.

Hörisch, Jochen 2005, *Brot und Wein. Die Poesie des Abendmahls*, Frankfurt am Main: Suhrkamp.

Hull, Isabel V. 1996, *Sexuality, State, and Civil Society in Germany, 1700–1815*, Ithaca: Cornell University Press.

Jameson, Fredric 1972, *Marxism and Form: Twentieth-Century Dialectical Theories of Literature*, Princeton: Princeton University Press.

Jameson, Fredric 1973, 'The Vanishing Mediator: Narrative Structure in Max Weber', *New German Critique*, 1: 52–89.

Jameson, Fredric 1979, 'Marxism and Historicism', *New Literary History*, 11, no. 1, 41–73.

Jameson, Fredric 1981, *The Political Unconscious: Narrative as a Socially Symbolic Act*, Ithaca: Cornell University Press.

Kautsky, Karl 1910 [1892], *The Class Struggle*, Chicago: Charles H. Kerr & Company.

Kautsky, Karl 1895, *Die Vorläufer des neueren Sozialismus 1:1*, Stuttgart: J.H.W. Dietz.

Kelly-Gadol, Joan 1987, 'The Social Relation of the Sexes. Methodological Implications of Women's History', in *Feminism and Methodology: Social Science Issues*, edited by Sandra G. Harding, Bloomington: Indiana University Press.

Knopp, Lawrence, and Mickey Lauria 1987, 'Gender Relations as a Particular Form of Social Relations', *Antipode*, 19, no. 1: 48–53.

Kocka, Jürgen 1990, *Weder Stand noch Klasse: Unterschichten um 1800*, Bonn: J.H.W. Dietz.

Kormann, Eva 2018, 'Schreiben als Netzwerk-, nicht als Werkpolitik: Zu Susanna Katharina von Klettenbergs religiöse Schriften', in *Pietismus und Adel: Genderhistorische Analysen*, edited by Ruth Albrecht, Ulrike Gleixner, Corinna Kirschstein, Eva Kormann and Pia Schmid, Halle: Verlag der Franckeschen Stiftungen.

Kröger, Rüdiger, Claudia Mai, and Olaf Nippe (eds) 2014, *Das Unitätsarchiv: Aus der Geschichte von Archiv, Bibliothek und Beständen*, Herrnhut: Comenius Buchhandlung.

Laclau, Ernesto, and Chantal Mouffe 1985, *Hegemony and Socialist Strategy: Towards a Radical Democratic Politics*, London: Verso.

Laqueur, Thomas W. 1990, *Making Sex: Body and Gender from the Greeks to Freud*, Cambridge, MA: Harvard University Press.

Laqueur, Thomas W. 2012, 'The Rise of Sex in the Eighteenth Century: Historical Context and Historiographical Implications', *Signs*, 37, no. 4: 802–13.

Leszczynski, Jozef 1964, *Der Klassenkampf der Oberlausitzer Bauern in den Jahren 1635–1720*, Bautzen: Domowina-Verlag.

Levering, Joseph Mortimer 1903, *A History of Bethlehem, Pennsylvania, 1741–1892*, Bethlehem: Times Publishing Company.

Lost, Christine 2006, 'Die Pädagogik der Lebensläufe', *Unitas Fratrum*, 57/58: 17–36.

Lost, Christine 2007, *Das Leben als Lehrtext: Lebensläufe aus der Herrnhuter Brüdergemeine*, Baltmannsweiler: Schneider Verlag Hohengehren.

Lost, Christine 2009, 'Formen und Normen des Selbstbildes in Herrnhuter Lebensläufen', in *Alter Adam und neue Kreatur. Pietismus und Anthropologie. Beiträge zum 11 Internationalen Kongress für Pietismusforschung 2005*, edited by Udo Sträter, Halle: Verlag der Franckeschen Stiftungen.

Losurdo, Domenico 2015, *War and Revolution: Rethinking the 20th Century*, London: Verso.

Lukács, Georg 1968, *Goethe and his Age*, London: Merlin.

Lukács, Georg 1975, *The Young Hegel: Studies in the Relations between Dialectics and Economics*, London: Merlin.

Lukács, Georg 1980, *The Destruction of Reason*, London: Merlin.

Lukács, Georg 1990, *History and Class Consciousness: Studies in Marxist Dialectics*, London: Merlin.

A Manual of Doctrine: Or, a Second Essay to Bring into the Form of Question and Answer as Well the Fundamental Doctrines, as the Other Scripture Knowledge of the Protestant Congregations Who for 300 Years Past Have Been Called the Brethren, London: James Hutton, 1742.

Marin, Louis 1989, *Food for Thought*, Baltimore: Johns Hopkins University Press.

Martin, Lucinda 2014, 'Jacob Böhme and the Anthropology of German Pietism', in *An Introduction to Jacob Boehme: Four Centuries of Thought and Reception*, edited by Ariel Hessayon and Sarah Apetrei, London: Routledge.

Marx, Karl 1975 [1843], 'On the Jewish Question', in Karl Marx and Friedrich Engels, *Collected Works*, Vol. 3, 146–74, Moscow: Progress Publishers.

Marx, Karl 1975 [1844], 'Contribution to the Critique of Hegel's Philosophy of Law: Introduction', in Karl Marx and Friedrich Engels, *Collected Works*, Vol. 3, Moscow: Progress Publishers.

Marx, Karl 1975 [1844], 'Economic and Philosophical Manuscripts of 1844', in Karl Marx and Friedrich Engels, *Collected Works*, Vol. 3, Moscow: Progress Publishers.

Marx, Karl 1979 [1852], 'The Eighteenth Brumaire of Louis Bonaparte', in Karl Marx and Friedrich Engels, *Collected Works*, Vol. 11, Moscow: Progress Publishers.

Marx, Karl, and Friedrich Engels 1972 [1845–46], *The German Ideology*, in *Collected Works*, Vol. 5, Moscow: Progress Publishers.

Marx, Karl, and Friedrich Engels 1976 [1848], *The Manifesto of the Communist Party*, in *Collected Works*, Vol. 6, Moscow: Progress Publishers.

McCullough, Thomas J. 2015, 'The Most Memorable Circumstances: Instructions for the Collection of Personal Data from Church Members, Circa 1752', *Journal of Moravian History*, 15, no. 2: 158–76.

McKeon, Michael 1995, 'Historicizing Patriarchy: The Emergence of Gender Difference in England, 1660–1760', *Eighteenth-Century Studies*, 28, no. 3: 295–322.

McKeon, Michael 2012, 'The Seventeenth- and Eighteenth-Century Sexuality Hypothesis', *Signs*, 37, no. 4: 791–801.

Mejrup, Kristian 2016, *Grand Prospects of Halle Pietism: The Acrobat, the Project-Maker and the Shepherd*, PhD thesis, University of Copenhagen.

Melton, Edgar 1988, 'Gutsherrschaft in East Elbian Germany and Livonia, 1500–1800: A Critique of the Model', *Central European History*, 21, no. 4: 315–49.

Melton, James van Horn 2001, *The Rise of the Public in Enlightenment Europe*, Cambridge: Cambridge University Press.

Mettele, Gisela 2005, 'Kommerz und fromme Demut. Wirtschaftsethik und Wirtschaftspraxis im Gefühlspietismus', *Vierteljahrschrift für Sozial- und Wirtschaftsgeschichte*, 92, no. 3: 301–21.

Mettele, Gisela 2009, *Weltbürgertum oder Gottesreich: Die Herrnhuter Brüdergemeine als Globale Gemeinschaft 1727–1857*, Göttingen: Vandenhoeck & Ruprecht.

Meyer, Dietrich 2000, *Zinzendorf und die Herrnhuter Brüdergemeine 1700–2000*, Göttingen: Vandenhoeck & Ruprecht.

Miller, Derrick R. 2013, 'Moravian Familiarities: Queer Community in the Moravian Church in Europe and North America in the Mid-Eighteenth Century', *Journal of Moravian History*, 13, no. 1: 54–75.

Miller, Derrick R. 2014, 'Alexander Volck's Anti-Moravian Polemics as Enlightenment Anxieties', *Journal of Moravian History*, 14, no. 2: 103–18.

Morgan, Ben 2013, *On Becoming God: Late Medieval Mysticism and the Modern Western Self*, New York: Fordham University Press.

Müller, Joseph Theodor 1907, 'Das Ältestenamt Christi in der erneuerten Brüderkirche', *Zeitschrift für Brüdergeschichte*.

Müller, Mogens 2008, *The Expression 'Son of Man' and the Development of Christology: A History of Interpretation*, Sheffield: Equinox.

Nachrichten aus der Brüder-Gemeine, Gnadau: C.E. Genft, 1825.

Ojakangas, Mika 2013, *The Voice of Conscience: A Political Genealogy of Western Ethical Experience*, London: Bloomsbury Academic.

Padgug, Robert A. 1979, 'Sexual Matters: On Conceptualizing Sexuality in History', *Radical History Review*, 20: 3–23.

Pateman, Carole 1988, *The Sexual Contract*. Cambridge: Polity Press.

Petterson, Christina 2014, '"Gar Nicht Biblisch!" Ephesians, Marriage, and Radical Pietism in 18th Century Germany', *Journal of the Bible and Its Reception*, 1, no. 2: 191–207.

Petterson, Christina 2015, 'Imagining the Body of Christ', in *Sexuality, Ideology and the Bible: Antipodean Engagements*, edited by Robert J. Myles and Caroline Blyth, Sheffield: Sheffield Phoenix Press.

Petterson, Christina 2016a, *From Tomb to Text: The Body of Jesus in the Book of John*, London: Bloomsbury T&T Clark.

Petterson, Christina 2016b, '"A Plague of the State and the Church": A Local Response to the Moravian Enterprise', *Journal of Moravian History*, 16, no. 1: 45–60.

Petterson, Christina 2016c, 'Response: The Ideology of Universalization', in *Psychoanalytic Mediations between Marxist and Postcolonial Readings of the Bible*, edited by Tat-siong Benny Liew and Erin Runions, Atlanta: Society of Biblical Literature.

Petterson, Christina 2018, 'From Communal Economy to Economic Community: Changes in Moravian Entrepreneurial Activities in the Eighteenth Century', *Journal for the History of Reformed Pietism*, 3, no. 1: 25–48.

Petterson, Christina 2019, 'Reading the Signs of the Times: The Moravian Brethren's Quiet Revolution', in *Reform, Revolution, and Crisis in Europe: Landmarks in History, Memory, and Thought*, edited by Bronwyn Winter and Cat Moir, New York: Routledge.

Petterson, Christina, and Katherine M. Faull 2017, 'Speaking About Marriage: Notes from the 1744 Married Choir Conferences', *Journal of Moravian History*, 17: 58–103.

Peucker, Paul M. 2000a, *Herrnhuter Wörterbuch. Kleines Lexikon von brüderischen Begriffen*, Herrnhut: Herrnhut Unitätsarchiv.

Peucker, Paul M. 2000b, 'Nikolaus Ludwig von Zinzendorf: Übersicht der wichtigsten Lebensdaten' in *Graf ohne Grenzen: Leben und Werk von Nikolaus Ludwig Graf von Zinzendorf; Ausstellung im Völkerkunde Museum Herrnhut, Außenstelle des Staatlichen Museums für Völkerkunde Dresden, und im Heimatmuseum der Stadt Herrnhut vom 26. Mai 2000 bis zum 7. Januar 2001*, edited by Paul Peucker, Dietrich Meyer, and Völkerkundemuseum, Herrnhut: Comenius-Buchh.

Peucker, Paul M. 2006, '"Inspired by Flames of Love": Homosexuality, Mysticism, and Moravian Brothers around 1750', *Journal of the History of Sexuality*, 15, no. 1: 30–64.

Peucker, Paul M. 2007, 'The Songs of the Sifting: Understanding the Role of Bridal Mysticism in Moravian Piety During the Late 1740s', *Journal of Moravian History*, 3: 51–87.

Peucker, Paul M. 2009, 'The Ideal of Primitive Christianity as a Source of Moravian Liturgical Practice', *Journal of Moravian History*, 6: 6–29.

Peucker, Paul M. 2010, 'Pink, White, and Blue: Function and Meaning of the Colored Choir Ribbons with the Moravians', in *Pietism and Community in Europe and North America 1650–1850*, Leiden: Brill.

Peucker, Paul M. 2011a, 'In the Blue Cabinet: Moravians, Marriage, and Sex', *Journal of Moravian History*, 10: 7–38.

Peucker, Paul M. 2011b, 'Wives of the Lamb: Moravian Brothers and Gender around 1750', in *Masculinity, Senses, Spirit*, edited by Katherine M. Faull, Lewisburg, PA: Bucknell University Press.

Peucker, Paul M. 2012, 'Herrnhuter Archive als Aufbewahrungsort pietistischer Erfahrungen', in *'Aus Gottes Wort und eigner Erfahrung Gezeiget' Erfahrung – Glauben, Erkennen und Handeln im Pietismus. Beiträge zum III Internationalen Kongress für Pietismusforschung 2009*, edited by Christian Soboth and Udo Sträter, Halle: Verlag der Franckeschen Stiftungen Halle.

Peucker, Paul M. 2015, *A Time of Sifting: Mystical Marriage and the Crisis of Moravian Piety in the Eighteenth Century*, Pennsylvania: Pennsylvania State University Press.

Plekhanov, Georgi [1907] 1969, *Fundamental Problems of Marxism*, New York: International Publishers.

Plett, Heinrich F. 2012, *Enargeia in Classical Antiquity and the Early Modern Age: The Aesthetics of Evidence*, Leiden: Brill.

Podmore, Colin 1998, *The Moravian Church in England, 1728–1760*, Oxford: Clarendon Press.

Podmore, Colin 2007, 'Zinzendorf and the English Moravians', *Journal of Moravian History*, 3: 31–50.

Poovey, Mary 1998, *A History of the Modern Fact: Problems of Knowledge in the Sciences of Wealth and Society*, Chicago: University of Chicago Press.

Prenter, Regin 1998, *Skabelse og Genløsning*, Frederiksberg: Anis.

Preston, Claire 2007, 'Ekphrasis: Painting in Words', in *Renaissance Figures of Speech*, edited by Sylvia Adamson, Gavin Alexander and Katrin Ettenhuber, Cambridge: Cambridge University Press.

REFERENCES

Reichel, Jörn 1969, *Dichtungstheorie und Sprache bei Zinzendorf*, Bad Homburg: Gehlen.
Rosenberg, Jordana 2011, *Critical Enthusiasm: Capital Accumulation and the Transformation of Religious Passion*, Oxford: Oxford University Press.
Rubin, Gayle 1975, 'The Traffic in Women: Notes on the "Political Economy" of Sex', in *Toward an Anthropology of Women*, edited by Rayna R. Reiter, New York: Monthly Review Press.
Sabean, David W. 1987, *Power in the Blood: Popular Culture and Village Discourse in Early Modern Germany*, Cambridge: Cambridge University Press.
Sayers, Sean 2011, *Marx and Alienation: Essays on Hegelian Themes*, New York: Palgrave Macmillan.
Schantz, Douglas H. 2013, *An Introduction to German Pietism: Protestant Renewal at the Dawn of Modern Europe*, Baltimore: Johns Hopkins University Press.
Schattkowsky, Martina 2013, *Adlige Lebenswelten in Sachsen: Kommentierte Bild- und Schriftquellen*, Böhlau Köln.
Schmid, Karl, Dieter Mertens, and Thomas Zotz 1998 [1961], *Geblüt, Herrschaft Geschlechterbeewußstsein: Grundfragen zum Verständnis des Adels im Mittelalter*, Sigmaringen.
Schmid, Pia 2002, 'Brüderische Schwestern. Frankfurter Herrnhuterinnen des 18. Jahrhunderts in ihren Lebensläufen', in *Frauen in der Stadt Frankfurt im 18. Jahrhundert*, edited by Gisela Engel, Ursula Kern, and Heide Wunder, Frankfurt am Main: Helmer Verlag.
Schmid, Pia 2004, 'Frömmigkeitspraxis und Selbstreflexion. Lebensläufe von Frauen der Herrnhuter Brüdergemeinde aus dem 18. Jahrhundert', in *Der Bildungsgang des Subjekts. Bildungstheoretische Analysen*, edited by Sonja Häder, Weinheim: Beltz Verlag.
Schmid, Pia 2009. ' „Wie Glücklich Man Sey, Wenn Man Sich Dem Heiland Ganz Ergebe" Selbstzweifel und Selbstgewissheit in Herrnhuter Lebensläufen des 18. Jahrhunderts. Zur Genese von Subjektivität im Medium religiöser Vergemeinschaftung', in *Alter Adam und neue Kreatur: Pietismus und Anthropologie. Beiträge Zum 11. Internationalen Kongress für Pietismusforschung 2005*, edited by Udo Sträter, Hartmut Lehmann, Thomas Müller-Bahlke, Christian Soboth, and Johannes Wallmann, Halle: Verlag der Franckeschen Stiftungen zu Halle.
Schmidt, Gottfried 1909, 'Die Banden oder Gesellschaften im alten Herrnhut', *Zeitschrift für Brüdergeschichte*, III: 145–207.
Schmidt, Theodor E. 1900, *Zinzendorfs soziale Stellung und ihr Einfluß auf seinen Character und sein Lebenswerk*, Basel: Adolf Geering.
Schneider, Hans 2004, 'Die „Zürnenden Mutterkinder". Der Konflikt zwischen Halle und Herrnhut' *Pietismus und Neuzeit*, 29: 37–66.
Scott, Joan W. 1986, 'Gender: A Useful Category of Historical Analysis', *The American Historical Review*, 91, no. 5: 1053–75.

Scott, Joan W. 1991, 'The Evidence of Experience', *Critical Inquiry*, 17, no. 4: 773–97.

Seibert, Dorette 2033, *Glaube, Erfahrung und Gemeinschaft: Der Junge Schleiermacher und Herrnhut*, Göttingen: Vandenhoeck & Ruprecht.

Seidel, Johann Gottlob 2000 [1755], *Haupt-Schlüssel zum Herrnhutischen Ehe-Sacrament*, in *Herrnhut im 18. Und 19. Jahrhundert*, 2, Hildesheim: Georg Olms Verlag.

Sepper, Dennis L. 2009, 'Goethe, Newton, and the Imagination of Modern Science', *Revue internationale de philosophie*, 249, no. 3: 261–77.

Sewell Jr, William H. 1990, 'How Classes Are Made: Critical Reflections on E.P. Thompson's Theory of Working-Class Formation', in *E.P. Thompson: Critical Perspectives*, edited by Harvey J. Kaye and Keith McClelland, Philadelphia: Temple University Press.

Sigurdson, Ola 2016, *Heavenly Bodies: Incarnation, the Gaze, and Embodiment in Christian Theology*, Grand Rapids: William B. Eerdmans.

Simmel, Georg 2009, *Sociology: Inquiries into the Construction of Social Forms*, Leiden: Brill.

Sommer, E.W. 2000, *Serving Two Masters: Moravian Brethren in Germany and North Carolina, 1727–1801*, Lexington: University Press of Kentucky.

Spangenberg, August Gottlieb 1772–75, *Leben des Herrn Nicolaus Ludwig Grafen von Zinzendorf und Pottendorf*, Barby.

Spangenberg, August Gottlieb 1838, *The Life of Nicholas Lewis Count Zinzendorf, Bishop and Ordinary of the Church of the United (or Moravian) Brethren*, London: Samuel Holdsworth.

Ste. Croix, G.E.M. de 1981, *The Class Struggle in the Ancient Greek World: From the Archaic Age to the Arab Conquests*, London: Duckworth.

Steinberg, Leo 1983, *The Sexuality of Christ in Renaissance Art and in Modern Oblivion*, New York: Pantheon Books.

Sterik, Edita 2006, 'Die Böhmischen Emigranten und Zinzendorf', in *Neue Aspekte der Zinzendorf-Forschung*, edited by Martin Brecht and Paul Peucker, Göttingen: Vandenhoeck & Ruprecht.

Sterik, Edita 2012, *Mährische Exulanten in der eneuerten Brüderunität im 18. Jahrhundert. Beiheft der Unitas Fratrum 20*, Herrnhut: Herrnhuter Verlag.

Tanner, Fritz 1952, *Die Ehe im Pietismus*, Zürich: Zwingli-Verlag.

Tarr, Zoltan 1989, 'A Note on Weber and Lukács', *International Journal of Politics, Culture, and Society*, 3, no. 1: 131–9.

Taylor, Charles 1989, *Sources of the Self: The Making of the Modern Identity*, Cambridge, MA: Harvard University Press.

Taylor, Michael Thomas 2015, 'Queer Moravians? Sexual Heterodoxy and the Historiography of Zinzendorf's *Ehereligion*', in *Gender im Pietismus. Netzwerke und Geschlechter-Konstruktionen*, edited by Pia Schmid, Halle: Verlag der Franckeschen Stiftungen.

Thompson, E.P. 1966, *The Making of the English Working Class*, New York: Vintage Books.
Thompson, E.P. 1993, *Witness Against the Beast: William Blake and the Moral Law*, New York: New Press.
Tribe, Keith 1978, *Land, Labour and Economic Discourse*, London: Routledge.
Tribe, Keith 1998, *Governing Economy: The Reformation of German Economic Discourse 1750–1840*, Cambridge: Cambridge University Press.
Tribe, Keith 1995, *Strategies of Economic Order: German Economic Discourse, 1750–1950*, Cambridge: Cambridge University Press.
Uttendörfer, Otto 1912, *Das Erziehungswesen Zinzendorfs und der Brüdergemeine in seinen Anfängen*, Berlin: Weidmannsche Buchhandlung.
Uttendörfer, Otto 1925, *Alt-Herrnhut. Wirtschaftsgeschichte und Religionssoziologie Herrnhuts während seiner ersten Zwanzig Jahre (1722–1742)*, Herrnhut: Verlag der Missionsbuchhandlung.
Uttendörfer, Otto 1926, *Wirtschaftsgeist und Wirtschaftsorganisation Herrnhuts und der Brüdergemeine von 1743 bis zum Ende des Jahrhunderts*, Herrnhut: Verlag der Missionsbuchhandlung.
Veit-Brause, Irmline 2003, 'Werner Conze (1910–1986): The Measure of History and the Historian's Measures', in *Paths of Continuity: Central European Historiography from the 1930s to the 1950s*, edited by Hartmut Lehmann and James Van Horn Melton, Cambridge: Cambridge University Press.
Vogt, Peter 2006, ' "Gloria Pleurae!": Die Seitenwunde Jesu in der Theologie des Grafen von Zinzendorf', in *Pietismus und Neuzeit Band 32*, Göttingen: Vandenhoeck & Ruprecht.
Vogt, Peter 2009, '"Honor to the Side": The Adoration of the Side Wound of Jesus in Eighteenth-Century Moravian Piety', *Journal of Moravian History*, 7: 83–106.
Vogt, Peter 2011, 'Zinzendorf's "Seventeen Points of Matrimony": A Fundamental Document on the Moravian Understanding of Marriage and Sexuality', *Journal of Moravian History*, 10: 39–67.
Vogt, Peter 2015, 'Christologie und Gender bei Zinzendorf', in *Gender im Pietismus: Netzwerke und Geschlechterkonstruktionen*, edited by Pia Schmid, Halle: Verlag der Frankeschen Stiftung.
Vogt, Peter 2018, ' "Als Christ ist man nicht Graf …". Paradoxien pietistisch-aristokratischer Identität bei Zinzendorf', in *Pietismus und Adel. Genderhistorische Analysen*, edited by Ruth Albrecht, Ulrike Gleixner, Corinna Kirschstein, Eva Kormann, and Pia Schmid, Halle: Verlag der Franckeschen Stiftungen.
Volck, Alexander 1748–51, *Das Entdecte Geheimnis der Bosheit der Herrnhutische Secte zu Errettung vieler Unschuldigen Seelen, zur Warnung der mit Vorurtheilen Eingenommenes Gtumeyner und zur Offenbarung der Verirreten und Verwirrten Verführer*, 7 vols., Frankfurt: Heinrich Ludwig Brönner.

Vološinov, Valentin N. 1973 [1930], *Marxism and the Philosophy of Language*, New York: Seminar Press.

Vosa, Aira 2009, 'Von der Tugend der Ehelosigkeit. Johann Georg Gichtels Einfluss auf August Gottlieb Spangenberg', *Unitas Fratrum*, 61/62: 9–21.

Wallerstein, Immanuel 2011 [1974], *The Modern World-System I. Capitalist Agriculture and the Origins of the European World Economy in the Sixteenth Century*, Berkeley: University of California Press.

Wallerstein, Immanuel 2011 [1974], *The Modern World-System II. Mercantilism and the Consolidation of the European World-Economy, 1600–1750*, Berkeley: University of California Press.

Ward, W.R 1987, 'Zinzendorf and Money', in *Church and Wealth*, edited by W.J. Shiels and Diana Wood, Oxford: Blackwell.

Webb, Ruth 2009, *Ekphrasis, Imagination and Persuasion in Ancient Rhetorical Theory and Practice*, Farnham: Ashgate.

Weber, Max 2013 [1905], *The Protestant Ethic and the Spirit of Capitalism*, Hoboken: Taylor and Francis.

Weckenbrock, Olga 2014, *Adel auf dem Prüfstand: Strategien der Selbstbehauptung bei Ernst (1738–1813) und Ludwig (1774–1844) Freiherren von Vincke*, Münster: Aschendorff Verlag.

Wickham, Chris 2008, 'Productive Forces and the Economic Logic of the Feudal Mode of Production', *Historical Materialism*, 16: 3–22.

Wollstadt, Hanns-Joachim 1966, *Geordnetes Dienen in der christlichen Gemeinde*, Göttingen: Vandenhoeck & Ruprecht.

Wood, Ellen Meiksins 1995, *Democracy Against Capitalism: Renewing Historical Materialism*, Cambridge: Cambridge University Press.

Young, Iris 1981, 'Beyond the Unhappy Marriage: A Critique of the Dual Systems Theory', in *Women and Revolution: A Discussion of the Unhappy Marriage of Marxism and Feminism*, edited by Lydia Sargent, Montreal: Black Rose Books.

Zaepernick, Gertraud 1982, 'Johann Georg Gichtels und seiner Nachfolger Briefwechsel mit den Hallischen Pietisten, Bes. mit A.M. Francke', *Pietismus und Neuzeit*, 8: 74–118.

Zimmerling, Peter 1991, *Gott in Gemeinschaft: Zinzendorfs Trinitätslehre*, Giessen.

von Zinzendorf, Nicholaus Ludwig 1763, *Auszüge aus des Seligen Ordinarii der Evangelischen Brüder-Kirche Sowol Ungedrukten als Gedrukten Reden über Biblische Texte: Erster Band über das Erste Buch Mose*, edited by Gottfried Clemens, Barby: Seminario Theologico.

von Zinzendorf, Nicholaus Ludwig 1963, *Hauptschriften 3*, edited by Erich Beyreuther and Gerhard Meyer, Hildesheim: Georg Olms.

von Zinzendorf, Nicholaus Ludwig 1963, *Hauptschriften 4*, edited by Erich Beyreuther and Gerhard Meyer, Hildesheim: Georg Olms.

von Zinzendorf, Nicholaus Ludwig 1963 [1748], '21 Diskurse über die Augsburger Konfession', in *Hauptschriften 6*, edited by Erich Beyreuther and Gerhard Meyer, Hildesheim: Georg Olms Verlag.

von Zinzendorf, Nicholaus Ludwig 1965, *Ergänzungsbände 6*, Ergänzungsbände zu den Hauptschriften, edited by Erich Beyreuther and Gerhard Meyer, Hildesheim: Georg Olms.

von Zinzendorf, Nicholaus Ludwig 1970, 'Zwey und Dreyßig Einzele Homiliae oder Gemein-Reden in denen Jahren 1744, 1745, 1746', in *Nikolaus Ludwig von Zinzendorf. Ergänzungsband 10*, edited by Erich Beyreuther and Gerhard Meyer, Hildesheim: Georg Olms.

Index

alienation 7, 19, 137, 285–286, 290
asscoiations (*Gesellschaften*) 39, 40–44, 46, 49–50, 51, 53, 55–59, 61–63, 78, 81, 97
  see also organisation, bonded groups/banden, choirs, and classes

Atwood, Craig 24n5, 25n8, 120, 121n76, 122–123, 146, 147–148, 150n43, 157, 170, 182n124, 213n199, 230n233, 235n6

Banaji, Jairus 10n24, 17n46
Bechler, Theodor 38n3, 40n12, 90, 91n240, 95
Berthelsdorf 59n114, 102, 242, 277n46, 294, 295
  church in 63, 87, 205
  outside free zone 3, 109–110, 112, 113n50, 205n176, 224n219
Bethlehem, Pennsylvania 22n, 38, 166, 206, 238, 329, 331
  Moravian Archives 25, 26, 28
Beyreuther, Erich 129, 132, 162, 192
Beyreuther, Gottfried 106n30, 235
Bible 224
  1 Corinthians 43n26, 131n, 173, 176, 177n112, 188, 223n, 258, 335n18
  2 Corinthians 351n39
  1 Timothy 222, 350n38
  Ephesians 242, 244
  Eucharist in 131n
  Hebrew bible 43n26, 138n19, 139, 163, 222, 246, 302, 304n, 331n12, 340n21, 349, 350n34–36
  Hebrews 156n
  James 188
  John, gospel 135n9, 139, 198n163, 227n228
  Luke, gospel 29n14, 131n, 198n163, 208n184, 219, 325n6, 336n19
  Mark, gospel 198n163, 131n
  Matthew, gospel 198n163, 131n
  New Testament 43n26, 163, 239, 246, 302, 349
  Romans 188, 190

blood 27, 68, 72, 79, 99, 115, 120, 139
  and class 118–120, 345
  and communion 131–132, 140, 143n20, 155–156, 167, 170
  and wounds devotion 20, 41, 52, 54, 74, 88, 97, 98–101, 105, 118–123, 127, 131, 146–147, 149, 170, 278, 280
  of brothers and sisters 175, 181, 187, 191, 337, 341
  of the Saviour 66–67, 85, 104, 123, 140, 155, 156, 167, 170, 186, 187, 189, 192, 246n32, 327–328
body 21, 119, 130, 134, 135, 138–142, 143, 160, 163, 173, 178, 181, 193, 212, 222, 231, 244, 265, 267, 281
  see also Hütte, corpse
  as corpse 71, 74, 143, 188–191, 211, 335–336
  as Hütte 81n210
  human 27, 133n5, 143–144, 150, 164, 321, 341
  individual/collective 132, 146n30, 176–177, 180, 181–182, 229, 280, 283, 284–286, 303
  of Christ 31, 122, 131–132, 149, 166, 170, 174, 176, 192, 241, 300
  of men 174–175, 177, 179n120, 181, 188–191, 273, 335–336
  of women 182, 185, 187, 191, 194, 200, 202–203, 226
Boer, Roland 14, 17n48, 19n55, 131n, 297n13, 298n14, 300n18
Bonded groups (*Banden*) 26, 39–40, 40–42, 43–44, 46, 47n42, 49–50, 52, 61, 63, 97, 131, 132, 184n134, 207n, 343, 345
bridal mysticism 220, 235
bride, church as 30, 69, 100, 106, 180, 196, 214, 235, 259, 264
  sister as 150, 195
bridegroom 30, 73, 106, 132, 185, 192, 194, 195, 196n159, 199, 201, 215n205, 216, 220, 235, 247, 255, 257, 264n83, 285n73
Bynum, Caroline Walker 120, 123, 160

INDEX

cabinet (intercourse)   212, 226, 248, 343, 345
capitalism   5, 13, 16, 146, 274, 285, 286, 289, 290, 302
   and Gutsherrschaft   12
   early   2, 15, 20, 27, 270, 287, 288, 290
   transition to   1, 7, 10, 17–18, 21, 36, 107, 234, 291, 296, 299, 300–301
choir   22, 23, 31, 36, 40–43, 45–46, 150, 284
see also ideology
   and *Stand*   35, 135–137, 195, 199, 219–222, 228–229, 231–232, 269
   as mediator between individual and collective   28–29, 34, 285, 292
   children's   22, 39, 76, 138–143
   Day of All Choirs   83–88
   diary   48, 113n51
   elder   47, 48, 49, 51, 53, 55, 60, 72n177, 76, 82, 86
   helper   86, 93, 103, 115, 127, 189
   houses   22n, 23, 38, 88–96, 97, 184
   married couples'   22, 34, 39, 77–79, 114–116, 162, 185, 207–208, 234, 236, 238, 239, 247, 248–254, 259–263
   (older) boys'   22, 30, 39, 76, 152–158
   (older) girls'   22, 39, 75, 133, 165–169
   point   176, 223–224, 231, 251
   relations   29, 184, 228
   single brothers'   22, 39, 70–71, 173–181, 184, 187, 191
   single sisters'   22, 39, 72–75, 107, 193–195, 202, 204–205
   speeches   21, 23, 24–27, 28, 33, 82, 130, 147, 149, 170–171, 182, 209–210, 218, 233, 235, 254, 274, 294, 301. See also Appendix 1–2
   structure   10, 27, 33, 39, 97, 98, 239, 296, 301
   system   7, 20, 21, 22n, 131, 161, 230, 234, 264, 270, 281–283
   terminology   20, 27–28, 49–70, 97
   transition   195, 219–222
   widowers'   22, 39, 81, 211, 216, 217
   widows'   22, 39, 80–81, 222–225, 227–228
   worker   42, 48–49, 50, 51, 62n135, 65, 67, 69, 71, 72, 73, 78n199, 102, 107, 115–117, 155, 174, 177, 180, 183, 187, 189, 231, 247–248, 253, 259

class (marxist)   7–11, 13–14, 15, 21, 39, 57, 98, 118, 136, 148, 182, 231, 242, 258, 265, 279, 304
   class and *Stand*   266–269
   class consciousness   11, 14, 15, 275
   class formation   12–13, 14
   class relations   10, 120, 163n81
   class struggle   1, 4, 7, 8, 11, 20, 23, 26, 27, 28, 34, 118, 128, 137, 232, 244, 254, 266, 275, 293
   ruling class   11, 120, 123, 231, 265, 269, 275–277
class, classes (organisation)   28n13, 44, 46n39, 49n50, 51, 52, 55, 58, 62, 78, 83, 85, 155, 211–212, 225, 327–328, 345, 350
corpse   27, 29, 73–74, 96, 122, 130, 132, 139–140, 143–144, 148, 149–150, 166, 170, 173, 175, 178, 181, 188, 190–192, 194, 206, 211–212, 217, 230, 256, 258, 300, 321
cultural revolution   18, 265, 266, 269, 270

dialectic, dialectical   28, 33, 130, 229, 271n24, 281, 283, 285, 290, 291
Dober, Leonhard   47, 123, 125n88, 127, 170
Dober, Martin   49, 50n55, 51, 52, 82, 83, 92n251, 95, 99–101, 105, 115, 118, 121, 126, 131, 147, 149, 251

Enlightenment   5, 6n, 32, 287, 288, 295n7, 302

Faull, Katherine M.   25n8, 79n202, 102n10, 103n11, 104n16, 105n24, 111n42, 112n47, 121n81, 150, 159n64, 180n122, 235n3, 288n80
feudalism   2, 10, 16–18, 36, 107, 134, 136, 219, 234, 291, 294, 296, 299–300

Gemüth   139, 144, 155, 167n, 175, 183, 187, 192, 203, 207, 255, 281, 318–319, 323–324, 327, 331, 336, 337
gender   27, 33, 44, 133, 164
   ahistorical concept of   159–163, 269–271
   as individualisation   34, 44, 137, 144, 150, 158, 228, 268–269, 274, 284, 285, 301
   organisation according to   4, 7, 22, 33, 35, 39, 44, 49, 60, 74, 97, 116, 152, 231, 266–267

production of   5, 10, 130, 136, 163, 173, 182, 184, 229, 230, 232
  relations   21, 35, 156, 202, 228, 243, 264, 269, 272–273, 274–275
genitals   133n5, 184
Gneuss, Rosina   56n90, 72n177, 102, 107, 113, 115, 117
Grassmann, Andreas   52n65, 55n83, 94, 100n6, 102, 116
Greenland   3, 10, 22n, 149n39, 195
Gutsherrschaft   10, 18, 293

Halle   4, 6, 34, 41–42, 98–99, 135n8, 277, 278, 290n
Hegel, Georg Wilhelm Friedrich   7n, 9, 19, 163, 271, 275, 282, 286–289, 290, 297–298, 301, 303
Herrnhaag (Wetterau)   23, 38, 41, 46n39, 47, 48, 49, 99, 113n51, 114, 115, 162, 208, 209, 235n3, 260
history
  see also class struggle, gender, Jameson, mode of production, transition
  discipline of   4–5
  end of   129
  fragmented (bourgeois)   150, 160, 270–271, 296–297
  historicization   6, 161
  horizon of   7–8, 21, 146, 285, 299–305
  materialist history   11–18, 19–20, 266, 271–272, 280, 297–299, 299–305
  of Christianity   150, 181
  of Moravian community   2, 26, 35n32, 37, 97, 147, 277, 290
household   2, 6n16, 9n22, 21, 33, 35, 36, 92, 94, 106, 195, 234, 238, 239n15, 250, 264, 270, 277, 284, 301, 326
Hull, Isabel V.   23, 36n36, 158–159, 181–182, 228, 232, 267, 295n8
Hütte   81n210, 107, 155, 165, 167, 174–175, 181–185, 187–190, 192, 194, 199, 221, 239, 243, 256, 264, 281, 324, 327–328, 330, 332–334, 335–337, 338, 340–341, 346

ideology   7, 12–15, 118, 130, 134, 164, 169, 170, 303–304
  bourgeois   32–33, 146, 233, 265, 270, 281, 287, 290, 299, 302

choir   4–5, 22–28, 37, 38–39, 41n15, 51, 54, 89, 97, 128, 233, 285, 291, 296, 301
  marital/spousal   107, 208, 264
  ruling class   123, 135n9, 265, 269
individual   4, 13, 28–29, 56, 70n168, 82, 98, 101, 107, 113n52, 122, 136, 146–148, 164, 171, 175, 190, 264, 266, 271, 275–276, 283, 303
  and collective   26, 28, 29, 33–34, 36–37, 39, 107, 130, 131–133, 137, 149, 166, 169, 201, 228–229, 233, 276, 284, 290–291, 301
  and gender   34, 45, 136, 155, 157, 159, 161, 166, 169, 181, 182, 200, 218, 230, 231, 269, 285
  and state/society   5, 11, 14, 15, 33, 181, 231, 265, 267–268, 272, 281–285, 287, 289
individualisation   230, 233, 274, 280n60
individualism   122, 149, 158, 280
intercourse, sexual   79, 103, 105, 106, 107, 110–111, 112, 203, 210, 212, 215, 221, 224–226, 236–237, 246, 249, 255–257
intercourse, social   8, 13, 151

Jameson, Fredric   11n29, 14n35, 17n47, 18, 19n54, 21, 32–33, 35–36, 145–146, 151–152, 265, 274, 280, 285, 300n17, 302–304

Langguth, Johann Michael   50n55, 51–52, 69, 88, 100, 102, 118–119, 121n78, 123, 127
  see also Watteville, Johannes von

language   61, 79, 87, 96, 146–152, 285
  affective   31, 98, 142, 149–152, 282
  and signification   171–172, 282
  as lived reality   147–149
  changes in   99–101, 131, 134
Litany of Wounds   70, 86, 87, 121–123, 147–148, 191
Losungen, watchword   46, 54, 63, 79, 138, 165, 173, 176, 177, 320, 330, 326
lot   6n124, 70, 75, 84, 86, 93, 103, 108, 113n52, 123, 124–127, 168n94, 170, 194, 238, 245, 250, 278
Lukács, Georg   32, 33, 162n77, 163n, 233, 271, 286–289, 301, 302

INDEX 377

marriage 21, 25n8, 63, 66n158, 77, 130, 135, 191, 211–213, 223, 225, 334–345, 349
   and class 119, 244–245
   as calling 194, 198–199, 201–202, 204–206, 214–216
   as subjectification of men and women 220–221, 254–259, 264
   change in 28, 79, 118, 209–210, 241–243, 300
   choir management 247, 251–252, 259–260
   community marriage 162, 169, 222, 234–236, 239–241, 249, 260, 263, 350
   cosmic 168, 180, 182, 213, 245–247, 249
   document 27, 102–107, 110–112, 115, 117, 250
   radical pietism and 105–106, 243–244
   Seidel and 162, 207–208, 296
   speaking 82–83, 88, 102
   symbolic 195, 219–220, 234–236, 252
   without lot 237–238
Marx, Karl
   Capital 131, 281, 303
   Eighteenth Brumarie of Louis Bonarparte 8, 12, 15, 270
   Introduction to *Contribution to the Critique of Hegel's Philosophy of Law* 19
   On the Jewish Question 5, 19, 283, 289–290
Marx, Karl, and Friedrich Engels
   The German Ideology 13, 120, 151, 265
   The Manifesto of the Communist Party 7, 233, 266
Marxism 5, 12–14, 16
Mary 29n14, 80n205, 82, 87, 136, 191, 201, 226–227, 228, 340
mediator, Saviour as 130, 197, 212, 282, 285
memoirs (*Lebenslauf*) 25n8, 27, 28, 49, 102, 113n50, 126n96, 143, 161, 205, 237, 280
mode of production 14, 16–18, 264, 272n27, 290, 300
   see also capitalism and feudalism and transition
Moravian (mährisch) 1, 3, 21, 27, 39, 40–41, 44, 62, 79, 99, 105, 118, 123, 125–127

Nitschmann, Anna 72n177, 74, 92, 94, 126, 127, 247
Nitschmann, David (Bishop) 126, 237

Nitschmann, David (Syndikus) 102, 114–115, 127, 238, 242, 244
Nitschmann, Johann 61, 69, 70, 76, 78, 115, 117, 126, 236, 248
Nitschmann, Rosina 237

office 51, 53, 80n209, 86, 100, 124, 125–127, 137, 169, 170, 174, 202, 203, 204, 215n206, 217, 218, 243, 256–267, 341, 350
organisation
   community 4, 9, 10, 20, 24, 31, 33, 36, 37, 40, 41, 43, 45, 47n42, 50, 51, 58, 60, 61, 72, 74, 76n189, 88, 91n249, 95, 96, 97n267, 123, 132, 178
   capitalism 5, 8, 9, 17, 161, 267, 270, 274n36

Peistel, Carl Heinrich von 60, 102, 107–110, 113, 115, 236, 293
Peucker, Paul 3n7, 24n7, 28n12, 34n29, 35n32, 38n5, 42n18, 45n36, 47n41, 48n44, 49n49, 52n64, 65n151, 81, 87n232, 98–99, 102n9, 107n37, 113n51, 120–121, 122n82, 146, 159n64, 209–210, 212, 224n220, 235n3, 236, 237, 238n14, 248n35, 254n49, 260n70, 277
Pietism 4, 6, 34, 41, 98, 99, 105, 106, 107, 134, 147, 277, 278, 290, 301–302
pilgrim congregation 47, 49, 65, 67–69, 81, 91
procurator marriage 221, 235, 249

Rubin, Gayle 158n57, 270n18, 272, 274

Schleiermacher 134, 164, 267–268
Scott, Joan W. 15, 159–161, 163, 270–271, 274
Seidel, Johann Gottlob 161, 162n73, 180n122, 208–209, 260, 294–296
sexuality 26, 32, 106, 159, 272, 274
side wound, side hole 67, 86–87, 101, 123, 132, 139–140, 141, 144, 147, 148, 252
sifting time 35, 120–121, 146, 207–209, 235, 260, 279, 301
Spangenberg, August Gottlieb 105n29, 126n96, 208n182
speakings 61, 71, 78n199, 80n204, 82, 88, 102–103

subjectification
see also choir and gender
  collective   37, 130, 133, 181, 264, 269, 300
  individual   37, 122, 130, 133, 161, 181, 200, 264, 269, 280
  practice   4, 133, 150, 228, 274
symbols (believers)
  bees   73, 194
  cross-air birds   204n173, 295
  doves   139–140, 321
  worm   101, 123

transition
  choir   21, 26, 27, 30, 34, 69, 84, 130, 143, 152–153, 157, 176, 184, 195, 201, 219–222, 223, 225, 232, 260, 263
  in mode of production   7, 10, 18, 21, 36, 107, 218, 233–234, 265–266, 270, 277, 291, 296, 299, 300–301

Uttendorfer, Otto   3n8, 9n22, 38n3, 40n12, 42, 90n240, 91, 92n250, 107, 110n39, 125, 126n95, 127, 224n220, 229n231, 277–278, 279

Vogt, Peter   103n15, 159n64, 161–163, 209–210, 235n5, 278–279

Watteville, Benigna von, nee Zinzendorf   52, 65, 68n, 69–70, 72n177, 81n212, 94, 180n122, 260
Watteville, Friedrich von   4, 44n27, 52, 83, 126, 185n134, 238n14, 277, 293n3
Watteville, Johannes von   52, 65, 67n159, 70, 71, 77n195, 79, 96, 121, 180n122, 247–248, 252n46, 259–260, 277
Weber, Max   4, 19, 35–36, 286, 288, 290, 301–302

Zinzendorf, Christian Renatus von, (Christel)   35n32, 64, 65, 69–70, 71, 87, 117n64, 121, 184, 209
Zinzendorf, Erdmuth Dorothea von, nee Reuss (Mama)   64n147, 65, 67, 68n161, 100, 110, 126, 238n14
Zinzendorf, Nikolaus Ludwig von
  and blood and wounds   99–100, 121, 123
  and body/hütte   181–193
  and choir speeches   21, 24–25, 26, 28, 30, 34n29, 89, chapter 4 and the appendices, 285
  and choirs   28–29, 40, 42, 45, 86, 228–232, 267, 285
  and language   31, 146–152
  and Moravians   99, 124–125
  and the Saviour   131–135, 169–173, 212, 220
  and Stand   9, 45, 135–137, 152–153, 156–158, 167–168, 178–179, 181, 183–184, 195, 198–202, 203, 211–222, 223–224, 225–228, 231–232, 245–246, 268–269
  as agent of history   129, 297–299
  as member of aristocracy   9, 12, 52, 102, 108, 113, 277–279, 282–283, 293
  banishment   52n65, 65n151, 86, 114
  entourage   49, 65, 70
  as landlord/leader   3–4, 33, 38, 41, 46, 60, 107, 108, 124, 125, 126
  on marriage   103n15, chapter 5
  publicity   207–209
  Sifting time   35n32, 208–209
  and local industry   294–296

CPSIA information can be obtained
at www.ICGtesting.com
Printed in the USA
JSHW010811020822
28650JS00004B/4